Ford Galaxy
Service and Repair Manual

Martynn Randall

Models covered

(3984 - 320)

Galaxy MPV models, including special/limited editions
Petrol engines: 2.0 litre (1998cc) & 2.3 litre (2295cc) 4-cyl
Turbo-Diesel engines: 1.9 litre (1896cc)

Does NOT cover 2.8 litre V6 petrol engine or 4x4 models
Does NOT cover revised model range introduced August 2000

© J H Haynes & Co. Ltd. 2003

A book in the **Haynes Service and Repair Manual Series**

ISBN **978 1 78521 445 5**

British Library Cataloguing in Publication Data
A catalogue record for this book is available from the British Library.

J H Haynes & Co. Ltd.
Haynes North America, Inc

www.haynes.com

Contents

LIVING WITH YOUR FORD GALAXY

MAINTENANCE

Routine maintenance and servicing

Contents

Advanced driving

Many people see the words 'advanced driving' and believe that it won't interest them or that it is a style of driving beyond their own abilities. Nothing could be further from the truth. Advanced driving is straightforward safe, sensible driving - the sort of driving we should all do every time we get behind the wheel.

An average of 10 people are killed every day on UK roads and 870 more are injured, some seriously. Lives are ruined daily, usually because somebody did something stupid. Something like 95% of all accidents are due to human error, mostly driver failure. Sometimes we make genuine mistakes - everyone does. Sometimes we have lapses of concentration. Sometimes we deliberately take risks.

For many people, the process of 'learning to drive' doesn't go much further than learning how to pass the driving test because of a common belief that good drivers are made by 'experience'.

Learning to drive by 'experience' teaches three driving skills:

☐ Quick reactions. (Whoops, that was close!)
☐ Good handling skills. (Horn, swerve, brake, horn).
☐ Reliance on vehicle technology. (Great stuff this ABS, stop in no distance even in the wet...)

Drivers whose skills are 'experience based' generally have a lot of near misses and the odd accident. The results can be seen every day in our courts and our hospital casualty departments.

Advanced drivers have learnt to control the risks by controlling the position and speed of their vehicle. They avoid accidents and near misses, even if the drivers around them make mistakes.

The key skills of advanced driving are **concentration,** effective all-round **observation, anticipation** and **planning.** When **good vehicle handling** is added to these skills, all driving situations can be approached and negotiated in a safe, methodical way, leaving nothing to chance.

Concentration means applying your mind to safe driving, completely excluding anything that's not relevant. Driving is usually the most dangerous activity that most of us undertake in our daily routines. It deserves our full attention.

Observation means not just looking, but seeing and seeking out the information found in the driving environment.

Anticipation means asking yourself what is happening, what you can reasonably expect to happen and what could happen unexpectedly. (One of the commonest words used in compiling accident reports is 'suddenly'.)

Planning is the link between seeing something and taking the appropriate action. For many drivers, planning is the missing link.

If you want to become a safer and more skilful driver and you want to enjoy your driving more, contact the Institute of Advanced Motorists on 0208 994 4403 or write to IAM House, Chiswick High Road, London W4 4HS for an information pack.

Working on your car can be dangerous. This page shows just some of the potential risks and hazards, with the aim of creating a safety-conscious attitude.

General hazards

Scalding

• Don't remove the radiator or expansion tank cap while the engine is hot.
• Engine oil, automatic transmission fluid or power steering fluid may also be dangerously hot if the engine has recently been running.

Burning

• Beware of burns from the exhaust system and from any part of the engine. Brake discs and drums can also be extremely hot immediately after use.

Crushing

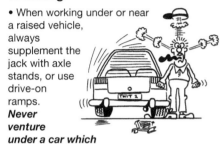

• When working under or near a raised vehicle, always supplement the jack with axle stands, or use drive-on ramps.
Never venture under a car which is only supported by a jack.
• Take care if loosening or tightening high-torque nuts when the vehicle is on stands. Initial loosening and final tightening should be done with the wheels on the ground.

Fire

• Fuel is highly flammable; fuel vapour is explosive.
• Don't let fuel spill onto a hot engine.
• Do not smoke or allow naked lights (including pilot lights) anywhere near a vehicle being worked on. Also beware of creating sparks (electrically or by use of tools).
• Fuel vapour is heavier than air, so don't work on the fuel system with the vehicle over an inspection pit.
• Another cause of fire is an electrical overload or short-circuit. Take care when repairing or modifying the vehicle wiring.
• Keep a fire extinguisher handy, of a type suitable for use on fuel and electrical fires.

Electric shock

• Ignition HT voltage can be dangerous, especially to people with heart problems or a pacemaker. Don't work on or near the ignition system with the engine running or the ignition switched on.

• Mains voltage is also dangerous. Make sure that any mains-operated equipment is correctly earthed. Mains power points should be protected by a residual current device (RCD) circuit breaker.

Fume or gas intoxication

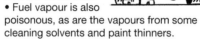

• Exhaust fumes are poisonous; they often contain carbon monoxide, which is rapidly fatal if inhaled. Never run the engine in a confined space such as a garage with the doors shut.
• Fuel vapour is also poisonous, as are the vapours from some cleaning solvents and paint thinners.

Poisonous or irritant substances

• Avoid skin contact with battery acid and with any fuel, fluid or lubricant, especially antifreeze, brake hydraulic fluid and Diesel fuel. Don't syphon them by mouth. If such a substance is swallowed or gets into the eyes, seek medical advice.
• Prolonged contact with used engine oil can cause skin cancer. Wear gloves or use a barrier cream if necessary. Change out of oil-soaked clothes and do not keep oily rags in your pocket.
• Air conditioning refrigerant forms a poisonous gas if exposed to a naked flame (including a cigarette). It can also cause skin burns on contact.

Asbestos

• Asbestos dust can cause cancer if inhaled or swallowed. Asbestos may be found in gaskets and in brake and clutch linings. When dealing with such components it is safest to assume that they contain asbestos.

Special hazards

Hydrofluoric acid

• This extremely corrosive acid is formed when certain types of synthetic rubber, found in some O-rings, oil seals, fuel hoses etc, are exposed to temperatures above 400°C. The rubber changes into a charred or sticky substance containing the acid. *Once formed, the acid remains dangerous for years. If it gets onto the skin, it may be necessary to amputate the limb concerned.*
• When dealing with a vehicle which has suffered a fire, or with components salvaged from such a vehicle, wear protective gloves and discard them after use.

The battery

• Batteries contain sulphuric acid, which attacks clothing, eyes and skin. Take care when topping-up or carrying the battery.
• The hydrogen gas given off by the battery is highly explosive. Never cause a spark or allow a naked light nearby. Be careful when connecting and disconnecting battery chargers or jump leads.

Air bags

• Air bags can cause injury if they go off accidentally. Take care when removing the steering wheel and/or facia. Special storage instructions may apply.

Diesel injection equipment

• Diesel injection pumps supply fuel at very high pressure. Take care when working on the fuel injectors and fuel pipes.

⚠️ *Warning: Never expose the hands, face or any other part of the body to injector spray; the fuel can penetrate the skin with potentially fatal results.*

Remember...

DO

• Do use eye protection when using power tools, and when working under the vehicle.

• Do wear gloves or use barrier cream to protect your hands when necessary.

• Do get someone to check periodically that all is well when working alone on the vehicle.

• Do keep loose clothing and long hair well out of the way of moving mechanical parts.

• Do remove rings, wristwatch etc, before working on the vehicle – especially the electrical system.

• Do ensure that any lifting or jacking equipment has a safe working load rating adequate for the job.

DON'T

• Don't attempt to lift a heavy component which may be beyond your capability – get assistance.

• Don't rush to finish a job, or take unverified short cuts.

• Don't use ill-fitting tools which may slip and cause injury.

• Don't leave tools or parts lying around where someone can trip over them. Mop up oil and fuel spills at once.

• Don't allow children or pets to play in or near a vehicle being worked on.

The Ford Galaxy models covered by this manual were first introduced to the UK in June 1995. This multi-personnel vehicle (MPV) is available in one body shape, and equipped with a variety of engine sizes. This manual covers the 4-cylinder petrol and diesel engine models. Two petrol engines were available, a 1998 cc DOHC 8-valve unit, and a 2295 cc DOHC 16-valve unit, equipped with balance shafts. The diesel engines, of VW origin, are SOHC 8-valve and turbocharged. Diesel engines with the code AFN are equipped with a variable geometry turbocharger, resulting in greater torque and power output.

Fully-independent front suspension is fitted, with the components attached to a subframe assembly; the rear suspension is semi-independent, with separate coil springs and dampers, and trailing arms.

A five-speed manual gearbox is fitted as standard to all models, with a four-speed automatic unit available on petrol models, and

diesel models (engine code AFN) from November 1997.

A wide range of standard and optional equipment is available within the model range to suit most tastes, including an anti-lock braking system and air conditioning.

For the home mechanic, the Galaxy is quite straightforward to maintain, and most of the items requiring frequent attention are easily accessible.

Your Ford Galaxy Manual

The aim of this manual is to help you get the best value from your vehicle. It can do so in several ways. It can help you decide what work must be done (even should you choose to get it done by a garage). It will also provide information on routine maintenance and servicing, and give a logical course of action and diagnosis when random faults occur. However, it is hoped that you will use the manual by tackling the work yourself. On

simpler jobs it may even be quicker than booking the car into a garage and going there twice, to leave and collect it. Perhaps most important, a lot of money can be saved by avoiding the costs a garage must charge to cover its labour and overheads.

The manual has drawings and descriptions to show the function of the various components so that their layout can be understood. Tasks are described and photographed in a clear step-by-step sequence. The illustrations are numbered by the Section number and paragraph number to which they relate – if there is more than one illustration per paragraph, the sequence is denoted alphabetically.

References to the 'left' or 'right' of the vehicle are in the sense of a person in the driver's seat, facing forwards.

Acknowledgements

Certain illustrations are the copyright of the Ford Motor Company, and are used with their permission. Thanks are due to Draper Tools Limited, who provided some of the workshop tools, and to all those people at Sparkford who helped in the production of this manual.

We take great pride in the accuracy of information given in this manual, but vehicle manufacturers make alterations and design changes during the production run of a particular vehicle of which they do not inform us. No liability can be accepted by the authors or publishers for loss, damage or injury caused by any errors in, or omissions from, the information given.

Project vehicles

The main vehicle used in the preparation of this manual, and which appears in many of the photographic sequences, was a 1998 Ford Galaxy 2.3 litre petrol. Also included was a 1999 1.9 litre turbo-diesel, and a 1997 2.0 litre petrol.

The following pages are intended to help in dealing with common roadside emergencies and breakdowns. You will find more detailed fault finding information at the back of the manual, and repair information in the main chapters.

If your car won't start and the starter motor doesn't turn

☐ IIf it's a model with automatic transmission, make sure the selector is in P or N.
☐ Open the bonnet and make sure that the battery terminals are clean and tight.
☐ Switch on the headlights and try to start the engine. If the headlights go very dim when you're trying to start, the battery is probably flat. Get out of trouble by jump starting (see next page) using a friend's car.

If your car won't start even though the starter motor turns as normal

☐ Is there fuel in the tank?
☐ Is there moisture on electrical components under the bonnet? Switch off the ignition, then wipe off any obvious dampness with a dry cloth. Spray a water-repellent aerosol product (WD-40 or equivalent) on ignition and fuel system electrical connectors like those shown in the photos. Pay special attention to the ignition coil wiring connector and HT leads. (Note that diesel engines don't normally suffer from damp.)

A Check the condition and security of the battery connections.

B Check the fuel injection system airflow sensor wiring is secure.

C Check the ignition system camshaft position sensor wiring is secure.

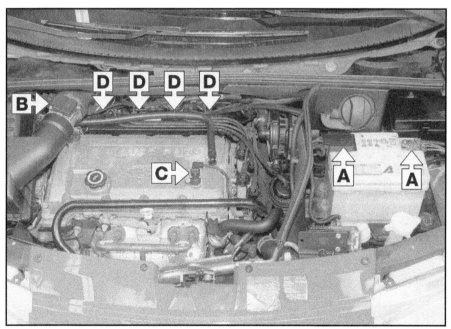

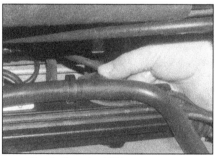

D Check that the HT leads are securely connected to the spark plugs on petrol engines.

Check that electrical connections are secure (with the ignition switched off) and spray them with a water dispersant spray like WD-40 if you suspect a problem due to damp.

Jump starting

When jump-starting a car using a booster battery, observe the following precautions:

✔ Before connecting the booster battery, make sure that the ignition is switched off.

✔ Ensure that all electrical equipment (lights, heater, wipers, etc) is switched off.

✔ Take note of any special precautions printed on the battery case.

✔ Make sure that the booster battery is the same voltage as the discharged one in the vehicle.

✔ If the battery is being jump-started from the battery in another vehicle, the two vehicles MUST NOT TOUCH each other.

✔ Make sure that the transmission is in neutral (or PARK, in the case of automatic transmission).

 Jump starting will get you out of trouble, but you must correct whatever made the battery go flat in the first place. There are three possibilities:

1 The battery has been drained by repeated attempts to start, or by leaving the lights on.

2 The charging system is not working properly (alternator drivebelt slack or broken, alternator wiring fault or alternator itself faulty).

3 The battery itself is at fault (electrolyte low, or battery worn out).

1 Connect one end of the red jump lead to the positive (+) terminal of the flat battery

2 Connect the other end of the red lead to the positive (+) terminal of the booster battery.

3 Connect one end of the black jump lead to the negative (-) terminal of the booster battery

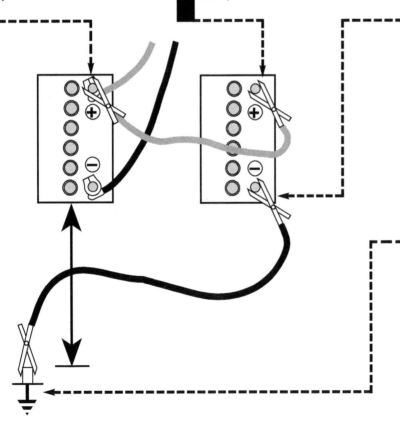

4 Connect the other end of the black jump lead to a bolt or bracket on the engine block, well away from the battery, on the vehicle to be started.

5 Make sure that the jump leads will not come into contact with the fan, drive-belts or other moving parts of the engine.

6 Start the engine using the booster battery and run it at idle speed. Switch on the lights, rear window demister and heater blower motor, then disconnect the jump leads in the reverse order of connection. Turn off the lights etc.

⚠️ **Warning: Do not change a wheel in a situation where you risk being hit by another vehicle. On busy roads, try to stop in a lay-by or a gateway. Be wary of passing traffic while changing the wheel – it is easy to become distracted by the job in hand.**

Wheel changing

Preparation

- ☐ When a puncture occurs, stop as soon as it is safe to do so.
- ☐ Park on firm level ground, if possible, and well out of the way of other traffic.
- ☐ Use hazard warning lights if necessary.

- ☐ If you have one, use a warning triangle to alert other drivers of your presence.
- ☐ Apply the handbrake and engage first or reverse gear (or Park on models with automatic transmission).

- ☐ Chock the wheel diagonally opposite the one being removed – a couple of large stones will do for this.
- ☐ If the ground is soft, use a flat piece of wood to spread the load under the jack.

Changing the wheel

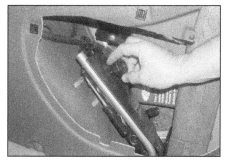

1 The vehicle jack and tools are stored behind the right-hand side luggage compartment side trim panel in the rear of the vehicle. Open the storage compartment, undo the retaining screw, and retrieve the jack, with the tools clipped to it.

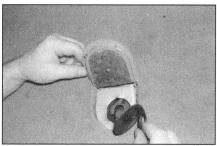

2 The spare wheel is located underneath the rear of the vehicle in a cradle. Lift the access cover in the floor covering in the luggage compartment, and remove the rubber cap. Use the wheelbrace to turn the hexagonal bolt anti-clockwise until the spare wheel has been completely lowered.

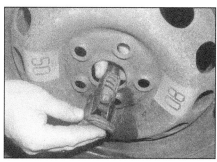

3 Lift the spare wheel, and compress (shorten) the steel retainer, which will allow the end of the retainer to swivel and be pushed through the centre of the wheel.

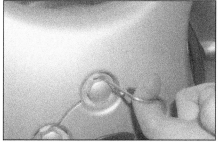

4 Where fitted, use the hook in the tool kit to pull the cover from the wheel. If caps are fitted to each bolt, use the tool to pull off the covers.

5 Loosen each wheel bolt by half a turn. Use the special adapter where a locking wheel bolt is fitted.

6 Locate the jack head below the reinforced jacking point nearest the wheel to be changed. The jacking point is indicated by a small indentations pressed into the sill. Turn the handle to raise the wheel clear of the ground. On vehicle fitted with sill trims, remove the jacking point covers from the sill by pulling them up, and out.

Finally . . .

- ☐ Remove the wheel chocks.
- ☐ Refit the steel cable retainer, and lay the spare wheel in the cradle valve side down. Use the wheelbrace to rotate the hexagonal bolt in the vehicle floor clockwise, until the cradle is fully raised.
- ☐ Stow the jack and tools in the correct locations in the car.
- ☐ Check the tyre pressure on the wheel just fitted. If it is low, or if you don't have a pressure gauge with you, drive slowly to the nearest garage and inflate the tyre to the right pressure.
- ☐ Have the damaged tyre or wheel repaired as soon as possible.

7 Remove the bolts and lift the wheel from the vehicle. Place the wheel beneath the sill as a precaution against the jack failing.

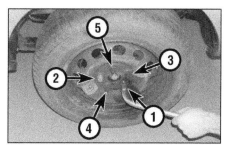

8 Fit the spare wheel, insert the bolts and then tighten them moderately with the wheel brace. Lower the vehicle to the ground, then finally tighten the wheel bolts in a diagonal sequence. Refit the wheel cover/cap as applicable. Note that the wheel bolts should be tightened to the specified torque at the earliest opportunity.

Identifying leaks

Puddles on the garage floor or drive, or obvious wetness under the bonnet or underneath the car, suggest a leak that needs investigating. It can sometimes be difficult to decide where the leak is coming from, especially if the engine bay is very dirty already. Leaking oil or fluid can also be blown rearwards by the passage of air under the car, giving a false impression of where the problem lies.

 Warning: Most automotive oils and fluids are poisonous. Wash them off skin, and change out of contaminated clothing, without delay.

 The smell of a fluid leaking from the car may provide a clue to what's leaking. Some fluids are distinctively coloured. It may help to clean the car carefully and to park it over some clean paper overnight as an aid to locating the source of the leak.
Remember that some leaks may only occur while the engine is running.

Sump oil

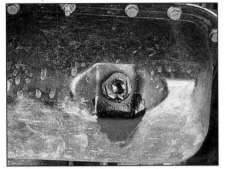

Engine oil may leak from the drain plug...

Oil from filter

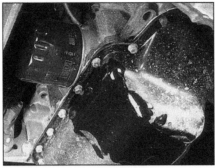

...or from the base of the oil filter.

Gearbox oil

Gearbox oil can leak from the seals at the inboard ends of the driveshafts.

Antifreeze

Leaking antifreeze often leaves a crystalline deposit like this.

Brake fluid

A leak occurring at a wheel is almost certainly brake fluid.

Power steering fluid

Power steering fluid may leak from the pipe connectors on the steering rack.

Towing

When all else fails, you may find yourself having to get a tow home – or of course you may be helping somebody else. Long-distance recovery should only be done by a garage or breakdown service. For shorter distances, DIY towing using another car is easy enough, but observe the following points:

☐ Use a proper tow-rope – they are not expensive. The vehicle being towed must display an ON TOW sign in its rear window.
☐ Always turn the ignition key to the 'on' position when the vehicle is being towed, so that the steering lock is released, and that the direction indicator and brake lights will work.
☐ A rear towing eye is provided below the right-hand side of the bumper. The front towing eye is provided behind the cover on the right-hand side of the front bumper –

carefully lever the cover from place **(see illustration)**.
☐ Before being towed, release the handbrake and select neutral on the transmission. **Note:** *On models with automatic transmission, special precautions apply. Selector lever must be in the N position, vehicle speed must not exceed 30mph (50 kmh), and towed distance must not exceed 30 miles (50 km).*
☐ Note that greater-than-usual pedal pressure will be required to operate the brakes, since the vacuum servo unit is only operational with the engine running.
☐ On models with power steering, greater-than-usual steering effort will also be required.
☐ The driver of the car being towed must keep the tow-rope taut at all times to avoid snatching.
☐ Make sure that both drivers know the route before setting off.

☐ Only drive at moderate speeds and keep the distance towed to a minimum. Drive smoothly and allow plenty of time for slowing down at junctions.

 Warning: To prevent damage to the catalytic converter on petrol models, do not tow or push-start a vehicle more than 50 yards. Where possible, use jump leads (see 'Jump starting').

Towing eye

Introduction

There are some very simple checks which need only take a few minutes to carry out, but which could save you a lot of inconvenience and expense.

These *Weekly checks* require no great skill or special tools, and the small amount of time they take to perform could prove to be very well spent, for example;

☐ Keeping an eye on tyre condition and pressures, will not only help to stop them wearing out prematurely, but could also save your life.

☐ Many breakdowns are caused by electrical problems. Battery-related faults are particularly common, and a quick check on a regular basis will often prevent the majority of these.

☐ If your car develops a brake fluid leak, the first time you might know about it is when your brakes don't work properly. Checking the level regularly will give advance warning of this kind of problem.

☐ If the oil or coolant levels run low, the cost of repairing any engine damage will be far greater than fixing the leak, for example.

Underbonnet check points

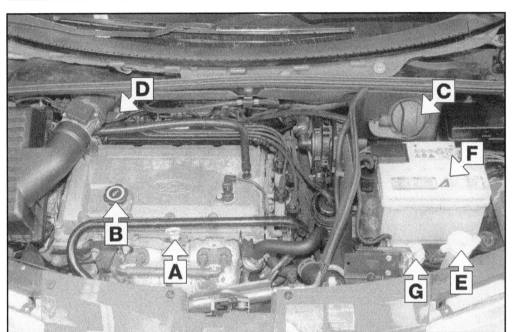

◀ 2.0 and 2.3 litre petrol

A *Engine oil level dipstick*

B *Engine oil filler cap*

C *Coolant expansion tank*

D *Brake fluid reservoir*

E *Screen washer fluid reservoir*

F *Battery*

G *Power steering fluid reservoir*

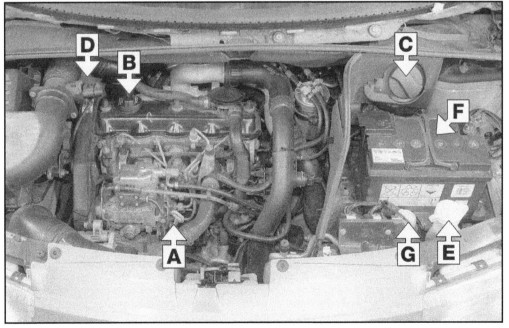

◀ 1.9 litre diesel

A *Engine oil level dipstick*

B *Engine oil filler cap*

C *Coolant expansion tank*

D *Brake fluid reservoir*

E *Screen washer fluid reservoir*

F *Battery*

G *Power steering fluid reservoir*

Engine oil level

Before you start

✔ Make sure that your car is on level ground.
✔ Check the oil level before the car is driven, or at least 5 minutes after the engine has been switched off.

HAYNES HiNT *If the oil is checked immediately after driving the vehicle, some of the oil will remain in the upper engine components, resulting in an inaccurate reading on the dipstick.*

The correct oil

Modern engines place great demands on their oil. It is very important that the correct oil for your car is used (see 'Lubricants and fluids').

Car care

● If you have to add oil frequently, you should check whether you have any oil leaks. Place some clean paper under the car overnight, and check for stains in the morning. If there are no leaks, the engine may be burning oil.
● Always maintain the level between the upper and lower dipstick marks (see photo 3). If the level is too low severe engine damage may occur. Oil seal and/or catalytic converter failure may result if the engine is overfilled by adding too much oil.

1 The dipstick is located on the front of the engine (see *Underbonnet check points* for exact location). Withdraw the dipstick.

2 Using a clean rag or paper towel, wipe all oil from the dipstick. Insert the clean dipstick into the tube as far as it will go, then withdraw it again.

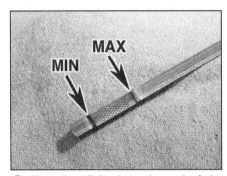
3 Note the oil level on the end of the dipstick, which should be between the upper and lower mark. Approximately 1.0 litre of oil will raise the level from the lower mark to the upper mark.

4 Oil is added through the filler cap on top of the engine. Turn the cap through a quarter-turn anti-clockwise and withdraw it. Top-up the level. A funnel may help to reduce spillage. Add the oil slowly, checking the level on the dipstick often. Do not overfill.

Coolant level

Warning: DO NOT attempt to remove the expansion tank pressure cap when the engine is hot, as there is a very great risk of scalding. Do not leave open containers of coolant about, as it is poisonous.

Car Care

● With a sealed-type cooling system, adding coolant should not be necessary on a regular basis. If frequent topping-up is required, it is likely there is a leak. Check the radiator, all hoses and joint faces for signs of staining or wetness, and rectify as necessary.

● It is important that antifreeze is used in the cooling system all year round, not just during the winter months. Don't top-up with water alone, as the antifreeze will become too diluted.
● It is also important to use the correct type of antifreeze; see *Lubricants and fluids*.

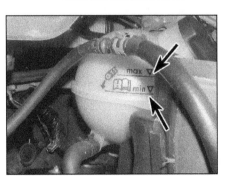
1 The coolant level varies with the temperature of the engine. When the engine is cold, the coolant level should be between the MIN and MAX marks.

2 If topping-up is necessary, wait until the engine is cold. Slowly unscrew the cap to release any pressure present in the cooling system, and remove the cap.

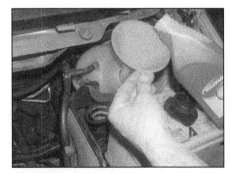
3 Add a mixture of water and antifreeze to the expansion tank until the coolant level is on the MAX mark.

Brake (and clutch) fluid level

Warning:
● *Brake fluid can harm your eyes and damage painted surfaces, so use extreme caution when handling and pouring it.*
● *Do not use fluid that has been standing open for some time, as it absorbs moisture from the air, which can cause a dangerous loss of braking effectiveness.*

HAYNES HiNT
● *Make sure that your car is on level ground.*
● *The fluid level in the reservoir will drop slightly as the brake pads wear down, but the fluid level must never be allowed to drop below the MIN mark.*

Safety first!

● If the reservoir requires repeated topping-up this is an indication of a fluid leak somewhere in the system, which should be investigated immediately.
● If a leak is suspected, the car should not be driven until the braking/clutch system has been checked. Never take any risks where brakes are concerned.

1 The MIN and MAX marks are indicated on the reservoir. The fluid level must be kept between the marks at all times.

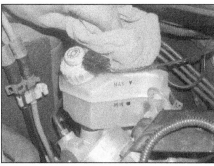

2 If topping-up is necessary, first wipe clean the area around the filler cap to prevent dirt entering the hydraulic system. Unscrew the reservoir cap. **Note:** *On right-hand drive models, it is necessary to remove the mass airflow sensor, and air intake ducting to gain access to the fluid reservoir – refer to the relevant Part of Chapter 4.*

3 Carefully add fluid, taking care not to spill it onto the surrounding components. Use only the specified fluid; mixing different types can cause damage to the system. On completion, securely refit the cap and wipe away any spilt fluid. With the ignition switched on, check the operation of the brake fluid low level warning lamp by having an assistant depress the button on the top of the reservoir cap.

Power steering fluid level

Before you start

✔ Park the vehicle on level ground.
✔ With the engine idling, turn the steering wheel slowly from lock-to-lock 2 or 3 times and set the front wheels at the straight-ahead position, then stop the engine.
✔ For the check to be accurate, the engine must be at operating temperature, and the steering must not be turned once the engine has been stopped.

Safety first!

● The need for frequent topping-up indicates a leak, which should be investigated immediately.

1 The power steering fluid reservoir is located on the left-hand side of the engine compartment. Slowly unscrew and remove the filler cap, which incorporates a fluid level dipstick.

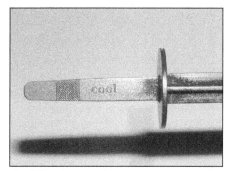

2 With the steering system at operating temperature, the level should lie in the 'hot' range on one side of the dipstick. If you are checking with the steering system cold, the level should lie in the 'cool' range on the other side of the dipstick. If necessary, wipe the dipstick with a clean cloth, then place it on the filler neck base and remove again.

3 Where topping-up is required, add the specified type of fluid until the level lies in the correct range, depending on the temperature of the steering system. On completion refit and tighten the cap.

Tyre condition and pressure

It is very important that tyres are in good condition, and at the correct pressure - having a tyre failure at any speed is highly dangerous. Tyre wear is influenced by driving style - harsh braking and acceleration, or fast cornering, will all produce more rapid tyre wear. As a general rule, the front tyres wear out faster than the rears. Interchanging the tyres from front to rear ("rotating" the tyres) may result in more even wear. However, if this is completely effective, you may have the expense of replacing all four tyres at once! Remove any nails or stones embedded in the tread before they penetrate the tyre to cause deflation. If removal of a nail does reveal that

the tyre has been punctured, refit the nail so that its point of penetration is marked. Then immediately change the wheel, and have the tyre repaired by a tyre dealer.

Regularly check the tyres for damage in the form of cuts or bulges, especially in the sidewalls. Periodically remove the wheels, and clean any dirt or mud from the inside and outside surfaces. Examine the wheel rims for signs of rusting, corrosion or other damage. Light alloy wheels are easily damaged by "kerbing" whilst parking; steel wheels may also become dented or buckled. A new wheel is very often the only way to overcome severe damage.

New tyres should be balanced when they are fitted, but it may become necessary to re-balance them as they wear, or if the balance weights fitted to the wheel rim should fall off. Unbalanced tyres will wear more quickly, as will the steering and suspension components. Wheel imbalance is normally signified by vibration, particularly at a certain speed (typically around 50 mph). If this vibration is felt only through the steering, then it is likely that just the front wheels need balancing. If, however, the vibration is felt through the whole car, the rear wheels could be out of balance. Wheel balancing should be carried out by a tyre dealer or garage.

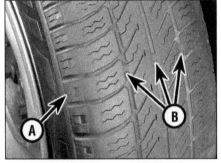

1 Tread Depth - visual check
The original tyres have tread wear safety bands (B), which will appear when the tread depth reaches approximately 1.6 mm. The band positions are indicated by a triangular mark on the tyre sidewall (A).

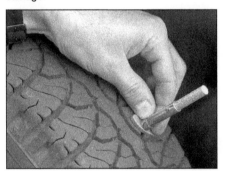

2 Tread Depth - manual check
Alternatively, tread wear can be monitored with a simple, inexpensive device known as a tread depth indicator gauge.

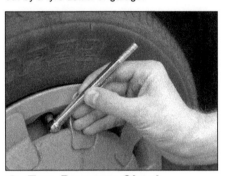

3 Tyre Pressure Check
Check the tyre pressures regularly with the tyres cold. Do not adjust the tyre pressures immediately after the vehicle has been used, or an inaccurate setting will result.

Tyre tread wear patterns

Shoulder Wear

Underinflation (wear on both sides)
Under-inflation will cause overheating of the tyre, because the tyre will flex too much, and the tread will not sit correctly on the road surface. This will cause a loss of grip and excessive wear, not to mention the danger of sudden tyre failure due to heat build-up.
Check and adjust pressures
Incorrect wheel camber (wear on one side)
Repair or renew suspension parts
Hard cornering
Reduce speed!

Centre Wear

Overinflation
Over-inflation will cause rapid wear of the centre part of the tyre tread, coupled with reduced grip, harsher ride, and the danger of shock damage occurring in the tyre casing.
Check and adjust pressures

If you sometimes have to inflate your car's tyres to the higher pressures specified for maximum load or sustained high speed, don't forget to reduce the pressures to normal afterwards.

Uneven Wear

Front tyres may wear unevenly as a result of wheel misalignment. Most tyre dealers and garages can check and adjust the wheel alignment (or "tracking") for a modest charge.
Incorrect camber or castor
Repair or renew suspension parts
Malfunctioning suspension
Repair or renew suspension parts
Unbalanced wheel
Balance tyres
Incorrect toe setting
Adjust front wheel alignment
Note: *The feathered edge of the tread which typifies toe wear is best checked by feel.*

Battery

Caution: Before carrying out any work on the vehicle battery, read the precautions given in 'Safety first!' at the start of this manual.

✔ Make sure that the battery tray is in good condition, and that the clamp is tight. Corrosion on the tray, retaining clamp and the battery itself can be removed with a solution of water and baking soda. Thoroughly rinse all cleaned areas with water. Any metal parts damaged by corrosion should be covered with a zinc-based primer, then painted.

✔ Periodically (approximately every three months), check the charge condition of the battery as described in Chapter 5A.

✔ If the battery is flat, and you need to jump start your vehicle, see *Roadside Repairs*.

HAYNES HINT

Battery corrosion can be kept to a minimum by applying a layer of petroleum jelly to the clamps and terminals after they are reconnected.

1 The battery is located on the left-hand side of the engine compartment.

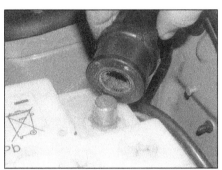

3 If corrosion (white, fluffy deposits) is evident, remove the cables from the battery terminals, clean them with a small wire brush, then refit them. Automotive stores sell a tool for cleaning the battery post . . .

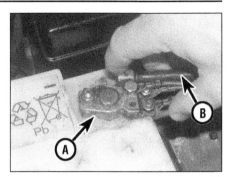

2 Check the tightness of battery clamps (A) to ensure good electrical connections. You should not be able to move them. Also check each cable (B) for cracks and frayed conductors.

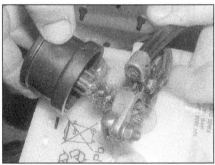

4 . . . as well as the battery cable clamps

Electrical systems

✔ Check all external lights and the horn. Refer to the appropriate Sections of Chapter 12 for details if any of the circuits are found to be inoperative.

✔ Visually check all accessible wiring connectors, harnesses and retaining clips for security, and for signs of chafing or damage.

HAYNES HINT

If you need to check your brake lights and indicators unaided, back up to a wall or garage door and operate the lights. The reflected light should show if they are working properly.

1 If a single indicator light, brake light or headlight has failed, it is likely that a bulb has blown and will need to be renewed. Refer to Chapter 12 for details. If both brake lights have failed, it is possible that the brake light switch operated by the brake pedal has failed. Refer to Chapter 9 for details.

2 If more than one indicator light or headlight has failed, it is likely that either a fuse has blown or that there is a fault in the circuit (see Chapter 12). The main fusebox is located beneath a cover on the driver's side of the facia panel; on diesel models further fuses may be located in the left-hand corner of the engine compartment.

3 To renew a blown fuse, pull it from its location in the fusebox. Fit a new fuse of the same rating, available from car accessory shops.

Screen washer fluid level

Screenwash additives not only keep the windscreen clean during foul weather, they also prevent the washer system freezing in cold weather – which is when you are likely to need it most. Don't top-up using plain water as the screenwash will become too diluted, and will freeze during cold weather. *On no account use coolant antifreeze in the washer system – this could discolour or damage paintwork.*

1 The reservoir for the windscreen and headlight washer systems is on the front left-hand side of the engine compartment.

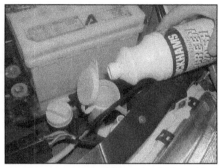

2 A screenwash additive should be added in the quantities recommended on the bottle.

Wiper blades

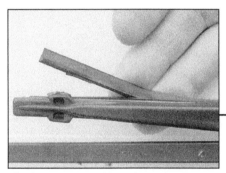

1 Check the condition of the wiper blades. If they are cracked or show any signs of deterioration, or if the glass swept area is smeared, renew them. For maximum clarity of vision, wiper blades should be renewed annually, as a matter of course.

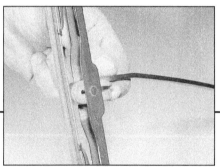

2 To remove a windscreen wiper blade, pull the arm fully away from the screen until it locks. Swivel the blade through 90°, then depress the locking tab with a screwdriver or your fingers.

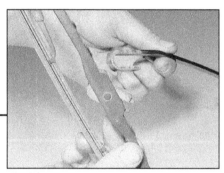

3 Slide the wiper blade out of the hooked end of the arm, then feed the arm through the hole in the blade. When fitting the new blade, make sure that the blade locks securely into the arm, and that the blade is orientated correctly.

Lubricants and fluids

Engine

Petrol . . . . Ford engine oil Formula E SAE 5W-30 (or to Ford specification WSS-M2C913-A, WSS-M2C912-A1) should be used for oil changes*

Diesel . . . . Engine oil to specification ACEA A3-96 and ACEA B3-96, SAE 10W-40

Cooling system . . . . Antifreeze to Ford specification ESDM-97B49-A (Motorcraft Super Plus 4 – blue/green in colour), or WSS-M97B44-D (Motorcraft Super Plus 2000 – orange in colour). **Do not** mix these two different types of coolant

Manual transmission . . . . Ford specification WSD-M2C200-C transmission fluid

Automatic transmission . . . . Ford specification N052162 VX00 transmission fluid

Final drive (automatic transmission) . . . . Ford specification N052145 VX00 gear oil, SAE 75W-90

Braking/clutch system . . . . Hydraulic fluid to DOT 4

Power steering system . . . . Ford specification N052146 VX00 lubricant

*Engine oil to specification ACEA A1/B1 viscosity SAE 5W-30 to 10W-40 may be used for topping-up in the absence of the above oil.

Choosing your engine oil

Engines need oil, not only to lubricate moving parts and minimise wear, but also to maximise power output and to improve fuel economy.

HOW ENGINE OIL WORKS

• Beating friction

Without oil, the moving surfaces inside your engine will rub together, heat up and melt, quickly causing the engine to seize. Engine oil creates a film which separates these moving parts, preventing wear and heat build-up.

• Cooling hot-spots

Temperatures inside the engine can exceed 1000° C. The engine oil circulates and acts as a coolant, transferring heat from the hot-spots to the sump.

• Cleaning the engine internally

Good quality engine oils clean the inside of your engine, collecting and dispersing combustion deposits and controlling them until they are trapped by the oil filter or flushed out at oil change.

OIL CARE - FOLLOW THE CODE

To handle and dispose of used engine oil safely, always:

OIL CARE

OIL BANK LINE
0800 66 33 66
www.oilbankline.org.uk

• *Avoid skin contact with used engine oil. Repeated or prolonged contact can be harmful.*
• *Dispose of used oil and empty packs in a responsible manner in an authorised disposal site. Call 0800 663366 to find the one nearest to you. Never tip oil down drains or onto the ground.*

Tyre pressures

Note: *The pressures given are for the original equipment tyres – the recommended pressures may vary if any other make or type of tyre is fitted; check with the tyre manufacturer or supplier for latest recommendations.*

Tyre size	Front	Rear
195/65:		
Up to 3 persons	38 psi (2.6 bar)	35 psi (2.4 bar)
Full load	39 psi (2.7 bar)	44 psi (3.0 bar)
205/60:		
Up to 3 persons	39 psi (2.7 bar)	36 psi (2.5 bar)
Full load	42 psi (2.9 bar)	46 psi (3.2 bar)
215/60:		
Up to 3 persons	33 psi (2.3 bar)	30 psi (2.1 bar)
Full load	36 psi (2.5 bar)	39 psi (2.7 bar)
215/55:		
Up to 3 persons	39 psi (2.7 bar)	36 psi (2.5 bar)
Full load	42 psi (2.9 bar)	48 psi (3.3 bar)

Chapter 1 Part A:
Routine maintenance and servicing – petrol models

Contents

Degrees of difficulty

Easy, suitable for novice with little experience		Fairly easy, suitable for beginner with some experience		Fairly difficult, suitable for competent DIY mechanic		Difficult, suitable for experienced DIY mechanic		Very difficult, suitable for expert DIY or professional	

Lubricants and fluids . . . . Refer to end of *Weekly checks*

Capacities

Engine oil (including filter)
2.0 litre engine . . . . 4.25 litres
2.3 litre engine . . . . 4.0 litres

Cooling system
2.0 litre engine:
   With one heater . . . . 8.3 litres approx
   With two heaters . . . . 10.1 litres approx
   With two heaters and auxiliary heater . . . . 10.8 litres approx
2.3 litre engine:
   With one heater . . . . 8.7 litres approx
   With two heaters . . . . 10.5 litres approx
   With two heaters and auxiliary heater . . . . 11.2 litres approx

Transmission
Manual transmission . . . . 2.0 litres
Automatic transmission:
   Initial filling . . . . 5.5 litres
      Fluid change . . . . 3.5 litres
Automatic transmission final drive (filled for life) . . . . 0.8 litres

Fuel tank
All models (approx) . . . . 70 litres

Cooling system

Antifreeze mixture:
   50% antifreeze . . . . Protection down to –35°C

Ignition system

Ignition timing . . . . Refer to Chapter 5B
Spark plugs:
   2.0 litre engine . . . . Bosch FR 5 DP 1 X or Motorcraft AGPR 12P
   2.3 litre engine . . . . Bosch FR 7 DPP 22 U or Motorcraft AGPR 22P1
Spark plug electrode gap . . . . 1.0 mm

Brakes

Front brake pad minimum thickness (including backing) . . . . 7.0 mm
Rear brake pad minimum thickness (including backing) . . . . 7.0 mm

Auxiliary drivebelt

Tension adjustment . . . . Automatically adjusted

Torque wrench settings

	Nm	lbf ft
Automatic transmission drain plug	15	11
Final drive filler plug (automatic transmission)	20	15
Ignition coils (2.3 litre engine)	10	7
Ignition coils cover (2.3 litre engine)	5	4
Manual transmission drain plug	35	26
Manual transmission filler/level plug	35	26
Roadwheel bolts:		
Except 16 in aluminium wheels	140	103
16 in aluminium wheels	170	125
Spark plugs	18	13
Sump drain plug	25	18

The maintenance intervals in this manual are provided with the assumption that you, not the dealer, will be carrying out the work. These are the minimum intervals recommended by us for vehicles driven daily. If you wish to keep your vehicle in peak condition at all times, you may wish to perform some of these procedures more often. We encourage frequent maintenance, since it enhances the efficiency, performance and resale value of your vehicle. **Note**: *The mileage conversions from kilometres are approximate.*

All Ford Galaxy models are equipped with a service interval display indicator in the instrument panel. Every time the engine is started the panel will illuminate for approximately 1 minute, displaying one of the following:

OIL – *Oil change service – every 10 000 miles (15 000 km) or 12 months whichever occurs first*

IN01 – *Inspection service – every 10 000 miles (15 000 km) or 12 months whichever occurs first*

IN02 – *Inspection service – every 30 000 miles (45 000 km) or 36 months whichever occurs first*

This is basically a reminder that a service is due, eg, when the Ford technician completes an oil change service, the display indicator is reprogrammed to show OIL when another 15 000 km have been covered. The indicator is programmed in km, even if the vehicle has mileage indication.

Every 250 miles (400 km) or weekly

☐ Refer to *Weekly checks*

Every 10 000 miles (15 000 km) or 12 months (whichever occurs first) – OIL or IN01 on interval display

☐ Renew the engine oil and filter (Section 3)

Note: *Frequent oil and filter changes are good for the engine. We recommend changing the oil more frequently than the mileage specified here, or at least twice a year.*

☐ Check condition of the auxiliary drivebelt (Section 4)
☐ Reset the service interval display (Section 5)
☐ Check the operation of the windscreen/tailgate washer system(s) (Section 6)
☐ Lubricate all hinges and locks (Section 7)
☐ Check the battery electrolyte level (Section 8)
☐ Check the cooling system for antifreeze content (Section 9)
☐ Engine management ECM memory fault code check (Section 10)
☐ Check the tyre wear (Section 11)
☐ Check all underbonnet components and hoses for fluid leaks (Section 12)
☐ Check all brake flexible hoses and rigid pipes for condition (Section 13)
☐ Check the front brake pad thickness and disc condition (Section 14)
☐ Check the rear brake pad thickness and disc condition (Section 15)
☐ Check the condition of the exhaust system and its mountings (Section 16)
☐ Check and if necessary adjust the handbrake (Section 17)
☐ Check the steering and suspension components for condition and security (Section 18)
☐ Carry out a road test (Section 19)
☐ Check the tightness of the roadwheel bolts (Section 20)
☐ Renew the pollen filter (Section 21)
☐ Check the underbody sealant (Section 22)

Every 2 years (regardless of mileage)

☐ Renew the remote handset battery (Section 23)
☐ Renew the brake/clutch fluid (Section 24)
☐ Renew the coolant (Section 25)

Every 30 000 miles (45 000 km) or 3 years (whichever occurs first) – IN02 on interval display

Note: *Carry out the following work in addition to that described for the 12 months interval.*

☐ Check manual transmission oil level (Section 26)
☐ Check the headlight beam adjustment (Section 27)
☐ Renew the spark plugs (Section 28)
☐ Check the automatic transmission final drive level (Section 29)
☐ Check the automatic transmission fluid level (Section 30)
☐ Renew the secondary air injection filter (Section 31)
☐ Carry out an exhaust emissions check (Section 32)

Every 40 000 miles (60 000 km) or 4 years (whichever occurs first)

☐ Renew the air filter element (Section 33)

Every 80 000 miles (120 000 km)

☐ Renew the auxiliary drivebelt (Section 34)

Underbonnet view of a 2.3 litre model

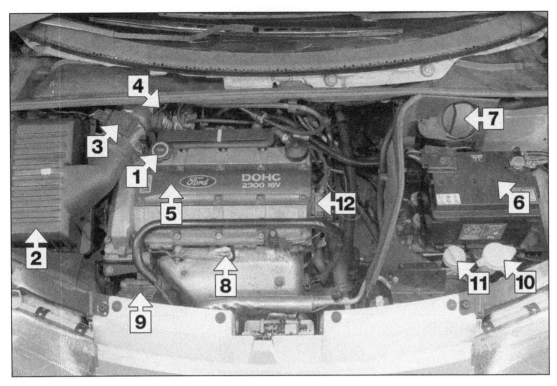

1 Engine oil filler cap
2 Air cleaner
3 Mass airflow meter
4 Brake/clutch fluid reservoir
5 Ignition coils/spark plugs cover
6 Battery
7 Coolant expansion tank
8 Engine oil level dipstick
9 Alternator
10 Washer fluid reservoir
11 Power steering fluid reservoir
12 Radio suppressor

Front underbody view of a 2.3 litre model

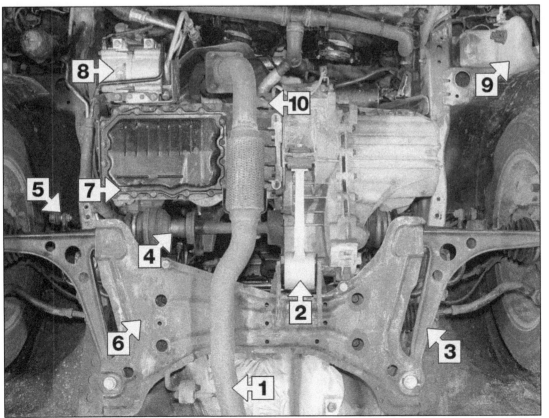

1 Exhaust front pipe
2 Engine roll restrictor
3 Lower suspension arm
4 Driveshaft
5 Anti-roll bar
6 Front crossmember
7 Engine sump oil drain plug
8 Air-conditioning compressor
9 Washer fluid reservoir
10 Oxygen sensor

Rear underbody view

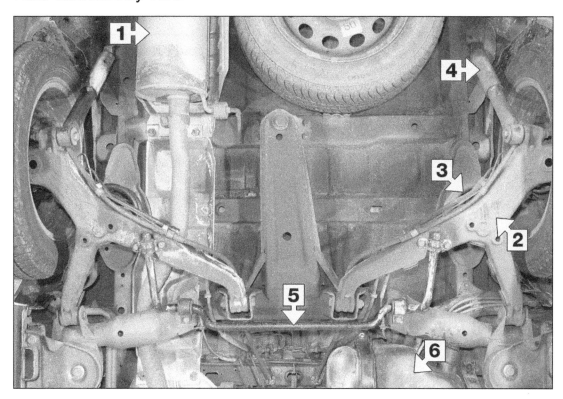

1 Exhaust tail pipe and
  silencer
2 Suspension trailing
  arm
3 Coil spring
4 Shock absorber
5 Anti-roll bar
6 Fuel tank

1 Introduction

This Chapter is designed to help the home mechanic maintain his/her vehicle for safety, economy, long life and peak performance.

The Chapter contains a master maintenance schedule, followed by Sections dealing specifically with each task in the schedule. Visual checks, adjustments, component renewal and other helpful items are included. Refer to the accompanying illustrations of the engine compartment and the underside of the vehicle for the locations of the various components.

Servicing your vehicle in accordance with the mileage/time maintenance schedule and the following Sections will provide a planned maintenance programme, which should result in a long and reliable service life. This is a comprehensive plan, so maintaining some items but not others at the specified service intervals, will not produce the same results.

As you service your vehicle, you will discover that many of the procedures can – and should – be grouped together, because of the particular procedure being performed, or because of the proximity of two otherwise unrelated components to one another. For example, if the vehicle is raised for any reason, the exhaust can be inspected at the same time as the suspension and steering components.

The first step in this maintenance programme is to prepare yourself before the actual work begins. Read through all the Sections relevant to the work to be carried out, then make a list and gather all the parts and tools required. If a problem is encountered, seek advice from a parts specialist, or a dealer service department.

2 Regular maintenance

1 If, from the time the vehicle is new, the routine maintenance schedule is followed closely, and frequent checks are made of fluid levels and high-wear items, as suggested throughout this manual, the engine will be kept in relatively good running condition, and the need for additional work will be minimised.
2 It is possible that there will be times when the engine is running poorly due to the lack of regular maintenance. This is even more likely if a used vehicle, which has not received regular and frequent maintenance checks, is purchased. In such cases, additional work may need to be carried out, outside of the regular maintenance intervals.
3 If engine wear is suspected, a compression test (refer to the relevant Part of Chapter 2) will provide valuable information regarding the overall performance of the main internal components. Such a test can be used as a basis to decide on the extent of the work to be carried out. If, for example, a compression test indicates serious internal engine wear, conventional maintenance as described in this Chapter will not greatly improve the performance of the engine, and may prove a waste of time and money, unless extensive overhaul work is carried out first.
4 The following series of operations are those most often required to improve the performance of a generally poor-running engine:

Primary operations

a) Clean, inspect and test the battery (See 'Weekly checks').
b) Check all the engine-related fluids (See 'Weekly checks').
c) Check the condition of the auxiliary drivebelt (Sections 4 and 34).
d) Renew the spark plugs (Section 28).
e) Inspect the ignition system components (Chapter 5B).
f) Check the condition of the air filter, and renew if necessary (Section 25).
g) Check the condition of all hoses, and check for fluid leaks (Sections 12 and 13).
5 If the above operations do not prove fully effective, carry out the following secondary operations:

Secondary operations

All items listed under *Primary operations*, plus the following:
a) Check the charging system (Chapter 5A).
b) Check the ignition system (Chapter 5B).
c) Check the fuel system (Chapter 4A).

Every 10 000 miles (15 000 km) or 12 months (whichever occurs first) – OIL or IN01 on interval display

3 Engine oil and filter renewal

1 Frequent oil and filter changes are the most important maintenance procedures which can be undertaken by the DIY owner. As engine oil ages, it becomes diluted and contaminated, which leads to premature engine wear.

2 Before starting this procedure, gather all the necessary tools and materials. Also make sure that you have plenty of clean rags and newspapers handy, to mop up any spills. Ideally, the engine oil should be warm, as it will drain better, and more built-up sludge will be removed with it. Take care, however, not to touch the exhaust or any other hot parts of the engine when working under the vehicle. To avoid any possibility of scalding, and to protect yourself from possible skin irritants and other harmful contaminants in used engine oils, it is advisable to wear gloves when carrying out this work. Access to the underside of the vehicle is possible if it can be raised on a lift, driven onto ramps, or jacked up and supported on axle stands (see *Jacking and vehicle support*). Whichever method is chosen, make sure that the vehicle remains level, or if it is at an angle, that the drain plug is at the lowest point. With the vehicle raised, remove the engine compartment undershield (four bolts, two nuts) **(see illustration)**.

3 Using a socket and wrench or a ring spanner, slacken the drain plug about half a turn. Position the draining container under the drain plug, then remove the plug completely **(see Haynes Hint)**. Recover the sealing ring from the drain plug **(see illustration)**.

4 Allow some time for the old oil to drain, noting that it may be necessary to reposition the container as the oil flow slows to a trickle.

5 After all the oil has drained, wipe off the drain plug with a clean rag, and fit a new sealing washer. Clean the area around the drain plug opening, and refit the plug. Tighten the plug to the specified torque.

6 If the filter is also to be renewed, move the container into position under the oil filter, which is located on the left-hand rear side of the cylinder block.

7 Using an oil filter removal tool if necessary, slacken the filter initially, then unscrew it by hand the rest of the way **(see illustration)**. Empty the oil in the filter into the container.

8 Use a clean rag to remove all oil, dirt and sludge from the filter sealing area on the engine. Check the old filter to make sure that the rubber sealing ring has not stuck to the engine. If it has, carefully remove it.

9 Apply a light coating of clean engine oil to the sealing ring on the new filter, then screw it into position on the engine. Tighten the filter firmly by hand only – **do not** use any tools.

10 Remove the old oil and all tools from under the car then refit the undershield and lower the car to the ground.

11 Remove the dipstick, then unscrew the oil

filler cap from the cylinder head cover **(see illustration)**. Fill the engine, using the correct grade and type of oil (see *Lubricants and fluids*). An oil can spout or funnel may help to reduce spillage. Pour in half the specified quantity of oil first, then wait a few minutes for the oil to settle in the sump. Continue adding oil a small quantity at a time until the level is up to the lower mark on the dipstick. Adding around 1.0 litre will bring the level up to the upper mark on the dipstick. Refit the filler cap.

12 Start the engine and run it at idle speed for a few minutes; check for leaks around the oil filter seal and the sump drain plug. Note that there may be a few seconds delay before the oil pressure warning light goes out when the engine is started, as the oil circulates through the engine oil galleries and the new oil filter before the pressure builds-up.

13 Switch off the engine, and wait a few minutes for the oil to settle in the sump once more. With the new oil circulated and the filter completely full, recheck the level on the dipstick, and add more oil as necessary.

14 Dispose of the used engine oil safely, with reference to *General repair procedures* in the *Reference* section of this manual.

3.2 Undo the nut and two bolts each side (arrowed), then remove the engine undershield

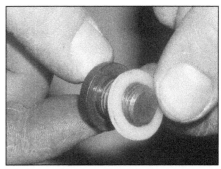

3.3 Recover the sealing ring from the drain plug

HAYNES HiNT

As the drain plug releases from the threads, move it away quickly so that the stream of oil running out of the sump goes into the drain pan and not up your sleeve.

3.7 Using a filter removal tool if necessary, slacken the filter

3.11 Unscrew the oil filler cap from the cylinder head cover

4 Auxiliary drivebelt condition and tension check

1 The auxiliary drivebelt drives the alternator, coolant pump, power steering pump, and where fitted, the air conditioning compressor.
2 For access to the drivebelt, apply the handbrake, then jack up the front of the vehicle and support it on axle stands (see *Jacking and vehicle support*). Undo the four bolts and two nuts, and remove the engine undershield **(see illustration 3.2)**.
3 Examine the auxiliary drivebelt along its entire length for damage and wear in the form of cuts and abrasions, fraying and cracking. The use of a mirror and possibly an electric torch will help, and the engine may be turned with a spanner on the crankshaft pulley in order to observe all areas of the belt.
4 If a drivebelt requires renewal, refer to Chapter 2A for the removal, refitting and adjustment procedure.

5 Service interval display resetting

1 In order to reset the service interval display, Ford technicians use specialist diagnostic equipment. However, in the absence of this equipment, the display can be reset as follows. With the ignition off, press the trip mileage reset button and hold it in. Turn the ignition on, and after approximately 4 seconds, the display should reset. Release the button, and turn off the ignition.

6 Washer system(s) operation check

1 Check that each of the washer jet nozzles are clear and that each nozzle provides a strong jet of washer fluid. The jets should be aimed to spray at a point slightly above the centre of the screen. The washer jets aim can be adjusted with a fine pin **(see illustration)**.
2 Carry out a check of all wiper blades. Look

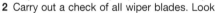
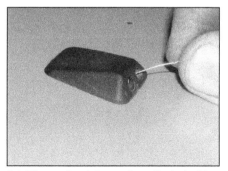

6.1 The washer jets can be adjusted with a fine pin

for splits or cracks on the wiping surface and renew as necessary. Check that the wipers clean efficiently across their entire sweep; any gaps in the swept area may be caused by defective wiper blade hinges, preventing the blade from following the contours of the screen/lens surface. Check that the wiper blades do not overshoot the edge of the screen/lens at the end of their sweep and that the blades park in the correct position when switched off. If this is not the case, or if the blades overlap each other at the midpoint of their stroke, the wiper arms may be incorrectly fitted (see Chapter 12).

7 Hinges and locks lubrication

1 Lubricate the hinges of the bonnet, doors and tailgate with a light general-purpose oil. Similarly, lubricate all latches, locks and lock strikers. At the same time, check the security and operation of all the locks, adjusting them if necessary (see Chapter 11).
2 Lightly lubricate the bonnet release mechanism and cable with a suitable grease.

8 Battery electrolyte level check

1 Where a standard (non-maintenance free) battery is fitted, the level of the electrolyte may be checked and if necessary topped-up. On some batteries, MIN and MAX marks are printed on the side of the battery and the level may be checked without removing the cell covers. Where there are no exterior marks, remove the cover(s) from the top of the cells and check that the level of the electrolyte is approximately 2 or 3 mm above the internal plates. Some batteries may have a plastic internal level indicator.
2 If necessary, top up the cells using distilled or de-ionised water.
3 Refit the cell cover(s).

9 Cooling system antifreeze concentration check

 Warning: Wait until the engine is cold before starting this procedure. Do not allow antifreeze to come in contact with your skin, or with the painted surfaces of the vehicle. Rinse off spills immediately with plenty of water.
1 Note that a tester will be required to check the coolant strength; these can be obtained relatively cheaply from most motor accessory shops.
2 With the engine completely cold, unscrew and remove the filler cap from the coolant

expansion tank. Follow the instructions supplied with the tester and check the coolant mixture is sufficient to give protection down to temperatures well below freezing. If the coolant has been renewed regularly this shouldn't be a problem. However, if the coolant mixture is not strong enough to provide sufficient protection it will be necessary to drain the cooling system and renew the coolant (see Section 25).
3 Once the test is complete, check the coolant level is correct (see *Weekly checks*) then securely refit the expansion tank cap.

10 Engine management ECM memory fault code check

This check can only be carried out by a Ford dealer or garage having the necessary equipment. If a fault code is evident, the problem must be corrected to ensure efficient operation of the engine.

11 Tyre wear check

1 Raise and securely support the relevant side of the car in turn to allow a thorough check of each tyre to be performed; refer to *Jacking and vehicle support* for reference.
2 Turn the tyre slowly by hand and carry out an inspection as described in *Weekly checks*.
3 Lower the vehicle to the ground.

12 Underbonnet/underbody components and hoses fluid leak check

1 For access to the bottom of the engine, jack up the front of the vehicle and support it on axle stands (see *Jacking and vehicle support*). Undo the two retaining nuts and four bolts (two each side), and remove the undershield. Visually inspect the engine joint faces, gaskets and seals for any signs of water or oil leaks. Pay particular attention to the areas around the camshaft cover, cylinder head, oil filter and sump joint faces. Bear in mind that, over a period of time, some very slight seepage from these areas is to be expected – what you are really looking for is any indication of a serious leak. Should a leak be found, renew the offending gasket or oil seal by referring to the appropriate Chapters in this manual.
2 Also check the security and condition of all the engine-related pipes and hoses. Ensure that all cable-ties or securing clips are in place and in good condition. Clips which are broken or missing can lead to chafing of the hoses, pipes or wiring, which could cause more serious problems in the future.
3 Carefully check the radiator hoses and

heater hoses along their entire length. Renew any hose which is cracked, swollen or deteriorated. Cracks will show up better if the hose is squeezed. Pay close attention to the hose clips that secure the hoses to the cooling system components. Hose clips can pinch and puncture hoses, resulting in cooling system leaks.

4 Inspect all the cooling system components (hoses, joint faces, etc) for leaks **(see Haynes Hint)**. Where any problems of this nature are found on system components, renew the component or gasket with reference to Chapter 3.

5 Where applicable, inspect the automatic transmission fluid cooler hoses for leaks or deterioration.

6 With the vehicle raised at the rear, inspect the petrol tank and filler neck for punctures, cracks and other damage. The connection between the filler neck and tank is especially critical. Sometimes a rubber filler neck or connecting hose will leak due to loose retaining clamps or deteriorated rubber.

7 Carefully check all rubber hoses and metal fuel lines leading away from the petrol tank. Check for loose connections, deteriorated hoses, crimped lines, and other damage. Pay particular attention to the vent pipes and hoses, which often loop up around the filler neck and can become blocked or crimped. Follow the lines to the front of the vehicle, carefully inspecting them all the way. Renew damaged sections as necessary.

8 From within the engine compartment, check the security of all fuel hose attachments and pipe unions, and inspect the fuel hoses and vacuum hoses for kinks, chafing and deterioration.

9 Check the condition of the power steering fluid hoses and pipes.

10 On completion, refit the undershield, and lower the vehicle to the ground.

13 Brake flexible hoses and rigid pipes condition check

1 Inspect all the braking system flexible hoses and metal pipes for signs of damage or deterioration. Any faulty pipe/hoses must be renewed (see Chapter 9).

14 Front brake pad thickness and disc condition check

1 Firmly apply the handbrake, loosen the front roadwheel bolts, then jack up the front of the car and support it securely on axle stands (see *Jacking and vehicle support*). Remove the front roadwheels.

2 For a comprehensive check, the brake pads should be removed and cleaned. The operation of the caliper can then also be checked, and the condition of the brake disc

A leak in the cooling system will usually show up as white- or rust- coloured crusty deposits on the area surrounding the leak.

itself can be fully examined on both sides. Refer to Chapter 9 **(see illustration)**.

3 If any pad's friction material is worn to the specified thickness or less, *all four pads must be renewed as a set*. **Note:** *If any pad is approaching the minimum thickness, consider renewal as a precautionary measure in case the pads wear out before the next service.*

4 On completion, refit the roadwheels and lower the vehicle to the ground.

15 Rear brake pad thickness and disc condition check

1 Firmly chock the front wheels and select first gear or PARK, then jack up the rear of the vehicle and support it securely on axle stands (see *Jacking and vehicle support*). Remove the rear roadwheels.

2 For a quick check, the pad thickness can be carried out via the inspection hole on the rear of the caliper. Using a steel rule, measure the thickness of the pad lining including the backing plate. This must not be less than that indicated in the Specifications.

3 The view through the caliper inspection hole gives a rough indication of the state of the brake pads. For a comprehensive check, the brake pads should be removed and cleaned. The operation of the caliper can then

14.2 The thickness of the brake pad, including the backing plate, must not be less than 7 mm

also be checked, and the condition of the brake disc itself can be fully examined on both sides. Chapter 9 contains a detailed description of how the brake disc should be checked for wear and/or damage.

4 If any pad's friction material is worn to the specified thickness or less, *all four pads must be renewed as a set*. **Note:** *If any pad is approaching the minimum thickness, consider renewal as a precautionary measure in case the pads wear out before the next service.* Refer to Chapter 9 for details.

5 On completion, refit the roadwheels and lower the vehicle to the ground.

16 Exhaust system and mountings condition check

1 With the engine cold, check the complete exhaust system from the engine to the end of the tailpipe. The exhaust system is most easily checked with the vehicle raised on a hoist, or suitably supported on axle stands, so that the exhaust components are readily visible and accessible.

2 Check the exhaust pipes and connections for evidence of leaks, severe corrosion and damage. Make sure that all brackets and mountings are in good condition, and that all relevant nuts and bolts are tight **(see illustration)**. Leakage at any of the joints or in other parts of the system will usually show up as a black sooty stain in the vicinity of the leak.

3 Rattles and other noises can often be traced to the exhaust system, especially the brackets and mountings. If the components are able to come into contact with the body or suspension parts, secure the system with new mountings. Otherwise separate the joints (if possible) and twist the pipes as necessary to provide additional clearance.

17 Handbrake check and adjustment

1 With the vehicle on level ground, chock the

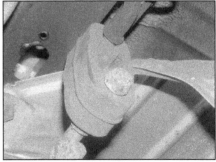

16.2 Check the condition of the exhaust mountings

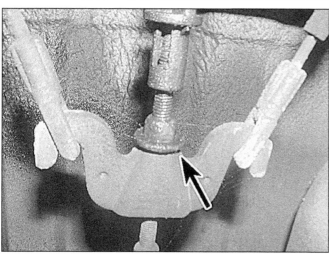

17.3 Turn the adjuster locknut (arrowed) to adjust the handbrake lever

18.4 Check for signs of wear in the hub bearings by grasping the roadwheel at the 12 o'clock and 6 o'clock positions, and trying to rock it

front wheels and release the handbrake lever. Gradually apply the handbrake, counting the number of clicks from the ratchet mechanism until the handbrake is fully applied. If the adjustment is correct, there should be 3 to 6 clicks before the handbrake is fully applied. If this is not the case, adjust as follows.

2 Ensure the front wheel chocks are still in place, jack up the rear of the vehicle and support it on axle stands (see *Jacking and vehicle support*). Fully release the handbrake lever.

3 Working underneath the vehicle, rotate the adjuster locknut in the required direction to achieve the correct lever adjustment **(see illustration)**.

4 With the handbrake fully released, check that the rear wheels rotate freely, with no signs of binding or resistance.

5 Once the adjustment is correct, lower the vehicle to the ground.

18 Steering and suspension components condition/security check

Suspension and steering

1 Raise the front of the vehicle, and securely support it on axle stands.

2 Visually inspect the balljoint dust covers and the steering rack gaiters for splits, chafing or deterioration. Any wear of these components will cause loss of lubricant, together with dirt and water entry, resulting in rapid deterioration of the balljoints or steering gear.

3 On vehicles with power steering, check the fluid hoses for chafing or deterioration, and the pipe and hose unions for fluid leaks. Also check for signs of fluid leakage under pressure from the steering gear rubber

gaiters, which would indicate failed fluid seals within the steering gear.

4 Grasp the roadwheel at the 12 o'clock and 6 o'clock positions, and try to rock it **(see illustration)**. Very slight free play may be felt, but if the movement is appreciable, further investigation is necessary to determine the source. Continue rocking the wheel while an assistant depresses the footbrake. If the movement is now eliminated or significantly reduced, it is likely that the hub bearings are at fault. If the free play is still evident with the footbrake depressed, then there is wear in the suspension joints or mountings.

5 Now grasp the wheel at the 9 o'clock and 3 o'clock positions, and try to rock it as before. Any movement felt now may again be caused by wear in the hub bearings or the steering track rod balljoints. If the inner or outer balljoint is worn, the visual movement will be obvious.

6 Using a large screwdriver or flat bar, check for wear in the suspension mounting bushes by levering between the relevant suspension component and its attachment point. Some movement is to be expected as the mountings are made of rubber, but excessive wear should be obvious. Also check the condition of any visible rubber bushes, looking for splits, cracks or contamination of the rubber.

7 With the car standing on its wheels, have an assistant turn the steering wheel back-and-forth about an eighth of a turn each way. There should be very little, if any, lost movement between the steering wheel and roadwheels. If this is not the case, closely observe the joints and mountings previously described, but in addition, check the steering column universal joints for wear, and the rack-and-pinion steering gear itself.

Strut/shock absorbers

8 Check for any signs of fluid leakage around

the suspension strut/shock absorber body, or from the rubber gaiter around the piston rod. Should any fluid be noticed, the suspension strut/shock absorber is defective internally, and should be renewed. **Note:** *Suspension struts/shock absorbers should always be renewed in pairs on the same axle.*

9 The efficiency of the suspension strut/shock absorber may be checked by bouncing the vehicle at each corner. Generally speaking, the body will return to its normal position and stop after being depressed. If it rises and returns on a rebound, the suspension strut/shock absorber is probably suspect. Examine also the suspension strut/shock absorber upper and lower mountings for any signs of wear.

Driveshafts

10 With the vehicle raised and securely supported on stands, turn the steering onto full lock then slowly rotate the roadwheel. Inspect the condition of the outer constant velocity (CV) joint rubber gaiters while squeezing the gaiters to open out the folds. Check for signs of cracking, splits or deterioration of the rubber which may allow the grease to escape and lead to water and grit entry into the joint. Also check the security and condition of the retaining clips. Repeat these checks on the inner CV joints. If any damage or deterioration is found, the gaiters should be renewed as described in Chapter 8, Section 3.

11 At the same time check the general condition of the CV joints themselves by first holding the driveshaft and attempting to rotate the wheel. Repeat this check by holding the inner joint and attempting to rotate the driveshaft. Any appreciable movement indicates wear in the joints, wear in the driveshaft splines or loose driveshaft retaining bolt.

19 Road test

Instruments/ electrical equipment

1 Check the operation of all instruments and electrical equipment.

2 Make sure that all instruments read correctly, and switch on all electrical equipment in turn, to check that it functions properly.

Steering and suspension

3 Check for any abnormalities in the steering, suspension, handling or road feel.

4 Drive the vehicle, and check that there are no unusual vibrations or noises.

5 Check that the steering feels positive, with no excessive sloppiness, or roughness, and check for any suspension noises when cornering and driving over bumps.

Drivetrain

6 Check the performance of the engine, clutch (where applicable), gearbox/transmission and driveshafts.

7 Listen for any unusual noises from the engine, clutch and gearbox/transmission.

21.2 **Pull out the battery compartment upper panel**

8 Make sure that the engine runs smoothly when idling, and that there is no hesitation when accelerating.

9 Check that, where applicable, the clutch action is smooth and progressive, that the drive is taken up smoothly, and that the pedal travel is not excessive. Also listen for any noises when the clutch pedal is depressed.

10 On manual gearbox models, check that all gears can be engaged smoothly without noise, and that the gear lever action is smooth and not abnormally vague or notchy.

11 On automatic transmission models, make sure that all gearchanges occur smoothly, without snatching, and without an increase in engine speed between changes. Check that all the gear positions can be selected with the vehicle at rest. If any problems are found, they should be referred to a Ford dealer.

Braking system

12 Make sure that the vehicle does not pull to one side when braking, and that the wheels do not lock when braking hard.

13 Check that there is no vibration through the steering when braking.

14 Check that the handbrake operates correctly without excessive movement of the lever, and that it holds the vehicle stationary on a slope.

15 Test the operation of the brake servo unit as follows. With the engine off, depress the footbrake four or five times to exhaust the vacuum. Hold the brake pedal depressed, then start the engine. As the engine starts, there should be a noticeable give in the brake pedal as vacuum builds-up. Allow the engine to run for at least two minutes, and then switch it off. If the brake pedal is depressed now, it should be possible to detect a hiss from the servo as the pedal is depressed. After about four or five applications, no further hissing should be heard, and the pedal should feel considerably harder.

20 Roadwheel bolts tightness check

1 With the vehicle wheels on the ground and the handbrake applied, prise off the wheel trims (where applicable), and check the tightness of the wheel bolts using a torque wrench. The correct torque setting is given at the start of this Chapter.

2 When all the bolts have been checked, refit the wheel trims (where applicable).

21 Pollen filter renewal

1 The pollen filter is located beneath the windscreen cowl panels; it is located on the right-hand side on left-hand drive models, and on the left-hand side on right-hand drive models.

2 Pull out the battery compartment upper panel (see illustration).

3 Undo the three screws and remove the bulkhead trim (see illustration). Slide the trim to the right-hand side and manoeuvre it from behind the coolant expansion tank.

4 Ensure that the area around the filter is cleared of all leaves, debris, etc, as when the filter is removed, this will be able to enter the vehicle interior.

5 Release the retaining clip, and slide the element with the frame out of the guide towards the centre of the vehicle. Manoeuvre the frame and element under the wiper linkage, and out from the engine compartment (see illustration).

6 Remove the filter element from the frame.

7 Fit the new element onto the frame, with the air flow arrows pointing towards the vehicle interior, ensuring that the left and right ends of the frame fit into the first laminations at each end of the element. Ensure also that the

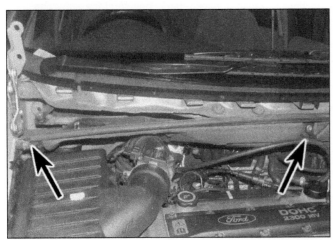

21.3 **Undo the screws (two arrowed) and remove the bulkhead panel**

21.5 **Release the pollen filter retaining clip (arrowed)**

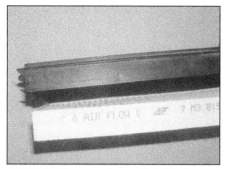

21.7a Fit the new element into the frame with the air flow arrows pointing to the vehicle interior . . .

21.7b . . . and the ends of the frame located into the first and last laminations of the filter

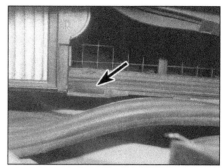

21.8 The lugs on the frame must engage with the guide slots in the housing (arrowed)

square pegs of the frame locate in the filter laminations **(see illustrations)**.

8 Guide the frame and element under the wiper linkage and slide it into position, ensuring that the guide lugs on the frame engage correctly with the guide slots in the housing, and the retaining clip locks the assembly in place **(see illustration)**.

9 The remainder of the refitting procedure is a reversal of removal.

22 Underbody sealant check

Raise and support the vehicle on axle stands (see *Jacking and vehicle support*). Using an electric torch or lead light, inspect the entire underside of the vehicle, paying particular attention to the wheelarches. Look for any damage to the flexible underbody coating, which may crack or flake off with age, leading to corrosion. Also check that the wheelarch liners (where fitted) are securely attached with any clips provided – if they come loose, dirt may get in behind the liners and defeat their purpose. If there is any damage to the underseal, or any corrosion, it should be repaired before the damage gets too serious.

Every 2 years (regardless of mileage)

23 Handset battery renewal

1 Carefully prise the handset body from the key blade **(see illustration)**.

2 Using a small screwdriver release the retaining clips and separate the halves of the handset body **(see illustration)**.

3 Gently push back the clips and lift the first battery, dividing plate, and second battery from the handset.

4 Insert the first new battery, positive side up, into the handset **(see illustration)**.

5 Place the dividing plate on top of the first battery **(see illustration)**.

6 Insert the second battery, again positive side up, making sure it is held in place by the retaining clips.

7 Fit the halves of the handset together, and slide it back into the key blade.

8 It may be the case that the handset will not function correctly after battery replacement. If this is the case the handset must be resynchronised. Unfortunately, this procedure varies from model year to model year, although the Owners Handbook supplied with the vehicle contains details of the procedure.

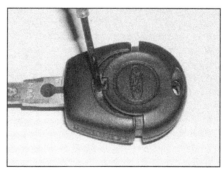

23.1 Prise the handset body from the key blade

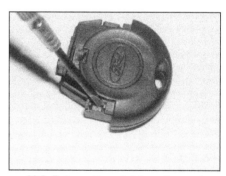

23.2 Release the retaining clips and separate the halves of the body

23.4 Insert the first battery, positive (+) side up

23.5 Place the dividing plate on the first battery

24 Brake/clutch fluid renewal

 Warning: Brake hydraulic fluid can harm your eyes and damage painted surfaces, so use extreme caution when handling and pouring it. Do not use fluid that has been standing open for some time, as it absorbs moisture from the air. Excess moisture can cause a dangerous loss of braking effectiveness.

Brakes

1 The procedure is similar to that for the bleeding of the hydraulic system as described in Chapter 9.

2 On right-hand drive models, remove the air ducting assembly as described in Chapter 4A, to gain access to the master cylinder reservoir.

3 Working as described in Chapter 9, open the first bleed screw in the sequence, and pump the brake pedal gently until nearly all the old fluid has been emptied from the master cylinder reservoir. Top-up to the MAX level with new fluid, and continue pumping until only the new fluid remains in the reservoir, and new fluid can be seen emerging from the bleed screw. Tighten the screw, and top the reservoir level up to the MAX level line.

 Old hydraulic fluid is invariably much darker in colour than the new, making it easy to distinguish the two.

4 Work through all the remaining bleed screws in the sequence until new fluid can be seen at all of them. Be careful to keep the master cylinder reservoir topped-up to above the MIN level at all times, or air may enter the system and greatly increase the length of the task. The bleed screw sequence is:
 a) Left-hand front brake.
 b) Right-hand front brake.
 c) Right-hand rear brake.
 d) Left-hand rear brake.

5 When the operation is complete, check that all bleed screws are securely tightened, and that their dust caps are refitted. Wash off all traces of spilt fluid, and recheck the master cylinder reservoir fluid level. Check the operation of the brakes before taking the car on the road.

Clutch

6 Because the clutch hydraulic system shares the same fluid reservoir as the brake system, we recommend that the clutch hydraulic fluid is renewed at the same time. Working as described in Chapter 6, remove the dust cap from the slave cylinder bleed screw. Fit a spanner and tube to the screw, place the other end of the tube in a jar, and

pour in sufficient fluid to cover the end of the tube.

7 Ensure that the fluid level is maintained at least above the lower level line in the reservoir throughout the procedure.

8 Have an assistant fully depress the clutch pedal several times to build-up pressure, then maintain it on the final downstroke.

9 While pedal pressure is maintained, unscrew the bleed screw (approximately one half of a turn) and allow the compressed fluid to flow into the jar. The assistant should maintain pedal pressure and should not release it until instructed to do so. When the flow stops, tighten the bleed screw again, have the assistant release the pedal slowly, and recheck the reservoir fluid level.

10 Repeat the steps given in paragraphs 8 and 9 until the new fluid emerges from the bleed screw. If the master cylinder has been drained and refilled allow approximately five seconds between cycles for the master cylinder passages to refill.

11 Tighten the bleed screw securely, remove the tube and spanner, and refit the dust cap. Do not overtighten the bleed screw.

12 Wash off all traces of spilt fluid, and recheck the fluid level.

25 Coolant renewal

 Warning: Wait until the engine is cold before starting this procedure. Do not allow antifreeze to come in contact with your skin, or with the painted surfaces of the vehicle. Rinse off spills immediately with plenty of water. Never leave antifreeze lying around in an open container, or in a puddle in the driveway or on the garage floor. Children and pets are attracted by its sweet smell, but antifreeze can be fatal if ingested.

Cooling system draining

1 With the engine completely cold, cover the expansion tank cap with a wad of rag, and slowly turn the cap anti-clockwise to relieve the pressure in the cooling system (a hissing

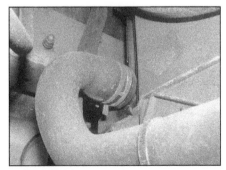

25.2 Release the retaining clip, and ease the bottom hose from the radiator stub

sound may be heard). Wait until any pressure remaining in the system is released, then continue to turn the cap until it can be removed.

2 Release the fasteners (four bolts, two nuts) and remove the engine/transmission undershield. Position a suitable container beneath the radiator bottom hose connection, then release the retaining clip and ease the hose from the radiator stub. If the hose joint has not been disturbed for some time, it will be necessary to gently manipulate the hose to break the joint. Do not use excessive force, or the radiator stub could be damaged. Allow the coolant to drain into the container **(see illustration)**.

3 If the coolant has been drained for a reason other than renewal, then provided it is clean and less than two years old, it can be re-used if there is no alternative, but this is not recommended. **Note:** *If an aluminium engine component which comes into contact with the coolant has been renewed, then the coolant must also be renewed. Used coolant will not protect new aluminium from corrosion.*

4 Once all the coolant has drained, reconnect the hose to the radiator and refit the retaining clip.

Cooling system flushing

5 If coolant renewal has been neglected, or if the antifreeze mixture has become diluted, then in time, the cooling system may gradually lose efficiency, as the coolant passages become restricted due to rust, scale deposits, and other sediment. Flushing the system clean can restore the cooling system efficiency.

6 The radiator should be flushed independently of the engine, to avoid unnecessary contamination.

Radiator flushing

7 To flush the radiator, disconnect the top and bottom hoses and any other relevant hoses from the radiator, with reference to Chapter 3.

8 Insert a garden hose into the radiator top inlet. Direct a flow of clean water through the radiator, and continue flushing until clean water emerges from the radiator bottom outlet.

9 If after a reasonable period, the water still does not run clear, the radiator can be flushed with a good proprietary cooling system cleaning agent. It is important that their manufacturer's instructions are followed carefully. If the contamination is particularly bad, insert the hose in the radiator bottom outlet, and reverse-flush the radiator.

Engine flushing

10 To flush the engine, remove the thermostat as described in Chapter 3, then temporarily refit the thermostat cover.

11 With the top and bottom hoses disconnected from the radiator, insert a garden hose into the radiator top hose. Direct a clean flow of water through the engine, and

continue flushing until clean water emerges from the radiator bottom hose.

12 On completion of flushing, refit the thermostat and reconnect the hoses with reference to Chapter 3.

Cooling system filling

13 Before attempting to fill the cooling system, make sure that all hoses and clips are in good condition, and that the clips/connections are secure. Note that an antifreeze mixture must be used all year round, to prevent corrosion of the engine components (see following sub-Section).

14 Remove the expansion tank filler cap, and fill the system by slowly pouring the coolant into the expansion tank to prevent airlocks from forming.

15 If the coolant is being renewed, begin by pouring in a couple of litres of water, followed by the correct quantity of antifreeze, then top-up with more water.

16 Once the level in the expansion tank starts to rise, squeeze the radiator top and bottom hoses to help expel any trapped air in the system. Once all the air is expelled, top-up the coolant level to the MAX mark, refit the expansion tank cap.

17 Start the engine and run it at a fast idle for about three minutes. After this, allow the engine to idle normally until the bottom hose becomes hot.

18 Check for leaks, particularly around disturbed components. Check the coolant level in the expansion tank, and top-up if necessary. Note that the system must be cold before an accurate level is indicated in the expansion tank. If the expansion tank cap is removed while the engine is still warm, cover the cap with a thick cloth, and unscrew the cap slowly to gradually relieve the system pressure (a hissing sound will normally be heard). Wait until any pressure remaining in the system is released, then continue to turn the cap until it can be removed. Never remove the cap when the engine is still hot.

Antifreeze mixture

Caution: Ford specify the use of two different coolants. Early models were filled with Motorcraft Super Plus 4 (blue/green in colour), whilst later models were filled with Motorcraft Super Plus 2000 (orange in colour). DO NOT mix these two different types of coolant. If the coolant visible in the expansion tank is any colour other than blue/green or orange, then the cooling system may have been topped-up with coolant containing the wrong type of antifreeze. If you are unsure of the type of antifreeze used, or if you suspect that mixing may have occurred, the best course of action is to drain, flush and refill the cooling system. Note that Ford specify the coolant should be changed after a period of two to ten years, depending on coolant type and model year. However, we consider it prudent to change the coolant after two years, regardless of coolant type.

19 The antifreeze should always be renewed at the specified intervals. This is necessary not only to maintain the antifreeze properties, but also to prevent corrosion, which would otherwise occur as the corrosion inhibitors become progressively less effective.

20 The quantity of antifreeze and levels of protection are indicated in the Specifications.

21 Before adding antifreeze, the cooling system should be completely drained, preferably flushed, and all hoses checked for condition and security.

22 After filling with antifreeze, a label should be attached to the expansion tank, stating the type and concentration of antifreeze used, and the date installed. Any subsequent topping-up should be made with the same type and concentration of antifreeze.

23 Do not use engine antifreeze in the windscreen/tailgate/headlight washer system, as it will cause damage to the vehicle paintwork.

Every 30 000 miles (45 000 km) or 3 years (whichever occurs first) – IN02 on interval display

26 Manual transmission oil level check

1 The oil filler/level plug is located on the front side of the manual transmission.

2 Apply the handbrake, then jack up the front and rear of the vehicle and support it on axle stands (see *Jacking and vehicle support*). To ensure an accurate check, make sure that the vehicle is level. Undo the two retaining nuts and four bolts (two each side), and remove the engine/transmission undershield.

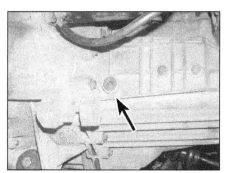

26.3 Unscrew and remove the filler/level plug (arrowed)

3 Unscrew and remove the filler/level plug (see illustration).

4 Check that the oil level is to the bottom lip of the filler hole.

5 If necessary, add the specified oil through the filler/level hole. If the level requires constant topping-up, check for leaks and repair.

6 Refit the plug and tighten to the specified torque. Refit the engine/transmission undershield, then lower the vehicle to the ground.

27 Headlight beam adjustment

1 Accurate adjustment of the headlight beam is only possible using optical beam setting equipment, and this work should therefore be carried out by a Ford dealer or suitably-equipped workshop.

2 For reference, the headlights can be adjusted using the adjuster screws, accessible via the top of each light unit (see the illustrations given in Chapter 12, Section 9).

3 Some models are equipped with an electrically-operated headlight beam adjustment system which is controlled through the switch in the facia. On these models, ensure that the switch is set to the basic 0 position before adjusting the headlight aim.

28 Spark plug renewal

1 The correct functioning of the spark plugs is vital for the correct running and efficiency of the engine. It is essential that the plugs fitted are appropriate for the engine (a suitable type is specified at the beginning of this Chapter). If this type is used and the engine is in good condition, the spark plugs should not need attention between scheduled replacement intervals. Spark plug cleaning is rarely necessary, and should not be attempted unless specialised equipment is available, as damage can easily be caused to the firing ends.

2.0 litre engines

2 If the marks on the original-equipment spark plug (HT) leads cannot be seen, mark the leads 1 to 4, to correspond to the cylinder the lead serves (No 1 cylinder is at the

28.3 Remove the cover (arrowed) from the ignition coils

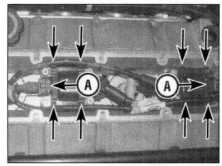

28.4 Release the wiring from the retaining clips (arrowed), then disconnect the wiring plugs (A) from the coils

28.5a Squeeze the retaining tabs and disconnect the HT leads from the coils . . .

timing chain end of the engine). Pull the leads from the plugs by gripping the end fitting, not the lead, otherwise the lead connection may be fractured.

2.3 litre engines

3 Undo the retaining bolts and remove the ignition coils cover from the top of the engine **(see illustration)**.
4 Release the wiring harness from the retaining clips on the coils, and disconnect the wiring plugs **(see illustration)**.
5 Release the HT leads from the retaining clips on the coils, and disconnect the HT lead connectors from the spark plugs. Pull the leads from the plugs by gripping the end fitting, not the lead, otherwise the lead connection may be fractured **(see illustrations)**.

6 Slacken and remove the retaining screws, and remove the ignition coils **(see illustration)**. Note that the HT connections on the underside of the coils locate directly onto the spark plugs beneath them.

All engines

7 It is advisable to remove the dirt from the spark plug recesses using a clean brush, vacuum cleaner or compressed air before removing the plugs, to prevent dirt dropping into the cylinders.
8 Unscrew the plugs using a spark plug spanner, suitable box spanner or a deep socket and extension bar **(see illustration)**. Keep the socket aligned with the spark plug – if it is forcibly moved to one side, the ceramic insulator may be broken off. As each plug is removed, examine it as follows.

9 Examination of the spark plugs will give a good indication of the condition of the engine. If the insulator nose of the spark plug is clean and white, with no deposits, this is indicative of a weak mixture or too hot a plug (a hot plug transfers heat away from the electrode slowly, a cold plug transfers heat away quickly).
10 If the tip and insulator nose are covered with hard black-looking deposits, then this is indicative that the mixture is too rich. Should the plug be black and oily, then it is likely that the engine is fairly worn, as well as the mixture being too rich.
11 If the insulator nose is covered with light tan to greyish-brown deposits, then the mixture is correct and it is likely that the engine is in good condition.
12 The spark plug electrode gap is of considerable importance as, if it is too large or too small, the size of the spark and its efficiency will be seriously impaired. On engines fitted with multi-electrode spark plugs, it is recommended that the plugs are renewed rather than attempting to adjust the gaps. With other spark plugs, the gap should be set to the value given by the manufacturer.
13 To set the gap, measure it with a feeler blade and then bend open, or closed, the outer plug electrode until the correct gap is achieved. The centre electrode should never be bent, as this may crack the insulator and cause plug failure, if nothing worse. If using feeler blades, the gap is correct when the appropriate-size blade is a firm sliding fit **(see illustrations)**.

28.5b . . . then pull the HT leads from the spark plugs

28.6 Undo the coil retaining screws (arrowed)

28.8 Unscrew the spark plugs using a deep socket or similar

28.13a Check the electrode gap using a feeler gauge . . .

28.13b . . . or wire gauge

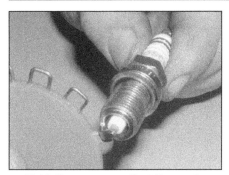

28.14 If necessary, adjust the gap by bending the electrode

14 Special spark plug electrode gap adjusting tools are available from most motor accessory shops, or from some spark plug manufacturers **(see illustration)**.

15 Before fitting the spark plugs, check that the threaded connector sleeves are tight, and that the plug exterior surfaces and threads are clean. It's often difficult to screw in new spark plugs without cross-threading them – this can be avoided using a piece of rubber hose **(see Haynes Hint)**.

16 Remove the rubber hose (if used), and tighten the plug to the specified torque using the spark plug socket and a torque wrench. Refit the remaining spark plugs in the same manner.

17 The remainder of refitting is a reversal of refitting.

29 Final drive oil level check and top-up (automatic transmission)

1 The final drive oil filler/level plug is located on the right-hand side of the automatic transmission, behind the right-hand driveshaft inner joint **(see illustration)**. Apply the handbrake, then jack up the front of the vehicle and support it on axle stands (see *Jacking and vehicle support*). Undo the two retaining nuts and four bolts (two each side), and remove the engine undershield. To ensure an accurate check, make sure that the vehicle is level.

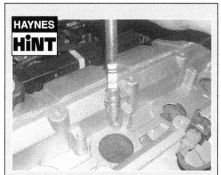

It is very often difficult to insert spark plugs into their holes without cross-threading them. To avoid this possibility, fit a short length of hose over the end of the spark plug. The flexible hose acts as a universal joint to help align the plug with the plug thread, the hose will slip on the spark plug, preventing thread damage to the aluminium cylinder head.

2 Unscrew and remove the filler/level plug and check that the oil level is on the bottom lip of the filler hole. If necessary, add the specified oil through the filler/level hole. If the level requires constant topping-up, check for leaks and repair.

3 Refit the plug and tighten to the specified torque, then lower the vehicle to the ground.

30 Automatic transmission fluid level check

Note: *For an accurate fluid level check, Ford technicians use an electronic tester which is plugged into the vehicles diagnostic socket, and establishes that the temperature of the fluid is between 35°C and 45°C via a sensor within the transmission casing. In view of this, it is recommended that the vehicle is taken to a Ford dealer or automatic transmission specialist to have the level checked.*

1 Jack up the front and rear of the vehicle and support it on axle stands (see *Jacking and*

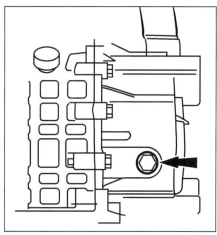

29.1 On automatic transmissions, the final drive oil filler/level plug is located on the right-hand side, behind the driveshaft inner joint (arrowed)

vehicle support). Undo the two retaining nuts and four bolts (two each side), and remove the engine undershield.

2 Note that the transmission must be refilled from below the vehicle, so make sure that the vehicle is supported in a level position.

3 Start the engine and move the selector lever through all gear positions. Switch off the engine.

4 At this point the Ford technician connects the FDS2000 tester to the vehicle's diagnostic socket, and establishes that the temperature of the transmission fluid is between 35°C and 45°C. **Note:** *If the level is checked when the temperature is too low, overfilling will occur. If the level is checked when the temperature is too high, underfilling will occur.*

5 With the vehicle still on level ground, start the engine and unscrew the level plug from under the transmission **(see illustration)**. If the level is too high, fluid will escape down the overflow pipe. Refit and tighten the level plug when the fluid ceases to drip. If the level is too low, no fluid will escape.

6 If the fluid level is too low, pull out the retaining clip and pull off the filler pipe blanking plug from the front of the transmission casing **(see illustration)**. On

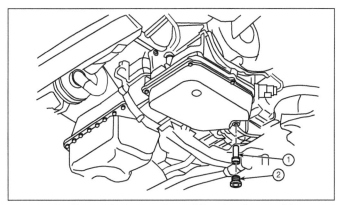

30.5 Transmission level plug (1) and drain plug (2)

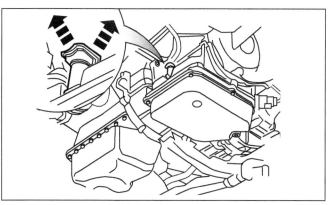

30.6 Pull out the filler cap

some models, the filler plug is secured by a cap. Prise the cap off with a s crewdriver. Using a funnel, add fluid until it begins to drip from the overflow pipe, then tighten the level plug. Always renew the sealing washer.

7 With the fluid level correct, refit the filler plug and secure it in place with the retaining clip or cap.

8 Refit the engine/transmission undertray, and lower the vehicle to the ground.

31 Secondary air injection pump filter renewal

1 Remove the battery compartment upper panel (see illustration 21.2).

2 Reach down and slacken the secondary air injection pump filter retaining clip (see illustration).

3 Pull the filter from the hose.

4 Refitting is a reversal of removal.

32 Exhaust emissions check

This check is part of the manufacturer's maintenance schedule, and involves testing the exhaust emissions using an exhaust gas analyser. Unless a fault is suspected, this test is not essential, although it should be noted that it is recommended by the manufacturers. Exhaust emissions testing is included as part of the MOT test.

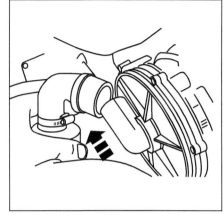

31.2 Slacken the secondary air injection pump filter retaining clip

Every 40 000 miles (60 000 km) or 4 years (whichever occurs first)

33 Air filter element renewal

1 Disconnect the mass airflow sensor wiring plug, then release the retaining clips, and

separate the sensor from the air filter cover (see illustrations).

2 On 2.3 litre engines, lift up and remove the right-hand headlight shield (see illustration).

3 On all models, release the air filter cover retaining clips, remove the cover, and lift out the element (see illustrations). Note which way around the element is fitted.

4 Wipe clean the main body, then fit the new air filter, making sure it is the correct way round.

5 Refit the upper cover and secure with the retaining clips. Where applicable refit the headlight shield.

6 Reconnect the mass airflow sensor, secure the retaining clips, then refit the wiring plug.

Every 80 000 miles (120 000 km)

34 Auxiliary drivebelt renewal

Refer to Chapter 2A, Section 6.

33.1a Disconnect the mass airflow sensor wiring plug . . .

33.1b . . . then release the retaining clips

33.2 On 2.3 litre models, slide up the headlight shield

33.3a Release the air filter cover retaining clips . . .

33.3b . . . then remove the filter

Chapter 1 Part B:
Routine maintenance and servicing – diesel models

Contents

Degrees of difficulty

| Easy, suitable for novice with little experience | | Fairly easy, suitable for beginner with some experience | | Fairly difficult, suitable for competent DIY mechanic | | Difficult, suitable for experienced DIY mechanic | | Very difficult, suitable for expert DIY or professional | |

Lubricants and fluids .... Refer to end of *Weekly checks*

Capacities

Engine oil (including filter)
All engines .... 4.3 litres (approx)

Cooling system
All models .... 9.2 litres (approx)

Transmission
Manual transmission:
   Diesel engine code AFN (81 kW) .... 2.25 litres
   All other engines .... 2.0 litres
Automatic transmission:
   Initial filling .... 5.5 litres
   Fluid change .... 3.5 litres
Automatic transmission final drive (filled for life) .... 0.8 litres

Fuel tank
All models (approx) .... 70 litres

Cooling system

Antifreeze mixture:
   50% antifreeze .... Protection down to –35°C

Brakes

Front brake pad minimum thickness (including backing) .... 7.0 mm
Rear brake pad minimum thickness (including backing) .... 7.0 mm

Auxiliary drivebelt

Tension adjustment:
   Main Poly-Vee drivebelt .... Automatically adjusted
   V-belt:
      Used belt .... 4 Nm
      New belt .... 7 Nm

Torque wrench settings	Nm	lbf ft
Automatic transmission drain plug	15	11
Final drive filler plug (automatic transmission)	20	15
Manual transmission drain plug	35	26
Manual transmission filler/level plug	35	26
Roadwheel bolts:		
Except 16 in aluminium wheels	140	103
16 in aluminium wheels	170	125
Sump drain plug	30	22

The maintenance intervals in this manual are provided with the assumption that you, not the dealer, will be carrying out the work. These are the minimum intervals recommended by us for vehicles driven daily. If you wish to keep your vehicle in peak condition at all times, you may wish to perform some of these procedures more often. We encourage frequent maintenance, since it enhances the efficiency, performance and resale value of your vehicle. **Note**: *The mileage conversions from kilometres are approximate.*

All Ford Galaxy models are equipped with a service interval display indicator in the instrument panel. Every time the engine is started the panel will illuminate for approximately 1 minute, displaying one of the following:

OIL – Oil change service – every 10 000 miles (15 000 km) or 12 months whichever occurs first
IN01 – Inspection service – every 10 000 miles (15 000 km) or 12 months whichever occurs first
IN02 – Inspection service – every 30 000 miles (45 000 km) or 36 months whichever occurs first

This is basically a reminder that a service is due, eg, when the Ford technician completes an oil change service, the display indicator is reprogrammed to show OIL when another 15 000 km have been covered. The indicator is programmed in km, even if the vehicle has mileage indication.

Every 250 miles (400 km) or weekly
☐ Refer to *Weekly checks*

Every 10 000 miles (15 000 km) or 12 months (whichever occurs first) – OIL or IN01 on interval display
☐ Renew the engine oil and filter (Section 3)
Note: *Frequent oil and filter changes are good for the engine. We recommend changing the oil more frequently than the mileage specified here, or at least twice a year.*
☐ Check condition of the auxiliary drivebelts (Section 4)
☐ Check the timing belt condition and wear (Section 5)
☐ Reset the service interval display (Section 6)
☐ Check the operation of the windscreen/tailgate washer system(s) (Section 7)
☐ Check the tyre wear (Section 8)
☐ Lubricate all hinges and locks (Section 9)
☐ Check the battery electrolyte level (Section 10)
☐ Check the cooling system for antifreeze content (Section 11)
☐ Drain water from the fuel filter (Section 12)
☐ Renew the pollen filter (Section 13)
☐ Check and if necessary adjust the handbrake (Section 14)
☐ Check the tightness of the roadwheel bolts (Section 15)
☐ Engine management ECM memory fault code check (Section 16)
☐ Check all underbonnet components and hoses for fluid leaks (Section 17)
☐ Check all brake flexible hoses and rigid pipes for condition (Section 18)
☐ Check the front brake pad thickness and disc condition (Section 19)
☐ Check the rear brake pad thickness and disc condition (Section 20)
☐ Check the condition of the exhaust system and its mountings (Section 21)
☐ Check the steering and suspension components for condition and security (Section 22)
☐ Carry out a road test (Section 23)
☐ Check the underbody sealant (Section 24)

Every 20 000 miles (30 000 km) or 2 years (whichever occurs first)
☐ Renew fuel filter (Section 25)

Every 2 years (regardless of mileage)
☐ Renew the remote control handset battery (Section 26)
☐ Renew the coolant (Section 27)
☐ Renew the brake/clutch fluid (Section 28)

Every 30 000 miles (45 000 km) or 3 years (whichever occurs first) – IN02 on interval display
Note: *Carry out the following work in addition to that described for the 12 months interval.*
☐ Check manual transmission oil level (Section 29)
☐ Check the headlight beam adjustment (Section 30)
☐ Check the automatic transmission fluid level (Section 31)
☐ Check the automatic transmission final drive level (Section 32)
☐ Carry out an exhaust emissions check (Section 33)

Every 40 000 miles (60 000 km) or 4 years (whichever occurs first)
☐ Renew the air filter element (Section 34)

Every 60 000 miles (90 000 km)
☐ Renew the timing belt (Section 35)
Note: *It is strongly recommended that the timing belt renewal interval is reduced to 30 000 miles (45 000 km) on vehicles which are subjected to intensive use, ie, mainly short journeys or a lot of stop-start driving. The actual belt renewal interval is therefore very much up to the individual owner, but bear in mind that severe engine damage will result if the belt breaks.*

Every 80 000 miles (120 000 km)
☐ Renew the auxiliary drivebelts (Section 36)

Underbonnet view of a 1.9 litre TDI model (code AFN)

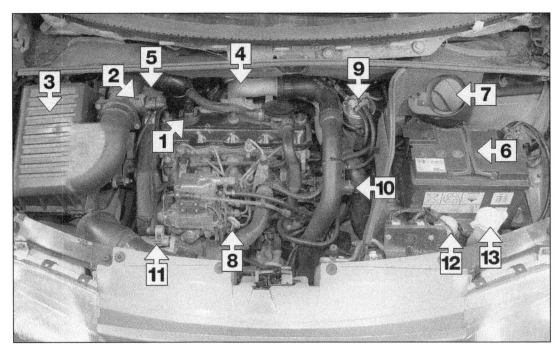

1 Engine oil filler cap
2 Mass airflow sensor
3 Air cleaner
4 EGR valve
5 Brake/clutch fluid reservoir
6 Battery
7 Coolant expansion tank
8 Engine oil level dipstick
9 Fuel filter
10 Charge pressure/temperature sensor
11 Alternator
12 Power steering fluid reservoir
13 Washer fluid reservoir

Front underbody view of a 1.9 litre TDI model

1 Exhaust front pipe
2 Engine roll restrictor
3 Suspension arm
4 Driveshaft
5 Anti-roll bar
6 Front crossmember
7 Intermediate support casing
8 Power steering pump
9 Engine sump oil drain plug
10 Intercooler
11 Oil filter
12 Air conditioning receiver/dryer
13 Washer fluid reservoir

Rear underbody view

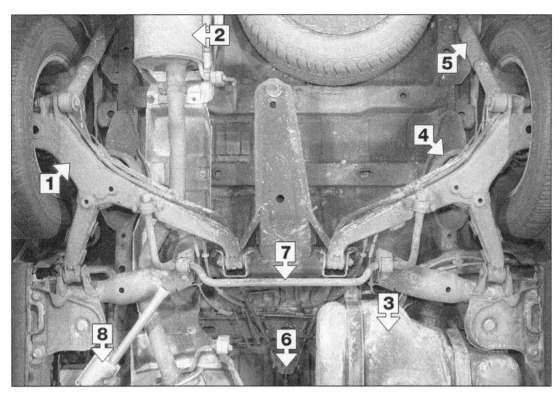

1 Suspension trailing arm
2 Exhaust tail pipe and silencer
3 Fuel tank
4 Coil spring
5 Shock absorber
6 Handbrake cable adjuster
7 Anti-roll bar
8 Booster heater silencer

1 Introduction

This Chapter is designed to help the home mechanic maintain his/her vehicle for safety, economy, long life and peak performance.

The Chapter contains a master maintenance schedule, followed by Sections dealing specifically with each task in the schedule. Visual checks, adjustments, component renewal and other helpful items are included. Refer to the accompanying illustrations of the engine compartment and the underside of the vehicle for the locations of the various components.

Servicing your vehicle in accordance with the mileage/time maintenance schedule and the following Sections will provide a planned maintenance programme, which should result in a long and reliable service life. This is a comprehensive plan, so maintaining some items but not others at the specified service intervals, will not produce the same results.

As you service your vehicle, you will discover that many of the procedures can – and should – be grouped together, because of the particular procedure being performed, or because of the proximity of two otherwise unrelated components to one another. For example, if the vehicle is raised for any reason, the exhaust can be inspected at the same time as the suspension and steering components.

The first step in this maintenance programme is to prepare yourself before the actual work begins. Read through all the Sections relevant to the work to be carried out, then make a list and gather all the parts and tools required. If a problem is encountered, seek advice from a parts specialist, or a dealer service department.

2 Regular maintenance

1 If, from the time the vehicle is new, the routine maintenance schedule is followed closely, and frequent checks are made of fluid levels and high-wear items, as suggested throughout this manual, the engine will be kept in relatively good running condition, and the need for additional work will be minimised.
2 It is possible that there will be times when the engine is running poorly due to the lack of regular maintenance. This is even more likely if a used vehicle, which has not received regular and frequent maintenance checks, is purchased. In such cases, additional work may need to be carried out, outside of the regular maintenance intervals.
3 If engine wear is suspected, a compression test (refer to the relevant Part of Chapter 2) will provide valuable information regarding the overall performance of the main internal components. Such a test can be used as a basis to decide on the extent of the work to

be carried out. If, for example, a compression test indicates serious internal engine wear, conventional maintenance as described in this Chapter will not greatly improve the performance of the engine, and may prove a waste of time and money, unless extensive overhaul work is carried out first.
4 The following series of operations are those most often required to improve the performance of a generally poor-running engine:

Primary operations

a) Clean, inspect and test the battery (See 'Weekly checks').
b) Check all the engine-related fluids (See 'Weekly checks').
c) Check the condition of the auxiliary drivebelts (Section 4).
d) Check the condition of the air filter, and renew if necessary (Section 34).
e) Renew the fuel filter (Section 25).
f) Check the condition of all hoses, and check for fluid leaks (Sections 17 and 18).
5 If the above operations do not prove fully effective, carry out the following secondary operations:

Secondary operations

All items listed under Primary operations, plus the following:
a) Check the charging system (Chapter 5A).
b) Check the preheating system (Chapter 5C)
c) Check the fuel system (Chapter 4B).

Every 10 000 miles (15 000 km) or 12 months (whichever occurs first) – OIL or IN01 on interval display

3 Engine oil and filter renewal

1 Frequent oil and filter changes are the most important maintenance procedures which can be undertaken by the DIY owner. As engine oil ages, it becomes diluted and contaminated, which leads to premature engine wear.

2 Before starting this procedure, gather all the necessary tools and materials. Also make sure that you have plenty of clean rags and newspapers handy, to mop up any spills. Ideally, the engine oil should be warm, as it will drain better, and more built-up sludge will be removed with it. Take care, however, not to touch the exhaust or any other hot parts of the engine when working under the vehicle. To avoid any possibility of scalding, and to protect yourself from possible skin irritants and other harmful contaminants in used engine oils, it is advisable to wear gloves when carrying out this work. Access to the underside of the vehicle is possible if it can be raised on a lift, driven onto ramps, or jacked up and supported on axle stands (see *Jacking and vehicle support*). Whichever method is chosen, make sure that the vehicle remains level, or if it is at an angle, that the drain plug is at the lowest point. With the vehicle raised, undo the two retaining nuts and four bolts (two each side), and remove the engine compartment undershield **(see illustration)**.

3 Using a socket and wrench or a ring spanner, slacken the drain plug about half a turn. Position the draining container under the drain plug, then remove the plug completely **(see Haynes Hint)**. Recover the sealing ring from the drain plug **(see illustration)**.

4 Allow some time for the old oil to drain, noting that it may be necessary to reposition the container as the oil flow slows to a trickle.

5 After all the oil has drained, wipe off the drain plug with a clean rag, and fit a new sealing washer. Clean the area around the drain plug opening, and refit the plug. Tighten the plug securely.

6 If the filter is also to be renewed, move the container into position under the oil filter, which is located on the left-hand front side of the cylinder block.

7 Using an oil filter removal tool if necessary, slacken the filter initially, then unscrew it by hand the rest of the way **(see illustration)**. Empty the oil in the filter into the container.

8 Use a clean rag to remove all oil, dirt and sludge from the filter sealing area on the engine. Check the old filter to make sure that the rubber sealing ring has not stuck to the engine. If it has, carefully remove it.

9 Apply a light coating of clean engine oil to the sealing ring on the new filter, then screw it into position on the engine. Tighten the filter firmly by hand only – **do not** use any tools.

10 Remove the old oil and all tools from under the car then refit the undershield and lower the car to the ground.

11 Remove the dipstick, then unscrew the oil filler cap from the cylinder head cover **(see illustration)**. Fill the engine, using the correct grade and type of oil (see *Lubricants and fluids*). An oil can spout or funnel may help to reduce spillage. Pour in half the specified quantity of oil first, then wait a few minutes for the oil to settle in the sump. Continue adding oil a small quantity at a time until the level is up to the lower mark on the dipstick. Adding around 1.0 litre will bring the level up to the upper mark on the dipstick. Refit the filler cap.

12 Start the engine and run it at idle speed for a few minutes; check for leaks around the oil filter seal and the sump drain plug. Note that there may be a few seconds delay before the oil pressure warning light goes out when the engine is started, as the oil circulates through the engine oil galleries and the new oil filter before the pressure builds-up.

13 Switch off the engine, and wait a few minutes for the oil to settle in the sump once more. With the new oil circulated and the filter completely full, recheck the level on the dipstick, and add more oil as necessary.

14 Dispose of the used engine oil safely, with reference to *General repair procedures* in the *Reference* section of this manual.

3.2 Undo the nut and two bolts each side (arrowed) to remove the engine undershield

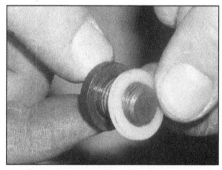

3.3 Recover the sealing ring from the drain plug

HAYNES HiNT

As the drain plug releases from the threads, move it away quickly so that the stream of oil running out of the sump goes into the drain pan and not up your sleeve.

3.7 The oil filter is located on the front of the cylinder block

3.11 Unscrew the oil filler cap from the cylinder head cover

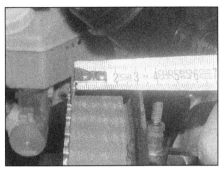

5.3 Measure the width of the timing belt to determine how worn it is

4 Auxiliary drivebelts condition and tension check

1 All models are fitted with two auxiliary drivebelts. On models without air conditioning, the main Poly-Vee drivebelt drives the alternator, and the coolant pump pulleys, whilst the V-belt drives the power steering pump. On models with air conditioning, the main Poly-Vee belt drives the alternator and air conditioning compressor pulleys, and the V-belt drives the power steering pump and coolant pump pulleys. Both belts are driven by a pulley bolted to the crankshaft.
2 For access to the drivebelts, apply the handbrake, then jack up the front of the vehicle and support it on axle stands (see *Jacking and vehicle support*). Undo the two nuts and four bolts (two each side) and remove the engine undershield.
3 Examine the auxiliary drivebelts along their entire length for damage and wear in the form of cuts and abrasions, fraying and cracking. The use of a mirror and possibly an electric torch will help, and the engine may be turned with a spanner on the crankshaft pulley in order to observe all areas of the belt. Whilst the presence of cracks across the ribs of the Poly-Vee belt does not automatically require its renewal, if the cracks occur more than once per 25 mm, per rib, the belt should be renewed.
4 If a drivebelt requires renewal, refer to Chapter 2B for the removal, refitting and adjustment procedure.

5 Timing belt condition and wear check

1 Release the spring clips and remove the upper timing cover from the front of the engine (refer to Chapter 2B, Section 4).
2 Inspect the timing belt for signs of excessive wear, fraying, cracking and damage. Also check for traces of oil which may have come from a faulty oil seal. The full length of the timing belt should be checked by

turning the engine with a spanner on the crankshaft pulley bolt.
3 Using a steel rule or vernier calipers, measure the width of the timing belt in several places. If it is less than 22.0 mm at any point, the timing belt must be renewed with reference to Chapter 2B **(see illustration)**.
4 On completion of the check, refit the upper timing cover.

6 Service interval display resetting

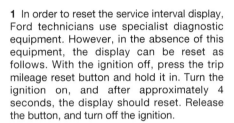

1 In order to reset the service interval display, Ford technicians use specialist diagnostic equipment. However, in the absence of this equipment, the display can be reset as follows. With the ignition off, press the trip mileage reset button and hold it in. Turn the ignition on, and after approximately 4 seconds, the display should reset. Release the button, and turn off the ignition.

7 Washer system(s) operation check

1 Check that each of the washer jet nozzles are clear and that each nozzle provides a strong jet of washer fluid. The jets should be aimed to spray at a point slightly above the centre of the screen. The washer jets aim can be adjusted with a fine pin **(see illustration)**.
2 Carry out a check of all wiper blades. Look for splits or cracks on the wiping surface and renew as necessary. Check that the wipers clean efficiently across their entire sweep; any gaps in the swept area may be caused by defective wiper blade hinges, preventing the blade from following the contours of the screen/lens surface. Check that the wiper blades do not overshoot the edge of the screen/lens at the end of their sweep and that the blades park in the correct position when switched off. If this is not the case, or if the blades overlap each other at the midpoint of their stroke, the wiper arms may be incorrectly fitted (see Chapter 12).

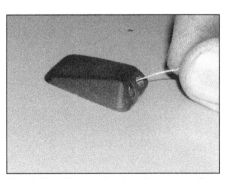

7.1 Adjust the washer jet aim using a fine pin

8 Tyre wear check

1 Raise and securely support the relevant side of the car in turn to allow a thorough check of each tyre to be performed; refer to *Jacking and vehicle support* for reference.
2 Turn the tyre slowly by hand and carry out an inspection as described in *Weekly checks*.

9 Hinges and locks lubrication

1 Lubricate the hinges of the bonnet, doors and tailgate with a light general-purpose oil. Similarly, lubricate all latches, locks and lock strikers. At the same time, check the security and operation of all the locks, adjusting them if necessary (see Chapter 11).
2 Lightly lubricate the bonnet release mechanism and cable with a suitable grease.

10 Battery electrolyte level check

1 Where a standard (non-maintenance free) battery is fitted, the level of the electrolyte may be checked and if necessary topped-up. On some batteries, MIN and MAX marks are printed on the side of the battery and the level may be checked without removing the cell covers. Where there are no exterior marks, remove the cover(s) from the top of the cells and check that the level of the electrolyte is approximately 2 or 3 mm above the internal plates. Some batteries may have a plastic internal level indicator.
2 If necessary, top up the cells using distilled or de-ionised water.
3 Refit the cell cover(s).

11 Cooling system antifreeze concentration check

⚠️ Warning: Wait until the engine is cold before starting this procedure. Do not allow antifreeze to come in contact with your skin, or with the painted surfaces of the vehicle. Rinse off spills immediately with plenty of water.
1 Note that a tester will be required to check the coolant strength; these can be obtained relatively cheaply from most motor accessory shops.
2 With the engine completely cold, unscrew and remove the filler cap from the coolant expansion tank. Follow the instructions supplied with the tester and check the coolant mixture is sufficient to give protection down to temperatures well below freezing. If the coolant has been renewed regularly this

12.1a Pull out the battery compartment upper panel . . .

12.1b . . . and remove the bulkhead trim panel (three screws – two arrowed)

12.2 Pull out the retaining clip and lift off the control valve

shouldn't be a problem. However, if the coolant mixture is not strong enough to provide sufficient protection it will be necessary to drain the cooling system and renew the coolant (see Section 27).

3 Once the test is complete, check the coolant level is correct (see *Weekly checks*) then securely refit the expansion tank cap.

12 Fuel filter draining

1 Pull out the upper section of the battery compartment panel. Undo the three bolts and remove the engine bulkhead trim panel. Slide the trim to the right-hand side and manoeuvre it from behind the coolant expansion tank **(see illustrations)**.

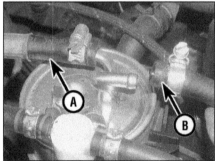

12.3 Disconnect the fuel supply (A) and outlet (B) hoses

2 Remove the control valve retaining clip, and lift off the valve with the hoses still attached **(see illustration)**.
3 Release the retaining clips and disconnect the fuel supply and outlet hoses from the top of the filter **(see illustration)**. Note the fitted positions of the hoses.
4 Slacken the fuel filter clamp screw, and lift the filter up and out of the clamp.
5 Loosen the drain cap under the filter, and drain off approximately 0.1 litre of liquid. Tighten the drain cap **(see illustration)**.
6 Refit the filter into the clamp and tighten the clamp screw. Reconnect the supply and outlet hoses, and tighten the retaining clips.
7 Refit the control valve, and secure it in place with the retaining clip.
8 Start the engine and press the accelerator pedal a few times to bleed the filter through. Check for leaks.

12.5 Slacken the cap to drain the water

9 Refit the bulkhead trim panel, and upper section of the battery compartment panel.

13 Pollen filter renewal

1 The pollen filter is located beneath the windscreen cowl panels; it is located on the right-hand side on left-hand drive models, and on the left-hand side on right-hand drive models.
2 Pull out the battery compartment upper panel **(see illustration 12.1a)**.
3 Undo the three screws and remove the bulkhead trim **(see illustration 12.1b)**. Slide the trim to the right-hand side and manoeuvre it from behind the coolant expansion tank.
4 Ensure that the area around the filter is cleared of all leaves, debris, etc, as when the filter is removed, this will be able to enter the vehicle interior.
5 Release the retaining clip, and slide the element with the frame out of the guide towards the centre of the vehicle. Manoeuvre the frame and element under the wiper linkage, and out from the engine compartment **(see illustration)**.
6 Remove the filter element from the frame.
7 Fit the new element onto the frame, with the air flow arrows pointing towards the vehicle interior, ensuring that the left and right ends of the frame fit into the first laminations at each end of the element. Ensure also that the square pegs of the frame locate in the filter laminations **(see illustrations)**.

13.5 Release the pollen filter retaining clip (arrowed)

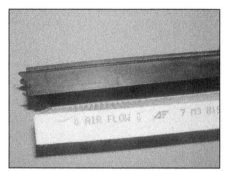

13.7a Fit the new element into the frame with the air flow arrows pointing to the vehicle interior . . .

13.7b . . . and the ends of the frame located into the first and last laminations of the filter

8 Guide the frame and element under the wiper linkage and slide it into position, ensuring that the guide lugs on the frame engage correctly with the guide slots in the housing, and the retaining clip locks the assembly in place **(see illustration)**.

9 The remainder of the refitting procedure is a reversal of removal.

14 Handbrake check and adjustment

1 With the vehicle on level ground, chock the front wheels and release the handbrake lever. Gradually apply the handbrake, counting the number of clicks from the ratchet mechanism until the handbrake is fully applied. If the adjustment is correct, there should be 3 to 6 clicks before the handbrake is fully applied. If this is not the case, adjust as follows.

2 Ensure the front wheel chocks are still in place, jack up the rear of the vehicle and support it on axle stands (see *Jacking and vehicle support*). Fully release the handbrake lever.

3 Working underneath the vehicle, rotate the adjuster locknut in the required direction to achieve the correct lever adjustment **(see illustration)**.

4 With the handbrake fully released, check that the rear wheels rotate freely, with no signs of binding or resistance.

5 Once the adjustment is correct, lower the vehicle to the ground.

15 Roadwheel bolts tightness check

1 With the vehicle wheels on the ground and the handbrake applied, prise off the wheel trims (where applicable), and check the tightness of the wheel bolts using a torque wrench. The correct torque setting is given at the start of this Chapter.

2 When all the bolts have been checked, refit the wheel trims (where applicable).

16 Engine management ECM memory fault code check

This check can only be carried out by an Ford dealer or garage having the necessary equipment. If a fault code is evident, the problem must be corrected to ensure efficient operation of the engine.

17 Underbonnet/underbody components and hoses fluid leak check

1 For access to the top and bottom of the engine, remove the engine top cover, then jack up the front of the vehicle and support it on

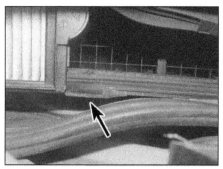

13.8 The lugs on the frame must engage with the guide slots in the housing (arrowed)

axle stands (see *Jacking and vehicle support*). Undo the two retaining nuts and four bolts (two each side), and remove the undershield. Visually inspect the engine joint faces, gaskets and seals for any signs of water or oil leaks. Pay particular attention to the areas around the camshaft cover, cylinder head, oil filter and sump joint faces. Bear in mind that, over a period of time, some very slight seepage from these areas is to be expected – what you are really looking for is any indication of a serious leak. Should a leak be found, renew the offending gasket or oil seal by referring to the appropriate Chapters in this manual.

2 Also check the security and condition of all the engine-related pipes and hoses. Ensure that all cable-ties or securing clips are in place and in good condition. Clips which are broken or missing can lead to chafing of the hoses, pipes or wiring, which could cause more serious problems in the future.

3 Carefully check the radiator hoses and heater hoses along their entire length. Renew any hose which is cracked, swollen or deteriorated. Cracks will show up better if the hose is squeezed. Pay close attention to the hose clips that secure the hoses to the cooling system components. Hose clips can pinch and puncture hoses, resulting in cooling system leaks.

4 Inspect all the cooling system components (hoses, joint faces etc) for leaks **(see Haynes Hint)**. Where any problems of this nature are found on system components, renew the

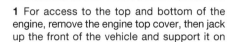

A leak in the cooling system will usually show up as white- or rust-coloured crusty deposits on the area surrounding the leak.

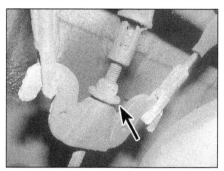

14.3 Rotate the locknut (arrowed) to adjust the handbrake lever

component or gasket with reference to Chapter 3.

5 Where applicable, inspect the automatic transmission fluid cooler hoses for leaks or deterioration.

6 With the vehicle raised at the rear, inspect the diesel tank and filler neck for punctures, cracks and other damage. The connection between the filler neck and tank is especially critical. Sometimes a rubber filler neck or connecting hose will leak due to loose retaining clamps or deteriorated rubber.

7 Carefully check all rubber hoses and metal fuel lines leading away from the diesel tank. Check for loose connections, deteriorated hoses, crimped lines, and other damage. Pay particular attention to the vent pipes and hoses, which often loop up around the filler neck and can become blocked or crimped. Follow the lines to the front of the vehicle, carefully inspecting them all the way. Renew damaged sections as necessary.

8 From within the engine compartment, check the security of all fuel hose attachments and pipe unions, and inspect the fuel hoses and vacuum hoses for kinks, chafing and deterioration.

9 Where applicable, check the condition of the power steering fluid hoses and pipes.

10 On completion, refit the undershield and engine top cover, and lower the vehicle to the ground.

18 Brake flexible hoses and rigid pipes condition check

1 Inspect all the braking system flexible hoses and metal pipes for signs of damage or deterioration. Any faulty pipe/hoses must be renewed (see Chapter 9).

19 Front brake pad thickness and disc condition check

1 Firmly apply the handbrake, loosen the front roadwheel bolts, then jack up the front of the car and support it securely on axle stands (see *Jacking and vehicle support*). Remove the front roadwheels.

2 For a comprehensive check, the brake pads should be removed and cleaned. The operation of the caliper can then also be checked, and the condition of the brake disc itself can be fully examined on both sides. Refer to Chapter 9 **(see illustration)**.

3 If any pad is worn to the specified thickness or less, *all four pads must be renewed as a set*. **Note:** *If any pad is approaching the minimum thickness, consider renewal as a precautionary measure in case the pads wear out before the next service.*

4 On completion, refit the roadwheels and lower the vehicle to the ground.

20 Rear brake pad lining thickness and disc condition check

1 Firmly chock the front wheels and select first gear or PARK, then jack up the rear of the vehicle and support it securely on axle stands (see *Jacking and vehicle support*). Remove the rear roadwheels.

2 For a quick check, the pad thickness can be carried out via the inspection hole on the rear of the caliper. Using a steel rule, measure the thickness of the pad lining including the backing plate. This must not be less than that indicated in the Specifications.

3 The view through the caliper inspection hole gives a rough indication of the state of the brake pads. For a comprehensive check, the brake pads should be removed and cleaned. The operation of the caliper can then also be checked, and the condition of the brake disc itself can be fully examined on both sides. Chapter 9 contains a detailed description of how the brake disc should be checked for wear and/or damage.

4 If any pad is worn to the specified thickness or less, *all four pads must be renewed as a set*. **Note:** *If any pad is approaching the minimum thickness, consider renewal as a precautionary measure in case the pads wear out before the next service.* Refer to Chapter 9 for details.

5 On completion, refit the roadwheels and lower the vehicle to the ground.

21 Exhaust system and mountings condition check

1 With the engine cold, check the complete exhaust system from the engine to the end of the tailpipe. The exhaust system is most easily checked with the vehicle raised on a hoist, or suitably supported on axle stands, so that the exhaust components are readily visible and accessible.

2 Check the exhaust pipes and connections for evidence of leaks, severe corrosion and damage. Make sure that all brackets and mountings are in good condition, and that all relevant nuts and bolts are tight. Leakage at

19.2 The thickness of the brake pad, including the backing plate, must not be less than 7 mm

any of the joints or in other parts of the system will usually show up as a black sooty stain in the vicinity of the leak.

3 Rattles and other noises can often be traced to the exhaust system, especially the brackets and mountings. If the components are able to come into contact with the body or suspension parts, secure the system with new mountings. Otherwise separate the joints (if possible) and twist the pipes as necessary to provide additional clearance.

22 Steering and suspension components condition/security check

Suspension and steering

1 Raise the front of the vehicle, and securely support it on axle stands.

2 Visually inspect the balljoint dust covers and the steering rack gaiters for splits, chafing or deterioration. Any wear of these components will cause loss of lubricant, together with dirt and water entry, resulting in rapid deterioration of the balljoints or steering gear.

3 On vehicles with power steering, check the fluid hoses for chafing or deterioration, and the pipe and hose unions for fluid leaks. Also check for signs of fluid leakage under pressure from the steering gear rubber gaiters, which would indicate failed fluid seals within the steering gear.

4 Grasp the roadwheel at the 12 o'clock and 6 o'clock positions, and try to rock it **(see illustration)**. Very slight free play may be felt, but if the movement is appreciable, further investigation is necessary to determine the source. Continue rocking the wheel while an assistant depresses the footbrake. If the movement is now eliminated or significantly reduced, it is likely that the hub bearings are at fault. If the free play is still evident with the footbrake depressed, then there is wear in the suspension joints or mountings.

5 Now grasp the wheel at the 9 o'clock and 3 o'clock positions, and try to rock it as before. Any movement felt now may again be caused by wear in the hub bearings or the

22.4 Check for signs of wear in the hub bearings by grasping the roadwheel at the 12 o'clock and 6 o'clock positions, and trying to rock it

steering track rod balljoints. If the inner or outer balljoint is worn, the visual movement will be obvious.

6 Using a large screwdriver or flat bar, check for wear in the suspension mounting bushes by levering between the relevant suspension component and its attachment point. Some movement is to be expected as the mountings are made of rubber, but excessive wear should be obvious. Also check the condition of any visible rubber bushes, looking for splits, cracks or contamination of the rubber.

7 With the car standing on its wheels, have an assistant turn the steering wheel back-and-forth about an eighth of a turn each way. There should be very little, if any, lost movement between the steering wheel and roadwheels. If this is not the case, closely observe the joints and mountings previously described, but in addition, check the steering column universal joints for wear, and the rack-and-pinion steering gear itself.

Strut/shock absorber

8 Check for any signs of fluid leakage around the suspension strut/shock absorber body, or from the rubber gaiter around the piston rod. Should any fluid be noticed, the suspension strut/shock absorber is defective internally, and should be renewed. **Note:** *Suspension struts/shock absorbers should always be renewed in pairs on the same axle.*

9 The efficiency of the suspension strut/shock absorber may be checked by bouncing the vehicle at each corner. Generally speaking, the body will return to its normal position and stop after being depressed. If it rises and returns on a rebound, the suspension strut/shock absorber is probably suspect. Examine also the suspension strut/shock absorber upper and lower mountings for any signs of wear.

Driveshafts

10 With the vehicle raised and securely supported on stands, turn the steering onto full lock then slowly rotate the roadwheel. Inspect the condition of the outer constant velocity (CV) joint rubber gaiters while squeezing the gaiters to open out the folds. Check for signs of cracking, splits or deterioration of the rubber which may allow the grease to escape and lead to water and grit entry into the joint. Also check the security and condition of the retaining clips. Repeat these checks on the inner CV joints. If any damage or deterioration is found, the gaiters should be renewed as described in Chapter 8, Section 3.

11 At the same time check the general condition of the CV joints themselves by first holding the driveshaft and attempting to rotate the wheel. Repeat this check by holding the inner joint and attempting to rotate the driveshaft. Any appreciable movement indicates wear in the joints, wear in the driveshaft splines or loose driveshaft retaining nut.

23 Road test

Instruments/ electrical equipment

1 Check the operation of all instruments and electrical equipment.
2 Make sure that all instruments read correctly, and switch on all electrical equipment in turn, to check that it functions properly.

Steering and suspension

3 Check for any abnormalities in the steering, suspension, handling or road feel.
4 Drive the vehicle, and check that there are no unusual vibrations or noises.

5 Check that the steering feels positive, with no excessive sloppiness, or roughness, and check for any suspension noises when cornering and driving over bumps.

Drivetrain

6 Check the performance of the engine, clutch (where applicable), gearbox/transmission and driveshafts.
7 Listen for any unusual noises from the engine, clutch and gearbox/transmission.
8 Make sure that the engine runs smoothly when idling, and that there is no hesitation when accelerating.
9 Check that, where applicable, the clutch action is smooth and progressive, that the drive is taken up smoothly, and that the pedal travel is not excessive. Also listen for any noises when the clutch pedal is depressed.
10 On manual gearbox models, check that all gears can be engaged smoothly without noise, and that the gear lever action is smooth and not abnormally vague or notchy.
11 On automatic transmission models, make sure that all gearchanges occur smoothly, without snatching, and without an increase in engine speed between changes. Check that all the gear positions can be selected with the vehicle at rest. If any problems are found, they should be referred to a Ford dealer.

Braking system

12 Make sure that the vehicle does not pull to one side when braking, and that the wheels do not lock when braking hard.
13 Check that there is no vibration through the steering when braking.
14 Check that the handbrake operates

correctly without excessive movement of the lever, and that it holds the vehicle stationary on a slope.
15 Test the operation of the brake servo unit as follows. With the engine off, depress the footbrake four or five times to exhaust the vacuum. Hold the brake pedal depressed, then start the engine. As the engine starts, there should be a noticeable give in the brake pedal as vacuum builds-up. Allow the engine to run for at least two minutes, and then switch it off. If the brake pedal is depressed now, it should be possible to detect a hiss from the servo as the pedal is depressed. After about four or five applications, no further hissing should be heard, and the pedal should feel considerably harder.

24 Underbody sealant check

Raise and support the vehicle on axle stands (see *Jacking and vehicle support*). Using an electric torch or lead light, inspect the entire underside of the vehicle, paying particular attention to the wheelarches. Look for any damage to the flexible underbody coating, which may crack or flake off with age, leading to corrosion. Also check that the wheelarch liners (where fitted) are securely attached with any clips provided – if they come loose, dirt may get in behind the liners and defeat their purpose. If there is any damage to the underseal, or any corrosion, it should be repaired before the damage gets too serious.

Every 20 000 miles (30 000 km) or 2 years (whichever occurs first)

25 Fuel filter renewal

1 Pull out the upper section of the battery compartment panel. Undo the three screws and remove the engine bulkhead trim panel **(see illustrations 12.1a and 12.1b)**. Slide the trim to the right-hand side and manoeuvre it from behind the coolant expansion tank.
2 Remove the control valve retaining clip, and lift off the valve with the hoses still attached **(see illustration 12.2)**.
3 Release the retaining clips and disconnect the fuel supply and outlet hoses from the top

of the filter **(see illustration 12.3)**. Note the fitted positions of the hoses.
4 Slacken the fuel filter clamp screw, and lift the filter up and out of the clamp **(see illustration)**.
Caution: Do not allow diesel fuel to contact any of the coolant hoses. Mop up any spilt fuel immediately.
5 Refit the filter into the clamp and tighten the clamp screw. Reconnect the supply and outlet hoses, and tighten the retaining clips.
6 Refit the control valve, and secure it in place with the retaining clip.
7 Start the engine and rev it a few times to bleed the filter through. Check for leaks.
8 Refit the bulkhead trim panel, and upper section of the battery compartment panel.

25.4 Slacken the fuel filter clamp screw (arrowed)

Every 2 years (regardless of mileage)

26 Handset battery renewal

1 Carefully prise the handset body from the key blade **(see illustration)**.
2 Using a small screwdriver release the retaining clips and separate the halves of the handset body **(see illustration)**.
3 Gently push back the clips and lift the first battery, dividing plate, and second battery from the handset.
4 Insert the first new battery, positive side up, into the handset **(see illustration)**.
5 Place the dividing plate on top of the first battery **(see illustration)**.
6 Insert the second battery, again positive side up, making sure it is held in place by the retaining clips.
7 Fit the halves of the handset together, and slide it back into the key blade.
8 It may be the case that the handset will not function correctly after battery replacement. If this is the case the handset must be resynchronised. Unfortunately, this procedure varies from model year to model year, although the Owners Handbook supplied with the vehicle contains details of the procedure.

27 Coolant renewal

 Warning: Wait until the engine is cold before starting this procedure. Do not allow antifreeze to come in contact with your skin, or with the painted surfaces of the vehicle. Rinse off spills immediately with plenty of water. Never leave antifreeze lying around in an open container, or in a puddle in the driveway or on the garage floor. Children and pets are attracted by its sweet smell, but antifreeze can be fatal if ingested.

Cooling system draining

1 With the engine completely cold, cover the expansion tank cap with a wad of rag, and slowly turn the cap anti-clockwise to relieve the pressure in the cooling system (a hissing sound will normally be heard). Wait until any pressure remaining in the system is released, then continue to turn the cap until it can be removed.
2 Release the fasteners (two nuts and four bolts) and remove the engine/transmission undershield. Undo the retaining clips and disconnect the intercooler right-hand hose.
3 Position a suitable container beneath the radiator bottom hose connection, then release the retaining clip and ease the hose from the radiator stub. If the hose joint has not been disturbed for some time, it will be necessary to gently manipulate the hose to break the joint. Do not use excessive force, or the radiator stub could be damaged. Allow the coolant to drain into the container.
4 If the coolant has been drained for a reason other than renewal, then provided it is clean and less than two years old, it can be re-used if there is no alternative, but this is not recommended. **Note:** *If an aluminium engine component which comes into contact with the coolant has been renewed, then the coolant must also be renewed. Used coolant will not protect new aluminium from corrosion.*
5 Once all the coolant has drained, reconnect the hose to the radiator and ensure the retaining clip is properly seated.

Cooling system flushing

6 If coolant renewal has been neglected, or if the antifreeze mixture has become diluted, then in time, the cooling system may gradually lose efficiency, as the coolant passages become restricted due to rust, scale deposits, and other sediment. Flushing the system clean can restore the cooling system efficiency.
7 The radiator should be flushed independently of the engine, to avoid unnecessary contamination.

Radiator flushing

8 To flush the radiator, disconnect the top and bottom hoses and any other relevant hoses from the radiator, with reference to Chapter 3.
9 Insert a garden hose into the radiator top inlet. Direct a flow of clean water through the radiator, and continue flushing until clean water emerges from the radiator bottom outlet.
10 If after a reasonable period, the water still does not run clear, the radiator can be flushed with a good proprietary cooling system

26.1 Prise the handset body from the key blade

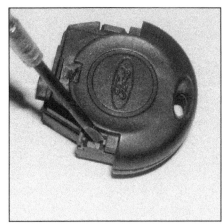

26.2 Release the retaining clips and separate the halves of the body

26.4 Insert the first battery, positive (+) side up

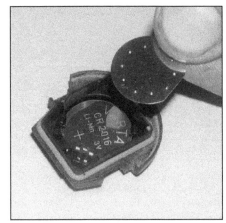

26.5 Place the dividing plate on the first battery

cleaning agent. It is important that their manufacturer's instructions are followed carefully. If the contamination is particularly bad, insert the hose in the radiator bottom outlet, and reverse-flush the radiator.

Engine flushing

11 To flush the engine, remove the thermostat as described in Chapter 3, then temporarily refit the thermostat cover.

12 With the top and bottom hoses disconnected from the radiator, insert a garden hose into the radiator top hose. Direct a clean flow of water through the engine, and continue flushing until clean water emerges from the radiator bottom hose.

13 On completion of flushing, refit the thermostat and reconnect the hoses with reference to Chapter 3.

Cooling system filling

14 Before attempting to fill the cooling system, make sure that all hoses and clips are in good condition, and that the clips/connections are secure. Note that an antifreeze mixture must be used all year round, to prevent corrosion of the engine components (see following sub-Section).

15 Remove the expansion tank filler cap, and fill the system by slowly pouring the coolant into the expansion tank to prevent airlocks from forming.

16 If the coolant is being renewed, begin by pouring in a litre of water, followed by the correct quantity of antifreeze, then top-up with more water.

17 Once the level in the expansion tank starts to rise, squeeze the radiator top and bottom hoses to help expel any trapped air in the system. Once all the air is expelled, top-up the coolant level to the MAX mark, refit the expansion tank cap, then refit the expansion tank to the bodywork.

18 Start the engine and run it at a fast idle for about three minutes. After this, allow the engine to idle normally until the bottom hose becomes hot.

19 Check for leaks, particularly around disturbed components. Check the coolant level in the expansion tank, and top-up if necessary. Note that the system must be cold before an accurate level is indicated in the expansion tank. If the expansion tank cap is removed while the engine is still warm, cover the cap with a thick cloth, and unscrew the cap slowly to gradually relieve the system pressure (a hissing sound will normally be heard). Wait until any pressure remaining in the system is released, then continue to turn the cap until it can be removed. Never remove the cap when the engine is still hot.

Antifreeze mixture

Caution: Ford specify the use of two different coolants. Early models were filled with Motorcraft Super Plus 4 (blue/green in colour), whilst later models were filled with Motorcraft Super Plus 2000 (orange in colour). DO NOT mix these two different types of coolant. If the coolant visible in the expansion tank is any colour other than blue/green or orange, then the cooling system may have been topped-up with coolant containing the wrong type of antifreeze. If you are unsure of the type of antifreeze used, or if you suspect that mixing may have occurred, the best course of action is to drain, flush and refill the cooling system. Note that Ford specify the coolant should be changed after a period of two to ten years, depending on coolant type and model year. However, we consider it prudent to change the coolant after two years, regardless of coolant type.

20 The antifreeze should always be renewed at the specified intervals. This is necessary not only to maintain the antifreeze properties, but also to prevent corrosion which would otherwise occur as the corrosion inhibitors become progressively less effective.

21 The quantity of antifreeze and levels of protection are indicated in the Specifications.

22 Before adding antifreeze, the cooling system should be completely drained, preferably flushed, and all hoses checked for condition and security.

23 After filling with antifreeze, a label should be attached to the expansion tank, stating the type and concentration of antifreeze used, and the date installed. Any subsequent topping-up should be made with the same type and concentration of antifreeze.

24 Do not use engine antifreeze in the windscreen/tailgate/headlight washer system, as it will cause damage to the vehicle paintwork.

28 Brake/clutch fluid renewal

⚠ *Warning: Brake hydraulic fluid can harm your eyes and damage painted surfaces, so use extreme caution when handling and pouring it. Do not use fluid that has been standing open for some time, as it absorbs moisture from the air. Excess moisture can cause a dangerous loss of braking effectiveness.*

Brakes

1 The procedure is similar to that for the bleeding of the hydraulic system as described in Chapter 9.

2 On right-hand drive models, remove the air ducting assembly as described in Chapter 4B, to gain access to the master cylinder reservoir.

3 Working as described in Chapter 9, open the first bleed screw in the sequence, and pump the brake pedal gently until nearly all the old fluid has been emptied from the master cylinder reservoir. Top-up to the MAX level with new fluid, and continue pumping until only the new fluid remains in the reservoir, and new fluid can be seen emerging from the bleed screw. Tighten the screw, and top the reservoir level up to the MAX level line.

HAYNES HiNT *Old hydraulic fluid is invariably much darker in colour than the new, making it easy to distinguish the two.*

4 Work through all the remaining bleed screws in the sequence until new fluid can be seen at all of them. Be careful to keep the master cylinder reservoir topped-up to above the MIN level at all times, or air may enter the system and greatly increase the length of the task. The bleed screw sequence is:
  a) *Left-hand front brake.*
  b) *Right-hand front brake.*
  c) *Right-hand rear brake.*
  d) *Left-hand rear brake.*

5 When the operation is complete, check that all bleed screws are securely tightened, and that their dust caps are refitted. Wash off all traces of spilt fluid, and recheck the master cylinder reservoir fluid level. Check the operation of the brakes before taking the car on the road.

Clutch

6 Because the clutch hydraulic system shares the same fluid reservoir as the brake system, we recommend that the clutch hydraulic fluid is renewed at the same time. Working as described in Chapter 6, remove the dust cap from the slave cylinder bleed screw. Fit a spanner and tube to the screw, place the other end of the tube in a jar, and pour in sufficient fluid to cover the end of the tube.

7 Ensure that the fluid level is maintained at least above the lower level line in the reservoir throughout the procedure.

8 Have an assistant fully depress the clutch pedal several times to build-up pressure, then maintain it on the final downstroke.

9 While pedal pressure is maintained, unscrew the bleed screw (approximately one half of a turn) and allow the compressed fluid to flow into the jar. The assistant should maintain pedal pressure and should not release it until instructed to do so. When the flow stops, tighten the bleed screw again, have the assistant release the pedal slowly, and recheck the reservoir fluid level.

10 Repeat the steps given in paragraphs 8 and 9 until the new fluid emerges from the bleed screw. If the master cylinder has been drained and refilled allow approximately five seconds between cycles for the master cylinder passages to refill.

11 Tighten the bleed screw securely, remove the tube and spanner, and refit the dust cap. Do not overtighten the bleed screw.

12 Wash off all traces of spilt fluid, and recheck the fluid level.

Every 30 000 miles (45 000 km) or 3 years (whichever occurs first) – IN02 on interval display

29 Manual transmission oil level check

1 The oil filler/level plug is located on the front side of the manual transmission.
2 Apply the handbrake, then jack up the front and rear of the vehicle and support it on axle stands (see *Jacking and vehicle support*). To ensure an accurate check, make sure that the vehicle is level. Undo the two retaining nuts and four bolts (two each side), and remove the engine/transmission undershield.
3 Unscrew and remove the filler/level plug.
4 Check that the oil level is to the bottom lip of the filler hole.
5 If necessary, add the specified oil through the filler/level hole **(see illustration)**. If the level requires constant topping-up, check for leaks and repair.

29.5 Add oil through the filler/level hole

6 Refit the plug and tighten to the specified torque. Refit the engine/transmission undershield, then lower the vehicle to the ground.

30 Headlight beam adjustment

1 Accurate adjustment of the headlight beam is only possible using optical beam setting equipment, and this work should therefore be carried out by a Ford dealer or suitably-equipped workshop.
2 For reference, the headlights can be adjusted using the adjuster screws, accessible via the top of each light unit (see the illustrations given in Chapter 12, Section 9).
3 Some models are equipped with an electrically-operated headlight beam adjustment system which is controlled through the switch in the facia. On these models, ensure that the switch is set to the basic 0 position before adjusting the headlight aim.

31 Automatic transmission fluid level check

Note: *For an accurate fluid level check, Ford technicians use an electronic tester which is plugged into the vehicles diagnostic socket, and establishes that the temperature of the fluid is between 35°C and 45°C via a sensor within the transmission casing. In view of this,* *it is recommended that the vehicle is taken to a Ford dealer or automatic transmission specialist to have the level checked.*

1 Jack up the front and rear of the vehicle and support it on axle stands (see *Jacking and vehicle support*). Undo the two retaining nuts and four bolts (two each side), and remove the engine undershield.
2 Note that the transmission must be refilled from below the vehicle, so make sure that the vehicle is supported in a level position.
3 Start the engine and move the selector lever through all gear positions. Switch off the engine.
4 At this point the Ford technician connects the FDS2000 tester to the vehicle's diagnostic socket, and establishes that the temperature of the transmission fluid is between 35°C and 45°C. **Note:** *If the level is checked when the temperature is too low, overfilling will occur. If the level is checked when the temperature is too high, underfilling will occur.*
5 With the vehicle still on level ground, start the engine and unscrew the level plug from under the transmission **(see illustration)**. If the level is too high, fluid will escape down the overflow pipe. Refit and tighten the level plug when the fluid ceases to drip. If the level is too low, no fluid will escape.
6 If the fluid level is too low, pull out the retaining clip and pull off the filler pipe blanking plug from the front of the transmission casing **(see illustration)**. On some models, the filler plug is secured by a cap. Prise the cap off with a screwdriver. Using a funnel, add fluid until it begins to drip from the overflow pipe, then tighten the level plug. Always renew the sealing washer.
7 With the fluid level correct, refit the filler

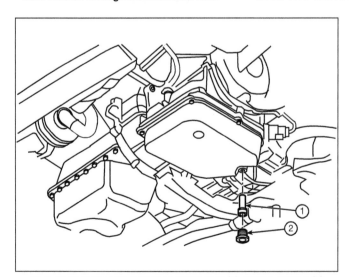

31.5 Automatic transmission drain plug (2) and level plug (1)

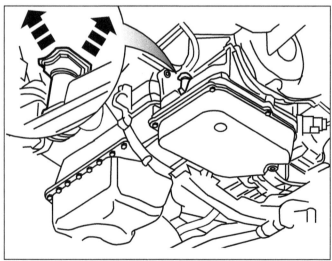

31.6 Pull off the filler pipe blanking plug

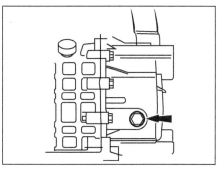

32.1 Final drive oil filler/level plug

plug and secure it in place with the retaining clip or cap.
8 Refit the engine/transmission undertray, and lower the vehicle to the ground.

32 Final drive oil level check and top-up (automatic transmission)

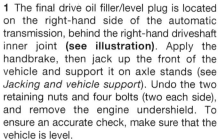

1 The final drive oil filler/level plug is located on the right-hand side of the automatic transmission, behind the right-hand driveshaft inner joint (see illustration). Apply the handbrake, then jack up the front of the vehicle and support it on axle stands (see *Jacking and vehicle support*). Undo the two retaining nuts and four bolts (two each side), and remove the engine undershield. To ensure an accurate check, make sure that the vehicle is level.
2 Unscrew and remove the filler/level plug and check that the oil level is on the bottom lip of the filler hole. If necessary, add the specified oil through the filler/level hole. If the level requires constant topping-up, check for leaks and repair.
3 Refit the plug and tighten to the specified torque, then lower the vehicle to the ground.

33 Exhaust emissions check

This check is part of the manufacturer's maintenance schedule, and involves testing the exhaust emissions using an exhaust gas analyser. Unless a fault is suspected, this test is not essential, although it should be noted that it is recommended by the manufacturers. Exhaust emissions testing is included as part of the MOT test.

Every 40 000 miles (60 000 km) or 4 years (whichever occurs first)

34.1 Disconnect the mass airflow sensor

34 Air filter element renewal

1 Disconnect the wiring plug from the mass airflow sensor. Release the wiring loom from the retaining clip on the air filter upper cover (see illustration).
2 Disconnect the vacuum pipe from the upper air filter cover.
3 Undo the two screws securing the mass airflow sensor to the upper air filter cover.
4 Release the three retaining clips, and lift away the upper air filter cover (see illustration).
5 Remove the air filter element, noting which way round it is fitted (see illustration).

6 Wipe clean the main body, then fit the new air filter, making sure it is the correct way round.
7 Refit the upper cover and secure with the retaining clips.
8 The remainder of refitting is a reversal of removal. Lubricate the air intake rubber seal with soap solution to help refitting.

Every 60 000 miles (90 000 km)

35 Timing belt renewal

Refer to Chapter 2B, Section 4.

Every 80 000 miles (120 000 km)

36 Auxiliary drivebelt renewal

Refer to Chapter 2B, Section 6.

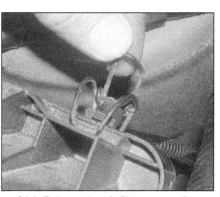

34.4 Release the air filter cover clips

34.5 Note which way around the air filter element is fitted

Chapter 2 Part A:
Petrol engine in-car repair procedures

Contents

Degrees of difficulty

Easy, suitable for novice with little experience	Fairly easy, suitable for beginner with some experience	Fairly difficult, suitable for competent DIY mechanic	Difficult, suitable for experienced DIY mechanic	Very difficult, suitable for expert DIY or professional

Specifications

General

Engine code*:
1998 cc, DOHC 8V .... NSE
2295 cc, DOHC 16V Y5B
Power output:
  NSE engine .... 85 kW @ 5500 rpm
  Y5B engine .... 107 kW @ 5500 rpm
Torque output:
  NSE engine .... 170 Nm @ 2300 rpm
  Y5B engine .... 203 Nm @ 2500 rpm
Bore:
  NSE engine .... 86.0 mm
  Y5B engine .... 89.6 mm
Stroke:
  NSE engine .... 86.0 mm
  Y5B engine .... 91.0 mm
Compression ratio:
  NSE engine .... 9.8 : 1
  Y5B engine .... 10.0 : 1
Firing order .... 1 – 3 – 4 – 2
No 1 cylinder location .... Timing chain end
* Note: See 'Vehicle identification' at the end of this manual for the location of code marking on the engine

Lubrication system

Oil pump type .... Bi-rotor, chain driven from the crankshaft
Oil pressure (oil temperature 80°C):
  At idle speed .... 1.6 bar
  At 2000 rpm .... 3.1 bar
Oil pressure relief valve opens at .... 3.7 to 4.6 bar
Oil pump clearances:
  Between rotor and housing .... 0.154 to 0.304 mm
  Between inner and outer rotor .... 0.05 to 0.2 mm
  Endfloat between mating face and rotor:
    NSE engine .... 0.014 to 0.079 mm
    Y5B engine .... 0.039 to 0.104 mm

Camshaft

Camshaft lift:
  NSE engine:
    Intake camshaft . . . . 10.83 mm
    Exhaust camshaft . . . . 10.83 mm
  Y5B engine:
    Intake camshaft . . . . 9.4 mm
    Exhaust camshaft . . . . 8.75 mm

Torque wrench settings

	Nm	lbf ft
Accessory bracket to cylinder block	47	35
Air conditioning compressor	23	17
Alternator mounting to cylinder head	23	17
Automatic auxiliary belt tensioner	44	32
Balancer shaft housing to cylinder block:		
Stage 1	5	4
Stage 2	17	13
Balancer shaft gears to shaft	19	14
Big-end bearing caps*:		
Stage 1	7	5
Stage 2	16	12
Stage 3	Angle-tighten a further 90°	
Camshaft bearing cap	24	18
Camshaft cover:		
Stage 1	3	2
Stage 2	9	7
Camshaft position sensor	5	4
Camshaft sprockets	59	44
Coolant outlet housing	10	7
Coolant pipe bracket to cylinder block	23	17
Coolant pump	23	17
Coolant pump blanking plug	16	12
Coolant pump pulley	23	17
Crankshaft oil seal housing	15	11
Crankshaft position sensor	4	3
Crankshaft pulley hub to crankshaft:		
Stage 1	52	38
Stage 2	Angle-tighten a further 85°	
Crankshaft pulley to hub (two-part pulley)	34	25
Cylinder head bolts:		
Stage 1	10	7
Stage 2	35	26
Stage 3	Angle-tighten a further 90°	
Stage 4	Angle-tighten a further 90°	
Three bolts at right-hand end (see text)	38	28
Driveshaft centre bearing to cylinder block bracket	27	20
EGR/air injection pipe to exhaust manifold	35	26
Engine coolant temperature sensor	12	9
Engine mountings:		
Engine support plate bracket to cylinder head	44	32
Engine support plate to engine	58	43
Left-hand mounting to body	54	40
Left-hand mounting to transmission:		
Long bolts	20	15
Torx bolts	98	72
Right-hand mounting bracket to engine support plate	61	45
Right-hand mounting bracket to rubber mounting	54	40
Right-hand rubber mounting to body	58	43
Engine-to-transmission bolts	44	32
Engine/transmission roll restrictor:		
To crossmember	98	72
To transmission:		
Aluminium	70	52
Aluminium bolt, 88 mm long:		
Stage 1	60	44
Stage 2	Angle-tighten a further 90°	
Steel	98	72

Torque wrench settings

	Nm	lbf ft
Exhaust manifold:		
Nuts	23	17
Studs	14	10
Exhaust pipe:		
To manifold:		
NSE engine	44	32
Y5B engine	35	26
Flywheel/driveplate mounting bolts*	87	64
Front arch to cylinder block	26	19
Front crossmember to body:		
Stage 1	150	111
Stage 2	Angle-tighten a further 90°	
Fuel rail	24	18
Inlet manifold:		
Studs	14	10
Nuts/bolts	22	16
Main bearing cap	97	72
Oil baffle plate to cylinder block	19	14
Oil drain plug	24	18
Oil filter mounting	21	15
Oil pick-up pipe to balance shaft housing/cylinder block	12	9
Oil pressure switch	27	20
Oil pump cover	10	7
Oil pump drive chain lower guide	12	9
Oil pump drive chain tensioner	12	9
Oil pump drive chain upper guide	26	19
Oil pump sprocket:		
NSE engine	18	13
Y5B engine	33	24
Oil pump to cylinder block	12	9
Power steering pump	23	17
Power steering pump pulley	25	18
Spark plugs	18	13
Sump to balancer shaft housing/cylinder block	12	9
Sump to cylinder block	12	9
Temperature gauge sender unit	6	4
Thermostat housing	20	15
Throttle body to intake manifold	10	7
Timing chain lower cover	11	8
Timing chain lower guide bolt	26	19
Timing chain upper cover	8	6
Timing chain upper guide bolt	12	9
Wheel bolts:		
Except 16 in aluminium wheels	140	103
16 in aluminium wheels	170	125

*Do not re-use

1 General information

Using this Chapter

Chapter 2 is divided into three Parts: A, B and C. Repair operations that can be carried out with the engine in the vehicle are described in Part A (petrol engines) and Part B (diesel engines). Part C covers the removal of the engine/transmission as a unit, and describes the engine dismantling and overhaul procedures.

In Parts A and B, the assumption is made that the engine is installed in the vehicle, with all ancillaries connected. If the engine has been removed for overhaul, the preliminary dismantling information which precedes each operation may be ignored.

Access to the engine compartment can be improved by removing the bonnet as described in Chapter 11.

Engine description

The engines are water-cooled, double-overhead camshaft, in-line four-cylinder units, with cast-iron cylinder blocks and aluminium-alloy cylinder heads. All are mounted transversely at the front of the vehicle, with the transmission bolted to the left-hand of the engine.

The crankshaft is of five-bearing type, and thrustwashers are fitted to the centre main bearing to control crankshaft endfloat.

The camshafts are driven by a simplex (single row) timing chain from the crankshaft sprocket. A hydraulic tensioner is fitted to the chain. The cylinder block-mounted oil pump is also driven by a simplex chain from the crankshaft sprocket. On 2.3 litre models, in order to smooth the running of the engine, a housing with two balancer shafts is fitted under the cylinder block. The shafts rotate in opposite directions at twice the speed of the crankshaft, and thus produce vibrations which counter those produced by the engine itself. The shafts are driven from the crankshaft sprocket, by the same chain that drives the oil pump.

On all engines, the valves are operated from the camshaft through hydraulic bucket-type tappets, and the valve clearances are adjusted automatically.

The cylinder head carries the double camshafts. It also houses the inlet and exhaust valves, which are closed by single or double coil springs, and which run in sintered guides pressed into the cylinder head. The camshaft actuates the valves directly via hydraulic tappets, mounted in the cylinder head. The cylinder head contains integral oilways which supply and lubricate the tappets. On 2.3 litre models, the exhaust valves are sodium-filled to provide better cooling.

Engine coolant is circulated by a pump, driven by an auxiliary drivebelt from the crankshaft pulley. For details of the cooling system, refer to Chapter 3.

Lubricant is circulated under pressure by means of a bi-rotor pump, driven by a chain from the crankshaft. Oil is drawn from the sump through a strainer, and then forced through an externally-mounted, renewable screw-on filter. From there, it is distributed to the cylinder head, where it lubricates the camshaft journals and hydraulic tappets, and also to the crankcase, where it lubricates the main bearings, connecting rod big-ends, gudgeon pins and cylinder bores.

Repairs possible with the engine installed in the vehicle

The following operations can be performed without removing the engine:
a) Auxiliary drivebelt – removal and refitting.
b) Camshafts – removal and refitting.
c) Camshaft sprockets – removal and refitting.
d) Coolant pump – removal and refitting (refer to Chapter 3).
e) Crankshaft oil seals – renewal.

f) Crankshaft sprocket – removal and refitting.
g) Cylinder head – removal and refitting.
h) Engine mountings – inspection and renewal.
i) Sump – removal and refitting.
j) Balancer shaft housing (2.3 litre engines) – removal, inspection and refitting.
k) Timing chain, sprockets and covers – removal, inspection and refitting.

2 Engine valve timing marks – general information and usage

General information

1 The crankshaft and camshafts are interconnected by the timing chain, and rotate in phase with each other. If the timing chain is removed, it is possible for the shafts to rotate independently of each other, and the correct phasing is then lost.
2 The design of the engines covered in this Chapter is such that piston-to-valve contact will occur if the crankshaft is turned with the timing chain removed. For this reason, it is important that the correct phasing between the camshafts and crankshaft is preserved whilst the timing chain is off the engine. This is

achieved by setting the engine in a reference condition (known as Top Dead Centre or TDC) before the timing chain is removed, and then preventing the shafts from rotating until the chain is refitted. Similarly, if the engine has been dismantled for overhaul, the engine can be set to TDC during reassembly to ensure that the correct shaft phasing is restored.
3 TDC is the highest position a piston reaches within its respective cylinder – in a four-stroke engine, each piston reaches TDC twice per cycle; once on the compression stroke, and once on the exhaust stroke. In general, TDC normally refers to No 1 cylinder on the compression stroke. Note that the cylinders are numbered one to four, starting from the timing chain end of the engine.
4 The crankshaft pulley has a marking which, when in the 12 o'clock position (vertical) in relation to the cylinder block, indicates that No 1 cylinder (and hence also No 4 cylinder) is at TDC (see illustration).
5 The camshaft sprockets are also equipped with timing marks (see illustration) – when these are aligned as shown, No 1 cylinder is at TDC compression.

Setting No 1 cylinder at TDC

6 Before starting work, make sure that the ignition is switched off.
7 Remove the timing chain upper cover (see Section 8).
8 Remove all of the spark plugs as described in Chapter 1A.
9 Using a socket or spanner on the crankshaft, rotate the engine clockwise until the mark on the crankshaft pulley is in the 12 o'clock position (vertical) in relation to cylinder block (see illustration 2.4).
10 Examine the camshaft sprockets, and check that the marks are aligned (see illustration 2.5). If the camshaft sprocket marks are adjacent to each other, and aligned with the cylinder head surface, the engine is set to TDC on cylinder No 4 (see illustration). Rotate the crankshaft pulley one complete turn to set the engine to TDC on No 1 cylinder.

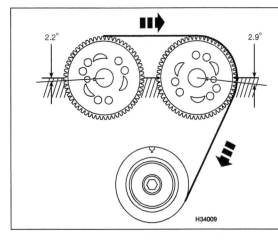

2.4 Rotate the crankshaft pulley until the notch on its circumference is in the 12 o'clock position, and the camshaft sprockets are positioned as shown

H34009

2.5 With the engine in position, the camshaft sprocket marks (arrowed) should be just below the upper edge of the cylinder head

2.10 If the camshaft sprocket marks (arrowed) are facing each other, the engine is at TDC on No 4 cylinder – rotate the crankshaft one complete turn

3 Cylinder compression test

1 When engine performance is down, or if misfiring occurs which cannot be attributed to the ignition or fuel systems, a compression test can provide diagnostic clues as to the engine's condition. If the test is performed regularly, it can give warning of trouble before any other symptoms become apparent.

2 The engine must be fully warmed-up to normal operating temperature, the battery must be fully charged. Remove the fuel pump fuse from below the central junction box behind the fusebox cover in the driver's side of the lower facia. The 20 amp (yellow) fuel pump fuse is No 18 on models up to '98 model year, and 14 on vehicles from '98 model year **(see illustration)**. Start the engine and allow it to stop.

3 Remove all the spark plugs (see Chapter 1A). **Note:** *In order to remove the spark plugs the ignition coils must be removed. Prior to removing the coils disconnect the wiring plugs.*

4 Fit a compression tester to the No 1 cylinder spark plug hole – the type of tester which screws into the plug thread is preferable.

5 Have an assistant hold the throttle wide open. Crank the engine on the starter motor several seconds. After one or two revolutions, the compression pressure should build-up to a maximum figure, and then stabilise. Record the highest reading obtained.

6 Repeat the test on the remaining cylinders, recording the pressure in each. Keep the throttle wide open.

7 All cylinders should produce very similar pressures; a difference of more than 3 bars between any two cylinders indicates a fault. Note that the compression should build-up quickly in a healthy engine. Low compression

3.2 Fuel pump fuse on vehicles up to '98 model year is No 18, and on vehicles from '98 model year, No 14 (arrowed)

on the first stroke, followed by gradually-increasing pressure on successive strokes, indicates worn piston rings. A low compression reading on the first stroke, which does not build-up during successive strokes, indicates leaking valves or a blown head gasket (a cracked head could also be the cause).

8 If the pressure in any cylinder is low, carry out the following test to isolate the cause. Introduce a teaspoonful of clean oil into that cylinder through its spark plug hole, and repeat the test.

9 If the addition of oil temporarily improves the compression pressure, this indicates that bore or piston wear is responsible for the pressure loss. No improvement suggests that leaking or burnt valves, or a blown head gasket, may be to blame.

10 A low reading from two adjacent cylinders is almost certainly due to the head gasket having blown between them.

11 If one cylinder is about 20 percent lower than the others and the engine has a slightly rough idle, a worn camshaft lobe could be the cause.

12 On completion of the test, refit the spark plugs, and fuel pump fuse.

4 Timing chain, sprockets and tensioner – removal, examination and refitting

General information

1 The primary function of the timing chain is to drive the camshafts. Should the chain break in service, the valve timing will be disturbed and piston-to-valve contact will occur, resulting in serious engine damage.

Removal

2 Before starting work, disconnect the battery negative (earth) lead (see Chapter 5A).

3 Set the engine at TDC on No 1 cylinder as described in Section 2.

4 Remove the oil pump/balancer shaft drive chain as described in Section 5.

5 Squeeze the upper timing chain guide securing lugs together, using pliers if necessary, and withdraw the guide from the plate at the front of the cylinder head **(see illustration)**. Discard the chain guide, a new one must be fitted.

6 Hold the inlet camshaft sprocket stationary using a peg spanner (or similar) which engages with the spokes of the camshaft sprocket. Unscrew the camshaft sprocket Torx bolt, taking care not to drop the washer from the bolt **(see illustration)**. Repeat the procedure on the exhaust camshaft sprocket. Slide the sprockets from the camshafts and the timing chain, and lay the chain over the exhaust side of the timing case, having eliminated the slack in the chain. Secure the chain in place using a cable tie or similar.

7 Using a suitable pair of pliers, extract the circlip from the chain tensioner arm pivot pin, taking care not to drop it into the timing case, then withdraw the pivot pin from the tensioner arm. If the pin is difficult to extract, an M6 bolt

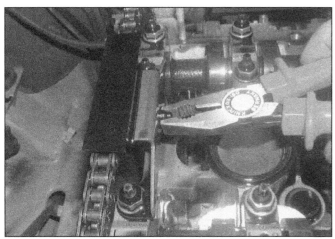

4.5 Squeeze together the retaining lugs, and remove the timing chain guide

4.6 Use a tool to hold the sprocket, and undo the Torx bolt – don't drop the washer

4.7a Pull out the circlip (arrowed) . . .

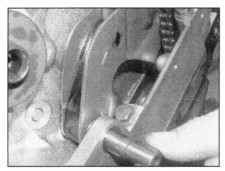

4.7b . . . and extract the pivot pin

4.7c If the pin is reluctant to move, screw in a 6 mm bolt, and pull it out

4.10a Undo the upper timing chain guide bolt (arrowed) . . .

4.10b . . . and the lower bolt (note the washers)

Refitting

15 Install the new tensioner plunger into the cylinder head. Before fitting the plunger, take note of the position of the piston **(see illustration)**. The assembly is normally supplied with the piston protruding slightly from the cylinder, or slightly below the top surface of the cylinder (A). If the new assembly is supplied with the piston partially unlatched (B), or fully unlatched (C), it must not be used.

> ⚠ **Warning: Take care when installing the plunger assembly, as there is a risk of personal injury if the piston flies out.**

16 Ensure that the slot for the Woodruff key in the end of the crankshaft is pointing vertically downwards. If necessary, temporarily refit the crankshaft pulley bolt in order to turn the crankshaft to the required position.

17 Insert the timing chain and chain guide down through the timing case. Ensure that the single copper coloured link is at the lower end **(see illustration)**. If desired, use a cable tie to prevent the timing chain from dropping into the timing case, as during removal.

18 Fit the chain to the inner row of teeth, aligning the coppered link in the chain with the timing mark on the sprocket **(see illustration)**. Slide the sprocket onto the crankshaft, ensuring the notch in the sprocket aligns with the groove in the crankshaft **(see**

can be screwed into the end to facilitate removal **(see illustrations)**.

8 Lift the tensioner arm from the timing case.

9 Lift the tensioner plunger assembly from the cylinder head, and discard it. A new one must be fitted.

10 Unscrew the two Torx bolts securing the timing chain guide, and withdraw the guide through the top of the timing case **(see illustrations)**.

11 Remove the Woodruff key from the end of the crankshaft, prising it free with a screwdriver if necessary, then slide the double

chain sprocket from the crankshaft, and lift the chain from the sprocket. Remove the chain from the top of the timing case.

Examination

12 Examine all the teeth on the camshafts and crankshaft sprockets. If the teeth are 'hooked' in appearance, renew the sprockets.

13 Check the tensioner sprocket for wear. If excessive wear is evident, the complete tensioner assembly must be renewed. Note that the tensioner plunger must be renewed whenever the chain is disturbed.

14 Examine the chain for wear. If the chain has been in operation for some time, if the chain can be pulled outwards from the sprocket teeth, or if when held horizontally (rollers vertical) it takes on a deeply bowed appearance, renew it.

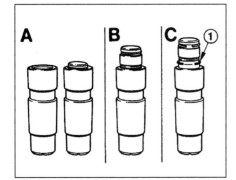

4.15 Timing chain plunger assembly

A Piston retracted – plunger assembly usable
B Piston partially unlatched – discard plunger assembly
C Latching ring (1) visible – discard plunger assembly

4.17 The copper-coloured link must be at the bottom (arrowed)

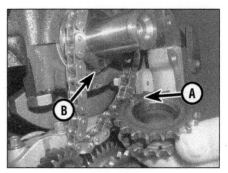

4.18a The notch on the sprocket (A) must align with the groove in the crankshaft (B)

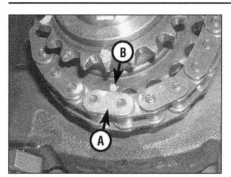

4.18b The copper-coloured link (A) must align with the mark on the sprocket (B)

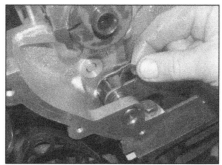

4.20 Insert the pivot pin, and secure it with the circlip

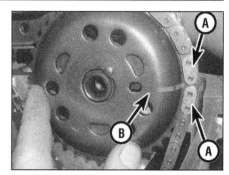

4.21 The copper-coloured links (A) must be centred around the mark on the sprocket (B)

illustration). Refit the Woodruff key into the end of the crankshaft.

19 Apply a little locking compound to the threads, and fit the bolts securing the chain guide in position. Tighten the bolts to the specified torque. Note that the upper bolt is fitted with a plain and a wave washer (see illustration 4.10b).

20 Refit the chain tensioner arm into position, then insert the pivot pin, and secure it with the circlip (see illustration). Take care not to drop the circlip into the timing case.

21 Release the cable tie securing the timing chain, take the slack out of the exhaust side of the chain, and fit the exhaust camshaft sprocket to the chain. The copper-coloured links must be centred around the mark on the sprocket (see illustration).

22 Fit the sprocket to the exhaust camshaft, with the camshaft in the TDC position (ie, with the exhaust camshaft sprocket timing mark in line with the top edge of the cylinder head, pointing to the exhaust side of the engine, refer to Section 2). If necessary, use a pair of pliers on one of the unmachined sections of the camshaft to turn the camshaft slightly. Take care not to damage the machined surfaces of the camshaft (see illustration). Note that the sprocket will only fit properly in one position – when the notch in the rear of the sprocket aligns with the groove in the end of the camshaft. Tighten the camshaft sprocket retaining bolt finger-tight only at this stage.

23 Fit the intake camshaft sprocket to the chain. Again, the copper-coloured links must be centred around the mark on the sprocket (see illustration).

24 Refit the sprocket to the intake camshaft, with the camshaft in the TDC position (ie, with the intake camshaft sprocket timing mark in line with the top edge of the cylinder head, pointing to the intake side of the engine – see Section 2). Again, if necessary, turn the camshaft to enable the sprocket to be fitted. Tighten the camshaft sprocket retaining bolt finger-tight only at this stage.

25 Turn the crankshaft clockwise slowly until the intake camshaft begins to turn.

26 If the chain tensioner plunger piston protrudes from the cylinder, unlatch the piston by gently tapping the piston with a brass drift.

27 If the plunger is below the top surface of the cylinder, a tool must be fabricated to unlatch the piston (see illustration). It is suggested that 2.5 mm diameter welding rod is used to manufacture the tool. Use the tool to release the piston as follows.

28 Carefully lift the chain tensioner arm with a screwdriver, and insert the tool between the tensioner arm and the piston. Remove the screwdriver, and release the piston by pressing down the tensioner arm by hand. Carefully withdraw the tool once the piston has been released.

29 Hold the camshaft sprockets using the same method as used during dismantling, and

tighten the sprocket bolts to the specified torque.

30 Temporarily refit the crankshaft pulley bolt, and rotate the crankshaft two full turns in a clockwise direction, and check that the sprocket marks align as described in Section 2.

31 Turn the crankshaft clockwise through another complete revolution, and check that the timing marks on the camshaft sprockets are facing each other, directly in line with the top face of the cylinder head (see illustration 2.10).

32 If the timing marks do not align as described, the chain has been incorrectly fitted, and should be removed and refitted. Note that a new tensioner plunger will be required if this is the case.

33 Once the timing marks correctly align, rotate the crankshaft clockwise one complete revolution until the crankshaft is the TDC position on No 1 cylinder (if necessary, refer to Section 2).

34 Push a new upper timing chain guide on to the bracket between the two camshaft sprockets.

35 Refit the oil pump/balancer shaft drive chain as described in Section 5.

36 Refit the timing chain upper cover and camshaft cover, as described in Sections 8 and 7 respectively.

37 Lower the vehicle to the ground, and reconnect the battery earth lead.

4.22 If necessary, use a pair of pliers on the unmachined surface to rotate the camshaft

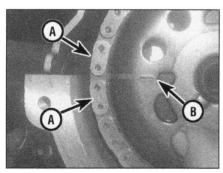

4.23 Centre the copper-coloured links (A) around the sprocket mark (B), and align the mark with the top edge of the cylinder head

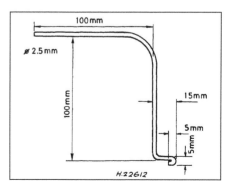

4.27 Fabricated tool used to unlatch the tensioner plunger piston

5.4 Compress the oil pump/balancer shaft chain tensioner, and lock it in place by inserting a drill bit (arrowed)

5.6a Undo the Torx bolts and remove the lower chain guide . . .

5.6b . . . and the upper guide

5 Oil pump/balancer shafts drive chain – removal and refitting

Removal

1 Apply the handbrake, then jack up the front of the vehicle and support it on axle stands (see *Jacking and vehicle support*). Undo the two retaining nuts and four bolts (two each side), and remove the undershield from under the engine compartment.
2 On 2.3 litre engines, set the engine at TDC as described in Section 2, then rotate the crankshaft a further half-a-turn to position it at TDC on cylinder No 2.
3 Remove the lower timing chain cover as described in Section 8.

2.3 litre engines

4 Compress the oil pump drive chain tensioner, and insert a 2.5 mm drill bit into the hole in the tensioner body, to secure the tensioner arm in place **(see illustration)**.
5 Undo the retaining Torx bolt and remove the tensioner from the engine.
6 Unscrew the Torx bolts and remove both oil pump chain guides. Remove the oil pump chain leaving the oil pump sprocket in place **(see illustrations)**. Note that the upper guide is slotted at its lower end to fit over the lower Torx bolt.

2.0 litre engines

7 Slacken and remove the retaining bolt, and carefully remove the oil pump chain tensioner **(see illustration)**.
8 Undo the Torx bolt and withdraw the oil pump sprocket complete with drive chain.

Refitting

2.3 litre engines

9 Fit the chain around the oil pump sprocket, balancer shaft sprocket, and outer row of teeth on the crankshaft sprocket. The copper-coloured links on the chain must be centred around the marks on the crankshaft and balance shaft sprocket **(see illustrations)**.
10 Refit the upper and lower oil pump chain guides, and tighten the bolts to the specified torque.
11 Check that the oil pump chain tensioner is still in its compressed state. If it is not, squeeze the arm into the tensioner body, and insert a 2.5 mm drill bit into the hole on the front face to hold the arm in place **(see illustration 5.4)**. Position the tensioner against the chain, insert and tighten the retaining bolts to the specified torque. Withdraw the drill bit, and allow the tensioner to extend.

2.0 litre engines

12 Fit the oil pump drive chain around the outer crankshaft sprocket and the oil pump sprocket, then refit the oil pump sprocket, and

tighten the securing bolt to the specified torque.
13 Refit the oil pump drive chain tensioner **(see illustration 5.7)**. Tighten the bolt to the specified torque.

All engines

14 Refit the lower timing cover as described in Section 8.
15 On all engines, refit the auxiliary drivebelt as described in Section 6.
16 On 2.3 litre engines, refit the timing chain upper cover and camshaft cover, as described in Sections 8 and 7 respectively.
17 Working underneath the vehicle, refit the engine undershield.
18 Lower the vehicle to the ground.

6 Auxiliary drivebelt – removal and refitting

1 Depending on the vehicle specification and engine type, the auxiliary drivebelt drives the alternator, coolant pump, power steering pump and, where fitted, the air conditioning compressor.
2 The drivebelt is of the Poly-Vee ribbed design.
3 On all engines, the drivebelt tension is adjusted automatically by a spring-tensioned idler.

5.7 Oil pump chain tensioner securing bolt (arrowed)

5.9a Fit the oil pump chain with the copper-coloured link (A) over the mark on the crankshaft sprocket (B)

5.9b Take up the slack to check the timing

6.6 Rotate the tensioner clockwise to relieve the tension

4 To remove the drivebelts first apply the handbrake, then jack up the front of the vehicle and support it on axle stands (see *Jacking and vehicle support*). Undo the four bolts and two nuts, then remove the undershield from under the engine compartment.

Removal

5 If the drivebelt is to be re-used, mark it for clockwise direction to ensure it is refitted the same way round.
6 Using a spanner on the hexagon in the centre of the tensioner pulley, rotate the tensioner clockwise to relieve the tension on the belt **(see illustration)**. Holding the tensioner in this position, disengage the belt from the pulleys.

Refitting

7 Route the drivebelt around the pulleys, holding the tensioner with a spanner. When the belt is correctly routed, release the tensioner **(see illustrations)**. If a used belt is being refitted, ensure the previously made direction of the rotation marks are observed.
8 Refit the engine undershield, and lower the vehicle to the ground.

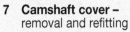

7 Camshaft cover –
removal and refitting

Removal

1 Pull out the upper part of the battery compartment panel **(see illustration)**.
2 Remove the air cleaner housing with reference to Chapter 4A.
3 Undo the three retaining bolts, and remove the bulkhead cover **(see illustration)**. Note that the centre bolt also secures the accelerator cable support bracket. Slide the trim to the right-hand side and manoeuvre it from behind the coolant expansion tank.
4 Pull the crankcase ventilation valve/

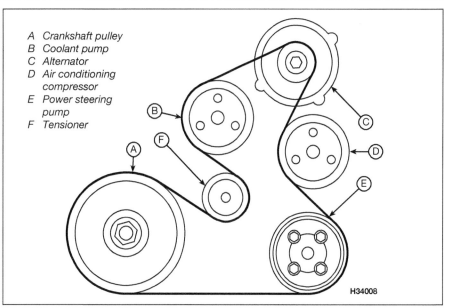

A Crankshaft pulley
B Coolant pump
C Alternator
D Air conditioning compressor
E Power steering pump
F Tensioner

6.7a Auxiliary belt routing – 2.0 litre

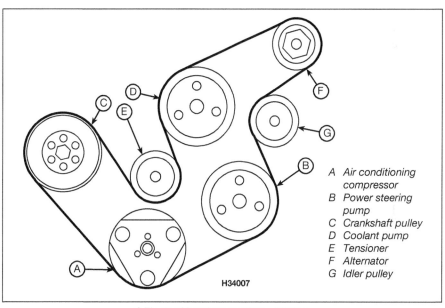

A Air conditioning compressor
B Power steering pump
C Crankshaft pulley
D Coolant pump
E Tensioner
F Alternator
G Idler pulley

6.7b Auxiliary belt routing – 2.3 litre

7.1 Pull out the upper battery compartment panel

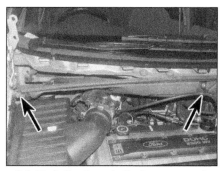

7.3 Undo the three bolts (two arrowed) and remove the bulkhead cover

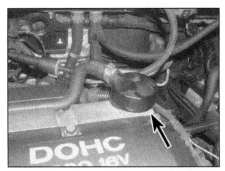

7.4 Pull out the ventilation valve (arrowed)

7.5 Undo the bolts and remove ignition coils cover

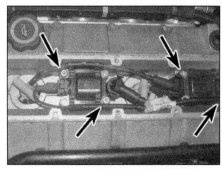

7.6a Undo the coil screws (arrowed) . . .

7.6b . . . and pull the HT connectors from the spark plugs

7.10 Disconnect the camshaft position sensor wiring plug – 2.3 litre

7.11 Disconnect the camshaft position sensor wiring plug – 2.0 litre

breather tube from the camshaft cover **(see illustration)**.

2.3 litre engines

5 Unscrew the ten bolts and remove the ignition coils cover **(see illustration)**.
6 Undo the coil retaining bolts, and disconnect the HT leads from the spark plugs **(see illustrations)**. **Note:** *Do not pull on the cable when disconnecting the plugs, only pull on the connectors. If the connectors are difficult to remove, twist the connector slightly prior to pulling.*
7 Remove the coils and lay them to one side.
8 If desired, using a spark plug socket and long extension, remove the spark plugs, if necessary refer to Chapter 1A.
9 Undo the two bolts securing the alternator wiring rail to the cylinder head.

10 Disconnect the camshaft position sensor wiring plug and unscrew the 15 camshaft cover retaining bolts/nuts **(see illustration)**.

2.0 litre engines

11 Disconnect the camshaft position sensor wiring plug **(see illustration)**.
12 Unscrew the 11 bolts securing the camshaft cover to the cylinder head.

All engines

13 Remove the camshaft cover, and recover the gasket(s).

Refitting

14 Clean the surfaces of the camshaft cover and cylinder head.
15 Carefully fit the gasket(s) to the camshaft cover, then fit the rubber washers over the

metal sleeves to hold them in place **(see illustrations)**. Position the cover on the cylinder head, then tighten the bolts/nuts progressively to the specified torque in the sequence shown **(see illustration)**.
16 The remainder of refitting is a reversal of removal. Note that prior to reconnecting the HT leads connectors to the spark plugs on 2.3 litre engines, smear a little silicone grease around the inside of the connectors.

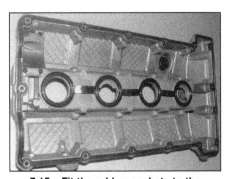

7.15a Fit the rubber gaskets to the camshaft cover . . .

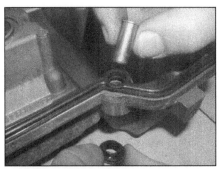

7.15b . . . then fit the metal sleeves with the rubber washers to hold them in place

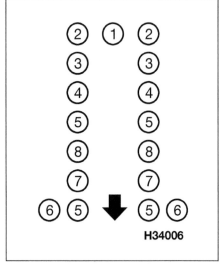

7.15c Progressively tighten the cover bolts in the sequence shown

8.3 Note the earth strap (arrowed) secured to the engine mounting bracket

8.4 Remove the small bracket from the corner of the cylinder head

8.5 Undo the three Torx screws and remove the engine mounting

8 Timing chain covers – removal and refitting

Upper cover

Removal

1 Remove the camshaft cover as described in Section 7. Undo the two retaining nuts and four bolts (two each side), and remove the engine undershield.

2 Position a jack under the engine sump, and take the weight of the engine. Use a block of wood on the jack head to prevent any damage to the sump casing.

3 Undo the three bolts and two nuts, then remove the engine mounting bracket. Where fitted, undo the nut securing the earth strap to the engine mounting bracket stud **(see illustration)**.

4 Undo the retaining bolt and stud, and remove the small engine support bracket from the front left-hand corner of the cylinder head **(see illustration)**.

5 Unscrew the three Torx screws, and remove the engine mounting from the right-hand side inner wing **(see illustration)**.

6 Using the jack, raise the engine, pushing back at the same time, until the engine support plate lower bolts are visible. Undo the retaining bolts and remove the engine support plate **(see illustration)**.

7 Remove the 7 bolts and withdraw the timing chain upper cover from the engine **(see illustration)**.

Refitting

8 Ensure the mating surfaces of the cover and cylinder head are clean and dry. Refit the upper timing cover using a new gasket. Before finally tightening the retaining bolts, align the top edge of the cover with the upper surface of the cylinder head. The step down from the cylinder head surface to the cover must be no more than 0.13 mm **(see illustration)**. Tighten the bolts to the specified torque.

9 The remainder of refitting is a reversal of removal.

Lower cover

Removal

10 Apply the handbrake, then jack up the front of the vehicle and support it on axle stands (see *Jacking and vehicle support*). Undo the two retaining nuts and four bolts

(two each side), and remove the engine undershield. With reference to Section 6, remove the auxiliary drivebelt.

11 On engines with a two-part crankshaft pulley, remove the outer ring of six bolts from the pulley, and use two M6 x 20 mm bolts in the holes provided to the force the pulley from the hub **(see illustration)**.

12 On all engines, slacken the crankshaft pulley bolt. Prevent the crankshaft from turning by engaging top gear (manual gearbox only) and having an assistant press the brake pedal hard, or by remove the starter motor and jamming the ring gear teeth with a lever or large flat-bladed screwdriver.

13 Unscrew the pulley bolt part-way, and use a suitable two-legged puller to draw the pulley hub from the crankshaft. We used two 6 mm bolts to attach the puller to the crankshaft pulley **(see illustration)**.

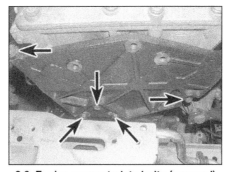

8.6 Engine support plate bolts (arrowed)

8.7 Undo the bolts and remove the upper timing chain cover

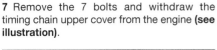

8.8 Check the step from the timing cover to the cylinder head with feeler gauges

8.11 Use two M6 bolts to force the pulley from the hub

8.13 Attach the puller to the hub using two M6 bolts and washers

8.19a Fit the hub to the crankshaft, aligning the Woodruff key with the slot in the hub

8.19b Use an M12 bolt, washer and nut to press the hub into place

8.19c The crankshaft pulley holes are offset so that it will only fit one way

14 Working underneath the vehicle, remove the bolt securing the power steering pipe to the support bracket.

15 Remove the bolts securing the lower timing chain cover.

Refitting

16 Using a punch (or similar) drive the seal out from the outside of the cover. Press the new oil seal into place from the inside of the cover, ensuring that the spring side of the seal faces the inside of the cover (see Section 10). Lubricate the inside lip of the seal with clean engine oil. On original covers the oil seal was bonded into place, and although it is possible to drive the seal out, there is a risk of distorting the cover. If this is the case, renewal of the cover is necessary.

17 Position a new timing cover gasket on the engine block. On 2.3 litre engines, the cover has an integral vulcanised gasket. Consequently, if the gasket is damaged, the cover must be renewed. Manoeuvre the cover over the crankshaft, and push it into place, taking care not to damage the inner edge of the oil seal on the shoulder of the crankshaft. Temporarily refit the crankshaft pulley/hub to 'centre' the cover and oil seal. Tighten the cover retaining bolts to the specified torque.

18 Where applicable, refit the power steering pipe to the support bracket and tighten the bolt securely.

19 On engines with a two-part crankshaft pulley, position the pulley hub over the end of the crankshaft, ensuring that the Woodruff key aligns with the slot in the hub, and press the pulley into place. It may be possible to gently tap the hub into place using a soft-faced

hammer, although Ford specify the use of special tool No 21-214 to press the hub into place. If necessary however, it is possible to fabricate a home-made equivalent using an M12 bolt, washer and nut. Screw the bolt, washer and nut into the end of the crankshaft, and up against the hub, then tighten the nut until the hub is against the shoulder of the crankshaft (see illustrations). Remove the tool. Screw in the hub retaining bolt and tighten it to the Stage 1 torque setting, and the Stage 2 angle tightening setting. Use the method employed during dismantling to prevent the crankshaft from rotating. Position the pulley on the hub, fit and tighten the retaining bolts to the specified torque. Note that one of the holes in the pulley and hub is slightly offset, so the pulley will only fit correctly in one position (see illustration).

20 On engines with a one-part crankshaft pulley, position the pulley over the end of the crankshaft, ensuring that the Woodruff key aligns with the slot in the pulley, and press the pulley into place. It may be possible to tap the pulley into place with a soft-faced hammer, although Ford specify the use of special tool No 16-057 to press the pulley into place. If necessary however, it is possible to fabricate a home-made equivalent using an M12 bolt, washer and nut. Screw the bolt, washer and nut into the end of the crankshaft, and up against the pulley, then tighten the nut until the pulley is against the shoulder of the crankshaft (see illustrations 8.19a and 8.19b). Remove the tool. Screw in the pulley retaining bolt and tighten it to the Stage 1 torque setting, and the Stage 2 angle tightening setting. Use the

method employed during dismantling to prevent the crankshaft from rotating.

21 On all engines, refit the auxiliary drivebelt as described in Section 6.

22 Working underneath the vehicle, refit the engine undershield.

23 Lower the vehicle to the ground.

9 Camshafts and hydraulic tappets – removal, inspection and refitting

Removal

1 Set the engine to TDC on No 1 cylinder, as described in Section 2.

2 Squeeze the upper timing chain guide securing lugs together, using pliers if necessary, and withdraw the guide from the plate at the front of the cylinder head (see illustration). Discard the chain guide, a new one must be fitted.

3 Hold the inlet camshaft sprocket stationary using a peg spanner (or similar) which engages with the spokes of the camshaft sprocket. Unscrew the camshaft sprocket Torx bolt, taking care not to drop the washer from the bolt. Repeat the procedure on the exhaust camshaft sprocket. Slide the sprockets from the camshafts and the timing chain, and lay the chain over the exhaust side of the timing case, having eliminated the slack in the chain. Secure the chain in place using a cable tie or similar.

4 Using a suitable pair of pliers, extract the circlip from the chain tensioner arm pivot pin, taking care not to drop it into the timing case, then withdraw the pivot pin from the tensioner arm. If the pin is difficult to extract, an M6 bolt can be screwed into the end to facilitate removal (see illustrations 4.7a, 4.7b and 4.7c).

5 Lift the tensioner arm from the timing case.

6 Withdraw the tensioner plunger assembly from the cylinder head, and discard it. A new one must be fitted.

7 Take note of the markings on the camshaft bearing caps. It is essential that they are refitted to their original positions. Evenly and progressively slacken the bearing cap nuts, until the caps can be removed. Note that the upper timing chain guide is retained by the No 1 intake and exhaust camshaft bearing caps (see illustration). Lift the camshafts from the cylinder head.

9.2 Squeeze the lugs (arrowed) together and remove the upper timing chain guide

9.7 The upper timing chain guide bracket is retained by No 1 intake and exhaust bearing cap nuts (arrowed)

9.14 Refit the hydraulic tappets to their original location

9.16a Position the camshaft, so that none of the lobes are at full lift

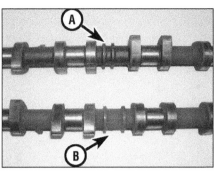

9.16b On 2.3 litre engines, rings identify the intake camshaft (A) and exhaust camshaft (B)

8 If the hydraulic tappets are to be removed proceed as follows. Obtain eight (2.0 litre engine) or sixteen (2.3 litre engine) small containers, or a large container divided into eight, or sixteen, compartments to store the tappets. Partially fill the container(s) so that the tappets will be immersed in oil.

9 Withdraw the tappets from the cylinder head bores – a tool fitted with a rubber suction cup (such as a valve grinding tool) will aid in this operation. Store the tappets in the order that they are removed from the cylinder head, to ensure they are refitted to the their original locations. Failure to do so could result in accelerated camshaft and tappet wear after reassembly.

10 After removing all the tappets, ensure that any excess oil accidentally spilled into the camshaft bearing caps securing bolt holes is removed, using compressed air or absorbent rag. This will prevent damage to the cylinder head by hydraulic action during reassembly.

Inspection

11 Examine the camshaft bearing surfaces and cam lobes for signs of wear ridges and scoring. Renew the camshaft if any of these conditions are apparent. Examine the condition of the bearing surfaces of the bearing caps and cylinder head.

12 If available, use a micrometer to measure the lift of the camshaft lobes. Measure the diameter of the camshaft at 90° to the camshaft lobe, and in line with the camshaft lobe. Subtract the first measurement from the second, and compare the dimension to that given in the Specifications at the start of this Chapter.

13 Inspect the tappet upper surfaces for signs of wear. If evident, examine the corresponding camshaft lobe as it is likely to be worn in the same manner. Check the sides of each tappet for signs of scoring.

Refitting

14 Lubricate the hydraulic tappets with clean engine oil, and refit them into their original locations **(see illustration)**.

15 Using a spanner on the crankshaft pulley, rotate the engine clockwise approximately 45°, to eliminate the possibility of accidental piston-to-valve contact.

16 Lubricate the bearing surfaces in the cylinder head, and the bearing surfaces and lobes of the camshaft with clean engine oil. Refit the camshafts into the cylinder head, in such a position that none of the lobes are at full lift **(see illustration)**. Note that on 2.0 litre engines the camshafts are identified with an R for intake, and an L for exhaust. On 2.3 litre

engines, the camshafts are marked with two identification rings between the second and third cylinder lobes **(see illustration)**.

17 Refit the camshaft bearing caps to their original locations, noting that the intake camshaft caps are numbered R1 to 5, and the exhaust camshaft caps are numbered L1 to 5, from the timing chain end of the cylinder head **(see illustrations)**. Note that the upper timing chain guide is fitted onto the studs of No 1 bearing cap **(see illustration 9.7)**.

18 Tighten the bearing cap nuts by hand evenly and progressively to lower the camshafts into position. Continue to tighten the bearing caps until they contact the cylinder head, then tighten them to the specified torque setting.

19 After the camshafts bearings have been tightened down, the crankshaft must not be moved for 15 minutes.

20 Install the new tensioner plunger into the cylinder head. Before fitting the plunger, take note of the position of the piston **(see illustration 4.15)**. The assembly is normally supplied with the piston protruding slightly from the cylinder, or slightly below the top surface of the cylinder (A). If the new assembly is supplied with the piston partially unlatched (B), or fully unlatched (C), it must not be used.

9.17a The intake camshaft caps are labelled R1 to R5 (arrowed) . . .

9.17b . . . and the exhaust caps are labelled L1 to L5 (arrowed) starting from the timing chain end

9.33 Check that the sprocket marks are facing each other

 Warning: Take care when installing the plunger assembly, as there is a risk of personal injury if the piston flies out.

21 Using a spanner or socket on the crankshaft pulley, rotate the crankshaft 45° anti-clockwise, to the TDC position.

22 Refit the chain tensioner arm into position, then insert the pivot pin, and secure it with the circlip **(see illustration 4.20)**. Take care not to drop the circlip into the timing case.

23 Release the cable tie securing the timing chain, take the slack out of the exhaust side of the chain, and fit the exhaust camshaft sprocket to the chain. The copper-coloured links must be centred around the mark on the sprocket **(see illustration 4.21)**.

24 Fit the sprocket to the exhaust camshaft, with the camshaft in the TDC position (ie, with the exhaust camshaft sprocket timing mark in line with the top edge of the cylinder head, pointing to the exhaust side of the engine, refer to Section 2). If necessary, use a pair of pliers on one of the unmachined sections of the camshaft to turn the camshaft slightly. Take care not to damage the machined surfaces of the camshaft. Note that the sprocket will only fit properly in one position – when the notch in the rear of the sprocket aligns with the groove in the end of the camshaft. Tighten the camshaft sprocket retaining bolt finger-tight only at this stage.

25 Fit the intake camshaft sprocket to the chain. Again, the copper-coloured links must be centred around the mark on the sprocket **(see illustration 4.23)**.

26 Refit the sprocket to the intake camshaft, with the camshaft in the TDC position (ie, with the intake camshaft sprocket timing mark in line with the top edge of the cylinder head, pointing to the intake side of the engine – see Section 2). Again, if necessary, turn the camshaft to enable the sprocket to be fitted. Tighten the camshaft sprocket retaining bolt finger-tight only at this stage.

27 Turn the crankshaft clockwise slowly until the intake camshaft begins to turn.

28 If the chain tensioner plunger piston protrudes from the cylinder, unlatch the piston by gently tapping the piston with a brass drift.

29 If the plunger is below the top surface of the cylinder, a tool must be fabricated to unlatch the piston **(see illustration 4.27)**. It is suggested that 2.5 mm diameter welding rod is used to manufacture the tool. Use the tool to release the piston as follows.

30 Carefully lift the chain tensioner arm with a screwdriver, and insert the tool between the tensioner arm and the piston. Remove the screwdriver, and release the piston by pressing down the tensioner arm by hand. Carefully withdraw the tool once the piston has been released.

31 Hold the camshaft sprockets using the same method as used during dismantling, and tighten the sprocket bolts to the specified torque.

32 Temporarily refit the crankshaft pulley bolt, and rotate the crankshaft two full turns in a clockwise direction, and check that the sprocket marks align as described in Section 2.

33 Turn the crankshaft clockwise through another complete revolution, and check that the timing marks on the camshaft sprockets are facing each other, directly in line with the top face of the cylinder head **(see illustration)**.

34 If the timing marks do not align as described, the chain has been incorrectly fitted, and should be removed and refitted. Note that a new tensioner plunger will be required if this is the case.

35 Once the timing marks correctly align, rotate the crankshaft clockwise one complete revolution until the crankshaft is the TDC position on No 1 cylinder (if necessary, refer to Section 2).

36 Push a new upper timing chain guide on to the bracket between the two camshaft sprockets.

37 Refit the upper timing chain cover and camshaft cover as described in Sections 8 and 7 respectively.

10 Crankshaft oil seals – renewal

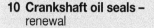

Timing chain end

1 Renewal of the seal is only possible once the lower timing cover has been removed (see Section 8).

2 With the cover on the bench, use a punch (or similar) to drive the seal from the cover from the outside. **Note:** *On original covers, the seal is bonded into place, and although the seal can be driven out, there is a high risk of distorting the cover. In which case the cover must be renewed.*

3 Clean the seal housing, and polish off any burrs or raised edges which may have caused the seal to fail in the first place.

4 Apply a smear of silicone sealant around the outside of the seal, and press the seal into place from the inside of the cover. Use a tubular drift (a socket) that bears only hard outer edge of the seal **(see illustrations)**.

5 Refit the lower timing cover as described in Section 8.

Flywheel/driveplate end

6 Remove the flywheel/driveplate, with reference to Section 12.

7 The oil seal must be renewed without removing the housing. Make a note of the fitted depth of the seal in its housing. Punch or drill two small holes opposite each other in the seal. Screw a self-tapping screw into each, and pull on the screws to extract the seal **(see illustration)**.

8 Clean the seal housing, and polish off any burrs or raised edges, which may have caused the seal to fail in the first place.

9 Lubricate the lip of the new seal with clean engine oil, and carefully locate the seal on the end of the crankshaft.

10 Using a suitable tubular drift, which bears only on the hard outer edge of the seal, drive the seal into position, to the same depth in the housing as the original was prior to removal.

10.4a From the inside of the cover, drive the seal into place . . .

10.4b . . . until it's flush with the cover outer edge

10.7 Pull on the self-tapping screws to extract the seal

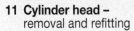
A tool can be improvised using a metal tube, a metal disc or flat bar, and two flywheel bolts. Draw the seal into position using the two flywheel bolts.

11 Wash off any traces of oil, and refit the flywheel/driveplate (with new bolts) as described in Section 12.

11 Cylinder head –
removal and refitting

Note: *Cylinder head dismantling and overhaul is covered in Chapter 2C.*

Warning: The cylinder head must have cooled to below 30°C before unscrew the cylinder head bolts.

Removal

1 Before starting work, disconnect the battery negative (earth) lead (see Chapter 5A). Depressurise the fuel system as described in Chapter 4A.
2 Remove the camshafts and hydraulic tappets as described in Section 9.
3 Undo the four nuts and disconnect the front exhaust pipe from the exhaust manifold.
4 Drain the cooling system as described in Chapter 1A.
5 On the rear side of the engine, disconnect the wiring plugs from the crankshaft position sensor, and the oil pressure switch. Unclip the harness from the retaining clip.

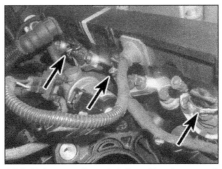
11.6 Prise out the retaining clips (arrowed) and remove injector wiring rail

6 Depress the retaining clips and pull off the connectors from the idle air control valve, No 4 injector and the throttle position sensor. Using a small screwdriver, prise out the retaining clips and lift off the injectors' power supply rail **(see illustration)**. Position the wiring harness to one side.
7 Where fitted, disconnect the hose from the secondary air injection filter.
8 Disconnect the coolant hose from the thermostat/coolant outlet housing at the left-hand end of the cylinder head **(see illustration)**.
9 Release the retaining clip and disconnect the heater hose from the thermostat/coolant outlet housing **(see illustration 11.8)**.
10 Disconnect the wiring plugs from the engine coolant temperature sensor, and temperature gauge sender, both located in the thermostat/coolant outlet housing. Where fitted, disconnect the wiring plug from the

11.8 Disconnect the hoses from the thermostat/coolant outlet housing

radio interference suppressor fitted above the thermostat housing.
11 Disconnect the inner end of the throttle cable from the quadrant, undo the three Torx screws and remove the cable from the engine complete with the support bracket **(see illustrations)**.
12 Release any retaining clips and disconnect the vacuum lines from the inlet manifold, idle air control valve and (where fitted) the EGR valve **(see illustrations)**. Note that the brake servo hose is disconnected by depressing the collar around the connection, and pulling the hose from the manifold **(see illustration)**.

2.0 litre engines

13 Disconnect the HT lead connectors from the spark plugs, unscrew the six retaining bolts and remove the ignition coils from the left-hand end of the cylinder head. Disconnect the wiring plugs from the coils as they are removed **(see illustration)**.

11.11a Disconnect the inner end of the accelerator cable from the quadrant

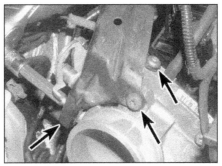
11.11b Undo the three accelerator cable bracket Torx screws (arrowed)

11.12a Disconnect the vacuum hoses from the inlet manifold . . .

11.12b . . . and the idle air control valve

11.12c The brake servo hose is released by depressing the collar

11.13 Undo the screws and remove the ignition coils (arrowed)

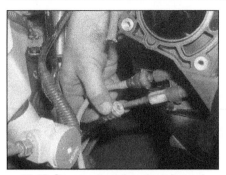

11.15 Squeeze together the tabs and disconnect the fuel supply and return couplings

11.20 Undo the three bolts at the right-hand end of the cylinder head

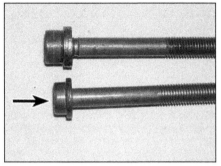

11.21a Only re-use bolt with integral washers (arrowed) . . .

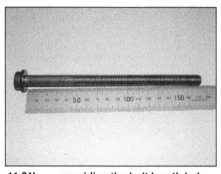

11.21b . . . providing the bolt length below the head does not exceed 174.3 mm

All engines

14 Unscrew the nut securing the alternator bracket to the cylinder head. Slacken the alternator top mounting nut and swivel the bracket away from the cylinder head.

15 Squeeze together the tabs of the quick-release connectors, and disconnect the fuel supply and return hoses **(see illustration)**. Note that the connectors are colour-coded to aid refitment.

16 Where fitted, undo the retaining bolts and remove the EGR valve and pipe.

17 Undo the nut securing the oil dipstick guide tube to the cylinder head. Carefully pull the dipstick guide tube from the engine block.

18 Unscrew the retaining bolts and remove the exhaust manifold heat shield.

19 Slacken and remove the upper bolt

securing the timing chain guide to the cylinder head **(see illustration 4.10a)**.

20 Undo and remove the three bolts at the right-hand end of the cylinder head **(see illustration)**.

21 Using a splined tool, unscrew the cylinder head bolts a turn at a time, in reverse order to the tightening sequence **(see illustration 11.29)** and remove them together with their washers. **Note:** *Only the cylinder head bolts with integral washers can be re-used, providing the length of the bolt below the head does not exceed 174.3 mm* **(see illustrations)**.

22 With all the bolts removed, lift the cylinder head from the block. If it is stuck, tap it free with a wooden mallet. Do not insert a lever into the gasket joint.

23 Remove the cylinder head gasket from the block.

24 If required, remove the inlet and exhaust manifolds from the cylinder head with reference to the relevant Part of Chapter 4.

Refitting

25 Thoroughly clean the contact faces of the cylinder head and block. Also clean any oil or coolant from the bolt holes in the block – if this precaution is not taken, not only will the tightening torque be incorrect but there is the possibility of damaging the block. Ensure the locating dowels are in place **(see illustrations)**. Where applicable (refer to paragraph 21), clean the threads of the used cylinder head bolts.

26 Where removed, refit the exhaust and intake manifolds to the cylinder head with reference to the relevant Part of Chapter 4.

27 Locate a new gasket on the block. The gasket will only fit one way around.

28 Carefully lower the head onto the block, making sure that it engages the location dowels correctly. Do not use any jointing compound on the cylinder head joint. Insert the cylinder head bolts, together with their integral washers, and initially hand-tighten them.

29 Using the sequence shown **(see illustration)** tighten all the bolts to the Stage 1 torque given in the Specifications.

30 Working in the same sequence, tighten the bolts to the Stage 2 torque, and the Stage 3 and 4 angles as given in the Specifications.

31 Insert the three bolts at the right-hand end of the cylinder head, and tighten them to the specified torque **(see illustration 11.20)**.

32 The remainder of refitting is a reversal of removal, bearing in mind the following points:

a) *After refitting the camshafts, allow 15 minutes before turning the crankshaft.*

b) *Tighten all nuts and bolts to their correct torque where specified.*

c) *Refill the cooling system as described in Chapter 1A.*

d) *Check the throttle cable adjustment as described in Chapter 4A.*

e) *Renew the oil dipstick guide tube O-ring.*

11.25a Ensure the locating dowels are in place at the timing chain end . . .

11.25b . . . and the flywheel end

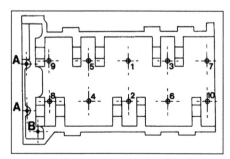

11.29 Cylinder head bolt tightening sequence

A Long M8 bolts   B Short M8 bolt

12.3 Flywheel locking tool

12 Flywheel/driveplate – removal, inspection and refitting

Removal

1 On manual gearbox models, remove the gearbox (see Chapter 7A) and clutch (see Chapter 6).

2 On automatic transmission models, remove the automatic transmission as described in Chapter 7B.

3 The flywheel/driveplate bolts are offset to ensure correct fitment. Unscrew the bolts while holding the flywheel/driveplate stationary. Temporarily insert a bolt in the cylinder block, and use a screwdriver to hold the flywheel/driveplate, or make up a holding tool as shown **(see illustration).**

4 Lift the flywheel/driveplate from the crankshaft. If removing a driveplate, note the location of the shim (next to the crankshaft) and the spacer.

Inspection

5 Check the flywheel/driveplate for wear and damage. Examine the starter ring gear for excessive wear to the teeth. If the driveplate or its ring gear are damaged, the complete driveplate must be renewed. The flywheel ring gear, however, may be renewed separately from the flywheel, but the work should be entrusted to a Ford dealer. If the clutch friction face is discoloured or scored excessively, it may be possible to regrind it, but this work

12.6 The flywheel bolts holes are slightly offset, so it will only fit one way around

should also be entrusted to a Ford dealer or specialist.

Refitting

6 Refitting is a reversal of removal **(see illustration)**. Use new bolts when refitting the flywheel or driveplate, and coat the threads of the bolts with locking fluid before inserting them. Tighten them to the specified torque.

13 Engine mountings – inspection and renewal

Inspection

1 If improved access is required, raise the front of the car and support it securely on axle stands. Undo the two retaining nuts and four bolts (two each side), and remove the engine undershield.

2 Check the mounting rubbers to see if they are cracked, hardened or separated from the metal at any point; renew the mounting if any such damage or deterioration is evident.

3 Check that all the mounting's fasteners are securely tightened; use a torque wrench to check if possible.

4 Using a large screwdriver or a crowbar, check for wear in the mounting by carefully levering against it to check for free play. Where this is not possible, enlist the aid of an assistant to move the engine/transmission back-and-forth, or from side-to-side, while you watch the mounting. While some free play

is to be expected even from new components, excessive wear should be obvious. If excessive free play is found, check first that the fasteners are correctly secured, then renew any worn components as described below.

Renewal

Right-hand engine mounting

5 Apply the handbrake then jack up the front of the vehicle and support it on axle stands (see *Jacking and vehicle support*). Undo the two retaining nuts and four bolts (two each side), and remove the undershield. Support the weight of the engine/transmission using a trolley jack with a block of wood placed on its head.

6 Remove the air cleaner housing as described in Chapter 4A.

7 Undo the three horizontal bolts securing the mounting bracket to the engine support plate, and the two nuts securing the mounting bracket to the engine mounting **(see illustration)**. Note the earth strap mounted on the foremost horizontal bolt.

8 Unscrew the three bolts and remove the mounting from the inner wing **(see illustration)**.

9 Fit the new engine mounting and bracket using a reversal of the removal procedure, tightening the nuts/bolts to the specified torque.

Left-hand engine mounting

10 Apply the handbrake then jack up the front of the vehicle and support it on axle stands (see *Jacking and vehicle support*). Undo the two retaining nuts and four bolts (two each side), and remove the undershield. Support the weight of the engine/transmission using a trolley jack with a block of wood placed on its head.

11 Remove the battery (see Chapter 5A).

12 Working in the battery tray area, slacken and remove the four bolts securing the engine/transmission mounting to the body **(see illustration)**.

13 Remove the starter motor as described in Chapter 5A.

14 Undo the retaining bolt and detach the engine roll restrictor from the transmission **(see illustration 13.19)**.

13.7 Undo the bolts/nuts and remove the mounting bracket

13.8 Lift out the rubber insert, and undo the Torx bolts

13.12 Undo the four mounting bolts

13.15 Four bolts secure the mounting to the bracket

13.19 Undo the roll restrictor transmission bolt and crossmember bolt (arrowed)

14.8 Undo the bolts and remove the sump plate

15 Using the jack, lower the engine/transmission slightly. Undo the four retaining bolts and remove the mounting from the bracket **(see illustration)**. If required, lower the transmission, unscrew the four Torx bolts, and remove the mounting bracket from the transmission.
16 Fit the new mounting using a reversal of the removal procedure, tightening the nuts/bolts to the specified torque.

Engine roll restrictor

17 Apply the handbrake, then jack up the front of the vehicle and support it on axle stands (see *Jacking and vehicle support*). Undo the two retaining nuts and four bolts (two each side), and remove the engine undershield.
18 Support the weight of the engine with a trolley jack and piece of wood beneath the sump.
19 Unscrew the bolt securing the roll restrictor to the transmission **(see illustration)**.
20 Slacken and remove the bolt securing the roll restrictor to the front crossmember.
21 Fit the new roll restrictor using a reversal of the removal procedure, noting the different specified torque applicable if the restrictor is made from steel or aluminium.

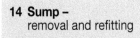

14 Sump –
removal and refitting

Removal

1 Apply the handbrake, then jack up the front of the vehicle and support it on axle stands (see *Jacking and vehicle support*).
2 Undo the two retaining nuts and four bolts (two each side), and remove the undershield from under the engine.
3 Position a container beneath the sump, then unscrew the drain plug and drain the engine oil. Clean the plug and if necessary renew the washer, then refit and tighten the plug after all the oil has drained. Remove the dipstick from the engine.

2.0 litre engine

4 Sump removal and refitting is much easier if

the engine is removed from the vehicle. However, if the engine is in the vehicle, proceed as follows.
5 Remove the front section of the exhaust system with reference to Chapter 4C.
6 Remove the flywheel/drive plate as described in Section 12. Remove the engine-to-transmission adapter plate.
7 Unscrew the sump retaining bolts and nuts, and withdraw the sump from the engine. Do not prise between the mating faces of the sump and cylinder block. Discard the old gasket.

2.3 litre engine

8 The sump plate is bolted to the underside of the balancer shaft housing. Undo the eighteen bolts and remove the sump plate **(see illustration)**.

All engines

9 If required, the baffle plate and oil pump pick-up tube can be removed by unscrewing the retaining nuts/bolts **(see illustration)**.

Refitting

10 Where removed, refit the oil pick-up tube (with a new gasket/O-ring where applicable) and oil baffle plate. Apply a little locking compound to the bolts, and tighten them to the specified torque **(see illustration)**.
11 Ensure the mating surfaces of the sump and cylinder block/balancer shaft housing are clean and dry.

2.0 litre engine

12 Apply a 3 to 5 mm thick bead of silicone sealer to the crankshaft seal housing **(see illustration)**.

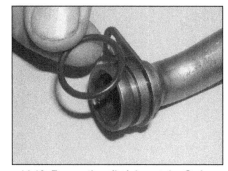

14.10 Renew the oil pick up tube O-ring

14.9 The oil pick-up tube and baffle plate is secured by five bolts (arrowed)

13 Position the new sump gasket over the cylinder block locating studs, and refit the sump casing. Do not fully tighten the retaining bolts/nuts at this stage.
14 Align the sump casing so that the end face of the sump is between 0.25 mm below and 0.1 mm proud of the cylinder block end face. If the sump cannot be fitted so that the

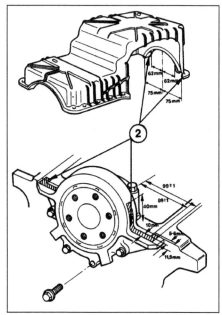

14.12 Apply sealing compound to the sump/cylinder block mating faces at the points indicated (2)

position is correct, measure the difference in height using a feeler gauge **(see illustration 15.12)**.

15 Tighten the sump securing nuts and bolts to the specified torque and repeat the measurement made in the previous paragraph. If the position is still not correct, suitable shims must be fitted (available from a Ford dealer) between the sump and the transmission to eliminate the clearance when mating the engine to the transmission. Note that the shims should be fitted at both sides of the sump casing. Select suitable shims from those listed in the following table.

Adjustment value	Available shims	Colour coding
0.0 to 0.25 mm	No adjustment	
0.26 to 0.29 mm	0.15 mm	Silver
0.30 to 0.44 mm	0.30 mm	Pale blue
0.45 to 0.59 mm	0.45 mm	Red
0.60 to 0.75 mm	0.60 mm	Black
0.76 to 0.90 mm	0.75 mm	Green

2.3 litre engine

16 The sump plate seal is integral with the plate, and is vulcanised into place. Providing the seal is in good condition the plate can be re-used. Refit the sump plate, tightening the bolts to the specified torque.

All engines

17 The remainder of refitting is a reversal of removal. Refill the engine with new oil as described in Chapter 1A.

15 Balancer housing and shafts
– removal, inspection and refitting

Removal

1 The balancer shaft housing is only fitted to the 2.3 litre DOHC 16V engine. Within the housing are two contra-rotating balancer shafts spinning at twice crankshaft speed, and produce vibrations which counter those produced by the engine. The rearmost shaft is driven by the crankshaft via a chain which

also drives the oil pump. The front shaft is geared to the rear shaft **(see illustration)**.

2 The balancer shaft housing removal and refitting is much easier if the engine is removed from the vehicle. However, if the engine is in the vehicle, proceed as follows.

3 Remove the front section of the exhaust system as described in Chapter 4C.

4 Remove the flywheel/driveplate as described in Section 12. Remove the engine-to-transmission adapter plate.

5 Remove the sump plate, baffle plate and oil pump pick-up tube as described in Section 14.

6 With reference to Section 5, remove the oil pump/balancer shaft drive chain.

7 Unscrew the balancer shaft housing retaining bolts and nuts, and withdraw the housing from the engine. Do not prise between the mating faces of the sump and cylinder block. Discard the old gasket. Note that the housing is aligned with the cylinder block by two guide sleeves. The sleeves must not be interchanged, because one has an oil supply hole.

Inspection

8 Although the balancer shafts can be removed for inspection, no parts are available separately. If any component shows sign of excessive wear or damage, the complete housing and shaft assembly must be renewed. At the time of writing, no specifications regarding shaft clearances, endfloat or dimensions were available.

Refitting

9 Ensure the mating surfaces of the cylinder block and balancer shaft housing are clean and dry. Apply a bead of silicone sealant to the crankshaft oil seal housing **(see illustration)**.

10 Fit the new gasket onto the housing, using the integral retaining tags to keep the gasket in place. Push the half-round section of the gasket into place. Apply a smear of sealant to both transition zones between the metal and rubber sections of the gasket **(see illustration)**.

11 Position the housing on the cylinder

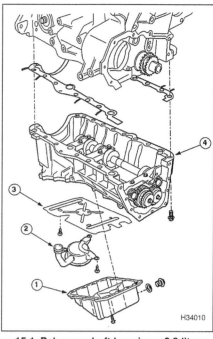

15.1 Balancer shaft housing – 2.3 litre

1 *Sump plate*
2 *Oil pick-up tube*
3 *Baffle plate*
4 *Balancer shaft housing*

block, but do not fully tighten the retaining nuts and bolts at this stage.

12 Align the balancer shaft housing so that its end face is between 0.25 mm below and 0.1 mm proud of the cylinder block end face. If the housing cannot be fitted so that the position is correct, measure the difference in height using a feeler gauge **(see illustration)**.

13 Tighten the housing securing nuts and bolts to the specified torque and repeat the measurement made in the previous paragraph. If the position is still not correct, suitable shims must be fitted (available from a Ford dealer) between the housing and the transmission to eliminate the clearance when mating the engine to the transmission **(see**

15.9 Apply sealant to the areas shown (arrowed)

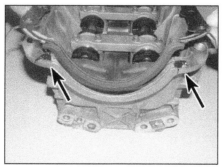

15.10 Apply sealant to the transition areas between the metal and rubber sections of the gasket (arrowed)

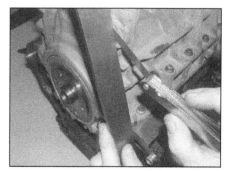

15.12 Using a straight-edge and feeler gauges, measure the difference in height between the cylinder block and the edge of the housing

15.13 If necessary, fit suitable shims to the edge of the balancer shaft housing (see text)

16.2 Undo the bolts (arrowed) and remove the oil pump

16.3 The oil pump cover is retained by two bolts

illustration). Note that the shims should be fitted at both sides of the housing. Select suitable shims from those listed in the table in Paragraph 15 of Section 14.

14 The remainder of refitting is a reversal of removal. Refill the engine with the correct specification and quantity of oil as described in Chapter 1A.

16 Oil pump – removal, inspection and refitting

Removal

1 Remove the oil pump/balancer shaft drive chain as described in Section 5.

2 Undo the retaining bolts and withdraw the pump from the cylinder block **(see illustration)**. On 2.3 litre engines, undo the Torx bolt and remove the pump sprocket to access the retaining bolts. Recover the gasket.

3 Slacken and remove the retaining bolts, and remove the outer cover from the pump assembly. Withdraw the pump rotors from the body **(see illustration)**.

Inspection

4 Clean the components and check them for wear and damage. Using a feeler blade, check the backlash between the gears, clearance between the outer rotor and pump body, and

compare with that given in the Specifications. Similarly check the endfloat of the gears, using a straight-edge across the end face of the pump. Note that the rotors should be fitted with the dot mark facing outwards. If outside the specified limits, the pump should be renewed, otherwise refit the cover and tighten the bolts to the specified torque **(see illustrations)**. To remove the oil pressure relief valve, slacken and remove the Torx retaining cap and washer, then pull out the spring and plunger **(see illustration)**. At the time of writing, no information was available concerning the free length or strength of the valve spring. When refitting the retaining cap, apply a few drops of locking compound to its threads, and tighten it securely.

16.4a Check for wear between the gears . . .

16.4b . . . between the outer rotor and body . . .

16.4c . . . and the rotor endfloat

16.4d The marks on the rotors (arrowed) must face outwards

16.4e Oil pressure relief valve components

16.5 Prime the oil pump before refitting

16.7 Fit the sprocket with FRONT facing outwards

Refitting

5 Prime the pump by pouring oil into the inlet aperture while turning the driveshaft **(see illustration)**.

6 Clean the contact faces, then refit the pump with a new gasket, into the cylinder block recess. Ensure that the gasket is fitted correctly, and does not obstruct any of the oil pump passages. Tighten the retaining bolts to the specified torque.

7 Refit the oil pump/balancer shaft drive chain as described in Section 5. On 2.3 litre engines refit the oil pump sprocket prior to refitting the drive chain. Note that to aid refitment, one side of the sprocket is marked FRONT **(see illustration)**.

8 The remainder of refitting is a reversal of removal.

17 Oil pressure switch – removal and refitting

Removal

1 The oil pressure switch is located on the rear of the cylinder block, adjacent to the oil filter **(see illustration)**.

2 Disconnect the wiring plug from the switch, and unscrew the switch from the cylinder block.

Refitting

3 If the original switch is to be refitted, apply a smear of sealant to the threads of the switch.

17.1 Oil pressure switch is on the rear of the cylinder block (arrowed)

Screw the switch into the cylinder block, and tighten it to the specified torque. Reconnect the wiring plug.

Notes

Chapter 2 Part B:
Diesel engine in-car repair procedures

Contents

Degrees of difficulty

| Easy, suitable for novice with little experience | 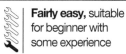 | Fairly easy, suitable for beginner with some experience | | Fairly difficult, suitable for competent DIY mechanic |  | Difficult, suitable for experienced DIY mechanic | | Very difficult, suitable for expert DIY or professional | |

Specifications

General

Engine code*:
1896 cc, electronic direct injection, turbocharged:

66 kW to 09.96	1Z
66 kW from 09.96	AHU
66 kW from 09.99	AVG
81 kW	AFN

Power output:
1Z, AHU, AVG	66 kW @ 4000
AFN	81 kW @ 4150

Torque output:
1Z, AHU, AVG	202 Nm @ 1900 rpm
AFN	235 Nm @ 1900 rpm

Bore	79.5 mm
Stroke	95.5 mm
Compression ratio	19.5 : 1
Compression pressures (wear limit)	19.0 bar
Firing order	1 – 3 – 4 – 2
Cylinder No 1 location	Timing belt end

* **Note:** See 'Vehicle Identification' for the location of the code marking on the engine

Lubrication system

Pump type	Sump-mounted, driven indirectly from intermediate shaft

Normal operating oil pressure (oil temperature 80°C):
At 2000 rpm	At least 2.0 bar
Pump pressure relief valve opening pressure	5.7 to 6.7 bar
Oil pump gear backlash	0.2 mm (wear limit)
Oil pump gear endfloat	0.15 mm (wear limit)

Auxiliary drivebelt tension

Main drivebelt (Poly-Vee)	Automatically adjusted by tensioner

V-belt:
New belt	7 Nm
Used belt	4 Nm

Torque wrench settings

	Nm	lbf ft
Accessory bracket to cylinder block	30	22
Air conditioning compressor drivebelt bracket	45	33
Alternator	25	18
Alternator bracket to cylinder block	25	18
Auxiliary Poly-Vee drivebelt tensioner	45	33
Big-end bearing caps bolts/nuts*:		
Stage 1	30	22
Stage 2	Angle-tighten a further 90°	
Camshaft bearing caps	20	15
Camshaft cover	10	7
Camshaft sprocket bolt	45	33
Coolant pump housing nuts:		
Stage 1	20	15
Stage 2	Angle-tighten a further 90°	
Coolant pump housing bolt	10	7
Coolant pump pulley	25	18
Crankcase breather connector to cylinder block	25	18
Crankshaft flywheel/driveplate end oil seal housing	10	7
Crankshaft position sensor	10	7
Crankshaft position sensor ring to crankshaft*:		
Stage 1	10	7
Stage 2	Angle-tighten a further 90°	
Crankshaft pulley/vibration damper to sprocket	25	18
Crankshaft sprocket bolt*		
Stage 1	90	66
Stage 2	Angle-tighten a further 90°	
Crankshaft timing belt end oil seal housing	25	18
Cylinder head bolts*:		
Stage 1	40	30
Stage 2	60	44
Stage 3	Angle-tighten a further 90°	
Stage 4	Angle-tighten a further 90°	
Driveplate (automatic transmission):		
Stage 1	60	44
Stage 2	Angle-tighten a further 90°	
Driveshaft centre bearing to cylinder block	43	32
Engine adapter plate	10	7
Engine mountings:		
Engine roll restrictor to transmission:		
Aluminium – 88 mm bolt:		
Stage 1	60	44
Stage 2	Angle-tighten a further 90°	
Steel	98	72
Engine support plate (outer part to inner)	23	17
Engine support plate to engine	58	43
Left-hand engine mounting to body	54	40
Right-hand bracket to engine support plate	61	45
Right-hand bracket to mounting	54	40
Engine-to-transmission bolts:		
M10	45	33
M12	65	48
Front crossmember to body:		
Stage 1	150	111
Stage 2	Angle-tighten a further 90°	
Flywheel (manual transmission)*:		
Stage 1	60	44
Stage 2	Angle-tighten a further 90°	
Intermediate shaft flange bolts	25	18
Intermediate shaft sprocket bolt	45	33
Main bearing cap bolts*:		
Stage 1	65	48
Stage 2	Angle-tighten a further 90°	
Oil filter housing to block	25	18
Oil cooler to filter housing	25	18
Oil jets	10	7
Oil pressure switches	25	18

Torque wrench settings

	Nm	lbf ft
Oil pump cover	10	7
Oil pump mounting bolt	25	18
Oil pump pick-up pipe to oil pump	10	7
Power steering pump	25	18
Power steering pump pulley	25	18
Sump	20	15
Sump drain plug	30	22
Timing belt covers	10	7
Timing belt small upper idler roller	25	18
Timing belt tensioner	20	15
Vacuum pump to cylinder block	20	15
Wheel bolts:		
Except 16 in aluminium wheels	140	103
16 in aluminium wheels only	170	125

Use new nuts/bolt(s)

1 General information

Using this Chapter

Chapter 2 is divided into three Parts: A, B and C. Repair operations that can be carried out with the engine in the vehicle are described in Part A (petrol engines) and Part B (diesel engines). Part C covers the removal of the engine/transmission as a unit, and describes the engine dismantling and overhaul procedures.

In Parts A and B, the assumption is made that the engine is installed in the vehicle, with all ancillaries connected. If the engine has been removed for overhaul, the preliminary dismantling information which precedes each operation may be ignored.

Access to the engine bay can be improved by removing the bonnet as described in Chapter 11.

Engine description

Throughout this Chapter, the engines are identified and referred to by manufacturer's code letters, rather than capacity. A listing of the engines covered, together with their code letters, is given in the Specifications at the start of this Chapter.

The engines are water-cooled, single-overhead camshaft, in-line four cylinder units with cast-iron cylinder blocks and aluminium-alloy cylinder heads. All are mounted transversely at the front of the vehicle, with the transmission bolted to the left-hand end of the engine.

The cylinder head carries the camshaft, which is driven by a toothed timing belt. It also houses the inlet and exhaust valves, which are closed by double coil springs, and which run in guides pressed into the cylinder head. The camshaft actuates the valves directly via hydraulic tappets, mounted in the cylinder head. The cylinder head contains integral oilways which supply and lubricate the tappets.

The engines are of direct injection design. Unlike indirect injection engines where the cylinder head incorporates swirl chambers, the piston crowns are shaped to form combustion chambers.

The crankshaft is supported by five main bearings, and endfloat is controlled by thrustwashers fitted each side of the centre (No 3) main bearing.

All engines are fitted with a timing belt-driven intermediate shaft, which provides drive for the brake servo vacuum pump and the oil pump. Engine coolant is circulated by a pump, driven by the auxiliary drivebelt. For details of the cooling system, refer to Chapter 3.

Lubricant is circulated under pressure by a pump, driven by the intermediate shaft. Oil is drawn from the sump through a strainer, and then forced through an externally-mounted, renewable screw-on filter. From there, it is distributed to the cylinder head, where it lubricates the camshaft journals and hydraulic tappets, and also to the crankcase, where it lubricates the main bearings, connecting rod big- and small-ends, gudgeon pins and cylinder bores. Oil jets are fitted to the base of each cylinder – these spray oil onto the underside of the pistons, to improve cooling. An oil cooler, supplied with engine coolant and mounted on the oil filter housing, reduces the temperature of the oil before it re-enters the engine.

Repairs possible with the engine installed in the vehicle

The following operations can be performed without removing the engine:

a) Auxiliary drivebelts – removal and refitting.
b) Camshaft – removal and refitting.
c) Camshaft oil seal – renewal.
d) Camshaft sprocket – removal and refitting.
e) Coolant pump – removal and refitting (refer to Chapter 3).
f) Crankshaft oil seals – renewal.
g) Crankshaft sprocket – removal and refitting.
h) Cylinder head – removal and refitting.*
i) Engine mountings – inspection and renewal.
j) Intermediate shaft oil seal – renewal.
k) Oil pump and pickup assembly – removal and refitting.
l) Sump – removal and refitting.
m) Timing belt, sprockets and cover – removal, inspection and refitting.

*Cylinder head dismantling procedures are in Chapter 2C.

Note: *It is possible to remove the pistons and connecting rods (after removing the cylinder head and sump) without removing the engine from the vehicle. However, this procedure is not recommended. Work of this nature is more easily and thoroughly completed with the engine on the bench – refer to Chapter 2C.*

2 Engine valve timing marks – locating TDC on No 1 cylinder

General information

1 The crankshaft, camshaft, intermediate shaft and injection pump sprockets are driven by the timing belt. The crankshaft and camshaft sprockets move in phase with each other to ensure correct valve timing.

2 The design of the engines covered in this Chapter is such that piston-to-valve contact will occur if the crankshaft is turned with the timing belt removed. For this reason, it is important that the correct phasing between the camshaft and crankshaft is preserved whilst the timing belt is off the engine. This is achieved by setting the engine in a reference condition (known as Top Dead Centre or TDC) before the timing belt is removed, and then preventing the shafts from rotating until the belt is refitted. Similarly, if the engine has been dismantled for overhaul, the engine can be set to TDC during reassembly to ensure that the correct shaft phasing is restored.

3 TDC is the highest position a piston reaches within its respective cylinder – in a four-stroke engine, each piston reaches TDC twice per cycle; once on the compression stroke, and once on the exhaust stroke. In general, TDC normally refers to No 1 cylinder on the compression stroke. Note that the cylinders are numbered one to four, starting from the timing belt end of the engine.

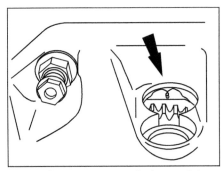

2.5a On manual transmission models, align the mark on the flywheel with the pointer on the transmission bellhousing

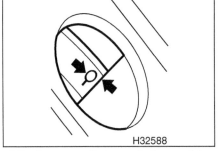

2.5b On automatic transmission models, align the mark on the flywheel with the edge of the inspection hole on the transmission bellhousing

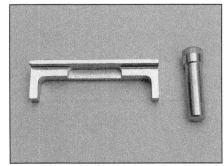

2.6 Engine locking tools

Setting No 1 cylinder at TDC

4 Remove the camshaft cover and auxiliary drivebelts as described in Sections 7 and 6 respectively. Also remove the timing belt upper outer cover with reference to Section 4. Remove the glow plugs as described in Chapter 5C, as an aid to turning the engine.

5 Rotate the crankshaft clockwise with a socket, or a spanner, until the timing mark machined onto the edge of the flywheel/driveplate lines up with the edge of the inspection hole on the bellhousing casting **and** the timing hole in the fuel injection sprocket lines up with the hole in the support bracket **(see illustrations)**. In order to see the flywheel inspection hole, the intercooler-to-manifold plastic pipe at the left-hand end of the engine must be disconnected and placed to one side.

6 To lock the engine in the TDC position, the camshaft (not the sprocket) and fuel injection pump sprocket must be secured in a reference position, using special locking tools. Improvised tools may be fabricated, but due to the exact measurements and machining involved, it is strongly recommended that a kit of locking tools is either borrowed or hired from a Ford dealer, or purchased from a reputable tool manufacturer **(see illustration)**.

7 Engage the edge of the locking bar with the slot in the end of the camshaft **(see illustration)**.

8 With the locking bar still inserted, turn the camshaft slightly (by turning the crankshaft

clockwise, as before), so that the locking bar rocks to one side, allowing one end of the bar to contact the cylinder head surface. At the other side of the locking bar, measure the gap between the end of the bar and the cylinder head using a feeler blade.

9 Turn the camshaft back slightly, then pull out the feeler blade. The idea now is to level the locking bar by inserting two feeler blades, each with a thickness equal to *half* the originally measured gap, on either side of the camshaft between each end of the locking bar and the cylinder head. This centres the camshaft, and sets the valve timing in reference condition **(see illustration)**.

10 Insert the locking pin through the fuel injection pump sprocket alignment hole, and into the support bracket behind the sprocket. This locks the fuel injection pump in the TDC reference condition **(see illustration)**.

3 Cylinder compression test

Compression test

Note: *A compression tester specifically designed for diesel engines must be used for this test.*

1 When engine performance is down, or if misfiring occurs, a compression test can provide diagnostic clues as to the engine's condition. If the test is performed regularly, it

can give warning of trouble before any other symptoms become apparent.

2 A compression tester specifically intended for diesel engines must be used, because of the higher pressures involved. The tester is connected to an adapter which screws into the glow plug hole. It is unlikely to be worthwhile buying such a tester for occasional use, but it may be possible to borrow or hire one – if not, have the test performed by a garage.

3 Unless specific instructions to the contrary are supplied with the tester, observe the following points:

 a) *The battery must be in a good state of charge, the air filter must be clean, and the engine should be at normal operating temperature.*

 b) *All the glow plugs should be removed before starting the test.*

 c) *The stop solenoid and fuel metering control wiring must be disconnected, to prevent the engine from running or fuel from being discharged.* **Note:** *As a result of the wiring being disconnected, faults will be stored in the ECU memory. These must be erased after the compression test.*

4 There is no need to hold the accelerator pedal down during the test, because the diesel engine air inlet is not throttled.

5 The manufacturers specify a wear limit for compression pressure – refer to the Specifications. Seek the advice of a Ford dealer or other diesel specialist if in doubt as

2.7 Engage the locking bar with the slot in the end of the camshaft

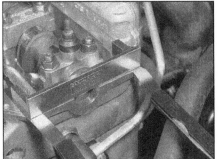

2.9 Camshaft centred and locked using the locking bar and feeler gauges

2.10 Injection pump sprocket locked using the locking pin (arrowed)

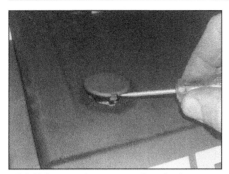

4.4 Prise out the caps and undo the nuts

4.6 The bulkhead cover is secured by three screws (two arrowed)

4.10 Undo the nuts and bolts securing the engine mounting bracket to the support plate

to whether a particular pressure reading is acceptable.

6 The cause of poor compression is less easy to establish on a diesel engine than on a petrol one. The effect of introducing oil into the cylinders (wet testing) is not conclusive, because there is a risk that the oil will sit in the recess on the piston crown, instead of passing to the rings. However, the following can be used as a rough guide to diagnosis.

7 All cylinders should produce very similar pressures; a difference of more than 5.0 bars between any two cylinders indicates the existence of a fault. Note that the compression should build-up quickly in a healthy engine; low compression on the first stroke, followed by gradually-increasing pressure on successive strokes, indicates worn piston rings. A low compression reading on the first stroke, which does not build-up during successive strokes, indicates leaking valves or a blown head gasket (a cracked head could also be the cause).

8 A low reading from two adjacent cylinders is almost certainly due to the head gasket having blown between them; the presence of coolant in the engine oil will confirm this.

Leakdown test

9 A leakdown test measures the rate at which compressed air fed into the cylinder is lost. It is an alternative to a compression test, and in many ways it is better, since the escaping air provides easy identification of where pressure loss is occurring (piston rings, valves or head gasket).

10 The equipment needed for leakdown testing is unlikely to be available to the home mechanic. If poor compression is suspected, have the test performed by a suitably-equipped garage.

---

4 Timing belt – removal, inspection and refitting

Removal

1 The primary function of the toothed timing belt is to drive the camshaft, but it also drives the fuel injection pump and intermediate shaft. Should the belt slip or break in service, the valve timing will be disturbed and piston-to-valve contact may occur, resulting in serious engine damage. For this reason, it is important that the timing belt is tensioned correctly, and inspected regularly for signs of wear or deterioration.

2 Note that the removal of the *inner* section of the timing belt cover is described as part of the cylinder head removal procedure; see Section 11 later in this Chapter.

3 Disconnect the battery as described in Chapter 5A.

4 Prise out the cover caps, undo the retaining nuts and remove the engine top cover **(see illustration)**.

5 Apply the handbrake, then jack up the front of the vehicle and support it on axle stands (see *Jacking and vehicle support*). Remove the splash guard from under the engine compartment.

6 Pull out the battery compartment upper panel. Release the three screws, and remove the bulkhead cover **(see illustration)**. Slide the trim to the right-hand side and manoeuvre it from behind the coolant expansion tank.

7 Remove the air cleaner housing, and the mass airflow meter, with reference to Chapter 4B.

8 Support the weight of the engine and transmission with a jack and a block of wood under the sump casing.

9 Where fitted, undo the nuts and remove the engine mounting damper from the right-hand engine mounting.

10 Undo the two nuts and three bolts securing the right-hand engine mounting bracket to the mounting and engine support plate **(see illustration)**.

11 Remove the auxiliary drivebelts with reference to Section 6.

12 Working through the right-hand front wheelarch, unscrew the bolt securing the power steering pipe to the engine support plate.

13 Undo the 7 retaining bolts, and remove both parts of the right-hand mounting engine support plate **(see illustration)**.

14 Release the two clips and remove the timing belt upper cover **(see illustration)**.

15 Set the engine to TDC on No 1 cylinder with reference to Section 2. This procedure includes removing the camshaft cover, and locking the fuel injection pump sprocket.

16 Unscrew and remove the retaining screws, then remove the pulley for the auxiliary belts from the crankshaft sprocket **(see illustration)**. On completion, check that

4.13 Undo the 7 bolts (one hidden – arrowed), and remove both parts of the engine support plate

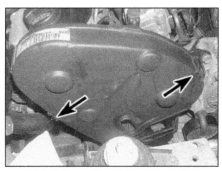

4.14 Release the timing cover clips (arrowed)

4.16a Unscrew the auxiliary belt pulleys from the crankshaft sprocket

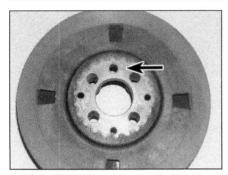

4.16b The larger of the four bolts holes (arrowed) fits over the raised edge of one of the sprocket holes

4.18 Lower timing cover upper bolt

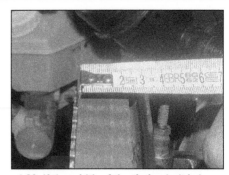

4.23 If the width of the timing belt is less than 22 mm at any point, it must be renewed

the engine is still set to TDC. To prevent the crankshaft from rotating, on manual transmission models, engage top gear and have an assistant apply the brakes firmly. On automatic transmission models, remove the starter motor, and lock the flywheel ring gear teeth using a large flat-bladed screwdriver or lever. Note that the pulley will only fit in one position, when the larger of the four bolts holes is fitted over the raised edge of one of the crankshaft sprocket bolt holes **(see illustration)**.

17 On non air-conditioned models, undo the retaining bolts and remove the coolant pump pulley. If necessary, use a strap-wrench to hold the pulley whilst slackening the bolts.

18 Remove the three retaining screws, and lift off the timing belt lower cover **(see illustration)**.

19 Relieve the tension on the timing belt by slackening the tensioner mounting nut slightly, allowing it to pivot away from the belt, with reference to Section 5.

20 Examine the timing belt for manufacturer's markings that indicate the direction of rotation. If none are present, make your own using typist's correction fluid or a dab of paint – do not cut or score the belt in any way.

Caution: If the belt appears to be in good condition and can be re-used, it is essential that it is refitted the same way around, otherwise accelerated wear will result, leading to premature failure.

21 Slide the belt off the sprockets, taking care to avoid twisting or kinking it excessively if it is to be re-used.

Inspection

22 Examine the belt for evidence of contamination by coolant or lubricant. If this is the case, find the source of the contamination before progressing any further. Check the belt for signs of wear or damage, particularly around the leading edges of the belt teeth. Renew the belt if its condition is in doubt; the cost of belt renewal is negligible compared with potential cost of the engine repairs, should the belt fail in service. The belt must be renewed if it has covered at least 40 000 miles, however if it has covered less it is prudent to renew it regardless of condition, as a precautionary measure.

23 Using a steel rule or vernier calipers, measure the width of the timing belt in several places. If it is less than 22.0 mm at any point, the timing belt must be renewed **(see illustration)**.

24 If the timing belt is not going to be refitted for some time, it is a wise precaution to hang a warning label on the steering wheel, to remind yourself (and others) not to attempt to start the engine.

Refitting

25 Ensure that the crankshaft and camshaft are still set to TDC on No 1 cylinder, as described in Section 2.

26 Carefully turn the crankshaft anti-clockwise 90°, to eliminate the possibility of

accidental piston-to-valve contact. Refer to Section 5 and slacken the camshaft sprocket bolt by half a turn. **Do not** use the timing locking bar to hold the camshaft stationary; it must be temporarily removed while loosening the sprocket bolt. Release the sprocket from the camshaft taper mounting by carefully tapping it with a soft metal drift inserted through the hole provided in the timing belt inner cover **(see illustration)**. Turn the crankshaft back to the TDC position.

27 Loop the timing belt loosely under the crankshaft sprocket. **Note:** *Observe the direction of rotation markings on the belt (where applicable).*

28 Engage the timing belt teeth with the crankshaft sprocket, then manoeuvre it into position around the intermediate shaft pulley, then over the injection pump and camshaft sprockets and around the tensioner pulley. Make sure that the belt teeth seat correctly on the sprockets. The upper run of the belt must be located beneath the small upper roller **(see illustrations)**. **Note:** *Slight adjustment to the position of the camshaft sprocket may be necessary to achieve this.* Avoid bending the belt back on itself or twisting it excessively as you do this.

29 Ensure that any slack in the belt is in the section of belt that passes over the tensioner roller.

30 Using a suitable tool engaged with the two holes in the tensioner hub, turn the tensioner pulley clockwise until the notch and the raised tab on the pulley and hub are aligned with

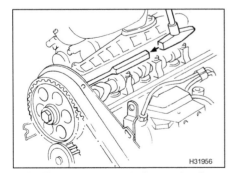

4.26 Release the camshaft sprocket from the taper using a pin punch

4.28a Locate the timing belt over the tensioner roller . . .

4.28b . . . and under the upper roller

each other **(see illustration)**. The tensioner is of semi-automatic type, and will correctly tension the timing belt when the notch and tab are aligned with each other. **Note:** *If the tensioner is turned too far clockwise, it must be completely slackened off before retensioning.*
31 With the tensioner marks aligned, tighten the tensioner locknut to the specified torque. Check the operation of the tensioner by pressing firmly on the timing belt with the thumb while checking that the pointers move away from each other – after releasing the belt the pointers must be aligned again.
32 Remove the locking pin from the fuel injection pump sprocket (see Section 2).
33 Remove the camshaft locking bar (see Section 2).
34 At this stage, check the crankshaft and injection pump are still set to TDC on No 1 cylinder (see Section 2).
35 Tighten the camshaft sprocket bolt to the specified torque while holding it stationary with the special tool as described in Section 5.
36 Using a spanner or wrench and socket on the crankshaft pulley centre bolt, rotate the crankshaft through two complete revolutions. Reset the engine to TDC on No 1 cylinder, with reference to Section 2 and check that the fuel injection pump sprocket locking pin and camshaft locking bar can still be inserted.
37 The remainder of refitting is a reversal of removal. Note that the offset of the crankshaft pulley mounting holes allows only one fitting position. Tighten all nuts/bolts to the specified torque where available.

5 Timing belt tensioner and sprockets – removal and refitting

1 Disconnect the battery (see Chapter 5A).
2 To gain access to the components detailed in this Section, first refer to Section 6 and remove the auxiliary drivebelts.

Timing belt tensioner

Removal

3 Set the engine to TDC on No 1 cylinder as described in Section 2.
4 Release the retaining clips and remove the timing belt upper cover.
5 Slacken the retaining nut at the hub of the tensioner pulley and turn the assembly anti-clockwise, relieving the tension on the timing belt. Remove the nut and recover the washer.
6 Slide the tensioner off its mounting stud.
7 Wipe the tensioner clean, but do not use solvents that may contaminate the bearings. Spin the tensioner pulley on its hub by hand. Stiff movement or excessive freeplay indicates that the tensioner is not serviceable and should be renewed.

Refitting

8 Slide the tensioner onto the mounting stud.
9 Refit the tensioner washer and retaining nut – do not fully tighten the nut at this stage.

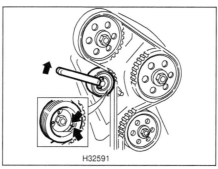

4.30 Alignment marks on the pulley and the hub on the automatic tensioner

10 With reference to Section 4, tension the timing belt.
11 Refit the upper timing belt cover, and secure it in place with the retaining clips.
12 Refit the auxiliary drivebelts (Section 6) and reconnect the battery (Chapter 5A).

Camshaft sprocket

Removal

13 Set the engine to TDC on No 1 cylinder with reference to Section 2. Release the retaining clips and remove the timing belt upper cover.
14 Remove the camshaft cover as described in Section 7.
15 Slacken the retaining nut at the hub of the tensioner pulley and allow the assembly to rotate anti-clockwise, relieving the tension on the timing belt. Slide the timing belt off the camshaft sprocket. In order to eliminate any possibility of accidental piston-to-valve contact, turn the crankshaft 90° anti-clockwise so that all the pistons are half-way up the cylinder bore.

To make a camshaft sprocket holding tool, obtain two lengths of steel strip about 6 mm thick by 30 mm wide, one 600 mm long, the other 200 mm long (all dimensions are approximate). Bolt the two strips together to form a forked end, leaving the bolt slack so that the shorter trip can pivot freely. At the end of each 'prong' of the fork, secure a bolt with a nut and a locknut, to act as the fulcrums; these will engage with the cut-outs in the sprocket, and should protrude by about 30 mm.

16 The camshaft sprocket must be held stationary whilst its retaining bolt is slackened; if access to the correct Ford special tool is not possible, a simple home-made tool using basic materials may be fabricated **(see Tool Tip)**. **Do not** use the timing locking bar to hold the camshaft stationary; it should be removed before loosening the sprocket bolt.
17 Using the home-made tool, brace the camshaft sprocket and slacken the retaining bolt half a turn. Release the sprocket from the camshaft taper mounting by carefully tapping it with a soft metal drift inserted through the hole provided in the timing belt inner cover **(see illustration 4.26)**
18 Remove the bolt then remove the camshaft sprocket from the end of the camshaft **(see illustration)**. Reset the crankshaft to TDC.
19 With the sprocket removed, examine the camshaft oil seal for signs of leaking. If necessary, refer to Section 8 and renew it.
20 Wipe the sprocket and camshaft mating surfaces clean.

Refitting

21 Locate the sprocket on the camshaft, then insert the retaining bolt hand-tight at this stage.
22 Check that the engine is still set to TDC on No 1 cylinder, then refit and tension the timing belt as described in Sections 2 and 4.
23 Refit the timing belt upper cover and the camshaft cover, then refit the auxiliary drivebelts (Section 6) and reconnect the battery (Chapter 5A).

Crankshaft sprocket

Removal

24 Remove the timing belt as described in Section 4. If the timing belt is to be re-used, make sure it is marked for direction of rotation.
25 The crankshaft sprocket must be held stationary whilst its retaining bolt is slackened. If access to the Ford flywheel/driveplate locking tool is not available, lock the crankshaft in position by removing the starter motor, as described in Chapter 5A, to expose the ring gear. Get an assistant to insert a wide-bladed screwdriver between the ring gear teeth and the transmission bellhousing whilst the sprocket

5.18 Remove the camshaft sprocket

retaining bolt is slackened. Exercise caution –
the bolt is extremely tight. Withdraw the bolt,
recover the washer (where fitted) and lift off
the sprocket.
26 With the sprocket removed, examine the
crankshaft oil seal for signs of leaking. If
necessary, refer to Section 10 and renew it.
27 Wipe the sprocket and crankshaft mating
surfaces clean.

Refitting

28 Offer up the sprocket to the crankshaft,
engaging the lug on the inside of the sprocket
with the recess in the end of the crankshaft.
Lubricate the threads of the new sprocket bolt
with a little clean engine oil. Insert the bolt and
tighten it to the specified Stage 1 torque while
holding the crankshaft stationary as described
for removal. Then angle-tighten the bolt by the
specified angle **(see illustration)**.
29 The remainder of refitting is a reversal of
removal.

Intermediate shaft sprocket

Removal

30 Remove the timing belt and the upper and
lower outer covers as described in Section 4.
If the timing belt is to be re-used, make sure it
is marked for direction of rotation.
31 The intermediate shaft sprocket must be
held stationary whilst its retaining bolt is
slackened; if access to the Ford special tool is
not possible, a simple home-made tool may
be fabricated as described in the camshaft
sprocket removal sub-Section. Alternatively,
insert a metal dowel rod or socket wrench
through one of the holes in the sprocket to
hold it stationary **(see illustration)**.
32 Slacken and remove the retaining bolt,
then slide the sprocket from the end of the
intermediate shaft. Recover the Woodruff key
from the keyway.
33 With the sprocket removed, examine the
intermediate shaft oil seal for signs of leaking.
If necessary, refer to Section 9 and renew it.
34 Wipe the sprocket and shaft mating
surfaces clean.

5.28 Refit the crankshaft sprocket with a new retaining bolt, and tighten to the specified torque and angle setting

Refitting

35 Fit the Woodruff key into the keyway with
the plain surface facing upwards. Offer up the
sprocket to the intermediate shaft, engaging
the slot in the sprocket with the Woodruff key.
36 Insert and tighten the sprocket retaining
bolt to the specified torque; hold the sprocket
using the method employed during removal.
37 Check that the engine is still set to TDC
on No 1 cylinder, then refit and tension the
timing belt as described in Sections 2 and 4.
Refit the timing belt outer covers, then refit the
auxiliary drivebelts (Section 6) and reconnect
the battery (Chapter 5A).

Fuel injection pump sprocket

38 Refer to Chapter 4B, Section 6.

6 Auxiliary drivebelts –
removal, refitting and tensioning

General information

1 On non-air conditioned models, one main
Poly-Vee drivebelt is fitted to drive the
alternator and coolant pump, whilst the V-belt
drives the power steering pump pulley. On
models with air conditioning, the main

5.31 Use a socket wrench to hold the intermediate shaft sprocket stationary whilst loosening the bolt

drivebelt drives the alternator, and air
conditioning compressor, whilst the V-belt
drives the power steering pump and coolant
pump pulleys. All drivebelts are driven from
pulleys mounted on the end of the crankshaft
(see illustrations).
2 The main drivebelt tension is adjusted
automatically by a spring-tensioned idler. The
V-belt is adjusted by rotating an adjuster bolt
on the lower power steering pump mounting.
3 To remove the drivebelts first apply the
handbrake, then jack up the front of the
vehicle and support it on axle stands (see
Jacking and vehicle support). Undo the two
retaining nuts and four bolts (two each side),
and remove the undershield from under the
engine compartment.

Removal

4 If any drivebelt is to be re-used, mark it for
clockwise direction to ensure it is refitted the
same way round.
5 Slacken the power steering pump mounting
bolts, rotate the adjuster nut clockwise, and
slip the drivebelt from the crankshaft.
6 To remove the main drivebelt, first note how
it is fitted to each pulley to ensure correct
refitting. The automatic tensioner must be
released using an adjustable spanner on the
tensioner arm **(see illustration)**. Turn the arm
clockwise to release the tension, then remove
the drivebelt from the tensioner, alternator,
crankshaft, and where fitted the air
conditioning compressor pulleys. Release the
tensioner after removing the drivebelt.

6.6 Rotate the tensioner using an adjustable spanner on the arm

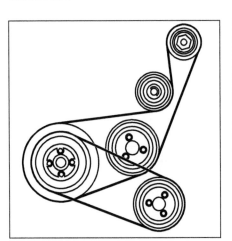

6.1a Auxiliary drivebelt routing – models without air conditioning

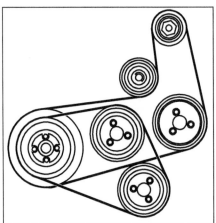

6.1b Auxiliary drivebelt routing – models with air conditioning

7.3 Disconnect the hose from the intercooler to the intake manifold

7.4a Undo the camshaft cover retaining nuts

7.4b Disconnect the breather hose

Refitting

7 Locate the main drivebelt on the alternator, crankshaft, and air conditioning compressor/ coolant pump pulleys as appropriate, making sure that each rib is correctly located in a groove. Turn the automatic tensioner clockwise and locate the drivebelt on the pulley, then release the tensioner to tension the drivebelt.

8 Refit the power steering pump and coolant pump belt (where applicable), rotate the adjuster bolt with a torque wrench and apply the specified torque. Hold the wrench in this position and tighten the pump mounting bolts to the specified torque. If a torque wrench is not available, depress the belt with firm thumb pressure at the midway point of the longest run between two pulleys. The belt should deflect approximately 6 mm. After a new drivebelt has covered a nominal mileage, recheck and if necessary, adjust the tension.

9 Replace the engine undershield, and lower the vehicle to the ground.

7 Camshaft cover – removal and refitting

Removal

1 Remove the air cleaner housing, as described in Chapter 4B.

2 Pull out the battery compartment upper panel. Remove the three screws and withdraw

the bulkhead cover from the engine compartment **(see illustration 4.6)**. Slide the trim to the right-hand side and manoeuvre it from behind the coolant expansion tank.

3 Prise out the cover caps, undo the retaining nuts and remove the engine top cover, then disconnect the hose from the intercooler to the intake manifold **(see illustration)**.

4 Unscrew and remove the three camshaft cover retaining nuts – recover the washers and seals noting the order of removal. Disconnect the crankcase breather hose to the intake ducting. Release the retaining clip and disconnect the cylinder block breather hose from the valve on the camshaft cover **(see illustrations)**.

5 Lift the cover away from the cylinder head **(see illustration)**; if it sticks, do not attempt to lever it off – instead free it by working around the cover and tapping it lightly with a soft-faced mallet.

6 Recover the camshaft cover gasket. Inspect the gasket carefully, and renew it if damage or deterioration is evident.

7 Clean the mating surfaces of the cylinder head and camshaft cover thoroughly, removing all traces of oil and old gasket – take care to avoid damaging the surfaces as you do this.

Refitting

8 Refit the camshaft cover by following the removal procedure in reverse, noting the following points:

a) *Before refitting the camshaft cover, at the*

left-hand end of the cylinder head apply suitable sealant to the top edges of the semi-circular cut-out in the cylinder head. At the right-hand end of the cylinder head, apply suitable sealant to the two points where the camshaft bearing cap contacts the cylinder head (see illustrations).

b) *Ensure that the gasket is correctly seated on the cylinder head, and take care to avoid displacing it as the camshaft cover is lowered into position.*

c) *Tighten the camshaft cover retaining nuts/bolts to the specified torque.*

8 Camshaft oil seal – renewal

1 Remove the camshaft sprocket as described in Section 5.

2 Note the fitted position of the seal in the housing, and drill two small holes into the existing oil seal, diagonally opposite each other. Take great care to avoid drilling through into the seal housing or camshaft sealing surface. Thread two self-tapping screws into the holes, and using two pairs of pliers, pull on the heads of the screws to extract the oil seal.

3 Clean out the seal housing and sealing surface of the camshaft by wiping it with a lint-free cloth. Remove any swarf or burrs that may cause the seal to leak.

4 Lubricate the inner lip of the new oil seal

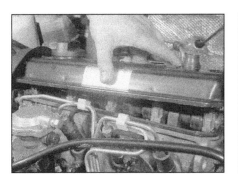

7.5 Lift the camshaft cover from the cylinder head

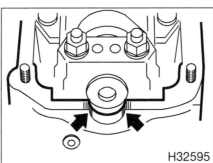

7.8a Apply sealant to the rear semi-circular cut-out . . .

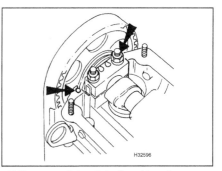

7.8b . . . and the right-hand bearing cap joint

with clean engine oil, and push it over the camshaft until it is positioned above its housing.

5 Using a hammer and a socket of suitable diameter, drive the seal squarely into its housing. **Note:** *Select a socket that bears only on the hard outer surface of the seal, not the inner lip which can easily be damaged.*

6 Refit the camshaft sprocket with reference to Section 5.

7 The remainder of refitting is a reversal of removal.

9 Intermediate shaft oil seal – renewal

1 Remove the intermediate shaft sprocket with reference to Section 5.

2 Remove the intermediate shaft flange (see Chapter 2C, Section 9) and renew the shaft and flange oil seals.

3 Refit the intermediate shaft sprocket with reference to Section 5.

10 Crankshaft oil seals – renewal

Timing belt end

1 Remove the crankshaft sprocket with reference to Section 5.

2 Note the fitted location of the seal, drill two small holes into the existing oil seal, diagonally opposite each other. Take great care to avoid drilling through into the seal housing or crankshaft sealing surface. Thread two self-tapping screws into the holes and using two pairs of pliers, pull on the heads of the screws to extract the oil seal **(see illustration)**.

3 Clean out the seal housing and sealing surface of the crankshaft by wiping it with a lint-free cloth – avoid using solvents that may enter the crankcase and affect component lubrication. Remove any swarf or burrs that could cause the seal to leak.

4 Smear the lip of the new oil seal with clean engine oil, and position it over the housing.

10.2 Remove the crankshaft right-hand oil seal using self-tapping screws

5 Using a hammer and a socket of suitable diameter, drive the seal squarely into its housing. **Note:** *Select a socket that bears only on the hard outer surface of the seal, not the inner lip, which can easily be damaged.*

6 Refit the crankshaft sprocket with reference to Section 5.

Seal housing gasket renewal

7 Remove the crankshaft sprocket with reference to Section 5.

8 Remove the sump as described in Section 16.

9 Progressively slacken and then remove the oil seal housing retaining bolts.

10 Lift the housing away from the cylinder block, together with the crankshaft oil seal, using a twisting motion to ease the seal along the shaft.

11 Recover the old gasket from the seal housing on the cylinder block. Clean the housing and block surfaces.

12 If necessary, prise the old oil seal from the housing using a screwdriver **(see illustration)**.

13 Wipe the oil seal housing clean, and check it visually for signs of distortion or cracking. Lay the housing on a work surface, with the mating surface face down. If removed, press in a new oil seal, using a block of wood as a press to ensure that the seal enters the housing squarely.

14 Lightly smear the crankcase mating surface with multi-purpose grease, and lay the new gasket in position **(see illustration)**.

15 Wrap the end of the crankshaft with tape to protect the oil seal as the housing is being fitted.

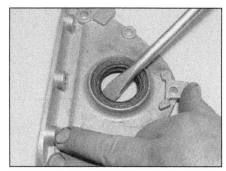

10.12 Prise the oil seal from the crankshaft oil seal housing

16 Lubricate the inner lip of the crankshaft oil seal with clean engine oil, then offer up the seal and its housing to the end of the crankshaft. Ease the seal along the shaft using a twisting motion, until the housing is flush with the crankcase **(see illustration)**.

17 Insert the bolts and tighten them progressively to the specified torque.

18 Refit the sump as described in Section 16.

19 Refit the crankshaft sprocket with reference to Section 5.

Flywheel/driveplate end

Note: *The oil seal is integral with the housing and must be renewed as one complete assembly.*

20 Remove the flywheel (manual transmission) or driveplate (automatic transmission) with reference to Section 14.

21 Remove the intermediate plate from the dowels on the cylinder block.

22 Remove the sump as described in Section 16.

23 Progressively slacken then remove the oil seal housing retaining bolts.

24 Lift the housing away from the cylinder block, together with the crankshaft oil seal, using a twisting motion to ease the seal off the shaft.

25 Recover the old gasket from the cylinder block, then wipe clean the block before fitting the new oil seal and housing.

26 Smear the block mating surface with a little multi-purpose grease, and lay the new gasket in position **(see illustration)**.

27 A protective plastic cap is supplied with genuine Ford crankshaft oil seals/housings;

10.14 Locate the new crankshaft oil seal housing gasket in position

10.16 Offer up the seal and its housing to the end of the crankshaft

10.26 Locate the new crankshaft oil seal housing in position

10.27 A protective cap is supplied with genuine Ford crankshaft oil seals

10.28 Locate the crankshaft oil seal housing over the protective plastic cap

11.7 Pull out the battery compartment upper panel

when fitted over the end of the crankshaft, the cap prevents damage to the inner lip of the oil seal as it is being fitted **(see illustration)**. Use adhesive tape wrapped around the end of the crankshaft if a cap is not available.

28 Lubricate the inner lip of the crankshaft oil seal with clean engine oil, then offer up the seal and its housing to the end of the crankshaft. Carefully ease the seal along the shaft using a twisting motion, until the housing is flush with the crankcase **(see illustration)**.

29 Insert the retaining bolts and tighten them progressively to the specified torque.

30 Refit the sump with reference to Section 16.

31 Refit the intermediate plate to the cylinder block, then insert and tighten the retaining bolts.

32 Refit the flywheel (manual transmission) or driveplate (automatic transmission) with reference to Section 14 of this Chapter.

11 Cylinder head –
removal and refitting

Note: *Cylinder head dismantling and overhaul is covered in Chapter 2C.*

Removal

1 Disconnect the battery negative (earth) lead (see Chapter 5A).

2 Drain the engine oil with reference to Chapter 1B.

3 Drain the cooling system with reference to Chapter 1B.

4 Refer to Section 6 and remove the auxiliary drivebelts.

5 Remove the camshaft cover with reference to Section 7.

6 Remove the camshaft sprocket as described in Section 5.

7 Unscrew the expansion tank cap, and pull out the upper part of the battery compartment panel **(see illustration)**.

8 Undo the turbocharger oil return pipe from the rear of the cylinder block, and recover the sealing washers. Be prepared for oil spillage.

9 Slacken and remove the retaining nuts, and separate the front exhaust pipe from the turbocharger. Refer to Chapter 4B if necessary.

10 Make a note of their fitted positions and detach the vacuum hoses from the turbocharger. Release the retaining clips, and disconnect the intake and pressure hoses from the turbocharger.

11 Disconnect the wiring plug from the vehicle speed sensor on the transmission casing, above the right-hand driveshaft.

12 Undo the retaining bolt, and vacuum hose (66 kW engine only), then remove the turbocharger intake pipe from the right-hand end of the engine.

13 Release the retaining clips and disconnect the coolant hoses from the housing on the front of the cylinder head.

14 On 81 kW engines, undo the nut and detach the turbocharger air charge pipe bracket, and disconnect the oil pressure switch from the left-hand end of the cylinder head **(see illustration)**.

15 Working at the left-hand side of the cylinder head, disconnect the wiring plugs for the needle lift sensor and the camshaft position sensor **(see illustration)**.

16 Release the retaining clip and disconnect the heater hose from the left-hand end of the cylinder head.

17 Separate the vacuum hose from the coolant hose clips, and disconnect it from the EGR valve.

18 Undo the retaining nuts/unions, and remove the turbocharger oil feed pipe from the oil filter housing, turbocharger, and retaining brackets.

19 Where fitted, undo the nuts and remove the engine mounting damper from the right-hand engine mounting.

20 Undo the two nuts and three bolts securing the right-hand engine mounting bracket to the mounting and engine support plate.

21 Undo the 7 retaining bolts, and remove both parts of the right-hand engine mounting engine support plate **(see illustration 4.13)**.

22 Working through the right-hand front wheelarch, unscrew the bolt securing the power steering pipe to the engine support plate.

23 Remove the retaining nut, and withdraw the timing belt tensioner from the mounting stud.

24 Remove the injection pump sprocket as described in Chapter 4B, Section 6.

25 Unscrew the retaining bolt, and remove the timing belt upper idler roller.

26 Undo the two bolts on the cylinder head, and the bolt on the injection pump securing the rear timing belt cover **(see illustration)**.

11.14 Disconnect the oil pressure switch and remove the bracket

11.15 Disconnect the needle lift sensor and camshaft position sensor wiring plugs

11.26 Undo the bolts securing the inner timing belt cover to the cylinder head

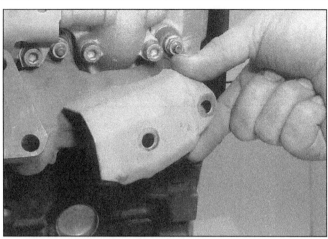

11.36 Remove the heat shield from the exhaust manifold

11.39 Fit the new exhaust manifold gaskets

27 Slacken the union nuts and remove the injector pressure pipes.

28 Remove the fuel injectors and glow plugs with reference to Chapters 4B and 5B.

29 Disconnect the engine coolant temperature sensor wiring plug.

30 Using a suitable splined tool, following the reverse of the tightening sequence **(see illustration 11.56)**, progressively slacken the cylinder head bolts, by half a turn at a time, until all bolts can be unscrewed by hand. Discard the bolts – new ones must be fitted on reassembly.

31 Check that nothing remains connected to the cylinder head, then lift the head away from the cylinder block; seek assistance if possible, as it is a heavy assembly, especially as it is being removed complete with manifolds.

32 Remove the gasket from the top of the block, noting the locating dowels. If the dowels are a loose fit, remove them for safe-keeping. Do not discard the gasket yet – it will be needed for identification purposes.

33 If the cylinder head is to be dismantled for overhaul, refer to Chapter 2C. For camshaft and hydraulic tappet removal, refer to Section 13.

Manifold

Separation

34 With the cylinder head on a workbench, remove the turbocharger (where applicable) with reference to Chapter 4B.

35 Remove the EGR valve with reference to Chapter 4C.

36 Where applicable, unscrew the nuts and remove the small heat shield from the front of the exhaust manifold **(see illustration)**.

37 Progressively unscrew the mounting bolts and remove the inlet manifold from the cylinder head. Remove the gasket and discard it.

38 Progressively unscrew the mounting nuts and remove the exhaust manifold from the cylinder head. Remove the gaskets and discard. Discard the self-locking mounting nuts and obtain new ones.

Reassembly

39 Ensure that the inlet and exhaust manifold mating surfaces are completely clean. Refit the exhaust manifold, using new gaskets and nuts. Ensure that the gaskets are fitted the correct way around, otherwise they will obstruct the inlet manifold gasket **(see illustration)**. Tighten the exhaust manifold retaining nuts to the specified torque (see Chapter 4C).

40 Fit a new inlet manifold gasket to the cylinder head, then lift the inlet manifold into position **(see illustration)**. Insert the retaining bolts and tighten them to the specified torque (see Chapter 4B).

41 Refit the heat shield to the studs on the exhaust manifold, then fit and tighten the retaining nuts.

42 Refit the EGR valve with reference to Chapter 4C.

43 Refit the turbocharger to the inlet and exhaust manifolds with reference to Chapter 4B.

Preparation for refitting

44 The mating faces of the cylinder head and cylinder block must be perfectly clean before refitting the head. Use a hard plastic or wood scraper to remove all traces of gasket and carbon; also clean the piston crowns. Take particular care during the cleaning operations, as aluminium alloy is easily damaged. Also,

11.40 Fit the new inlet manifold gasket to the cylinder head

make sure that the carbon is not allowed to enter the oil and water passages – this is particularly important for the lubrication system, as carbon could block the oil supply to the engine's components. Using adhesive tape and paper, seal the water, oil and bolt holes in the cylinder block/crankcase.

45 Check the mating surfaces of the cylinder block/crankcase and the cylinder head for nicks, deep scratches and other damage. If slight, they may be removed carefully with abrasive paper, but note that head machining will not be possible – refer to Chapter 2C.

46 If warpage of the cylinder head gasket surface is suspected, use a straight-edge to check it for distortion. Refer to Part C of this Chapter if necessary.

47 Clean out the cylinder head bolt drillings using a suitable tap. If a tap is not available, make a home-made substitute **(see Tool Tip)**.

48 On the engines covered in this Chapter, it is possible for the piston crowns to strike the

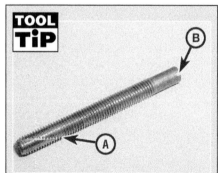

If a tap is not available, make a home-made substitute by cutting a slot (A) down the threads of one of the oil cylinder head bolts. After use, the bolt head can be cut-off, and the shank can then be used as an alignment dowel to assist cylinder head refitting. Cut a screwdriver slot (B) in the top of the bolt, to allow it to be unscrewed.

valve heads, if the camshaft is rotated with the timing belt removed and the crankshaft set to TDC. For this reason, the camshaft must be locked at its TDC position using the locking bar engaged with the slot in the end of the camshaft while the cylinder head is being refitted. Turn the crankshaft to TDC on No 1 cylinder, and then anti-clockwise 90° so that all pistons are half-way up the cylinders.

Refitting

49 Examine the old cylinder head gasket for manufacturer's identification markings. These will either be in the form of notches or holes, and a part number, on the edge of the gasket **(see illustration)**. Unless new pistons have been fitted, the new cylinder head gasket must be the same type as the old one.
50 If new piston assemblies have been fitted as part of an engine overhaul, before purchasing the new cylinder head gasket, refer to Chapter 2C and measure the piston projection. Purchase a new gasket according to the results of the measurement (see Chapter 2C Specifications).
51 Lay the new head gasket on the cylinder block, engaging it with the locating dowels. Ensure that the manufacturer's TOP or OBEN and part number markings are facing upwards.
52 Cut the heads from two of the old cylinder head bolts. Cut a slot, big enough for a screwdriver blade, in the end of each bolt. These can be used as alignment guides to assist in cylinder head refitting **(see illustration)**.
53 With the help of an assistant, place the cylinder head and manifolds centrally on the cylinder block, ensuring that the locating dowels engage with the recesses in the cylinder head.
54 Unscrew the home-made alignment dowels using a screwdriver and remove them.
55 Oil the bolt threads, then carefully enter each new bolt (with washers where applicable) into its relevant hole (*do not drop them in*) and screw in, by hand only, until finger-tight.
56 Working progressively and in the sequence shown, tighten the cylinder head bolts to their Stage 1 torque setting, using a torque wrench and socket **(see illustration)**. Repeat the exercise in the same sequence for the Stage 2 torque setting.
57 Once all the bolts have been tightened to their Stage 2 settings, working again in the given sequence, angle-tighten the bolts through the specified Stage 3 angle, using a socket and extension bar. It is recommended that an angle-measuring gauge is used during this stage of the tightening, to ensure accuracy. If a gauge is not available, use white paint to make alignment marks between the bolt head and cylinder head prior to tightening; the marks can then be used to check the bolt has been rotated through the correct angle during tightening. Repeat for the Stage 4 setting **(see illustration)**. **Note:** *No*

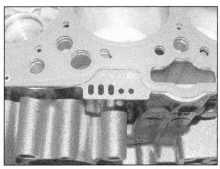
11.49 The thickness of the cylinder head gasket can be identified by notches or holes

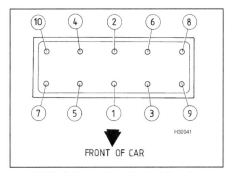
11.56 Cylinder head bolt tightening sequence

further tightening of the cylinder head bolts is required after the engine has been started.
58 Turn the crankshaft 90° clockwise (to TDC), and check that the TDC timing marks are still aligned with reference to Section 2.
59 The remainder of refitting is a reversal of the removal procedure, but on completion carry out the following:
a) Refill the cooling system with the correct quantity of new coolant with reference to Chapter 1B.
b) Refill the engine with the correct grade and quantity of oil with reference to Chapter 1B.

12 Hydraulic tappets – operation check

⚠ **Warning: After fitting hydraulic tappets, wait a minimum of 30 minutes (or preferably, leave overnight) before starting the engine, to allow the tappets time to settle, otherwise the valve heads will strike the pistons.**
1 The hydraulic tappets are self-adjusting, and require no attention whilst in service.
2 If the hydraulic tappets become excessively noisy, their operation can be checked as described below.
3 Run the engine until it reaches its normal operating temperature, then increase the engine speed to approximately 2500 rpm for 2 minutes.

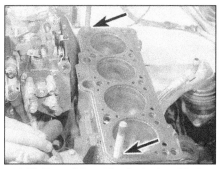
11.52 Two of the old cylinder head bolts (arrowed) can be used as alignment guides

11.57 Angle-tighten the cylinder head bolts

4 If irregular noisy tappets occur mainly when driving the car on short distances, but disappear after running the engine as described in paragraph 3, renew the oil retention valve located in the oil filter housing.
5 In the case of a regular noisy tappet, the faulty tappet must be renewed. To determine which one is faulty, switch off the engine, then refer to Section 7 and remove the camshaft cover.
6 Rotate the camshaft by turning the crankshaft with a socket or spanner, until the first cam lobe over No 1 cylinder is pointing upwards.
7 Using a non-metallic tool, press the tappet downwards then use a feeler blade to check the free travel. If this is more than 0.2 mm, the tappet should be renewed.
8 Hydraulic tappet removal and refitting is described as part of the camshaft removal sequence – see Section 13 for details.

13 Camshaft and hydraulic tappets – removal and refitting

Removal

1 Remove the camshaft sprocket with reference to Section 5.
2 Remove the camshaft cover as described in Section 7.
3 Remove the injection pump sprocket as described in Chapter 4B, Section 6.
4 Remove the retaining nut, and withdraw the timing belt tensioner from the mounting stud.

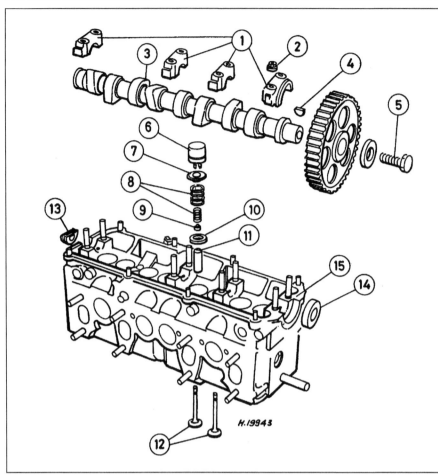

13.6 Cylinder head components

1 Camshaft bearing cap	6 Hydraulic tappet	11 Valve guides
2 Nut	7 Upper valve spring seat	12 Valves
3 Camshaft	8 Valve springs	13 Plug
4 Woodruff key	9 Valve stem seal	14 Camshaft oil seal
5 Camshaft sprocket bolt	10 Lower valve spring seat	15 Cylinder head

5 Undo the two bolts on the cylinder head, and the bolt on the injection pump securing the timing belt inner cover **(see illustration 11.26)**.
6 Slacken the nuts from bearing caps 5, 1, and 3 first, then from bearing caps 2 and 4 **(see illustration)**. Slacken the nuts alternatively and diagonally half a turn at a time until they can be removed, then remove the bearing caps. Keep the caps in order and note their fitted positions. **Note:** *The camshaft bearing caps are numbered 1 to 5 from the timing belt end.*
7 Slide the seal from the camshaft and

discard it – a new one must be fitted on reassembly **(see illustration)**.
8 Carefully lift the camshaft from the cylinder head, keeping it level and supported at both ends as it is removed, so that the journals and lobes are not damaged.
9 Lift the hydraulic tappets from their bores and store them with the valve contact surface downwards to prevent the oil from draining out **(see illustration)**. It is recommended that the tappets are kept immersed in oil for the period they are removed from the cylinder head. Make a note of the position of each tappet, as they must be fitted to the same valves on reassembly. If required, check the camshaft condition, endfloat and bearing clearances as described in Chapter 2C, Section 6. Inspection of the hydraulic tappets is detailed in Section 12.

Refitting

10 Check that the crankshaft is still at TDC on No 1 cylinder, then turn it anti-clockwise 90° so that all pistons are half-way up the cylinders, to prevent any accidental valve-to-piston contact.
11 Lubricate the camshaft and cylinder head bearing journals with clean engine oil.
12 Carefully lower the camshaft into position in the cylinder head making sure that the cam lobes for No 1 cylinder are pointing upwards. Support the ends of the shaft as it is fitted, to avoid damaging the lobes and journals **(see illustration)**.
13 Lubricate the inner lip of the new camshaft oil seal with clean engine oil, then locate it on the end of the camshaft. Make sure that the closed end of the seal faces outwards from the camshaft, and take care not to damage the seal lip. Locate the seal against the seat in the cylinder head.
14 The bearing caps have their respective cylinder numbers stamped onto them, and have an elongated lug on one side. When correctly fitted, the numbers should be readable from the exhaust side of the cylinder head, and the lugs should face the intake side of the cylinder head. Oil the upper surfaces of the camshaft bearing journals, then fit Nos 2 and 4 bearing caps. Ensure they are fitted the right way around and in the correct locations, then progressively tighten down the retaining

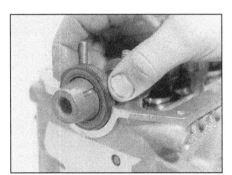

13.7 Remove the camshaft oil seal

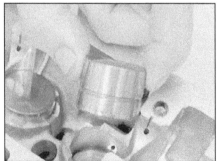

13.9 Lift the hydraulic tappets from their bores

13.12 Lower the camshaft into position on the cylinder head

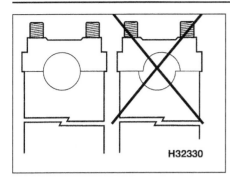

13.14a The camshaft bearing caps are drilled off-centre

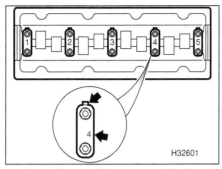

13.14b The bearing caps are fitted as shown

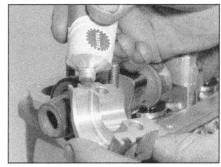

13.15 Smear the mating surfaces of cap No 1 with sealant

nuts to the specified torque **(see illustrations)**.
15 Smear the mating surfaces of bearing cap No 1 with sealant, then fit caps 1, 3 and 5 over the camshaft and progressively tighten the nuts to the specified torque **(see illustration)**.
16 The remainder of refitting is a reversal of removal, noting the following points.
  a) *After installing the camshaft, do not rotate the crankshaft or camshaft for at least 30 minutes.*
  b) *Tighten all nuts/bolts to their specified torque setting where available.*

14 Flywheel/driveplate – removal, inspection and refitting

Removal

1 On manual gearbox models, remove the gearbox (see Chapter 7A) and clutch (see Chapter 6).
2 On automatic transmission models, remove the automatic transmission as described in Chapter 7B.
3 The flywheel/driveplate bolts are offset to ensure correct fitment. Unscrew the bolts while holding the flywheel/driveplate stationary. Temporarily insert a bolt in the cylinder block, and use a screwdriver to hold the flywheel/driveplate, or make up a holding tool.
4 Lift the flywheel/driveplate from the crankshaft. If removing a driveplate, note the location of the shim and spacer.

Inspection

5 Check the flywheel/driveplate for wear and damage. Examine the starter ring gear for excessive wear to the teeth. If the driveplate or its ring gear are damaged, the complete driveplate must be renewed. The flywheel ring gear, however, may be renewed separately from the flywheel, but the work should be entrusted to an Ford dealer or specialist. If the clutch friction face is discoloured or scored excessively, it may be possible to regrind it,

but this work should also be entrusted to an Ford dealer or specialist. Always renew the flywheel/driveplate bolts.

Refitting

6 Refitting is a reversal of removal, but coat the threads of the (new) bolts with locking fluid before inserting them and tightening them to the specified torque. If a replacement driveplate is to be fitted, its position must be checked and adjusted if necessary.

15 Engine mountings – inspection and renewal

Inspection

1 If improved access is required, raise the front of the car and support it securely on axle stands. Undo the two retaining nuts and four bolts (two each side), then remove the undershield.
2 Check the mounting rubbers to see if they are cracked, hardened or separated from the metal at any point; renew the mounting if any such damage or deterioration is evident.
3 Check that all the mounting's fasteners are securely tightened; use a torque wrench to check if possible.
4 Using a large screwdriver or a crowbar, check for wear in the mounting by carefully levering against it to check for free play. Where this is not possible, enlist the aid of an assistant to move the engine/transmission back-and-forth, or from side-to-side, while you watch the mounting. While some free play is to be expected even from new components, excessive wear should be obvious. If excessive free play is found, check first that the fasteners are correctly secured, then renew any worn components as described below.

Renewal

Right-hand engine mounting

5 Apply the handbrake then jack up the front of the vehicle and support it on axle stands

(see *Jacking and vehicle support*). Undo the two retaining nuts and four bolts (two each side), and remove the undershield. Support the weight of the engine/transmission using a trolley jack with a block of wood placed on its head.
6 Remove the air cleaner housing as described in Chapter 4A.
7 Undo the three horizontal bolts securing the mounting bracket to the engine support plate, and the two nuts securing the mounting bracket to the engine mounting **(see illustration 4.10)**.
8 Unscrew the three bolts and remove the mounting from the inner wing **(see illustration)**.
9 Fit the new engine mounting and bracket using a reversal of the removal procedure, tightening the nuts/bolts to the specified torque.

Left-hand engine mounting

10 Apply the handbrake then jack up the front of the vehicle and support it on axle stands (see *Jacking and vehicle support*). Undo the two retaining nuts and four bolts (two each side), and remove the undershield. Support the weight of the engine/transmission using a trolley jack with a block of wood placed on its head.
11 Remove the battery as described in Chapter 5A.
12 Working in the battery tray area, slacken and remove the four bolts securing the

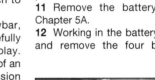

15.8 Undo the three bolts and remove the engine mounting

15.12 Undo the four bolts

15.14 Undo the engine roll restrictor-to-transmission bolt

15.15 Four bolts secure the mounting to the bracket

engine/transmission mounting to the body **(see illustration)**.

13 Remove the starter motor as described in Chapter 5A.

14 Undo the retaining bolt and detach the engine roll restrictor from the transmission **(see illustration)**.

15 Using the jack, lower the engine/transmission slightly. Undo the retaining bolts and remove the mounting from the mounting bracket **(see illustration)**. If required, undo the four Torx bolts, and remove the bracket from the transmission casing.

16 Fit the new mounting using a reversal of the removal procedure, tightening the nuts/bolts to the specified torque.

Engine roll restrictor

17 Apply the handbrake, then jack up the front of the vehicle and support it on axle stands (see *Jacking and vehicle support*). Undo the two retaining nuts and four bolts (two each side), and remove the engine undershield.

18 Support the weight of the engine with a trolley jack and piece of wood beneath the sump.

19 Unscrew the bolt securing the roll restrictor to the transmission **(see illustration 15.14)**.

20 Slacken and remove the bolt(s) securing the roll restrictor to the crossmember.

21 Fit the new roll restrictor using a reversal of the removal procedure, noting the different specified torque applicable if the restrictor is made from steel or aluminium.

16 Sump – removal, inspection and refitting

Removal

1 Apply the handbrake, then jack up the front of the vehicle and support it on axle stands (see *Jacking and vehicle support*). Undo the two retaining nuts and four bolts (two each side), and remove the engine undershield.

2 Position a container beneath the sump, then unscrew the drain plug (refer to Chapter 1B) and drain the engine oil. Clean, refit, and tighten the plug after all the oil has drained. Remove the dipstick from the engine.

3 The plastic sump cover is secured by one bolt, and two retaining clips. To release the clip at the left-hand end, push the centre pin up through the clip **(see illustration)**.

4 Undo the bolts and remove the lower flywheel cover plate.

5 Unscrew and remove the sump bolts **(see illustration)**.

6 Remove the sump and gasket. If it is stuck, tap it gently with a mallet to free it.

Refitting

7 Clean the contact faces of the sump and block. Apply a little suitable sealant to the joint areas where the crankshaft oil seal housings contact the cylinder block.

8 Locate a new gasket on the sump, then offer it up to the block and fit the bolts. Tighten the bolts to the specified torque in diagonal sequence.

9 The remaining refitting procedure is a reversal removal, but tighten the nuts and bolts to the specified torque where given in the Specifications. On completion, fill the engine with the correct quantity of oil as described in Chapter 1B.

17 Oil pump and pick-up – removal, inspection and refitting

Removal

1 Remove the sump as described in Section 16.

2 Unscrew and remove the large oil pump mounting bolts, then withdraw the pump from the block **(see illustration)**.

3 With the pump on the bench, unscrew the bolts and remove the suction tube from the oil pump. Recover the O-ring.

4 Unscrew the two bolts, and lift off the cover.

Inspection

5 Clean the components, and check them for wear and damage.

6 Using a feeler blade as shown **(see illustrations)**, check the backlash between the gears, and compare with that given in the Specifications. Similarly check the endfloat of the gears, using a straight-edge across the end face of the pump. If outside the specified limits, the pump should be renewed, otherwise refit the cover and tighten the bolts.

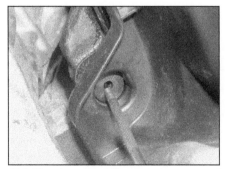

16.3 To release the clip, push the centre of the clip up

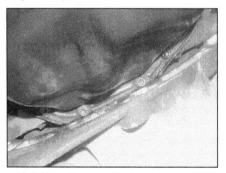

16.5 Note the securing bolts at the left-hand end of the sump

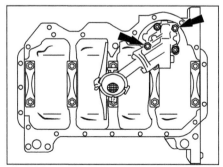

17.2 Undo the large oil pump mounting bolts (arrowed)

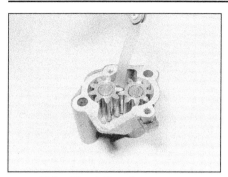

17.6a Check the oil pump gear backlash . . .

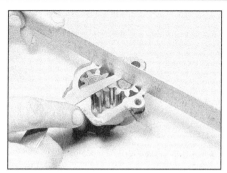

17.6b . . . and endfloat

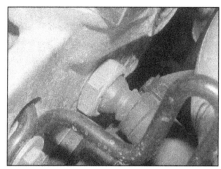

18.1 Oil pressure switch at the left-hand end of the cylinder head

Refitting

7 Prime the pump with oil by immersing it in oil and turning the driveshaft.

8 Clean the contact faces, then fit the oil pump to the block, insert the mounting bolts, and tighten them to the specified torque.

9 Locate a new O-ring seal on the end of the suction tube. Fit the tube to the oil pump, insert the bolts and tighten them to the specified torque.

10 Refit the sump with reference to Section 16.

18 Oil pressure switches – removal and refitting

Removal

1 The oil pressure switches are located on the top of the oil filter housing, and the left-hand end of the cylinder head **(see illustration)**. The blue switch (where fitted) on the cylinder head is designed to switch at 0.25 bar pressure, whilst the grey switch operates at 0.9 bar. For improved access, prise out the cover cap, undo the retaining nuts/bolts and remove the plastic cover from the top of the engine.

2 Disconnect the wiring plug from the relevant switch.

3 Unscrew the switch from the housing.

Refitting

4 If the original switch is to be refitted, apply a smear of sealant to the threads of the switch. Screw the switch into the housing, and tighten it to the specified torque.

Notes

Chapter 2 Part C:
Engine removal and overhaul procedures

Contents

Crankshaft – refitting 13
Crankshaft – removal and inspection 8
Cylinder block/crankcase – cleaning and inspection 10
Cylinder head – dismantling, cleaning, inspection and reassembly . 6
Engine – initial start-up after overhaul and reassembly 16
Engine – removal and refitting 4
Engine overhaul – general information 2
Engine overhaul – preliminary information 5
Engine overhaul – reassembly sequence 12
Engine removal – preparation and precautions 3
General information 1
Intermediate shaft – removal and refitting 9
Main and big-end bearings – inspection and selection 11
Piston/connecting rod assemblies – refitting 15
Piston/connecting rod assemblies – removal and inspection 7
Pistons and piston rings – assembly 14

Degrees of difficulty

Easy, suitable for novice with little experience	**Fairly easy,** suitable for beginner with some experience	**Fairly difficult,** suitable for competent DIY mechanic 	**Difficult,** suitable for experienced DIY mechanic	**Very difficult,** suitable for expert DIY or professional

Specifications

Engine codes*

Petrol engines:
1998 cc, 85 kW	NSE
2295 cc, 107 kW	Y5B

Diesel engines:
1896 cc:
66 kW to 09.96	1Z
66 kW from 09.96	AHU
66 kW from 09.99	AVG
81 kW	AFN

* **Note:** *See 'Vehicle Identification' for the location of the code marking on the engine.*

Cylinder head

Cylinder head gasket surface maximum distortion	0.1 mm

Minimum cylinder head height:
Petrol engines:
Code NSE	147.45 mm
Code Y5B	147.25 mm
Diesel engines	Head resurfacing not possible

Cylinder head gasket selection (diesel engines):
Piston projection 0.91 to 1.00 mm	1 hole/notch*
Piston projection 1.01 to 1.10 mm	2 holes/notches*
Piston projection 1.11 to 1.20 mm	3 holes/notches*
Maximum crack width between valve seats (diesel engines)	0.5 mm

Disregard single and double oval holes

Camshaft

Maximum endfloat:
Petrol engines	0.02 to 0.26 mm
Diesel engines	0.15 mm maximum

Intermediate shaft
Maximum endfloat .... 0.25 mm

Pistons and piston rings
Piston diameter:
  Petrol engines:
    Code NSE:
      Standard .... 85.97 85.99 mm
      0.15 and 0.50 mm oversizes available
    Code Y5B .... 89.58 to 89.62 mm
  Diesel engines .... 79.47 to 79.97 mm
Piston ring end gap clearance (ring 15 mm from bottom of bore):
  Petrol engines:
    Code NSE:
      Top compression ring .... 0.30 to 0.60 mm
      Middle compression ring .... 0.50 to 0.80 mm
      Oil scraper rings .... 0.40 to 1.50 mm
    Code Y5B:
      Top compression ring .... 0.30 to 0.46 mm
      Middle compression ring .... 0.50 to 0.76 mm
      Oil control ring .... 0.15 to 0.71 mm
  Diesel engines:
    New:
      Compression rings .... 0.20 to 0.40 mm
      Oil scraper ring .... 0.25 to 0.50 mm
    Wear limit .... 1.0 mm

Valves
Valve spring free length:
  Petrol engines:
    Code NSE:
      Inner spring .... 49.2 mm
      Outer spring .... 48.2 mm
    Code Y5B .... 43.6 mm
  Diesel engines .... Not available
Maximum valve head deflection (end of stem flush with top of guide):
  Petrol engines .... Not available
  Diesel engines .... 1.3 mm

Cylinder block
Bore diameter:
  Petrol engines:
    Code NSE .... 86.00 mm (nominal)
    Code Y5B .... 89.60 mm (nominal)
  Diesel engines .... 79.51 mm (nominal)

Connecting rods
Big-end shell-to-journal clearance:
  Petrol engines .... 0.006 to 0.060 mm
  Diesel engines .... 0.080 mm maximum
Big-end bearing endfloat:
  Petrol engines .... 0.09 to 0.31 mm
  Diesel engines .... 0.37 mm

Crankshaft
Endfloat:
  Petrol engines .... 0.093 to 0.303 mm
    Wear limit .... Not specified
  Diesel engines .... 0.070 to 0.170 mm
    Wear limit .... 0.37 mm
Main bearing running clearance:
  Petrol engines .... 0.020 to 0.039 mm
    Wear limit .... 0.15 mm
  Diesel engines .... 0.030 to 0.080 mm
    Wear limit .... 0.17 mm

Torque wrench settings
Refer to Chapters 2A or 2B.

1 General information

1 Included in this Part of Chapter 2 are details of removing the engine from the car and general overhaul procedures for the cylinder head, cylinder block and all other engine internal components.
2 The information given ranges from advice concerning preparation for an overhaul and the purchase of replacement parts, to detailed step-by-step procedures covering removal, inspection, renovation and refitting of engine internal components.
3 After Section 5, all instructions are based on the assumption that the engine has been removed from the car. For information concerning in-car engine repair, as well as the removal and refitting of those external components necessary for full overhaul, refer to the relevant in-car repair procedure section (Chapters 2A or 2B) and to Section 5 of this Chapter. Ignore any preliminary dismantling operations described in the relevant in-car repair sections that are no longer relevant once the engine has been removed from the car.
4 Apart from torque wrench settings, which are given at the beginning of the relevant in-car repair procedure in Chapters 2A or 2B, all specifications relating to engine overhaul are at the beginning of this Part of Chapter 2.

2 Engine overhaul – general information

1 It is not always easy to determine when, or if, an engine should be completely overhauled, as a number of factors must be considered.
2 High mileage is not necessarily an indication that an overhaul is needed, while low mileage does not preclude the need for an overhaul. Frequency of servicing is probably the most important consideration. An engine which has had regular and frequent oil and filter changes, as well as other required maintenance, should give many thousands of miles of reliable service. Conversely, a neglected engine may require an overhaul very early in its life.
3 Excessive oil consumption is an indication that piston rings, valve seals and/or valve guides are in need of attention. Make sure that oil leaks are not responsible before deciding that the rings and/or guides are worn. Perform a compression test, as described in the relevant Part A or B of this Chapter, to determine the likely cause of the problem.
4 Check the oil pressure with a gauge fitted in place of the oil pressure switch, and compare it with that specified (see Chapter 2A or 2B). If

it is extremely low, the main and big-end bearings, and/or the oil pump, are probably worn out.
5 Loss of power, rough running, knocking or metallic engine noises, excessive valve gear noise, and high fuel consumption may also point to the need for an overhaul, especially if they are all present at the same time. If a complete service does not remedy the situation, major mechanical work is the only solution.
6 An engine overhaul involves restoring all internal parts to the specification of a new engine. During an overhaul, the pistons and the piston rings are renewed. New main and big-end bearings are generally fitted; if necessary, the crankshaft may be renewed, to restore the journals. The valves are also serviced as well, since they are usually in less-than-perfect condition at this point. While the engine is being overhauled, other components, such as the starter and alternator, can be overhauled as well. The end result should be an as-new engine that will give many trouble-free miles. **Note:** *Critical cooling system components such as the hoses, thermostat and coolant pump should be renewed when an engine is overhauled. The radiator should be checked carefully, to ensure that it is not clogged or leaking. Also, it is a good idea to renew the oil pump whenever the engine is overhauled.*
7 Before beginning the engine overhaul, read through the entire procedure, to familiarise yourself with the scope and requirements of the job. Overhauling an engine is not difficult if you follow carefully all of the instructions, have the necessary tools and equipment, and pay close attention to all specifications. It can, however, be time-consuming. Plan on the car being off the road for a minimum of two weeks, especially if parts must be taken to an engineering works for repair or reconditioning. Check on the availability of parts and make sure that any necessary special tools and equipment are obtained in advance. Most work can be done with typical hand tools, although a number of precision measuring tools are required for inspecting parts to determine if they must be renewed. Often the engineering works will handle the inspection of parts and offer advice concerning reconditioning and renewal. **Note:** *Always wait until the engine has been completely dismantled, and until all components (especially the cylinder block and the crankshaft) have been inspected, before deciding what service and repair operations must be performed by an engineering works. The condition of these components will be the major factor to consider when determining whether to overhaul the original engine, or to buy a reconditioned unit. Do not, therefore, purchase parts or have overhaul work done on other components until they have been thoroughly inspected. As a general rule, time is the primary cost of an overhaul, so it does not pay to fit worn or sub-standard parts.*

8 As a final note, to ensure maximum life and minimum trouble from a reconditioned engine, everything must be assembled with care, in a spotlessly-clean environment.

3 Engine removal – preparation and precautions

If you have decided that the engine must be removed for overhaul or major repair work, several preliminary steps should be taken.
Locating a suitable place to work is extremely important. Adequate work space, along with storage space for the vehicle, will be needed. If a workshop or garage is not available, at the very least a solid, level, clean work surface is required.
If possible, clear some shelving close to the work area and use it to store the engine components and ancillaries as they are removed and dismantled. In this manner, the components stand a better chance of staying clean and undamaged during the overhaul. Laying out components in groups together with their fixings, bolts, screws, etc, will save time and avoid confusion when the engine is refitted.
Clean the engine compartment and engine before beginning the removal procedure; this will help visibility and help to keep tools clean.
The help of an assistant is essential; there are certain instances when one person cannot safely perform all of the operations required to remove the engine from the vehicle. Safety is of primary importance, considering the potential hazards involved in this kind of operation. A second person should always be in attendance to offer help in an emergency. If this is the first time you have removed an engine, advice and aid from someone more experienced would also be beneficial.
Plan the operation ahead of time. Before starting work, obtain (or arrange for the hire of) all of the tools and equipment you will need. Access to the following items will allow the task of removing and refitting the engine to be completed safely and with relative ease: a heavy-duty trolley jack – rated in excess of the weight of the engine, complete sets of spanners and sockets as described in the rear of this Manual, wooden blocks, and plenty of rags and cleaning solvent for mopping-up spilled oil, coolant and fuel. A selection of different sized plastic storage bins will also prove useful for keeping dismantled components grouped together. If any of the equipment must be hired, make sure that you arrange for it in advance, and perform all of the operations possible without it beforehand; this may save you time and money.
Plan on the vehicle being out of use for quite a while, especially if you intend to carry out an engine overhaul. Read through the whole of this Section and work out a strategy based on your own experience and the tools, time and workspace available to you. Some of the overhaul processes may have to be

carried out by an Ford dealer or an engineering works – these establishments often have busy schedules, so it would be prudent to consult them before removing or dismantling the engine, to get an idea of the amount of time required to carry out the work.

When removing the engine from the vehicle, be methodical about the disconnection of external components. Labelling cables and hoses as they are removed will greatly assist the refitting process.

Always be extremely careful when lifting the engine from the engine bay. Serious injury can result from careless actions. If help is required, it is better to wait until it is available rather than risk personal injury and/or damage to components by continuing alone. By planning ahead and taking your time, a job of this nature, although major, can be accomplished successfully and without incident.

4 Engine – removal and refitting

Note: *The engine can be removed from the car only as a complete unit with the transmission; the two are then separated for overhaul. The engine/transmission unit is lowered out of position, and withdrawn from under the vehicle. Bearing this in mind, ensure the vehicle is raised sufficiently so that there is enough clearance between the front of the vehicle and the floor to allow the engine/transmission assembly to be slid out once it has been lowered out of position. The distance from the top of the camshaft cover to the lower edge of the oil sump is 66 cm, consequently, the use of a wheels-free vehicle lift is recommended, but not essential.*

Removal

1 Select a solid, level surface to park the vehicle on. Give yourself enough space to move around it easily.
2 Disconnect the negative (earth) lead, and remove the battery, battery compartment upper and lower panels (see Chapter 5A).
3 Apply the handbrake, slacken both front

wheel bolts, then jack up the front of the vehicle and support it on axle stands (see *Jacking and vehicle support*). Remove both front wheels.
4 Remove the engine/transmission undershield, and where applicable, the top cover.
5 Remove the bonnet (see Chapter 11).
6 Carry out the following with reference to the relevant Part of Chapter 1:
  a) Drain the cooling system.
  b) Drain the engine oil.
7 Unbolt the power steering pump and tie it to one side (see Chapter 10). **Note:** *There is no need to disconnect the fluid pipes.*
8 On models with air conditioning, unbolt the compressor and tie it to one side (see Chapter 3). **Note:** *Although not strictly necessary, we found it preferable to remove the alternator (Chapter 5A) and the alternator/power steering pump/compressor mounting bracket (seven bolts) from the front of the engine block. This gave much greater clearance when lowering the engine/transmission.*

⚠️ **Warning: Do not disconnect the air conditioning refrigerant circuit.**

9 Remove the bulkhead trim panel.
10 Remove the air cleaner housing and intake ducting with reference to the relevant Part of Chapter 4.
11 Depressurise the fuel system, and disconnect the fuel supply and return pipes from the fuel rail/injection pump. Plug or cap the open pipes/fittings to prevent fuel loss/dirt ingress.
12 Label all vacuum hoses, wiring connections, and coolant hoses to ensure correct refitment, then disconnect them. Pieces of masking tape with numbers or letters written on them work well **(see illustration)**. If there is a possibility of confusion regarding connects or routing, make a sketch or notes.
13 Where fitted, disconnect the accelerator cable from the engine (see the relevant Part of Chapter 4).
14 On manual transmission models, prise out the spring clip and disconnect the clutch hydraulic pipe (see Chapter 6). Release the pipe from the selector cable bracket, and plug

the pipe openings to prevent dirt ingress and fluid loss.
15 Prise the selector cable end(s) from the balljoint(s) on the transmission, and undo the bolts securing the cable support bracket to the transmission housing (see the relevant Part of Chapter 7). Note the fitted positions of the cable(s).
16 Remove the front section of the exhaust system with reference to Chapter 4C.
17 Remove the starter motor (see Chapter 5A).
18 Remove both front driveshafts as described in Chapter 8.
19 Remove the front crossmember with reference to Chapter 10.
20 Attach lifting chains/straps to the lifting eyes on the cylinder head. Attach the chains to a lifting crane or engine support beam, and take the weight of the engine and transmission **(see illustration)**.
21 Disconnect and remove the engine/transmission mountings (see the relevant Part of Chapter 2).
22 If available, a low trolley should be placed under the engine/transmission assembly, to facilitate its easy removal from under the vehicle. Make a final check to ensure that nothing else remains connected to the engine/transmission. Lower the engine/transmission assembly, making sure that nothing is trapped, taking great care not to damage the radiator/cooling fan assembly. Enlist the help of an assistant during this procedure, as it may be necessary to tilt the assembly slightly to clear the body panels. Great care must be taken to ensure that no components are trapped and damaged during the removal procedure.
23 Detach the hoist and withdraw the engine/transmission unit from under the vehicle.

Separation

24 With the engine/transmission assembly removed, support the assembly on suitable blocks of wood, on a workbench (or failing that, on a clean area of the workshop floor).
25 On automatic transmission models, prise out the engine adapter plate plug from the front of the engine, and unscrew the three torque converter nuts. Turn the crankshaft to align each nut in turn with the adapter plate hole – see Chapter 7B.
26 Ensure that both engine and transmission are adequately supported, then slacken and remove the remaining bolts securing the transmission housing to the engine. Note the correct fitted positions of each bolt (and the relevant brackets) as they are removed, to use as a reference on refitting.
27 Carefully withdraw the transmission from the engine, ensuring that the weight of the transmission is not allowed to hang on the input shaft while it is engaged with the clutch friction disc.
28 If they are loose, remove the locating dowels from the engine or transmission, and keep them in a safe place.

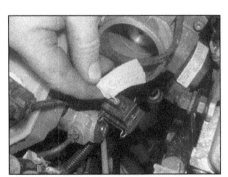

4.12 Label the wiring and hoses as they are disconnected (TPS = Throttle Position Sensor)

4.20 Attach chains/straps to the lifting eyes on the cylinder head

Refitting

29 Refitting is a reversal of removal, but note the following points:

a) *On manual transmission models first smear the splines of the input shaft with a little 'white grease', manufactured specifically for this application, and normally supplied with a replacement clutch kit. Do not use copper grease.*

b) *On automatic transmission models, check that the torque converter is fully entered on the input shaft by checking that the distance between the bellhousing mounting flange and the torque converter is approximately 16.1 mm. If it is less, the torque converter is not fully entered.*

c) *Ensure that all engine and transmission mountings are fitted free of strain.*

d) *Tighten all nuts and bolts to the specified torque where given.*

e) *Refit, and where applicable adjust, all engine related components and systems with reference to the Chapters concerned.*

f) *Ensure that the engine is filled with oil and that the cooling system is refilled as described in the relevant Part of Chapter 1 before starting the engine.*

5 Engine overhaul – preliminary information

It is much easier to dismantle and work on the engine if it is mounted on a portable engine stand. These stands can often be hired from a tool hire shop. Before the engine is mounted on a stand, the flywheel should be removed, so that the stand bolts can be tightened into the end of the cylinder block/crankcase. **Note:** *Do not measure cylinder bore dimensions with the engine mounted on this type of stand.*

If a stand is not available, it is possible to dismantle the engine with it blocked up on a sturdy workbench, or on the floor. Be very careful not to tip or drop the engine when working without a stand.

If you intend to obtain a reconditioned engine, all ancillaries must be removed first to be transferred to the new engine (just as they

will if you are doing a complete engine overhaul yourself). These components include the following:

Petrol engines

a) *Alternator (including mounting brackets) and starter motor (Chapter 5A).*

b) *The ignition system and HT components including all sensors, distributor, HT leads and spark plugs (Chapters 1A and 5B).*

c) *The fuel injection system components (Chapter 4A).*

d) *All electrical switches, actuators and sensors, and the engine wiring harness (Chapters 4A and 5B).*

e) *Inlet and exhaust manifolds (Chapters 4A and 4C).*

f) *Engine oil dipstick and tube.*

g) *Engine mountings (Chapter 2A).*

h) *Flywheel/driveplate (Chapter 2A).*

i) *Clutch components (Chapter 6).*

Diesel engines

a) *Alternator (including mounting brackets) and starter motor (Chapter 5A).*

b) *The glow plug/preheating system components (Chapter 5C).*

c) *All fuel system components, including the fuel injection pump, all sensors and actuators (Chapter 4C).*

d) *The vacuum pump (Chapter 9).*

e) *All electrical switches, actuators and sensors, and the engine wiring harness (Chapter 4B and Chapter 5C).*

f) *Inlet and exhaust manifolds, and turbocharger (Chapter 4B and 4C).*

g) *The engine oil level dipstick and its tube.*

h) *Engine mountings (Chapter 2B).*

i) *Flywheel/driveplate (Chapter 2B).*

j) *Clutch components (Chapter 6).*

All engines

Note: *When removing the external components from the engine, pay close attention to details that may be helpful or important during refitting. Note the fitted position of gaskets, seals, spacers, pins, washers, bolts, and other small components.*

If you are obtaining a short engine (the engine cylinder block/crankcase, crankshaft, pistons and connecting rods, all fully assembled), then the cylinder head, sump, oil pump, timing chain/belt (together with its

tensioner and covers), auxiliary belt (together with its tensioner), coolant pump, thermostat housing, coolant outlet elbows, oil filter housing and, where applicable, oil cooler will also have to be removed.

If you are planning a full overhaul, the engine can be dismantled in the order given below:

a) *Inlet and exhaust manifolds (see the relevant part of Chapter 4).*

b) *Timing belt, sprockets and tensioner (see Chapter 2B).*

c) *Cylinder head (see Chapter 2A or 2B).*

d) *Timing chains and sprockets (see Chapter 2A).*

e) *Flywheel/driveplate (see Chapter 2A or 2B).*

f) *Sump (see Chapter 2A or 2B).*

g) *Oil pump (see Chapter 2A or 2B).*

h) *Piston/connecting rod assemblies (see Section 7).*

i) *Crankshaft (see Section 8).*

6 Cylinder head – dismantling, cleaning, inspection and reassembly

Note: *New and reconditioned cylinder heads are available from Ford, and from engine specialists. Specialist tools are required for the dismantling and inspection procedures, and new components may not be readily available. It may, therefore, be more practical for the home mechanic to buy a reconditioned head, rather than to dismantle, inspect and recondition the original head.*

Dismantling

1 Remove the cylinder head from the engine block as described in Part A or B of this Chapter. Also remove the camshaft(s) and hydraulic tappets as described in Part A or B of this Chapter.

2 On diesel models, remove the injectors and glow plugs (see Chapters 4B and 5C).

3 Where applicable, remove the rear coolant outlet housing together with its gasket/O-ring.

4 It is important that groups of components are kept together when they are removed and, if still serviceable, refitted in the same groups. If they are refitted randomly, accelerated wear leading to early failure will occur. Stowing groups of components in plastic bags or storage bins will help to keep everything in the right order – label them according to their fitted location, eg, No 1 exhaust, No 2 inlet, etc **(see illustration)**. Note that No 1 cylinder is nearest the timing chain/belt end of the engine.

5 With the cylinder head resting on one side, using a valve spring compressor, compress each valve spring in turn, extracting the split collets when the upper valve spring seat has been pushed far enough down the valve stem to free them. If the spring seat sticks, tap the upper jaw of the compressor with a hammer to free it **(see illustration)**.

6.4 Keep groups of components together in labelled bags or boxes

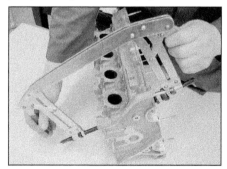

6.5 Compress the valve springs with a compressor tool

6 Release the valve spring compressor and remove the upper spring seat, and single valve springs (2.3 litre petrol engines) or double valve springs (2.0 litre petrol and diesel engines) **(see illustrations)**.

7 Use a pair of pliers or a special removal tool to extract the valve stem oil seal, then remove the lower spring seat from the valve guide. Withdraw the valve itself from the head gasket side of the cylinder head. Repeat this process for the remaining valves **(see illustrations)**.

Cleaning

8 Using a suitable degreasing agent, remove all traces of oil deposits from the cylinder head, paying particular attention to the journal bearings, hydraulic tappet bores, valve guides and oilways. Scrape off any traces of old gasket from the mating surfaces, taking care not to score or gouge them. If using emery paper, do not use a grade of less than 100. Turn the head over and using a blunt blade, scrape any carbon deposits from the combustion chambers and ports. Finally, wash the entire head casting with a suitable solvent to remove the remaining debris.

9 Clean the valve heads and stems using a fine wire brush. If the valve is heavily coked, scrape off the majority of the deposits with a blunt blade first, then use the wire brush. On 2.3 litre petrol models, the exhaust valve stems are filled with sodium to aid cooling. If the exhaust valves

are to be renewed, the old valves must be treated as special waste, and disposed of accordingly.

10 Thoroughly clean the remainder of the components using solvent and allow them to dry completely. Discard the oil seals, as new ones must be fitted when the cylinder head is reassembled.

Inspection

Cylinder head

Note: *On diesel engines the cylinder heads and valves cannot be reworked (although valves may be lapped-in); new or exchange units must be obtained.*

11 Examine the head casting closely to identify any damage or cracks that may have developed. Pay particular attention to the areas around the valve seats and spark plug holes. If cracking is discovered in this area, Ford state that the diesel cylinder head may be re-used, provided the cracks between the valves are no larger than 0.5 mm wide. More serious damage will mean the renewal of the cylinder head casting.

12 Moderately pitted and scorched valve seats can be repaired by lapping the valves in during reassembly, as described later in this Section. Badly worn or damaged valve seats may be restored by recutting, however this work should be entrusted to an engineering works.

13 Measure any distortion of the gasket surfaces using a straight-edge and a set of feeler

blades. Take one measurement longitudinally on both the inlet and exhaust manifold mating surfaces. Take several measurements across the head gasket surface, to assess the level of distortion in all planes **(see illustration)**. Compare the measurements with the figures in the Specifications. On petrol engines, if the head is distorted out of specification, it may be possible to have it machined by an engineering works.

14 Minimum cylinder head heights (measured between the cylinder head gasket surface and the cylinder head cover gasket surface) are listed in Specifications.

Camshaft

15 Visually inspect the camshaft for evidence of wear on the surfaces of the lobes and journals. Normally their surfaces should be smooth and have a dull shine; look for scoring, erosion or pitting and areas that appear highly polished, indicating excessive wear. Accelerated wear will occur once the hardened exterior of the camshaft has been damaged, so always renew worn items. **Note:** *If these symptoms are visible on the tips of the camshaft lobes, check the corresponding tappet, as it will probably be worn as well.*

16 If the machined surfaces of the camshaft appear discoloured or blued, it is likely that it has been overheated at some point, probably due to inadequate lubrication. This may have distorted the shaft, so have the camshaft inspected at an automotive engineering workshop.

17 To measure the camshaft endfloat, temporarily refit the camshaft to the cylinder head, then fit the first and last bearing caps (and shell bearings where applicable) and tighten the retaining nuts to the specified torque setting. Anchor a DTI gauge to the timing belt end of the cylinder head and align the gauge probe with the camshaft axis. Push the camshaft to one end of the cylinder head as far as it will travel, then rest the DTI gauge probe on the end of the camshaft, and zero the gauge display. Push the camshaft as far as it will go to the other end of the cylinder head, and record the gauge reading. Verify the reading by pushing the

6.6a **Remove the upper spring seat . . .**

6.6b **. . . and the valve spring**

6.7a **Use a removal tool to extract the stem oil seal . . .**

6.7b **. . . then remove the lower spring seat**

6.13 **Measure the distortion of the cylinder head**

6.17 Check the camshaft endfloat using a DTI gauge

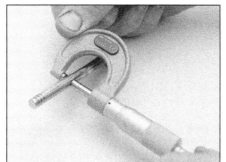

6.20 Measure the diameter of the valve stems with a micrometer

6.23 Measure the maximum deflection of the valve in its guide, using a DTI gauge

camshaft back to its original position and checking that the gauge indicates zero again **(see illustration)**. **Note:** *The hydraulic tappets must not be fitted whilst this measurement is being taken.*

18 Check that the camshaft endfloat measurement is within the limit listed in the Specifications. Wear outside of this limit is unlikely to be confined to any one component, so renewal of the camshaft, cylinder head and bearing caps must be considered.

19 If it is considered necessary to establish the camshaft bearing running clearance, take the camshaft and cylinder head to an automotive engineering workshop. If the camshaft journals or cylinder head bearing surfaces are worn, they may be able to offer a solution. Otherwise renewal of the camshaft and/or cylinder head is the only course of action.

Valves & associated components

Note: *On all engines, the valve heads cannot be recut, although they may be lapped-in.*

20 Examine each valve closely for signs of wear. Inspect the valve stems for wear ridges, scoring or variations in diameter; measure their diameters at several points along their lengths with a micrometer **(see illustration)**.

21 The valve heads should not be cracked, badly pitted or charred. Note that light pitting of the valve head can be rectified by lapping-in the valves during reassembly, as described later in this Section.

22 Check that the valve stem end face is free from excessive pitting or indentation; this

would be caused by defective hydraulic tappets.

23 Insert each valve into its respective guide in the cylinder head and set up a DTI gauge against the edge of the valve head. With the end of the valve stem flush with the top of the valve guide, measure the maximum side-to-side deflection of the valve in its guide **(see illustration)**.

24 If the measurement exceeds that given in the Specifications, the valve and valve guide should be renewed as a pair. **Note:** *Valve guides are an interference fit in the cylinder head and their removal requires access to a hydraulic press. For this reason, it would be wise to entrust the job to an engineering workshop.*

25 Using vernier calipers, measure the free length of each of the valve springs. Compare the measurement obtained with that given in the Specifications. Note that valve springs are usually renewed during a major engine overhaul **(see illustration)**.

26 Stand each spring on its end on a flat surface, against an engineer's square **(see illustration)**. Check the squareness of the spring visually, and renew it if it appears distorted.

Reassembly

27 To achieve a gas-tight seal between the valves and their seats, it will be necessary to lap-in (or grind-in) the valves. To complete this process you will need a quantity of fine/coarse grinding paste and a grinding tool – this can either be of the rubber sucker type,

or the automatic type which is driven by a rotary power tool.

28 Smear a small quantity of *fine* grinding paste on the sealing face of the valve head. Turn the cylinder head over so that the combustion chambers are facing upwards and insert the valve into the correct guide. Attach the grinding tool to the valve head and, using a backward/forward rotary action, grind the valve head into its seat. Periodically lift the valve and rotate it to redistribute the grinding paste **(see illustration)**.

29 Continue this process until the contact between valve and seat produces an unbroken, matt grey ring of uniform width, on both faces. Repeat the operation on the remaining valves.

30 If the valves and seats are so badly pitted that coarse grinding paste must be used, bear in mind that there is a maximum protrusion of the end of the valve stem from the valve guide. If this dimension is outside the limit due to excessive grinding-in, the hydraulic tappets may not operate correctly. Have the cylinder head inspected by an automotive engineering workshop.

31 Assuming the repair is feasible, work as described previously but use coarse grinding paste initially, to achieve a dull finish on the valve face and seat. Wash off the coarse paste with solvent and repeat the process using fine grinding paste to obtain the correct finish.

32 When all the valves have been lapped-in, remove all traces of grinding paste from the cylinder head and valves with solvent, and allow them to dry completely.

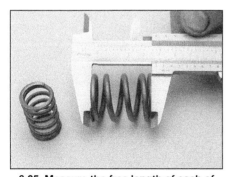

6.25 Measure the free length of each of the valve springs

6.26 Check the squareness of the valve springs

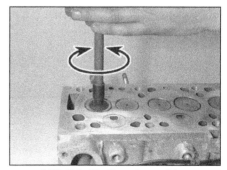

6.28 Grind in the valves with a reciprocating rotary motion

6.33 Fit the lower spring seat with the convex face facing the cylinder head

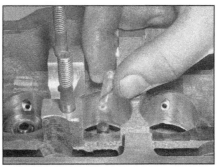

6.34 Fit a protective sleeve over the valve stem before fitting the stem seal

6.35a Push the stem seal over the valve and onto the top of the valve guide . . .

6.35b . . . then use a long reach socket to seat the seal

6.36 Fit the valve spring(s)

33 Turn the head on its side. Fit the first lower spring seat into place, with the convex side facing the cylinder head **(see illustration)**.
34 Working on one valve at a time, lubricate the valve stem with clean engine oil, and insert it into the guide. Fit one of the protective plastic sleeves supplied with the new valve stem oil seals over the valve end face – this will protect the oil seal whilst it is being fitted **(see illustration)**.
35 Dip a new valve stem seal in clean engine oil, and carefully push it over the valve and onto the top of the valve guide – take care not to damage the stem seal as it passes over the valve end face. Use a suitable long reach socket or special installer to press it firmly into position **(see illustrations)**. Remove the protective sleeve.
36 Locate the valve spring(s) over the valve stem **(see illustration)**. Ensure that the springs locate correctly on the lower seat.

37 Fit the upper seat over the top of the springs, then using a valve spring compressor, compress the springs until the upper seat is pushed beyond the collet grooves in the valve stem. Refit the split collet, using a dab of grease to hold the two halves in the grooves **(see illustrations)**. Gradually release the spring compressor, checking that the collet remains correctly seated as the spring extends. When correctly seated, the upper seat should force the two halves of the collet together, and hold them securely in the grooves in the end of the valve.
38 Repeat this process for the remaining sets of valve components. To settle the components after installation, strike the end of each valve stem with a mallet, using a block of wood to protect the stem from damage. Check before progressing any further that the split collets remain firmly held in the end of the valve stem by the upper spring seat.

39 Refit the hydraulic tappets and camshaft as described in Part A or B of this Chapter.
40 Where applicable, refit the coolant sensor and oil pressure switch to the cylinder head.
41 Where applicable, refit the thermostat/coolant outlet housing together with a new gasket/O-ring **(see illustration)**.
42 On diesel models, refit the injectors, and glow plugs (see Chapters 4B and 5C).
43 Refit the cylinder head with reference to Parts A or B of this Chapter. Also refit the camshaft sprocket as described in Part A or B of this Chapter.

7 Piston/connecting rod assemblies – removal and inspection

Removal

1 Refer to Part A or B of this Chapter (as applicable) and remove the cylinder head, flywheel, sump/balancer shaft housing and baffle plate, oil pump and pick-up.
2 Inspect the tops of the cylinder bores for ridges at the point where the pistons reach top dead centre. These must be removed otherwise the pistons may be damaged when they are pushed out of their bores. Use a scraper or ridge reamer to remove the ridges.
3 Using a set of feeler blades, measure the big-end-to-crankpin web thrust clearance at each connecting rod, and record the measurements for later reference.
4 Rotate the crankshaft until piston No 1 is at bottom dead centre; piston No 4 will also be

6.37a Fit the upper seat over the top of the valve spring

6.37b Use grease to hold the two halves of the split collet in the groove

6.41 On 2.3 litre engines, the coolant outlet seal is integral with the housing

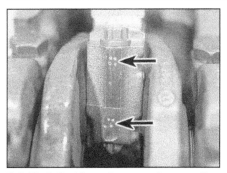

7.4 Mark the big-end caps and connecting rods with their numbers (arrowed)

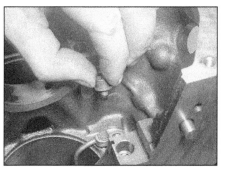

7.8a Remove the piston cooling jets retaining screws . . .

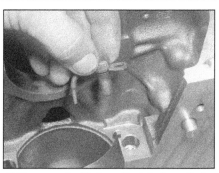

7.8b . . . and withdraw the jets from their mounting holes

at bottom dead centre. Unless they are already identified, mark the big-end bearing caps and connecting rods with their respective piston numbers, using a centre-punch or a scribe **(see illustration)**. Note the orientation of the bearing caps in relation to the connecting rod; it may be difficult to see the manufacturer's markings at this stage, so scribe alignment arrows on them both to ensure correct reassembly.

5 Unscrew the bearing cap bolts half a turn at a time, until they can be removed and the cap withdrawn. Recover the bottom shell bearing, and tape it to the cap for safe-keeping. Note that if the shell bearings are to be re-used, they must be refitted to the same connecting rod.

6 Drive the piston out of the top of the bore using a piece of wooden dowel or a hammer handle. As the piston and connecting rod emerge, recover the top shell bearing and tape it to the connecting rod for safe-keeping. On engines fitted with piston cooling jets at the bottom of the cylinders, take care not to allow the connecting rod to damage the jet as the piston is being removed.

7 Remove No 4 piston and connecting rod in the same manner, then turn the crankshaft through half a turn and remove No 2 and 3 pistons and connecting rods. Remember to maintain the components in their cylinder groups, whilst they are in a dismantled state.

8 If applicable, remove the retaining screws and withdraw the piston cooling jets from the bottom of the cylinder **(see illustrations)**.

Inspection

9 On petrol engines, the gudgeon pin is an interference fit in the connecting rod. If new pistons are to be fitted to existing connecting rods, the work should be carried out be a Ford dealer or specialist. Note that the F cast into the side of the connecting rod must face in the same direction as the arrow on the piston crown (the arrow on the piston crown faces towards the timing chain end).

10 On diesel engines, remove the circlips, push out the gudgeon pin, and separate the piston and connecting rod **(see illustrations)**. Discard the circlips as new items must be fitted on reassembly. If the pin proves difficult to remove, heat the piston to 60°C with hot water – the resulting expansion will then allow the two components to be separated.

11 Before an inspection of the pistons can be carried out, the existing piston rings must be removed, using a removal/installation tool, or an old feeler blade if such a tool is not available. Always remove the upper piston rings first, expanding them to clear the piston crown. The rings are very brittle and will snap if they are stretched too much – sharp edges are produced when this happens, so protect your eyes and hands. Discard the rings on removal, as new items must be fitted when the engine is reassembled **(see illustration)**.

12 Use a section of old piston ring to scrape the carbon deposits out of the ring grooves, taking care not to score or gouge the edges of the groove.

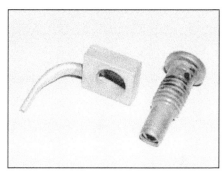

7.8c Piston cooling jet and retainer

13 Carefully scrape away all traces of carbon from the tops of the pistons. A hand-held wire brush (or a piece of fine emery cloth) can be used, once the majority of the deposits have been scraped away. Be careful not to remove any metal from the piston, as it is relatively soft. **Note:** *Make sure each piston is kept identified for position during cleaning.*

14 Once the deposits have been removed, clean the pistons and connecting rods with paraffin or a suitable solvent, and dry thoroughly. Make sure that the oil return holes in the ring grooves are clear.

15 Examine the pistons for signs of excessive wear or damage. Some normal wear will be apparent, in the form of a vertical 'grain' on the piston thrust surfaces and a slight looseness of the top compression ring in its groove. Abnormal wear should be carefully examined, to assess whether the

7.10a Insert a small screwdriver into the slot and prise off the gudgeon pin circlips

7.10b Push out the gudgeon pin to separate the piston and connecting rod

7.11 Piston rings can be removed using an old feeler gauge

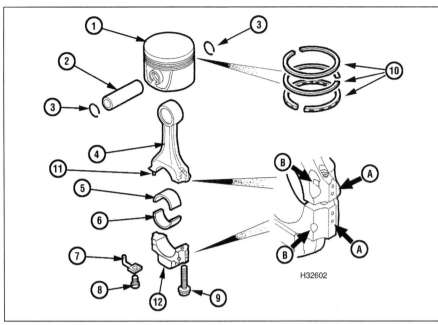

H32602

7.19 Piston assembly (AFN engine – other diesel engines similar)

1 Piston	7 Oil jet for piston cooling	11 Locating dowel
2 Gudgeon pin	(where applicable)	12 Big-end bearing cap
3 Circlip	8 Oil jet retaining screw	A Connecting rod/bearing
4 Connecting rod	9 Big-end bearing cap	cap identification marks
5 Big-end bearing shell	bolts	B Connecting rod/bearing
6 Big-end bearing shell	10 Piston rings	cap orientation marks

component is still serviceable and what the cause of the wear might be.

16 Scuffing or scoring of the piston skirt may indicate that the engine has been overheating, through inadequate cooling or lubrication. Scorch marks on the skirt indicate that blow-by has occurred, perhaps caused by worn bores or piston rings. Burnt areas on the piston crown are usually an indication of pre-ignition, pinking or detonation. In extreme cases, the piston crown may be melted by operating under these conditions. Corrosion pit marks in the piston crown indicate that coolant has seeped into the combustion chamber. The faults causing these symptoms must be corrected before the engine is brought back into service, or the same damage will recur.

17 Check the pistons, connecting rods,

gudgeon pins and bearing caps for cracks. Lay the connecting rods on a flat surface, and look along the length to see if it appears bent or twisted. If you have doubts about their condition, get them measured at an engineering workshop. Inspect the small-end bush bearing in the connecting rod for signs of wear or cracking.

18 Have the cylinder bores, pistons, rings and connecting rods examined and measured by an automotive engineering workshop. If replacement is necessary, they will be able to supply piston kits to match the cylinder bores.

19 The orientation of the piston with respect to the connecting rod must be correct when the two are reassembled. The piston crown is marked with an arrow (which may be obscured by carbon deposits); this must point towards the timing chain/belt end of the

engine when the piston is installed. On diesel engines, the connecting rod and its bearing cap both have recesses/lugs machined into them, close to their mating surfaces – these recesses/lugs must both face the same way as the arrow on the piston crown (ie, towards the timing belt end of the engine) when correctly installed **(see illustration)**. On petrol engines, the connecting rod has an F cast into the side which faces the timing chain end of the engine.

20 On diesel engines, lubricate the gudgeon pin and small-end bush with clean engine oil. Slide the pin into the piston, engaging the connecting rod small-end. Fit two new circlips to the piston at either end of the gudgeon pin. Repeat this operation for the remaining pistons.

8 Crankshaft – removal and inspection

Note: *If no work is to be done on the pistons and connecting rods, then removal of the pistons will not be necessary. Instead, the pistons need only be pushed far enough up the bores so that the connecting rods are positioned clear of the crankpins. The use of an engine stand is strongly recommended.*

Removal

1 With reference to Chapter 2A or 2B as applicable, carry out the following:
  a) Remove the timing chain/belt and crankshaft sprocket.
  b) Remove the clutch components and flywheel or driveplate (as applicable).
  c) Remove the sump/balancer shaft housing, baffle plate **(see illustrations)**, oil pump and pick-up tube.
  d) Remove the crankshaft oil seals and housings.

2 On 2.0 litre petrol engines, undo the two screws and remove the front arch from the underside of the cylinder block **(see illustration)**.

3 Remove the pistons and connecting rods or disconnect them from the crankshaft as described in Section 7 (see Note above).

4 With the cylinder block upside down on the

8.1a Oil baffle plate – petrol engines

8.1b Oil baffle plate – diesel engines

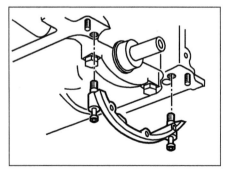

8.2 Remove the front arch from the underside of the cylinder block

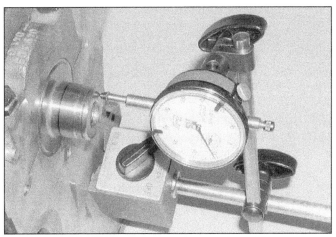

8.4 Measure the crankshaft endfloat using a DTI gauge

8.5 If a DTI gauge is not available, measure the endfloat using feeler gauges

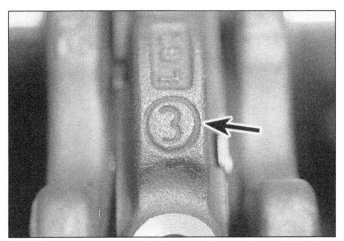

8.6a Manufacturer's identification markings on the main bearing caps (arrowed) – diesel engines

8.6b On petrol engines, the caps also have an arrow to indicate which side faces the timing chain end (arrowed)

bench, carry out a check of the crankshaft endfloat as follows. **Note:** *This can only be accomplished when the crankshaft is still installed in the cylinder block/crankcase, but is free to move.* Set up a DTI gauge so that the probe is in line with the crankshaft axis and is in contact with a fixed point on the end of the crankshaft. Push the crankshaft along its axis to the end of its travel, and then zero the gauge. Push the crankshaft fully the other way, and record the endfloat indicated on the dial **(see illustration)**. Compare the result with the figure given in the Specifications and establish whether new thrustwashers are required.

5 If a dial gauge is not available, feeler blades can be used. First push the crankshaft fully towards the flywheel end of the engine, then use a feeler blade to measure the gap between cylinder No 3 crankpin web and the main bearing thrustwasher **(see illustration)**. Compare the results with the Specifications.

6 Observe the manufacturer's identification marks on the main bearing caps. The number indicates the cap position in the crankcase, as counted from the timing chain/belt end of the engine **(see illustrations)**.

7 Loosen the main bearing cap bolts half a turn at a time, until they can be removed. Using a soft-faced mallet, strike the caps lightly to free them from the crankcase. Recover the lower main bearing shells, using tape to attach them to the cap for safe-keeping. Mark them to aid identification, but do not score or scratch them in any way. Note that on diesel engines, thrustwashers are fitted either side of the upper and lower centre main bearing cap/saddle.

8 Carefully lift the crankshaft out, taking care not to dislodge the upper main bearing shells.

9 Extract the upper main bearing shells from the crankcase, and tape them to their respective bearing caps. Remove the two thrustwasher bearings from either side of No 3 bearing saddle.

10 With the shell bearings removed, observe the recesses machined into the bearing caps and crankcase – these provide location for the lugs which protrude from the shell bearings and so prevent them from being fitted incorrectly.

Inspection

11 Wash the crankshaft in a suitable solvent and allow it to dry. Flush the oil holes thoroughly, to ensure they are not blocked.

12 Inspect the main bearing and crankpin journals carefully. If uneven wear, cracking, scoring or pitting are evident then the crankshaft should be reground by an engineering workshop, and refitted to the engine with undersize bearings.

13 Rather than attempt to determine the crankshaft journal sizes, and the bearing clearances, take the crankshaft to an automotive engineering workshop. Have them perform the necessary measurements, grind the journals if necessary, and supply the appropriate new shell bearings.

14 Check the oil seal journals at either end of the crankshaft. If they appear excessively scored or damaged, they may cause the new seals to leak when the engine is reassembled. It may be possible to repair the journal; seek the advice of an engineering workshop or your Ford dealer.

9 Intermediate shaft – removal and refitting

Note: *This Section applies to diesel engines only.*

Removal

1 Refer to Chapters 2B and 9 as applicable and carry out the following. Note that as the engine is out of the car, some of the preliminary procedures will not be necessary:
   a) *Remove the timing belt.*
   b) *Remove the intermediate shaft sprocket.*
   c) *Remove the brake vacuum pump.*
2 Before the shaft is removed, the endfloat must be checked. Anchor a DTI gauge to the cylinder block with its probe in line with the intermediate shaft centre axis. Push the shaft into the cylinder block to the end of its travel, zero the DTI gauge and then draw the shaft out to the opposite end of its travel. Record the maximum deflection and compare the figure with that listed in Specifications – renew the shaft if the endfloat exceeds this limit **(see illustration)**.
3 Slacken the retaining bolts and withdraw the intermediate shaft flange. Recover the O-ring seal, then press out the oil seal **(see illustrations)**.
4 Withdraw the intermediate shaft from the cylinder block and inspect the drive gear at the end of the shaft; if the teeth show signs of excessive wear, or are damaged in any way, the shaft should be renewed.

5 If the oil seal has been leaking, check the shaft mating surface for signs of scoring or damage.

Refitting

6 Liberally oil the intermediate shaft bearing surfaces and drive gear, then guide the shaft into the cylinder block and engage the journal at the leading end with its support bearing.
7 Press a new shaft oil seal into its housing in the intermediate shaft flange and fit a new O-ring seal to the inner sealing surface of the flange.
8 Lubricate the inner lip of the seal with clean engine oil, and slide the flange and seal over the end of the intermediate shaft. Ensure that the O-ring is correctly seated, then fit the flange retaining bolts and tighten them to the specified torque. Check that the intermediate shaft can rotate freely.
9 With reference to Chapters 2B and 9 as applicable, carry out the following:
   a) *Refit the brake vacuum pump.*
   b) *Refit the sprocket to the intermediate shaft and tighten the centre bolt to the specified torque.*
   c) *Refit the timing belt.*

10 Cylinder block/crankcase – cleaning and inspection

Cleaning

1 Remove all external components as applicable including lifting eyes, mounting brackets, the coolant pump, oil cooler and filter mounting housing, fuel injection pump mounting bracket (where applicable) and electrical switches/sensors from the block. For complete cleaning, the core plugs should ideally be removed. Drill a small hole in the plugs, then insert a self-tapping screw into the hole. Extract the plugs by pulling on the screw with a pair of grips, or by using a slide hammer.
2 Scrape all traces of gasket and sealant from the cylinder block/crankcase, taking care not to damage the sealing surfaces.
3 Remove all oil gallery plugs (where fitted). The plugs are usually very tight – they may have to be drilled out, and the holes retapped. Use new plugs when the engine is reassembled.
4 If the casting is extremely dirty, it should be steam-cleaned. After this, clean all oil holes and galleries one more time. Flush all internal passages with warm water until the water runs clear. Dry thoroughly, and apply a light film of oil to all mating surfaces and cylinder bores, to prevent rusting. If you have access to compressed air, use it to speed up the drying process, and to blow out all the oil holes and galleries.

⚠️ *Warning: Wear eye protection when using compressed air.*

5 If the castings are not very dirty, you can do an adequate cleaning job with hot, soapy water and a stiff brush. Take plenty of time, and do a thorough job. Regardless of the cleaning method used, be sure to clean all oil holes and galleries very thoroughly, and to dry all components well. Protect the cylinder bores as described above, to prevent rusting.
6 All threaded holes must be clean, to ensure accurate torque readings during reassembly. To clean the threads, run the correct-size tap into each of the holes to remove rust, corrosion, thread sealant or sludge, and to restore damaged threads. If possible, use compressed air to clear the holes of debris produced by this operation. **Note:** *Take extra care to exclude all cleaning liquid from blind tapped holes, as the casting may be cracked by hydraulic action if a bolt is threaded into a hole containing liquid.*

9.2 Check the intermediate shaft endfloat using a DTI gauge

9.3a Slacken the retaining bolts (arrowed) . . .

9.3b . . . and withdraw the intermediate shaft flange

9.3c Press out the oil seal . . .

9.3d . . . then recover the O-ring seal

7 Apply suitable sealant to the new oil gallery plugs, and insert them into the holes in the block. Tighten them securely. Similarly fit new core plugs – driving them into place with a suitable close-fitting tube or socket.

8 If the engine is not going to be reassembled immediately, cover it with a large plastic bag to keep it clean; protect all mating surfaces and the cylinder bores as described above, to prevent rusting.

Inspection

9 Visually check the casting for cracks and corrosion. Look for stripped threads in the threaded holes. If there has been any history of internal water leakage, it may be worthwhile having an engine overhaul specialist check the cylinder block/crankcase with professional equipment. If defects are found, have them renewed or if possible, repaired.

10 Check the cylinder bores for scuffing or scoring. Any evidence of this kind of damage should be cross-checked with an inspection of the pistons (see Section 7 of this Chapter). If the damage is in its early stages, it may be possible to repair the block by reboring it. Seek the advice of an engineering workshop.

11 Place the cylinder block on a level work surface, crankcase downwards. Use a straight-edge and a set of feeler blades to measure the distortion of the cylinder head mating surface in both planes. A maximum figure is not quoted by the manufacturer, but use the figure of 0.05 mm as a rough guide. If the measurement exceeds this figure, repair may be possible by machining – consult an engineering workshop for advice.

12 To allow an accurate assessment of the wear in the cylinder bores to be made, take the cylinder block (and pistons) to an automotive engineering workshop, and have them carry out the measurement procedures.

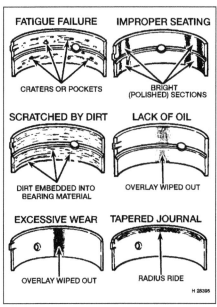

FATIGUE FAILURE   **IMPROPER SEATING**

CRATERS OR POCKETS   BRIGHT (POLISHED) SECTIONS

SCRATCHED BY DIRT   **LACK OF OIL**

DIRT EMBEDDED INTO BEARING MATERIAL   OVERLAY WIPED OUT

EXCESSIVE WEAR   **TAPERED JOURNAL**

OVERLAY WIPED OUT   RADIUS RIDE

H 28395

11.1 Typical bearing failures

If necessary, they will be able to rebore the cylinders, and supply appropriate piston kits.

13 Even if the cylinder bores are not excessively worn, the cylinder bores must be honed. This process involves using an abrasive tool to produce a fine, cross-hatch pattern on the inner surface of the bore. This has the effect of seating the piston rings, resulting in a good seal between the piston and cylinder. Again, an engineering workshop will be able to carry out the job for you at a reasonable cost.

14 Refit all the components removed in paragraph 1.

11 Main and big-end bearings – inspection and selection

Inspection

1 Even though the main and big-end bearings should be renewed during the engine overhaul, the old bearings should be retained for close examination, as they may reveal valuable information about the condition of the engine **(see illustration)**.

2 Bearing failure can occur due to lack of lubrication, the presence of dirt or other foreign particles, overloading the engine, or corrosion. Regardless of the cause of bearing failure, the cause must be corrected before the engine is reassembled, to prevent it from happening again.

3 When examining the bearing shells, remove them from the cylinder block/crankcase, the main bearing caps, the connecting rods and the connecting rod big-end bearing caps. Lay them out on a clean surface in the same general position as their location in the engine. This will enable you to match any bearing problems with the corresponding crankshaft journal. *Do not* touch any shell's internal bearing surface with your fingers while checking it, or the delicate surface may be scratched.

4 Dirt and other foreign matter gets into the engine in a variety of ways. It may be left in the engine during assembly, or it may pass through filters or the crankcase ventilation system. It may get into the oil, and from there into the bearings. Metal chips from machining operations and normal engine wear are often present. Abrasives are sometimes left in engine components after reconditioning, especially when parts are not thoroughly cleaned using the proper cleaning methods. Whatever the source, these foreign objects often end up embedded in the soft bearing material, and are easily recognised. Large particles will not embed in the bearing, but will score or gouge the bearing and journal. The best prevention for this cause of bearing failure is to clean all parts thoroughly, and keep everything spotlessly-clean during engine assembly. Frequent and regular engine oil and filter changes are also recommended.

5 Lack of lubrication (or lubrication breakdown) has a number of interrelated causes. Excessive heat (which thins the oil), overloading (which squeezes the oil from the bearing face) and oil leakage (from excessive bearing clearances, worn oil pump or high engine speeds) all contribute to lubrication breakdown. Blocked oil passages, which usually are the result of misaligned oil holes in a bearing shell, will also oil-starve a bearing, and destroy it. When lack of lubrication is the cause of bearing failure, the bearing material is wiped or extruded from the steel backing of the bearing. Temperatures may increase to the point where the steel backing turns blue from overheating.

6 Driving habits can have a definite effect on bearing life. Full-throttle, low-speed operation (labouring the engine) puts very high loads on bearings, tending to squeeze out the oil film. These loads cause the bearings to flex, which produces fine cracks in the bearing face (fatigue failure). Eventually, the bearing material will loosen in pieces, and tear away from the steel backing.

7 Short-distance driving leads to corrosion of bearings, because insufficient engine heat is produced to drive off the condensed water and corrosive gases. These products collect in the engine oil, forming acid and sludge. As the oil is carried to the engine bearings, the acid attacks and corrodes the bearing material.

8 Incorrect bearing installation during engine assembly will lead to bearing failure as well. Tight-fitting bearings leave insufficient bearing running clearance, and will result in oil starvation. Dirt or foreign particles trapped behind a bearing shell result in high spots on the bearing, which lead to failure.

9 *Do not* touch any shell's internal bearing surface with your fingers during reassembly as there is a risk of scratching the delicate surface, or of depositing particles of dirt on it.

10 As mentioned at the beginning of this Section, the bearing shells should be renewed as a matter of course during engine overhaul. To do otherwise is false economy.

Bearings selection

11 Main and big-end bearings for the engines described in this Chapter are available in standard sizes and a range of undersizes to suit reground crankshafts. Refer to your Ford dealer or automotive engineering workshop for details.

12 Engine overhaul – reassembly sequence

1 Before reassembly begins, ensure that all new parts have been obtained, and that all necessary tools are available. Read through the entire procedure to familiarise yourself with the work involved, and to ensure that all items necessary for reassembly of the engine

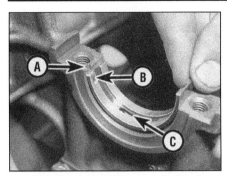

13.3 Bearing shells correctly fitted

A Recesses in bearing saddle
B Lug on bearing shell
C Oil hole

are at hand. In addition to all normal tools and materials, thread-locking compound will be needed. A suitable tube of liquid sealant will also be required for the joint faces that are without gaskets. It is recommended that the manufacturer's own products are used, which are specially formulated for this purpose; the relevant product names are quoted in the text of each Section where they are required.

2 In order to save time and avoid problems, engine reassembly should ideally be carried out in the following order:

a) Crankshaft (see Section 13).
b) Piston/connecting rod assemblies (see Section 14 and 15).
c) Oil pump (see Chapter 2A or 2B).
d) Sump/balancer shaft housing (see Chapter 2A or 2B).
e) Flywheel/driveplate (see Chapter 2A or 2B).
f) Cylinder head (see Chapter 2A or 2B).
g) Timing chain/belt tensioner, sprockets and timing chain/belt (see Chapter 2A or 2B).
h) Inlet and exhaust manifolds (see the relevant part of Chapter 4).
i) Engine external components and ancillaries (see list in Section 5 of this Chapter).

3 At this stage, all engine components should be absolutely clean and dry, with all faults repaired. The components should be laid out (or in individual containers) on a completely clean work surface.

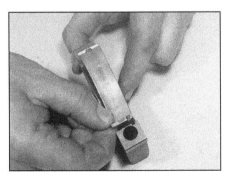

13.8 Ensure the bearing shell locating lugs engage with the recesses in the caps

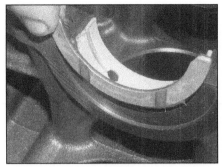

13.4a Fit the thrustwashers to the bearing saddle . . .

13 Crankshaft – refitting

1 Crankshaft refitting is the first stage of engine reassembly following overhaul. At this point, it is assumed that the crankshaft, cylinder block/crankcase and bearings have been cleaned, inspected and reconditioned or renewed. Where removed, the oil jets must be refitted at this stage and their mounting bolts tightened to the specified torque.

2 Place the cylinder block on a clean, level work surface, with the crankcase facing upwards. Wipe out the inner surfaces of the main bearing caps and crankcase with a clean cloth – they must be kept spotlessly clean.

3 Clean the rear surface of the new bearing shells with a cloth and lay them on the bearing saddles in the crankcase. Ensure that the orientation lugs on the shells engage with the recesses in the saddles, and that the oil holes are correctly aligned **(see illustration)**. Do not hammer or otherwise force the bearing shells into place. It is critically important that the surfaces of the bearings are kept free from damage and contamination.

4 Fit the thrustwashers either side of the No 3 bearing saddle and/or bearing cap. On petrol engines the thrustwashers are fitted to either side of the central bearing saddle, and on diesel engines they are fitted to either side of both the central bearing saddle and the central main bearing cap. Use a small quantity of grease to hold them in place. Ensure that

13.9a No 3 main bearing cap – diesel engines

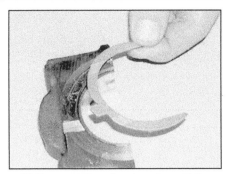

13.4b . . . and on diesel engines, fit the thrustwashers to the bearing cap

they are seated correctly in the machined recesses, with the oil grooves facing outwards **(see illustrations)**.

5 Give the newly-fitted main bearing shells and the crankshaft journals a final clean with a cloth. Check that the oil holes in the crankshaft are free from dirt, as any left here will become embedded in the new bearings when the engine is first started.

6 Liberally coat the bearing shells in the crankcase with clean engine oil of the appropriate grade.

7 Lower the crankshaft into position so that No 1 cylinder crankpin is at BDC, ready for fitting No 1 piston.

8 Lubricate the lower bearing shells in the main bearing caps with clean engine oil. Make sure that the locating lugs on the shells are still engaged with the corresponding recesses in the caps **(see illustration)**.

9 Fit the main bearing caps in the correct order and orientation – No 1 bearing cap must be at the timing chain/belt end of the engine and the bearing shell locating recesses in the bearing saddles and caps must be adjacent to each other **(see illustrations)**. Insert the bearing cap bolts and hand-tighten them only. The main bearing caps are labelled 1 to 5, and on petrol engines, the arrow mark points towards the timing chain end.

10 Working from the centre bearing cap outwards, tighten the new retaining bolts to their specified torques and angles in the stages given.

11 Check that the crankshaft rotates freely by turning it manually. If resistance is felt,

13.9b No 1 main bearing cap – diesel engines

13.14 The housing must be installed with a step of up to 0.46 mm on each side – petrol engines

having the running clearances and crankshaft measurements rechecked.

12 Carry out a check of the crankshaft endfloat as described at the beginning of Section 8. If the thrust surfaces of the crankshaft have been checked and new thrustwashers have been fitted, then the endfloat should be within specification.

13 Refit the pistons and connecting rods or reconnect them to the crankshaft as described in Section 15.

14 On petrol engines, refit the flywheel end oil seal housing to the cylinder block. Note that the housing must not be installed flush with the lower edge of the block, but with a step of up to 0.46 mm on each side **(see illustration)**.

15 With reference to Chapter 2A or 2B as applicable, carry out the following:

a) On 2.0 litre petrol engines, refit the front arch to the underside of the cylinder block.
b) Refit the crankshaftr oil seals/housing.
c) Refit the oil pump and pick-up tube, baffle plate and sump/balancer shaft housing.
d) Refit the flywheel and clutch or driveplate (as applicable).
e) Refit the crankshaft sprocket and timing chain/belt.

14 Pistons and piston rings – assembly

1 At this point it is assumed that the pistons

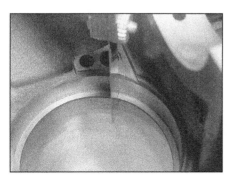

14.5 Check the piston ring end gap using feeler gauges

have been correctly assembled to their respective connecting rods.

2 Before the rings can be fitted to the pistons, the end gaps must be checked with the rings fitted into the cylinder bores.

3 Lay out the piston assemblies and the new ring sets on a clean work surface so that the components are kept together in their groups during and after end gap checking. Place the crankcase on the work surface on its side, allowing access to the top and bottom of the bores.

4 Take the No 1 piston top ring and insert it into the top of the bore. Using the No 1 piston, push the ring close to the bottom of the bore, at the lowest point of the piston travel. Ensure that it is perfectly square in the bore.

5 Use a set of feeler blades to measure the gap between the ends of the piston ring. The correct blade will just pass through the gap with a minimal amount of resistance **(see illustration)**. Compare this measurement with that listed in Specifications. Check that you have the correct ring before deciding that a gap is incorrect. Repeat the operation for the remaining rings.

6 If new rings are being fitted, it is unlikely that the end gaps will be too small. If a measurement is found to be undersize, it must be corrected or there is the risk that the ends of the ring may contact each other during operation, possibly resulting in engine damage. This is achieved by gradually filing down the ends of the ring, using a file clamped in a vice. Fit the ring over the file such that both its ends contact opposite faces of the file. Move the ring along the file, removing small amounts of material at a time. Take great care as the rings are brittle and form sharp edges if they fracture. Remember to keep the rings and piston assemblies in the correct order.

7 When all the piston ring end gaps have been verified, they can be fitted to the pistons. Work from the lowest ring groove (oil control ring) upwards. Note that the oil control ring may comprise of two side rails separated by an expander ring, or a one-piece oil control ring with a internal expander spring. Note also that the two compression rings are different in cross-section, and so must be fitted in the

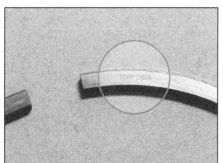

14.7 Piston ring top markings

correct groove and the right way up, using a piston ring fitting tool. Both of the compression rings may have marks stamped on one side to indicate the top facing surface. Ensure that these marks face up when the rings are fitted **(see illustration)**.

8 Distribute the end gaps around the piston, spaced at 120° intervals to the each other.
Note: *If the piston ring manufacturer supplies specific fitting instructions with the rings, follow these exclusively.*

15 Piston/connecting rod assemblies – refitting

Note: *At this point, it is assumed that the crankshaft has been measured, renewed/reground as necessary, and has been fitted to the engine, as described in Section 13.*

2 Place the cylinder block on a clean, level work surface. Position the crankshaft such that crankpin No 1 is at BDC.

3 Fit the upper big-end bearing shell to the connecting rod, ensuring that the locating lug and recess engage correctly. If new shells are being fitted, ensure that all traces of the protective grease are cleaned off using paraffin. Wipe dry the shells and connecting rods with a lint-free cloth. **Note:** *On engine codes AFN, the upper bearing shell is more wear resistant than the lower – identified by a black line on the bearing surface in the area of the bearing joint.*

4 Lubricate the cylinder bores, the pistons, piston rings and upper bearing shells with clean engine oil. Lay out each piston/connecting rod assembly in order on a work surface. Where the bearing caps are secured with nuts, pad the threaded ends of the bolts with insulating tape to prevent them scratching the crankpins and bores when the pistons are refitted.

5 Start with piston/connecting rod assembly No 1. Make sure that the piston rings are still spaced as described in Section 14, then clamp them in position with a piston ring compressor.

6 Insert the piston/connecting rod assembly into the top of cylinder No 1. Lower the big-end in first, guiding it to protect the cylinder bores. Where oil jets are located at the bottoms of the bores, take particular care not to break them off when guiding the connecting rods onto the crankpins.

7 Ensure that the orientation of the piston in its cylinder is correct – the piston crown, connecting rods and big-end bearing caps have markings which must point towards the timing chain/belt end of the engine when the piston is installed in the bore – refer to Section 7 for details.

8 Using a block of wood or hammer handle against the piston crown, tap the assembly into the cylinder until the piston crown is

15.8 Use a hammer handle to tap the piston into its bore

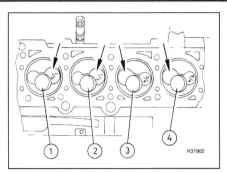

15.10 Piston orientation and coding on diesel engines

15.16 Measure the piston projection with a DTI gauge

flush with the top of the cylinder **(see illustration)**.

9 Ensure that the bearing shell is still correctly installed. Liberally lubricate the crankpin and both bearing shells with clean engine oil. Taking care not to mark the cylinder bores, tap the piston/connecting rod assembly down the bore and onto the crankpin. Oil the threads and undersides of the bolt heads. Fit the big-end bearing cap, tightening its new retaining nuts/bolts finger-tight at first. Note that the orientation of the bearing cap with respect to the connecting rod must be correct when the two components are reassembled. On diesel engines, the connecting rod and its corresponding bearing cap both have recesses/lugs machined into them – these recesses/lugs must both face in the same direction as the arrow on the piston crown (ie, towards the timing belt end of the engine) when correctly installed – refer to the illustrations in Section 7 for details.

10 On diesel engines, the piston crowns are specially shaped to improve the engine's combustion characteristics. Because of this, pistons 1 and 2 are different to pistons 3 and 4. When correctly fitted, the larger inlet valve chambers on pistons 1 and 2 must face the flywheel/driveplate end of the engine, and the larger inlet valve chambers on the remaining pistons must face the timing belt end of the engine. New pistons have number markings on their crowns to indicate their type – 1/2 denotes piston 1 or 2, 3/4 indicates piston 3 or 4 **(see illustration)**.

11 Tighten the retaining bolts/nuts to the specified Stage 1 torque.

12 Tighten the retaining bolts/nuts to the specified Stage 2 setting. On petrol engines, tighten the bolts to the Stage 3 setting.

13 Refit the remaining three piston/connecting rod assemblies in the same way.

14 Rotate the crankshaft by hand. Check that it turns freely; some stiffness is to be expected if new parts have been fitted, but there should be no binding or tight spots.

Diesel engines

15 If new pistons are fitted or if a new short engine is installed, the projection of the piston crowns above the cylinder head at TDC must be measured, to determine the type of head gasket that should be fitted.

16 Turn the cylinder block over (so that the crankcase is facing downwards) and rest it on a stand or wooden blocks. Anchor a DTI gauge to the cylinder block, and zero it on the head gasket mating surface. Rest the gauge probe on No 1 piston crown and turn the crankshaft slowly by hand so that the piston reaches TDC. Measure and record the maximum projection at TDC **(see illustration)**.

17 Repeat the measurement for the remaining pistons and record.

18 If the measurements differ from piston-to-piston, take the highest figure and use this to determine the head gasket type that must be used – refer to the Specifications for details.

19 Note that if the original pistons have been refitted, then a new head gasket of the same type as the original item must be fitted.

All engines

20 Refer to Part A or B of this Chapter (as applicable) and refit the oil pump and pick-up, sump/balancer shaft housing and baffle plate, flywheel and cylinder head.

---

16 Engine – initial start-up after overhaul and reassembly

---

1 Refit the remainder of the engine components in the order listed in Section 12 of this Chapter. Refit the engine to the vehicle as described in Section 4 of this Chapter. Double-check the engine oil and coolant levels and make a final check that everything has been reconnected. Make sure that there are no tools or rags left in the engine compartment.

Petrol models

2 Remove the spark plugs, referring to Chapter 1A for details.

3 The engine must be immobilised such that it can be turned over using the starter motor, without starting – disable the fuel pump by removing the fuel pump fuse from the fusebox with reference to Chapter 2A, illustration 3.2, and disconnect the wiring plugs from the ignition coils with reference to Chapter 5B.

Caution: To prevent damage to the catalytic converter, it is important to disable the fuel system.

4 Turn the engine using the starter motor until the oil pressure warning lamp goes out. If the lamp fails to extinguish after several seconds of cranking, check the engine oil level and oil filter security. Assuming these are correct, check the security of the oil pressure switch cabling – do not progress any further until you are satisfied that oil is being pumped around the engine at sufficient pressure.

5 Refit the spark plugs, coil wiring plugs, and the fuel pump fuse.

Diesel models

6 Disconnect the electrical cable from the fuel cut-off solenoid at the fuel injection pump – refer to Chapter 4B, Section 8, for details.

7 Turn the engine using the starter motor until the oil pressure warning lamp goes out.

8 If the lamp fails to extinguish after several seconds of cranking, check the engine oil level and oil filter security. Assuming these are correct, check the security of the oil pressure switch cabling – do not progress any further until you are satisfied that oil is being pumped around the engine at sufficient pressure.

9 Reconnect the fuel cut-off solenoid cable.

All models

10 Start the engine, but be aware that as fuel system components have been disturbed, the cranking time may be a little longer than usual.

11 While the engine is idling, check for fuel, water and oil leaks. Don't be alarmed if there are some odd smells and the occasional plume of smoke as components heat-up and burn-off oil deposits.

12 Assuming all is well, keep the engine idling until hot water is felt circulating through the top hose.

13 After a few minutes, recheck the oil and coolant levels, and top-up as necessary.

14 There is no need to retighten the cylinder head bolts once the engine has been run following reassembly.

15 If new pistons, rings or crankshaft bearings have been fitted, the engine must be treated as new, and run-in for the first 600 miles (1000 km). *Do not* operate the engine at full-throttle, or allow it to labour at low engine speeds in any gear. It is recommended that the engine oil and filter are changed at the end of this period.

Chapter 3
Cooling, heating and ventilation systems

Contents

Degrees of difficulty

| **Easy,** suitable for novice with little experience | | **Fairly easy,** suitable for beginner with some experience | | **Fairly difficult,** suitable for competent DIY mechanic | | **Difficult,** suitable for experienced DIY mechanic | | **Very difficult,** suitable for expert DIY or professional | |

Specifications

Thermostat

Opening temperature . . . . 85°C (approx)

Air conditioning system

Refrigerant R134a . . . . Ford specification WSH-M17B19-A
Refrigerant oil . . . . Ford specification WSH-M1C231-B
Refrigerant capacity:
  Front air conditioning only . . . . 950 ± 50 g
  Front and rear air conditioning . . . . 1350 ± 50 g
Refrigerant oil capacity:
  Front air conditioning only:
    Petrol engines . . . . 205 ml
    Diesel engines . . . . 135 ml
  Front and rear air conditioning . . . . 240 ml

Torque wrench settings

	Nm	lbf ft
Petrol engines		
Compressor bolts	25	18
Coolant outlet housing bolts (2.3 litre)	10	7
Coolant pump pulley bolts	25	18
Coolant pump retaining bolts	19	14
Coolant temperature gauge sensor	12	9
Engine mounting nuts	65	48
High-pressure switch	8	6
Radiator	10	7
Reaction rod retaining bolt	72	53
Refrigerant pipe to compressor:		
2.0 litre models	20	15
2.3 litre models	30	22
Refrigerant pipe- to expansion valve	7	5
Thermostat housing bolts (2.0 litre)	10	7
Diesel engines		
Accessory drive bracket bolts	30	22
Auxiliary drivebelt tensioner bolt	24	18
Compressor bolts	45	33
Coolant pump housing bolt	10	7
Coolant pump housing nuts:		
Stage 1	20	14
Stage 2	Angle-tighten a further 90°	
Coolant pump pulley bolts	25	18
Engine mounting nuts	65	48
High-pressure switch	8	6
Power steering pump bolts	25	18
Radiator	10	7
Reaction rod retaining bolt	72	53
Refrigerant pipe to compressor	30	22
Refrigerant pipe to expansion valve	7	5
Thermostat housing retaining bolts	10	7

1 General information and precautions

General information

1 The cooling system is of the pressurised type, comprising a coolant pump, an aluminium radiator, cooling fan(s), a thermostat, heater matrix, and all associated hoses and switches. The coolant pump is driven by the auxiliary drivebelt. All models are fitted with one or two electric cooling fans, located behind the radiator. The system functions as follows.

2 When the engine is cold, the coolant in the engine is pumped around the cylinder block and head passages, and through an engine oil cooler (where fitted). After cooling the cylinder bores, combustion surfaces and valve seats, the coolant passes through the heater, and is returned via the cylinder block to the coolant pump. The thermostat is initially closed, preventing the cold coolant from the radiator entering the engine.

3 When the coolant in the engine reaches a predetermined temperature, the thermostat opens. The cold coolant from the radiator is then allowed to enter the engine through the bottom hose and the hot coolant from the engine flows through the top hose to the radiator. As the coolant circulates through the radiator, it is cooled by the inrush of air when the car is in forward motion. The airflow is supplemented by the action of the cooling fan(s) when necessary. As the coolant reduces in temperature, it passes to the bottom of the radiator and the cycle is repeated.

4 On some models, the operation of the electrically-operated auxiliary cooling fan(s) is controlled by a thermostatic switch. Whilst on others, the fans are controlled by the engine management ECM, receiving its signal from the engine coolant temperature sensor. At a predetermined coolant temperature, the switch/sensor actuates the fan. The switch then cuts the power supply to the fan when the coolant temperature has reduced sufficiently.

Precautions

 Warning: Do not attempt to remove the expansion tank filler cap, or to disturb any part of the cooling system, while the engine is hot, as there is a high risk of scalding. If the expansion tank filler cap must be removed before the engine and radiator have fully cooled (even though this is not recommended), the pressure in the cooling system must first be relieved. Cover the cap with a thick layer of cloth to avoid scalding, and slowly unscrew the filler cap until a hissing sound is heard. When the hissing has stopped, indicating that the pressure has reduced, slowly unscrew the filler cap until it can be removed; if more hissing sounds are heard, wait until they have stopped before unscrewing the cap completely. At all times, keep well away from the filler cap opening, and protect your hands.

 Warning: Do not allow antifreeze to come into contact with your skin, or with the painted surfaces of the vehicle. Rinse off spills immediately, with plenty of water. Never leave antifreeze lying around in an open container, or in a puddle in the driveway or on the garage floor. Children and pets are attracted by its sweet smell, but antifreeze can be fatal if ingested.

 Warning: If the engine is hot, the electric cooling fan may start rotating even if the engine is not running. Be careful to keep your hands, hair, and any loose clothing well clear when working in the engine compartment.

 Warning: Refer to Section 10 for precautions to be observed when working on models equipped with air conditioning.

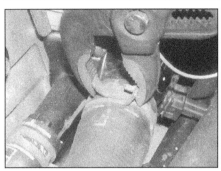

2.3 To release the clip, squeeze together the ends

2 Cooling system hoses –
disconnection and renewal

Note: *Refer to the warnings given in Section 1 of this Chapter before proceeding. Hoses should only be disconnected once the engine has cooled sufficiently to avoid scalding.*

1 If the checks described in the relevant Part of Chapter 1 reveal a faulty hose, it must be renewed as follows.
2 First drain the cooling system (see the relevant Part of Chapter 1). If the coolant is not due for renewal, it may be re-used, providing it is collected in a clean container.
3 To disconnect a hose, release the retaining

3.4a Remove the control unit screws (arrowed) . . .

clips, then move them along the hose, clear of the relevant inlet/outlet **(see illustration)**. Carefully work the hose free. The hoses can be removed with relative ease when new – on an older car, they may have stuck.
4 If a hose proves to be difficult to remove, try to release it by rotating its ends before attempting to free it. Gently prise the end of the hose with a blunt instrument (such as a flat-bladed screwdriver), but do not apply too much force, and take care not to damage the pipe stubs or hoses. Note in particular that the radiator inlet stub is fragile; do not use excessive force when attempting to remove the hose. If all else fails, cut the hose with a sharp knife, then slit it so that it can be peeled off in two pieces. Although this may prove expensive if the hose is otherwise undamaged, it is preferable to buying a new radiator. Check first, however, that a new hose is readily available.
5 When fitting a hose, first slide the clips onto the hose, then work the hose into position. On some hose connections alignment marks are provided on the hose and union; if marks are present, ensure they are correctly aligned.

> **TOOL TIP** *If the hose is stiff, use a little soapy water as a lubricant, or soften the hose by soaking it in hot water. Do not use oil or grease, which may attack the rubber.*

3.4b . . . then release the upper radiator cover screw

6 Ensure the hose is correctly routed, then slide each clip back along the hose until it passes over the flared end of the relevant inlet/outlet, before tightening the clip securely.
7 Refill the cooling system with reference to the relevant Part of Chapter 1.
8 Check thoroughly for leaks as soon as possible after disturbing any part of the cooling system.

3 Radiator – removal, inspection and refitting

Note: *Due to the size of the radiator and the restricted access space, the help of an assistant is recommended.*

Removal

1 Remove the battery, upper and lower battery compartment panels (see Chapter 5A).
2 Remove the front bumper bar and radiator grille as described in Chapter 11.
3 Drain the cooling system as described in the relevant Part of Chapter 1.
4 On air conditioned models, undo the two screws and move the control unit/relay bracket to one side, then undo the screws securing the refrigerant pipes to the brackets on the top of the cooling fan shroud. On all models, unscrew the single bolt and remove the upper radiator cover **(see illustrations)**.
5 Unplug the wiring connectors from the cooling fans and thermal switch (where fitted), which is screwed into the radiator. Release the cable harness from the retaining clips **(see illustration)**.
6 Disconnect the radiator top and bottom coolant hoses (see Section 2). Release the hoses from their retaining clips noting the correct fitted locations.
7 Undo the two bolts and remove the cooling fan shroud strut from the right-hand side of the assembly **(see illustration)**.
8 Undo the four retaining bolts, and manoeuvre the cooling fan(s) and shroud

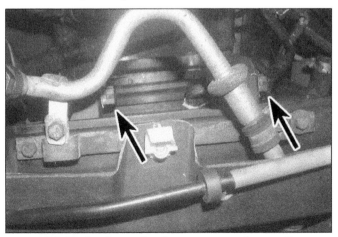

3.5 Unplug the cooling fans connectors (arrowed)

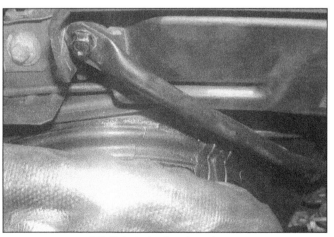

3.7 Unbolt the fan shroud strut

3.8a Cooling fan shroud left-hand upper fixing bolt (arrowed) . . .

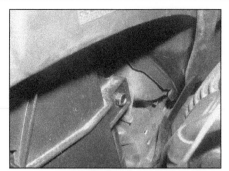

3.8b . . . and right-hand upper fixing bolt

3.9a Right-hand radiator mounting bolt . . .

3.9b . . . and left-hand mounting bolt

assembly down and out of the engine compartment (see illustrations).

9 Unscrew the two mounting bolts and manoeuvre the radiator from its mountings (see illustrations).

10 On models equipped with air conditioning, slacken and remove the nuts and bolts securing the condenser to the radiator and any nuts/bolts securing the refrigerant pipe clips in position. On some models the condenser is secured using plastic pins – depress the lug in the end of the pin and pull it free. Release the condenser from the radiator and support it to prevent excessive strain being placed on the pipes. Do not disconnect the refrigerant pipes (see Section 10).

11 On models equipped with air conditioning, unplug the wiring from the pressure switch (where fitted) at the right-hand side of the radiator.

12 On all models, manoeuvre the radiator down and out of the engine compartment.

Inspection

13 If the radiator has been removed due to suspected blockage, reverse-flush it as described in Section 25 of Chapter 1A (petrol engines) or Section 27 of Chapter 1B (diesel engines). Clean dirt and debris from the radiator fins, using an air line (in which case, wear eye protection) or a soft brush. Be careful, as the fins are sharp, and easily damaged.

14 If necessary, a radiator specialist can perform a flow test on the radiator, to establish whether an internal blockage exists.

15 A leaking radiator must be referred to a specialist for permanent repair. Do not attempt to weld or solder a leaking radiator, as damage to the plastic components may result.

16 If the radiator is to be sent for repair or renewed, remove all hoses and switches.

17 Inspect the condition of the radiator mounting rubbers, and renew them if necessary.

Refitting

18 Refitting is a reversal of removal, bearing in mind the following points.

a) Ensure that the lugs on the top edge of the radiator engage correctly with their corresponding locating holes in the front panel (see illustration).

b) Make sure all coolant hoses are correctly reconnected and securely retained by their clips.

c) Refill the cooling system as described in the relevant Part of Chapter 1.

d) On models with automatic transmission, on completion check the transmission fluid level and, if necessary, top-up as described in the relevant Part of Chapter 1.

4 Thermostat – removal, testing and refitting

1 On 2.0 litre and 2.3 litre (up to '98) petrol models, the thermostat is located on the left-hand end of the cylinder head. 2.3 litre models from '98 are equipped with a thermostat in a housing acting as a 'T-piece' fitted into the radiator top hose. The thermostat is integral with its housing, and if faulty the complete assembly must be renewed. On diesel models, the thermostat is located on the front right-hand corner of the cylinder block.

Removal

Petrol engines

2 Disconnect the battery negative lead, and remove the battery compartment upper and lower panels (see Chapter 5A).

3 Drain the cooling system as described in Chapter 1A.

4 On 2.0 litre and 2.3 litre (up to '98 model year), disconnect the wiring plugs for the engine coolant temperature sensor, located on the thermostat housing (see illustration).

3.18 Ensure the radiator lugs engage in the upper mounting holes

4.4 Disconnect the coolant temperature sensors wiring plugs (arrowed)

4.5a Disconnect the thermostat housing hoses – 2.0 litre and 2.3 litre models (up to '98)

4.5b Disconnect the thermostat housing hoses – 2.3 litre models ('98-on)

4.6a Undo the thermostat housing Torx screws (arrowed)

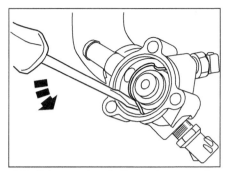

4.6b Prise out the circlips and remove the thermostat

4.13a Unscrew the retaining bolts and remove the thermostat housing cover . . .

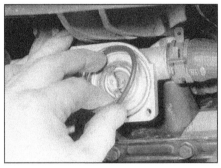

4.13b . . . then remove the sealing ring

4.14 Remove the thermostat from its housing

5 On all models, release the retaining clips and disconnect the coolant hoses from the thermostat housing (see illustrations).

6 On 2.0 litre and 2.3 litre (up to '98 model year), slacken and withdraw the three securing bolts and remove the thermostat housing cover. Using a screwdriver, prise out the retaining circlip and lift the thermostat from its housing and recover the sealing ring. A new sealing ring must be used on refitting (see illustrations).

Diesel engines

7 Disconnect the battery negative lead (see Chapter 5A). Where applicable, undo the retaining bolts and remove the engine top cover.

8 Drain the cooling system as described in Chapter 1B.

9 Slacken the power steering pump mounting bolts, and remove the drivebelt (see Chapter 2B)

10 Remove the power steering pump from the engine, and tie it to one side.

11 Undo the three bolts and remove the power steering pump mounting bracket.

12 If necessary, to improve access, release the retaining clip and disconnect the coolant hose from the thermostat cover.

13 Unscrew the retaining bolts and remove the thermostat housing cover and sealing ring from the engine (see illustrations). Discard the sealing ring; a new one must be used on refitting.

14 Remove the thermostat, noting which way around it is fitted (see illustration).

Testing

15 A rough test of the thermostat may be made by suspending it with a piece of string in a container full of water. Heat the water to bring it to the boil – the thermostat must be fully open by the time the water boils. If not, renew it.

16 If a thermometer is available, the precise opening temperature of the thermostat may be determined; compare with the figure given in the Specifications. The opening temperature should also be marked on the thermostat.

17 A thermostat which fails to close as the water cools, must also be renewed.

Refitting

18 Refitting is a reversal of removal, noting the following points:
  a) Use a new thermostat housing cover sealing ring (all except 2.3 litre '98-on).
  b) Tighten the housing retaining bolts to the specified torque setting (all except 2.3 litre).
  c) Refill the cooling system as described in the relevant Part of Chapter 1.
  d) On completion reconnect the battery.

5 Cooling fan(s) – testing, removal and refitting

Testing

1 On some models, current supply to the cooling fan(s) is via the ignition switch, a fuse, and a thermostatic switch which is mounted in the left-hand side of the radiator. On some models, the cooling fans' operation is managed by a radiator fan control unit located in the front left-hand corner of the engine compartment. Whilst on others, two relays are used to operate the fan motor(s). One low-speed relay, and one high-speed relay operated by the engine electronic control module, which receives information from the engine coolant temperature sensor. On some models, an engine cooling fan run-on relay is used to operate the cooling fan(s) after the engine is switched off. Depending on the vehicle model specification, engine, and geographical market, the cooling fans could be controlled by any combination of the above. If a fault develops have the vehicle's self-diagnosis system interrogated by a Ford dealer or suitably-equipped specialist. Any faults recognised should be stored in the engine management control module. With the fault pin-pointed, corrective action should be limited to component repair or renewal.

Removal

2 Remove the battery compartment upper and lower panels (see Chapter 5A).

3 Disconnect the cooling fan(s) wiring plug (see illustration 3.5).

4 Undo the two screws and remove the fan shroud strut (see illustration 3.7)

5 Slacken and remove the retaining bolts and remove the fan shroud assembly from the rear of the radiator (see illustrations 3.8a and 3.8b).

5.6 The cooling fan motor is secured the shroud be three nuts

6 Unclip the motor wiring from the rear of the shroud then undo the retaining nuts and pull the motor assembly away from the shroud. On some models it will be necessary to detach the fan blade from the motor to gain the necessary clearance required; and unscrew the retaining nut **(left-hand thread)** to free the fan **(see illustration)**. If the motor is faulty, the complete unit must be renewed, as no spares are available.

Refitting

7 Fit the motor assembly to the shroud and securely tighten its retaining nuts. Ensure the motor wiring is correctly routed and clipped securely in position. Where necessary, seat the fan blade on the motor spindle then refit the retaining nut. Tighten the nut securely.
8 Refit the shroud assembly to the radiator and securely tighten its retaining bolts.
9 The remainder of refitting is a reversal of removal.

6 Cooling system electrical switches and sensors – testing, removal and refitting

Cooling fan(s) thermal switch

Testing

1 Testing of the switch is described in Section 5, as part of the electric cooling fan test procedure.

Removal

Note: *The engine and radiator should be allowed to cool completely before the switch is removed.*

2 On some models, the switch is clipped into the radiator upper hose, whilst on others, the switch is located in the left-hand side of the radiator, just above the bottom hose stub **(see illustrations)**. On 2.3 litre manual models, the function of the switch is incorporated into the engine management ECM.
3 Disconnect the battery negative lead (see Chapter 5A).
4 Drain the cooling system to just below the level of the switch (as described in the relevant Part of Chapter 1). Alternatively, have ready a suitable bung to plug the switch aperture in the radiator/hose when the switch is removed. If this method is used, take great care not to damage the radiator/hose, and do not use anything which will allow foreign matter to enter the radiator/hose.
5 Disconnect the wiring plug from the switch.
6 Carefully unscrew the switch from the radiator, or pull out the retaining clip and remove the switch (as applicable), and recover the seal. If the system has not been drained, plug the switch aperture to prevent further coolant loss.

Refitting

7 If the switch was originally fitted using a sealing ring, use a new sealing ring on refitting. Where no sealing ring was fitted, clean the switch threads (where applicable) thoroughly and coat them with fresh sealing compound.
8 Refitting is a reversal of removal. Where applicable, tighten the switch securely and refill (or top-up) the cooling system as described in the relevant Part of Chapter 1.
9 On completion, start the engine and run it until it reaches normal operating temperature. Continue to run the engine, and check that the cooling fan cuts in and out correctly.

Temperature gauge sender

Testing

10 On all petrol models, the coolant temperature gauge sender is located on the underside of the thermostat housing on the left-hand end of the cylinder head **(see illustration)**. Where two sensors are present, the lower of the two is the coolant temperature gauge sender. On diesel models, the engine coolant temperature sensor also provides the signal for the temperature gauge and warning light.
11 The sender contains a thermistor – an electronic component whose electrical resistance decreases at a predetermined rate as its temperature rises. When the coolant is cold, the sender resistance is high, current flow through the gauge is reduced, and the gauge needle points towards the blue (cold) end of the scale. As the coolant temperature rises and the sender resistance falls, current flow increases, and the gauge needle moves towards the upper end of the scale. If the sender is faulty, it must be renewed.
12 If a fault develops, have the vehicles self-diagnosis memory interrogated by a Ford dealer or specialist. A faulty sender or gauge should register a fault code.

Removal

13 Either partially drain the cooling system to just below the level of the sender (as described in the relevant Part of Chapter 1), or have ready a suitable plug which can be used to plug the sender aperture whilst it is removed. If a plug is used, take great care not to damage the sender unit aperture, and do not use anything which will allow foreign matter to enter the cooling system.
14 Disconnect the wiring connector from the sender.
15 On petrol models, unscrew the sender from the engine. On diesel models pull out the retaining clip, remove the sensor and recover the sealing ring.

Refitting

16 Fit a new sealing washer then fit the sender, tightening it securely.
17 On diesel models, renew the sealing ring and secure the sensor in place with the retaining clip.
18 Reconnect the wiring connector then refill the cooling system as described in the relevant Part of Chapter 1 or top-up as described in *Weekly checks*.

6.2b . . . or the radiator itself

6.2a The thermal switch may be fitted to the upper radiator hose . . .

6.10 The coolant temperature gauge sender is on the underside of the thermostat/coolant outlet housing

6.19a Engine coolant temperature sensor (ECT) – petrol models

6.19b Engine coolant temperature sensor (ECT) – diesel models

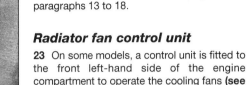

6.23a Radiator cooling fans control unit – petrol models . . .

6.23b . . . and diesel models

Engine management system temperature sensor

19 On petrol models, the engine management system coolant temperature sensor (ETC) is located in the in the thermostat housing on the left-hand end of the cylinder head. The upper of the two sensors is the ETC sensor. On diesel models, the sensor is located in the coolant outlet union on the front side of the cylinder head **(see illustrations)**.

20 The sensor is a thermistor (see paragraph 11). The fuel injection/engine management electronic control module (ECM) supplies the sensor with a set voltage and then, by measuring the current flowing in the sensor circuit, it determines the engine's temperature. This information is then used, in

conjunction with other inputs, to control the injector timing, the idle speed, etc. It is also used to determine the glow plug preheating and post-heating times.

21 If the sensor circuit should fail to provide adequate information, the ECM's back-up facility will override the sensor signal. In this event, the ECM assumes a predetermined setting which will allow the fuel injection/engine management system to run, albeit at reduced efficiency. When this occurs, the warning light on the instrument panel will come on, and the advice of a Ford dealer should be sought. The sensor itself can only be tested using special Ford diagnostic equipment. *Do not* attempt to test the circuit using any other equipment, as there is a high risk of damaging the ECM.

Removal and refitting

22 Refer to the information given in paragraphs 13 to 18.

Radiator fan control unit

23 On some models, a control unit is fitted to the front left-hand side of the engine compartment to operate the cooling fans **(see illustrations)**. To remove the unit, release the retaining clips, and disconnect the wiring plugs.

24 Undo the retaining screws and remove the unit.

25 Refitting is a reversal of removal.

---

7 Coolant pump – removal and refitting

Petrol engines

Removal

1 Drain the cooling system as described in Chapter 1A. **Note:** *If an aluminium engine component which comes into contact with the coolant has been renewed, then the coolant must also be renewed. Used coolant will not protect new aluminium from corrosion.*

2 With reference to Chapter 4A, remove the air cleaner assembly.

3 Remove the radiator grille and right-hand headlamp, With reference to Chapters 11 and 12 respectively,

4 Undo the headlamp shield upper and lower fixing bolts. Release the wiring harness cable tie.

5 In order to remove the clips securing the trim panel adjacent to the alternator, press in the centre of the clips and prise them from the panel **(see illustration)**. Note that the lower three clips are inserted from the headlamp side of the panel. Remove the trim panel.

6 Unscrew the remaining headlamp shield fixing bolt, release the two clips and manoeuvre the shield from the engine compartment.

7 Disconnect the front exhaust pipe from the exhaust manifold, as described in Chapter 4C. Do not allow the front exhaust pipe to hang down and possibly distort the flexible section of the pipe.

8 Working underneath the vehicle, undo the bolt and disconnect the engine roll restrictor from the transmission casing.

9 Using a jack and block of wood under the engine sump, take the weight of the engine.

10 Slacken the coolant pump pulley bolts **(see illustration)**.

11 Using a spanner on the tensioner pulley, slacken the auxiliary belt, and slip the belt from the coolant pump pulley.

12 Undo the two nuts securing the right-hand engine mounting bracket to the mounting, and

7.5 Push the centre pin out, then remove the clip

7.10 Undo the coolant pump pulley bolts

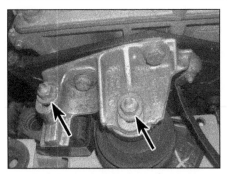

7.12 Undo the two mounting nuts (arrowed)

7.13 The coolant pump is secured by five bolts

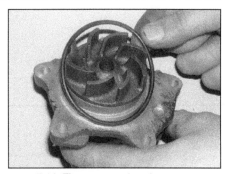

7.14 Fit a new seal to the pump

remove the coolant pump pulley bolts. Lift the pulley from the pump **(see illustration)**.

13 Using the jack, raise the engine sufficiently to gain access to the coolant pump securing bolts. Undo the five bolts and manoeuvre the pump from the engine. Recover the sealing ring **(see illustration)**.

Refitting

14 Ensure that the pump and cylinder block mating surfaces are clean and dry and position a new seal on the pump **(see illustration)**.

15 Fit the coolant pump to the cylinder block and evenly tighten its retaining bolts to the specified torque setting. Note that due to the offset of the bolt holes, the pump will only fit correctly in one position.

16 The remainder of refitting is a reversal of removal, noting to tighten all nuts/bolts to their specified torque (where available), and refill the cooling system as described in Chapter 1A.

Diesel engines

Removal

17 Drain the cooling system as described in Chapter 1B. **Note:** *If an aluminium engine component which comes into contact with the coolant has been renewed, then the coolant must also be renewed. Used coolant will not protect new aluminium from corrosion.*

18 Prise out the covers, undo the retaining screws and remove the plastic cover from the top of the engine.

19 Remove the air cleaner assembly as described in Chapter 4B.

20 Apply the handbrake, slacken both front wheel bolts, then jack up the front of the vehicle and support it on axle stands (see *Jacking and vehicle support*). Remove engine compartment undershield.

21 On models with air conditioning, disconnect the compressor wiring plug.

22 On models with air conditioning, unscrew the bolt securing the refrigerant pipe bracket to the front of the engine block.

23 Slacken and remove the power steering belt (see Chapter 2B).

24 Remove the auxiliary Poly-Vee drivebelt with reference to Chapter 2B.

25 On models equipped with air conditioning, remove the compressor mounting bolts and move it to one side. Tie the compressor in place.

 Warning: Do not disconnect the air conditioning refrigerant circuit.

26 Unscrew the two mounting bolts, and manoeuvre the power steering pump bracket (complete with pump) to one side. There is no need to disconnect any of the pump hoses.

27 Remove the alternator with reference to Chapter 5A.

28 Undo the bolt and remove the auxiliary drivebelt tensioner pulley.

29 Undo the five nuts/bolts, and remove the accessory drive bracket from the side of the engine **(see illustration)**. As the bracket is withdrawn, release the retaining clips, and disconnect the coolant hoses from the coolant pump.

30 With the coolant pump pulley held in a vice, undo the three pulley retaining bolts, and remove the pulley. Unscrew the eight bolts and remove the coolant pump from the housing **(see illustration)**. Recover the O-ring and the gasket.

Refitting

31 Ensure that the pump and housing mating surfaces are clean and dry, then position a new sealing ring and gasket on the pump.

32 Insert the pump retaining bolts, then tighten them evenly and progressively to the specified torque.

33 The remainder of refitting is a reversal of removal

34 On completion refill the cooling system as described in the relevant Part of Chapter 1B.

8 Heating and ventilation system – general information

1 The heating/ventilation system consists of a fully adjustable blower motor (housed behind the facia), face level vents in the centre and at each end of the facia, and air ducts to the front footwells. A second heater unit for the rear passenger compartment was available as an option.

2 The heater control unit is located in the facia, and the controls operate flap valves to deflect and mix the air flowing through the various parts of the heating/ventilation system. The flap valves are contained in the air distribution housing, which acts as a central distribution unit, passing air to the various ducts and vents.

3 Cold air enters the system through the grille at the lower front edge of the windscreen. If required, the airflow is boosted by the blower, and then flows through the various ducts,

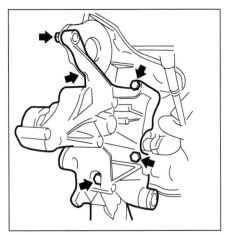

7.29 Remove the accessory drive bracket bolts from the side of the engine

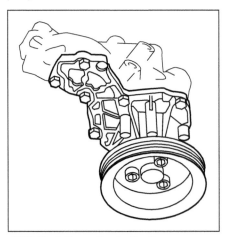

7.30 Undo the pulley bolts, then unscrew the pump retaining bolts

9.4 Carefully prise the trim from around the heater control knobs

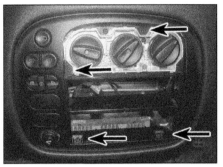

9.5 Undo the screws and remove the panel trim (arrowed)

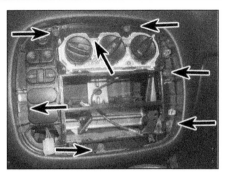

9.6 Undo the screws and remove the heater control unit retaining frame (arrowed)

according to the settings of the controls. Stale air is expelled through ducts at the rear of the vehicle. If warm air is required, the cold air is passed over the heater matrix, which is heated by the engine coolant.

4 The outside air supply to the vehicle can be closed off which is useful to prevent unpleasant odours entering from outside the vehicle. This facility should only be used briefly, as the recirculated air inside the vehicle will soon become stale.

9 Heater/ventilation components – removal and refitting

General information

1 The information in this Section is only applicable to models equipped with a manually-operated conventional heating system, without air conditioning. On models with air conditioning, removal and refitting of the heater/ventilation/air conditioning system components is described in Section 11. Optional extra equipment includes a rear heater unit, where heat from the engine coolant is passed through a heat exchanger, in the same manner as the front heater. The controls for the rear heater are set in the headlining above the second row of seats. Also available as options are a booster heater on the 1.9 TDI models, and an additional heater, available for all diesel models. Both

heaters ignite fuel supplied from the main tank. Due to the efficiency of the direct injection diesel engine, not enough heat output is available to provide adequate heating. The booster heater increases the coolant temperature, by burning diesel metered by a separate pump from the main fuel return pipe. If the outside temperature is below 5°C, or the engine coolant temperature is below 75°C, the heater starts automatically. As soon as the coolant temperature reaches 80°C, the heater output is reduced from 3 kW to 1.5 kW. If the temperature reaches 85°C, the heater is switched off. There is no manual control of the booster heater. The additional heater is supplied with fuel from the tank via a separate metering pump, with an additional battery providing the power supply. The switch-on time of the heater can be preset, so that the heater will operate with the engine running, switched off before the engine is started, or switched on or off manually for immediate heat output.

Front control unit

Removal

2 Disconnect the battery negative lead (see Chapter 5A).

3 Remove the audio unit as described in Chapter 12, and the storage compartment below the audio unit.

4 Carefully prise the trim from around the heater control knob **(see illustration)**. Pad the screwdriver blade with tape to avoid damaging the trim panel and facia.

5 Undo the four screws, and remove the heater control/audio compartment panel trim **(see illustration)**.

6 Undo the screws, and remove the heater control unit retaining frame **(see illustration)**.

7 Note the correct fitted location of each control cable, then squeeze together the outer cable end fitting retaining clip lugs, detach the outer and inner cables from the panel **(see illustration)**. The red cable is fitted on the right-hand lever, and the blue to the left. Disconnect the wiring plugs and vacuum hoses, again noting their fitted positions.

8 Once the wiring and cables are detached, remove the control panel from the vehicle.

Refitting

9 Refitting is a reversal of removal, but ensure that the control cables (where fitted) are securely reconnected to their original locations. Check the operation of the controls prior to refitting the centre console.

Rear control unit

10 The rear control unit is fitted into the headlining above the rear doors. Carefully prise the trim from the controls **(see illustration)**.

11 Release the three retaining clips, and manoeuvre the control panel from the headlining **(see illustration)**. Disconnect the wiring plugs as the unit is withdrawn. Refitting is a reversal of removal.

Front blower motor

12 Remove the passenger side glovebox and

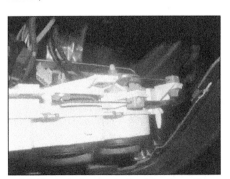

9.7 Detach the control cables from the control panel

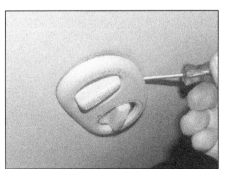

9.10 Carefully prise the trim from the controls

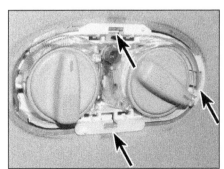

9.11 Release the three retaining clips (arrowed)

9.13 Disconnect the blower motor wiring plug

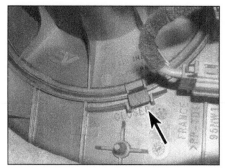

9.14 Release the retaining tab (arrowed)

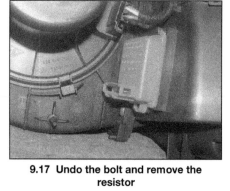

9.17 Undo the bolt and remove the resistor

lower facia panel as described in Chapter 11, Sections 28 and 31.

13 Disconnect the wiring plug from the blower motor (see illustration).

14 Release the retaining tab, turn the motor anti-clockwise, and withdraw it from the housing (see illustrations).

15 Refitting is a reversal of removal.

Front blower motor resistor

16 Remove the passenger side glovebox and lower facia panel as described in Chapter 11, Sections 28 and 31.

17 Disconnect the wiring plug, undo the retaining bolt, and remove the resistor (see illustration).

18 Refitting is the reverse of removal.

Rear blower motor

19 Remove the left-hand rear luggage

9.20 Undo the three screws and remove the rear blower motor

9.23 Undo the screw and remove the resistor

compartment side trim as described in Chapter 11, Section 31.

20 Disconnect the wiring plug, undo the three screws, and remove the blower motor (see illustration).

21 Refitting is a reversal of removal.

Rear blower motor resistor

22 Remove the left-hand rear luggage compartment trim panel as described in Chapter 11, Section 31.

23 Disconnect the wiring plug, undo the retaining screw, and remove the resistor (see illustration).

24 Refitting is a reversal of removal.

Front heater unit

Removal

25 Ensure that engine has cooled completely before starting work, and disconnect the battery negative lead as described in Chapter 5A.

26 Remove the windscreen wiper linkage with reference to Chapter 12.

27 At the rear of the engine compartment, locate the heater matrix hoses and trace them back to the point where they connect to bulkhead stub pipes.

28 Place a draining container underneath the hoses, to catch the coolant that will escape when they are disconnected.

29 Apply proprietary hose clamps to both heater hoses, then release the clips and disconnect the hoses from the bulkhead stubs (see illustration). Allow the coolant from the heater circuit to collect in the draining

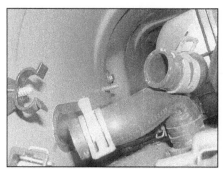

9.29 Disconnect the hoses from the bulkhead stubs

container. Alternatively, drain the coolant system as described in the relevant Part of Chapter 1).

30 If you have access to a source of compressed air, apply it carefully at *low pressure* to the left-hand bulkhead stub and blow the remainder of the coolant from the heater matrix.

> ⚠ **Warning: Always wear eye protection when working with compressed air.**

31 If you do not have access to compressed air, bear in mind that a larger volume of coolant will remain in the heater circuit and that this may escape as the heater unit is removed from the inside of the car.

32 Remove the heater controls, as described in Paragraphs 2 to 8.

33 Remove the entire facia panel and crossmember as described in Chapter 11.

34 Undo the two bolts securing the brake and clutch pedal bracket to the facia strut.

35 Press in the locking tab, pull out the retaining clip, and tilt the central junction box towards the rear of the car. Undo the two plastic clips (one each side), manoeuvre the junction box from its fitted position, and lay to one side (see illustration).

36 On models up to '98, disconnect the wiring plug, undo the retaining bolt, and remove the ABS module.

37 With the ABS module removed, undo the three retaining bolts and remove the module bracket from the bulkhead and facia struts.

38 The heater housing retaining nuts are accessed from the engine compartment. The

9.35 Press in the locking tab (arrowed)

9.51 Prise off the metal clips

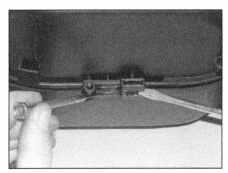

9.52 Release the plastic retaining clips

Rear heater matrix

Removal

50 Remove the rear heater unit as described in the Paragraphs 44 to 48.
51 With the unit on the bench, prise off the metal retaining clips **(see illustration)**.
52 Working around the circumference of the heater unit, release the plastic retaining clips with a small screwdriver **(see illustration)**. Separate the two halves of the heater unit, and lift the matrix from the casing.

Refitting

53 Refitting is a reversal of removal. New heater matrices may be supplied with self-adhesive foam padding strips – these should be affixed to the outer circumference of the matrix.

Fresh air/recirculation flap servo

Removal

54 Remove the complete facia panel as described in Chapter 11.
55 Unhook the operating lever, disconnect the vacuum hose, undo the two screws, and remove the servo from the heater unit **(see illustration)**.

Refitting

56 Refitting is a reversal of removal.

Booster heater

Removal

57 Chock the front wheels, then jack up the rear of the vehicle and support on axle stands (see *Jacking and vehicle support*).
58 Working underneath the vehicle on the left-hand side in front of the rear wheel, undo the clamp bolt, disconnect the air intake pipe from the heater and pull the pipe from the sill **(see illustration)**.
59 Undo the bolt securing the silencer pipe.
60 Unscrew the two mounting bolts, and lower the unit.
61 Apply proprietary hose clamps to both coolant hoses, then release the clips and disconnect the hoses from the heater stubs. Disconnect the fuel supply pipe.
62 Disconnect the wiring plug, and manoeuvre the heater from under the vehicle **(see illustration)**. No dismantling of the heater is advised.

nuts are located behind premade flaps in the sound insulation material fixed to the bulkhead **(see illustrations 11.20a and 11.20b)**. Undo the nuts.
39 Pull the heater housing from the bulkhead, and manoeuvre it from the passenger cabin. Disconnect the vacuum pipe as the heater is withdrawn.

Refitting

40 Refitting is the reverse of removal, noting the following points.
  a) Ensure the ducts, elbows and gaiter are all securely joined to the housing and the wiring/cables are correctly routed before securing the housing in position.
  b) Ensure the coolant hoses are securely reconnected to the matrix.
  c) On completion, top-up and bleed the cooling system as described in the relevant Part of Chapter 1.

Front heater matrix

Removal

41 Remove the heater unit as described earlier in this Section, noting that it is only necessary to move the heater unit 30 to 40 mm away from the bulkhead to provide sufficient clearance for the matrix pipes.
42 Undo the screws, and withdraw the heater matrix from the top of the heater unit **(see illustrations 11.20c and 11.20d)**. Protect

your hands as you do this – the matrix fins are sharp and can cause injury.

Refitting

43 Refitting is a reversal of removal. New heater matrices will be supplied with self-adhesive foam padding strips – these should be affixed to the edges of the core and the upper flange before the matrix is inserted into the heater unit.

Rear heater unit

Removal

44 Remove the left-hand rear luggage compartment side panel as described in Chapter 11, Section 31.
45 Place a draining container underneath the heater hoses, to catch the coolant that will escape when they are disconnected.
46 Apply proprietary hose clamps to both heater hoses, then release the clips and disconnect the hoses from the heater stubs. Allow the coolant from the heater to collect in the draining container. Alternatively, drain the coolant system as described in the relevant Part of Chapter 1.
47 Disconnect the wiring plugs from the blower motor, resistor and temperature control valve.
48 Unscrew the four retaining bolts, and remove the heater from the vehicle.

Refitting

49 Refitting is a reversal of removal. If necessary, top up the cooling system as described in the relevant Part of Chapter 1.

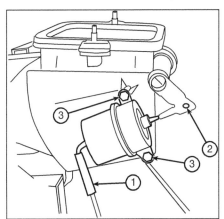

9.55 Unhook the operating lever (2), disconnect the hose (1) and undo the screws (3)

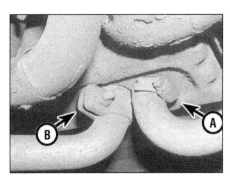

9.58 Booster heater intake pipe clamp (A) and silencer pipe clamp (B)

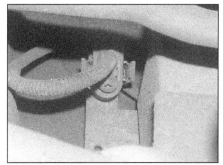

9.62 Disconnect the wiring plug located just behind the booster heater

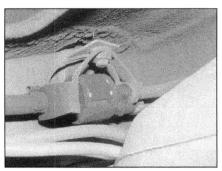

9.65 Disconnect the booster heater fuel metering pump

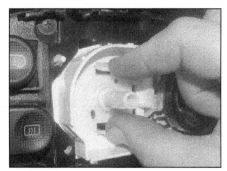

9.71a Squeeze together the retaining tabs and pull switch from the panel . . .

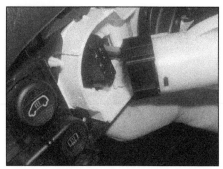

9.71b . . . then disconnect the wiring plug and vacuum connection

Refitting

63 Refitting is a reversal of removal. Top-up the coolant level as described in the relevant Part of Chapter 1.

Booster heater fuel metering pump

Removal

64 Chock the front wheels, then jack up the rear of the vehicle and support on axle stands (see *Jacking and vehicle support*).
65 The pump is located just in front of the fuel tank, on the right-hand side of the vehicle. Disconnect the wiring plug from the pump, and remove the retaining nut **(see illustration)**.
66 Release the retaining clips, and disconnect the fuel pipes from the pump. Note the fitted positions of the pipes, and be prepared for fuel spillage.

Refitting

67 Refitting is a reversal of removal.

Additional heater

68 At the time of writing, no information concerning the additional heater was available.

Heater blower motor switch

69 Use a small screwdriver to gently prise out the heater control panel trim. Use a pad of soft material between the screwdriver and the panel to prevent any accidental damage.
70 Pull the knob from the switch.
71 Depress the two retaining tabs (one at the top, and one at the bottom of the switch), and pull the switch from the panel. Disconnect the wiring plugs as the switch is withdrawn **(see illustrations)**.

10 Air conditioning system – general information and precautions

General information

1 An air conditioning system is available on certain models. It combines a conventional air heating system with an air cooling and dehumidifying system. This allows greater control over the temperature and humidity of the air inside the car, giving increased comfort and rapid window demisting. On models equipped with automatic climate control, a rear passenger cabin air conditioning system is available. The heater/air conditioning unit is located behind the left-hand rear panel trim, with the conditioned air being routed through ducting by the rear pillar to emerge through vents in the rear passenger headlining **(see illustration)**.
2 The cooling side of the system works in the same way as a domestic refrigerator. Refrigerant gas, contained in a sealed network of alloy pipes, is drawn into a belt-driven compressor, and is forced through a condenser mounted on the front of the radiator. On entering the condenser, the refrigerant changes state from gas to liquid and releases heat, which is absorbed by the air flowing into the front of the engine compartment through the condenser. The liquid refrigerant passes through an expansion valve to an evaporator, where it changes from liquid under high pressure to gas under low pressure. This change in state is accompanied by a drop in temperature, which cools the evaporator. Air passing through the evaporator is cooled before flowing into the air distribution unit. The refrigerant then returns to the compressor, and the cycle begins again.
3 The cooled air passes to the air distribution unit, where it is blended with hot air blown through the heater matrix, to achieve the desired temperature in the passenger compartment. When the air conditioning system is operating in Automatic mode, a series of air valves controlled by servo motors automatically regulate the cabin temperature by blending hot and cold air.

10.1 Models with front and rear air conditioning

1 Second row air vents	4 Rear air conditioning unit	7 Refrigerant hoses
2 Third row air vents	5 Rear lower air vents	8 Front air conditioning
3 D-pillar air ducting	6 Heater coolant hoses	unit

4 The heating side of the system works in the same way as on models without air conditioning (see Section 8).

5 The operation of the system can be manually controlled, or automatically managed by an electronic control unit, which controls the electric cooling fan, the compressor, and the facia-mounted warning light. Any problems with the system should be referred to a Ford dealer. The system has a built-in, self-diagnostic capability, but specialist equipment is needed to interpret the information it produces.

Precautions

6 When working on a vehicle equipped with air conditioning, it is necessary to observe special precautions whenever dealing with any part of the air conditioning system, or its associated components. If for any reason the refrigerant lines must be disconnected, you must entrust this task to a Ford dealer or an air conditioning specialist. Similarly, the system can only be evacuated and recharged by a dealer or air conditioning specialist.

 Warning: The air conditioning system contains a pressurised liquid refrigerant. If the system is discharged in an uncontrolled manner without the aid of specialist equipment, the refrigerant will boil as soon as it is exposed to the atmosphere, causing severe frostbite if it comes into contact unprotected skin. In addition, certain refrigerants, in the presence of a naked flame (including a lit cigarette), will oxidise to form a highly poisonous gas. It is

therefore extremely dangerous to disconnect any part of the air conditioning system without specialised knowledge and equipment.

7 Uncontrolled discharging of the refrigerant can also be damaging to the environment, as certain refrigerants contain CFCs.

8 Do not operate the air conditioning system if it is known to be short of refrigerant, as this will damage the compressor.

11 Air conditioning system components – removal and refitting

 Warning: Do not attempt to discharge the refrigerant circuit yourself (refer to the precautions given in Section 10). Have the air conditioning system discharged by a qualified refrigeration engineer. The quick-release discharge couplings are in the top refrigerant pipe behind the bonnet slam panel, and behind the right-hand indicator. On completion, have the engineer fit new O-rings to the line connections and evacuate and recharge the system.

Compressor

Removal

1 Disconnect the negative cable from the battery terminal (see Chapter 5A).

2 Have the air conditioning system discharged by a qualified engineer.

3 Remove the auxiliary drivebelt as described in the relevant Part of Chapter 2.

4 Unscrew the retaining bolt and disconnect the refrigerant lines from the compressor. Remove the O-ring seals and discard them – new ones must be used on reconnection. Plug the open pipes and ports to prevent the ingress of moisture **(see illustration)**.

5 Disconnect the compressor wiring plug **(see illustration)**.

6 Unscrew the securing bolts, then remove the compressor from its mounting bracket **(see illustration)**.

Refitting

7 Refitting is a reversal of the removal procedure; ensure that all fixings are tightened to the specified torque, where given. On completion, have the refrigerant engineer fit new O-rings to the line connections and then evacuate and recharge the refrigerant circuit.

Front evaporator/heater matrix

Removal

8 Have the air conditioning system discharged by a qualified engineer.

9 Ensure that engine has cooled completely before starting work.

10 Drain the cooling system as described in the relevant Part of Chapter 1.

11 Disconnect the negative cable from the battery terminal (see Chapter 5A).

12 Pull out the battery compartment upper panel, then release the retaining screws, and remove the bulkhead cover panel **(see illustration)**. Slide the panel to the right-hand side and manoeuvre it from behind the coolant expansion tank.

13 Working in the left-hand corner of the engine compartment, release the retaining clips and disconnect the hose from the coolant expansion tank. Undo the mounting bolts, and remove the tank from the engine compartment. Disconnect the wiring plug as the tank in withdrawn.

14 At the rear of the engine compartment, locate the heater matrix hoses and trace them back to the point where they connect to bulkhead stub pipes. Release the retaining clips and disconnect the hoses **(see illustration)**.

15 If you have access to a source of

11.4 Undo the bolt and disconnect the refrigerant pipes (arrowed)

11.5 Disconnect the compressor wiring plug

11.6 Undo the bolts and remove the compressor (arrowed)

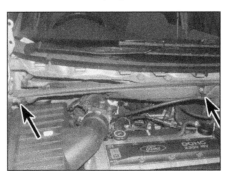

11.12 The bulkhead panel is secured by three bolts (two arrowed)

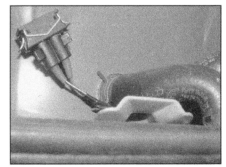

11.14 Release the retaining clips and disconnect the heater hoses

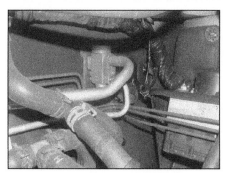

11.19 The refrigerant pipes union is at the rear of the engine compartment

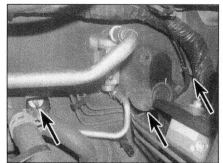

11.20a Three of the heater unit nuts are behind flaps in the bulkhead material (arrowed) . . .

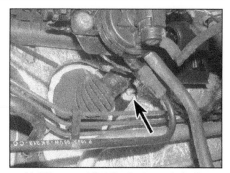

11.20b . . . whilst the last one is in the centre of the bulkhead (arrowed)

compressed air, apply it carefully at *low pressure* to the left hand bulkhead stub and blow the remainder of the coolant from the heater matrix. Be prepared for coolant spillage.

 Warning: Always wear eye protection when working with compressed air.

16 If you do not have access to compressed air, bear in mind that a larger volume of coolant will remain in the heater circuit and that this may escape as the housing is removed from the inside of the car.

17 Remove the entire facia panel and crossmember as described in Chapter 11.

18 Note their fitted positions (label each connection to avoid confusion on refitting), then disconnect the seven wiring plugs from the evaporator/heater housing.

19 Working in the engine compartment, locate the aluminium air conditioning refrigerant pipes and trace them back to the bulkhead. Unscrew the centre bolt and disconnect the pipes at the union **(see illustration)**. Remove the O-ring seals and discard them – new ones must be used on reconnection. Plug the open pipes to prevent the ingress of moisture.

20 The heater/evaporator housing retaining nuts are accessed from the engine compartment. Three of the nuts are located behind premade flaps in the sound insulation material fixed to the bulkhead, and one is located in the centre of the bulkhead **(see illustrations)**. Undo the nuts. **Note:** *If only the heater matrix is to be removed, the housing*

only needs to be pulled 30 to 40 mm from the bulkhead. The matrix Torx screws can then be undone and the matrix lifted out **(see illustrations)**.

21 Lift the evaporator/heater matrix housing away from the bulkhead. Disconnect the vacuum hose as the unit is withdrawn.

22 Remove the housing from the vehicle, keeping it upright to avoid spilling the residual coolant.

Refitting

23 Refitting is the reverse of removal, noting the following points.
a) Ensure that the condenser drain pipe is correctly positioned on the rear of the evaporator/heater matrix housing.
b) Ensure the wiring/cables are correctly routed before securing the housing in position.
c) Ensure the coolant hoses are securely reconnected to the matrix.
d) Top-up and bleed the cooling system as described in the relevant Part of Chapter 1.
e) On completion, have the refrigerant engineer fit new O-rings to the line connections and then evacuate and recharge the refrigerant circuit.

Rear evaporator/heater matrix

Removal

24 Have the air conditioning system discharged by a qualified engineer.

25 Ensure that engine has cooled completely before starting work.

26 Drain the cooling system as described in the relevant Part of Chapter 1.

27 Disconnect the negative cable from the battery terminal (see Chapter 5A).

28 Remove the left-hand luggage compartment trim panel as described in Chapter 11, Section 31.

29 Note their fitted positions (label each connection to avoid confusion on refitting), then disconnect the four wiring plugs from the evaporator/heater housing. Disconnect the water drain pipe from the housing **(see illustration)**.

30 Where fitted, release the cable ties, unscrew the retaining bolt, and remove the headlining air duct by pulling it out at the base, and down from the headlining guide.

31 Undo the bolt and detach the refrigerant pipes from the rear expansion valve.

32 Release the retaining clips and disconnect the coolant pipes.

33 Unscrew the four bolts and remove the heater/evaporator housing.

Refitting

34 Refitting is the reverse of removal, noting the following points.
a) Ensure that the condenser drain pipe is correctly positioned.
b) Ensure the wiring/cables are correctly routed before securing the housing in position.

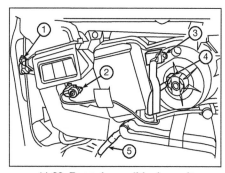

11.29 Rear air conditioning unit

1 Air distribution servo motor
2 Temperature flap servo motor
3 Blower control unit
4 Blower motor
5 Water drain pipe

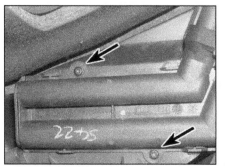

11.20c Undo the Torx screws (arrowed) . . .

11.20d . . . and remove the heater matrix

c) *Ensure the coolant hoses are securely reconnected to the matrix.*

d) *Top-up and bleed the cooling system as described in the relevant Part of Chapter 1.*

e) *On completion, have the refrigerant engineer fit new O-rings to the line connections and then evacuate and recharge the refrigerant circuit.*

Front blower motor

Removal

35 Remove the passenger side glovebox and lower facia panel as described in Chapter 11, Sections 28 and 31.

36 Disconnect the wiring plug from the blower motor.

37 Release the retaining tab, turn the motor clockwise, and withdraw it from the housing **(see illustrations)**.

Refitting

38 Refitting is a reversal of removal.

Rear blower motor

Removal

39 Remove the left-hand luggage compartment trim panel as described in Chapter 11, Section 31.

40 Disconnect the blower motor wiring plug.

41 Release the locking tab, twist the motor and remove it from the housing.

Refitting

42 Refitting is a reversal of removal.

Receiver/dryer

Removal

43 Have the air conditioning system discharged by a qualified engineer.

44 Apply the handbrake, then jack up the front of the vehicle and support it on axle stands (see *Jacking and vehicle support*). The receiver/dryer is located to the right of the radiator.

45 Undo the single bolt and disconnect the refrigerant pipes from the receiver/dryer **(see illustration)**. Discard the O-ring(s) a new one must be fitted.

46 Disconnect the high-pressure switch wiring plug.

47 Undo the two retaining bolts, and remove

11.37a Release the retaining tab (arrowed) . . .

the receiver/dryer **(see illustration)**. If required, detach the high-pressure switch.

Refitting

48 Refitting is a reversal of removal. On completion, have the refrigerant engineer fit new O-rings to the line connections and then evacuate and recharge the refrigerant circuit.

High-pressure switch

Removal

49 The high-pressure switch is located on the receiver/dryer. There is no need to have the refrigerant evacuated from the system, as a non-return valve in the receiver/dryer seals the port as the switch is removed.

50 Disconnect the wiring plug from the switch.

51 Unscrew the switch from the receiver/dryer **(see illustration 11.47)**.

Refitting

52 Install the switch, tightening it to the specified torque.

53 Reconnect the wiring plug, and lower the vehicle to the ground.

Front expansion valve

Removal

54 Have the air conditioning system discharged by a qualified engineer. The expansion valve is located on the engine compartment rear bulkhead.

55 Undo the single bolt, and disconnect the refrigerant pipe from the valve **(see illustration)**. Discard the O-ring seals, new ones must be fitted.

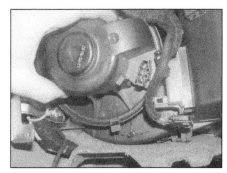

11.37b . . . then turn the motor clockwise and remove it

56 Slacken and remove the two retaining bolts, and remove the expansion valve.

Refitting

57 Refitting is a reversal of removal, noting that the new O-ring seals should be lubricated with refrigerant oil prior to installation.

Rear expansion valve

Removal

58 Have the air conditioning system discharged by a qualified engineer.

59 Remove the left-hand seat from the second and third row of seats.

60 Remove the left-hand D-pillar trim and left-hand luggage compartment panel as described in Chapter 11, Section 31.

61 Undo the single bolt and detach the refrigerant pipes from the expansion valve. Discard the O-ring seals, new ones must be fitted.

62 Undo the retaining bolts, and remove the expansion valve.

Refitting

63 Refitting is a reversal of removal, noting that the new O-ring seals should be lubricated with refrigerant oil prior to installation.

De-icing switch

Removal

64 On petrol engine models, in order to prevent the compressor from icing up, a de-icing switch probe measures the surface temperature of the evaporator cooling fins. If the temperature of the fins drops below 1°C,

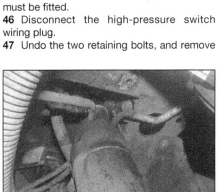

11.45 Disconnect the receiver/dryer pipes

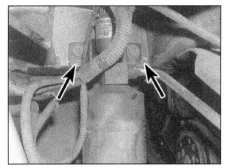

11.47 The receiver/dryer is secured by two bolts (arrowed)

11.55 Undo the bolt and disconnect the pipes from the expansion valve

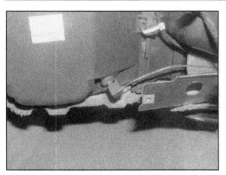

11.70 Pull the de-icing switch probe from the evaporator

11.77 Condenser refrigerant pipe fixings (arrowed)

the switch disengages the electromagnetic clutch of the compressor. As soon as the temperature rises above 2.5°, the clutch re-engages.

65 Where fitted, refer to Chapter 12, and remove the passenger air bag or upper glovebox as applicable.

66 Working through the airbag/glovebox aperture, disconnect the de-icing switch wiring plug.

67 Undo the retaining bolts, and remove the lower centre console trim.

68 Remove the passenger glovebox as described in Chapter 11.

69 Carefully prise out the glovebox light, undo the five screws, release the retaining clip and remove the glovebox frame.

70 Pull out the probe from the evaporator. Undo the two Torx screws and remove the switch relay. Remove the switch and harness **(see illustration)**.

Refitting

71 Refitting is a reversal of removal.

Condenser

Removal

72 Have the air conditioning system discharged by a qualified engineer.

73 With reference to the relevant Part of Chapter 1, drain the coolant. **Note:** *Do not reconnect the lower radiator hose.*

74 Remove the front radiator grille with reference to Chapter 11.

75 Undo the two screws on the bonnet slam

panel, and detach the bracket for the coolant fan/run-on control module **(see illustration 3.4a)**.

76 Unscrew the single bolt and remove the upper radiator cover **(see illustration 3.4b)**.

77 Undo the bolt and remove the upper refrigerant pipe from the condenser, then undo the single bolt and remove the lower refrigerant pipe **(see illustration)**.

78 On diesel models, detach the engine air intake pipe from the bonnet slam panel.

79 Release the retaining clip, and disconnect the radiator top hose.

80 Unscrew the two bolts, and remove the strut from the cooling fan assembly.

81 On diesel models, working underneath the vehicle, undo the two retaining bolts and remove the intercooler air guide.

82 Undo the four retaining bolts, disconnect the wiring plugs, and manoeuvre the cooling fan and shroud assembly out from the bottom of the engine compartment.

83 On diesel models, again, working underneath the vehicle, release the retaining clips, and remove the left- and right-hand intercooler hoses.

84 Disconnect the radiator thermal switch (where fitted) wiring plug.

85 Undo the two retaining bolts, and pull the bottom of the radiator backwards, and manoeuvre the radiator from the engine compartment.

86 Remove the four screws and detach the condenser from the radiator **(see illustrations)**.

Refitting

87 Refitting is a reversal of removal, noting the following points:

a) *Ensure that the lugs on the top edge of the radiator engage correctly with the corresponding locating holes in the front panel.*

b) *Ensure the coolant hoses are securely reconnected.*

c) *Top-up and bleed the cooling system as described in the relevant Part of Chapter 1.*

d) *On completion, have the refrigerant engineer fit new O-rings to the line connections and then evacuate and recharge the refrigerant circuit. Note that all air conditioning O-rings should be lubricated with refrigerant oil prior to being fitted.*

Control panel

Manual air conditioning

88 Refer to the non-air conditioning heater control panel removal procedure in Section 9 of this Chapter.

Automatic air conditioning

89 Disconnect the battery negative terminal (see Chapter 5A).

90 Remove the audio unit from the facia with reference to Chapter 12.

91 Reaching through the audio unit aperture, unlatch the locking tab underneath the control unit, and gently pull unit from the facia. Disconnect the three wiring plugs as the unit is withdrawn **(see illustration)**.

92 No further dismantling of the control panel is possible.

93 Refitting is a reversal of removal. A click should be audible as the unit is slid into place, and the locking tab engages.

Flap valve positioning motors

Automatic air conditioning

94 The various flap valve positioning motors are only accessible after the facia panel has been removed (front air conditioning), or the rear left-hand luggage compartment side trim has been removed (rear air conditioning) – see Chapter 11.

11.86a The condenser is secured to the radiator by two screws one the left-hand side (one arrowed – one hidden) . . .

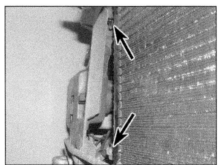

11.86b . . . and two on the right-hand side (arrowed)

11.91 Release the automatic air conditioning control panel locking tab (arrowed)

95 Unplug the wiring connector, then undo the Torx screws and lift the motor from the unit **(see illustration)**.

96 Refitting is a reversal of removal.

Sunlight photo-sensor

97 Carefully prise from the defrosting vent in the centre of the facia **(see illustration)**. Disconnect the wiring and tie the connector back to prevent it from disappearing down inside the facia.

98 Refitting is a reversal of removal.

Thermal cut-off switch

99 The switch (where fitted) is located in the upper radiator hose. To remove the switch, drain the cooling system to just below the level of the switch, as described in the relevant Part of Chapter 1, or be prepared for coolant spillage.

100 Remove the battery compartment upper and lower panels (see Chapter 5A). Disconnect the wiring plug from the switch.

101 Prise the retaining clip out, and remove the switch. Recover the O-ring seal.

11.95 Undo the screws and remove the flap positioning motor

102 Refitting is a reversal of removal. The O-ring seal can be re-used, provided it is in good condition.

Radiator fan third speed switch

103 The switch (where fitted) is located in the upper radiator hose. To remove the switch, drain the cooling system to just below the level of the switch, as described in the

11.97 Sunlight sensor

relevant Part of Chapter 1, or be prepared for coolant spillage.

104 Remove the battery compartment upper and lower panels (see Chapter 5A). Disconnect the wiring plug from the switch.

105 Prise the retaining clip out, and remove the switch. Recover the O-ring seal.

106 Refitting is a reversal of removal. The O-ring seal can be re-used, provided it is in good condition.

Notes

Chapter 4 Part A:
Fuel system – petrol

Contents

Degrees of difficulty

Easy, suitable for novice with little experience		Fairly easy, suitable for beginner with some experience		Fairly difficult, suitable for competent DIY mechanic		Difficult, suitable for experienced DIY mechanic		Very difficult, suitable for expert DIY or professional	

Specifications

System type
All models . . . . Ford EEC V sequential multipoint injection

Recommended fuel
Minimum octane rating . . . . 95 RON unleaded only

Fuel system data
Fuel pump type . . . . Electric, immersed in fuel tank
Regulated fuel pressure at idling speed:
    Vacuum hose fitted . . . . 3.5 bar (approx)
    Vacuum hose disconnected . . . . 4.0 bar (approx)
Minimum holding pressure (after 10 minutes) . . . . 2.0 bar
Engine idle speed (non-adjustable, ECM controlled):
    2.0 litre engine . . . . 865 rpm
    2.3 litre engine . . . . 875 rpm
Engine maximum speed . . . . 6175 rpm
Idle CO content . . . . Not adjustable, ECM controlled
Fuel tank capacity . . . . 70 litres

Torque wrench settings	Nm	lbf ft
Camshaft position sensor	5	4
Crankshaft position sensor	4	3
Engine coolant temperature sensor	23	17
Fuel injector bolts	6	4
Fuel pressure regulator	6	4
Fuel rail	10	7
Idle air control valve to intake manifold	10	7
Intake manifold:		
Nuts and bolts	23	17
Studs	14	10
Throttle body to intake manifold	10	7

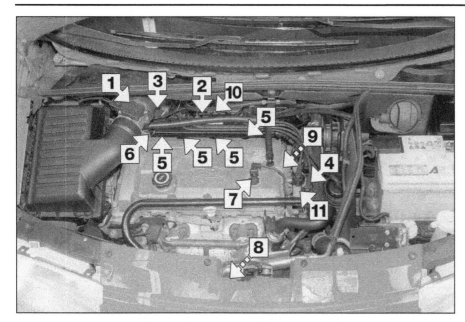

1.1a 2.0 litre engine management components

1 Mass airflow sensor
2 Throttle position sensor
3 Intake air temperature sensor
4 Coolant temperature sensor
5 Fuel injectors and fuel rail
6 Fuel pressure regulator
7 Camshaft position sensor
8 Oxygen sensor
9 Crankshaft position sensor
10 Idle air control valve
11 Ignition coils

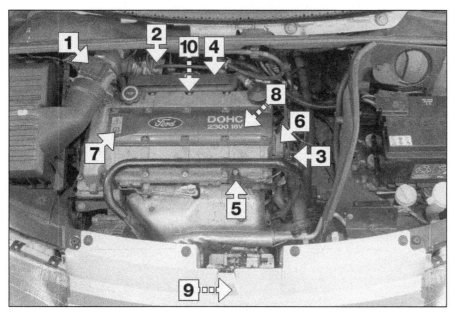

1.1b 2.3 litre engine management components

1 Mass airflow sensor
2 Throttle position sensor
3 Coolant temperature sensor
4 Fuel injectors wiring rail
5 Camshaft position sensor
6 Radio suppressor
7 Ignition coils/spark plugs cover
8 Crankshaft position sensor (rear of engine)
9 Oxygen sensor
10 Idle air control valve

1 General information and precautions

General information

The Ford EEC V sequential multipoint petrol injection system described in this Chapter is a self-contained engine management system, which controls both the fuel injection and, via a separate module, ignition **(see illustrations)**. This Chapter deals with the fuel system components only, however refer to Chapter 5B for details of the ignition system.

The fuel injection system comprises a fuel tank, an electric fuel pump, a fuel filter, fuel supply and return lines, a throttle body, an air mass sensor, a fuel rail and four electronic injectors, a fuel pressure regulator, and an electronic control module (ECM), together with its associated sensors, actuators and wiring.

The air mass sensor is located on the air cleaner outlet to the throttle body. Fuel is supplied under pressure to a fuel rail, and then passes to four electronic injectors. The duration of the injection period is determined by the ECM which switches the injectors on and off as required.

The tank immersed fuel pump delivers a constant supply of fuel through a cartridge filter. The fuel is supplied to a fuel rail, and the fuel pressure regulator maintains a constant fuel pressure to the fuel injectors and returns excess fuel to the tank via the return line. The constant fuel flow system helps to reduce fuel temperature and prevents vaporisation.

The ECM controls starting and warm-up enrichment together with idle speed regulation and Lambda control. Idle speed control is achieved by an idle air control valve on the side of the throttle body, and partly by the ignition system. Manual adjustment of the idle speed is not possible.

Intake air is drawn into the engine through the air cleaner, which contains a renewable paper filter element.

The exhaust gas oxygen content is constantly monitored by the ECM via the oxygen sensor, which is mounted in the front section of the exhaust pipe, before the catalytic converter. On models for some markets, a second oxygen sensor is mounted

2.3 Detach the air intake pipe from the filter housing

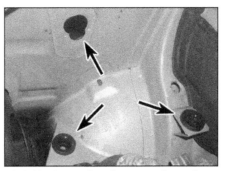

2.4 Air cleaner housing mounting points (arrowed)

2.5 Disconnect the breather hose from the housing

after the catalytic converter. The ECM then uses this information to adjust the air/fuel ratio. Manual adjustment of the idle speed exhaust CO content is not possible. A catalytic converter is fitted to the exhaust system on all models. A secondary air injection system is fitted, where air is introduced into the exhaust manifold during the warm-up phase, to shorten the amount of time taken for the catalytic converter to reach operating temperature, thus reducing harmful exhaust emissions (see Chapter 4C). A fuel evaporative control system is fitted, and the ECM controls the operation of the activated charcoal canister – refer to Chapter 4C for further details.

It should be noted that fault diagnosis of all the engine management systems described in this Chapter is only possible with dedicated electronic test equipment. Problems with the system operation should therefore be referred to an Ford dealer or engine management specialist for assessment. Once the fault has been identified, the removal and refitting sequences detailed in the following Sections will then allow the appropriate component(s) to be renewed as required.

Precautions

 Warning: Many of the procedures in this Chapter require the removal of fuel lines and connections, which may result in some fuel spillage. Before carrying out any operation on the fuel system, refer to the precautions given in 'Safety first!' at

the beginning of this manual, and follow them implicitly. Always switch off the ignition before working on the fuel system. Petrol is a highly-dangerous and volatile liquid, and the precautions necessary when handling it cannot be overstressed.
Note: *Residual pressure will remain in the fuel lines long after the vehicle was last used. Before disconnecting any fuel line, first depressurise the fuel system as described in Section 8.*

2 Air cleaner and intake ducts – removal and refitting

Removal

1 Release the clips securing the air cleaner ducting to the mass airflow sensor (see illustration 4.2).

2.3 litre models

2 Remove the right-hand headlamp as described in Chapter 12.
3 Detach the air intake pipe from the lower section of the air cleaner housing (see illustration).

All models

4 The air cleaner housing is secured by three lugs which locate in corresponding grommets in the inner wing. Gently pull the housing until the lugs disengage from the grommets (see illustration).
5 As the air cleaner housing is withdrawn,

release the retaining clip and disconnect the crankcase breather hose from the housing (see illustration).

Refitting

6 Refitting is a reversal of removal.

3 Accelerator cable – removal, refitting and adjustment

Removal

1 Pull out the battery compartment upper panel (see Chapter 5A), undo the three retaining screws and slide the bulkhead trim panel to the right and manoeuvre it from behind the coolant expansion tank. Note that the centre panel screw also retains the accelerator cable support bracket.
2 Disconnect the accelerator cable from the segment on the throttle body by turning the segment to open the throttle, then releasing the cable and end fitting (see illustration).
3 Disconnect the air intake temperature sensor wiring plug (where fitted), undo the two retaining clips and remove the air intake ducting (see illustration 4.15).
4 Undo the three Torx screws and remove the accelerator cable bracket from the throttle body, complete with the cable (see illustration).
5 Using a pair of pliers, squeeze together the retaining tags and remove the outer cable end fitting from the bracket (see illustration).

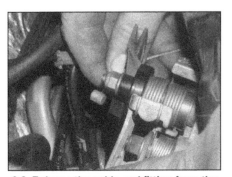

3.2 Release the cable end fitting from the quadrant

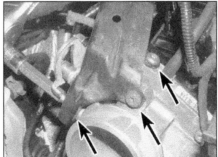

3.4 The accelerator cable bracket is secured by three Torx screws (arrowed)

3.5 Squeeze together the retaining tags and remove the end fitting from the bracket

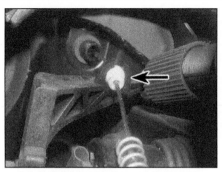

3.6 Pull the ferrule (arrowed) from the pedal and disconnect the cable

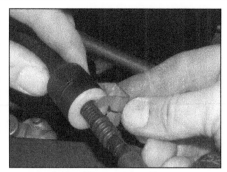

3.10a Remove the clip . . .

3.10b . . . and pull the adjuster and outer cable away from each other

6 Working in the passenger compartment, reach up under the facia, pull the cable ferrule from the top of the accelerator pedal, and disconnect the inner cable (see illustration).

7 On automatic transmission models, where fitted, disconnect the kick-down switch wiring from the outer cable on the engine compartment rear panel in the engine compartment.

8 In the engine compartment, pull the outer cable (complete with plastic end fitting) from the rubber grommet in the bulkhead, and remove it from the vehicle.

Refitting

9 Refitting is a reversal of removal, but adjust the cable as follows. Make sure that the outer cable is located securely in the bulkhead.

4.2 Disconnect the mass airflow sensor wiring plug

Adjustment

10 At the throttle body, pull the clip from the adjuster, and pull the adjuster and outer cable away from each other (see illustrations).

11 Fully depress the throttle pedal, then slowly release it.

12 Refit the clip to the adjuster and outer cable. Depress the throttle pedal fully, and check that full travel is achieved at the throttle body quadrant.

4 Engine management system components – removal and refitting

Note: Observe the precautions in Section 1 before working on any component in the fuel system. The ignition must be switched off at all times.

Mass airflow sensor

1 The mass airflow sensor is located on the air ducting from the air cleaner housing.

2 Disconnect the wiring plug from the sensor (see illustration).

3 Slacken the retaining clip, and disconnect the intake hose from the sensor.

4 Release the retaining clips and remove the sensor from the air ducting. Check that the sensor sealing ring is in good condition (see illustration).

5 Refitting is a reversal of removal.

Throttle position sensor

Note: On automatic transmission models, the ECM 'basic set-up' procedure must be carried out following disconnection of the sensor. This necessitates the use of FDS2000 dedicated diagnostic equipment, and should be entrusted to your local Ford dealer or suitably-equipped specialist.

6 Remove the mass airflow sensor, as described earlier in this Section. Undo the three screws and remove the bulkhead panel trim. Slide the panel to the right-hand side and manoeuvre it from behind the coolant expansion tank.

7 Disconnect the wiring plug from the intake air temperature sensor (see illustration 4.15).

8 Slacken the retaining clip and remove the intake ducting from the throttle body (see illustration).

9 On 2.0 litre models, disconnect the wiring multiplugs from the injectors and position to one side.

10 Unplug the throttle position sensor wiring, and disconnect the inner accelerator cable from the throttle valve. On 2.3 litre models, undo the retaining bolts and position the accelerator cable bracket to one side (see illustrations 3.2 and 3.4).

11 Disconnect the vacuum hose from the throttle body, undo the retaining Torx screws, and remove the throttle body (see illustrations).

12 With the throttle body removed, undo the

4.4 Check that the sensor sealing ring is in good condition (arrowed)

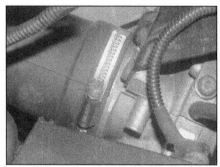

4.8 Slacken the retaining clip and disconnect the hose from the throttle body

4.11a Disconnect the vacuum hose

4.11b The throttle body is secured by four Torx screws (two arrowed – two hidden)

4.12 Undo the screws and detach the throttle position sensor

4.13 The rubber gasket can be re-used if it is in good condition

two Torx screws, and remove the throttle position sensor (see illustration).

13 Refitting is a reversal of removal, ensuring that the sensor is correctly located on the throttle valve shaft. Before refitting the throttle body, check the sealing gasket is in good condition (see illustration). On automatic transmission models, it will now be necessary to carry out the 'basic set-up' procedure using FDS2000 diagnostic equipment.

Intake air temperature sensor

14 The intake air temperature sensor is located on the intake ducting between the mass airflow sensor and the throttle body. On 2.0 litre models, remove the mass airflow sensor as described earlier in this Section.

15 Disconnect the wiring plug from the intake air temperature sensor (see illustration).

16 Carefully prise the sensor from the ducting. If required, the sensor can be tested by checking the output voltage and resistance, and comparing the values obtained with those given below.

Air temp °C	Resistance kΩ	Voltage V
–10	183	4.20
0	95	3.87
10	66	3.55
20	38	3.10
30	27	2.70
40	16	2.10

17 Refitting is a reversal of removal, tightening the sensor securely.

Vehicle speed sensor

18 Where fitted, the roadspeed sensor is fitted into the back of the gearbox. Refer to Chapter 7A or 7B as applicable, for the removal and refitting procedure. Any fault with the sensor must be checked by a Ford dealer or suitably-equipped specialist, and if necessary renewed.

Coolant temperature sensor

19 The engine coolant temperature sensor is located on the rear of the thermostat/coolant outlet housing on the left-hand end of the cylinder head (see illustration). The upper sensor is the engine coolant temperature sensor, and the lower sensor is the coolant temperature gauge sender.

20 Disconnect the wiring plug from the sensor.

21 Either drain the cooling system (as described in Chapter 1A) to below the level of the sensor, or be prepared for coolant spillage.

22 Unscrew the sensor from the housing. If required, the sensor can be tested by checking the output voltage and resistance. The values obtained should be identical to those given for the intake air temperature sensor in Paragraph 16.

23 Refitting is a reversal of removal, tightening the sensor to the specified torque. Refer to Chapter 1A and top-up the cooling system.

Crankshaft position sensor

24 The engine speed sensor is mounted on the rear of the cylinder block, adjacent to the mating surface of the block and transmission bellhousing, just behind the oil filter. Apply the handbrake, then jack up the front of the vehicle and support it on axle stands (see Jacking and vehicle support). Where applicable, remove the splash guard from under the engine compartment.

25 Disconnect the wiring plug from the sensor (see illustration).

26 Unscrew the retaining bolt and withdraw the sensor from the cylinder block. If required, the sensor can be tested as follows. Ensure the ignition is turned off, and disconnect the sensor wiring plug. Connect a multimeter between the two sensor terminals, and set the meter to measure resistance. A sensor in good condition should register a resistance of 200 to 450 ohms. If the resistance is outside the range specified, it is likely the sensor is defective.

27 Refitting is a reversal of removal. Tighten the securing bolt to the specified torque.

Throttle body

28 The throttle body removal procedure is incorporated into the throttle position sensor removal procedure described in Paragraph 6 of this Section.

Fuel injectors and fuel rail

2.0 litre models

29 Disconnect the battery negative lead, as described in Chapter 5A.

30 Carefully release the wiring multiplug rail

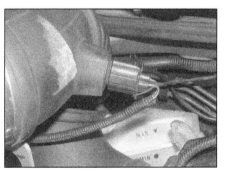

4.15 Disconnect the intake air temperature sensor wiring plug

4.19 Engine coolant temperature sensor

4.25 The crankshaft position sensor is adjacent to the oil filter

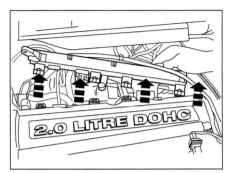

4.30 Release the wiring multiplug rail from the injectors

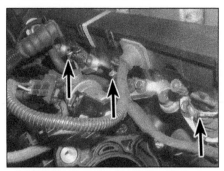

4.40 Release the retaining clips and place the wiring multiplug rail to one side (arrowed)

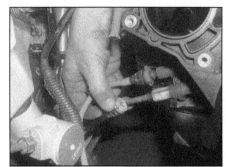

4.42 Squeeze together the locking tabs and disconnect the fuel supply and return pipes

from the top of the injectors, and place it to one side **(see illustration)**.

31 Depressurise the fuel system as described in Section 8.

32 Unscrew the fuel pressure regulator retaining bolts at the right-hand end of the fuel rail, and disconnect the regulator from the fuel rail. Be prepared for fuel spillage.

33 Undo the fuel supply hose union bolts at the left hand end of the fuel rail, disconnect the hose and recover any sealing washers/O-rings.

34 Unscrew the mounting bolts, then carefully lift the fuel rail together with the injectors from the intake manifold.

35 With the assembly on the bench, undo the retaining bolts and release each of the injectors from the fuel rail. Recover the O-ring seals. Check the availability of new O-ring seals before discarding the old ones.

4.43 Undo the hose retaining clip Torx screw (arrowed)

2.3 litre models

36 Disconnect the battery negative lead as described in Chapter 5A.

37 Remove the air cleaner housing as described in Section 2.

38 Disconnect the intake air temperature sensor wiring plug.

39 Slacken the retaining clip and remove the air intake ducting from the throttle body.

40 Carefully release the wiring multiplug rail from the top of the injectors, and place it to one side **(see illustration)**.

41 Depressurise the fuel system as described in Section 8.

42 Squeeze together the locking tabs and disconnect the fuel supply and return pipes **(see illustration)**.

43 Undo the Torx screw and remove the fuel pipes retaining clip **(see illustration)**.

44 Disconnect the vacuum pipe from the fuel pressure regulator.

45 Undo the retaining bolts and remove the fuel rail complete with pressure regulator and injectors **(see illustration)**.

46 If required, the pressure regulator can be removed by unscrewing the two retaining bolts. Check the availability of a new O-ring seal before discarding the old one.

47 Undo the retaining bolts and carefully prise the injectors from the fuel rail. Check the availability of new O-ring seals before discarding the old ones **(see illustrations)**.

All models

48 Refit the injectors, regulator (where applicable) and fuel rail by following the

removal procedure in reverse, noting the following points:

a) *The No 4 injector electrical socket must point to the rear of the engine, whilst the remainder face the front.*

b) *Where available, renew the injector O-ring seals, and smear them with a little clean engine oil before fitting them.*

c) *Check that the fuel supply and return pipes is reconnected correctly.*

d) *Check that all vacuum and electrical connections are remade correctly and securely.*

e) *Reconnect the battery as described in Chapter 5A.*

f) *On completion, start the engine and check for fuel leaks.*

Fuel pressure regulator

2.0 litre models

49 Depressurise the fuel system as described in Section 8.

50 Disconnect the vacuum hose from the pressure regulator at the right-hand end of the fuel rail.

51 Undo the two regulator retaining bolts, and remove the pressure regulator from the fuel rail. Be prepared for fuel spillage.

52 Disconnect the fuel hose from the regulator. Check the availability of a new O-ring seal before discarding the old one

2.3 litre models

53 Remove the fuel rail assembly as described earlier in this Section.

4.45 The fuel rail is secured by two bolts

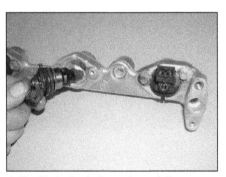

4.47a Undo the bolts and carefully remove the injectors

4.47b Where available, renew the O-ring seals

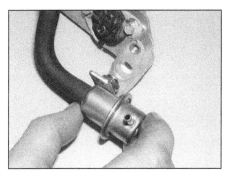

4.54 Undo the bolts and remove the pressure regulator

4.57a Camshaft position sensor – 2.0 litre

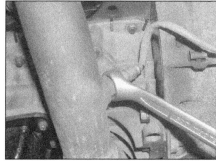

4.57b Camshaft position sensor – 2.3 litre

54 Undo the two retaining bolts, and remove the regulator from the fuel rail (see illustration). Check the availability of a new O-ring seal before discarding the old one.

All models

55 Refit the fuel pressure regulator by following the removal procedure in reverse, tightening the retaining bolts to the specified torque.

Camshaft position sensor

56 Disconnect the battery negative lead as described in Chapter 5A.
57 Disconnect the wiring plug from the sensor (see illustrations).
58 Unscrew the mounting bolt and withdraw the sensor from the camshaft cover. Recover the seal. If required, the sensor can be tested as follows. Ensure the ignition is turned off, and disconnect the sensor wiring plug. Connect a multimeter between the two sensor terminals, and set the meter to measure resistance. A sensor in good condition should register a resistance of 200 to 900 ohms. If the resistance is outside the range specified, it is likely the sensor is defective.
59 Refitting is a reversal of removal, tightening the mounting bolt to the specified torque.

Oxygen sensor(s)

60 Disconnect the battery negative lead as described in Chapter 5A.
61 Apply the handbrake, then jack up the front of the vehicle and support it on axle stands (see *Jacking and vehicle support*). Undo the two retaining nuts and four bolts (two each side) and remove the engine undershield.
62 Disconnect the wiring plug from the sensor (see illustration).
63 Unscrew and remove the sensor, taking care to avoid damaging the sensor probe as it is removed (see illustration).
64 Apply a little anti-seize grease to the sensor threads, but avoid contaminating the probe tip. Note: *New Oxygen sensors may be supplied with fitting paste on the threads.*
65 Refit the sensor and tighten it securely.
66 Reconnect the wiring plug, refit the engine undershield, and lower the vehicle to the ground.

Electronic control module (ECM)

Caution: *Always wait at least 30 seconds after switching off the ignition before disconnecting the wiring from the ECM. When the wiring is disconnected, all the learned values may be erased, however any contents of the fault memory are retained. After reconnecting the wiring, the vehicle must be driven for several miles so that the ECM can learn its basic settings. If the engine still runs erratically, the basic settings may be reinstated by an Ford dealer or specialist using special diagnostic equipment. Note also that if the ECM is renewed, the identification of the new ECM must be transferred to the immobiliser control unit by a Ford dealer or specialist. If a new ECM is fitted, or on automatic transmission models even if the original ECM is refitted, the 'basic set-up'*

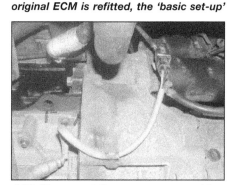

4.62 Disconnect the oxygen sensor wiring plug

procedure must be carried out using FDS2000 diagnostic equipment, which should be entrusted to a Ford dealer or suitably-equipped specialist.
67 The electronic control module is located behind the facia in the passenger compartment.
68 Disconnect the battery negative (earth) lead (see Chapter 5A).
69 Remove the instrument panel as described in Chapter 12.

Vehicles up to 1998

70 Remove the driver's side lower facia trim panel with reference to Chapter 11, Section 31.
71 Where fitted, unscrew the bulb failure module retaining nut, disconnect the wiring plugs, and remove the module (see illustration).

4.63 Unscrew the sensor from the exhaust pipe

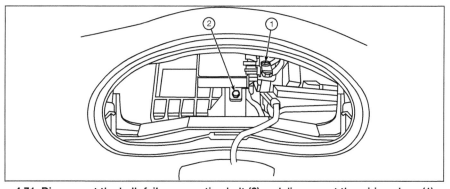

4.71 Disconnect the bulb failure mounting bolt (2) and disconnect the wiring plugs (1)

4.74 Undo the two screws and remove the bracket (shown with facia removed)

4.75 Undo the bolt and disconnect the ECM wiring plug (shown with facia removed)

4.81 The idle air control valve is secured to the top of the inlet manifold by two bolts

72 Slacken the ECM retaining band bolt.
73 Unscrew the retaining bolt and disconnect the ECM wiring plug. Slide the ECM from the retaining band, and manoeuvre it through the instrument panel aperture **(see illustration 4.75)**.

Vehicles from 1998

74 Working through the instrument panel aperture, undo the two ECM plug bracket screws **(see illustration)**.
75 Unscrew the retaining bolt and disconnect the ECM wiring plug **(see illustration)**.
76 Slacken the ECM retaining bracket bolt, and remove the ECM.
77 Refitting is a reversal of removal. If a new ECM has been fitted, or on automatic transmission models, it will now be necessary to carry out the 'basic set-up' procedure using FDS2000 diagnostic equipment.

Idle air control valve

78 Disconnect the battery negative lead as described in Chapter 5A.
79 Release the retaining clips, carefully pull the wiring multiplug rail from the top of the injectors, and position it to one side.
80 Disconnect the wiring plug from the idle air control valve.
81 Unscrew the two retaining bolts and remove the valve **(see illustration)**.
82 Refitting is a reversal of removal. Tighten the valve retaining bolts to the specified torque.

5 Fuel filter – renewal

Note: *Observe the precautions in Section 1 before working on fuel system components.*
1 The fuel filter is situated underneath the centre of the vehicle, in front of the fuel tank. Firmly apply the handbrake, then jack up the front of the vehicle and support it securely on axle stands.
2 If available, fit hose clamps to the filter intake and outlet flexible hoses. Even with hose clamps fitted, the old filter will contain some fuel, so have some rags ready to soak up any spillage.
3 Release the hose clips and detach the hoses from the filter **(see illustration)**. If the fuel hoses show any sign of perishing or cracking, particularly at the hose ends or where the hose enters the metal end fitting, renew the hoses.
4 Before removing the filter, note any direction-of-flow markings on the filter body, and check against the new filter – the arrow should point in the direction of fuel flow (towards the front of the car) **(see illustration)**.
5 Unscrew the two fuel filter housing retaining nuts.
6 Lower the filter and housing from the vehicle body, noting the housing retaining clips need to be pulled down over the

mounting studs with the housing. Remove the filter from the housing.
7 Fit the new filter into position in the housing, with the flow marking arrows correctly orientated **(see illustration)**. Push the housing over the retaining studs, and tighten the retaining nuts.
8 Reconnect the fuel hoses using new clips if necessary. Ensure that no dirt is allowed to enter the hoses or filter connections. Where applicable, remove the hose clamps.
9 Start the engine noting that there may be a delay as the system repressurises and the new filter fills with fuel. Let the engine run for several minutes while you check the filter hose connections for leaks, then switch it off.

> ⚠ **Warning: Dispose safely of the old filter; it will be highly flammable, and may explode if thrown on a fire.**

6 Fuel pump and gauge sender unit – removal and refitting

Note: *Observe the precautions in Section 1 before working on fuel system components.*

Removal

1 The fuel pump and gauge sender unit are combined in one assembly, mounted in the fuel tank. Access is via a hatch provided in the load space floor. Removal of the unit exposes

5.3 Release the fuel hose retaining clips

5.4 The arrows on the filter housing points to the front of the vehicle (arrowed)

5.7 Install the new filter with the arrow to the front of the vehicle

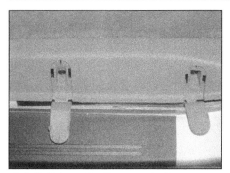

6.5 Pull down the flaps, undo the screws and remove the door sill trim panels

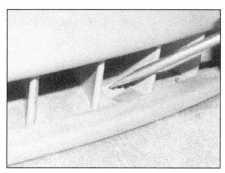

6.6a Depress the retaining clips and lift the cover away . . .

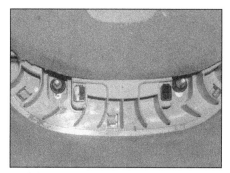

6.6b . . . then undo the two nuts and remove the centre vent

the contents of the tank to the atmosphere, so extreme care must be exercised to prevent fire. The area inside and around the car must be well-ventilated to prevent a build-up of fuel fumes. If possible, remove the unit when the fuel tank is nearly empty, or alternatively syphon the fuel from the tank into a suitable container.

2 Depressurise the fuel system as described in Section 8.

3 Ensure that the vehicle is parked on a level surface, then disconnect the battery negative lead (see Chapter 5A).

4 Pull the weatherstrips from the door apertures adjacent to the sill trim panels.

5 Lever open the plastic flaps, undo the two screws each side, and remove both door sill trim panels **(see illustration)**.

6 Depress the three retaining clips, and lift

the floor-mounted centre rear air vent cover. Undo the two nuts and remove the vent **(see illustrations)**.

7 Undo the screws securing seat mounting trims to the floor for the second row of seats.

8 Carefully prise up the trims at the front edge of the rear carpet, and fold the front half of the carpet to the rear **(see illustration)**.

9 Undo the retaining bolts and remove the seat mounting rail over the access hatch.

10 Slacken and remove the access hatch screws and lift the hatch away from the floorpan **(see illustration)**.

11 Unplug the wiring connector from the pump/sender unit **(see illustration)**.

12 Release the clips and disconnect the fuel supply and return hoses **(see illustration)**. Identify each hose for position – the blue hose is the return circuit.

13 Unscrew the plastic ring securing the pump/sender unit cover to the tank. Ford technicians use a special tool to unscrew the ring, however two screwdrivers engaged with the slots in the ring and crossed over each other may be used with success. Alternatively use a pair of large water pump pliers **(see illustration)**.

14 Lift the sender/pump unit from the tank taking care not to bend or damage the float or arm **(see illustration)**. On some models, the sender unit cover is separate from the pump unit. On these, lift the unit cover and push down and twist the pump unit anti-clockwise, then lift out the assembly. Discard the aperture seal, a new one must be fitted.

15 Inspect the float on the sender unit swinging arm for punctures and fuel ingress, and renew it if it appears damaged. Inspect

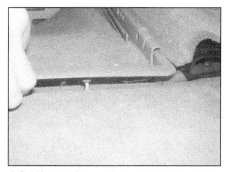

6.8 Lift the trims and peel back the carpet

6.10 Undo the three screws and remove the access hatch

6.11 Disconnect the pump/sender unit wiring plug

6.12 Note the arrows on the cover indicating supply and return (arrowed)

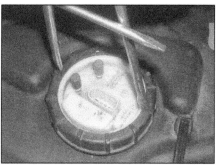

6.13 Unscrew the plastic ring

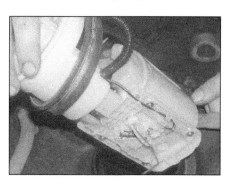

6.14 Lift the pump/sender unit from the tank

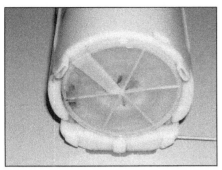

6.15 At the base of the pump is a fine mesh filter

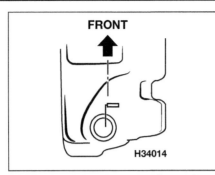

6.17 Install the sender unit with the float arm pointing to the front of the vehicle

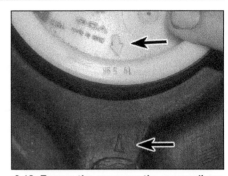

6.18 Ensure the arrow on the cover aligns with the arrow on the tank (arrowed)

the sender unit wiper and track; clean off any dirt and debris that may have accumulated and look for breaks in the track. Note the fine mesh filter on the base of the pump unit (see illustration). At the time of writing, it would appear that the pump/sender unit is only available as a complete unit.

Refitting

16 Smear the new rubber seal with clean fuel, then locate it on the flange.
17 Where applicable, insert the fuel pump/sender unit into the tank, then press down and twist it clockwise, or insert the pump/sender unit into the tank aperture. Ensure that the unit is fitted into its original position (see illustration).
18 Ensure that the arrow on the cover aligns with the mark on the fuel tank (see illustration).
19 Refit and tighten the plastic ring. To ensure the alignment arrows are opposite each other when the ring is fully tight, turn the

cover slightly anti-clockwise while the ring is being tightened.
20 Reconnect the fuel supply and return hoses and tighten the clips.
21 Reconnect the wiring connector to the pump/sender unit.
22 Refit the access hatch and tighten the screws.
23 Refit the trim to the load space floor.
24 Reconnect the battery negative (earth) lead (see Chapter 5A).

7 Fuel tank – removal and refitting

Note: *Observe the precautions in Section 1 before working on fuel system components.*

Removal

1 Before the tank can be removed, it must be

drained of as much fuel as possible. As no drain plug is provided, it is preferable to remove the tank when it is nearly empty. Alternatively, syphon or hand-pump the fuel from the tank into a suitable safe container.
2 Disconnect the battery negative lead (see Chapter 5A).
3 Fold back the front section of the carpet from the load space floor as described in Paragraphs 4 to 9 of the previous Section.
4 Slacken and remove the access hatch screws and lift the hatch away from the floorpan (see illustration 6.10).
5 Unplug the wiring connector from the pump/sender unit, and disconnect the fuel supply and return hoses. Identify each hose for position. The blue hose is the return circuit.
6 Chock the front wheels, then jack up the rear of the vehicle and support on axle stands (see *Jacking and vehicle support*).
7 Support the fuel tank with a trolley jack and a suitable piece of wood, to prevent the jack head damaging the tank.
8 Undo the four securing bolts, and remove the fuel tank retaining straps (see illustrations).
9 Using the jack, lower the tank slightly, and release the fuel supply and return pipes from the retaining clips on the tank.
10 Release the retaining clips and disconnect the breather pipes from the fuel tank (see illustrations).
11 Slide the fuel filler pipe out as the tank is lowered out of position. Take care not to damage the non-return valve fitted on the end of the fuel filler pipe (see illustration).

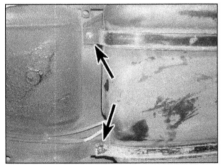

7.8a Fuel tank straps bolts at the front . . .

7.8b . . . and rear of the tank

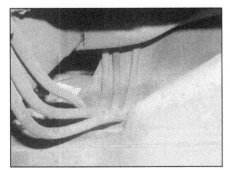

7.10a Release the fuel and breather hoses from the clips on the tank . . .

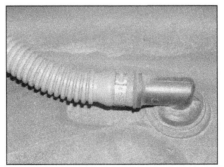

7.10b . . . and the breather hose from the connection on the tank

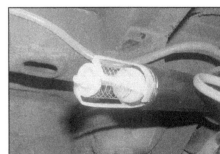

7.11 Take care not to damage the non-return valve on the filler neck as the tank is removed

8.4 Unscrew the cap from the valve on the fuel rail (arrowed)

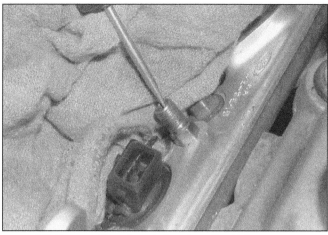

8.5 Depress the valve pin to relieve the fuel pressure

12 With the help of an assistant, lower the fuel tank to the ground and remove from under the vehicle.

13 If the tank is contaminated with sediment or water, remove the fuel pump/sender unit (see Section 6) and swill the tank out with clean fuel. The tank is injection-moulded from a synthetic material and if damaged, it should be renewed. However, in certain cases it may be possible to have small leaks or minor damage repaired by a suitable specialist. If required, the filler neck seal can be prised from its location and renewed.

Refitting

14 Refitting is the reverse of the removal procedure noting the following points:

9.4 To disconnect the brake servo pipe, depress the collar and pull the hose out

9.5a Pull the crankcase breather pipe from the valve at the front of the engine block . . .

a) When lifting the tank back into position take care to ensure none of the hoses get trapped between the tank and vehicle underbody.
b) Ensure that all pipes and hoses are correctly routed and secured.
c) Tighten the tank retaining strap bolts.
d) On completion, refill the tank with fuel and thoroughly check for signs of leakage prior to taking the vehicle out on the road.
e) Reconnect the battery as described in Chapter 5A.

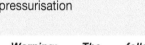

8 Fuel injection system – depressurisation

> ⚠ **Warning: The following procedure will merely relieve the pressure in the fuel system – remember that fuel will still be present in the system components and take precautions accordingly before disconnecting any of them.**

Note: *Observe the precautions in Section 1 before working on fuel system components.*

1 The fuel system referred to in this Section comprises the tank-mounted fuel pump and sender, the fuel filter, the fuel rail and injectors, the fuel pressure regulator and the metal pipes and flexible hoses of the fuel lines

9.5b . . . and from the inlet manifold

between these components. All these contain fuel which will be under pressure while the engine is running and/or while the ignition is switched on. The pressure will remain for some time after the ignition has been switched off and must be relieved before any of these components are disturbed for servicing work.

2 Disconnect the battery negative lead (see Chapter 5A).

3 Open the fuel filler flap and briefly remove the filler cap to relieve any pressure in the fuel tank. Refit the cap.

4 Place some cloth rags around the Schrader valve on the right-hand end of the fuel rail **(see illustration)**.

5 Unscrew the valve cap, and depress the valve pin using a small screwdriver (or similar). Try to absorb the fuel spray with the rags **(see illustration)**.

6 On completion, refit the valve cap.

9 Intake manifold – removal and refitting

Note: *Observe the precautions in Section 1 before working on fuel system components.*

Removal

1 Disconnect the battery negative lead (see Chapter 5A). Drain the cooling system as described in Chapter 1A.

2 Remove the fuel injectors and throttle body as described in Section 4 of this Chapter.

3 Disconnect the vacuum hose(s) from the manifold. Label the hoses for identification, and note their fitted positions.

4 Disconnect the brake servo vacuum hose from the intake manifold **(see illustration)**.

5 Undo the bolt securing the crankcase breather pipe to the left-hand end of the engine block. Carefully pull the pipe from the connection at the front of the engine block, and from the connection on the manifold **(see illustrations)**.

6 Disconnect the idle air control valve wiring

9.8a The inlet manifold is secured by five fasteners (arrowed)

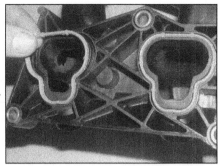

9.8b Fit new seals to the manifold

plug with reference to Section 4.

7 Slacken and remove the nut securing the power steering pipe bracket to the rear of the engine block.

8 Unscrew the nuts and bolts securing the manifold to the cylinder head, and manoeuvre it from the engine compartment. Recover the manifold-to-cylinder rubber seals. Discard the seals, new ones must be fitted (see illustrations).

Refitting

9 Refitting is the reverse of the removal procedure noting the following points:

a) Clean the contact faces of the intake manifold and cylinder head, and fit new seals.

b) Tighten nuts and bolts to the specified torque where given.

c) Renew the injector O-rings.

d) Check and if necessary adjust the accelerator cable as described in Section 3.

e) Refill/top-up the cooling system with reference to Chapter 1A.

f) Reconnect the battery as described in Chapter 5A.

10 Fuel injection system – testing and adjustment

1 If a fault appears in the fuel injection system first ensure that all the system wiring connectors are securely connected and free of corrosion. Then ensure that the fault is not due to poor maintenance; ie, check that the air cleaner filter element is clean, the spark plugs are in good condition and correctly gapped, the cylinder compression pressures are correct, the ignition timing is correct and the engine breather hoses are clear and undamaged, referring to Chapters 1A, 2A and 5B for further information. Bear in mind that if the battery has been disconnected, the stored values within the engine management ECM will be lost. These values will be relearnt after the vehicle has been driven for 10 to 25 miles.

During this period, erratic engine performance may be experienced.

2 If the engine management ECM detects a fault, or if a fault develops within the ECM itself, set values may be substituted by the module which then enters a 'limited operation strategy' or 'limp home' mode. In this condition some management operations are limited, and engine performance may be reduced. Vehicle speed may be limited to 38 mph on level ground. Once the fault(s) is rectified, and the battery reconnected, the ECM should relearn the necessary operating values over a distance of approximately 10 to 25 miles.

3 If these checks fail to reveal the cause of the problem the vehicle should be taken to a Ford dealer or suitably-equipped specialist for testing. A diagnostic connector, located under the ashtray/storage tray in the centre console (see illustration), is incorporated in the engine management system wiring harness, into which dedicated electronic test equipment can be plugged. The test equipment is capable of 'interrogating' the engine management system ECM electronically and accessing its internal fault log. In this manner, faults can be pinpointed quickly and simply, even if their occurrence is intermittent. Testing all the system components individually in an attempt to locate the fault by elimination is a time-

consuming operation that is unlikely to be fruitful (particularly if the fault occurs dynamically) and carries high risk of damage to the ECM's internal components.

4 Experienced home mechanics equipped with an accurate tachometer and a carefully-calibrated exhaust gas analyser may be able to check the exhaust gas CO content and the engine idle speed. If these are found to be out of specification, then the vehicle must be taken to a Ford dealer for assessment. Neither the air/fuel mixture (exhaust gas CO content) nor the engine idle speed are manually adjustable, therefore incorrect test results indicate a fault within the fuel injection system.

11 Fuel inertia shut-off switch – removal, refitting and resetting

Removal

1 In the event of an accident, this switch is designed to shut-off the fuel supply. Consequently, the switch can also be triggered by sudden vibrations as well, eg, a parking collision. The switch is located in the storage compartment beneath the front passenger seat. Slide the seat as far forward as possible, and remove the storage compartment panel.

2 Ensure the ignition is off, and disconnect the wiring plug from the switch.

3 Undo the two retaining screws and remove the switch (see illustration).

Refitting

4 Refitting is a reversal of removal.

Resetting

5 To reset the switch, ensure the ignition is off, and depress the button on the switch. Turn the ignition switch to position II, pause for a few seconds, then turn the ignition switch to position I.

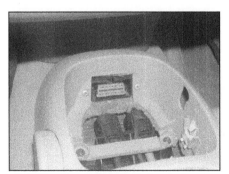

10.3 The diagnostic plug is located under the front ashtray/storage box in the centre console

11.3 Undo the screws and remove the fuel inertia shut-off switch

Chapter 4 Part B:
Fuel system – diesel

Contents

Degrees of difficulty

Easy, suitable for novice with little experience	Fairly easy, suitable for beginner with some experience	Fairly difficult, suitable for competent DIY mechanic 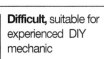	Difficult, suitable for experienced DIY mechanic	Very difficult, suitable for expert DIY or professional

Specifications

General
Maximum engine speed	5100 rpm (not adjustable ECM controlled)
Engine idle speed	900 rpm (not adjustable ECM controlled)

Fuel injectors
Injection pressure	170 bar minimum

Turbocharger
Type	Garrett
Maximum boost pressure:	
Engine code 1Z, AHU and AVG	1.7 to 1.9 bar
Engine code AFN	1.7 to 2.2 bar

Torque wrench settings
	Nm	lbf ft
Accelerator pedal position sensor	10	7
Crankshaft position sensor	10	7
Fuel cut-off solenoid	40	30
Fuel pipe unions to injection pump and injectors	25	18
Fuel tank retaining strap bolts	25	18
Heat shield to exhaust manifold	25	18
Injection pump bracket*:		
Stage 1	20	15
Stage 2	Angle-tighten a further 90°	
Injection pump mounting bolts	25	18
Injection pump sprocket	55	41
Injector clamp bolt	22	16
Intake manifold to cylinder head	25	18
Oil supply pipe bracket to exhaust manifold	25	18
Turbocharger oil return pipe to cylinder block	30	22
Turbocharger oil supply pipe	25	18
Turbocharger to catalytic converter	25	18
Turbocharger to exhaust manifold*	35	26

*Do not re-use

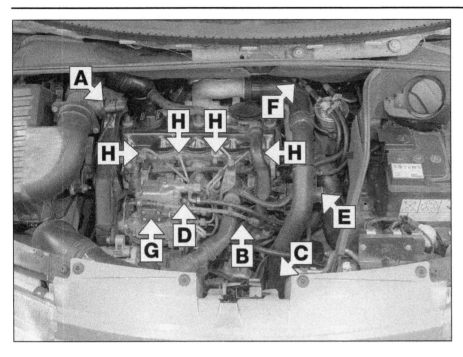

1.1 Diesel injection components

A *Mass airflow sensor*
B *Coolant temperature sensor*
C *Engine speed sensor*
D *Fuel cut-off solenoid*
E *Charge pressure/temperature sensor*
F *Charge pressure control valve*
G *Fuel injection pump*
H *Fuel injectors*

1 General information and precautions

General information

The fuel system comprise of a fuel tank, an engine-bay mounted fuel filter with an integral water separator, fuel supply and return lines, fuel injection pump and four fuel injectors. The commencement of injection is controlled by the engine management electronic control module (ECM) and a solenoid valve on the injection pump. The pump is driven at half crankshaft speed by the camshaft timing belt. Fuel is drawn from the fuel tank, through the filter by the injection pump, which then distributes the fuel under very high pressure to the injectors via separate delivery pipes. All engines are fitted with a turbocharger and an intercooler. However, on engine code AFN the turbocharger is equipped with variable vanes which change the shape of the inlet port. This increases the speed of the incoming exhaust gases at low engine speed, and the result is that full boost pressure is available over almost all of the engine speed range, decreasing fuel consumption and improving torque/power output. The operation of the guide vanes is controlled by the engine management ECM via a charge pressure sensor, and vacuum-operated actuator.

Basic injection timing is set mechanically by the position of the pump on its mounting bracket. Dynamic timing and injection duration are controlled by the ECM and are dependant on engine speed, throttle position and rate of opening, intake air flow, intake air temperature, coolant temperature, fuel temperature, ambient pressure (altitude) and manifold depression information, received from sensors mounted on and around the engine. Closed loop control of the injection timing is achieved by means of an injector needle lift sensor. Note that injector No 3 is fitted with the needle lift sensor. Two-stage injectors are used, which improve the engine's combustion characteristics, leading to quieter running and better exhaust emissions. The direct-injection fuelling system is controlled electronically by a diesel engine management system, comprising an ECM and its associated sensors, actuators and wiring (see illustration).

On all engines, the ECM also manages the operation of the Exhaust Gas Recirculation (EGR) emission control system, the turbocharger boost pressure control system and the glow plug control system.

It should be noted that fault diagnosis of the diesel engine management system is only possible with dedicated electronic test equipment. Problems with the system's operation should therefore be referred to a Ford dealer or suitably-equipped specialist for assessment. Once the fault has been identified, the removal/refitting sequences detailed in the following Sections will then allow the appropriate component(s) to be renewed as required.

Note: *Throughout this Chapter, vehicles are frequently referred to by their engine code, rather than by their engine capacity – refer to Chapter 2B for engine code listings.*

Precautions

Many of the operations described in this Chapter involve the disconnection of fuel lines, which may cause an amount of fuel spillage. Before commencing work, refer to the warnings below and the information in *Safety first!* at the beginning of this manual.

Warning: When working on any part of the fuel system, avoid direct contact skin contact with diesel fuel – wear protective clothing and gloves when handling fuel system components. Ensure that the work area is well-ventilated to prevent the build-up of diesel fuel vapour.

Fuel injectors operate at extremely high pressures and the jet of fuel produced at the nozzle is capable of piercing skin, with potentially fatal results. When working with pressurised injectors, take care to avoid exposing any part of the body to the fuel spray. It is recommended that a diesel fuel systems specialist should carry out any pressure testing of the fuel system components.

Under no circumstances should diesel fuel be allowed to come into contact with coolant hoses – wipe off accidental spillage immediately. Hoses that have been contaminated with fuel for an extended period should be renewed. Diesel fuel systems are particularly sensitive to contamination from dirt, air and water. Pay particular attention to cleanliness when working on any part of the fuel system, to prevent the ingress of dirt. Thoroughly clean the area around fuel unions before disconnecting them. Store dismantled components in sealed containers to prevent contamination and the formation of condensation. Only use lint-free cloths and clean fuel for component cleansing.

2.1a Disconnect the wiring from the mass airflow sensor . . .

2.1b . . . and disconnect the vacuum hose

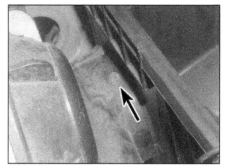

2.5 Undo the screw and remove the intake pipe

2.6 Air cleaner mounting points (arrowed)

2.10 Release the clips and disconnect the rear air ducts

2 Air cleaner and intake ducts – removal and refitting

Removal

1 Disconnect the wiring from the mass airflow sensor on the air cleaner outlet ducting. Also disconnect the small hose from the air cleaner upper housing **(see illustrations)**.
2 Release the wiring harness from the clip on the air cleaner cover.
3 Undo the retaining screws and detach the mass airflow sensor from the air cleaner assembly.
4 Release the three spring clips and withdraw the air cleaner cover, then remove the filter element (see Chapter 1B for more details).
5 Undo the screw and remove the air cleaner intake pipe **(see illustration)**.

6 The air cleaner housing is secured by three lugs, which locate in corresponding grommets in the inner wing. Gently pull the housing until the lugs disengage from the grommets **(see illustration)**. Manoeuvre the housing from the engine compartment.
7 To remove the remaining ducting, apply the handbrake, then jack up the front of the vehicle and support it on axle stands (see *Jacking and vehicle support*). Undo the two nuts and four bolts (two each side), and remove the engine undershield.
8 Loosen the clips and disconnect the hose from the intercooler and air pipe on the left-hand side of the engine compartment.
9 Loosen the clip and disconnect the air cleaner hose from the right-hand side of the turbo, then unbolt and remove the air pipe.

10 Loosen the clips and disconnect the rear air ducts from the intercooler and intake manifold. Disconnect the wiring and hoses as applicable, then unscrew the mounting bolts and remove the ducts **(see illustration)**.

Refitting

11 Refitting is a reversal of removal.

3 Accelerator pedal position sensor – removal and refitting

Models up to 09.97

Removal

1 Open the fusebox on the driver's side of the facia, pulling the panel downwards, then outwards, and remove it from the vehicle. Pull the lower fusebox cover downwards, and remove it **(see illustration)**.
2 Undo the single screw and remove the cover from the accelerator pedal position sensor.
3 Release the sensor wiring plug from the retaining bracket, and disconnect it.
4 Unscrew the bolts and remove the accelerator pedal position sensor **(see illustration)**.
5 Detach the operating cable from the pedal, then lift the sensor from the bracket **(see illustration)**.

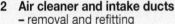

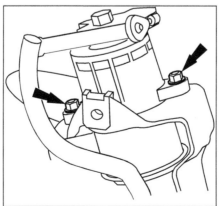

3.1 Pull the lower fusebox cover downwards and remove it

3.4 Undo the sensor retaining bolts (arrowed)

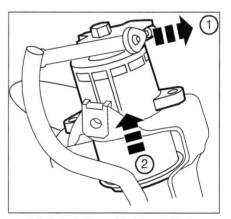

3.5 Detach the cable (1) and lift the sensor (2)

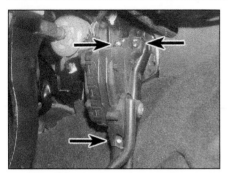

3.13 Undo the bolts (arrowed), then remove the pedal, bracket and sensor

Refitting

6 Locate the position sensor on the bracket, then insert and tighten the screws to the specified torque.
7 Locate the operating cable on the pedal.
8 Reconnect the wiring for the position sensor.
9 Position the cover over the sensor, and tighten the single securing screw.
10 Refit the trim panels beneath the steering column.

Models from 09.97

Removal

11 Open the fusebox on the driver's side of the facia, pulling the panel downwards, then outwards, and remove it from the vehicle. Pull the lower fusebox cover downwards, and remove it **(see illustration 3.1)**.
12 Disconnect the wiring from the accelerator pedal position sensor.
13 Undo the bolts, and remove the pedal, bracket and sensor **(see illustration)**.
14 No further dismantling of the sensor is recommended – at the time of writing the sensor was only available as a complete assembly with the pedal and bracket. If the sender if faulty, a new assembly must be fitted.

Refitting

15 Position the assembly in place on the bulkhead.
16 Insert and tighten the bolts to the specified torque. Reconnect the wiring plug, and refit the under dash trim panels.

4.8 Undo the three screws and remove the access hatch

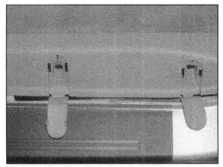

4.3 Pull down the flaps, undo the screws, and remove the door sill trim panels

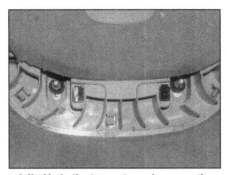

4.4b Undo the two nuts and remove the centre vent

4 Fuel gauge sender unit – removal and refitting

Note: *Observe the precautions in Section 1 before working on fuel system components.*

Removal

1 The fuel gauge sender unit is mounted in the fuel tank. Access is via a hatch provided in the load space floor. Removal of the unit exposes the contents of the tank to the atmosphere, so extreme care must be exercised to prevent fire. The area inside and around the car must be well-ventilated to prevent a build-up of fuel fumes. If possible, remove the unit when the fuel tank is nearly empty, or alternatively syphon the fuel from the tank into a suitable container.
2 Pull the weatherstrips from the door apertures adjacent to the sill trim panels.

4.9 Disconnect the sender unit wiring plug

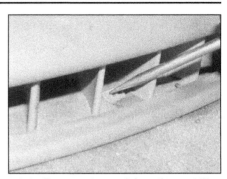

4.4a Depress the retaining clips and lift the cover away

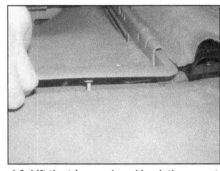

4.6 Lift the trims and peel back the carpet

3 Lever open the plastic flaps, undo the two screws each side, and remove both door sill trim panels **(see illustration)**.
4 Depress the three retaining clips, and lift the floor-mounted centre rear air vent cover. Undo the two nuts and remove the vent **(see illustrations)**.
5 Undo the screws securing seat mounting trims to the floor for the second row of seats.
6 Carefully prise up the trims at the front edge of the rear carpet, and fold the front half of the carpet to the rear **(see illustration)**.
7 Undo the retaining bolts and remove the seat mounting rail over the access hatch.
8 Slacken and remove the access hatch screws and lift the hatch away from the floorpan **(see illustration)**.
9 Unplug the wiring connector from the sender unit **(see illustration)**.
10 Release the clips and disconnect the fuel supply and return hoses **(see illustration)**. Identify each hose for position.

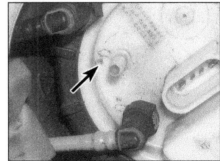

4.10 Note the arrows on the cover indicating supply and return (arrowed)

11 Unscrew the plastic ring securing the pump/sender unit cover to the tank. Ford technicians use a special tool to unscrew the ring, however two screwdrivers engaged with the slots in the ring and crossed over each other may be used with success. Alternatively use a pair of large water pump pliers **(see illustration)**.

12 Lift out the sender assembly. Discard the aperture seal, a new one must be fitted.

13 Inspect the float on the sender unit swinging arm for punctures and fuel ingress, and renew it if it appears damaged. Inspect the sender unit wiper and track; clean off any dirt and debris that may have accumulated and look for breaks in the track. At the time of writing, it would appear that the sender unit is only available as a complete unit.

Refitting

14 Smear the new rubber seal with clean fuel, then locate it in the tank aperture.

15 Lower the sender unit into the tank. Ensure that the arrow on the flange aligns with the mark on the fuel tank **(see illustration)**.

16 Screw on and tighten the plastic ring. To ensure the alignment arrows are opposite each other when the ring is fully tight, turn the flange slightly anti-clockwise while the ring is being tightened.

17 Reconnect the fuel supply and return hoses and tighten the clips.

18 Reconnect the wiring connector to the sender unit.

19 Refit the access hatch and tighten the screws.

20 Refit the trim to the load space floor.

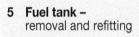

5 Fuel tank – removal and refitting

Note: *Observe the precautions in Section 1 before working on fuel system components.*

Removal

1 Before the tank can be removed, it must be drained of as much fuel as possible. As no drain plug is provided, it is preferable

4.11 Unscrew the plastic ring

to remove the tank when it is nearly empty.

2 Remove the carpet from the load space floor as described in Chapter 11, Section 31.

3 Slacken and remove the access hatch screws and lift the hatch away from the floorpan.

4 Unplug the wiring connector from the sender unit, and disconnect the fuel supply and return hoses. Identify each hose for position.

5 Chock the front wheels, then jack up the rear of the vehicle and support on axle stands (see *Jacking and vehicle support*).

6 Support the fuel tank with a trolley jack and a suitable piece of wood, to prevent the jack head damaging the tank.

7 Undo the four securing bolts, and remove the fuel tank retaining straps **(see illustrations)**.

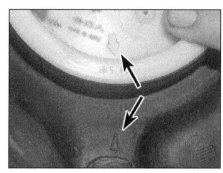

4.15 Ensure the arrows align (arrowed)

8 Using the jack, lower the tank slightly, and release the fuel supply and return pipes from the retaining clips on the tank.

9 Release the retaining clips and disconnect the breather pipes from the fuel tank **(see illustrations)**.

10 Detach the fuel filler pipe as the tank is lowered out of position **(see illustration)**.

11 With the help of an assistant, lower the fuel tank to the ground and remove from under the vehicle.

12 If the tank is contaminated with sediment or water, remove the fuel sender unit (see Section 4) and swill the tank out with clean fuel. The tank is injection-moulded from a synthetic material and if damaged, it should be renewed. However, in certain cases it may be possible to have small leaks or minor damage repaired by a suitable specialist.

5.7a Fuel tank straps bolts at the front . . .

5.7b . . . and at the rear

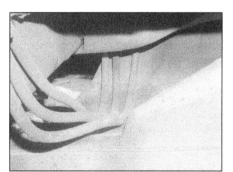

5.9a Release the fuel and breather hoses from the clips on the tank . . .

5.9b . . . and the breather hose from the connection on the tank

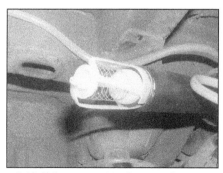

5.10 Take care not to damage the non-return valve on the filler neck as the tank is removed

6.4 Hold the sprocket and slacken the nut

6.6a Pull the sprocket . . .

6.6b . . . remove it from the shaft . . .

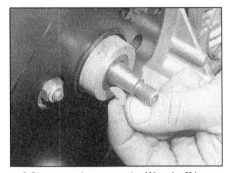

6.6c . . . and recover the Woodruff key

6.7a Disconnect the fuel inlet . . .

6.7b . . . and return hoses

Refitting

13 Refitting is the reverse of the removal procedure noting the following points:
  a) *When lifting the tank back into position take care to ensure none of the hoses get trapped between the tank and vehicle underbody.*
  b) *Ensure that all pipes and hoses are correctly routed and secured.*
  c) *Tighten the tank retaining strap bolts.*
  d) *On completion, refill the tank with fuel and thoroughly check for signs of leakage prior to taking the vehicle out on the road.*

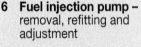

6 Fuel injection pump –
removal, refitting and adjustment

Note: *Observe the precautions in Section 1 before working on fuel system components. In order to check and adjust the injection timing, dedicated test equipment is required to access the ECM's built-in self diagnostic facilities. If such equipment is not available, the pump should be refitted as described here, and the vehicle taken to a Ford dealer or diesel injection specialist to have the timing checked, and if necessary, adjusted.*

Removal

1 Remove the air cleaner housing with reference to Section 2.
2 Prise out the cover caps, undo the retaining nuts and remove the plastic cover from the top of the engine.
3 Remove the timing belt, as described in Chapter 2B.

4 Slacken the injection pump sprocket retaining nut/bolt by holding the injection pump sprocket stationary using a suitable tool engaged with the holes in the sprocket **(see illustration)**.
5 Unscrew the injection pump sprocket nut approximately 1 turn.
6 Using a suitable puller, release the sprocket from the injection pump shaft. **Do not** strike the puller hard in an attempt to release the sprocket, otherwise the injection pump may be damaged. Unscrew the nut and remove the sprocket. Recover the Woodruff key from the slot in the shaft **(see illustrations)**.
7 Unscrew the union bolts and disconnect the fuel inlet and return hoses from the injection pump **(see illustrations)**. Recover the sealing washers.
8 Note and identify the wiring connections on the fuel injection pump, then disconnect them.

6.9 Unscrew the fuel pipe union nuts

9 Unscrew the union nuts securing the fuel pipes to the injectors and fuel injection pump, and remove them as a complete set **(see illustration)**. Hold the adapters stationary with a further spanner. Take care not to bend the pipes.
10 Cover the open pipes and ports to prevent the ingress of dust and dirt **(see Haynes Hint)**.
11 Mark the position of the injection pump in relation to the mounting bracket as a guide to refitting. Unscrew the nuts/bolt securing the injection pump to the inner timing cover. The two inner nuts are accessed from the front of the inner timing cover, and the remaining bolt is accessed from the injection pump side of the mounting bracket.
12 Unscrew the rear mounting bolt/nut and

HAYNES HiNT

Fit a short length of hose over the banjo bolt (arrowed) so that the drillings are covered, then thread the bolt back into its injection pump port withdraw the injection pump from the mounting bracket **(see illustration)**.

Refitting and adjustment

13 Locate the injection pump in the mounting bracket, refit the rear mounting bolt finger tight only at this stage.

14 Rotate the injection pump body as necessary to centralise it within the slotted holes at the front of the mounting bracket, then refit and tighten the front mounting bolt/nuts. If the original pump is being refitted, align the previously made marks and tighten the mounting bolts. Unless the dynamic timing adjustment procedure is to be carried out straightaway using Ford diagnostic equipment, tighten the pump mounting nuts/bolts to the specified torque.

15 Insert the Woodruff key in the slot in the shaft, then refit the sprocket and nut. Hold the sprocket stationary with the tool used for removal, and tighten the nut to the specified torque.

16 Align the TDC pin holes, and insert the pin to lock the sprocket in the TDC position.

17 Refit the timing belt and tensioner as described in Chapter 2B.

18 Reconnect the wiring plugs and fuel pipes to the injection pump.

19 Refit the fuel inlet and return hoses together with new sealing washers and tighten the union bolts to the specified torque. Make sure that the union bolt with the non-return valve is fitted to the return line.

20 Refit the camshaft cover with reference to Chapter 2B, then refit the upper outer timing cover.

21 Reconnect the battery negative (earth) lead (see Chapter 5A).

22 The injection pump must now be bled using a hand-operated vacuum pump. The Ford vacuum pump includes a container in the hose to receive the fuel as it is drawn from the pump. Connect the pump to the return union on the injection pump and operate the vacuum pump until fuel free of bubbles flows into the container. Do not allow the fuel to enter the vacuum pump.

23 Refit the return hose, then start the engine and check for fuel leaks.

24 There is no static pump adjustment procedure recommended by the manufacturer. The injection timing can only be checked and adjusted dynamically by a Ford

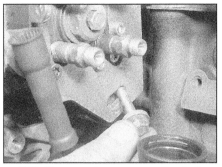

6.12 Unscrew the rear mounting bolt

dealer or injection specialist, who will have the equipment necessary to carry out the check.

25 After making an adjustment to the injection pump timing, always loosen the fuel pipe union nuts and retighten them to relieve any tension which may cause them to fracture after constant vibration.

26 Refit the plastic cover to the top of the engine.

7 Injectors – general information, removal and refitting

Note: *Observe the precautions in Section 1 before working on fuel system components.*

⚠️ *Warning: Exercise extreme caution when working on the fuel injectors. Never expose the hands or any part of the body to injector spray, as the high working pressure can cause the fuel to penetrate the skin, with possibly fatal results. You are strongly advised to have any work which involves testing the injectors under pressure carried out by a dealer or fuel injection specialist.*

General information

1 Injectors do deteriorate with prolonged use and it is reasonable to expect them to need reconditioning or renewal after 100 000 miles (160 000 km) or so. Accurate testing, overhaul and calibration of the injectors must be left to a specialist. A defective injector which is causing knocking or smoking can be located without dismantling as follows.

2 Run the engine at a fast idle. Slacken each injector union in turn, placing rag around the

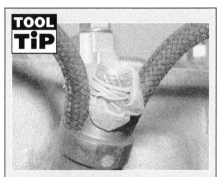

Cut the fingertips from an old pair of rubber gloves and secure them over the fuel ports with elastic bands.

union to catch spilt fuel and being careful not to expose the skin to any spray. When the union on the defective injector is slackened, the knocking or smoking will stop.

Removal

Note: *Take care not to allow dirt into the injectors or fuel pipes during this procedure. Do not drop the injectors or allow the needles at their tips to become damaged. The injectors are precision-made to fine limits and must not be handled roughly.*

3 Cover the alternator with a clean cloth or plastic bag to prevent the possibility of fuel being spilt onto it.

4 Carefully clean around the injectors and pipe union nuts and disconnect the return pipes from the injectors.

5 Wipe clean the pipe unions then slacken the union nuts securing the injector pipes to the injectors and the union nuts securing the pipes to the rear of the injection pump (the pipes are removed as one assembly); as each pump union nut is slackened, retain the adapter with a suitable open-ended spanner to prevent it being unscrewed from the pump. With the union nuts undone, remove the injector pipes from the engine. Cover the injector and pipe unions to prevent the entry of dirt into the system **(see Haynes Hint)**.

6 Disconnect the wiring for the needle lift sensor from injector No 3.

7 Carefully pull the wiring plugs from the glow plugs.

8 Unscrew the injector clamp retaining bolts. Remove the washers, then remove the clamps and spacers **(see illustrations)**.

7.8a Unscrew the bolt . . .

7.8b . . . and remove the clamp . . .

7.8c . . . and spacer

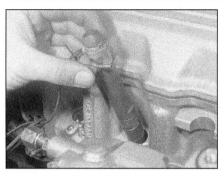

7.9 Remove the injector from the cylinder head

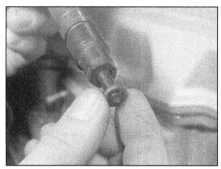

7.11a Locate a new heat shield washer on the injector before refitting it

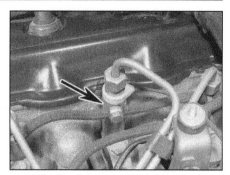

7.11b The injector with the needle lift sensor (arrowed) is second from the left

9 Withdraw the injectors from the cylinder head **(see illustration)**. If they are tight, ease them out by turning them with a spanner on their flats. If they are seized in position, Ford technicians use a slide hammer tool which is screwed onto the pipe union thread. Note that the injector second from the left is higher than the rest (No 3 cylinder), and incorporates a needle lift sensing device which sends a signal to the engine management ECM.

10 Using a screwdriver, hook out the copper heat shield washers from the injector recesses in the cylinder head. New ones must be obtained for refitting.

Refitting

11 Insert the injectors into position, using new copper heat shield washers. Make sure that the injector with the needle lift sensor is located in No 3 position **(see illustrations)**.

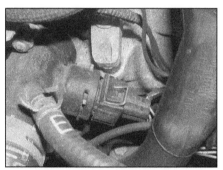

8.1 The coolant temperature sensor is located on the front of the cylinder head

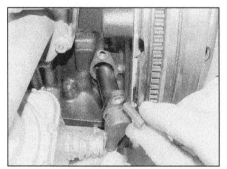

8.5 Engine speed sensor (shown with the engine removed)

12 Fit the mounting collars and retaining clamps, and secure in position with the washers and bolts, tightened to the specified torque.

13 Reconnect the wiring for the needle stroke transmitter on injector No 3.

14 Refit the injector pipes and tighten the union nuts to the specified torque setting.

15 Reconnect the return pipes to the injectors.

16 Start the engine and check that it runs correctly.

8 Engine management system components – removal and refitting

Note: *Observe the precautions in Section 1 before working on the fuel system.*

Coolant temperature sensor

Removal

1 The coolant temperature sensor is located on the front of the cylinder head **(see illustration)**. Prise out the cover caps, undo the retaining nuts and remove the engine cover.

2 Drain approximately one quarter of the coolant from the engine with reference to Chapter 1B.

3 Disconnect the wiring, pull out the retaining clip, and remove the sensor. The sensor can be tested using a multimeter. Connect the multimeter leads to the terminals of the sensor and set the meter to measure resistance

8.10 Unscrew the nut and disconnect the wiring

(ohms). As the temperature increases, the resistance of the sensor decreases. So at 30°C the resistance should be 1500 to 2000 ohms, and at 80°C the resistance should be 275 to 375 ohms. If the resistance value of the sensor does not match these values, or fails to change, it must be renewed.

Refitting

4 Refitting is a reversal of removal. Top-up the cooling system with reference to Chapter 1B.

Crankshaft position sensor

Removal

5 The crankshaft position sensor is mounted on the front left-hand side of the cylinder block, adjacent to the mating surface of the block and transmission bellhousing **(see illustration)**. Prise out the cover caps, undo the retaining nuts and remove the engine cover.

6 Trace the wiring back from the sensor to the connector and disconnect it.

7 Undo the retaining screw and withdraw the sensor from the cylinder block. The sensor can be tested using a multimeter. Connect the multimeter leads to terminals 1 (adjacent to the square side of the plug) and 2 (centre terminal) of the sensor plug, and set the meter to measure resistance (ohms). If the sensor is usable, the resistance should be 1000 to 1500 ohms. If the sensor resistance is outside this range, renew the sensor.

Refitting

8 Refitting is a reversal of removal. Tighten the sensor retaining bolt to the specified torque.

Fuel cut-off solenoid

Removal

9 The fuel cut-off solenoid is located on top of the distributor head on the fuel injection pump. Prise out the cover caps, undo the retaining nuts and remove the engine cover. Clean the area around the solenoid to prevent dust and dirt entering the fuel system.

10 To remove the solenoid, unscrew the nut and disconnect the wiring **(see illustration)**.

11 Unscrew the solenoid and remove the O-ring, spring and plunger.

8.18 Charge pressure control valve

Refitting

12 Refitting is a reversal of removal, but clean all components before fitting and tighten the solenoid to the specified torque.

Start of injection valve
Removal

13 The start of injection valve is located just below the distributor head on the fuel injection pump. Prise out the cover caps, undo the retaining nuts and remove the engine cover. Clean the area around the valve to prevent dust and dirt entering the fuel system.
14 Undo the screw and withdraw the valve from the injection pump. Be prepared for some loss of fuel.
15 Recover the outer O-ring, strainer and inner O-ring.
16 Disconnect the wiring at the connector.

Refitting

17 Refitting is a reversal of removal, but clean all components before fitting and tighten the screw securely.

Charge pressure control valve
Removal

18 The charge pressure control valve is located on the bulkhead in the left-hand rear corner of the engine compartment (see illustration).
19 Disconnect the wiring from the valve.
20 Remove the vacuum hoses, noting their order of connection carefully to aid correct refitting.

8.28 Release the clip (arrowed) and disconnect the air ducting

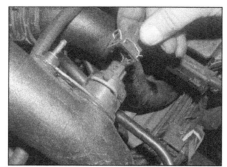

8.23 Disconnect the charge pressure sensor fitted to the air ducting

21 Unscrew the mounting nuts and withdraw the valve.

Refitting

22 Refitting is a reversal of removal.

Air intake charge pressure/temperature sensor

Note: The charge pressure sensor pipe take-off port is incorporated into the temperature sensor assembly. However, the charge pressure sensor is incorporated into the engine management ECM, and is not available separately.

Removal

23 The air intake charge pressure port/temperature sensor is located on the air duct leading from the intercooler to the intake manifold, on the left-hand side of the engine compartment. First disconnect the wiring and the pressure hose (see illustration).
24 Undo the screws and remove the sensor from the air duct.

Refitting

25 Refitting is a reversal of removal.

Mass airflow sensor
Removal

26 The mass airflow sensor is located in the ducting from the air cleaner.
27 Disconnect the wiring plug from the sensor (see illustration 2.1a).

28 Loosen the clip and disconnect the air ducting from the airflow sensor (see illustration).
29 Undo the two bolts and remove the sensor. Recover the O-ring seal.

Refitting

30 Refitting is a reversal of removal. The O-ring seal can be re-used, providing it is in good condition. Tighten the retaining bolts securely.

Electronic control module (ECM)

Caution: Always wait at least 30 seconds after switching off the ignition before disconnecting the wiring from the ECM. When the wiring is disconnected, all the learned values may be erased, however any contents of the fault memory are retained. After reconnecting the wiring, the values will be relearned after approximately 10 to 25 miles. During this period, engine performance may be erratic. Note also that if the ECM is renewed, the identification of the new ECM must be transferred to the immobiliser control unit by an Ford dealer or specialist.

Removal

31 The ECM is located behind the instrument panel.
32 Disconnect the battery negative (earth) lead (see Chapter 5A).
33 Remove the instrument panel as described in Chapter 12.
34 Where fitted, unscrew the retaining bolt and move the bulb monitor unit to one side (see illustration).
35 Remove the driver's side lower facia panel trim as described in Chapter 11, Section 31.

⚠ Warning: Wait a minimum of 30 seconds after switching off the ignition, before disconnecting the ECM wiring connector.

36 Working under the facia, undo the ECM clip retaining screw, and pull the clip sideways.
37 Release the wiring plug(s) and disconnect it from the ECM. Disconnect the vacuum pipe and remove the ECM.

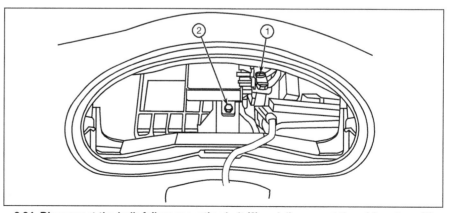

8.34 Disconnect the bulb failure mounting bolt (2) and disconnect the wiring plugs (1)

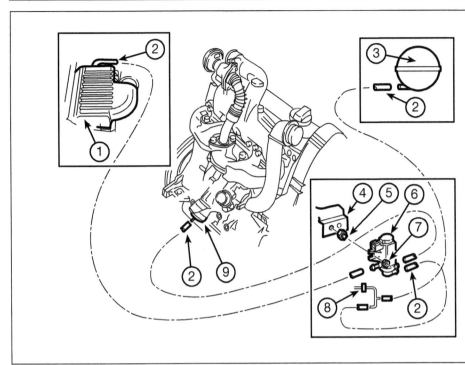

1 Air cleaner
2 Vacuum pipe
3 Vacuum canister
4 Vacuum canister bracket
5 Rubber mounting
6 Charger pressure control valve
7 Nut
8 One-way valve
9 Vacuum actuator diaphragm

9.1 Turbocharger vacuum connections

Refitting

38 Refitting is a reversal of removal. Reconnect the battery as described in Chapter 5A.

Fuel temperature sensor

Removal

39 The fuel temperature sender is located in the top of the injection pump, below the cover.
40 Undo the screws and lift the top cover from the injection pump. Recover the gasket.
41 Undo the screws and remove the fuel temperature sensor.

Refitting

42 Refitting is a reversal of removal.

Altitude sensor

43 The altitude sensor is built into the engine management ECM. It is not available as a separate part. If the sensor is defective, the ECM must be replaced.

---

9 Turbocharger – general information, removal and refitting

General information

1 A turbocharger is fitted to all diesel engines, and is mounted directly on the exhaust manifold. Lubrication is provided by an oil supply pipe that runs from the engine oil filter mounting. Oil is returned to the sump via a return pipe that connects to the side of the cylinder block. The turbocharger unit has an integral wastegate valve or variable intake vane (depending on model) and vacuum actuator diaphragm, which is used to control the boost pressure applied to the intake manifold **(see illustration)**.
2 The turbocharger's internal components rotate at a very high speed, and as such are very sensitive to contamination; a great deal of damage can be caused by small particles of dirt, particularly if they strike the delicate turbine blades.
Caution: Thoroughly clean the area around all oil pipe unions before disconnecting them, to prevent the ingress of dirt. Store dismantled components in a sealed container to prevent contamination. Cover the turbocharger air intake ducts to prevent debris entering, and clean using lint-free cloths only.

Removal

3 Apply the handbrake, then jack up the front of the vehicle and support it on axle stands (see *Jacking and vehicle support*). Undo the two retaining nuts and four bolts (two each side), and remove the engine compartment undershield.
4 Prise out the cover caps, undo the retaining bolts and remove the engine top cover. Pull out the battery compartment upper panel, then undo the three retaining screws and remove the engine compartment bulkhead cover **(see illustration)**. Slide the cover to the right-hand side and manoeuvre it from behind the coolant expansion tank.

5 Unscrew the air intake pipe retaining bolts from the right-hand rear corner of the cylinder head.
6 Slacken and remove the nut securing the turbocharger oil supply pipe bracket to the manifold at the rear left-hand side of the cylinder head.
7 Unscrew the union nut and disconnect the oil supply pipe from the turbocharger **(see illustration)**. Release the oil supply pipe supporting bracket from its mounting point.
8 Unscrew the union bolts and disconnect the oil return pipe from the turbocharger. Plug or cover the pipe and aperture to prevent entry of dust and dirt. Be prepared for oil spillage.
9 Unscrew the turbocharger-to-exhaust manifold mounting bolts but leave the two front bolts loose to support the unit.
10 Slacken and remove the nuts/bolts securing the front section of the exhaust pipe

9.4 The bulkhead cover is secured by three screws (two shown)

Fuel system - diesel 4B•11

to the turbocharger and the catalytic converter **(see illustration)**. Release the front section of the exhaust pipe from the rubber mountings, and remove the pipe.

11 Loosen the clips and disconnect the air outlet hose from the turbocharger.

12 Undo the two bolts and disconnect the air intake pipe from the turbocharger.

13 Note the location of the vacuum hose then disconnect it from the wastegate actuator **(see illustration)**.

14 Undo the nut and bolt securing the turbocharger support bracket. Remove the last two mounting bolts, and withdraw the turbocharger from the exhaust manifold. Recover the gasket.

Refitting

15 Refit the turbocharger by following the removal procedure in reverse, noting the following points:

a) Renew the gaskets.

b) Renew all self-locking nuts.

c) Before reconnecting the oil supply pipe, fill the turbocharger with fresh oil using an oil can.

d) Tighten all nuts and bolts to the specified torque where given.

e) When the engine is started after refitting, allow it to idle for approximately one minute to give the oil time to circulate around the turbine shaft bearings.

10 Intercooler – removal and refitting

Removal

1 Apply the handbrake, then jack up the front of the vehicle and support it on axle stands (see *Jacking and vehicle support*). Remove the engine compartment undertray.

2 The intercooler is located below the radiator. Release the retaining clips and

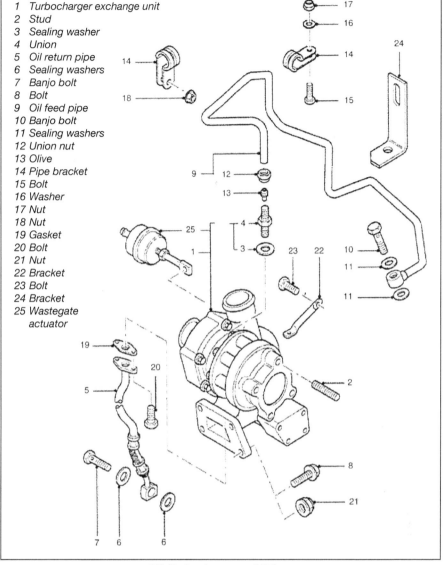

1 Turbocharger exchange unit
2 Stud
3 Sealing washer
4 Union
5 Oil return pipe
6 Sealing washers
7 Banjo bolt
8 Bolt
9 Oil feed pipe
10 Banjo bolt
11 Sealing washers
12 Union nut
13 Olive
14 Pipe bracket
15 Bolt
16 Washer
17 Nut
18 Nut
19 Gasket
20 Bolt
21 Nut
22 Bracket
23 Bolt
24 Bracket
25 Wastegate actuator

9.7 Turbocharger and fittings

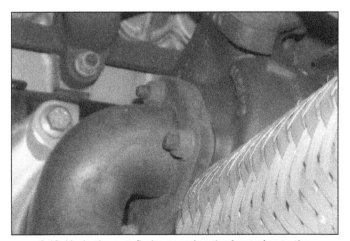

9.10 Undo the nuts/bolts securing the front pipe to the turbocharger

9.13 Disconnect the vacuum pipe from the wastegate actuator

disconnect the intercooler inlet and outlet hoses **(see illustrations)**.

3 Working as described in Chapter 3, remove the radiator mounting bolts, and move the radiator to the rear sufficiently to gain access to the intercooler mounting bolts.

4 Undo the intercooler mounting bolts.

5 Manoeuvre the intercooler from underneath the vehicle.

Refitting

6 Refitting is a reversal of removal.

11 Intake manifold – removal and refitting

Removal

1 Pull out the upper part of the battery compartment panel. Undo the retaining screws and remove the bulkhead panel cover from the rear of the engine compartment **(see illustration 9.4)**. Slide the panel to the right-hand side and manoeuvre it from behind the coolant expansion tank.

10.2a Release the clips and disconnect the intercooler inlet hose . . .

2 Prise out the cover caps, undo the retaining nuts and remove the engine top cover.

3 Release the retaining clips and detach the air intake pipe from the intake manifold.

4 Remove the bolt securing the air intake pipe support bracket to the right-hand end of the intake manifold.

5 Unbolt the EGR valve and pipe from the intake and exhaust manifolds and move the assembly to one side. It is not necessary to disconnect the vacuum hose from the EGR valve.

10.2b . . . and outlet hose

6 Unbolt the oil supply pipe bracket from the exhaust manifold and cylinder head. Undo the unions on the oil filter housing and turbocharger, and remove the supply pipe.

7 Slacken and remove the six nuts, and manoeuvre the manifold from the engine. Recover the gasket.

Refitting

8 Refitting is a reversal of removal, using a new manifold gasket. Tighten all nuts/bolts to the specified torque where given.

4C•1

Chapter 4 Part C:
Emission control and exhaust systems

Contents

Catalytic converter – general information and precautions 7
Crankcase emission system – general information 3
Evaporative loss emission control system – information and
    component renewal 2
Exhaust Gas Recirculation (EGR) system – component removal . . . 4
Exhaust manifold – removal and refitting 5
Exhaust system – component renewal 6
General information 1
Secondary air injection system – information and
    component renewal 8

Degrees of difficulty

Easy, suitable for novice with little experience	**Fairly easy,** suitable for beginner with some experience	**Fairly difficult,** suitable for competent DIY mechanic 	**Difficult,** suitable for experienced DIY mechanic	**Very difficult,** suitable for expert DIY or professional

Specifications

Torque wrench settings	Nm	lbf ft
Catalytic converter to front pipe:		
Diesel engines	25	18
Petrol engines	35	26
EGR valve to inlet manifold	25	18
EGR/secondary air injection pipe to exhaust manifold:		
Diesel engines	25	18
Petrol engines	35	26
Exhaust manifold to cylinder head:		
Diesel engines	25	18
Petrol engines:		
Studs	14	10
Nuts	23	17
Front exhaust pipe to manifold:		
2.0 litre engines	35	26
2.3 litre engines	44	32
Front exhaust pipe to turbocharger	25	18
Oxygen sensor	42	31
Turbocharger to exhaust manifold	35	26

1 General information

Emission control systems

All petrol engine models are designed to use unleaded petrol and are controlled by engine management systems that are programmed to give the best compromise between driveability, fuel consumption and exhaust emission production. In addition, a number of systems are fitted that help to minimise other harmful emissions. A crankcase emission control system is fitted, which reduces the release of pollutants from the engines lubrication system, and a catalytic converter is fitted which reduces exhaust gas pollutant. An evaporative loss emission control system is fitted which reduces the release of gaseous hydrocarbons from the fuel tank, and a secondary injection system is fitted to reduce the catalytic converter warm-up time.

Diesel-engined models have a crankcase emission control system, and in addition are fitted with a catalytic converter, and an Exhaust Gas Recirculation (EGR) system to reduce exhaust emissions.

Crankcase emission control

To reduce the emission of unburned hydrocarbons from the crankcase into the atmosphere, the engine is sealed and the blow-by gases and oil vapour are drawn from inside the crankcase, through a wire mesh oil separator, into the inlet tract to be burned by the engine during normal combustion. All diesel engines have a pressure regulating valve on the camshaft cover, to control the flow of gases from the crankcase. On petrol models the valve is fitted into the tubing from the cylinder block.

Exhaust emission control
Petrol models

To minimise the amount of pollutants which escape into the atmosphere, all petrol models are fitted with a three-way catalytic converter in the exhaust system. The fuelling system is of the closed-loop type, in which an oxygen sensor in the exhaust system provides the engine management system ECM with constant feedback, enabling the ECM to adjust the air/fuel mixture to optimise combustion. Some models are also fitted with a second oxygen sensor after the catalytic converter, to inform the ECM of the oxygen content of the post-catalyst gases.

The oxygen sensor(s) has a heating element built-in that is controlled by the ECM through the oxygen sensor relay to quickly bring the sensor's tip to its optimum operating temperature. The sensor's tip is sensitive to oxygen and relays a voltage signal to the ECM that varies according on the amount of oxygen in the exhaust gas. If the inlet air/fuel mixture is too rich, the exhaust gases are low in oxygen so the sensor sends a low-voltage signal, the voltage rising as the mixture

weakens and the amount of oxygen rises in the exhaust gases. Peak conversion efficiency of all major pollutants occurs if the inlet air/fuel mixture is maintained at the chemically-correct ratio for the complete combustion of petrol of 14.7 parts (by weight) of air to 1 part of fuel (the stoichiometric ratio). The sensor output voltage alters in a large step at this point, the ECM using the signal change as a reference point and correcting the inlet air/fuel mixture accordingly by altering the fuel injector pulse width. Details of the oxygen sensor removal and refitting are given in Chapter 4A, Section 4.

An Exhaust Gas Recirculation (EGR) system is also fitted to some models. This reduces the level of nitrogen oxides produced during combustion by introducing a proportion of the exhaust gas back into the inlet manifold, under certain engine operating conditions, via a plunger valve. The system is controlled electronically by the engine management ECM.

In order to work efficiently, the catalytic converter needs to heated to a temperature of at least 300°C. So that the exhaust gases can heat the catalyst up faster, petrol models are equipped with a secondary air injection system. During the initial warm-up stage, fresh air is injected behind the exhaust valves, this enriches the exhaust gases with oxygen, which causes an 'afterburning' effect, which shortens the catalyst warm-up phase. The activation of the secondary air injection pump and inlet valve, is controlled by the engine management ECM.

Diesel models

An oxidation catalyst is fitted in the exhaust system of all diesel engined models. This has the effect of removing a large proportion of the gaseous hydrocarbons, carbon monoxide and particulates present in the exhaust gas.

An Exhaust Gas Recirculation (EGR) system is also fitted to all diesel engined models. This reduces the level of nitrogen oxides produced during combustion by introducing a proportion of the exhaust gas back into the inlet manifold, under certain engine operating conditions, via a plunger valve. The system is controlled electronically by the diesel engine management ECM.

Evaporative emission control
Petrol models

To minimise the escape of unburned hydrocarbons into the atmosphere, an evaporative loss emission control system (EVAP) is fitted to all petrol models. The fuel tank filler cap is sealed and a charcoal canister is mounted underneath the right-hand wing to collect the petrol vapours released from the fuel contained in the fuel tank. It stores them until they can be drawn from the canister (under the control of the engine management system ECM) via the purge valve(s) into the inlet tract, where they are then burned by the engine during normal combustion.

To ensure that the engine runs correctly

when it is cold and/or idling and to protect the catalytic converter from the effects of an over-rich mixture, the purge control valve(s) are not opened by the ECM until the engine has warmed-up, and the engine is under load; the valve solenoid is then modulated on and off to allow the stored vapour to pass into the inlet tract.

Exhaust systems

On petrol models up to 04.97, the exhaust system comprises the exhaust manifold, front pipe (with oxygen sensor), catalytic converter, a short connecting pipe, intermediate pipe and silencer, and tailpipe and silencer. From 04.97, the short connecting pipe is incorporated into the catalytic converter.

On all diesel models, the exhaust system comprises the exhaust manifold, turbo-charger, front pipe, catalytic converter, intermediate pipe and silencer, and tailpipe and silencer. The system is supported by rubber bushes and/or rubber mounting rings.

2 Evaporative loss emission control system – information and component renewal

Information

1 The evaporative loss emission control system consists of the purge valve, the activated charcoal filter canister and a series of connecting vacuum hoses.
2 The purge valve is located on the bulkhead of the engine compartment, in the vacuum line between the charcoal canister and the inlet manifold. The charcoal canister is mounted inside the right-hand front wheel housing behind the wheelarch liner, in front of the A-pillar.

Component renewal

Purge valve

3 Ensure that the ignition is switched off, then unplug the wiring harness from the purge valve at the connector **(see illustration)**.
4 Undo the valve retaining bolts.
5 Note the fitted locations of the vacuum and vapour hoses, and disconnect them from the valve.
6 Refitting is a reversal of removal.

2.3 Evaporative loss emission control purge valve

Charcoal canister

7 Apply the handbrake, then jack up the front of the vehicle and support it on axle stands (see *Jacking and vehicle support*). Remove the right-hand front roadwheel.

8 Partially remove the rear of the right-hand front wheelarch liner to give access to the charcoal canister with reference to Chapter 11.

9 Disconnect the vapour hoses, noting which ports they connect to.

10 Undo the mounting bolt and remove the charcoal canister **(see illustration)**.

11 Refitting is a reversal of removal.

3 Crankcase emission system – general information

1 The crankcase emission control system consists of hoses, and separating valves, connecting the crankcase to the camshaft cover, and the air cleaner or inlet manifold **(see illustrations)**.

2 The systems requires no attention other than to check at regular intervals that the hoses, valve and oil separator are free of blockages and in good condition.

4 Exhaust Gas Recirculation (EGR) system – component removal

EGR valve

Petrol engines

1 Pull out the battery compartment upper panel.

2 Release the retaining clips/screws and remove the bulkhead cover from the engine compartment. Slide the cover to the right-hand side and manoeuvre it from behind the coolant expansion tank.

3 Unscrew the EGR supply pipe union, and disconnect the pipe from the valve.

4 Slacken and remove the two bolts securing the EGR valve. Disconnect the vacuum hose as the valve is withdrawn. Ford recommend that the exhaust manifold-to-EGR valve pipe

2.10 Undo the bolt and remove the charcoal canister

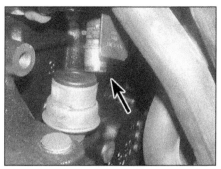

3.1a The crankcase emission regulating valve (arrowed) is fitted to the front of the cylinder block – petrol engines

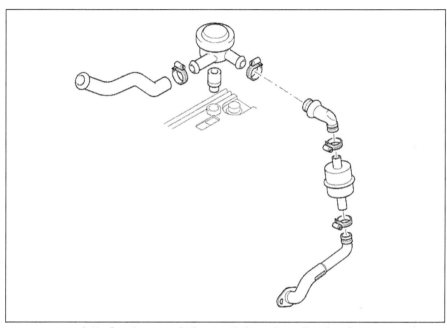

3.1b Crankcase emission regulating valve – diesel engines

is renewed whenever the connecting unions are disturbed – see later in this Section.

5 Refitting is a reversal of removal.

Diesel engines

6 Prise out the cover caps, undo the retaining nuts and remove the plastic cover from the top of the engine.

7 Disconnect the vacuum hose from the top of the valve **(see illustration)**.

8 Undo the bolts securing the EGR pipe to the valve, and recover the gasket.

9 Slacken and remove the retaining bolts, and detach the valve from the manifold. Recover the gasket.

10 Refitting is a reversal of removal. Renew the gaskets and tighten the bolts to the specified torque where given.

EGR control valve

Petrol engines

11 Disconnect the valve wiring plug, located on the engine compartment bulkhead.

12 Undo the two retaining bolts, and disconnect the vacuum pipe as the valve is removed.

13 Refitting is a reversal of removal.

Diesel engines

14 The EGR valve is located on the engine compartment bulkhead. The valve is the right-hand of the two vacuum control solenoids **(see illustration)**.

4.7 Pull the vacuum hose from the EGR valve

4.14 The EGR control valve is located on the engine compartment bulkhead

4.19 Disconnect the secondary air injection hose from the EGR pipe

4.21 Undo the EGR pipe-to-manifold unions

4.37 Undo the bolts securing the EGR pipe to the intake manifold

15 Note their fitted positions, and disconnect the valve vacuum hoses. Disconnect the wiring plug, undo the two nuts and remove the valve.

16 Refitting is a reversal of removal.

EGR pipe

2.0 litre engines

17 Remove the battery compartment upper panel. Undo the three screws and remove the bulkhead cover panel. Slide the panel two the right-hand side and manoeuvre it from behind the coolant expansion tank.

18 Unscrew the union nut securing the EGR pipe to the EGR valve.

19 Slacken the retaining clip and disconnect the secondary air injection hose from the EGR pipe **(see illustration)**.

20 Disconnect the EGR pressure transducer system hoses.

21 Undo the EGR pipe-to-exhaust manifold unions **(see illustration)**.

22 Unscrew the EGR pipe support bracket bolt and remove the pipe from the engine. Ford recommend that the EGR pipe should not be re-used.

23 Refitting is a reversal of removal, using a new EGR pipe and gasket.

2.3 litre engines

24 Drain the cooling system as described in Chapter 1A.

25 At the left-hand end of the cylinder head, disconnect the pressure transducer pipes from the EGR pipe.

26 Release the retaining clips and disconnect the coolant pipes from the outlet housing on the left-hand end of the cylinder head.

27 Disconnect the wiring plug from the engine coolant temperature sensor on the under side of the coolant outlet housing.

28 Disconnect the vacuum hose, and undo the two EGR valve retaining bolts.

29 Undo the two bolts securing the coolant pipe to the left-hand end of the cylinder head.

30 Slacken and remove the two EGR pipe retaining bolts.

31 Release the retaining clip and disconnect the secondary air injection pipe from the EGR pipe.

32 Undo the unions and separate the EGR pipe from the exhaust manifold.

33 Manoeuvre the EGR pipe from the engine complete with the EGR valve. If required, unscrew the union and separate the pipe from the valve. Ford recommend that the EGR pipe should not be re-used.

34 Refitting is a reversal of removal, using a new EGR pipe and gaskets. Tighten the nuts/bolts to the specified torque where given. Refill the cooling system as described in Chapter 1A.

Diesel engines

35 Prise out the cover caps, undo the retaining nuts, and remove the plastic cover from the top of the engine.

36 For improved access, undo the three screws, and remove the bulkhead cover from the rear of the engine compartment. Slide the cover to the right-hand side and manoeuvre it from behind the coolant expansion tank.

37 Slacken and remove the bolts/nuts securing the EGR pipe to the intake and exhaust manifolds, and manoeuvre the pipe from the engine **(see illustration)**. Recover the gaskets.

38 Refitting is a reversal of removal, using new gaskets, and tightening the nuts/bolts to the specified torque where given.

EGR transducer

Note: *No EGR pressure transducer is fitted to diesel engines.*

39 Ensure that the ignition is switched off. Unscrew the two transducer retaining nuts **(see illustration)**.

40 Disconnect the wiring plug and system hoses, as the transducer is withdrawn.

41 Refitting is a reversal of removal.

---

5 Exhaust manifold –
removal and refitting

Petrol engine models

Removal

1 Remove the EGR pipe (where fitted) as described in the previous Section.

2 Remove the auxiliary drivebelt with reference to Chapter 2A.

3 Where fitted, undo the retaining bolts and remove the exhaust manifold heat shield.

4 Undo the retaining nuts and disconnect the front exhaust pipe from the exhaust manifold.

5 Undo the bolt/nuts securing the bracket to

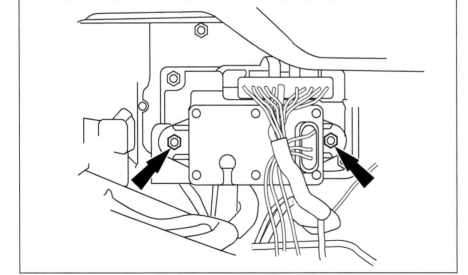

4.39 The pressure transducer is held in place by two nuts (arrowed)

5.5 Remove the bracket from the engine mounting plate to the cylinder head

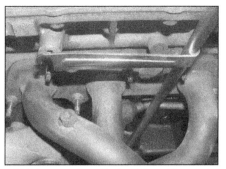

5.7 Remove the oil dipstick and bracket

5.8 Undo the exhaust manifold nuts (engine removed for clarity)

the engine mounting support plate and cylinder head **(see illustration)**.

6 Slacken and remove the alternator top mounting bolt. Pivot the alternator forwards. Undo the nut and bolt, and remove the small bracket above the alternator

7 Unscrew the nut securing the oil dipstick guide tube bracket, and carefully pull the guide tube from the engine block **(see illustration)**.

8 Undo the retaining nuts and remove the exhaust manifold from the engine **(see illustration)**. Recover the gaskets.

Refitting

9 Clean thoroughly the mating surfaces of the manifold and cylinder head.

10 Refitting is a reversal of removal, but fit new gaskets, renew self-locking nuts, and tighten the nuts to the specified torque.

Diesel engine models

Removal

11 Remove the turbocharger as described in Chapter 4B.

12 Unbolt and remove the heat shield.

13 Unscrew the bolt securing the turbo oil supply pipe to the exhaust manifold.

14 Unbolt and remove the EGR recirculation pipe. Recover the gaskets. **Note:** *On models fitted with automatic transmission, undo the bolts securing the EGR flexible pipe to the inlet flange housing, and the exhaust manifold, undo the bolts securing the EGR cooler to the inlet manifold and position it to one side.*

15 Working underneath the vehicle, progressively unscrew and remove the nuts and washers, and withdraw the exhaust manifold from the studs on the cylinder head, and lower it from the engine. Recover the gaskets.

Refitting

16 Clean thoroughly the mating surfaces of the manifold and cylinder head.

17 Refitting is a reversal of removal, but fit new gaskets, renew self-locking nuts, and tighten the nuts to the specified torque.

6 Exhaust system – component renewal

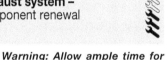 **Warning: Allow ample time for the exhaust system to cool before starting work. In particular, note that the catalytic converter runs at very high temperatures. If there is any chance that the system may still be hot, wear suitable gloves.**

Removal

1 Each exhaust section can be removed individually, although because the system is located above the rear axle, the system cannot be removed complete.

2 To remove part of the system, first jack up the front or rear of the car and support it on axle stands (see *Jacking and vehicle support*). Alternatively position the car over an inspection pit or on car ramps.

Front pipe

Note: *Handle the flexible, braided section of the front pipe carefully, and do not bend it excessively.*

3 On petrol models, trace the oxygen sensor wiring back to the multiplug, and disconnect it.

4 Unscrew the nuts and disconnect the front pipe from the exhaust manifold. Recover the gasket **(see illustrations)**.

5 Support the catalytic converter/short pipe exhaust section on a trolley jack, then unscrew the flange bolts/clamp bolt and separate the front pipe. Recover the gasket.

Catalytic converter

6 Working under the car, support the front pipe and intermediate section on axle stands or trolley jacks.

7 Unscrew the flange bolts and separate the catalytic converter from the front pipe. Recover the gasket **(see illustration)**.

8 Note the fitted position of the clamp, then unscrew the clamp bolts and separate the catalytic converter from the intermediate section. On 2.0 litre engines up to 04.97, undo the flange bolts and separate the catalytic converter from the short pipe. Recover the gasket.

Short pipe (2.0 litre up to 04.97)

9 Unscrew the flange bolts and separate the short pipe from the catalytic converter.

10 Unscrew the clamp bolts and separate the short pipe from the intermediate section. Withdraw the short pipe from under the car.

6.4a Undo the nuts to disconnect the front pipe . . .

6.4b . . . and recover the gasket – 2.3 litre model

6.7 Recover the gasket between the catalytic converter and the intermediate pipe

6.16 Tail pipe/silencer mountings

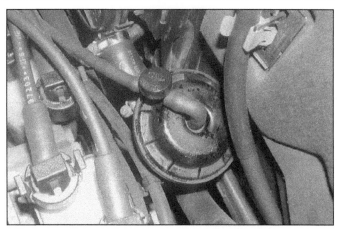

8.2 Secondary air injection switching valve

Intermediate pipe and silencer

11 Working under the car, support the front pipe on an axle stand or trolley jack.
12 Unscrew the clamp bolts and separate the intermediate pipe from the tailpipe.
13 Note the fitted position of the clamp attaching the intermediate pipe to the catalytic converter or short pipe (the bolts should be on the left-hand side of the clamp, and the lower ends of the bolts should not be below the bottom of the pipe), then unscrew the clamp bolts and separate the catalytic converter.
14 Disconnect the rubber mountings and withdraw the intermediate pipe and silencer from under the car.

Tailpipe and silencer

15 Unscrew the clamp bolts and separate the tailpipe from the intermediate pipe. Note that the fitted position of the clamp should be with the bolts facing the rear of the car, and the bolt ends should not be below the bottom of the pipe.
16 Disconnect the rubber mountings and withdraw the tailpipe and silencer from under the car **(see illustration)**.

Refitting

17 Each section is refitted by a reversal of the removal sequence, noting the following points.
  a) *Ensure that all traces of corrosion have been removed from the flanges or pipe ends and renew all necessary gaskets.*
  b) *Inspect the rubber mountings for signs of damage or deterioration and renew as necessary.*
  c) *Prior to tightening the exhaust system mounting, ensure that all rubber mountings are correctly located and that there is adequate clearance between the exhaust system and vehicle underbody.*
  d) *Do not use any form of jointing compound on the exhaust system upstream of the catalytic converter, as any residue could cause irreparable damage to its internal components.*

7 Catalytic converter – general information and precautions

1 The catalytic converter is a reliable and simple device which needs no maintenance in itself, but there are some facts which an owner should be aware of if the converter is to function properly for its full service life.

Petrol models

  a) *DO NOT use leaded petrol – the lead will coat the internal precious metals, reducing their converting efficiency and will eventually destroy the converter.*
  b) *Always keep the ignition and fuel systems well-maintained in accordance with the manufacturer's schedule.*
  c) *If the engine develops a misfire, do not drive the car at all (or at least as little as possible) until the fault is cured.*
  d) *DO NOT push- or tow-start the car further than 50 yards – this will soak the catalytic converter in unburned fuel, causing it to overheat when the engine does start.*
  e) *DO NOT switch off the ignition at high engine speeds.*
  f) *The catalytic converter, used on a well-maintained and well-driven car, should last between 50 000 and 100 000 miles – if the converter is no longer effective it must be renewed.*

Petrol and diesel models

  a) *DO NOT use fuel or engine oil additives – these may contain substances harmful to the catalytic converter.*
  b) *Remember that the catalytic converter operates at very high temperatures. DO NOT, therefore, park the car in dry undergrowth, over long grass or piles of dead leaves after a long run.*
  c) *Remember that the catalytic converter is FRAGILE – do not strike it with tools during servicing work.*

8 Secondary air injection system – information and component renewal

Information

Petrol engined models may be equipped with a system which is designed to shorten the amount of time the catalytic converter takes to warm-up. In order to function correctly, the catalytic converter needs to be at a temperature of at least 300°C. This temperature level is achieved by the action of the exhaust gases passing through. In order to reduce the catalyst warm-up phase, a secondary air injection pump injects fresh air just behind the exhaust valves in the exhaust manifold. This oxygen-rich mixture causes an 'afterburning' effect in the exhaust, greatly increasing the gas temperature, and therefore the catalyst temperature. The system is only active during cold starts (up to 33°C coolant temperature), and only operates for approximately 2 minutes.

Component renewal

1 Ensure the ignition is switched off.

Switching valve

2 The switching valve is located in the air secondary air injection pipe between the pump and the EGR pipe. Disconnect the vacuum hose from the valve **(see illustration)**.
3 Slacken the retaining clips and disconnect the inlet and outlet hoses from the valve. Note the fitted positions of the hoses.
4 Refitting is a reversal of removal.

Diverter valve

5 The diverter valve is located on the engine compartment bulkhead, just to the right-hand side of the EGR control valve. Disconnect the wiring plug from the valve.
6 Lift the valve from the mounting bracket, and disconnect the vacuum hoses. Note the fitted positions of the hoses.
7 Refitting is a reversal of removal.

Air pump

8 Undo the three screws and remove the bulkhead cover and the battery compartment upper panel. Slide the bulkhead panel to the right-hand side and manoeuvre it from behind the coolant expansion tank **(see illustration)**.

9 Disconnect the pump wiring plug **(see illustration)**.

10 Slacken the retaining clips and disconnect the air inlet and outlet hoses from the pump. Note the fitted positions of the hoses **(see illustrations)**.

11 Undo the three nuts, and remove the pump from its retaining bracket.

12 Refitting is a reversal of removal.

8.8 The bulkhead cover is secured by three screws (two arrowed)

8.9 Disconnect the pump wiring plug (arrowed)

8.10a Disconnect the pump inlet hose (arrowed) . . .

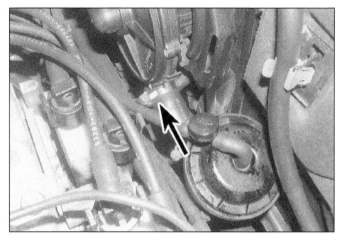

8.10b . . . and outlet hose (arrowed)

Notes

Chapter 5 Part A:
Starting and charging systems

Contents

Degrees of difficulty

Easy, suitable for novice with little experience	Fairly easy, suitable for beginner with some experience	Fairly difficult, suitable for competent DIY mechanic	Difficult, suitable for experienced DIY mechanic	Very difficult, suitable for expert DIY or professional

Specifications

General
System type . . . . 12 volt, negative earth

Starter motor
Type . . . . Bosch, Pre-engaged

Battery
Ratings:
  Main battery . . . . 44 to 92 Ah (depending on model and market)
  Auxiliary battery . . . . 61 Ah

Alternator
Type . . . . Bosch
Rating . . . . 70, 90 or 120 amp
Minimum brush length . . . . 5.0 mm

Torque wrench settings	Nm	lbf ft
Alternator mounting bolts	53	39
Auxiliary drivebelt tensioner bolts	25	18
Battery mounting clamp	35	26
Starter motor	35	26

1 General information and precautions

General information

The engine electrical system consists mainly of the charging and starting systems. Because of their engine-related functions, these are covered separately from the body electrical devices such as the lights, instruments, etc, which are covered in Chapter 12. On petrol engine models refer to Part B of this Chapter for information on the ignition system, and on diesel models refer to Part C for the preheating system.

The electrical system is of the 12 volt negative earth type.

The battery may be of the low maintenance or maintenance-free (sealed for life) type and is charged by the alternator, which is belt-driven from the crankshaft pulley. On some models, an auxiliary battery is fitted in a floor-level storage compartment, to provide electrical power for the additional heater/air conditioning unit.

The starter motor is of the pre-engaged type, with an integral solenoid. On starting, the solenoid moves the drive pinion into engagement with the flywheel/driveplate ring gear before the starter motor is energised. Once the engine has started, a one-way clutch prevents the motor armature being driven by the engine until the pinion disengages from the flywheel. Two primary earth straps are fitted; one from the battery negative terminal to the body, and one from the engine to the body (see illustrations).

Further details of the various systems are given in the relevant Sections of this Chapter. While some repair procedures are given, the usual course of action is to renew the component concerned. The owner whose interest extends beyond mere component renewal should obtain a copy of the *Automotive Electrical & Electronic Systems Manual*, available from the publishers of this manual.

Precautions

⚠️ **Warning:**
• **It is necessary to take extra care when working on the electrical system to avoid damage to semi-conductor devices (diodes and transistors), and to avoid the risk of personal injury. In addition to the precautions given in 'Safety first!', observe the following when working on the system:**
• **Always remove rings, watches, etc, before working on the electrical system.** Even with the battery disconnected, capacitive discharge could occur if a component's live terminal is earthed through a metal object. This could cause a shock or nasty burn.
• **Do not reverse the battery connections.** Components such as the alternator, electronic control units, or any other components having semi-conductor circuitry could be irreparably damaged.
• **Never disconnect the battery terminals, the alternator, any electrical wiring or any test instruments when the engine is running.**
• **Do not allow the engine to turn the alternator when the alternator is not connected.**
• **Never test for alternator output by 'flashing' the output lead to earth.**
• **Always ensure that the battery negative lead is disconnected when working on the electrical system.**
• If the engine is being started using jump leads and a slave battery, connect the batteries **positive-to-positive** and **negative-to-negative** (see *Jump starting* at the beginning of the manual). This also applies when connecting a battery charger.
• Before using electric-arc welding equipment on the car, **disconnect the battery, alternator and components such as electronic control units** to protect them from the risk of damage.
Caution:
• **The radio/cassette fitted as standard equipment has a built-in security code to deter thieves. If the power source to the unit is cut, the anti-theft system will activate. Even if the power source is immediately reconnected, the radio/cassette unit will not function until the correct security code has been entered. Therefore, if you do not know the correct security code for the radio/cassette unit, do not disconnect the battery negative terminal or remove the radio/cassette unit from the vehicle.-**
• **Disconnecting the main battery will also cause the engine management electronic control module (ECM) to lose its stored values. After reconnection, a journey of approximately 10 to 25 miles may be necessary for the ECM to relearn those values. During this period, the engine performance may be erratic.-**
• **To avoid losing the ECM data, radio code and clock settings, a device known as a 'code saver' may be used in some circumstances. This usually plugs into the** cigarette lighter socket, and provides the electrical system with a small 12 volt supply. For details of their recommended usage, refer to your Ford dealer or automotive accessory specialist.

2 Battery – testing and charging

Caution 1: Battery acid is caustic and corrosive. Wash spillages off skin, clothing or surfaces immediately with plenty of water. If acid gets into the eyes, seek medical advice.
Caution 2: The gas given off by the battery during charging is explosive. Do not smoke or allow naked lights near the battery. Connect the charger to the battery before switching on at the mains, and switch off at the mains before disconnecting the charger when charging is complete.

Testing

1 If the battery cell caps can be removed, a hydrometer may be used to check the state of charge. The specific gravity of the electrolyte in a fully-charged battery should be around 1.270. A reading of 1.130 or below indicates a discharged battery. A difference of 0.040 or more between cells suggests a defective cell.
2 Most modern batteries are sealed for life and maintenance-free. Topping-up and testing of the electrolyte in each cell is not possible. The condition of the battery can therefore only be tested using a battery condition indicator or a digital voltmeter.
3 Certain maintenance-free batteries have a built-in battery condition indicator. The indicator is located in the top of the battery casing, and indicates the condition of the battery from its colour. If the indicator shows green, then the battery is in a good state of charge. If the indicator turns darker, eventually to black, then the battery requires charging, as described later in this Section. If the indicator shows clear or yellow, the electrolyte level in the battery is too low to allow further use, and the battery should be renewed. **Do not** attempt to charge, load or jump start a battery when the indicator shows clear or yellow.

1.4a Battery earth connection . . .

1.4b . . . and engine earth connection

4 If testing the battery using a digital voltmeter, connect the voltmeter across the battery and note the voltage. The test is only accurate if the battery has not been subjected to charge for the previous six hours. If this is not the case, switch on the headlights for 30 seconds, then switch them off and wait 5 minutes before testing the battery. All other electrical circuits must be switched off, so check that the doors and tailgate are fully shut when making the test.

5 A fully-charged battery should give a reading of at least 12.6 volts. If the reading is less than 12.2 volts the battery is discharged, whilst a reading of 12.2 to 12.4 volts indicates a partially-discharged condition.

6 If the battery is to be charged, remove it from the vehicle unless the battery charger is specifically stated to be safe for use with the battery connected, otherwise there is a risk of damaging the vehicle's electronics.

Charging

Note: *The following is intended as a guide only. Always refer to the manufacturer's recommendations (often printed on a label attached to the battery) before charging a battery.*

7 Charge the battery at a rate equivalent to no more than 10% of the battery capacity (eg, for a 45 Ah battery charge at 4.5 A maximum) for no more than 12 hours. Stop at once if gasing (a fizzing noise coming from the cells) becomes apparent.

8 Alternatively, a trickle charger charging at the rate of 1.5 A can safely be used overnight.

9 Rapid boost charges can restore the power of the battery in 1 to 2 hours, but they must be strictly controlled to avoid damage through overheating. Suitable equipment is generally found in garage workshops.

10 While charging the battery, note that the temperature of the electrolyte should never exceed 38°C (100°F).

Maintenance-free battery

11 This battery type takes considerably longer to fully recharge than the standard type, the time taken being dependent on the extent of discharge, but it can take anything up to three days.

12 A constant voltage type charger is required, to be set, when connected, to 13.9 to 14.9 volts with a charger current below 25 amps. Using this method, the battery should be useable within three hours, giving a voltage reading of 12.5 volts, but this is for a partially-discharged battery and, as mentioned, full charging can take far longer.

13 If the battery is to be charged from a fully-discharged state (condition reading less than 12.2 volts), have it recharged by your local automotive electrician, as the charge rate is higher and constant supervision during charging is necessary.

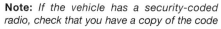

3 Battery – disconnection, removal and refitting

Note: *If the vehicle has a security-coded radio, check that you have a copy of the code*

number before disconnecting the battery cable; refer to the caution in Section 1.
Note: *Disconnecting the main battery will also cause the engine management electronic control module (ECM) to lose its stored values. Again, refer to the caution in Section 1.*

Disconnection and removal
Main battery

1 The battery is located at the left-hand side of the engine compartment **(see illustration)**.
2 Loosen the clamp nut and disconnect the battery negative (–) lead from the terminal **(see illustrations)**.
3 Lift the plastic flap where fitted, then loosen the clamp nut and disconnect the battery positive (+) lead from the terminal **(see illustration)**.
4 At the base of the battery, unscrew the retaining bolt and remove the clamp **(see illustration)**.
5 Where fitted, disconnect the vent pipe from the battery. Note on some models the vent incorporates a flashback arrester.
6 Lift out the battery and withdraw it from the engine compartment **(see illustration)**.

Additional battery

7 Vehicles equipped with an auxiliary heater are fitted with an additional battery under the passenger seat. At the time of writing, no information concerning removal and refitting of the additional battery was available.

Refitting

8 Clean the battery mounting and apply a little grease to the threads of the clamp bolt.

3.1 Battery location

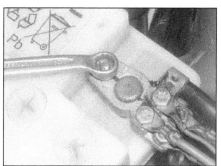
3.2a Undo the negative terminal clamp nut . . .

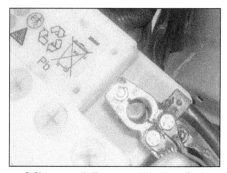
3.2b . . . and disconnect the terminal

3.3 Disconnect the positive terminal

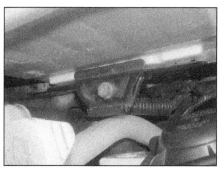
3.4 Undo the bolt and remove the clamp

3.6 Lift the battery from the engine compartment

4.1 The upper panel simply pulls out

4.4 Release the hose clips and pull the lower panel out

9 Place the battery in position and refit the clamp. Tighten the bolt to the specified torque.
10 Where fitted, refit the vent pipe.
11 Reconnect the battery positive (+) lead to the terminal and tighten the clamp nut.
12 Reconnect the battery negative (–) lead to the terminal and tighten the clamp nut.
13 Re-activate the radio by inserting the security code where applicable. Refer to Section 1 and the notes at the start of this Section.

4 Battery compartment panels – removal and refitting

Upper panel

Removal
1 The upper panel simply pulls from its location **(see illustration)**.

Refitting
2 Refitting is a reversal of removal, ensuring that the panel edges locate in the grooves of the adjoining panels.

Lower panel

Removal
3 Remove battery compartment upper panel, as described in Paragraph 1.
4 Release the hose(s) from any retaining clips on the engine side of the panel, and pull the panel up and out of the engine compartment **(see illustration)**.

6.5 To remove the clips, push the centres out

Refitting
5 Refitting is a reversal of removal, ensuring that the panel edges locate in the grooves of the adjoining panels.

5 Alternator/charging system – testing in vehicle

Note: *Refer to Section 1 of this Chapter before starting work.*

1 If the charge warning light fails to illuminate when the ignition is switched on, first check the alternator wiring connections for security. If satisfactory, check that the warning light bulb has not blown, and that the bulbholder is secure in its location in the instrument panel. If the light still fails to illuminate, check the continuity of the warning light feed wire from the alternator to the bulbholder. Check the condition of the auxiliary drivebelt. Check the condition of the regulator within the alternator as described in Section 7 of this Chapter. If all is satisfactory, the alternator is at fault and should be renewed or taken to an auto-electrician for testing and repair.
2 Similarly, if the charge warning light comes on with the ignition, but is then slow to go out when the engine is started, this may indicate an impending alternator problem. Check all the items listed in the preceding Paragraph, and refer to an auto-electrical specialist if no obvious faults are found.
3 If the charge warning light illuminates when the engine is running, stop the engine and check that the drivebelt is correctly tensioned (see Chapter

6.9 Unscrew the two alternator mounting bolts (arrowed)

1A or 1B) and that the alternator connections are secure. If all is so far satisfactory, check the alternator brushes and slip rings as described in Section 7. If the fault persists, the alternator should be renewed, or taken to an auto-electrician for testing and repair.
4 If the alternator output is suspect even though the warning light functions correctly, the regulated voltage may be checked as follows.
5 Connect a voltmeter across the battery terminals, and start the engine.
6 Increase the engine speed until the voltmeter reading remains steady; the reading should be approximately 12 to 13 volts, and no more than 14 volts.
7 Switch on as many electrical accessories (eg, the headlights, heated rear window and heater blower) as possible, and check that the alternator maintains the regulated voltage at around 13 to 14 volts.
8 If the regulated voltage is not as stated, this may be due to worn brushes, weak brush springs, a faulty voltage regulator, a faulty diode, a severed phase winding or worn or damaged slip rings. The brushes and slip rings may be checked (see Section 7), but if the fault persists, the alternator should be renewed or taken to an auto-electrician.

6 Alternator – removal and refitting

Removal

Petrol engines
1 Disconnect the battery negative lead and position it away from the terminal – refer to the precautions in Section 1.
2 Remove the air cleaner assembly as described in Chapter 4A.
3 Remove the right-hand side headlamp as described in Chapter 12, Section 7.
4 Undo the headlamp shield upper and lower fixing bolts. Release the wiring harness cable tie.
5 In order to remove the clips securing the trim panel adjacent to the alternator, press in the centre of the clips and prise them from the panel **(see illustration)**. Note that the lower three clips are inserted from the headlamp side of the panel. Remove the trim panel.
6 Unscrew the remaining headlamp shield fixing bolt, release the two clips and manoeuvre the shield from the engine compartment.
7 Apply the handbrake, then jack up the front of the vehicle and support it on axle stands (see *Jacking and vehicle support*). Undo the four bolts and two nuts, and remove the engine undershield.
8 With a spanner, rotate the auxiliary drivebelt tensioner clockwise, and remove the belt from the alternator pulley.
9 Unscrew the two alternator mounting bolts, and lift the alternator slightly to gain access to the electrical connections **(see illustration)**.

6.10 Disconnect the alternator wiring

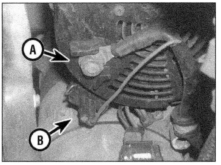

6.12 Disconnect the alternator main cable (A) and charge light wire (B)

6.15 Alternator upper mounting bolt (arrowed)

10 Undo the electrical connections and manoeuvre the alternator from the engine compartment **(see illustration)**.

Diesel engines

11 Disconnect the battery negative lead and position it away from the terminal – refer to the precautions in Section 1.
12 Undo the nuts and disconnect the main cable and charging warning light (D+) wire from the rear of the alternator **(see illustration)**. **Note:** *On some models the D+ connection is a push-on plug.*
13 Detach the air intake pipe adjacent to the alternator.
14 Using an adjustable spanner on the tensioner arm, rotate the tensioner clockwise and detach the drivebelt from the alternator pulley (see Chapter 2B).
15 Support the alternator, then unscrew and

remove the mounting bolts **(see illustration)**. Manoeuvre the alternator from the engine compartment.

Refitting

16 Refitting is a reversal of removal. Refer to Chapter 2A or 2B as applicable for details of refitting the main drivebelt. Tighten the alternator mounting bolts to the specified torque.

7 Alternator – brush holder/regulator module renewal

1 Remove the alternator, as described in Section 6.
2 Place the alternator on a clean work surface, with the pulley facing down.

3 Undo the cover screws, remove the harness retaining bracket (where fitted), then prise open the clips and lift the plastic cover from the rear of the alternator **(see illustrations)**.
4 Undo the two screws and carefully remove the voltage regulator/brush holder from the alternator **(see illustrations)**.
5 Measure the free length of the brush contacts – where applicable, take the measurement from the manufacturer's emblem (A) etched on the side of the brush contact, to the shallowest part of the curved end face of the brush (B) **(see illustration)**. Check the measurement with the Specifications; renew the module if the brushes are worn below the minimum limit.
6 Clean and inspect the surfaces of the slip rings, at the end of the alternator shaft **(see illustration)**. If they are excessively worn, or damaged, the alternator must be renewed.

7.3a Undo the screws, release the clips . . .

7.3b . . . then remove the cover

7.4a Undo the screws . . .

7.4b . . . and remove the voltage regulator/brush holder

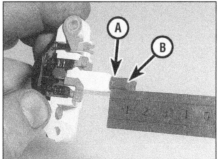

7.5 Measure the alternator brush length from the manufacturer's emblem (A) to the shallowest part of the curved end face of the brush (B)

7.6 Inspect the surface of the slip rings (arrowed) at the end of the alternator shaft

7 Reassemble the alternator by following the dismantling procedure in reverse. On completion, refer to Section 3 and refit the alternator.

8 Starting system – testing

Note: *Refer to Section 1 of this Chapter before starting work.*

1 If the starter motor fails to operate when the ignition key is turned to the appropriate position, the following possible causes may be to blame:

a) *The battery is faulty.*
b) *The electrical connections between the switch, solenoid, battery and starter motor are somewhere failing to pass the necessary current from the battery through the starter to earth.*
c) *The solenoid is faulty.*
d) *The starter motor is mechanically or electrically defective.*

2 To check the battery, switch on the headlights. If they dim after a few seconds, this indicates that the battery is discharged – recharge (see Section 2) or renew the battery. If the headlights glow brightly, operate the ignition switch and observe the lights. If they dim, then this indicates that current is reaching the starter motor, therefore the fault must lie in the starter motor. If the lights continue to glow brightly (and no clicking sound can be heard from the starter motor

solenoid), this indicates that there is a fault in the circuit or solenoid – see following Paragraphs. If the starter motor turns slowly when operated, but the battery is in good condition, then this indicates that either the starter motor is faulty, or there is considerable resistance somewhere in the circuit.

3 If a fault in the circuit is suspected, disconnect the battery leads (including the earth connection to the body), the starter/solenoid wiring and the engine/transmission earth strap. Thoroughly clean the connections, and reconnect the leads and wiring, then use a voltmeter or test light to check that full battery voltage is available at the battery positive lead connection to the solenoid, and that the earth is sound. Smear petroleum jelly around the battery terminals to prevent corrosion – corroded connections are amongst the most frequent causes of electrical system faults.

4 If the battery and all connections are in good condition, check the circuit by disconnecting the wire from the solenoid blade terminal. Connect a voltmeter or test light between the wire end and a good earth (such as the battery negative terminal), and check that the wire is live when the ignition switch is turned to the start position. If it is, then the circuit is sound – if not the circuit wiring can be checked as described in Chapter 12.

5 The solenoid contacts can be checked by connecting a voltmeter or test light between the battery positive feed connection on the starter side of the solenoid, and earth. When

the ignition switch is turned to the start position, there should be a reading or lighted bulb, as applicable. If there is no reading or lighted bulb, the solenoid is faulty and should be renewed.

6 If the circuit and solenoid are proved sound, the fault must lie in the starter motor. It may be possible to have the starter motor overhauled by a specialist, but check on the availability and cost of spares before proceeding, as it may prove more economical to obtain a new or exchange motor.

9 Starter motor – removal and refitting

Removal

1 Disconnect the battery negative (earth) lead (see Section 3).

2 Apply the handbrake, then jack up the front of the vehicle and support it on axle stands (see *Jacking and vehicle support*). Undo the two retaining nuts and four bolts (two each side), then remove the engine undershield.

3 Working underneath the vehicle, disconnect the starter motor wiring connections **(see illustration)**.

4 Undo the two starter motor retaining bolts. Remove the wiring harness brackets from the bolts, and manoeuvre the starter motor from under the vehicle **(see illustration)**.

Refitting

5 Refit the starter motor by following the removal procedure in reverse. Tighten the mounting bolts to the specified torque.

10 Starter motor – testing and overhaul

If the starter motor is thought to be defective, it should be removed from the vehicle and taken to an auto-electrician for assessment. In the majority of cases, new starter motor brushes can be fitted at a reasonable cost. However, check the cost of repairs first as it may prove more economical to purchase a new or exchange motor.

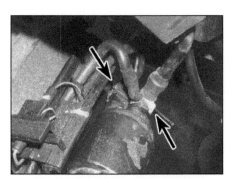

9.3 Disconnect the starter motor connections (arrowed)

9.4 Undo the two bolts (arrowed) and remove the motor (engine removed for clarity)

Chapter 5 Part B:
Ignition system – petrol engines

Contents

Degrees of difficulty

Easy, suitable for novice with little experience		Fairly easy, suitable for beginner with some experience		Fairly difficult, suitable for competent DIY mechanic		Difficult, suitable for experienced DIY mechanic		Very difficult, suitable for expert DIY or professional	

Specifications

Ignition timing .... Not adjustable, ECM controlled

Spark plugs .... See Chapter 1A Specifications

1 General information

The Ford system described in this Chapter is a self-contained engine management system. Whilst the EEC V electronic control module (ECM) has overall control of the both the fuel injection and ignition systems, on 2.0 litre models a separate ignition module is fitted to control the ignition system. This Chapter deals with the ignition system components only – refer to Chapter 4A for details of the fuel system components.

The ignition system comprises the spark plugs, HT (High Tension) leads, electronic ignition coils, and an electronic ignition module (where applicable) together with its associated sensors, actuators and wiring.

The basic operation is as follows: the module supplies a voltage to the input stage of the ignition coil which causes the primary windings in the coil to be energised. The supply voltage is periodically interrupted by the ECM/module and this results in the collapse of primary magnetic field, which then induces a much larger voltage in the secondary coil, called the HT voltage. This voltage is directed, via the HT leads, to the spark plugs whose pistons rise and fall together, ie, cylinders 1 and 4, 2 and 3. This is known as a wasted-spark DIS (distributorless ignition system). The spark plug electrodes form a gap small enough for the HT voltage to arc across, and the resulting spark ignites the fuel/air mixture in the cylinder. The timing of this sequence of events is critical and is regulated solely by the module.

On 2.0 litre models, the module, in conjunction with the engine management ECM, calculates and controls the ignition timing according to engine speed, crankshaft position, throttle position, inlet air temperature and engine coolant temperature, received from sensors mounted on and around the engine. On all engines, ignition timing angle is determined by the engine management ECM, and sent to the ignition module, which compares this signal with that from the crankshaft position sensor, and then determines the optimum exact ignition timing. If the ignition module fails to receive a signal from the engine management ECM, the module determines the ignition timing using the last data received. If no signals are received by the ignition module for five consecutive cycles (10 crankshaft rotations), the module implements a 'limited operation' strategy, and engine performance may be reduced. No manual adjustment of the ignition timing is possible.

On 2.3 litre models, all ignition functions are under the control of the engine management EEC V ECM. The DIS coils are fitted directly above Nos 2 and 4 spark plugs, with conventional HT connecting these coils to cylinders No 3 and 1 respectively.

It should be noted that comprehensive fault diagnosis of all the engine management systems described in this Chapter is only possible with dedicated electronic test equipment. Problems with the systems operation that cannot be pinpointed by following the basic guidelines in Section 2 should therefore be referred to a Ford dealer or suitably-equipped specialist for assessment. Once the fault has been identified, the removal/refitting sequences detailed in the following Sections will then allow the appropriate component(s) to be renewed as required.

2 Ignition system – testing

Warning: Extreme care must be taken when working on the system with the ignition switched on; it is possible to get a substantial electric shock from a vehicle's ignition system. Persons with cardiac pacemaker devices should keep well clear of the ignition circuits, components and test equipment. Always switch off the ignition before disconnecting or connecting any component and when using a multi-meter to check resistances.

General

1 Most ignition system faults are likely to be due to loose or dirty connections or to 'tracking' (unintentional earthing) of HT voltage due to dirt, dampness or damaged insulation, rather than by the failure of any of the system's components. Always check all wiring thoroughly before condemning an electrical component and work methodically to eliminate all other possibilities before deciding that a particular component is faulty.

3.1 Squeeze together the locking lugs and disconnect the HT leads

2 The practice of checking for a spark by holding the live end of an HT lead a short distance away from the engine is definitely not recommended.

Engine will not start

3 If the engine either will not turn over at all, or only turns very slowly, check the battery and starter motor. Connect a voltmeter across the battery terminals (meter positive probe to battery positive terminal), then disable the ignition by disconnecting the wiring from the coil(s). Note the voltage reading obtained while turning over the engine on the starter for a maximum of ten seconds. If the reading obtained is less than approximately 10.0 volts, first check the battery, starter motor and charging systems (see Chapter 5A).
4 Check the HT leads and ignition coil with reference to Section 3 of this Chapter.
5 If there is still no spark, then the problem must lie within the engine management system. The vehicle should be referred to a Ford dealer or specialist for assessment.

Engine misfires

6 An irregular misfire suggests either a loose connection or intermittent fault on the primary circuit.
7 With the ignition switched off, check carefully through the system ensuring that all

3.2 Disconnect the coil wiring plug (arrowed)

connections are clean and securely fastened. Check the LT circuit as described above.
8 Check that the HT coil, and the HT leads are clean and dry. Check the leads themselves and the spark plugs (by substitution, if necessary).
9 Regular misfiring is almost certainly due to a fault in the HT leads, or spark plugs.
10 If HT voltage is not present on one particular lead, the fault will be in that lead. If HT is present on all leads, the fault will be in the spark plugs.

Other problems

11 Problems with the system's operation that cannot be pinpointed by following the guidelines in the preceding Paragraphs should be referred to a Ford dealer or specialist for assessment.

3 HT coil – removal and refitting

Removal

2.0 litre engines

1 The ignition coils are located at the left-hand end of the cylinder head. Ensure that the ignition is switched off, then squeeze together the locking lugs of the HT lead terminals, and disconnect the HT leads from the coils **(see illustration)**.
2 Disconnect the wiring plug from each coil **(see illustration)**.
3 Unscrew the two Torx screws securing each coil, and pull the coils horizontally from the locating dowels **(see illustration)**.

2.3 litre engines

4 On these engines, the coils are fitted directly above the spark plugs, into the camshaft cover. Ensure that the ignition is switched off, then unscrew the 10 bolts securing the coils cover on the camshaft cover **(see illustration)**.

3.3 Undo the screws and remove the coils (arrowed)

3.4 Unscrew the ten bolts and remove the coils cover

3.5 Release the wiring harness from the clips and disconnect the wiring plugs

3.6 Squeeze the locking tabs and disconnect the HT leads

3.7 Undo the Torx screws and remove the coils

5 Release the wiring harness from the retaining clips on the coils, and disconnect the wiring plugs **(see illustration)**.

6 Release the HT leads from the retaining clips on the coils, squeeze together the locking tabs and disconnect the HT lead connectors **(see illustration)**.

7 Slacken and remove the retaining screws, and remove the ignition coils **(see illustration)**. Note that the HT connection on the underside of the coil locates directly onto the spark plug beneath it.

Refitting

8 Refitting is a reversal of removal.

---

4 Ignition timing – checking and adjusting

The ignition timing is under the control of the engine management system ECM and is not manually adjustable. The vehicle must be taken to a Ford dealer or suitably-equipped specialist if the timing requires checking.

---

5 Electronic ignition module – removal and refitting

Note: *Only models equipped with the 2.0 litre engine are fitted with a separate electronic ignition module. On 2.3 litre models, the function of the ignition module is incorporated into the EEC V engine management ECM.*

Removal

1 Disconnect the battery negative lead as described in Chapter 5A.

2 The module is located to the right of the brake fluid reservoir on the engine compartment bulkhead. Undo the two

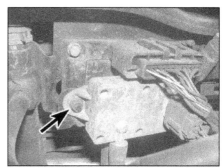

5.2 Undo the bolts and remove the ignition module (arrowed – one bolt hidden)

retaining bolts and remove the module from the bulkhead **(see illustration)**.

3 Disconnect the wiring plug as the module is withdrawn.

Refitting

4 Refitting is a reversal of removal.

Notes

Chapter 5 Part C:
Preheating systems – diesel models

Contents

Degrees of difficulty

Easy, suitable for novice with little experience	**Fairly easy,** suitable for beginner with some experience	**Fairly difficult,** suitable for competent DIY mechanic	**Difficult,** suitable for experienced DIY mechanic	**Very difficult,** suitable for expert DIY or professional

Specifications

Glow plugs

Current consumption .... 8 amps per glow plug
Type .... Bosch 0 250 202 022

Torque wrench setting	**Nm**	**lbf ft**
Glow plug to cylinder head	15	11

1 General information

To assist cold starting, diesel engined models are fitted with a preheating system, which comprises four glow plugs, a glow plug control unit (incorporated in the engine management ECM), a facia-mounted warning lamp and the associated electrical wiring.

The glow plugs are miniature electric heating elements, encapsulated in a metal case with a probe at one end and electrical connection at the other. Each combustion chamber has a glow plug threaded into it, which is positioned directly in line with the incoming spray of fuel. When the glow plug is energised, the fuel passing over it is heated, allowing its optimum combustion temperature to be achieved more quickly.

The duration of the preheating period is governed by the glow plug control unit, which monitors the temperature of the engine via the coolant temperature sensor and alters the preheating time to suit the conditions. Plug 'after glow' occurs regardless of the engine or ambient temperature, to reduce harmful exhaust emissions.

A facia-mounted warning lamp informs the driver that preheating is taking place. The lamp extinguishes when sufficient preheating has taken place to allow the engine to be started, but power will still be supplied to the glow plugs for a further period until the engine is started. If no attempt is made to start the engine, the power supply to the glow plugs is switched off to prevent battery drain and glow plug burn-out. Note that if a fault occurs in the engine management system while the car is moving, the glow plug warning lamp will start flashing and the system will then switch to fail-safe mode. Should this occur, the car must be taken to a Ford dealer or suitably-equipped specialist for fault diagnosis.

2 Glow plugs –
testing, removal and refitting

Testing

1 If the system malfunctions, testing is ultimately by substitution of known good units, but some preliminary checks may be made as described in the following Paragraphs.

2 Connect a voltmeter or 12 volt test lamp between the glow plug supply cable and a good earth point on the engine.

Caution: Make sure that the live connection is kept well clear of the engine and bodywork.

3 Have an assistant activate the preheating system by turning on the ignition, and check that the battery voltage is applied to the glow plug electrical connection. Note that the voltage will drop to zero when the preheating period ends.

4 If no supply voltage can be detected at the glow plug, then the supply cabling must be faulty.

5 To locate a faulty glow plug, remove the supply cabling from the glow plug terminal, and connect an ammeter between the cable and terminal. Disconnect the coolant

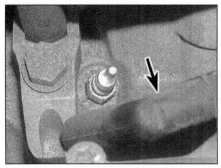

2.8 Pull the connector (arrowed) from the glow plug

temperature sensor at the back of the cylinder head, to simulate a cold start, and turn the ignition switch to 'on'. Measure the steady state current consumption (ignore the initial current surge which will be about 50% higher). Compare the result with the Specifications – high current consumption (or no current draw at all) indicates a faulty glow plug.

6 As a final check, remove the glow plugs and inspect them visually, as described in the next sub-Section.

Removal

7 Disconnect the battery negative (earth) lead

2.9 Remove the glow plug from the cylinder head

(see Chapter 5A). Prise out the cover caps, undo the retaining nuts/bolts, and remove the engine top cover.

8 Carefully pull the connector(s) from the relevant glow plug(s) **(see illustration)**.

9 Unscrew and remove the glow plug(s) **(see illustration)**.

10 Inspect the glow plug stems for signs of damage. A badly burned or charred stem may be an indication of a faulty fuel injector; refer to Chapter 4B, Section 7, for greater detail.

Refitting

11 Refitting is a reversal of removal, but tighten the glow plug to the specified torque.

Chapter 6
Clutch

Contents

Degrees of difficulty

Easy, suitable for novice with little experience		Fairly easy, suitable for beginner with some experience		Fairly difficult, suitable for competent DIY mechanic		Difficult, suitable for experienced DIY mechanic		Very difficult, suitable for expert DIY or professional	

Specifications

General

Type	Single dry plate, diaphragm spring with spring-loaded hub
Operation	Hydraulic with slave and master cylinders
Friction disc diameter	228 mm
Clutch pedal travel	133 ± 5 mm
Friction disc nominal thickness	7.3 mm

Torque wrench settings

	Nm	lbf ft
Clutch slave cylinder mounting bolt	11	8
Pressure plate-to-flywheel bolt	30	22

1 General information

The clutch is of single dry disc type, incorporating a diaphragm spring pressure plate, and is hydraulically-operated.

The clutch cover (pressure plate) is bolted to the rear face of the flywheel, and the friction disc is located between the pressure plate and the flywheel friction surface. The disc hub is splined to the transmission input shaft and is free to slide along the splines. Friction lining material is riveted to each side of the disc, and the disc hub incorporates cushioning springs to absorb transmission shocks and ensure a smooth take-up of drive. On all engines except the 2.0 litre engine, the flywheel is manufactured in two parts instead of the conventional single unit; the friction surface has a limited buffered movement in relation to the main flywheel mass bolted to the rear of the crankshaft. This has the effect of absorbing the initial clutch engagement shock and makes for a smoother gearchange.

When the clutch pedal is depressed, the centrally-mounted slave cylinder forces the release bearing onto the diaphragm spring fingers. As the centre of the spring is pushed in, the outer part of the spring moves out and releases the pressure plate from the friction disc. Drive then ceases to be transmitted to the transmission.

When the clutch pedal is released, the diaphragm spring forces the pressure plate into contact with the linings on the friction disc, and at the same time pushes the disc slightly forward along the input shaft splines into engagement with the flywheel. The friction disc is now firmly sandwiched between the pressure plate and flywheel. This causes drive to be taken up.

As the linings wear on the friction disc, the pressure plate rest position moves closer to the flywheel resulting in the 'rest' position of the diaphragm spring fingers being raised. The hydraulic system requires no adjustment since the quantity of hydraulic fluid in the circuit automatically compensates for wear every time the clutch pedal is operated.

2 Hydraulic system – bleeding

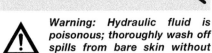

⚠️ **Warning: Hydraulic fluid is poisonous; thoroughly wash off spills from bare skin without delay. Seek immediate medical advice if any fluid is swallowed or gets into the eyes. Certain types of hydraulic fluid are inflammable and may ignite when brought into contact with hot components. Hydraulic fluid is also an effective paint stripper. If spillage occurs onto painted**

bodywork or fittings, it should be washed off immediately, using copious quantities of cold water. It is also hygroscopic (ie, it can absorb moisture from the air) which lowers the boiling point of the fluid, rendering it dangerous to use in the hydraulic system. Old fluid will have suffered contamination, and should never be re-used.

1 The correct operation of any hydraulic system is only possible after removing all air from the components and circuit; this is achieved by bleeding the system.

2 During the bleeding procedure, add only clean, unused hydraulic fluid of the recommended type; never re-use fluid that has already been bled from the system. Ensure that sufficient fluid is available before starting work.

3 If there is any possibility of incorrect fluid being already in the system, the hydraulic circuit must be flushed completely with uncontaminated, correct fluid.

4 If hydraulic fluid has been lost from the system, or air has entered because of a leak, ensure that the fault is cured before continuing further.

5 On right-hand drive models, with reference to the relevant Part of Chapter 4, remove the mass airflow sensor and air intake ducting to gain access to the fluid reservoir.

6 Check that all pipes and hoses are secure, unions tight and the bleed screw is closed. The bleed screw is located on the top of the transmission, adjacent to the clutch hydraulic pipe where it enters the transmission casing. Clean any dirt from around the bleed screw.

7 Unscrew the master cylinder fluid reservoir cap (the clutch has the same fluid reservoir as the braking system), and top the master cylinder reservoir up to the upper (MAX) level line. Refit the cap loosely, and remember to maintain the fluid level at least above the lower (MIN) level line throughout the procedure, or there is a risk of further air entering the system.

8 There are a number of one-man, do-it-yourself bleeding kits currently available from motor accessory shops. It is recommended that one of these kits is used whenever possible, as they greatly simplify the bleeding operation, and reduce the risk of expelled air and fluid being drawn back into the system. If such a kit is not available, the basic (two-man) method must be used, which is described in detail below.

9 If a kit is to be used, prepare the vehicle as described previously, and follow the kit manufacturer's instructions, as the procedure may vary slightly according to the type being used; generally, they are as outlined below in the relevant sub-Section.

Bleeding

Basic (two-man) method

10 Collect a clean glass jar, a suitable length

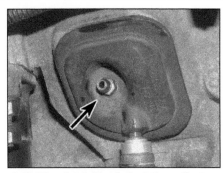

2.10 The clutch bleed nipple is on the top of the transmission bellhousing (arrowed)

of plastic or rubber tubing which is a tight fit over the bleed screw located on the top of the transmission bellhousing (see illustration), and a ring spanner to fit the screw. The help of an assistant will also be required.

11 Remove the dust cap from the bleed screw. Fit the spanner and tube to the screw, place the other end of the tube in the jar, and pour in sufficient fluid to cover the end of the tube.

12 Ensure that the fluid level is maintained at least above the lower level line in the reservoir throughout the procedure.

13 Have the assistant fully depress the clutch pedal several times to build-up pressure, then maintain it on the final downstroke.

14 While pedal pressure is maintained, unscrew the bleed screw (approximately one turn) and allow the compressed fluid and air to flow into the jar. The assistant should maintain pedal pressure and should not release it until instructed to do so. When the flow stops, tighten the bleed screw again, have the assistant release the pedal slowly, and recheck the reservoir fluid level.

15 Repeat the steps given in paragraphs 13 and 14 until the fluid emerging from the bleed screw is free from air bubbles. If the master cylinder has been drained and refilled allow approximately five seconds between cycles for the master cylinder passages to refill.

16 When no more air bubbles appear, tighten the bleed screw securely, remove the tube and spanner, and refit the dust cap. Do not overtighten the bleed screw.

Using a one-way valve kit

17 As their name implies, these kits consist of a length of tubing with a one-way valve fitted, to prevent expelled air and fluid being drawn back into the system; some kits include a translucent container, which can be positioned so that the air bubbles can be more easily seen flowing from the end of the tube.

18 The kit is connected to the bleed screw, which is then opened. The user returns to the driver's seat, depresses the clutch pedal with a smooth, steady stroke, and slowly releases it; this is repeated until the expelled fluid is clear of air bubbles.

19 Note that these kits simplify work so much that it is easy to forget the fluid reservoir

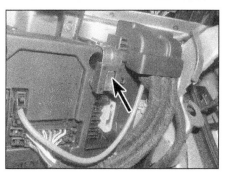

3.4 Depress the locking tab, and release the upper clip (arrowed)

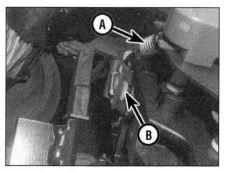

3.5 Unhook the pedal return spring (A) and remove the pivot shaft clip (B)

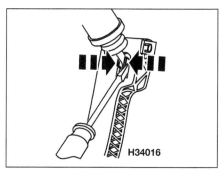

3.6 Unclip the master cylinder pushrod and slide the pedal from the shaft

level; ensure that this is maintained at least above the lower level line at all times.

Using a pressure-bleeding kit

20 These kits are usually operated by the reservoir of pressurised air contained in the spare tyre. However, note that it will probably be necessary to reduce the pressure to a lower level than normal; refer to the instructions supplied with the kit.

21 By connecting a pressurised, fluid-filled container to the hydraulic fluid reservoir, bleeding can be carried out simply by opening the bleed screw and allowing the fluid to flow out until no more air bubbles can be seen in the expelled fluid.

22 This method has the advantage that the large reservoir of fluid provides an additional safeguard against air being drawn into the system during bleeding.

All methods

23 When bleeding is complete, and correct pedal feel is restored, tighten the bleed screw securely and wash off any spilt fluid. Refit the dust cap to the bleed screw, and refit the air cleaner housing and airflow sensor, where necessary.

24 Check the hydraulic fluid level in the master cylinder reservoir, and top-up if necessary (see *Weekly Checks*).

25 Discard any hydraulic fluid that has been bled from the system; it will not be fit for re-use.

26 Check the operation of the clutch pedal. If the clutch is still not operating correctly, air must still be present in the system, and further bleeding is required. Failure to bleed satisfactorily after a reasonable repetition of the bleeding procedure may be due to worn master cylinder/release cylinder seals.

3 Clutch pedal – removal and refitting

Removal

1 Disconnect the battery negative lead (see Chapter 5A).

2 Where fitted, disconnect the wiring and unscrew the switch above the clutch pedal,

counting the number of turns, to aid refitment.

3 Remove the lower facia panels from the right-hand side of the facia – see Chapter 11, Section 31.

4 Depress the locking tab, and release the upper clip, then release the clips either side and remove the central junction box from its mountings. Using a cable tie or similar, tie it up to allow access to the pedal pivot **(see illustration)**.

5 Unhook the pedal return spring, and remove the pivot shaft retaining clip **(see illustration)**. Slide the pivot shaft to the right.

6 Unclip the master cylinder pushrod from the pedal, and slide the pedal from the shaft **(see illustration)**. The two sides of the pushrod retaining clip must be pushed in before the clip will release.

Refitting

7 Refitting is a reversal of removal, noting that the pushrod retaining clip must be fitted to the pushrod prior to refitting the pedal. Reconnect the battery negative lead as described in Chapter 5A.

4 Master cylinder – removal, overhaul and refitting

Note: *Refer to the warning at the beginning of Section 2 regarding the hazards of working with hydraulic fluid.*

Removal

1 The clutch master cylinder is located inside

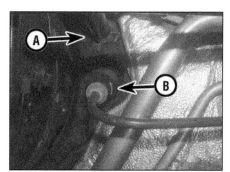

4.2 Clutch cylinder supply hose clip (A) and pressure hose clip (B)

the car on the clutch and brake pedal mounting bracket. Hydraulic fluid for the unit is supplied from the brake master cylinder reservoir.

2 Working at the engine compartment bulkhead, clamp the supply hose from the brake master cylinder (or be prepared for fluid spillage), release the clip and disconnect the hose from the clutch master cylinder. Prise out the clip and pull the pressure pipe from the cylinder **(see illustration)**.

3 Remove the clutch pedal as described the previous Section.

4 Undo the two mounting bolts and manoeuvre the cylinder from under the driver's side facia **(see illustration)**.

Overhaul

5 At the time of writing no overhaul kits or information was available. Consult your Ford dealer or local motor factors.

Refitting

6 Refitting is a reversal of removal. Apply a little grease to the clevis pin eye before refitting it. Bleed the clutch hydraulic system as described in Section 2.

5 Slave cylinder/release bearing – removal, overhaul and refitting

Note: *Refer to the warning at the beginning of Section 2 regarding the hazards of working with hydraulic fluid.*

4.4 Clutch cylinder mounting bolts (arrowed)

Removal

1 The slave cylinder is located within the bellhousing of the transmission. Remove the transmission as described in Chapter 7A.
2 Undo the three bolts and manoeuvre the slave cylinder, complete with release bearing and fluid pipes, from the transmission input shaft and bellhousing aperture **(see illustration)**. No further dismantling is possible, the release bearing is integral with the slave cylinder.

Overhaul

3 Repair kits are not available from Ford. If a fault develops, the complete cylinder/release bearing must be renewed. Note that cylinder assemblies should be supplied with an input shaft seal already fitted. If not, refer to Chapter 7A and fit a new seal.

Refitting

4 Refitting is a reversal of removal, but renew the cylinder-to-transmission casing O-ring seal **(see illustration)**. Tighten the mounting bolts to the specified torque, refit the transmission (Chapter 7A), and finally bleed the system as described in Section 2.

6 Clutch disc and pressure plate – removal, inspection and refitting

⚠ *Warning: Dust created by clutch wear and deposited on the clutch components may contain asbestos, which is a health hazard. DO NOT blow it out with compressed air or inhale any of it. DO NOT use petrol or petroleum-based solvents to clean off the dust. Brake system cleaner or methylated spirit should be used to flush the dust into a suitable receptacle. After the clutch components are wiped clean with clean rags, dispose of the contaminated rags and cleaner in a sealed container.*

Removal

1 Access to the clutch is obtained by removing the transmission as described in Chapter 7A.

6.4 Remove the pressure plate and friction disc from the flywheel

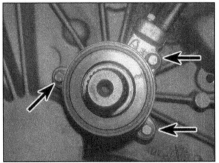
5.2 Undo the slave cylinder mounting bolts (arrowed) and manoeuvre it from the bellhousing complete with pipes and bleed nipple

2 Mark the clutch pressure plate and flywheel in relation to each other.
3 Hold the flywheel stationary, then unscrew the clutch pressure plate bolts progressively in diagonal sequence. With the bolts unscrewed two or three turns, check that the pressure plate is not binding on the dowel pins. If necessary, use a screwdriver to release the pressure plate.
4 Remove all the bolts, then lift the clutch pressure plate and friction disc from the flywheel **(see illustration)**.

Inspection

Note: *Due to the amount of work necessary to remove and refit clutch components, it is usually considered good practice to renew the clutch friction disc, pressure plate assembly and release bearing as a matched set, even if only one of these is actually worn enough to require renewal. It is also worth considering the renewal of the clutch components on a preventative basis if the engine and/or transmission have been removed for some other reason.*
5 Clean the pressure plate, disc and flywheel. Do not inhale the dust, as it may contain asbestos which is dangerous to health.
6 Examine the fingers of the diaphragm spring for wear or scoring **(see illustration)**. If the depth of wear exceeds half the thickness of the fingers, a new pressure plate assembly must be fitted.
7 Examine the pressure plate for scoring, cracking and discoloration. Light scoring is

6.6 Examine the fingers of the diaphragm spring for wear or scoring

5.4 Renew the slave cylinder O-ring

acceptable, but if excessive, a new pressure plate assembly must be fitted.
8 Examine the friction disc linings for wear and cracking, and for contamination with oil or grease **(see illustration)**. The linings are worn excessively if they are worn down to, or near, the rivets. Check the disc hub and splines for wear, by temporarily fitting it on the transmission input shaft. Renew the friction disc as necessary.
9 Examine the flywheel friction surface for scoring, cracking and discoloration (caused by overheating). If excessive, it may be possible to have the flywheel machined by an engineering works, otherwise it should be renewed.
10 Ensure that all parts are clean, and free of oil or grease, before reassembling. Apply just a small amount of lithium-based grease to the splines of the friction disc hub. Do **not** use copper-based grease. Note that new pressure plates and clutch covers may be coated with protective grease. It is only permissible to clean the grease away from the friction disc lining contact area. Removal of the grease from other areas will shorten the service life of the clutch.

Refitting

11 Commence reassembly by locating the friction disc on the flywheel, with the raised, torsion spring side of the hub facing outwards. One side of the disc may be marked 'Flywheel side'. If possible, the centralising tool (see paragraph 14) should be used to hold the disc on the flywheel at this stage **(see illustration)**.

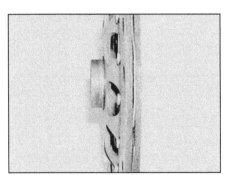
6.8 Examine the friction disc linings for wear and cracking

6.11 Locate the friction disc on the flywheel

12 Locate the clutch pressure plate on the disc, and fit it onto the location dowels **(see illustration)**. If refitting the original pressure plate, make sure that the previously-made marks are aligned.

13 Insert the bolts finger-tight to hold the pressure plate in position.

14 The friction disc must now be centralised, to ensure correct alignment of the transmission input shaft with the spigot bearing in the crankshaft. To do this, a proprietary tool may be used, or alternatively, use a wooden mandrel made to fit inside the friction disc and flywheel spigot bearing. Insert the tool through the friction disc into the spigot bearing, and make sure that it is central.

15 Tighten the pressure plate bolts progressively and in diagonal sequence, until the specified torque setting is achieved, then remove the centralising tool.

6.12 Locate the clutch pressure plate over the friction disc

16 Check the release bearing in the transmission bellhousing for smooth operation, and if necessary renew it with reference to Section 5.

17 Refit the transmission with reference to Chapter 7A.

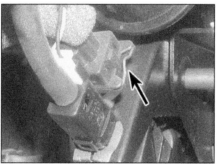

7.1 Clutch pedal switch (arrowed)

7 Clutch pedal switch –
removal, refitting and adjustment

Removal

1 Inside the car, remove the storage compartment/panel from below the steering column (refer to Chapter 11, Section 31, if necessary). Unclip the cover then undo the retaining screws and pull the storage compartment from the clips in the facia. This will allow access to the pedal switch **(see illustration)**.

2 Depress the retaining clip and disconnect the switch wiring plug.

3 Rotate the switch 90 degrees anti-clockwise and remove the switch **(see illustration)**.

Refitting

4 Refitting is a reversal of removal.

7.3 Turn the switch 90° anti-clockwise and remove it

Chapter 7 Part A:
Manual transmission

Contents

Degrees of difficulty

Easy, suitable for novice with little experience	**Fairly easy,** suitable for beginner with some experience	**Fairly difficult,** suitable for competent DIY mechanic 	**Difficult,** suitable for experienced DIY mechanic	**Very difficult,** suitable for expert DIY or professional

Specifications

General

Type	Manual, five forward speeds and reverse. Synchromesh on all forward speeds
Identification code	VXT 75
Torque capacity	250 Nm

Lubrication

Fluid type	Refer to *Lubricants and fluids*
Oil capacity (approximate):	
Diesel engine code AFN (81 kW)	2.25 litres
All other engines	2.0 litres

Ratios (:1)

	1st	2nd	3rd	4th	5th
Petrol:					
2.0 litre	3.58	2.05	1.35	0.97	0.81
2.3 litre petrol	3.58	2.05	1.35	0.97	0.81
Diesel	3.58	2.05	1.35	0.92	0.67
Reverse	3.46				
Differential	4.24				

Torque wrench settings

	Nm	lbf ft
Adaptor plate to transmission (diesel)	11	8
Engine-to-transmission unit bolts	44	32
Engine roll restrictor to transmission:		
Aluminium	70	52
Steel	98	72
Front crossmember to body:		
Stage 1	150	111
Stage 2	Angle-tighten a further 90°	
Gearchange cable bracket to transmission	31	23
Gearchange mechanism to transmission	26	19
Left-hand transmission mounting central bolt (2.0 litre petrol)	106	78
Oil drain plug	35	26
Oil filler plug	35	26
Right-hand engine mounting bracket to engine support plate	61	45
Right-hand engine mounting to bracket	54	40
Roadwheel bolts:		
All except 16 in aluminium wheels	140	103
16 in aluminium wheels	170	125
Starter motor bolts	44	32
Transmission mounting long bolts	20	15
Transmission mounting to body	54	40
Transmission mounting Torx bolts	98	72

1 General information

1 The transmission is contained in a cast-aluminium alloy casing bolted to the engine's left-hand end, and consists of the gearbox and final drive differential – often called a transaxle **(see illustration)**.

2 Drive is transmitted from the crankshaft via the clutch to the input shaft, which has a splined extension to accept the clutch friction disc, and rotates in tapered roller bearings. From the input shaft, drive is transmitted to the output shaft, which also rotates in tapered roller bearings. From the output shaft, the drive is transmitted to the differential crownwheel, which rotates with the differential case and planetary gears, thus driving the sun gears and driveshafts. The rotation of the planetary gears on their shaft allows the inner roadwheel to rotate at a slower speed than the outer roadwheel when the car is cornering.

3 The input and output shafts are arranged side-by-side, parallel to the crankshaft and driveshafts, so that their gear pinion teeth are in constant mesh. In the neutral position, the output shaft gear pinions rotate freely, so that drive cannot be transmitted to the crownwheel.

4 Gear selection is via a floor-mounted lever and selector cables. The selector cables cause the appropriate selector fork to move its respective synchro-sleeve along the shaft, to lock the gear pinion to the synchro-hub. Since the synchro-hubs are splined to the output shaft, this locks the pinion to the shaft, so that drive can be transmitted. To ensure that gearchanging can be made quickly and quietly, a synchromesh system is fitted to all gears, consisting of baulk rings and spring-loaded fingers, as well as the gear pinions and synchro-hubs. The synchromesh cones are formed on the mating faces of the baulk rings and gear pinions.

5 The VXT 75 identification stands for:

V = Vehicle
X = Transaxle
T = Transmission
75 = The distance between the input and output shafts in mm

2 Transmission oil – draining and refilling

1 This operation is much more efficient if the car is first taken on a journey of sufficient length to warm the engine/transmission up to normal operating temperature.
Caution: If the procedure is to be carried out on a hot transmission unit, take care not to burn yourself on the hot exhaust or the transmission/engine unit.

2 Park the car on level ground, switch off the

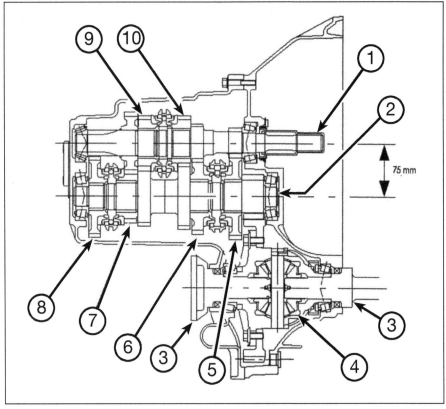

1.1 VTX 75 transmission

1 Transmission input shaft	5 1st gear	8 Reverse gear
2 Output shaft	6 2nd gear	9 4th gear
3 Front driveshafts	7 5th gear	10 3rd gear
4 Differential		

ignition and apply the handbrake firmly. Jack up the front of the car and support it securely on axle stands. Undo the retaining bolts/nuts and remove the undercover from beneath the engine/transmission unit.

3 Wipe clean the area around the drain plug (located on the end of the transmission) and position a suitable container underneath.

4 Unscrew the drain plug and allow the transmission oil to drain into the container **(see illustration)**.

5 Allow the oil to drain completely into the container. If the oil is hot, take precautions against scalding.

6 Once the oil has finished draining, ensure the drain plug is clean and refit it to the transmission with a new washer. Tighten the drain plug to the specified torque. Lower the vehicle to the ground.

7 The transmission is refilled via the level plug on the front of the transmission casing. Wipe clean the area around the level plug, and unscrew it from the casing. Refill the transmission with the specified type and amount of oil given in the Specifications, until the fluid begins to trickle out of the level hole **(see illustration)**. Refit the plug and tighten it to the specified torque.

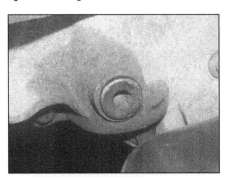

2.4 The drain plug is located on the end of the transmission

2.7 Fill the transmission until the fluid begins to trickle out

3.3 Pull the collars back, and turn them to the left to lock them in place

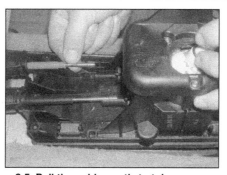

3.5 Pull the cable gently to take up any free play

8 Take the vehicle on a short journey so that the new oil is distributed fully around the transmission components.
9 On your return, park the vehicle on level ground and check the transmission oil level as described in Section 9. Refit the engine/transmission undertray.

3 Gearchange mechanism – adjustment

Note: *Ford special tool No.16-083 will be required to hold the position of the gear lever in neutral. If the tool is not available, adjustment is still possible by proceeding on a trial-and-error basis, preferably with the help*

of an assistant to hold the gear lever in the neutral position.
1 Adjustment of the gearchange mechanism is not a routine operation and should only be needed if the mechanism has been removed. If the gearchange action is stiff or imprecise, check that it is correctly adjusted as follows.
2 Remove the centre console as described in Chapter 11.
3 Ensure that the transmission is in neutral. Pull the shift and selector cable locking mechanisms back, and lock them in place by turning the collars to the left **(see illustration)**.
4 Position the gear lever in the neutral position. Ford specify the use of special tool No 16-083 to ensure the lever is in the correct place. If the tool is available, fit it around the lever, and push it down as far as it will go. If

the tool is not available, the lever is in the correct position when it lies between the 3rd and 4th gear gates.
5 Gently pull the selector cable (blue) into the end fitting to take up any free play, and turn the cable locking mechanism to the right to release it **(see illustration)**. Repeat this procedure for the shift cable (black).
6 If fitted, remove the gear lever positioning tool, and check the operation of the lever several times. If the action of the lever is not satisfactory, repeat the adjustment procedure until it is.
7 Refit the centre console as described in Chapter 11.

4 Gearchange mechanism – removal and refitting

Removal

1 The gearchange mechanism consists of the gearchange lever, the selector cables and the linkage assembly on the transmission **(see illustration)**. The lever and selector cables can be removed separately.

Gearchange lever and housing

2 Firmly apply the handbrake then jack up the front of the vehicle and support it on axle stands. Undo the retaining bolts and remove

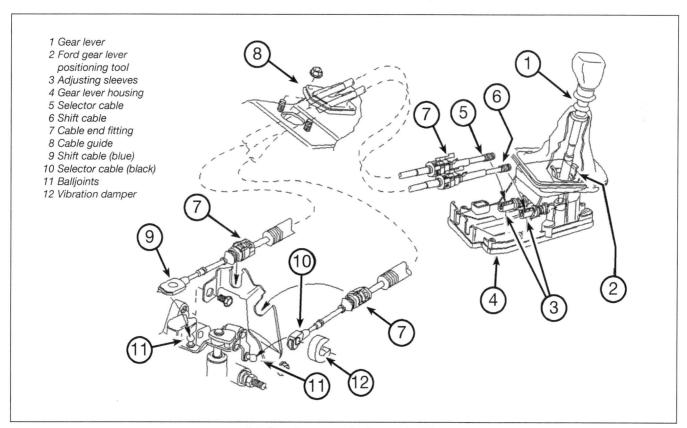

1 Gear lever
2 Ford gear lever positioning tool
3 Adjusting sleeves
4 Gear lever housing
5 Selector cable
6 Shift cable
7 Cable end fitting
8 Cable guide
9 Shift cable (blue)
10 Selector cable (black)
11 Balljoints
12 Vibration damper

4.1 Gearchange mechanism and cables

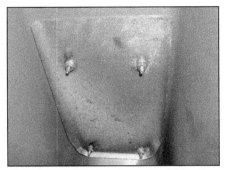

4.4 Remove the gearchange housing plate from under the vehicle

4.7 Squeeze together the tangs and remove the cable end fittings

4.9 Lever out the rectangular-headed bolts

the undercover from beneath the engine/transmission unit.

3 Undo the retaining nuts, and remove the exhaust system front heat shield.

4 Unscrew the four retaining nuts and remove the gearchange housing strengthening plate from under the vehicle **(see illustration)**.

5 Remove the centre console as described in Chapter 11.

6 Ensure that the gear lever and transmission is in neutral. Pull back the cable locking mechanisms, and lock them in place by turning the collars to the left **(see illustration 3.3)**.

7 Squeeze in the tangs of the outer cables end fittings, and press them out from the retaining bracket **(see illustration)**.

8 Lift the lever housing from the floor, disengaging the cables as the housing is withdrawn.

9 To dismantle the lever and housing assembly, unscrew the gear knob and recover the compression spring. Lever out the rectangular-headed bolts and seals, and unclip the housing gasket **(see illustration)**.

10 Invert the housing and note the fitted location of the shank spring. Remove the retaining clip and the spring **(see illustration)**.

11 Carefully lever the cable end fittings from the balljoints. Undo the three screws and remove the upper section of the housing.

12 Using a punch, drive out the cranked lever pivot pin. The lever can now be removed from the housing along with the various components **(see illustration)**. Examine all components for signs of wear or damage, paying particular attention to the selector rod

and lever locating pivot bushes, and renew as necessary.

Selector and shift cables

13 Firmly apply the handbrake then jack up the front of the vehicle and support it on axle stands. Remove the engine undertray.

14 Undo the retaining nuts, and remove the exhaust system front heat shield.

15 On diesel engine models, detach the left-hand air charge pipe from the intercooler, and release it from the bracket on the transmission. Unclip the fuel pipes from the pipe and pull it downwards.

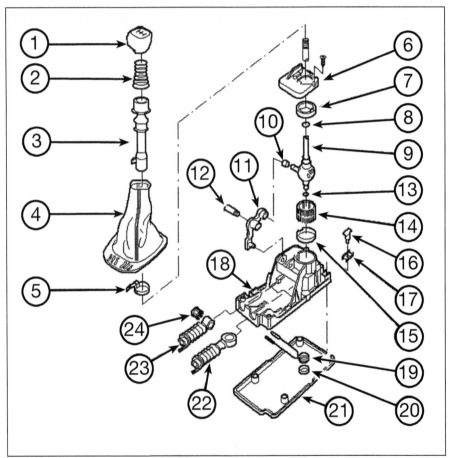

4.12 Gearchange lever and housing

1 Gear knob
2 Compression spring
3 Reverse gear sleeve
4 Gaiter
5 Cable tie
6 Housing upper part
7 Upper rubber mounting
8 O-ring
9 Gear lever
10 Cranked lever bush
11 Cranked lever
12 Pivot pin
13 O-ring
14 Gearchange lever ball seat
15 Lower rubber mounting
16 Rectangular-headed bolt
17 Seal
18 Housing lower part
19 Shank spring
20 Circlip
21 Gasket
22 Selector cable mounting
23 Shift cable mounting
24 Mounting bush

4.10 Remove the clip (arrowed) and spring

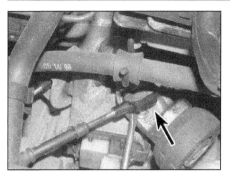

4.17a Carefully prise the gearchange cables from the balljoints (arrowed) . . .

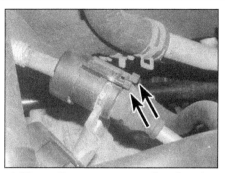

4.17b . . . then squeeze together the tabs of the clip and lift the cable end fittings from the bracket (arrowed)

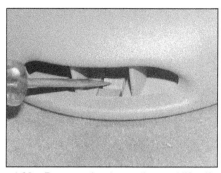

4.22a Depress the three clips and lift off the bezel . . .

16 On vehicles with secondary air injection, release the retaining clip and detach the air hose from the secondary injection pump.
17 Carefully prise the selector and shift cables from the transmission shift levers. Unclip the outer cables from the retaining bracket **(see illustrations)**. **Note:** *Take care not to pull on the blue and black sleeves of the cables.*
18 Remove both front seats as described in Chapter 11.
19 Lift the flaps and undo the retaining screws, then remove the door sill scuff panel from the front passenger side.
20 Unclip the left-hand, right-hand and centre heater covers.
21 With reference to Chapter 11, remove the centre console.
22 Depress the three retaining clips, lift off the bezel, undo the two nuts, and remove the rear footwell heating nozzle **(see illustrations)**.
23 Pull off the handbrake lever cover. Unclip the handbrake lever floor covering and remove it.
24 Fold the carpet from passenger side to the driver's side to expose the rear footwell heating channel.
25 Undo the bolts, and remove the strut from the front of the shift assembly baseplate **(see illustration)**.
26 Slacken and remove the three retaining nuts (two at the front and one at the rear), and slide the rear footwell heating channel to the rear **(see illustrations)**.
27 Undo the two bolts and remove the

gearchange cables' aperture cover **(see illustration)**.
28 Ensure that the gear lever and transmission are in neutral. Pull back the cable locking mechanisms, and lock them in place by turning the collars to the left **(see illustration 3.3)**.
29 Squeeze in the tangs of the outer cables end fittings, and press them out from the retaining bracket **(see illustration 4.7)**.
30 Manoeuvre the cables from the vehicle, noting the routing.
31 Examine the cables closely for signs of wear or damage, renewing worn components as necessary.

Refitting

Gearchange lever and housing

32 If necessary, reassemble the lever in the housing, reversing the dismantling procedure.

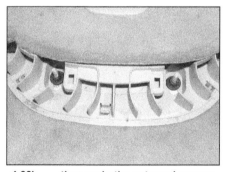

4.22b . . . then undo the nuts and remove the vent

33 Lubricate all pivot points and bearing surfaces with silicone grease then manoeuvre the assembly into position. Working underneath the vehicle refit the housing strengthen plate, and tighten the retaining nuts securely.
34 Position the exhaust front heat shield, and tighten the nuts securely.
35 Working inside the vehicle, clip the outer cables end fittings into the retaining bracket.
36 Insert the selector and shift cables into the locking mechanisms, and adjust them as described in the pervious Section.
37 Once the gearchange action is satisfactory, refit the centre console and lower the vehicle to the ground.

Selector and shift cables

38 Working from the passenger compartment, guide the cables through the aperture, and into the engine compartment.

4.25 Remove the strut from the baseplate

4.26a Undo the two nuts at the front . . .

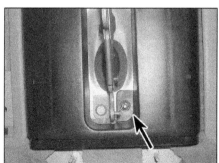

4.26b . . . and one at the rear (arrowed)

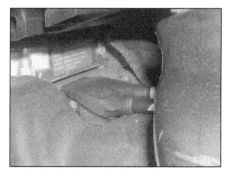

4.27 Undo the two bolts and remove the cable aperture cover

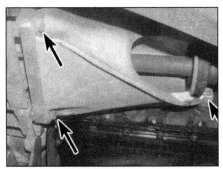

5.2a Intermediate support casing lower bolts (arrowed) . . .

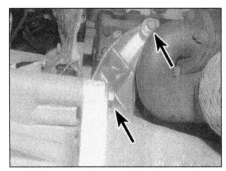

5.2b . . . and upper bolts (arrowed)

5.3 Carefully prise the driveshaft oil seal from position

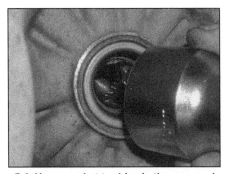

5.4 Use a socket to drive in the new seal

5.8 Prise the input shaft seal from the rear of the slave cylinder

5.9 Use a socket to drive in the new seal

Note that the cables can only be fitted as a pair.

39 Install the cables in place at the transmission. Note that the shift cable crosses over the selector cable. The outer cables end fittings must clip into place on the retaining bracket, and the inner cable ends push onto the transmission balljoints. The balljoints are different sizes, so it should not be possible to install ther cables incorrectly.

40 The remainder of refitting is a reversal of removal. If necessary adjust the cables as described in the previous Section.

5 Oil seals – renewal

Driveshaft oil seals

1 Chock the rear wheels, apply the handbrake, then jack up the front of the car and support it on axle stands. Remove the appropriate front roadwheel.

2 Remove the driveshaft as described in Chapter 8. Be prepared for oil spillage. On diesel models, if renewing the right-hand drive shaft seal, undo the bolts and remove driveshaft intermediate support casing from the transmission and cylinder block **(see illustrations)**.

3 Carefully prise the oil seal out of position using a large flat-bladed screwdriver **(see illustration)**. Note that to improve access to the right-hand side oil seal, we found it helpful

to remove the front section of the exhaust pipe (see the relevant Part of Chapter 4).

4 Remove all traces of dirt from the area around the oil seal aperture, then apply a smear of grease to the outer lip of the new oil seal. Ensure the seal is correctly positioned, with its sealing lip and spring facing inwards, and tap it squarely into position, using a suitable tubular drift (such as a socket) which bears only on the hard outer edge of the seal **(see illustration)**. Ensure the seal is fitted flush with the seal housing.

5 Refit the driveshaft as described in Chapter 8.

6 Refill the transmission with the specified type and amount of oil, as described in Section 2.

Input shaft oil seal

7 The input shaft oil seal is fitted into the rear of the clutch slave cylinder. Remove the cylinder as described in Chapter 6.

8 Carefully prise the seal from the cylinder using a flat-bladed screwdriver **(see illustration)**.

9 Remove all traces of dirt from the seal contact area, and using a tubular drift, press the new seal into place, with the sealing lip and spring facing the rear of the cylinder **(see illustration)**.

10 Refit the cylinder as described in Chapter 6.

Vehicle speed sensor O-ring

11 The procedure if covered in Section 10 of this Chapter.

6 Reversing light switch – testing, removal and refitting

Testing

1 The reversing light circuit is controlled by a switch mounted on the gearchange housing located on the top of the transmission casing **(see illustration)**.

2 To test the switch, disconnect the wiring connector. Use a multimeter (set to the resistance function) or a battery-and-bulb test circuit to check that there is continuity between the switch terminals only when reverse gear is selected. If this is not the case, and there are no obvious breaks or other damage to the wires, the switch is faulty, and must be renewed.

6.1 The reversing light switch is on the top of the transmission casing (arrowed)

6.5 Release the retaining clips and remove the switch

7.10 Prise up the retaining clip and disconnect the clutch hydraulic pipe

7.15 Undo the nuts and bolts and remove the engine mounting plate

Removal

3 On diesel engine models, detach the left-hand air charge pipe from the intercooler, and release it from the bracket on the transmission (if necessary refer to Chapter 4B). Unclip the fuel pipes from the pipe and pull it downwards.

4 On vehicles with secondary air injection, release the retaining clip and detach the air hose from the secondary injection pump.

5 Disconnect the wiring connector, then release the retaining clips and remove the switch from the gearchange housing **(see illustration)**.

Refitting

6 Refit the switch to the gearchange housing, and secure it in place with the retaining clips. Reconnect the wiring connector, and the secondary air injection hose, or intercooler pipe as applicable.

7 Transmission – removal and refitting

Note: *Removal of the transmission with the engine in place is an involved task. For the small amount of extra work involved, it may be prudent to remove the engine and transmission as a complete assembly, as described in Chapter 2C. This would greatly reduce the risk of damage to various hoses, pipes, etc, as the engine is manoeuvred to facilitate transmission removal.*

Removal

1 Chock the rear wheels, then firmly apply the handbrake. Slacken both front roadwheel bolts and the driveshaft hub bolts. Jack up the front of the vehicle, and securely support it on axle stands. There must be sufficient clearance below the car for the transmission to be lowered and removed. Remove both front roadwheels then remove the engine undertray. On diesel engines, remove the engine top plastic cover.

2 Remove the air cleaner housing and intake trunking (see the relevant Part of Chapter 4)

3 Drain the transmission oil as described in

Section 2 or be prepared for oil loss as the transmission is removed.

4 Remove the battery as described in Chapter 5A. Remove the battery compartment upper panel, and the bulkhead panel trim panel.

5 On vehicles with secondary air injection, release the retaining clip and disconnect the hose from the pump.

6 Where fitted, release the retaining clip and disconnect the air cooling hose from the alternator.

7 Remove the front section of the exhaust pipe with reference to Chapter 4C.

8 Remove both front driveshafts as described in Chapter 8. On diesel models, unbolt the right-hand driveshaft intermediate support casing from the transmission and cylinder block **(see illustrations 5.2a and 5.2b)**.

9 Remove the front crossmember as described in Chapter 11.

10 Use suitable clamp on the clutch hydraulic flexible hose in front of the engine compartment bulkhead. Prise out the retaining clip securing the clutch hydraulic pipe/hose end fitting and separate the quick-release coupling **(see illustration)**. Plug/cover both the union and pipe ends to minimise fluid loss and prevent the entry of dirt into the hydraulic system. **Note:** *Whilst the hose/pipe is disconnected, do not depress the clutch pedal.*

11 Carefully prise the gearchange cables end fittings from the balljoints on the transmission linkage. Undo the nut and bolt securing the gearchange cable retaining bracket to the transmission casing, and position the cables/bracket to one side **(see illustration 4.17a)**.

12 The engine and transmission must now be supported, as the left-hand mounting must be disconnected. Ford technicians use a support bar which locates in the tops of the inner wings – proprietary engine support bars are available from tool outlets.

13 If a support bar is not available, an engine hoist should be used. With an engine hoist the engine/transmission can be manoeuvred more easily and safely. We found the best solution was to suspend the engine with the hoist, and support the transmission with a

trolley jack from below. As both the engine and transmission mountings are removed during this procedure, balancing the engine on a jack is not recommended.

14 Completely remove the transmission mounting assembly (see the relevant Part of Chapter 2).

15 Undo the nuts and bolts securing the right-hand engine mounting plate to the mounting and engine. Remove the plate **(see illustration)**.

16 Ensure all the transmission electrical wiring is disconnected. On diesel models, undo the bolts and remove the lower flywheel cover plate.

17 Undo the upper engine-to-transmission nuts, which also secure the coolant pipe and earth lead (where fitted). Unscrew the studs noting their fitted locations.

18 Slacken and remove the remaining engine-to-transmission bolts and carefully pull the transmission from the engine and free it from its locating dowels. Once the transmission is free, lower the jack and manoeuvre the unit out from under the car. Remove the locating dowels from the transmission or engine if they are loose, and keep them in a safe place. **Note:** *If the transmission is to be renewed, check if a starter motor pinion bush is fitted into the casing of the old transmission. If one was, then a new bush must be fitted into the casing of the new transmission, using a suitable drift.*

Refitting

19 The transmission is refitted by a reversal of the removal procedure, bearing in mind the following points.
 a) *Ensure the locating dowels are correctly positioned prior to installation.*
 b) *Tighten all nuts and bolts to the specified torque (where given).*
 c) *Renew the driveshaft oil seals (see Section 5) before refitting the driveshafts.*
 d) *Refit the driveshafts as described in Chapter 8.*
 e) *Refill the transmission with the correct quantity and specification oil as described in Section 2.*
 f) *On completion, adjust the gearchange mechanism as described in Section 3.*

8 Transmission overhaul – general information

1 Overhauling a manual transmission unit is a difficult and involved job for the DIY home mechanic. In addition to dismantling and reassembling many small parts, clearances must be precisely measured and, if necessary, changed by selecting shims and spacers. Internal transmission components are also often difficult to obtain, and in many instances, extremely expensive. Because of this, if the transmission develops a fault or becomes noisy, the best course of action is to have the unit overhauled by a specialist repairer, or to obtain an exchange reconditioned unit.

2 Nevertheless, it is not impossible for the more experienced mechanic to overhaul the transmission, provided the special tools are available, and the job is done in a deliberate step-by-step manner, so that nothing is overlooked.

3 The tools necessary for an overhaul include internal and external circlip pliers, bearing pullers, a slide hammer, a set of pin punches, a dial test indicator, and possibly a hydraulic press. In addition, a large, sturdy workbench and a vice will be required.

4 During dismantling of the transmission, make careful notes of how each component is fitted, to make reassembly easier and more accurate.

5 Before dismantling the transmission, it will help if you have some idea what area is malfunctioning. Certain problems can be closely related to specific areas in the transmission, which can make component

10.2 Vehicle speed sensor (arrowed)

examination and replacement easier. Refer to the *Fault finding* Section of this manual for more information.

9 Transmission oil level check

Refer to the relevant Part of Chapter 1.

10 Vehicle speed sensor – removal and refitting

Removal

1 Chock the rear wheels, apply the handbrake, then jack up the front of the vehicle and support it on axle stands (see *Jacking and vehicle support*). Undo the two retaining nuts and four bolts (two each side), and remove the undertray from under the engine compartment.

10.3 Unscrew the sensor from the drive pinion

2 The sensor is fitted on the rear of the transmission casing, above the driveshafts. Lift up the heat shield (where fitted), and disconnect the sensor wiring plug **(see illustration)**.

3 Unscrew and remove the sensor **(see illustration)**.

4 If required, withdraw the roll pin and pull the sensor drive from the casing, complete with the drive pinion. Discard the O-ring seal, a new one must be fitted.

Refitting

5 If the sensor drive was previously removed, fit the new O-ring to the drive body, and insert it, complete with pinion, into the transmission casing.

6 Ensure that the drive is fully seated, then insert the roll pin.

7 Screw the sensor onto the drive, tightening it securely.

8 Reconnect the sensor wiring plug, and slide the heat shield (where fitted) over the sensor.

9 Refit the engine/transmission undertray, and lower the vehicle to the ground.

Chapter 7 Part B:
Automatic transmission

Contents

Degrees of difficulty

Easy, suitable for novice with little experience		**Fairly easy,** suitable for beginner with some experience		**Fairly difficult,** suitable for competent DIY mechanic		**Difficult,** suitable for experienced DIY mechanic		**Very difficult,** suitable for expert DIY or professional	

Specifications

General

Transmission type number	AG4
Application	All models
Description	Electro-hydraulically controlled planetary gearbox providing four forward speeds and one reverse speed. Drive transmitted through hydrokinetic torque converter. Lock-up clutch on all four forward speeds, controlled by electronic control module (ECM). Shift points controlled by the ECM using 'Fuzzy logic'
Automatic transmission fluid	Refer to *Lubricants and fluids*
Automatic transmission final drive fluid	Refer to *Lubricants and fluids*
Automatic transmission fluid capacity:	
Dry (new transmission)	5.5 litres
Final drive	0.8 litres

Ratios

1st	2.714:1
2nd	1.441:1
3rd	1.000:1
4th	0.742:1
Reverse	2.884:1
Final drive:	
Petrol:	
2.0 litre	4.235:1
2.3 litre	3.944:1
Diesel	3.684:1

Torque wrench settings

	Nm	lbf ft
Engine mountings:		
Left-hand mounting bracket to body	54	40
Left-hand mounting to transmission	61	45
Right-hand mounting bracket to engine mounting plate	61	45
Right-hand mounting bracket to mounting	54	40
Roll restrictor to transmission:		
Aluminium	70	52
Steel	98	72
Final drive fluid drain/filler plug	20	15
Front crossmember to body:		
Stage 1	150	111
Stage 2	Angle-tighten a further 90°	
Heater coolant pipe to transmission	23	17
Oil cooler to transmission	35	26
Right-hand driveshaft oil seal carrier	8	6
Selector cable bracket to transmission	10	7
Steering rack to crossmember	48	35
Starter motor to transmission	11	8
Sump	12	9
Torque converter-to-driveplate nuts	57	42
Transmission bellhousing-to-engine bolts	44	32
Transmission fluid drain/level plug	15	11
Transmission range sensor	14	10
Wheel bolts:		
Except 16 in alloy wheels	140	103
16 in alloy wheels	170	125

1 General information

The Ford AG4 automatic transmission has four forward speeds and one reverse. The automatic gearchanges are electronically-controlled, rather than hydraulically as with previous conventional types. The advantage of electronic management is to provide a faster gearchange response. The ECM employs 'Fuzzy logic' to determine the gear up-shift and down-shift points. Instead of having predetermined points for up-shift and down-shift, the ECM takes into account several influencing factors before deciding to shift up or down. These factors include engine speed, driving 'resistance' (engine load), brake pedal position, throttle position, and the rate at which the throttle pedal position is changed. This results in an almost infinite number of shift points, which the ECM can tailor to match the driving style, be that sporty or economic. A kickdown facility is also provided, to enable a faster acceleration response when required.

The transmission consists of three main assemblies, these being the torque converter, which is directly coupled to the engine; the final drive unit, which incorporates the differential unit; and the planetary gearbox, with its multi-disc clutches and brake bands. The transmission is lubricated with automatic transmission fluid (ATF), and is regarded by the manufacturers as being 'filled for life', with no requirement for the fluid to be changed at regular intervals.

The torque converter incorporates an automatic lock-up feature, which eliminates any possibility of converter slip in all four forward gears; this aids performance and economy.

Another feature of this transmission is the selector lever lock, with which the selector lever can be set in the P or N position when the engine is running, below about 3 mph. Under these conditions, selection from P or N can only be made by depressing the brake pedal. Correct functioning of the brake stop-light switch is therefore vital for this system to work correctly – see Chapter 9.

The transmission kickdown switch, which acts to select a lower gear (where possible) on full-throttle acceleration, is incorporated into the accelerator cable. The switch itself is mounted on the bulkhead in the engine compartment. No adjustment of the switch is possible, beyond ensuring that the basic accelerator cable adjustment is correct – see Chapter 4A or 4B, as applicable.

A starter inhibitor/reversing light relay is fitted, to prevent starter motor operation unless the transmission is in P or N, and switch on the reversing lights when signalled to do so by the transmission range sensor. The relay is located in the left-hand corner of the engine compartment, marked 150.

A transmission range sensor is fitted, and sends signals to the ECM to inform it of the selector shaft position, so that the ECM can initiate such functions as reversing lights, starter inhibition, and cruise control applications. On RHD models, a separate starter inhibitor switch is also fitted on the selector lever. Transmission output speed and turbine shaft speed sensors are also fitted, to inform the ECM of the speed of the output gear, and sun wheel in the planetary gear train. The ECM uses this information to monitor the gear ratio, decide gearchanges, and regulate torque converter slip. The AG4 ECM also instructs the engine management ECM to retard the ignition timing during gearchanges to reduce engine torque output, to produce a smooth transition from one ratio to the next.

A fault diagnosis system is integrated into the control module, but analysis can only be undertaken with specialised equipment. There is also an emergency running mode, in which only 1st, 3rd and reverse gears can be selected. In any event, it is important that any transmission fault be identified and rectified at the earliest possible opportunity. Delay in doing so will only cause further problems. A Ford dealer or suitably-equipped specialist can 'interrogate' the ECM fault memory for stored fault codes, enabling him to pinpoint the fault quickly. Once the fault has been corrected and any fault codes have been cleared, normal transmission operation should be restored.

Because of the need for special test equipment, the complexity of some of the parts, and the need for scrupulous cleanliness when servicing automatic transmissions, the amount which the owner can do is limited. Repairs to the final drive differential are also not recommended. Most major repairs and overhaul operations should be left to a Ford dealer or specialist, who will be equipped with the necessary equipment for fault diagnosis and repair. The information in this Chapter is therefore limited to a description of the removal and refitting of the transmission as a

2.5 Undo the three bolts and remove the bulkhead cover (two arrowed)

complete unit, the transmission range sensor, and the starter inhibitor switch. The removal, refitting and adjustment of the selector cable is also described.

In the event of a transmission problem occurring, consult a Ford dealer or transmission specialist before removing the transmission from the vehicle, since the majority of fault diagnosis is carried out with the transmission *in situ*.

2 Automatic transmission – removal and refitting

Removal

1 Select a solid, level surface to park the vehicle upon. Give yourself enough space to move around it easily. Apply the handbrake and chock the rear wheels.
2 Remove both front driveshafts (see Chapter 8).
3 Remove the battery, and battery compartment panels as described in Chapter 5A.
4 Drain the cooling system (see the relevant Part of Chapter 1).
5 Undo the three bolts and remove the bulkhead cover from the rear of the engine compartment **(see illustration)**. Slide the cover to the right-hand side and manoeuvre it from behind the coolant expansion tank. Where fitted remove the plastic cover from the top of the engine.
6 Remove the air cleaner housing and intake ducting (see the relevant Part of Chapter 4).
7 Where fitted, remove the secondary air injection pump (see Chapter 4C).
8 Disconnect the hoses from the coolant pipe at the left-hand end of the cylinder head. Undo the two retaining nuts, and move the coolant pipe to one side.
9 Disconnect all the transmission wiring plugs, and release the harnesses from their retaining clips **(see illustrations)**. Note the routing of the harnesses.
10 Remove the front section of the exhaust pipe (see Chapter 4C).
11 On 2.3 litre models, disconnect the various vacuum hoses from the intake

manifold, and where fitted, the EGR valve (see Chapter 4C).
12 On all models, ensure the selector lever is in the P position, and unclip the selector inner cable from the lever on the transmission. Unclip the cable outer from the retaining bracket, and position the cable to one side **(see illustration 4.7)**.
13 Remove the front crossmember (see Chapter 10)
14 The engine and transmission must now be supported, as the left-hand mounting must be disconnected. Ford technicians use a support bar which locates in the tops of the inner wings – proprietary engine support bars are available from tool outlets.
15 If a support bar is not available, an engine hoist should be used. With an engine hoist the engine/transmission can be manoeuvred more easily and safely. We found the best solution was to suspend the engine with the hoist, and support the transmission with a trolley jack from below.
16 Completely remove left-hand transmission mounting (see the relevant Part of Chapter 2).
17 Undo the nuts and bolts securing the engine mounting plate to the mounting and engine. Remove the plate **(see illustration)**.
18 Using a combination of the hoist/and or trolley jack, lower the engine and transmission unit slightly. Take care not to strain any wiring or hoses.

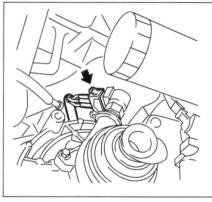

1 Valve control solenoid
2 Large sungear sensor
3 Transmission range sensor

2.9a Disconnect the wiring plugs from the transmission

2.9b Disconnect the wiring plug from the vehicle speed sensor (arrowed)

19 Prise out the rubber plug from front side of the transmission-to-engine adaptor plate, and undo the three torque converter-to-driveplate nuts. Use a spanner or socket on the crankshaft pulley nut to rotate the driveplate, and unscrew each nut as it becomes accessible **(see illustration)**.
20 Slacken and remove the bolts securing the transmission to the engine. Note the fitted locations of each bolt to aid refitting.
21 With the help of an assistant, withdraw the transmission from the locating dowels, making sure that the torque converter remains

2.17 Remove the engine mounting plate

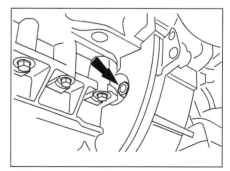

2.19 Unscrew each torque converter nut as it becomes available (arrowed)

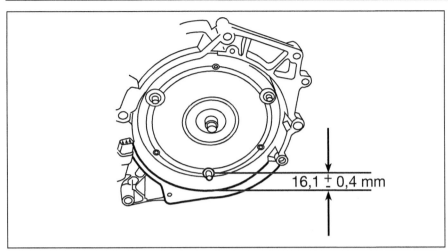

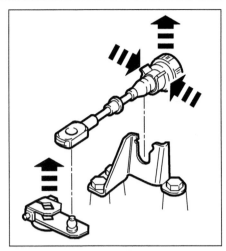

2.23 The distance from the converter face to the bellhousing mating surface must be 16.1 ± 0.4 mm

4.7 Disconnect the inner and outer selector cable from the transmission

fully engaged with the transmission input shaft. If necessary, use a lever to release the torque converter from the driveplate.

22 When the locating dowels are clear of their mounting holes, lower the transmission to the ground and remove it from under the vehicle. Strap a retaining bar across the front of the bellhousing to keep the torque converter in place.

 Warning: Take care to prevent the torque converter from falling out as the transmission is removed.

Refitting

23 Refitting is a reversal of the removal procedure, but note the following special points:

a) *Check the fitted depth of the torque converter. The distance from the converter face to the bellhousing mating surface must be 16.1 ± 0.4 mm (see illustration).*

b) *When reconnecting the transmission to the engine, ensure that the location dowels are in position, and the adaptor plate is correctly positioned. Check that the transmission is correctly aligned with the locating dowels, before pushing it fully into engagement with the engine.*

c) *Tighten all retaining bolts to their specified torque wrench settings (where given).*

d) *Reconnect and adjust the selector cable, as described in Section 4.*

e) *If a new transmission unit has been fitted, it may be necessary to have the transmission ECM 'matched' to the engine management ECM electronically, to ensure correct operation – seek the advice of your Ford dealer or automatic transmission specialist..*

3 Automatic transmission overhaul – general information

In the event of a fault occurring, it will be necessary to establish whether the fault is electrical, mechanical or hydraulic in nature, before repair work can be contemplated. Diagnosis requires detailed knowledge of the transmission's operation and construction, as well as access to specialised test equipment, and so is deemed to be beyond the scope of this manual. It is therefore essential that problems with the automatic transmission are referred to a Ford dealer or automatic transmission specialist for assessment.

Note that a faulty transmission should not be removed before the vehicle has been assessed by a dealer or specialist, as fault diagnosis is carried out with the transmission *in situ.*

4 Selector cable – removal, refitting and adjustment

Removal

1 Remove the battery as described in Chapter 5A.

2 Move the selector lever to the P position.

3 Firmly apply the handbrake then jack up the front of the vehicle and support it on axle stands. Undo the retaining bolts and remove the undercover from beneath the engine/transmission unit.

4 Undo the retaining nuts, and remove the exhaust system front heat shield.

5 On diesel engine models, detach the left-hand air charge pipe from the intercooler, and release it from the bracket on the transmission. Unclip the fuel pipes from the pipe and pull it downwards.

6 On vehicles with secondary air injection, release the retaining clip and detach the air hose from the secondary injection pump.

7 Carefully prise the selector inner cable end from the lever on the transmission. Squeeze together the outer cable end fitting retaining tabs, and pull it up from the retaining bracket on the transmission (see illustration).

8 Remove both front seats as described in Chapter 11.

9 Lift the flaps and undo the retaining screws, then remove the sill scuff panel from the passenger side.

10 Remove the left-hand, right-hand and centre heater covers.

11 Remove the centre console as described in Chapter 11.

12 Depress the retaining clips and lift of the bezel, then undo the two nuts, and remove the footwell heating nozzle (see illustrations).

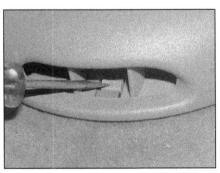

4.12a Depress the clips and lift off the bezel . . .

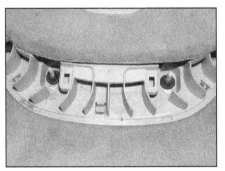

4.12b . . . then undo the nuts and remove the nozzle

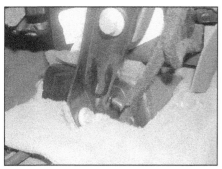

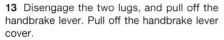

4.15 Undo the bolts and remove the strut

4.16a Undo the two nuts at the front . . .

4.16b . . . and one at the rear, then slide the channel to the rear

13 Disengage the two lugs, and pull off the handbrake lever. Pull off the handbrake lever cover.
14 Unclip the handbrake lever floor covering and remove it.
15 Undo the bolts, and remove the strut from the front of the shift assembly baseplate **(see illustration)**.
16 Slacken and remove the three retaining nuts, and slide the rear footwell heating channel backwards **(see illustrations)**.
17 Undo the two bolts and remove the gearchange cable aperture cover.
18 Slacken and remove the bolt securing the selector cable to the selector lever. Squeeze together the outer cable end fitting retaining tabs and remove the cable from the bracket **(see illustration)**.
19 Manoeuvre the cable from the vehicle, noting the routing.
20 Examine the cable closely for signs of wear or damage, renew as necessary.

Refitting

21 Working from the passenger

compartment, guide the cable through the aperture, and into the engine compartment.
22 Install the cable in place at the transmission. The outer cable end fittings must clip into place on the retaining brackets and the inner cable end pushes onto the transmission ball joints.
23 If necessary adjust the cable as described below. The remainder of refitting is a reversal of removal.

Adjustment

24 Ensure the selector lever is in position P.
25 Remove the centre console as described in Chapter 11.
26 Slacken the selector cable clamp bolt sufficiently to release the cable **(see illustration 4.18)**.
27 Firmly apply the handbrake then jack up the front of the vehicle and support it on axle stands. Undo the retaining bolts and remove the undercover from beneath the engine/transmission unit.
28 Check that the transmission selector shaft is in position P. If not, move it to this position.
29 Refit the engine/transmission undercover, and lower the vehicle to the ground.
30 Ensure that the selector lever is still is position P, then tighten the selector lever clamp bolt.
31 Refit the centre console as described in Chapter 11.
32 Verify the operation of the selector lever by shifting through all gear positions and checking that every gear can be selected smoothly and without delay.

5 Automatic transmission fluid – renewal

Note: *For an accurate fluid level check, Ford technicians use an electronic tester which is plugged into the vehicles diagnostic socket, and establishes that the temperature of the fluid is between 35°C and 45°C via a sensor within the transmission casing. In view of this, it is recommended that the vehicle is taken to a Ford dealer or automatic transmission specialist to have the level checked after renewing the fluid.*
1 Firmly apply the handbrake then jack up the front of the vehicle and support it on axle stands. Undo the retaining bolts and remove the undercover from beneath the engine/transmission unit.
2 Position a container beneath the combined drain/level plug. Unscrew the centre level plug using an Allen key, then using the same Allen key unscrew the overflow pipe **(see illustration)**. Allow the fluid to drain completely.
3 Refit the overflow pipe, and tighten it securely. **Note:** *The overflow pipe is made of plastic. Do not overtighten it.* Refit the level plug and tighten it to the specified torque.
4 Pull out the retaining clip and pull off the filler pipe blanking plug from the front of the transmission casing **(see illustration)**. On some models, the filler plug is secured by a cap. Prise the cap off with a screwdriver.

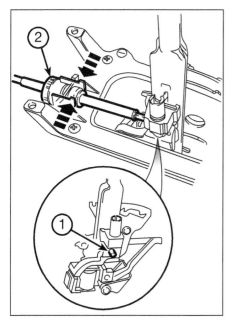

4.18 Selector cable retaining bolt (1) and outer cable end fitting (2)

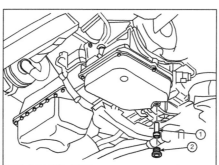

5.2 Drain plug (1) and overflow pipe (2)

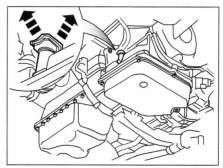

5.4 Pull out the retaining clip and remove the filler pipe plug

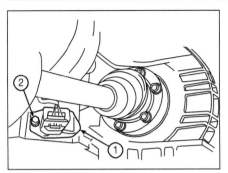

6.4 Disconnect the wiring plug (1), undo the bolts (2) and remove the transmission range sensor

5 Using a suitable funnel, pour in three litres of the correct specification automatic transmission fluid. Lower the vehicle to the ground.

6 Start the engine and move the selector lever through all gear positions. Switch off the engine.

7 At this point the Ford technician connects the FDS2000 tester to the vehicles diagnostic socket, and establishes that the temperature of the transmission fluid is between 35°C and 45°C. **Note:** *If the level is checked when the temperature is too low, overfilling will occur. If the level is checked when the temperature is too high, underfilling will occur.*

8 With the vehicle still on level ground, start the engine and unscrew the level plug from under the transmission **(see illustration 5.2)**. If the level is too high, fluid will escape down the overflow pipe. Refit and tighten the level plug when the fluid ceases to drip. If the level is too low, no fluid will escape. Add fluid until it begins to drip from the overflow pipe, then tighten the level plug. Always renew the sealing washer.

9 With the fluid level correct, refit the filler plug and secure it in place with the retaining clip or cap.

10 Refit the engine/transmission undercover.

6 Transmission range sensor – removal and refitting

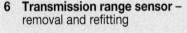

Removal

1 Firmly apply the handbrake then jack up the front of the vehicle and support it on axle stands. Undo the retaining bolts and remove the undercover from beneath the engine/transmission unit.

2 Disconnect the battery negative lead as described in Chapter 5A.

3 Drain the automatic transmission fluid as described in the previous Section.

4 The sensor is located on the rear of the transmission casing in front of the left-hand driveshaft. Disconnect the sensor wiring plug, undo the two retaining bolts, and remove the sensor **(see illustration)**.

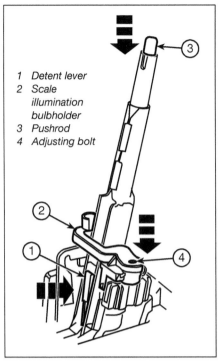

1 Detent lever
2 Scale illumination bulbholder
3 Pushrod
4 Adjusting bolt

7.5 Selector lever assembly

Refitting

5 Fit a new O-ring to the sensor, and position it in the transmission casing. Tighten the retaining bolts to the specified torque, and reconnect the wiring plug.

6 Refill the transmission with the correct specification of fluid as described in the previous Section.

7 The remainder of refitting is a reversal of removal.

7 Starter inhibitor switch – removal and refitting

Note: *On RHD models, an additional starter inhibitor switch is fitted to the selector lever assembly which prevents the starter being operated when the selector lever button is*

8.2 Screw a bolt through the driveshaft flange and onto a distance piece placed against the transmission casing

pressed. This switch is not fitted to LHD vehicles.

Removal

1 Remove the centre console as described in Chapter 11.

2 Carefully pull off the selector display illumination bulbholder. The switch is integral with the bulbholder.

Refitting

3 Press the display illumination bulbholder onto the mounting as far as it will go.

4 With the selector lever in position P, depress the selector lever button and attempt to start the engine.

5 Screw in the switch adjusting bolt until the starter motor operates, then screw the bolt out until the starter can no longer be operated **(see illustration)**. Now turn the bolt one quarter of a turn anti-clockwise. Check the operation of the switch and selector lever.

6 Refit the centre console.

8 Driveshaft oil seals – renewal

1 Remove the relevant driveshaft as described in Chapter 8.

Left hand driveshaft

2 To remove the output flange from the final drive casing, attach a slide hammer to the flange and pull it from the casing. It may take several sharp blows to free the flange. Take care not to pull the vehicle from the axle stands. Alternatively, locate a suitable distance piece (such as a chisel) between the flange and the final drive cover or transmission casing (as applicable), then screw a bolt through the flange onto the distance piece. As the bolt is tightened, the flange will be forced outwards and the circlip released from its groove **(see illustration)**. If the flange is tight, turn it 180° and repeat the removal procedure. Be prepared for oil spillage.

3 With the flange out, note the fitted depth of the oil seal in the housing, then prise it out using a large flat-bladed screwdriver **(see illustration)**.

8.3 Lever the oil seal from the casing

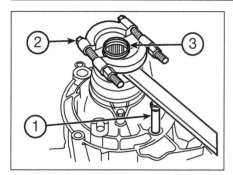

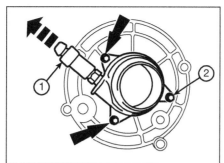

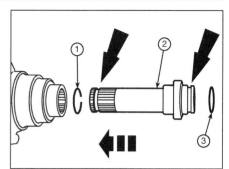

8.7 Output shaft removal

1 *M10 x 100 mm bolt*
2 *Separator in O-ring groove*
3 *Output shaft*

4 Clean all traces of dirt from the area around the oil seal aperture, then apply a smear of grease to the lips of the new oil seal.
5 Ensure the seal is correctly positioned, with its sealing lip facing inwards, and tap it squarely into position, using a suitable tubular drift (such as a socket) which bears only on the hard outer edge of the seal. If the surface of the flange is good, make sure the seal is fitted at the same depth in its housing as originally fitted.

8.8 Disconnect the vehicle speed sensor (1), undo the retaining bolts (2) and remove the seal carrier

6 Refit the driveshaft as described in Chapter 8.

Right-hand driveshaft

7 Clamp a bearing separator to the final drive output shaft, and lever the intermediate shaft from the casing **(see illustration)**. Be prepared for oil spillage.
8 Disconnect the vehicle speed sensor wiring plug, undo the three retaining bolts, and remove the oil seal carrier **(see illustration)**.
9 Using a punch, drive the oil seal from the carrier.

8.13 Output shaft (2), circlips (1) and O-ring (3)

10 Ensure the oil seal carrier is clean and dry, and fit the seal into the carrier using a tubular drift that bears only on the hard outer edge of the seal. Fit the seal with the sealing lip facing inwards.
11 Fit a new O-ring seal to the final drive casing.
12 Refit the oil seal carrier to the casing, and tighten the retaining bolts securely. Reconnect the vehicle speed sensor wiring plug.
13 With a new O-ring and circlip fitted, insert the intermediate shaft into the casing, and give it a tap with a wooden mallet or similar, to ensure that the shaft circlip engages positively in the differential **(see illustration)**.
14 Refit the driveshaft as described in Chapter 8.

9 Electronic control module (ECM) – removal and refitting

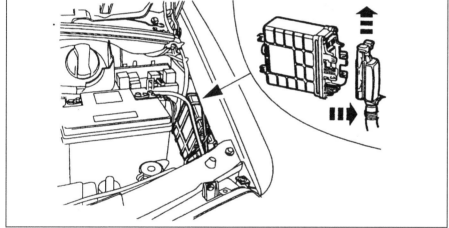

9.2 Disconnect the ECM wiring plug

Removal

1 Remove the battery (see Chapter 5A).
2 Working in the left-hand front corner of the engine compartment, disconnect the ECM wiring plug **(see illustration)**.
3 Undo the securing screw, slide the module to the front and remove it.

Refitting

4 Refitting is a reversal of removal.

Notes

Chapter 8
Driveshafts

Contents

Degrees of difficulty

| Easy, suitable for novice with little experience | | Fairly easy, suitable for beginner with some experience | | Fairly difficult, suitable for competent DIY mechanic | | Difficult, suitable for experienced DIY mechanic | | Very difficult, suitable for expert DIY or professional |  |

Specifications

Lubrication

Type of grease	VW G-6.3 high durability grease
Quantity of grease per joint:	
Outer joint	120 g
Inner joint:	
Manual transmission	120 g (60 g each side of the joint)
Automatic transmission	140 g (70 g each side of the joint)

Torque wrench settings

	Nm	lbf ft
Anti-roll bar link to suspension strut	100	74
Driveshaft-to-hub bolt*:		
Stage 1	150	111
Stage 2	Angle-tighten a further 90°	
Driveshaft-to-transmission flange bolts (automatic transmission)	80	59
Lower arm balljoint to hub carrier	55	41
Right-hand driveshaft intermediate bearing bracket to cylinder block .	47	35
Right-hand driveshaft intermediate bearing to bracket	27	20
Right-hand driveshaft oil seal carrier	8	6
Wheel bolts:		
Except 16 in aluminium wheels	140	103
16 in aluminium wheels	170	125

*Do not re-use

1 General information

Drive is transmitted from the differential to the front wheels by means of two steel driveshafts of either solid or hollow construction (depending on model). Both driveshafts are splined at their outer ends, to accept the wheel hubs, and are secured to the hub by a large bolt. The inner end of each driveshaft is bolted to the transmission drive flanges on automatic transmission models, or is a push-fit secured by a circlip on manual models. The right-hand intermediate driveshaft is supported by a bearing and bracket bolted to the rear of the cylinder block.

Constant velocity (CV) joints are fitted to each end of the driveshafts, to ensure the smooth and efficient transmission of drive at all the angles possible as the roadwheels move up-and-down with the suspension, and as they turn from side-to-side under steering. On all models with manual transmission, both inner and outer constant velocity joints are of the ball-and-cage type. On models with automatic transmission, the outer joint is of the ball-and-cage type, but the inner joint is of the tripod type.

Rubber or plastic gaiters are secured over both CV joints with steel clips. The gaiters contain the grease which lubricates the joints, and also protect the joints from the entry of dirt and debris.

2.4 Use a open-ended spanner to stop the balljoint from rotating

2.6 Undo the two Allen bolts – one each side of the balljoint

2.7 Remove the driveshaft bolt and washer

2 Driveshafts – removal and refitting

Left-hand driveshaft removal

1 Remove the wheel trim/hub cap (as applicable) then apply the handbrake, and partially slacken the relevant hub bolt with the vehicle resting on its wheels – note that the nut is very tight, and a suitable extension bar will probably be required to aid slackening. Also slacken the roadwheel securing bolts.

2 Apply the handbrake, then jack up the front of the vehicle and support it on axle stands (see *Jacking and vehicle support*). Remove the appropriate front roadwheel.

3 Remove the two retaining nuts and four screws (two each side), then remove the undershields from beneath the engine/transmission unit to gain access to the driveshafts.

4 Undo the retaining nut and detach the anti-roll bar link rod from the suspension strut. Use an open-ended spanner to stop the link rod balljoint from rotating **(see illustration)**.

5 Release the brake hose and ABS harness from the retaining brackets on the suspension strut.

6 Slacken and remove the two retaining Allen bolts, and separate the lower arm balljoint from the hub carrier **(see illustration)**.

7 Fully unscrew the driveshaft-to-hub bolt and washer, and pull the hub carrier from the driveshaft end **(see illustration). Do not allow the driveshaft to hang down under its own weight, or the joint may be damaged.**

Automatic transmission models

8 Disconnect the transmission range sensor wiring plug from the rear of the casing.

9 Using a multi-splined tool, slacken and remove the bolts securing the inner driveshaft joint to the transmission flange and, where applicable, recover the retaining plates from underneath the bolts. Manoeuvre the driveshaft from under the vehicle

Manual transmission models

10 Using a lever, carefully prise the inner joint from the final drive casing. Ensure the lever does not damage the seal surfaces of the inner joint. Manoeuvre the driveshaft from under the vehicle. Be prepared for oil spillage.

Right-hand driveshaft removal

11 Proceed as described in Paragraphs 1 to 7.

Automatic transmission models

12 Undo the three bolts securing the intermediate bearing support bracket to the cylinder block.

13 Carefully lever the inner driveshaft from the final drive casing. Be prepared for oil spillage.

Manual transmission models

14 On petrol models, undo the two nuts/bolts securing the driveshaft intermediate bearing to the cylinder block bracket **(see illustration)**. On diesel models, undo the bolts securing the driveshaft intermediate bearing to the support casing **(see illustrations)**.

15 Pull the inner joint from the final drive casing. Manoeuvre the driveshaft from under the vehicle. Be prepared for oil spillage.

Left-hand driveshaft refitting

Automatic transmission models

16 Position the driveshaft inner joint against the transmission output flange, and insert the six retaining bolts. Take care not to damage the transmission range sensor. Tighten the bolts to the specified torque. Reconnect the transmission range sensor wiring plug.

Manual transmission models

17 Fit a new circlip to the inner end of the shaft **(see illustration)**. Insert the driveshaft into the final drive casing, until it can be felt to

2.14a Undo the nuts (arrowed – one hidden) and slide the intermediate bearing flange from the bracket

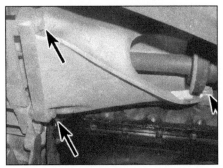

2.14b Intermediate support casing lower bolts (arrowed) . . .

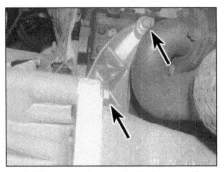

2.14c . . . and upper bolts (arrowed)

2.17 Fit a new circlip to the inner end of the driveshaft

2.27 Refit the intermediate bearing flange to the bracket

3.4 Use an old driveshaft bolt to force the outer CV joint from the shaft

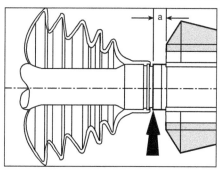

3.10 Position the damper so that the gap (a) between the groove and the damper edge is 8.6 ± 1 mm

positively engage. Take care not to damage the oil seal in the casing.

All models

18 Manoeuvre the driveshaft into position, and engage the outer joint with the hub. Fit the new hub bolt and washer, then use it to draw the joint fully into position (a new bolt is normally included in a gaiter kit – check with your supplier.

19 Align the suspension lower arm balljoint, and the hub assembly, then fit lower arm balljoint securing bolts, and tighten them to the specified torque setting.

20 Connect the anti-roll bar link to the suspension strut and tighten the retaining nut to the specified torque.

21 Refit the brake hose and ABS harness into the retaining bracket on the suspension strut.

22 Check the transmission oil level (manual models) or final drive oil level (automatic models) as described in the relevant Part of Chapter 1.

23 Refit the engine/transmission undershield, and front roadwheel(s), then lower the vehicle to the ground.

24 Tighten the driveshaft-to-hub bolt in the two Stages given in the Specifications.

25 Once the driveshaft nut is correctly tightened, tighten the wheel bolts to the specified torque and refit the wheel trim/hub cap.

Right-hand driveshaft refitting

Automatic transmission models

26 Fit a new circlip to the inner end of the shaft. Insert the driveshaft into the final drive casing, ensuring the circlip positively engages. Take care not to damage the casing oil seal. Position the intermediate bearing bracket against the cylinder block. Insert the retaining bolts and tighten them to the specified torque.

Manual transmission models

27 Fit a new circlip to the inner end of the shaft. Insert the driveshaft into the final drive casing, ensuring the circlip positively engages. Take care not to damage the casing oil seal. Position the intermediate bearing against the support bracket. Insert the

retaining bolts and tighten them to the specified torque **(see illustration)**.

All models

28 Proceed as described in Paragraphs 18 to 25.

---

3 Driveshaft rubber gaiters – renewal

1 Remove the driveshaft from the car, as described in Section 2.

Outer CV joint gaiter

2 Secure the driveshaft in a vice equipped with soft jaws, and release the two outer joint gaiter retaining clips. If necessary, the retaining clips can be cut to release them.

3 Slide the rubber gaiter down the shaft to expose the constant velocity joint, and scoop out excess grease.

4 Using a soft-faced mallet, tap the joint off the end of the driveshaft. Alternatively, use the old driveshaft bolt and screw it down into the end of the joint shaft, and force the joint from the driveshaft **(see illustration)**. Check to see if the circlip has been forced from the end of the shaft – if so remove it from the outer joint. Recover the plastic spacer and dished washer.

5 Slide the gaiter from the shaft.

6 Thoroughly clean the constant velocity

joint(s) using paraffin, or a suitable solvent, and dry thoroughly. Carry out a visual inspection as follows.

7 Move the inner splined driving member from side-to-side to expose each ball in turn at the top of its track. Examine the balls for cracks, flat spots or signs of surface pitting.

8 Inspect the ball tracks on the inner and outer members. If the tracks have widened, the balls will no longer be a tight fit. At the same time, check the ball cage windows for wear or cracking between the windows.

9 If on inspection any of the constant velocity joint components are found to be worn or damaged, it will be necessary to renew the complete joint assembly. If the joint is in satisfactory condition, obtain a new gaiter and retaining clips, a constant velocity joint circlip and the correct type of grease. Grease is often supplied with the joint repair kit – if not, use a good-quality molybdenum disulphide grease.

10 Tape over the splines on the end of the driveshaft, to protect the new gaiter as it is slid into place. Where fitted, ensure the vibration damper is fitted correctly **(see illustration)**

11 Slide the new gaiter onto the end of the driveshaft, then remove the protective tape from the driveshaft splines. Fit the dished washer and plastic spacer **(see illustrations)**.

12 Fit a new circlip to the driveshaft groove, and using a soft-faced hammer, drive the joint onto the end of the driveshaft until the circlip

3.11a Fit the dished washer . . .

3.11b . . . and plastic spacer

3.12a Fit the new circlip . . .

3.12b . . . and refit the CV joint

3.15a Secure the large retaining clip . . .

3.15b . . . and the small one

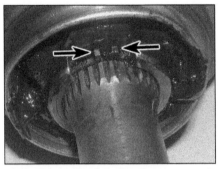

3.18 Use a pair of circlip pliers to spread the ends of the circlips (arrowed)

positively engages in the groove (see illustrations).

13 Pack the joint with the specified type of grease. Work the grease well into the bearing tracks whilst twisting the joint, and fill the rubber gaiter with any excess.

14 Ease the gaiter over the joint, and ensure that the gaiter lips are correctly located on both the driveshaft and constant velocity joint. Lift the outer sealing lip of the gaiter to equalise air pressure within the gaiter.

15 Fit the large metal retaining clip to the gaiter. Pull the clip as tight as possible, and locate the hooks on the clip in their slots. Remove any slack in the gaiter retaining clip by carefully compressing the raised section of the clip. In the absence of the special tool, a pair of side-cutters may be used, taking care not to cut the clip (see illustrations). Secure the small retaining clip using the same procedure.

16 Check the constant velocity joint moves freely in all directions, then refit the driveshaft as described in Section 2.

Inner CV joint

Manual transmission models

17 Secure the driveshaft in a vice equipped with soft jaws, then release the gaiter outer securing clip, securing the gaiter to the driveshaft. If necessary, the clip can be cut to release it.

18 Use circlip pliers to open the circlip securing the inner joint to the driveshaft (see illustration).

19 Using a hammer and a small drift, carefully drive the inner joint from the driveshaft. Discard the circlip.

20 Slide the old gaiter from the shaft.

21 Thoroughly clean the constant velocity joint(s) using paraffin, or a suitable solvent,

and dry thoroughly. Carry out a visual inspection as follows.

22 Move the inner splined driving member from side-to-side to expose each ball in turn at the top of its track. Examine the balls for cracks, flat spots or signs of surface pitting.

23 Inspect the ball tracks on the inner and outer members. If the tracks have widened, the balls will no longer be a tight fit. At the same time, check the ball cage windows for wear or cracking between the windows.

24 If on inspection any of the constant velocity joint components are found to be worn or damaged, it will be necessary to renew the complete joint assembly. If the joint is in satisfactory condition, obtain a new gaiter and retaining clips, a constant velocity joint circlip and the correct type of grease. Grease is often supplied with the joint repair kit – if not, use a good-quality molybdenum disulphide grease.

25 Tape over the splines on the end of the driveshaft, to protect the new gaiter as it is slid into place.

26 Slide the new gaiter onto the end of the driveshaft, then remove the protective tape from the driveshaft splines (see illustrations).

27 Fit a new circlip into the inner joint, and using a soft-faced hammer, drive the inner joint onto the end of the driveshaft until the circlip positively engages in the groove (see illustration).

28 Pack the joint with the specified type of grease. Work the grease well into the bearing tracks whilst twisting the joint, and fill the rubber gaiter with any excess.

3.26a Slide the new gaiter on . . .

3.26b . . . until the inner end sits in the groove

3.27 Fit a new circlips to the inner joint

29 Ease the gaiter over the joint, and ensure that the gaiter lips are correctly located on both the driveshaft and constant velocity joint. Lift the outer sealing lip of the gaiter to equalise air pressure within the gaiter.
30 Fit the large metal retaining clip to the gaiter. Pull the clip as tight as possible, and locate the hooks on the clip in their slots. Remove any slack in the gaiter retaining clip by carefully compressing the raised section of the clip. In the absence of the special tool, a pair of side-cutters may be used, taking care not to cut the clip **(see illustrations 3.15a and 3.15b)**. Secure the small retaining clip using the same procedure.
31 Check the constant velocity joint moves freely in all directions, then refit the driveshaft to the vehicle, as described in Section 2.

Automatic transmission models

32 Remove the outer CV joint and gaiter as described earlier in this Section.
33 Release the two inner joint gaiter retaining clips. If necessary, the retaining clips can be cut to release them. Slide the rubber gaiter off the end of the shaft, away from the joint inner member.
34 Thoroughly clean the constant velocity joint(s) using paraffin, or a suitable solvent, and dry thoroughly.
35 Tape over the splines on the end of the driveshaft, to protect the new gaiter as it is slid into place. Slide the new gaiter onto the outer end of the driveshaft, then remove the

protective tape from the driveshaft splines.
36 Pack the joint with the specified type of grease. Work the grease well into the bearing tracks whilst twisting the joint, and fill the rubber gaiter with any excess.
37 Ease the gaiter over the joint, and ensure that the gaiter lips are correctly located on both the driveshaft and constant velocity joint. Lift the outer sealing lip of the gaiter to equalise air pressure within the gaiter.
38 Fit the large metal retaining clip to the gaiter. Pull the clip as tight as possible, and locate the hooks on the clip in their slots. Remove any slack in the gaiter retaining clip by carefully compressing the raised section of the clip. In the absence of the special tool, a pair of side-cutters may be used, taking care not to cut the clip **(see illustrations 3.15a and 3.15b)**. Secure the small retaining clip using the same procedure.
39 Refit the outer CV gaiter and joint as described earlier in this Section.

4 Driveshaft overhaul – general information

If any of the checks described in Chapter 1A or 1B reveal wear in any driveshaft joint, first remove the roadwheel trim or centre cap (as applicable) and check that the hub bolt is tight. If the bolt is loose, obtain a new bolt, and tighten it to the specified torque. If the

bolt is tight, refit the centre cap/trim, and repeat the check on the other hub bolt.

Road test the vehicle, and listen for a metallic clicking from the front of the vehicle as the vehicle is driven slowly in a circle on full-lock. If a clicking noise is heard, this indicates wear in the outer constant velocity joint; this means that the joint must be renewed.

If vibration consistent with road speed is felt through the car when accelerating, there is a possibility of wear in the inner constant velocity joints.

To check the joints for wear, remove the driveshafts, then dismantle them as described in Section 3. If any wear or free play is found, the affected joint must be renewed. Refer to a Ford dealer for information on the availability of driveshaft components.

5 Intermediate driveshaft support bearing – renewal

1 Renewal of the intermediate driveshaft support bearing requires access to a hydraulic press and heat treatment equipment to temporarily shrink the diameter of the driveshaft. If the bearing requires renewal, we recommend that the driveshaft is removed as described in Section 2, and taken to a Ford dealer or specialist.

Chapter 9
Braking system

Contents

Degrees of difficulty

Easy, suitable for novice with little experience	Fairly easy, suitable for beginner with some experience	Fairly difficult, suitable for competent DIY mechanic	Difficult, suitable for experienced DIY mechanic	Very difficult, suitable for expert DIY or professional

Specifications

Front brakes

Type	Ventilated disc, with single-piston sliding caliper
Disc diameter	288 mm
Disc thickness:	
New	25 mm
Minimum	21 mm
Maximum disc run-out	0.10 mm
Brake pad wear limit (all types – including backing plate)	7.0 mm

Rear brakes

Type	Solid disc, with single-piston sliding caliper
Disc diameter	268 mm
Disc thickness:	
New	10 mm
Minimum thickness	8 mm
Maximum disc run-out	0.05 mm
Brake pad wear limit (including backing plate)	7.0 mm

Torque wrench settings

	Nm	lbf ft
ABS hydraulic unit nuts/bolts:		
Up to '98 model year	10	7
From '98 model year	21	15
Brake disc retaining screw	9	7
Brake pipe union nut	14	10
Front brake caliper:		
Guide pins	28	21
Mounting bracket bolts	190	140
Wiring/brake hose bracket bolt	10	7
Handbrake lever mounting bolts	24	18
Hydraulic pipe union nuts	15	11
Master cylinder retaining nuts	25	18
Pedal bracket:		
Bolts	21	15
Nuts	27	20
Rear brake caliper:		
Guide pin bolt	25	18
Mounting bracket bolt	106	78
Servo retaining nuts*	27	20
Splash shield retaining bolts	8	6
Vacuum pump clamp retaining bolt	23	17
Wheel bolts:		
Except 16 in aluminium wheels	140	103
16 in aluminium wheels	170	125
Wheel sensor retaining bolt	10	7

* Use new fasteners

1 General information

1 The braking system is of the servo-assisted, dual-circuit hydraulic type. The arrangement of the hydraulic system is such that each circuit operates one front and one rear brake from a tandem master cylinder. Under normal circumstances, both circuits operate in unison. However, in the event of hydraulic failure in one circuit, full braking force will still be available at two diagonally-opposite roadwheels.

2 All models have disc brakes fitted at the front and rear wheels as standard. ABS is also fitted as standard on all models (refer to Section 18 for further information on ABS operation). Traction control is available as an option (refer to Section 18).

3 The front and rear disc brakes are actuated by single-piston sliding type calipers, which ensure that equal pressure is applied to each disc pad. The handbrake mechanism is built into the rear calipers.

4 On all models, the handbrake provides an independent mechanical (rather than hydraulic) means of rear brake application.

5 Because these diesel engines have no throttle valve, there is insufficient vacuum in the inlet manifold to operate the braking system servo effectively at all times. To overcome this problem, a vacuum pump is fitted to models with diesel engines, to provide sufficient vacuum to operate the servo unit. The pump is mounted to the side of the cylinder block and is driven by the auxiliary shaft.

Note: *When servicing any part of the system, work carefully and methodically; also observe scrupulous cleanliness when overhauling any part of the hydraulic system. Always renew components (in axle sets, where applicable) if in doubt about their condition, and use only genuine Ford replacement parts, or at least those of known good quality. Note the warnings given in 'Safety first!' and at relevant points in this Chapter concerning the dangers of asbestos dust and hydraulic fluid.*

2 Hydraulic system – bleeding

⚠️ *Warning: Hydraulic fluid is poisonous; wash off immediately and thoroughly in the case of skin contact, and seek immediate medical advice if any fluid is swallowed or gets into the eyes. Certain types of hydraulic fluid are inflammable, and may ignite when allowed into contact with hot components; when servicing any hydraulic system, it is safest to assume that the fluid is inflammable, and to take precautions against the risk of fire as though it is petrol that is being handled. Hydraulic fluid is also an effective paint stripper, and will attack plastics; if any is spilt, it should be washed off immediately, using copious quantities of fresh water. Finally, it is hygroscopic (it absorbs moisture from the air) – old fluid may be contaminated and unfit for further use. When topping-up or renewing the fluid, always use the recommended type, and ensure that it comes from a freshly-opened sealed container.*

Note: *Ford state that if the ABS hydraulic unit needs to be bled, special test equipment (FDS2000) must be used. Bearing this in mind it is recommended that the removal and refitting of the unit is entrusted to a Ford dealer or suitably-equipped specialist. If you do decide to remove and refit the unit yourself, bleed the system as described in Section 2, then have the operation of the unit checked at the earliest opportunity by a Ford dealer or specialist.*

General

1 The correct operation of any hydraulic system is only possible after removing all air from the components and circuit; this is achieved by bleeding the system.

2 During the bleeding procedure, add only clean, unused hydraulic fluid of the recommended type; *never* re-use fluid that has already been bled from the system. Ensure that a sufficient quantity of new fluid is available before starting work.

3 If there is any possibility of incorrect fluid being already in the system, the brake

components and circuit must be flushed completely with uncontaminated, correct fluid, and new seals should be fitted to the various components.

4 If hydraulic fluid has been lost from the system, or air has entered because of a leak, ensure that the fault is cured before proceeding further.

5 Park the vehicle on level ground, securely chock the wheels then release the handbrake.

6 Check that all pipes and hoses are secure, unions tight and bleed screws closed. Clean any dirt from around the bleed screws.

7 Remove the air intake ducting to gain access to the master cylinder reservoir with reference to the relevant Part of Chapter 4. Unscrew the master cylinder reservoir cap, and top the master cylinder reservoir up to the MAX level line; refit the cap loosely, and remember to maintain the fluid level at least above the MIN level line throughout the procedure, or there is a risk of further air entering the system.

8 There are a number of one-man, do-it-yourself brake bleeding kits currently available from motor accessory shops. It is recommended that one of these kits is used whenever possible, as they greatly simplify the bleeding operation, and also reduce the risk of expelled air and fluid being drawn back into the system. If such a kit is not available, the basic (two-man) method must be used, which is described in detail below.

9 If a kit is to be used, prepare the vehicle as described previously, and follow the kit manufacturer's instructions, as the procedure may vary slightly according to the type being used; generally, they are as outlined below in the relevant sub-Section.

10 Whichever method is used, the same sequence must be followed (see paragraphs 11 to 13) to ensure the removal of all air from the system.

Bleeding sequence

11 If the system has been only partially disconnected, and suitable precautions were taken to minimise fluid loss, it should be necessary only to bleed that part of the system (ie, the primary or secondary circuit).

12 If the complete system is to be bled, then it should be done working in the following sequence:
   a) Left-hand front brake.
   b) Right-hand front brake.
   c) Right-hand rear brake.
   d) Left-hand rear brake.

Bleeding

Basic (two-man) method

13 Collect a clean glass jar, a suitable length of plastic or rubber tubing which is a tight fit over the bleed screw, and a ring spanner to fit the screw. The help of an assistant will also be required.

14 Remove the dust cap from the first screw in the sequence. Fit the spanner and tube to

the screw, place the other end of the tube in the jar, and pour in sufficient fluid to cover the end of the tube.

15 Ensure that the master cylinder reservoir fluid level is maintained at least above the MIN level line throughout the procedure.

16 Have the assistant fully depress the brake pedal several times to build-up pressure, then maintain it on the final downstroke.

17 While pedal pressure is maintained, unscrew the bleed screw (approximately one turn) and allow the compressed fluid and air to flow into the jar.

18 The assistant should maintain pedal pressure, following it down to the floor if necessary, and should not release it until instructed to do so. When the flow stops, tighten the bleed screw again, have the assistant release the pedal slowly, and recheck the reservoir fluid level.

19 Repeat the steps given in paragraphs 16 to 18 inclusive until the fluid emerging from the bleed screw is free from air bubbles. If the master cylinder has been drained and refilled, and air is being bled from the first screw in the sequence, allow approximately five seconds between cycles for the master cylinder passages to refill.

20 When no more air bubbles appear, tighten the bleed screw securely, remove the tube and spanner, and refit the dust cap. Do not overtighten the bleed screw.

21 Repeat the procedure on the remaining screws in the sequence, until all air is removed from the system and the brake pedal feels firm again. On completion, lower the vehicle to the ground (where necessary).

Using a one-way valve kit

22 As their name implies, these kits consist of a length of tubing with a one-way valve fitted, to prevent expelled air and fluid being drawn back into the system; some kits include a translucent container, which can be positioned so that the air bubbles can be more easily seen flowing from the end of the tube.

23 The kit is connected to the bleed screw, which is then opened (see illustrations). The user returns to the driver's seat, depresses the brake pedal with a smooth, steady stroke, and slowly releases it; this is repeated until the expelled fluid is clear of air bubbles.

24 Note that these kits simplify work so much that it is easy to forget to watch the master cylinder reservoir fluid level; ensure that this is maintained at least above the MIN level line at all times, otherwise air will be reintroduced into the system.

Using a pressure-bleeding kit

25 These kits are usually operated by the reservoir of pressurised air contained in the spare tyre. However, note that it will probably be necessary to reduce the pressure to a lower level than normal; refer to the instructions supplied with the kit.

26 By connecting a pressurised, fluid-filled container to the master cylinder reservoir, bleeding can be carried out simply by opening each screw in turn (in the specified sequence), and allowing the fluid to flow out until no more air bubbles can be seen in the expelled fluid.

27 This method has the advantage that the large reservoir of fluid provides an additional safeguard against air being drawn into the system during bleeding.

28 Pressure-bleeding is particularly effective when bleeding difficult systems, or when bleeding the complete system at the time of routine fluid renewal.

All methods

29 When bleeding is complete, and firm pedal feel is restored, wash off any spilt fluid, tighten the bleed screws securely, and refit their dust caps.

30 Check the hydraulic fluid level in the master cylinder reservoir, and top-up if necessary (see *Weekly checks*).

31 Discard any hydraulic fluid that has been bled from the system; it will not be fit for re-use.

32 Check the feel of the brake pedal. If it feels at all spongy, air must still be present in the system, and further bleeding is required. Failure to bleed satisfactorily after a reasonable repetition of the bleeding procedure may be due to worn master cylinder seals. **Note:** *If difficulty is experienced in bleeding the braking circuit, this maybe due to air being trapped in the ABS hydraulic unit. If this is the case then the vehicle should be taken to a Ford dealer so that the system can be bled using special electronic test equipment.*

2.23a Remove the dust cap . . .

2.23b . . . and open the bleed nipple with a spanner

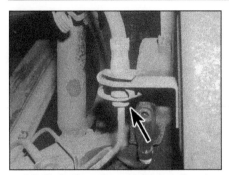

3.2 Undo the union nut (arrowed) and remove the spring clip

4.2a Prise out the retaining clip . . .

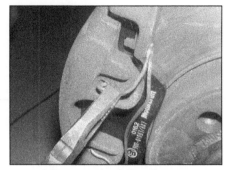

4.2b . . . and pull the clip away

3 Hydraulic pipes and hoses – renewal

Caution: Disconnect the battery before disconnecting any braking system hydraulic union and do not reconnect the battery until after the hydraulic system has been reconnected and the fluid reservoir is topped-up. Failure to do this could lead to air entering the hydraulic unit requiring the unit to be bled using special Ford test equipment (see Section 2).
Note: *Before starting work, refer to the note at the beginning of Section 2 concerning the dangers of hydraulic fluid.*

1 If any pipe or hose is to be renewed, minimise fluid loss by first removing the master cylinder reservoir cap, then tightening it down onto a piece of polythene to obtain an airtight seal. Alternatively, flexible hoses can be sealed, if required, using a proprietary brake hose clamp; metal brake pipe unions can be plugged (if care is taken not to allow dirt into the system) or capped immediately they are disconnected. Place a wad of rag under any union that is to be disconnected, to catch any spilt fluid.

2 If a flexible hose is to be disconnected, unscrew the brake pipe union nut and remove the spring clip which secures the hose to its mounting bracket **(see illustration)**.

3 To unscrew the union nuts, it is preferable to obtain a brake pipe spanner of the correct size; these are available from most large

motor accessory shops. Failing this, a close-fitting open-ended spanner will be required, though if the nuts are tight or corroded, their flats may be rounded-off if the spanner slips. In such a case, a self-locking wrench is often the only way to unscrew a stubborn union, but it follows that the pipe and the damaged nuts must be renewed on reassembly. Always clean a union and surrounding area before disconnecting it. If disconnecting a component with more than one union, make a careful note of the connections before disturbing any of them.

4 If a brake pipe is to be renewed, it can be obtained, cut to length and with the union nuts and end flares in place, from Ford dealers. All that is then necessary is to bend it to shape, following the line of the original, before fitting it to the car. Alternatively, most motor accessory shops can make up brake pipes from kits, but this requires very careful measurement of the original, to ensure that the replacement is of the correct length. The safest answer is usually to take the original to the shop as a pattern.

5 On refitting, do not overtighten the union nuts. It is not necessary to exercise brute force to obtain a sound joint.

6 Ensure that the pipes and hoses are correctly routed, with no kinks, and that they are secured in the clips or brackets provided. After fitting, remove the polythene from the reservoir, and bleed the hydraulic system as described in Section 2. Wash off any spilt fluid, and check carefully for fluid leaks.

4 Front brake pads – renewal

⚠️ *Warning: Renew both sets of front brake pads at the same time – never renew the pads on only one wheel, as uneven braking may result. Note that the dust created by wear of the pads may contain asbestos, which is a health hazard. Never blow it out with compressed air, and don't inhale any of it. An approved filtering mask should be worn when working on the brakes. DO NOT use petrol or petroleum-based solvents to clean brake parts; use brake cleaner or methylated spirit only.*

1 Apply the handbrake, slacken the roadwheel bolts, then jack up the front of the vehicle and support it on axle stands. Remove the front roadwheels.

2 Insert a small screwdriver under the top of the caliper retaining clip and lever it from the locating hole. Use a pair of pliers to pull the clip out. Repeat the procedure for the lower end of the clip **(see illustrations)**.

3 Remove the dust caps from the guide bushes to gain access to the caliper guide pins **(see illustration)**.

4 Use a 7 mm hexagon key to slacken and remove the caliper guide pins, then lift the caliper away from the mounting bracket **(see illustrations)**. Tie the caliper to the suspension strut using a suitable piece of

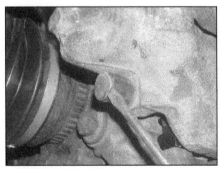

4.3 Remove the plastic end caps from the guide bushes

4.4a Use a 7 mm Allen key to remove the guide pins . . .

4.4b . . . then remove the caliper

4.6 The thickness of each pad must exceed 7 mm, including the backing plate

4.8 Check the caliper guide pins move freely

4.9 Ideally, use a piston retraction tool to push the caliper piston back

wire; do not allow it to hang unsupported from the flexible brake hose.

5 Pull the inner pad from the caliper piston and remove the outer pad from the mounting bracket.

6 First measure the thickness of each brake pad, including the metal backing plate **(see illustration)**. If either pad is worn at any point to the specified minimum thickness or less, **all four** pads must be renewed. Also, the pads should be renewed if any are fouled with oil or grease; there is no satisfactory way of degreasing friction material, once contaminated. If any of the brake pads are worn unevenly, or are fouled with oil or grease, trace and rectify the cause before reassembly.

7 If the brake pads are still serviceable, carefully clean them using a clean, fine wire brush or similar, paying particular attention to the sides and back of the metal backing. Clean out the grooves in the friction material, and pick out any large embedded particles of dirt or debris. Carefully clean the pad locations in the caliper mounting bracket.

8 Prior to fitting the pads, check that the guide pins are free to slide easily in the caliper body bushes, and are a reasonably tight fit **(see illustration)**. Brush the dust and dirt from the caliper and piston, but **do not** inhale it, as it is injurious to health. Inspect the dust seal around the piston for damage, and the piston for evidence of fluid leaks, corrosion or damage. If any of these components requires attention, refer to Section 8.

9 If new brake pads are to be fitted, the caliper piston must be pushed back into the cylinder to make room for them. Either use a piston retraction tool, a G-clamp or use suitable pieces of wood as levers. Clamp off the flexible brake hose leading to the caliper then connect a brake bleeding kit to the caliper bleed nipple. Open the bleed nipple as the piston is retracted; the surplus brake fluid will then be collected in the bleed kit vessel **(see illustration)**. When the piston is fully retracted, close the bleed nipple and remove the brake pipe clamp. **Note:** *The ABS unit contains hydraulic components that are very sensitive to impurities in the brake fluid. Even the smallest particles can cause the system to*

fail through blockage. The pad retraction method described here prevents any debris in the brake fluid expelled from the caliper from being passed back to the ABS hydraulic unit.

10 Clip the inner pad into the caliper piston and fit the outer pad to the mounting bracket, ensuring its friction material is against the brake disc **(see illustrations)**.

11 Manoeuvre the caliper into position then refit the caliper guide pins and tighten them to the specified torque setting **(see illustration 4.4a)**.

12 Refit the end caps to the caliper guide bushes.

13 Fit the retaining spring ends into the locating holes in the caliper body, then use a pair of pliers to force the sides of the springs over the caliper mounting bracket lugs **(see illustration)**.

4.10a Fit the inner pad . . .

4.10c . . . and the outer pad to the mounting bracket

14 Depress the brake pedal repeatedly, until the pads are pressed into firm contact with the brake disc, and normal (non-assisted) pedal pressure is restored.

15 Repeat the above procedure on the remaining front brake caliper.

16 Refit the roadwheels, then lower the vehicle to the ground and tighten the roadwheel bolts to the specified torque setting.

17 Check (and if necessary top-up) the hydraulic brake fluid level as described in *Weekly checks*.

⚠ *Warning: New pads will not give full braking efficiency until they have bedded-in. Be prepared for this, and avoid hard braking as much as possible for the first hundred miles or so after pad renewal.*

4.10b . . . to the caliper piston . . .

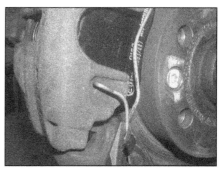

4.13 Ensure the ends of the springs are correctly located

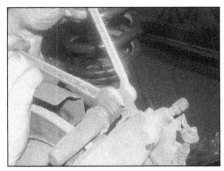

5.3 Slacken and remove the caliper guide pin bolts

5.9a Rotate the piston retraction tool clockwise . . .

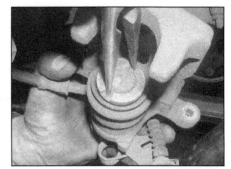

5.9b . . . or use a pair of pliers and push the piston back at the same time

5 Rear brake pads – renewal

⚠ *Warning: Renew both sets of rear brake pads at the same time – never renew the pads on only one wheel, as uneven braking may result. Note that the dust created by wear of the pads may contain asbestos, which is a health hazard. Never blow it out with compressed air, and don't inhale any of it. An approved filtering mask should be worn when working on the brakes. DO NOT use petrol or petroleum-based solvents to clean brake parts; use brake cleaner or methylated spirit only.*

1 Chock the front wheels, slacken the rear roadwheel bolts, then jack up the rear of the vehicle and support it on axle stands. Remove the rear wheels.
2 Release the handbrake lever then back off the handbrake cable adjuster to obtain maximum freeplay in the cables and ensure both caliper handbrake levers are against their stops (see Section 14).
3 Slacken and remove the caliper guide pin bolts **(see illustration)**.
4 Lift the caliper away from the brake pads, and tie it to the suspension strut using a suitable piece of wire. Do not allow the caliper to hang unsupported on the flexible brake hose.
5 Withdraw the two brake pads from the caliper mounting bracket.

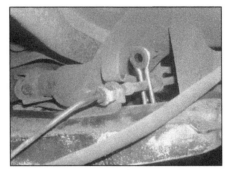

5.9c Clamp the flexible rubber pipe . . .

6 First measure the thickness of each brake pad (including the backing plate) **(see illustration 4.6)**. If either pad is worn at any point to the specified minimum thickness or less, **all four** pads must be renewed. Also, the pads should be renewed if any are fouled with oil or grease; there is no satisfactory way of degreasing friction material, once contaminated. If any of the brake pads are worn unevenly, or fouled with oil or grease, trace and rectify the cause before reassembly.
7 If the brake pads are still serviceable, carefully clean them using a clean, fine wire brush or similar, paying particular attention to the sides and back of the metal backing. Clean out the grooves in the friction material (where applicable), and pick out any large embedded particles of dirt or debris. Carefully clean the pad locations in the caliper body/mounting bracket.
8 Prior to fitting the pads, check that the

5.9d . . . and open the bleed nipple (arrowed) as the piston is retracted

guide pins are free to slide easily in the caliper bracket, and check that the rubber guide pin gaiters are undamaged. Brush the dust and dirt from the caliper and piston, but **do not** inhale it, as it is injurious to health. Inspect the dust seal around the piston for damage, and the piston for evidence of fluid leaks, corrosion or damage. If attention to any of these components is necessary, refer to Section 9.
9 If new brake pads are to be fitted, it will be necessary to retract the piston fully into the caliper bore, by rotating it in a clockwise direction and pressing the piston in at the same time, using a retraction tool, or a pair of pliers **(see illustrations)**. Clamp off the flexible brake hose leading to the caliper then connect a brake bleeding kit to the caliper bleed nipple. Open the bleed nipple as the piston is retracted; the surplus brake fluid will then be collected in the bleed kit vessel **(see illustrations)**. When the piston is fully retracted, close the bleed nipple and remove the brake pipe clamp. **Note:** *The ABS unit contains hydraulic components that are very sensitive to impurities in the brake fluid. Even the smallest particles can cause the system to fail through blockage. The pad retraction method described here prevents any debris in the brake fluid expelled from the caliper from being passed back to the ABS hydraulic unit.*
10 Fit the pads in the mounting bracket, ensuring that each pad's friction material is facing the brake disc **(see illustrations)**.
11 Slide the caliper back into position over the pads ensuring the pad anti-rattle springs are correctly positioned against the inner

5.10a Fit the outer pad . . .

5.10b . . . then the inner pad

5.11 Refit the caliper over the pads

6.5 Using a DTI gauge to measure disc run-out

6.8 Undo the countersunk screw

surface of the caliper body and are not jammed in the inspection aperture **(see illustration)**.

12 Press the caliper into position, then install the guide pin bolts, tightening them to the specified torque setting **(see illustration 5.3)**.

13 Repeat the above procedure on the remaining rear brake caliper.

14 Depress the brake pedal repeatedly to force the pads into firm contact with the discs. Once normal pedal feel has returned, check that the discs rotate freely. Adjust the handbrake as described in Section 14.

15 Refit the roadwheels then lower the vehicle to the ground and tighten the roadwheel bolts to the specified torque setting.

16 Check (and if necessary top-up) the hydraulic fluid level as described in *Weekly checks*.

 Warning: New pads will not give full braking efficiency until they have bedded-in. Be prepared for this, and avoid hard braking as much as possible for the first hundred miles or so after pad renewal.

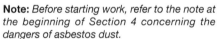

6 Front brake disc – inspection, removal and refitting

Note: *Before starting work, refer to the note at the beginning of Section 4 concerning the dangers of asbestos dust.*
Note: *If either disc requires renewal, BOTH should be renewed at the same time, to ensure even and consistent braking. New brake pads should also be fitted.*

Inspection

1 Apply the handbrake, slacken the front roadwheel bolts, then jack up the front of the car and support it on axle stands. Remove the appropriate front roadwheel.

2 Slowly rotate the brake disc so that the full area of both sides can be checked; remove the brake pads if better access is required to the inboard surface. Light scoring is normal in the area swept by the brake pads, but if heavy scoring or cracks are found, the disc must be renewed.

3 It is normal to find a lip of rust and brake

dust around the disc's perimeter; this can be scraped off if required. If, however, a lip has formed due to excessive wear of the brake pad swept area, then the disc's thickness must be measured using a micrometer. Take measurements at several places around the disc, at the inside and outside of the pad swept area; if the disc has worn at any point to the specified minimum thickness or less, the disc must be renewed.

4 If the disc is thought to be warped, it can be checked for run-out. First secure the disc firmly to the hub by refitting at least two roadwheel bolts – fit plain washers to the roadwheel bolts to ensure that the disc is properly seated on the hub.

5 Either use a dial gauge mounted on any convenient fixed point, while the disc is slowly rotated, or use feeler blades to measure (at several points all around the disc) the clearance between the disc and a fixed point, such as the caliper mounting bracket **(see illustration)**. If the measurements obtained are at the specified maximum or beyond, the disc is excessively warped, and must be renewed; however, it is worth checking first that the wheel bearing is in good condition (Chapter 10).

6 Check the disc for cracks, especially around the wheel bolt holes, and any other wear or damage, and renew if necessary.

Removal

7 Slacken and remove the two bolts securing the brake caliper mounting bracket to the hub carrier. Slide the whole caliper assembly off the hub and away from the disc and tie the assembly to the front coil spring, using a piece of wire or string, to avoid placing any strain on the hydraulic brake hose. The caliper mounting bracket can be unbolted and removed separately if required (see Section 8).

8 Unscrew the countersunk disc retaining screw **(see illustration)**. If the bolt is tight, use an impact driver. Remove the disc, lightly tap its rear face with a hide or plastic mallet to free it from the hub.

Refitting

9 Refitting is the reverse of the removal procedure, noting the following points:

a) *Ensure that the mating surfaces of the disc and hub are clean and flat.*
b) *Tighten the disc retaining screw to the specified torque.*
c) *If a new disc has been fitted, use a suitable solvent to wipe any preservative coating from the disc, before refitting the caliper. Note that new brake pads should always be fitted when the disc is renewed.*
d) *Prior to installation, clean the caliper bracket mounting bolts. Slide the caliper into position, making sure the pads pass either side of the disc, and tighten the caliper bracket bolts to the specified torque setting.*
e) *Refit the roadwheel then lower the vehicle to the ground and tighten the wheel bolts to the specified torque. Apply the footbrake several times to force the pads back into contact with the disc before driving the vehicle.*

 Warning: New pads will not give full braking efficiency until they have bedded-in. Be prepared for this, and avoid hard braking as much as possible for the first hundred miles or so after pad renewal.

7 Rear brake disc – inspection, removal and refitting

Note: *Before starting work, refer to the note at the beginning of Section 5 concerning the dangers of asbestos dust.*
Note: *If either disc requires renewal, BOTH should be renewed at the same time, to ensure even and consistent braking. New brake pads should be fitted also.*

Inspection

1 Firmly chock the front wheels, engage 1st gear (or P), slacken the rear roadwheel bolts, then jack up the rear of the car and support it on axle stands (see *Jacking and vehicle support*). Remove the appropriate rear roadwheel.

2 Inspect the disc as described in Section 6.

Removal

3 Unscrew the two bolts securing the brake caliper in position, then slide the whole caliper assembly off the disc. Using a piece of wire or string, tie the caliper to the rear suspension coil spring, to avoid placing any strain on the hydraulic brake hose. The caliper mounting bracket must be unbolted and removed **(see illustration)**.

4 Undo the countersunk disc retaining screw. If the screw is tight, slacken it using an impact driver **(see illustration)**. Remove the disc, lightly tapping its rear face with a hide or plastic mallet to free it from the hub.

Refitting

5 Refitting is the reverse of the removal procedure, noting the following points:

  a) *Ensure that the mating surfaces of the disc and hub are clean and flat.*

  b) *Tighten the disc retaining screw to the specified torque.*

  c) *If a new disc has been fitted, use a suitable solvent to wipe any preservative coating from the disc, before refitting the caliper. Note that new brake pads should always be fitted when the disc is renewed.*

  d) *Prior to installation, clean the caliper bracket mounting bolts. Slide the caliper into position, making sure the pads pass either side of the disc, and tighten the caliper bracket bolts to the specified torque setting.*

  e) *Refit the roadwheel then lower the vehicle to the ground and tighten the wheel bolts to the specified torque. Apply the footbrake several times to force the pads back into contact with the disc before driving the vehicle.*

⚠️ *Warning: New pads will not give full braking efficiency until they have bedded-in. Be prepared for this, and avoid hard braking as much as possible for the first hundred miles or so after pad renewal.*

---

8 Front brake caliper –
removal, overhaul and refitting

Note: *Before starting work, refer to the note at the beginning of Section 2 concerning the*

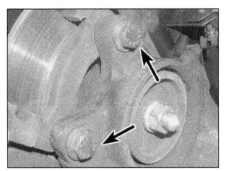

7.3 In order to remove the rear disc, the caliper mounting bracket must be removed – two bolts (arrowed)

dangers of hydraulic fluid, and to the warning at the beginning of Section 4 concerning the dangers of asbestos dust.

Removal

1 Apply the handbrake, slacken the front roadwheel bolts, then jack up the front of the vehicle and support it on axle stands. Remove the front roadwheels.

2 Minimise fluid loss by using a brake hose clamp, a G-clamp or a similar tool to clamp the flexible hose.

3 Where applicable, disconnect the wiring connector from the brake pad wear sensor connector. Unclip the connector from the caliper bracket.

4 Clean the area around the caliper brake pipe union then slacken the union nut.

5 Carefully lever the pad retaining spring out position and remove it from the brake caliper using a flat-bladed screwdriver **(see illustrations 4.2a and 4.2b)**. Remove the dust caps from the guide bushes then slacken and remove the caliper guide pins (see Section 4).

6 Lift the caliper out of position. Remove the inner brake pad from the piston and the outer brake pad from the caliper mounting bracket. Disconnect the flexible brake hose by rotating the caliper off the end of the hose. Unbolt and remove the caliper mounting bracket **(see illustrations)**.

Overhaul

7 With the caliper on the bench, wipe away all

7.4 The disc is secured by a countersunk screw

traces of dust and dirt, but *avoid inhaling the dust, as it is injurious to health.*

8 Withdraw the partially ejected piston from the caliper body, and remove the dust seal.

> **HAYNES HiNT** *If the piston cannot be withdrawn by hand, it can be forced out by applying compressed air to the brake hose union hole. Only low pressure should be required, such as that generated by a foot pump. Even using low pressure, the piston will be ejected with considerable force; place a block of soft wood in the caliper to prevent damage to the end of the piston, and avoid getting your fingers trapped between the piston and caliper.*

9 Using a soft flat-bladed instrument, such as a plastic spatula, extract the piston hydraulic seal, taking great care not to damage the caliper bore **(see illustration)**.

10 Thoroughly clean all components, using only methylated spirit, isopropyl alcohol or clean brake fluid as a cleaning medium. Never use mineral-based solvents such as petrol or paraffin, as they will attack the hydraulic system's rubber components. Dry the components immediately, using compressed air or a clean, lint-free cloth. Use compressed air to blow clear the fluid passages.

11 Check all components, and renew any that are worn or damaged. Check particularly the cylinder bore and piston; these should be

8.6a Rotate the caliper off the brake hose

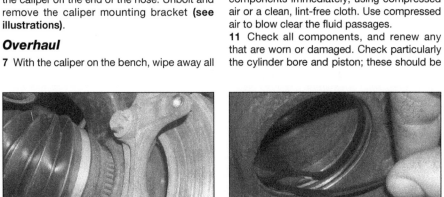

8.6b Undo the bolts and remove the caliper mounting bracket

8.9 Use a plastic tool to carefully prise out the piston hydraulic seal

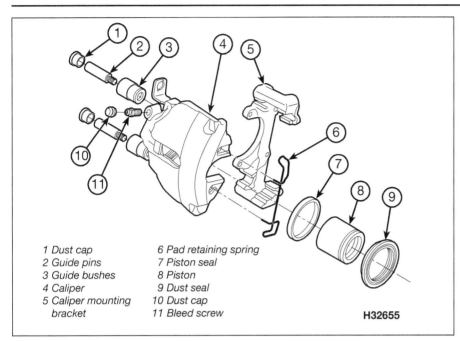

1 Dust cap
2 Guide pins
3 Guide bushes
4 Caliper
5 Caliper mounting
   bracket

6 Pad retaining spring
7 Piston seal
8 Piston
9 Dust seal
10 Dust cap
11 Bleed screw

H32655

8.11 Exploded view of the front brake caliper

renewed (note that this means the renewal of the complete body assembly) if they are scratched, worn or corroded in any way. Similarly check the condition of the guide pins and the bushes in the caliper body; both pins should be undamaged and (when cleaned) a reasonably tight sliding fit in the bushes. If there is any doubt about the condition of any component, renew it **(see illustration)**.

12 If the assembly is fit for further use, obtain the appropriate repair kit; the components are available from Ford dealers in various combinations. All rubber seals should be renewed as a matter of course; these should never be re-used.

13 On reassembly, ensure that all components are clean and dry.

14 Soak the piston and the new piston (fluid) seal in clean hydraulic fluid. Smear clean fluid on the cylinder bore surface.

15 Fit the new piston (fluid) seal, using only your fingers (no tools) to manipulate it into the cylinder bore groove **(see illustration)**.

16 Fit the new dust seal to the piston groove.

Carefully ease the piston squarely into the cylinder bore using a twisting motion. Press the piston fully into position and seat the outer lip of the dust seal in the caliper body groove **(see illustrations)**.

17 Prior to refitting, fill the caliper with fresh hydraulic fluid by slackening the bleed screw and pumping the fluid through the caliper until bubble-free fluid is expelled from the union hole.

Refitting

18 Bolt the caliper mounting bracket to the hub carrier; and tighten to the specified torque.

19 Reconnect the brake pipe by rotating the caliper onto the pipe.

20 Refit the brake pads to the piston and caliper mounting bracket, with reference to Section 4.

21 Manoeuvre the caliper into position.

22 Fit the caliper guide pins, tightening them to the specified torque setting, and refit the dust caps to the guide bushes.

23 Tighten the brake pipe union nut securely.

24 Fit the pad retaining spring, ensuring its ends are correctly located in the caliper body holes.

25 Remove the brake hose clamp and bleed the hydraulic system as described in Section 2. Note that, providing the precautions described were taken to minimise brake fluid loss, it should only be necessary to bleed the relevant front brake.

26 Refit the roadwheel, then lower the vehicle to the ground and tighten the roadwheel bolts to the specified torque.

9 Rear brake caliper – removal, overhaul and refitting

Note: *Before starting work, refer to the note at the beginning of Section 2 concerning the dangers of hydraulic fluid, and to the warning at the beginning of Section 5 concerning the dangers of asbestos dust.*

Removal

1 Chock the front wheels, slacken the rear wheel bolts, then jack up the rear of the vehicle and support it on axle stands. Remove the relevant rear wheel.

2 Release the handbrake lever then back off the handbrake cable adjuster to obtain maximum freeplay in the cables with reference to Section 14.

3 Release the retaining clip and free the handbrake cable from the caliper lever, then free the outer cable from the caliper body.

4 Minimise fluid loss by using a brake hose clamp, a G-clamp or a similar tool to clamp the flexible hose **(see illustration 5.9c)**.

5 Clean the area around the caliper brake hose then slacken the union.

6 Slacken and remove the caliper guide pin bolts.

7 Lift the brake caliper away from the its mounting bracket and unscrew it from the end of the brake hose. Plug/cover the hose end and caliper union to minimise fluid loss and prevent the entry of dirt into the hydraulic system. Wash off any spilt fluid immediately with cold water. Remove the inner and outer brake pads from the caliper mounting bracket.

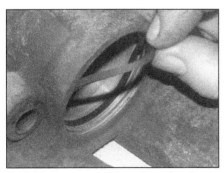

8.15 Fit the new seal into the caliper body

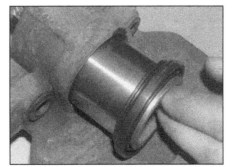

8.16a Insert the piston with the seal fitted into the caliper body . . .

8.16b . . . and seat the outer edge of the seal in the caliper body groove

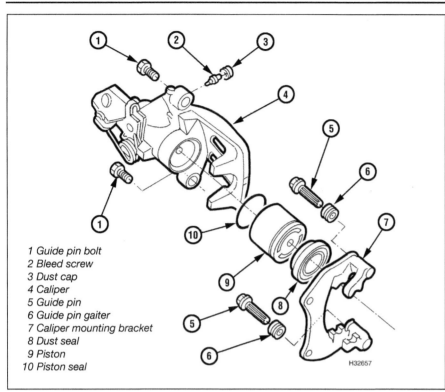

1 Guide pin bolt
2 Bleed screw
3 Dust cap
4 Caliper
5 Guide pin
6 Guide pin gaiter
7 Caliper mounting bracket
8 Dust seal
9 Piston
10 Piston seal

H32657

9.13 Exploded view of a rear brake caliper

Unbolt and remove the caliper mounting bracket.

Overhaul

Note: *It is not possible to overhaul the brake caliper handbrake mechanism. If the mechanism is faulty, or fluid is leaking from the handbrake lever seal the caliper assembly must be renewed.*

8 With the caliper on the bench, wipe away all traces of dust and dirt, but *avoid inhaling the dust, as it is injurious to health.*

9 Remove the piston from the caliper bore by rotating it in an anti-clockwise direction. This can be achieved using a suitable pair of circlip pliers engaged in the caliper piston slots. Once the piston turns freely but does not come out any further, the piston is held in only by its seal and can be withdrawn by hand.

10 Remove the dust seal from the piston then, using a blunt flat-bladed instrument, carefully extract the piston hydraulic seal from the caliper bore. Take great care not to mark the caliper surface.

11 Withdraw the guide pins from the caliper mounting bracket, and remove the guide pin gaiters.

12 Inspect all the caliper components (as described for the front brake caliper in Section 8), and renew as necessary, noting that the handbrake mechanism must **not** be dismantled.

13 On reassembly, ensure all components are clean and dry **(see illustration)**.

14 Soak the piston and the new piston (fluid) seal in clean hydraulic fluid. Smear clean fluid on the cylinder bore surface. Fit the new piston (fluid) seal, using only your fingers (not

tools) to manipulate into the cylinder bore groove.

15 Fit the new dust seal to the piston groove. Carefully ease the piston squarely into the cylinder bore using a twisting motion. Turn and push the piston in a clockwise direction, using the method employed on dismantling, until it is fully retracted into the caliper bore then seat the outer lip of the dust seal in the caliper groove.

16 Apply the grease supplied in the repair kit, or a copper-based brake grease or anti-seize compound, to the guide pins. Ensure that the gaiters are correctly located in the grooves on the caliper bracket.

17 Prior to refitting, fill the caliper with fresh hydraulic fluid by slackening the bleed screw and pumping the fluid through the caliper until bubble-free fluid is expelled from the union hole.

Refitting

18 Bolt the caliper mounting bracket to the rear hub carrier; and tighten to the specified torque. Refit the brake pads to the caliper mounting bracket with reference to Section 5.

19 Screw the caliper fully onto the brake hose, then manoeuvre the caliper into position over the pads then fit the new guide pin bolts, tightening them to the specified torque setting. Ensure that the pin gaiters are correctly fitted.

20 Tighten the brake hose union, and remove the brake hose clamp.

21 Bleed the hydraulic system as described in Section 2. Note that, providing the precautions described were taken to minimise brake fluid loss, it should only be necessary to bleed the relevant rear brake.

22 Reconnect the handbrake cable to the caliper **(see illustration)**, securing it in position with the retaining clip, and adjust the cable as described in Section 14.

23 Refit the roadwheel, then lower the vehicle to the ground and tighten the roadwheel bolts to the specified torque.

10 Master cylinder – removal, overhaul and refitting

Note: *Before starting work, refer to the warning at the beginning of Section 2 concerning the dangers of hydraulic fluid.*

Removal

1 Slacken both front roadwheel bolts, raise the front of the vehicle and rest it securely on axle stands. Remove both front roadwheels.

2 Remove the air cleaner housing, mass airflow sensor, and intake ducting to access the master cylinder, located on the right-hand side of the engine compartment bulkhead (see the relevant Part of Chapter 4).

3 Pull out the battery compartment upper panel **(see illustration)**.

4 Release the three retaining screws, and

9.22 Reconnect the handbrake cable to the caliper lever

10.3 Remove the battery compartment upper panel

10.4 Undo the three screws (two arrowed) and remove the bulkhead cover

10.7 Disconnect the level sensor wiring plug

10.8 Release the clip and disconnect the clutch master cylinder feed hose (arrowed)

remove the bulkhead cover **(see illustration)**. Slide the cover to the right-hand side and manoeuvre it from behind the coolant expansion tank.

5 On petrol models, remove the throttle body as described in Chapter 4A, Section 4.

6 Connect a length of hose to the right-hand front brake caliper bleed screw, then direct the other end of the hose into a suitable receptacle, as described in Section 2. Open the bleed screw and then depress the brake pedal repeatedly until the level of fluid in the right-hand side of the master cylinder reservoir is below that of the clutch master cylinder supply hose. Close the bleed screw. Repeat the procedure for the left-hand front caliper, to reduce the fluid level in the left-hand side of the reservoir.

7 Pad the area underneath the master cylinder with absorbent rags, to catch any fluid spills. Disconnect the wiring plug from the brake fluid level sensor **(see illustration)**.

8 On manual transmission models, disconnect the clutch master cylinder feed hose from the side of the brake master cylinder and plug the outlet to minimise fluid loss **(see illustration)**.

9 If required, release the retaining tabs, and pull the reservoir up and off the master cylinder **(see illustration)**.

10 Wipe clean the area around the brake pipe unions on the side of the master cylinder, and place absorbent rags beneath the pipe unions to catch any surplus fluid. Make a note

of the correct fitted positions of the unions, then unscrew the union nuts and carefully withdraw the pipes **(see illustration)**. Plug or tape over the pipe ends and master cylinder orifices, to minimise the loss of brake fluid, and to prevent the entry of dirt into the system. Wash off any spilt fluid immediately with cold water.

11 Undo the two nuts and remove the master cylinder **(see illustration)**. Recover the sealing ring.

Overhaul

12 If the master cylinder is faulty, it must be renewed. Repair kits are not available from Ford dealers, so the cylinder must be treated as a sealed unit.

13 The only items which can be renewed are the mounting seals for the fluid reservoir; if these show signs of deterioration, pull out and remove the old seals. Lubricate the new seals with clean brake fluid, and ease them into the master cylinder ports.

Refitting

14 Remove all traces of dirt from the master cylinder and servo unit mating surfaces, and where necessary, fit a new sealing ring to the rear of the master cylinder body.

15 Fit the master cylinder to the servo unit, ensuring that the servo unit pushrod enters the master cylinder bore centrally. Have an assistant depress the brake pedal slightly, so that pushrod is moved towards the master cylinder.

16 Refit the master cylinder mounting nuts and tighten them to the specified torque.

17 Wipe clean the brake pipe unions, then refit them to the master cylinder ports and tighten them to the specified torque.

18 Refit the reservoir into the seals on the top of the master cylinder.

19 On manual transmission models, reconnect the clutch master cylinder hose to the fluid reservoir and securely tighten the retaining clip.

20 Reconnect the fluid level sender unit wiring connector.

21 Refill the master cylinder reservoir with new fluid, and bleed the brake and (if necessary) the clutch hydraulic systems, as described in Section 2 and Chapter 6 respectively.

22 The remainder of refitting is a reversal of removal.

11 Brake pedal – removal and refitting

Removal

1 Disconnect the battery negative lead – see Chapter 5A.

2 Remove the driver's side lower facia panel as described in Chapter 11, Section 31.

3 Lower the central junction box, release the retaining clips each side and at the top, and

10.9 Release the reservoir retaining tabs

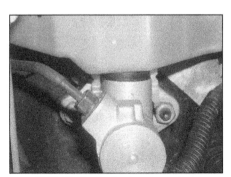

10.10 Undo the brake pipe unions

10.11 Undo the two nuts (one each side) and remove the master cylinder

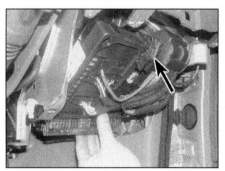

11.3 The central junction box is secured by a clip each side, and one at the top (arrowed)

11.5 Release the retaining clip from the servo pushrod

11.6 Remove the pedal shaft retaining clip (arrowed)

pull the junction box up and out. Tie the junction box to one side **(see illustration)**.

4 Release the stop-light switch from its mounting bracket and position it to one side (see Section 17).

5 Remove the servo pushrod pin retaining clip, and slide out the pivot pin **(see illustration)**.

6 Detach the pedal pivot shaft retaining clip, slide the shaft towards the clutch pedal, and remove the brake pedal **(see illustration)**.

7 Examine all components for signs of wear or damage, renewing them as necessary.

Refitting

8 Apply a smear of multi-purpose grease to the pedal pivot bore.

9 The remainder of the refitting procedure is a reversal of the removal procedure, noting the following points:
  a) Tighten all fixings to the correct torque, where specified.
  b) Refit and adjust the stop-light switch as described in Section 17.

---

12 Vacuum servo unit – testing, removal and refitting

Testing

1 To test the operation of the servo unit, depress the footbrake several times to

exhaust the vacuum, then start the engine whilst keeping the pedal firmly depressed. As the engine starts, there should be a noticeable give in the brake pedal as the vacuum builds-up. Allow the engine to run for at least two minutes, then switch it off. If the brake pedal is now depressed it should feel normal, but further applications should result in the pedal feeling firmer, with the pedal stroke decreasing with each application.

2 If the servo does not operate as described, first inspect the servo unit check valve as described in Section 13. On diesel engine models, also check the vacuum pump as described in Section 20.

3 If the servo unit still fails to operate satisfactorily, the fault may lie within the unit itself. Repairs to the unit are not possible – if faulty, the servo unit must be renewed.

Removal

4 Remove the master cylinder as described in Section 10.

5 On petrol models, depress the locking tabs, and disconnect the fuel pipes at their quick-release couplings behind the cylinder head **(see illustration)**. Disconnect the evaporative emission pipe below the master cylinder location.

6 Carefully ease the vacuum hose connection out from the servo unit, taking care not to damage the grommet.

7 Working underneath the facia, disconnect the accelerator cable from the pedal, or the wiring plug from the accelerator pedal

position sensor – as applicable (see the relevant Part of Chapter 4).

8 Pull out the retaining clip, and pull the pressure pipe from the end of the clutch master cylinder in the engine compartment. Plug the end of the cylinder to prevent fluid loss and dirt ingress.

9 Working underneath the facia, locate the servo unit pushrod and release the retaining clip, and remove the pushrod pin **(see illustration 11.5)**.

10 Slacken and remove the four nuts securing the servo unit to the bulkhead **(see illustration)**.

11 Manoeuvre the servo unit out of position. Recover the gasket which is fitted between the servo and bulkhead. Examine the gasket for signs of wear or damage and renew if necessary.

Refitting

12 Manoeuvre the pedal bracket back into position, and tighten the retaining bolts/nuts to the specified torque.

13 Ensure the servo unit and bulkhead mating surfaces are clean, fit the gasket to the rear of the servo unit and manoeuvre the unit into position. Fit the new servo unit retaining nuts, and tighten them to the specified torque.

14 The remainder of refitting is a reversal of removal, noting the following points:
  a) Tighten all nuts and bolts to their specified torque where given.
  b) Bleed the braking system as described in Section 2.
  c) On manual transmission models, if necessary, bleed the clutch hydraulic system as described in Chapter 6.
  d) Establish that the braking system is working satisfactorily before driving on the road.

---

13 Vacuum servo unit check valve – removal, testing and refitting

Note: The valve is an integral part of the servo unit vacuum hose and is not available separately.

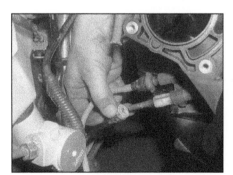

12.5 Disconnect the fuel supply and return couplings

12.10 Undo the four servo retaining nuts (arrowed)

13.1 Carefully prise the hose connection from the servo unit

13.3 Depress the retaining collar and pull the vacuum hose from the manifold

Removal

1 Carefully ease the vacuum hose connection out from the servo unit, taking care not to damage the grommet **(see illustration)**.
2 Work back along the hose, freeing it from all the relevant retaining clips whilst noting its correct routing.
3 Slacken the retaining clip then disconnect the vacuum hose from the manifold and/or vacuum pump (as applicable) and remove it from the vehicle. On petrol models depress the collar and pull the hose from the manifold **(see illustration)**.

Testing

4 Examine the vacuum hose for signs of damage, and renew if necessary. The valve may be tested by blowing through it in both directions. Air should flow through the valve in one direction only – when blown through from the servo unit end of the valve. Renew the valve if this is not the case.
5 Examine the servo unit rubber sealing grommet and hose(s) linking the main hose to the manifold/pump (as applicable) for signs of damage or deterioration, and renew as necessary.

Refitting

6 Ensure the sealing grommet is in position in the servo unit then carefully ease the vacuum

hose end fitting into position, taking great care not to displace or damage the grommet.
7 Ensure the hose is correctly routed then connect it to the pump/manifold and securely tighten the retaining clip(s).
8 On completion, start the engine and check the check valve-to-servo unit connection for signs of air leaks.

14 Handbrake – adjustment

1 Depress the brake pedal firmly, to settle the rear brake self adjustment mechanism.
2 Chock the front wheels, then jack up the rear of the vehicle and support it on axle stands. Fully release the handbrake lever.
3 Working underneath the vehicle, locate the adjuster locknut at the point where the two handbrake cables join the equaliser plate, and slacken the locknut until the cable levers on the rear calipers return to their stops **(see illustration)**.
4 From inside the vehicle, pull the handbrake on, then release it.
5 Tighten adjuster locknut until the cable levers on the calipers begin to move from the stops.
6 Adjust the locknut so that both brakes

securely lock the wheels, when the lever has travelled between three and six clicks of the ratchet mechanism. Check that when the lever is released, the rear wheels spin freely.
7 Lower the vehicle to the ground.

15 Handbrake lever – removal and refitting

Removal

1 Chock the front wheels, then jack up the rear of the vehicle and support it on axle stands. Fully release the handbrake lever.
2 Working underneath the vehicle, locate the adjuster locknut at the point where the two handbrake cables join the equaliser plate, and slacken the locknut until the cable levers on the rear calipers return to their stops **(see illustration 14.3)**.
3 Remove the rear centre console as described in Chapter 11. On models without a rear centre console, remove the handbrake lever trim.
4 Undo the two lever retaining bolts **(see illustration)**.
5 Release the retaining clip, and disengage the handbrake cable from the base of the lever, then disconnect the wiring switch and remove it from the vehicle.

Refitting

6 Refitting is a reversal of removal, but adjust the handbrake, as described in Section 14, before the rear section of the centre console is refitted.

16 Handbrake cables – removal and refitting

Removal

1 The handbrake cable consists of three sections, a right- and a left-hand section, which

14.3 Handbrake cable adjuster locknut (arrowed)

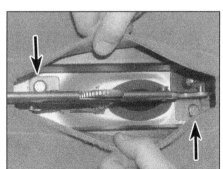

15.4 Undo the handbrake lever bolts (arrowed)

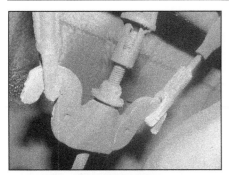

16.5 Unhook the inner cables from the equaliser plate

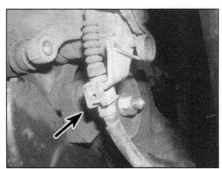

16.6a Pull out the cable retaining clip (arrowed) . . .

16.6b . . . then pull the inner cable end from the caliper lever

17.3 Twist the stop-light switch *clockwise* to remove it

are linked to the front cable by a equaliser plate. Each section can be removed individually as follows. Chock the front wheels, then jack up the rear of the vehicle and support it on axle stands. Fully release the handbrake lever.

2 Working underneath the vehicle, locate the adjuster locknut at the point where the two handbrake cables join the equaliser plate, and slacken the locknut until the cable levers on the rear calipers return to their stops.

Front cable

3 Remove the handbrake lever assembly as described in the previous Section.

4 Pull the cable from the rubber gaiter, and disengage it from the equaliser plate rod.

Rear cables

5 Unhook the cable inner from the equaliser plate, and release the outer cable from the retaining bracket **(see illustration)**. If required, repeat this operation on the remaining rear cable.

6 Working at the first rear brake caliper, remove the retaining clip and disconnect the handbrake cable from the caliper lever and retaining bracket **(see illustrations)**. If required, repeat this operation at the remaining caliper.

7 Work back along the length of each handbrake cable, noting its correct routing, and free it from all the relevant retaining clips and fixings.

Refitting

8 Refitting is a reversal of the removal procedure, ensuring that the cable is correctly routed and retained by all the necessary clips and ties. On completion, adjust the operation of the handbrake as described in Section 14.

17 Braking system switches – removal and refitting

Stop-light switch

Removal

1 The stop-light switch is located on the pedal bracket behind the facia. On models with cruise control there are two switches on the brake pedal, the stop-light switch is the lower of the two.

2 Remove the driver's side lower facia panel as described in Chapter 11, Section 31.

3 Twist the switch **clockwise** and release it from the mounting bracket. Disconnect the wiring plug as the switch is withdrawn **(see illustration)**.

Refitting

4 Before refitting, pull the switch plunger out to its full extent **(see illustration)**.

5 Depress the brake pedal, insert the switch into the hole in the mounting bracket and rotate it anti-clockwise to lock it in place. Slowly release the brake pedal.

6 Reconnect the switch wiring plug.

7 Refit the lower facia panel as described in Chapter 11.

Handbrake warning switch

Removal

8 Remove the rear centre console as described in Chapter 11. On models without a centre console, remove the handbrake lever trim **(see illustration)**.

9 Squeeze together the lugs of the retaining

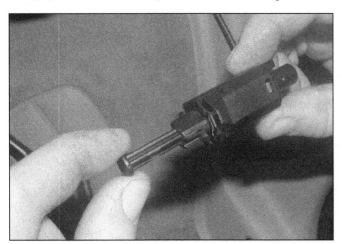

17.4 Pull the stop-light switch plunger out to its full extent

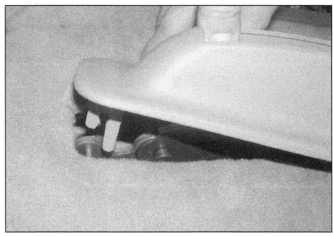

17.8 The handbrake lever trim is clipped to the lever assembly

17.9a Squeeze together the lugs of the retaining clip . . .

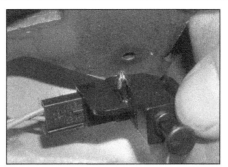

17.9b . . . and remove the switch

17.14 Brake pedal cruise control switch (stop-light switch removed)

clip and remove the switch from the lever **(see illustrations)**.

10 Disconnect the wiring plug as the switch is withdrawn.

Refitting

11 Refitting is a reversal of removal. Adjustment of the switch is not possible.

Cruise control pedal switch

Removal

12 The brake pedal switch is located on the pedal bracket behind the facia. The upper of the two switches is the cruise control pedal switch.

13 Remove the driver's side lower facia panel as described in Chapter 11, Section 31.

14 Disconnect the switch vacuum hose and wiring plug, then unscrew the switch from the bracket **(see illustration)**.

Refitting

15 Refitting is a reversal of removal. With the pedal in the 'at rest' position, screw the switch in until the pedal begins to move, then unscrew the switch a quarter of a turn.

18 Anti-lock braking system (ABS) – general information

Note: *On models equipped with traction control, the ABS unit is a dual function unit, controlling both the Anti-Lock Braking system (ABS), and the Traction Control (TC) system.*

1 ABS is fitted as standard to all models in the range. The system comprises a hydraulic unit, an electronic control module (ECM) and four roadwheel sensors. The hydraulic unit contains the eight hydraulic solenoid valves and the electrically-driven pressure pump. The purpose of the system is to prevent the roadwheels locking during heavy braking. This is achieved by automatic release of the brake on the relevant wheel, followed by re-application of the brake.

2 The solenoid valves are controlled by the ECM, which itself receives signals from the four wheel sensors, which monitor the speed of rotation of each wheel. By comparing these signals, the ECM can determine the speed at which the vehicle is travelling. It can then use this speed to determine when a wheel is decelerating at an abnormal rate, compared

to the speed of the vehicle, and therefore predicts when a wheel is about to lock. During normal operation, the system functions in the same way as a non-ABS braking system. The ABS system only functions at speeds in excess of 3 mph.

3 If the ECM senses that a wheel is about to lock, it activates the relevant solenoid valve in the hydraulic unit, effectively dropping the hydraulic pressure to that caliper, which allows the wheel rotational speed to increase.

4 Once the speed of rotation of the wheel returns to an acceptable rate, the ABS pressure pump is activated, rapidly increasing the pressure to the caliper in accordance with the brake pressure applies by the brake pedal. The ABS unit solenoid valves are de-activated during the pressure build-up phase. This cycle can be carried out many times a second.

5 The action of the solenoid valves and pressure pump creates pulses in the hydraulic circuit. When the ABS system is functioning, these pulses can be felt through the brake pedal.

6 On models with traction control, the ABS system components are used to prevent wheel spin in low traction conditions, such as wet or icy roads. If under acceleration the ECM senses that a wheel is spinning, it uses the hydraulic unit to gradually apply the brake on that wheel until traction is regained. Once the wheel regains traction, the brake is released. With traction control, an extra pair of solenoids are incorporated in to the hydraulic control unit, to supply hydraulic pressure to each of the front brake calipers. The traction control system is active at roads speeds of up to 30 mph (50 kph).

7 The operation of the ABS system is entirely dependent on electrical signals. To prevent the system responding to any inaccurate signals, a built-in safety circuit monitors all signals received by the ECM. If an inaccurate signal or low battery voltage is detected, the ABS system is automatically shut down, and the warning light on the instrument panel is illuminated, to inform the driver that the ABS system is not operational. Normal braking should still be available, however.

8 If a fault does develop in the ABS system, the vehicle must be taken to a Ford dealer or suitably-equipped specialist for fault diagnosis and repair.

19 Anti-lock braking system (ABS) components – removal and refitting

Hydraulic unit

Note: *Ford state that if the ABS hydraulic unit needs to be bled, special test equipment (FDS2000) must be used. Bearing this in mind it is recommended that the removal and refitting of the unit is entrusted to a Ford dealer or suitably-equipped specialist. If you do decide to remove and refit the unit yourself, bleed the system as described in Section 2, then have the operation of the unit checked at the earliest opportunity by a Ford dealer or specialist.*

Removal

1 Remove the battery as described in Chapter 5A.

2 Undo the two bolts securing the coolant expansion tank to the mounting bracket, and disconnect the low coolant level warning switch wiring plug. Place the expansion tank to one side.

3 Pull out the battery compartment upper panel. Release the retaining screws, and remove the engine compartment bulkhead cover. Slide the cover to the right-hand side and manoeuvre it from behind the coolant expansion tank. On vehicles from '98 model year, remove the battery compartment lower panel (see Chapter 5A).

4 Release the locking element and disconnect the ABS hydraulic unit wiring plug **(see illustration)**.

19.4 Pull out the locking element (arrowed) and disconnect the wiring plug

19.8 Undo the pipe union nuts and the unit mounting nuts

19.17 Wheel speed sensor

20.7 On refitting, ensure the slot in the vacuum pump drive gear (arrowed) aligns with the dog on the driveshaft

5 On diesel engined models, undo the two retaining bolts, and move the relay box to one side.

6 Slacken both front roadwheel bolts. Raise the front of the vehicle and rest it securely on axle stands, then remove both front roadwheels.

7 Connect a length of hose to the right-hand front brake caliper bleed screw, then direct the other end of the hose into a suitable receptacle, as described in Section 2. Open the bleed nipple and then depress and release the brake pedal until the right-hand side of the brake master cylinder fluid reservoir is empty. Close the bleed screw. Repeat this procedure on the left-hand caliper/reservoir chamber.

8 Wipe clean the area around all the pipes unions and mark the locations of the hydraulic fluid pipes to ensure correct refitting. Unscrew the union nuts and disconnect the pipes from the hydraulic unit **(see illustration)**. Be prepared for fluid spillage, and plug the open ends of the pipes and the hydraulic unit unions, to prevent dirt ingress and further fluid loss.

9 Where necessary, release the air conditioning pipes from their retaining clips to gain access to the ABS hydraulic unit mounting bolts.

10 Slacken and remove the hydraulic unit mounting bracket nuts and bolts, then remove the assembly from the engine compartment.

Refitting

Note: *New hydraulic units are supplied pre-filled and fully bled; it is vitally important that the union plugs are not removed until the brake pipes are reconnected, as loss of fluid will introduce air into the unit.*

11 Manoeuvre the hydraulic unit into position, and refit mounting bracket. Tighten the mounting nuts to the specified torque setting.

12 Remove the plugs and reconnect the

hydraulic pipes to the correct unions on the hydraulic unit and tighten the union nuts to the specified torque.

13 Reconnect the wiring connector to the hydraulic unit and engage the locking element.

14 The remainder of refitting is a reversal of removal. Bleed the brakes as described in Section 2 – refer to the note at the start of this sub-Section. If necessary, bleed the clutch hydraulic system as described in Chapter 6.

Wheel speed sensor

Removal

15 Apply the handbrake, then jack up the front or rear of the vehicle as applicable, and support securely on axle stands. To improve access, remove the roadwheel.

16 Trace the wiring back from the sensor, releasing it from all the relevant clips and ties whilst noting its correct routing, and disconnect the wiring connector.

17 Slacken and remove the retaining bolt, then carefully pull the sensor out from the hub carrier assembly and remove it from the vehicle **(see illustration)**.

Refitting

18 Ensure that the mating faces of the sensor and hub carrier are clean and dry then lubricate the wheel sensor surfaces with a small quantity of copper-based grease.

19 Insert the wheel speed sensor and tighten the retaining bolt to the specified torque.

20 Ensure the sensor is securely retained then work along the sensor wiring, making sure it is correctly routed, securing it in position with all the relevant clips and ties. Reconnect the wiring connector.

21 Refit the wheel (where removed) then lower the vehicle and (where necessary) tighten the wheel bolts to the specified torque.

20 Vacuum pump (diesel engine models) – removal and refitting

Removal

1 Prise out the covers then unscrew the retaining nuts and remove the plastic cover from the top of the engine. The vacuum pump is situated on the left-hand side of the front face of the cylinder block.

2 Release the retaining clip, and disconnect the vacuum hose from the top of pump.

3 Slacken the retaining clips and remove the charge air pipe from the intercooler to the intake manifold.

4 Undo the retaining bolt and remove the pump retaining clamp from the cylinder block.

5 Withdraw the vacuum pump from the cylinder block, and recover the sealing ring. Discard the sealing ring, a new one should be used on refitting. According to Ford, no parts are available. If the pump is defective, it must be renewed.

Refitting

6 Fit the new sealing to the vacuum pump and apply a smear of oil to it to aid installation.

7 Manoeuvre the vacuum pump into position, making sure that the slot in the drive gear aligns with the dog on the drive shaft **(see illustration)**.

8 Refit the retaining clamp and tighten its retaining bolt to the specified torque.

9 Reconnect the vacuum hose to the pump, and secure it in position with the retaining clip.

10 Reconnect the air charge pipe, and tighten the retaining clips.

11 Refit the top cover to the engine and securely tighten its retaining nuts/bolts.

Chapter 10
Suspension and steering

Contents

Degrees of difficulty

Easy, suitable for novice with little experience	Fairly easy, suitable for beginner with some experience	Fairly difficult, suitable for competent DIY mechanic	Difficult, suitable for experienced DIY mechanic	Very difficult, suitable for expert DIY or professional

Specifications

Front suspension
Type . . . . Independent MacPherson strut, coil springs, lower suspension arms mounted to the front crossmember, anti-roll bar

Rear suspension
Type . . . . Semi-trailing arm, coil springs, shock absorbers, and anti-roll bar, mounted to the rear crossmember

Steering
Type . . . . Rack-and-pinion, power-assisted

Front wheel alignment and steering angles
Note: *All measurements should be taken with the vehicle unladen*
Camber angle (negative) . . . . –0° 20' ± 0° 45'
Castor angle . . . . 3° 20' ± 0° 40'
Front wheel alignment – total toe-out . . . . 0° 10' ± 0° 20'

Rear wheel alignment
Note: *All measurements should be taken with the vehicle unladen*
Camber angle (negative) . . . . –0° 20' ± 0° 30'
Rear wheel alignment – total toe-in . . . . 0° 05' ± 0° 30'

Roadwheels

Type . . . .   Pressed-steel or aluminium alloy

Tyres

Size . . . .   195/65 R 15, 205/60 R 15, 215/60 R 15
or 215/55 R16 (depending on model)

Pressures . . . .   *See end of Weekly checks*

Torque wrench settings	Nm	lbf ft
Front suspension		
Anti-roll bar clamp bolts	55	41
Anti-roll bar drop link balljoint nuts*	100	74
Brake caliper mounting bracket	190	140
Driveshaft bolt*:		
Stage 1	150	111
Stage 2	Angle-tighten a further 90°	
Engine roll restrictor	98	72
Front crossmember bolts*:		
Stage 1	150	111
Stage 2	Angle-tighten a further 90°	
Lower arm balljoint retaining bolts	55	41
Lower arm front pivot bolt†:		
Stage 1	90	66
Stage 2	Angle-tighten a further 90°	
Lower arm-to-balljoint locknut*†:		
Stage 1	30	22
Stage 2	Angle-tighten a further 90°	
Strut damper rod locknut	60	44
Strut-to-hub carrier bolt	110	81
Strut top mount retaining nut*	60	44
Wheel bolts:		
Except 16 in aluminium wheels	140	103
16 in aluminium wheels	170	125
Rear suspension		
Anti-roll bar bolts	30	22
Brake pipe unions	14	10
Rear axle support bracket-to-body bolts	110	81
Rear hub retaining nut/bolt*	200	148
Rear subframe roll restrictor bolt*	260	192
Rear subframe-to-body bolts*	170	125
Shock absorber-to-trailing arm nuts/bolts**	130	96
Shock absorber upper retaining bolts*	110	81
Trailing arm retaining bolts*†	170	125
Wheel bolts:		
Except 16 in aluminium wheels	140	103
16 in aluminium wheels	170	125
Steering		
PAS pipe unions:		
Aluminium pipe	12	9
Pump high pressure union bolt	41	30
Steel pipe	32	24
PAS pump mounting bolts	23	18
PAS pump pulley bolts	25	18
Steering column lower retaining bolt	11	8
Steering column-to-steering rack pinion pinch-bolt*	24	17
Steering rack mounting bolts	48	35
Steering rack shield nut	10	7
Steering wheel bolt*	40	30
Track rod end balljoint nut*:		
Stage 1	30	22
Stage 2	Angle-tighten a further 90°	
Track rod end adjuster locknut	55	41
Track rod locking collar	80	59

* *Use new nut/bolt*
† *Tighten when vehicle is resting on its wheels*

Note: *Many of the suspension and steering components are secured in position with self-locking 'Nyloc' nuts, recognisable by having a plastic thread insert (often coloured blue). Whenever a self-locking nut is disturbed, it must be discarded and a new nut fitted.*

2.2 Bulkhead cover screws – one each side, and one in the centre (two arrowed)

2.3 Insert an Allen key into the damper rod (arrowed)

1 General information

The independent front suspension is of the MacPherson strut type, incorporating coil springs and integral telescopic shock absorbers. The struts are located by transverse lower suspension arms, which use rubber inner mounting bushes. The front wheel bearing housings/hub carriers, which carry the wheel bearings, brake calipers and the hub/disc assemblies, are attached to the MacPherson struts by clamp bolts, and connected to the lower arms through balljoints bolted to the under side of the assembly. A front anti-roll bar is fitted to all models. The anti-roll bar is rubber mounted on the crossmember, and connected to both lower suspension arms by balljointed drop links.

The rear suspension is of the semi-trailing arm type. These arms pivot from a tubular subframe bolted to the floor pan. A coil spring is fitted between the trailing arms and the floor pan, with separate telescopic shock absorbers fitted to the ends of the arms. The rear hub carriers/wheel bearing housings are incorporated into the trailing arm, with an anti-roll bar clamped to the subframe and trailing arms to prevent excessive body roll.

The steering system comprises an impact-absorbing telescopic steering column, power-assisted steering rack and engine-driven fluid pump, with a fluid reservoir, and connecting pipes and hoses. The adjustable steering column has upper mountings which are designed to detach or deform in the event of a collision, allowing the column to collapse and reduce the risk of injuring the driver. The upper section of the column is splined to accept the steering wheel; the intermediate shaft is joined to the lower shaft by a universal joint, and a further universal joint at the base of the column joins to the splined adaptor

which attaches the column to the rack pinion. The steering column fitted to vehicles from late '98 model year onwards, incorporates a 'clutch' which allows the steering wheel to rotate independently of the column if a force in excess of 145 ± 35 Nm (107 ± 26 lbf ft) is applied at the wheel. This is designed to prevent would-be car thieves from damaging the steering column lock by force.

The steering rack, which is mounted on the front crossmember, is of conventional design and is connected by two track rods, with balljoints at their outer ends, to bosses projecting rearwards from the hub carriers/wheel bearing housings. The track rod ends are threaded to facilitate adjustment.

Power-assisted steering is standard on all models. The hydraulic steering system is powered by a vane-type pump, which is belt-driven off the crankshaft pulley. Rotary movement of the steering wheel is transferred via the steering column to the valve unit mounted on the steering rack; depending on direction of rotation, fluid pressure is applied to one side of the valve or the other, to boost the turning force applied to the pinion, which in turn moves the rack left or right.

2 Front suspension strut – removal, overhaul and refitting

Removal

1 Apply the handbrake, slacken the roadwheel bolts and the hub retaining bolt, then jack up the front of the vehicle and support it on axle stands. Remove the front roadwheels.
2 Pull out the battery compartment upper panel. Release the three retaining bolts, and remove the engine compartment bulkhead cover **(see illustration)**. Slide the cover to the right-hand side and manoeuvre it from behind the coolant expansion tank. On the left-hand side strut, to improve access, remove the

battery (see Chapter 5A) and the plastic panel in front of the coolant expansion tank.
3 With an Allen key to prevent the damper rod from rotating, slacken but do not remove, the suspension unit top mount nut **(see illustration)**.
4 Disengage the flexible brake hose from the retaining bracket on the strut **(see illustration)**.
5 Undo the retaining bolt and remove the wheel speed sensor from the hub carrier, freeing the wiring from any retaining clips – see Chapter 9, Section 19, for details. Rather than risk damaging the sensor if it has corroded in place, disconnect the wiring harness at the connector on the inner wing.
6 Slacken and remove the two bolts securing the brake caliper mounting bracket to the hub carrier, and suspend the caliper under the wheelarch using a length of wire, or a cable tie – see Chapter 9 for details. Ensure that no strain is placed on the flexible hose. Do **not** disconnect the brake hose.
7 Unscrew the track rod end balljoint nut, and using a balljoint splitter, detach the balljoint from the hub carrier (see Section 23).
8 Remove and discard the hub retaining bolt. A new one must be fitted.
9 Using an Allen key to prevent the balljoint from rotating, slacken but do not remove, the lower arm balljoint locknut.

2.4 Disengage the wheel speed sensor and brake hose from the bracket on the strut

2.10 Use a balljoint splitter to separate the balljoint from the lower arm

2.11 Use an open-ended spanner to prevent the balljoint from rotating whilst slackening the locknut

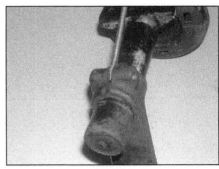

2.13 Use a screwdriver to gently open the hub carrier clamp

10 Using a balljoint splitter, separate the balljoint from the lower arm. Remove the locknut, push the lower arm down, pull the hub carrier outwards and over the end of the driveshaft **(see illustration)**.
Caution: Support the driveshaft by suspending it with wire or string – do not allow it to hang under its own weight, or the joint may be damaged.
11 Slacken and remove the anti-roll bar link upper locknut, and detach the balljoint from the strut **(see illustration)**.
12 Support the strut, and remove the top mount nut. Manoeuvre the strut, complete with the hub carrier, from under the wheelarch.
13 With the assembly on the bench, unscrew the hub carrier clamp bolt and remove the strut. If the strut is reluctant to move, use a

screwdriver to gently open the hub carrier clamp **(see illustration)**.

Overhaul

 Warning: Before attempting to dismantle the suspension strut, a suitable tool to hold the coil spring in compression must be obtained. Adjustable coil spring compressors are readily available, and are recommended for this operation. Any attempt to dismantle the strut without such a tool is likely to result in damage or personal injury.

14 Fit the spring compressors to the coils of the spring **(see illustration)**. Tighten the compressors evenly until the load is taken off the spring seats.
15 Hold the strut piston with an Allen key,

then use a spanner to unscrew the damper rod locknut **(see illustration)**.
16 Take off the thrust bearing, followed by the upper spring seat, spring, gaiter and bump stop **(see illustrations)**.
17 With the shock absorber assembly now dismantled, examine all the components for wear and damage. Check the rubber components for deterioration. Examine the shock absorber for damage and signs of fluid leakage, and check the piston rod for pitting along its entire length. While holding it in an upright position, test the operation of the shock absorber by moving the rod through a full stroke, and then through short strokes of 50 to 100 mm. In both cases, the resistance felt should be smooth and continuous. If the resistance is jerky, or uneven, or if there is any visible sign of wear

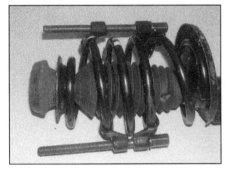

2.14 Compressors must be used to relieve the pressure on the spring seats

2.15 Use an Allen key to prevent the damper rod from rotating whilst slackening the locknut

2.16a Remove the locknut and thrust bearing . . .

2.16b . . . followed by the upper spring seat and spring . . .

2.16c . . . then the gaiter . . .

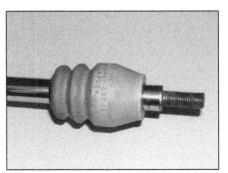

2.16d . . . and bump stop

2.21 When refitting, the spring end must fit correctly against the lower spring seat (arrowed)

or damage to the shock absorber, renewal is necessary.

18 If any doubt exists about the condition of the coil spring, gradually release the spring compressor, and check the spring for distortion and signs of cracking. Renew the spring if it is damaged or distorted, or if there is any doubt as to its condition. Note that springs should only be replaced with those that have the same colour-coding – mixing them up will result in a difference in ride heights; springs, like shock absorbers, should be renewed in axle pairs.

19 Inspect all other components for signs of damage or deterioration, and renew any that are suspect.

20 If a new shock absorber is being fitted, hold it vertically and pump the piston a few times to prime it.

21 Reassembly is a reversal of dismantling, noting the following points:
  a) *Compress the spring before fitting it.*
  b) *Use a new damper rod locknut, and using a torque wrench and adapter, tighten it to the specified torque while holding the strut piston against rotation with an Allen key.*
  c) *Ensure that when the spring is decompressed, the spring ends fit correctly against the lower spring seat (see illustration).*

Refitting

22 Refitting is a reversal of the removal procedure, noting the following points:

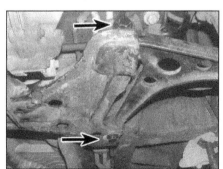

3.4 Undo the lower arm bolts (arrowed)

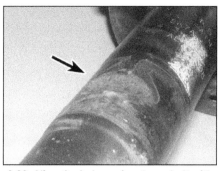

2.22 Align the hub carrier clamp bolt with the cutaway in the strut leg (arrowed)

  a) *Note the cutaway in the strut leg to accommodate the clamp bolt (see illustration).*
  b) *Renew the strut top mounting nut, but only tighten it once the weight of the vehicle is back on its wheels.*
  c) *Tighten all fixings to the specified torque where given.*
  d) *Refit the ABS wheel sensor and brake caliper as described in Chapter 9.*
  e) *Refit the driveshaft using a new hub bolt.*

3 Front suspension lower arm – removal, overhaul and refitting

Removal

1 Loosen the wheel bolts, apply the handbrake, then jack up the relevant front wheel and support on axle stands (see *Jacking and vehicle support*). Remove the relevant front wheel.

2 Undo the two retaining nuts and four bolts (two each side), then remove the engine/transmission undertray.

3 Slacken, but do not remove, the lower arm balljoint locknut. Use a balljoint splitter to separate the balljoint. With the balljoint separated, remove the locknut and push the lower arm down and disengage it from the balljoint (see Section 4).

4 Unscrew the lower arm front and rear bolts,

3.6 Draw the bush from the arm using a length of threaded rod, washers, nuts and large sockets

and manoeuvre the arm from the vehicle (see illustration).

Overhaul

5 Overhaul is limited to renewing the bush at the front of the arm. At the time of writing, the rear bush was only available complete with the lower arm – check availability with a Ford dealer. If the arm has suffered damage (from, for example, careless jacking-up or a collision), the arm is best renewed complete. It is advisable to consider renewing both arms in an axle set, rather than just one.

6 To renew the front bush, mount the arm in a vice, and draw the bush from the arm using a length of threaded rod, with several large washers and large sockets (see illustration). If the DIY approach fails, entrust bush renewal to a Ford dealer or specialist.

Refitting

7 Refitting is a reversal of the removal procedure, noting the following points:
  a) *Tighten all fixings to the specified torque where given.*
  b) *Do not fully tighten the lower arm mounting/pivot bolts until the vehicle is resting on its wheels.*

4 Front suspension lower arm balljoint – renewal

1 Loosen the wheel bolts, apply the handbrake, then jack up the relevant front wheel and support on axle stands (see *Jacking and vehicle support*). Remove the front wheel.

2 Slacken, but do not remove, the lower arm balljoint locknut. Use an Allen key in the end of the balljoint to prevent it rotating as the locknut is undone.

3 Use a balljoint splitter to separate the balljoint (see illustration 2.10). With the balljoint separated, remove the locknut and push the lower arm down and disengage it from the balljoint.

4 Slacken and remove the two Allen bolts securing the balljoint to the underside of the hub carrier (see illustration).

5 Refitting is a reversal of removal. Tighten all fixings to the specified torque where given.

4.4 Undo the Allen bolts (one each side) and separate the balljoint from the hub carrier

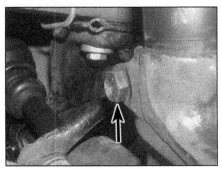

5.10 Undo the hub carrier clamp pinch-bolt (arrowed)

5.13 Drive the flange from the hub

5.14 Remove the bearing inner race from the hub flange

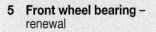

5 Front wheel bearing – renewal

1 Loosen the wheel bolts, and the driveshaft-to-hub bolt, apply the handbrake, then jack up the relevant front wheel and support on axle stands (see *Jacking and vehicle support*). Remove the front wheel.
2 Remove the two retaining nuts and four bolts (two each side), and remove the engine/transmission undertray.
3 Release the flexible brake hose from the retaining bracket on the suspension strut. Do **not** disconnect the brake hose.
4 Undo the retaining bolt and remove the ABS wheel speed sensor (see Chapter 9, Section 19).
5 Undo the two bolts securing the brake caliper mounting bracket to the hub carrier.

Slide the caliper from the disc, and using wire or cable ties, suspend it under the wheelarch.
6 Slacken the track rod balljoint locknut, and using a balljoint splitter, separate the track rod balljoint from the hub carrier. Undo the locknut and lift the track rod balljoint from the hub carrier (see Section 23).
7 Remove and discard the driveshaft-to-hub bolt, a new one must be fitted.
8 Undo the retaining screw, and remove the brake disc. Remove the two retaining bolts, and remove the disc shield from the hub carrier. If necessary, refer to Chapter 9.
9 Slacken and remove the two bolts securing the balljoint to the under side of the hub carrier (see illustration 4.4).
10 Unscrew the hub carrier-to-strut clamp pinch-bolt **(see illustration)**.
11 Pull the hub carrier out and over the end of the driveshaft.

12 Using a screwdriver in the gap, spread the hub carrier clamp, and detach the strut **(see illustration 2.13)**.
13 Mount the hub carrier securely in a vice, and using a suitable drift (such as a large socket) drive out the hub flange from the inboard side **(see illustration)**.
14 Mount the drive flange in a vice, then with careful use of a chisel, progressively tap off the bearing race **(see illustration)**. If a bearing puller is available, this is preferable, to avoid risking any damage to the drive flange surfaces.
15 Remove the bearing retaining circlip from the outboard side of the hub **(see illustration)**.
16 Mount the hub carrier in a vice, and drive out the bearing from the inboard side, using a suitable drift.
17 Clean up the hub and drive flange, removing all old grease, and any metal debris from removing the old bearing.
18 Support the inboard side of the hub below the bearing location, and progressively press in the new bearing using a suitable socket or tube which bears only on the bearing outer race. Make sure that the bearing is kept square in the hub until it is fully seated **(see illustration)**.
19 Secure the bearing using a new circlip (usually supplied with the new bearing), then refit the brake disc shield and secure with the bolts **(see illustration)**.
20 Again supporting the inboard side of the hub below the bearing location, align the drive flange squarely into the hub, and tap/press it fully into position **(see illustrations)**.

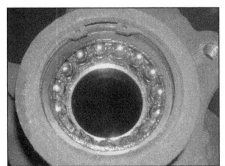

5.15 Remove the bearing retaining circlip

5.18 Try to keep the bearing square to the hub whilst driving it in

5.19 Secure the bearing using a new circlips

5.20a Align the drive flange with the bearing . . .

5.20b . . . and drive it squarely in

21 Refitting the hub is a reversal of removal, noting the following points:

a) *Tighten all fasteners to the specified torque where given.*

b) *Use a new hub-to-driveshaft bolt. Tighten the bolt when the weight of the vehicle is on its wheels again.*

c) *Refit the brake disc and ABS wheel sensor as described in Chapter 9.*

6 Front anti-roll bar bushes – renewal

1 Loosen the wheel bolts, apply the handbrake, then jack up the front of the car and support it securely on axle stands (see *Jacking and vehicle support*). Remove the front wheels.

2 Release the two retaining nuts and four bolts (two each side), then remove the engine/transmission undertray.

3 Loosen and remove the nut and bolt for each clamp, and remove the clamp plates from the top of the crossmember **(see illustrations)**.

4 The rubber bushes are of split design, so they can be twisted around and removed with the bar *in situ* **(see illustration)**. Once the old bushes are removed, clean up their locations on the bar, and also clean the inner surfaces of the clamp plates.

 When fitting the new bushes, it is helpful to coat them in soapy water (such as washing-up liquid) prior to fitting. This will make it much easier to slip them into place, and to twist them round into position on the bar.

5 Locate the new bushes in place, then refit the clamp plates and tighten the nuts and bolts to the specified torque.

6 Refit the engine/transmission undertray and the front wheels, then lower the car to the ground.

7 Front anti-roll bar drop links – removal and refitting

Removal

1 Loosen the wheel bolts, apply the handbrake, then jack up the front of the car and support it securely on axle stands (see *Jacking and vehicle support*). Remove the front wheels.

2 Unscrew the nut securing the lower end of each drop link to the anti-roll bar. It may be necessary to use a second spanner on the inboard side of the roll bar, to prevent the drop link balljoint shank from turning as the nut is unscrewed **(see illustration)**.

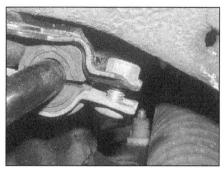

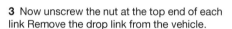
6.3a Undo the clamp bolts . . .

3 Now unscrew the nut at the top end of each link Remove the drop link from the vehicle.

Refitting

4 If a new link is not being fitted, clean up the balljoint tapers and their mating faces in their fitted locations on the strut and anti-roll bar. Do not apply any lubricant to the tapers, or tightening the balljoint nuts will be made more difficult.

5 Offer the links into position, making sure they are the right way up. Holding the balljoint shanks against rotation as necessary, tighten the upper and lower balljoint nuts to the specified torque.

6 Refit the front wheels, then lower the car to the ground and tighten the wheel bolts to the specified torque.

8 Front anti-roll bar – removal and refitting

Removal

1 Remove the front crossmember as described in Section 9.

2 Loosen and remove the nut and bolt for each anti-roll bar clamp, and remove the clamp plates from the top of the crossmember **(see illustrations 6.3a and 6.3b)**.

3 Lift the anti-roll bar from the crossmember, and remove the bushes as described in Section 6.

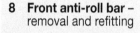
7.2 Anti-roll bar drop link lower end (arrowed)

6.3b . . . and remove the clamp plates

6.4 As the bushes are split, they can be renewed with the anti-roll bar in place

Refitting

4 Refitting is a reversal of removal, noting the following points:

a) *Tighten all fasteners to the specified torque where given.*

b) *If a new anti-roll bar has been fitted, it is advisable to fit new bushes, as described in Section 6.*

9 Front crossmember – removal and refitting

Note: *New crossmember mounting bolts will be required*

Removal

1 Loosen the wheel bolts, apply the handbrake, then jack up the front of the car and support it securely on axle stands (see *Jacking and vehicle support*). Do not support under the front crossmember, for obvious reasons. Remove the front wheels.

2 Undo the two retaining nuts and four bolts (two each side), then remove the engine/transmission undertray.

3 Remove the front section of the exhaust pipe as described in Chapter 4C.

4 Unscrew the nuts securing the anti-roll bars drop links to the ends of the anti-roll bar (see Section 7).

5 Undo the two Allen bolts each side securing the lower arm balljoints to the underside of the

9.6 Undo the four bolts securing the steering rack to the crossmember (arrowed)

9.7 Remove the bolt securing the roll restrictor to the transmission (arrowed)

9.9 Two large bolts each side secure the front crossmember (arrowed)

hub carriers. Separate the balljoints from the carriers (see illustration 4.4).

6 Undo the four bolts securing the steering rack to the crossmember (see illustration).

7 Slacken and remove the bolt securing the engine roll restrictor to the transmission (see illustration).

8 Before proceeding further, securely support the weight of the crossmember. It may also be useful to have an assistant on hand, to help with lowering the crossmember.

9 Remove the four large bolts (two each side) securing the crossmember to the underside of the vehicle. Carefully lower the crossmember, and remove it from under the vehicle (see illustration).

10 If required, undo the clamp bolts and remove the anti-roll bar (see Section 8). The lower arms can be removed by unscrewing the remaining front pivot bolts (see Section 3).

Refitting

11 Where necessary, refit the lower arms and anti-roll bar as described in Sections 3 and 8 respectively. Do not fully tighten the lower arm pivot bolts at this stage.

12 With the help of an assistant, offer up the crossmember, and secure it by the four new crossmember-to-body bolts.

13 Tighten the crossmember-to-body bolts to the specified torque.

14 The remainder of refitting is a reversal of removal. Tighten all fixings to the specified torque where given.

15 Refit the wheels, and lower the car to the ground. Tighten the wheel bolts to the specified torque.

16 With the weight of the car on its wheels, tighten the lower arm pivot bolts to the specified torques.

10 Rear suspension shock absorber – removal, examination and refitting

Removal

1 Loosen the relevant rear wheel bolts, then chock the front wheels and jack up the rear of the car and support on axle stands (see *Jacking and vehicle support*). Remove the relevant rear wheel. Undo the two lower wheelarch liner bolts, and pull the liner out a little.

2 Support the trailing arm with a trolley jack or similar, and slightly compress the suspension spring.

3 Undo the nut and bolt securing the shock absorber to the trailing arm, and the bolt securing the shock absorber to the vehicle body (see illustrations).

4 Manoeuvre the shock absorber from under the vehicle.

Examination

5 Examine the shock absorber for damage and signs of fluid leakage. While holding it in an upright position, test the operation of the shock absorber by moving the rod through a full stroke, and then through short strokes of 50 to 100 mm. In both cases, the resistance felt should be smooth and continuous. If the resistance is jerky, or uneven, or if there is any visible sign of wear or damage to the shock absorber, renewal is necessary.

6 If a new shock absorber is being fitted, hold it vertically and pump the piston a few times to prime it.

Refitting

7 Position the shock absorber against its mounting holes, then insert the upper mounting bolt, and lower nut and bolt. Finger tighten the lower bolt/nut only at this stage.

8 Slowly lower the trailing arm, and remove the support.

9 Refit the roadwheel, lower the vehicle to the ground. Tighten the shock absorber lower mounting bolt/nut and the roadwheel bolts to their specified torque.

10.3a Undo the nut and bolt securing the shock absorber to the trailing arm . . .

10.3b . . . and the bolt securing it to the vehicle body

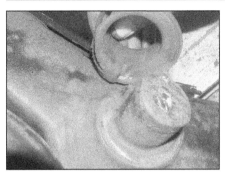

11.5 Rubber inserts are fitted between the spring and its seats

11 Rear suspension spring – removal and refitting

Removal

1 Loosen the relevant rear wheel bolts, chock the front wheels, then jack up the rear of the vehicle and support it on axle stands (see *Jacking and vehicle support*). Remove the relevant rear roadwheel. If you're using a normal, DIY-type trolley jack, the outer trailing arm pivot bolt needs to be at least 43 cm from the ground to provide enough clearance.
2 Remove the rear anti-roll bar as described in Section 12.
3 Support the trailing arm with a trolley jack or similar, and slightly compress the suspension spring.

12.2 Rear anti-roll bar clamp bolts (arrowed)

12.3b . . . and remove the inner bushes . . .

4 Undo the lower retaining nut/bolt, and remove the shock absorber **(see illustration 10.3a)**.
5 Lower the trailing arm until all tension is removed from the spring, and it can be manoeuvred out from its locating seats **(see illustration)**.
6 Check the spring for distortion and signs of cracking. Renew the spring if it is damaged or distorted, or if there is any doubt as to its condition. Note that springs should only be replaced with those that have the same colour-coding – mixing them up will result in a difference in ride heights; springs, like shock absorbers, should be renewed in axle pairs.

Refitting

7 Refitting is a reversal of removal. Tighten all fixings to their specified torque where given. Only fully tighten the shock absorber nuts/bolts fully once the weight of the vehicle is on its roadwheels.

12 Rear anti-roll bar and bushes – removal and refitting

Removal

1 Chock the front wheels, then jack up the rear of the vehicle and support it on axle stands (see *Jacking and vehicle support*).
2 Slacken and remove the bolts securing the anti-roll bar clamps to the trailing arms and the rear subframe **(see illustration)**.

12.3a Remove the clamp plates . . .

12.3c . . . and outer bushes

3 If required, the anti-roll bar bushes can now be removed **(see illustrations)**. If the anti-roll bar is being renewed, the bushes should also be renewed as a matter of course.

Refitting

4 Once the old bushes are removed, clean up their locations on the bar, and also clean the inner surfaces of the clamp plates.

  HAYNES HiNT *When fitting the new bushes, it is helpful to coat them in soapy water (such as washing-up liquid) prior to fitting. This will make it much easier to slip them into place, and to twist them round into position on the bar.*

5 Locate the new bushes in place on the bar. Manoeuvre the anti-roll bar into place, then refit the clamp plates and tighten the bolts to the specified torque.

13 Rear trailing arms and bushes – removal and refitting

Removal

1 Loosen the relevant rear wheel bolts, chock the front wheels, then jack up the rear of the vehicle and support it on axle stands (see *Jacking and vehicle support*). There must be at least 43 cm between the trailing arm outer pivot bolt and the ground to provide enough clearance to lower the arm and remove the spring. Remove the relevant rear roadwheel.
Note: *If the trailing arm is to be renewed but the wheel bearing retained, slacken the rear hub nut and bolt prior to jacking the vehicle up.*
2 Remove the rear brake caliper as described in Chapter 9. Clamp the flexible hose and disconnect the brake pipe at the retaining bracket **(see illustration)**. Free the brake pipe/hose and handbrake cable from any retaining clips on the trailing arm.
3 Unbolt the rear wheel speed sensor, and

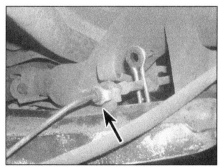

13.2 Clamp the flexible hose, and disconnect the brake pipe at the retaining bracket (arrowed)

13.5 The brake disc splash shield is retained by three bolts (arrowed – one hidden)

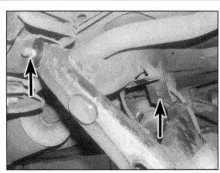

13.9 Slacken and remove the inner and outer trailing arm bolts (arrowed)

13.10a Use a nut and bolt, several washers and large sockets to remove the trailing arm bushes

13.10b If bushes with eccentric holes were originally fitted, the same type must be fitted, in exactly the same position

Refitting

12 With the new bearing and hub in place where applicable, draw the new bushes into place using a combination of sockets, washers, and a nut and bolt.

> **HAYNES HiNT** *When fitting the new bushes, it is helpful to coat them in soapy water (such as washing-up liquid) prior to fitting. This will make it much easier to slip them into position.*

13 The remainder of refitting is a reversal of removal, tightening all fixings to their specified torque where given. **Note:** *Final tightening of the trailing arm pivot bolts, and lower shock absorber nut/bolt should be carried out with the weight of the vehicle on its wheels.*

14 Rear wheel bearing – renewal

1 Loosen the wheel nuts, chock the front wheels, then jack up the relevant rear wheel and support on axle stands (see *Jacking and vehicle support*). Remove the rear wheel.
2 Undo the retaining bolt and remove the rear wheel speed sensor.
3 Undo the caliper bracket retaining bolts, slide the caliper (and mounting bracket) from the disc, and using a length of wire or a cable tie, suspend the caliper under the wheelarch. Do **not** place the flexible hose under any strain.
4 Undo the retaining screw, and remove the rear brake disc.
5 Slacken and remove the hub securing bolt, nut and washer. Remove the ABS sensor ring **(see illustrations)**. Discard the nut and bolt, new ones must be fitted.
6 Using a slide hammer, pull the hub from the bearings. A DIY slide hammer can be made from a length of threaded rod, four nuts, a suitably sized socket, a large

free the wiring harness from any retaining clips on the arm.
4 Slacken and remove the brake disc retaining screw, and remove the disc (see Chapter 9).
5 Unscrew the three retaining bolts and remove the brake disc splash shield **(see illustration)**.
6 Undo the clamp bolts and remove the rear anti-roll bar as described in Section 12.
7 Position a trolley jack to support the end of the trailing arm, undo and remove the lower shock absorber nut and bolt.
8 Lower the trailing arm until all tension is removed from the spring, and it can be manoeuvred out from its locating seats.
9 Slacken and remove the inner and outer

trailing arm retaining bolts, then manoeuvre the arm from under the vehicle **(see illustration)**.
10 If required, the bushes can be removed by making up your own puller, using a nut and bolt, with several large washers and large sockets **(see illustration)**. If the DIY approach fails, entrust bush renewal to a Ford dealer or specialist. **Note:** *If the original bushes have an eccentric centre hole, they must be replaced with the same type of bush, fitted in exactly the same position, otherwise the rear wheel geometry will be altered* **(see illustration)**.
11 If the trailing arm is to be renewed, fit the rear hub bearing as described in Section 14.

14.5a Remove the hub bolt . . .

14.5b . . . and nut . . .

14.5c . . . followed by the sensor ring

14.6a Use a home-made slide hammer . . .

14.6b . . . with a large socket pulling the hub from the bearings

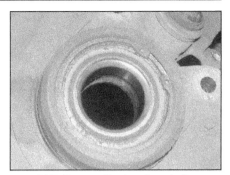

14.7 Remove the bearing circlip

14.8 Use the slide hammer to extract the wheel bearing

14.10a Draw the new bearing into the housing . . .

14.10b . . . and fit a new circlip

washer, and a suitable weight **(see illustrations)**.

7 Use a pair of circlip pliers to remove the bearing retaining clip **(see illustration)**. Discard the circlip, a new one must be fitted.

8 With the slide hammer used to remove the hub, and a suitably-sized socket, pull the inner and outer bearing assemblies from the bearing housing **(see illustration)**. If the bearing refuses to be removed by this method, remove the trailing arm as described in Section 13, and either press the bearings out or have the bearing renewed by a Ford dealer or suitably-equipped specialist.

9 With the bearing removed, ensure the bearing housing internal surface is clean. Also check the hub surface for cleanliness.

10 Using the threaded rod and suitably-sized washers, socket and nuts, draw the bearing into the housing until the complete circlip groove is visible. Fit the new bearing circlip **(see illustrations)**.

11 Again, using the threaded rod, nuts, washers and sockets, draw the hub into the bearings, until the inner race of the outer bearing is up against the hub inner shoulder **(see illustration)**.

12 Insert the new hub retaining bolt and washer, install the ABS sensor ring, and tighten the new nut to the specified torque. *Caution: The hub retaining nut is very tight. Take great care not to pull the vehicle from the axle stands.*

13 The remainder of refitting is a reversal of removal. Tighten all fixings to their specified torque where given.

15 Rear subframe – removal and refitting

Removal

1 Remove both rear trailing arms as described in Section 13.

2 Slacken and remove the bolt securing the subframe to the roll restrictor **(see illustration)**.

3 Support the weight of the subframe on a jack (or preferably, a pair of jacks). The help of an assistant will also prove useful in lowering the subframe.

4 Undo the three bolts each side securing the support brackets and subframe to the vehicle body **(see illustration)**.

14.11 Use the threaded rod, nuts and washers to draw the hub into the bearings

15.2 Undo the roll restrictor bolt

15.4 Remove the three bolts and the support brackets

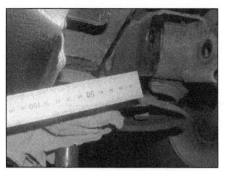

15.7 The gap between the subframe and the edge of the sill must be the same on both sides

16.3a Undo the steering column shrouds upper screws (arrowed) . . .

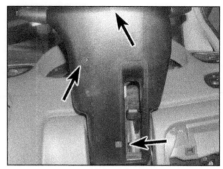

16.3b . . . and lower screws (arrowed)

5 With the help of an assistant, lower the subframe and remove from under the car.

Refitting

6 Position the subframe against its mounting points, and support it with a trolley jack or similar. Refit the support brackets and new securing bolts. Only finger tighten the bolts at this stage.

7 Using a ruler, measure the distance between the edge of the subframe and the inner sill (see illustration). The measurement should be equal on both sides. If the gap is not equal, carefully lever the subframe in the direction of the largest gap, until the position is correct. Tighten the subframe and support brackets retaining bolts to the specified torque.

16.5 Disconnect the air bag contact unit wiring plug

16.6 Undo and discard the steering wheel retaining bolt

8 The remainder of refitting is a reversal of removal, noting the following points:

a) *Ford do not state that new subframe-to-body bolts must be used, but they are done up to an extremely high torque, and it would seem sensible to fit new ones. New ones should certainly be fitted if there is any doubt about the old ones' condition.*

b) *Tighten all fasteners to the specified torque. The trailing arm, and shock absorber mounting bolts should not be fully tightened until the weight of the vehicle is on its wheels.*

16 Steering wheel – removal and refitting

Removal

1 Release the steering lock by inserting the ignition key.

2 Remove the airbag unit as described in Chapter 12, then return the steering wheel to the straight-ahead position, and engage the steering lock.

3 Undo the two upper screws and three lower screws, and remove both steering column shrouds (see illustrations).

4 Where fitted, slide the audio unit remote control switch from the lock casing.

5 Disconnect the airbag contact unit wiring plug (see illustration).

16.10a Depress the red locking plunger (arrowed) . . .

6 Hold the steering wheel to prevent it turning (don't rely on the steering lock for this, as it may not be strong enough, and damage could result), and undo the steering wheel retaining bolt (see illustration). Discard the bolt, a new one must be fitted.

7 Make an alignment mark between the wheel boss and the top of the column, to ensure the wheel goes back on straight. Pull the steering wheel from the splined end of the steering column feeding the wiring through as it is withdrawn. This should not require great effort, but if it sticks, put the wheel bolt back on by a few threads (to prevent it flying off), and tap the wheel off from behind the boss.

Refitting

8 Locate the steering wheel on the column splines, aligning the marks made on removal.

9 Route the airbag rotary contact unit wiring alongside the steering column and reconnect the plug.

10 Regardless of whether or not the airbag contact unit has been removed, prior to refitting the wheel, carry out the following centralisation procedure: depress the locking plunger, and rotate the outer rotor anti-clockwise until it becomes tight. Rotate the outer rotor clockwise approximately 2.75 turns. Release the locking plunger, and make sure that the plunger locks the contact unit in this position (see illustrations).

11 Fit a new retaining nut, and tighten it to the specified torque setting, holding the wheel against rotation as before.

16.10b . . . then rotate the contact unit anti-clockwise until it stops, then back 2.75 turns

12 Reconnect the contact unit, feed the airbag wiring back into the steering wheel, then refit the airbag unit as described in Chapter 12.

17 Ignition switch, lock barrel and steering column lock – removal and refitting

Ignition switch

Removal

1 Remove the steering column upper and lower shrouds. Two screws retain the upper shroud, and the lower shroud is retained by three screws (see illustrations 16.3a and 16.3b).
2 Disconnect the switch wiring plug (see illustration).
3 Depress the two retaining clips and slide the switch from the lock casing (see illustrations).

Refitting

4 Refitting is the reverse of removal.

Lock barrel

Removal

5 Disconnect the battery negative lead (see Chapter 5A). Remove the ignition key.
6 Remove the steering column upper and lower shrouds. The upper shroud is retained by two screws, and the lower shroud is retained by three screws (see illustrations 16.3a and 16.3b).
7 Gently pull the anti-theft transceiver coil from the switch (see illustration).
8 Very carefully drill a 4 mm hole in the side of the lock barrel casing as shown (see illustration).
9 Insert the ignition key and turn it to position II. Use a small screwdriver to depress the locking detent and pull the key, with the lock barrel, from the barrel casing.

Refitting

10 Insert the ignition key into the lock barrel, align the key with the locking detent, and insert it into the barrel casing.

17.2 Release the retaining clip and disconnect the wiring plug

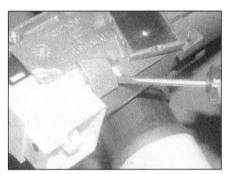

17.3b . . . and rear . . .

11 Push the anti-theft transceiver coil over the end of the switch.
12 The remainder of refitting is a reversal of removal.

Steering column lock

13 Remove the steering wheel as described in Section 16.
14 Remove the airbag rotary contact unit, and the steering column combination switch as described in Chapter 12.
15 Note the fitted location of the lock casing. Ensure the steering lock is not engaged, and using a soft-faced hammer, drive the lock casing up off the end of the steering column (see illustration).

Refitting

16 Refitting is a reversal of removal.

17.3a Depress the clip at the front . . .

17.3c . . . then slide the switch from the casing

18 Steering column – removal and refitting

Removal

1 Remove the steering wheel as described in Section 16.
2 Remove the steering column multi-function switches, and airbag rotary contact unit as described in Chapter 12. Note their fitted positions, then cut the cables tie(s) securing the wiring harnesses to the steering column.
3 Disconnect the multi-plugs from the ignition switch and slide the anti-theft transceiver coil over the end of the ignition switch (see illustrations 17.2 and 17.7).

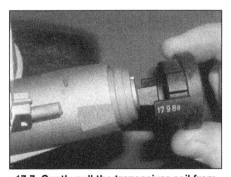

17.7 Gently pull the transceiver coil from the casing

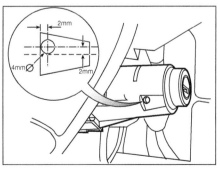

17.8 Drill a 4 mm hole in the casing as shown

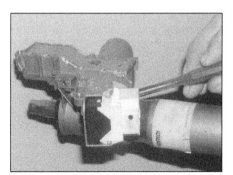

17.15 Drive the steering lock from the column

18.5 Make alignment marks, then undo the pinch-bolt

18.6 Slacken and remove the column lower Allen bolt (arrowed)

18.7a Steering column shear bolts (arrowed)

18.7b Careful use of a chisel should unscrew the bolts

4 Remove the driver's side lower facia trim panel as described in Chapter 11, Section 31.

5 At the base of the steering column, make an alignment mark between the flexible coupling clamp and the steering rack pinion shaft. Slacken and remove the coupling-to-pinion shaft clamp bolt **(see illustration)**. Discard the bolt, a new one must be fitted.

6 Slacken and remove the lower steering column retaining Allen bolt **(see illustration)**.

7 The upper column retaining bolts are 'shear' bolts. To remove these, drill a hole in the centre of each bolt, and use an extractor to unscrew the bolts. Alternatively, careful use of a chisel should unscrew the bolts **(see illustrations)**.

8 Ease the column upwards to disengage the flexible coupling from the steering rack pinion.

Refitting

9 Refitting is a reversal of removal, noting the following points:

a) When the column is first offered in, only tighten the mounting nuts and bolts hand-tight until the column has been engaged correctly with the rack pinion, and the new pinch-bolt tightened to the specified torque.

b) If the original column is being refitted, align the previously made marks on the clamp and pinion.

c) Use new steering column upper mounting shear bolts, and tighten them until the heads of the bolts shear off.

d) Tighten all fasteners to the specified torque where given.

e) On completion, check the operation of the steering column lock and indicator self-cancelling before taking the car out on the road.

19 Steering rack – removal and refitting

Removal

1 Loosen the wheel bolts, apply the handbrake, then jack up the front of the car and support it securely on axle stands (see *Jacking and vehicle support*). Do not support under the front crossmember. Remove the front wheels.

2 Remove the front crossmember as described in Section 9.

19.4a Disconnect the pipe unions at the front . . .

3 Working in the passenger cabin, slacken and remove the bolt securing the base of the steering column to the steering rack pinion **(see illustration 18.5)**.

4 Undo the power steering pipe unions from the steering rack, and release the pipes from the clamp on the rack **(see illustrations)**. Discard the O-ring seals, new ones must be fitted.

5 Disconnect the wiring plug from the power steering pressure switch on the rack **(see illustration 19.4b)**.

6 Carefully lower the steering rack to the ground.

7 Where fitted, undo the retaining nut, release the two retaining clips, and remove the shield from the steering rack.

Refitting

8 Refitting is a reversal of removal, noting the following points:

a) Ensure that the steering rack pinion gaiter is correctly located on the rack before refitting.

b) Likewise, engage the rack pinion with the steering column as the crossmember is refitted.

c) Renew the fluid pipe union O-ring seals.

d) Tighten all fasteners and unions to the specified torque where given.

e) On completion, top-up and bleed the power steering system as described in Section 22. Have the front wheel alignment checked and if necessary adjusted as soon as possible.

20 Steering rack gaiter – renewal

1 Remove the track rod end balljoint as described in Section 23.

2 Remove the two gaiter securing clips, and slide the gaiter off the rack.

3 Refit in the reverse order of removal. Smear the inner bore of the gaiter with lubricant (often supplied with the gaiter kit) prior to fitting. Renew the balljoint locknut. Use new clips to secure the gaiter, and ensure that the outer end of the gaiter locates correctly in the

19.4b . . . and rear of the rack pinion housing

20.3a Ensure the inner (arrowed) . . .

20.3b . . . and outer ends of the gaiter are correctly located

21.3 Rotate the tensioner clockwise to relieve the tension

groove machined into the track rod, without twisting **(see illustrations)**.

4 On completion, have the front wheel alignment checked and if necessary adjusted (see Section 25).

21 Power steering pump – removal and refitting

Petrol models

Removal

1 Disconnect the battery negative lead as described in Chapter 5A.

2 Apply the handbrake, then jack up the front of the vehicle and support it on axle stands (see *Jacking and vehicle support*). Release the two retaining nuts and four bolts (two each side), and remove the engine/transmission undertray.

3 With a spanner or socket in the centre of the pulley, rotate the pump drivebelt tensioner clockwise, and remove the belt from the pump pulley **(see illustration)**.

4 Slacken and remove the pump pulley retaining bolts. Prevent the pump from rotating with an Allen key in the centre of the shaft **(see illustration)**.

5 On models with air conditioning, disconnect the compressor wiring plug.

6 Position a container under the fluid inlet

hose connection on the pump – be prepared for the contents of the fluid reservoir to drain into it.

7 Undo the bolt securing the high pressure pipe bracket to the right-hand end of the engine block.

8 Unscrew the high-pressure pipe union bolt on the pump, and recover the two sealing washers **(see illustration)**. Clean the connection on the pump, then plug it or tape over it to prevent dirt getting in.

9 Slacken the retaining clamp and disconnect the low-pressure hose from the pump **(see illustration 21.8)**. Allow the fluid to drain into the container. Again, clean the connection on the pump, then plug it or tape over it to prevent dirt getting in.

10 Loosen and remove the three mounting bolts, and manoeuvre the pump from the engine bay **(see illustration)**.

Refitting

11 Refitting is a reversal of removal, noting the following points:
 a) *Tighten all fasteners and unions to the specified torque where given.*
 b) *Renew the high-pressure pipe union sealing washers*
 c) *Refit the drivebelt as described in Chapter 2A.*
 d) *On completion, fill the fluid reservoir and bleed the system as described in Section 22.*

Diesel models

Removal

12 Disconnect the battery negative lead as described in Chapter 5A.

13 Apply the handbrake, then jack up the front of the vehicle and support it on axle stands (see *Jacking and vehicle support*). Release the two retaining nuts and four bolts (two each side), and remove the engine/transmission undertray.

14 With a spanner or socket in the centre of the pulley, rotate the pump drivebelt tensioner clockwise, and remove the belt from the pump pulley.

15 Slacken and remove the pump pulley retaining bolts. Prevent the pump from rotating with an Allen key in the centre of the shaft.

16 Position a container under the fluid inlet hose connection on the pump – be prepared for the contents of the fluid reservoir to drain into it.

17 Unscrew the high-pressure pipe union bolt on the pump, and recover the two sealing washers. Clean the connection on the pump, then plug it or tape over it to prevent dirt getting in.

18 Slacken the retaining clip and disconnect the low-pressure hose from the pump. Allow the fluid to drain into the container. Again, clean the connection on the pump, then plug it or tape over it to prevent dirt getting in.

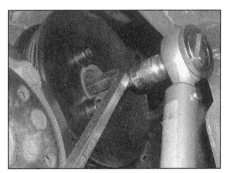

21.4 Prevent the pump pulley from rotating by inserting an Allen key in the centre

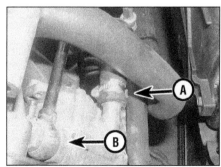

21.8 Power steering pump low-pressure hose (A) and high-pressure pipe (B)

21.10 Undo the three bolts and remove the pump

21.19 Power steering pump – diesel models

23.3 Slacken the track rod end balljoint

23.4 Use a balljoint splitter to separate the track rod end balljoint from the hub carrier

19 Loosen and remove the three mounting bolts on the right-hand end of the pump, and the two on the left-hand end, and manoeuvre the pump from the engine bay **(see illustration)**.

Refitting

20 Refitting is a reversal of removal, noting the following points:
  a) *Tighten all fasteners and unions to the specified torque where given.*
  b) *Renew the high-pressure pipe union sealing washers*
  c) *Refit the drivebelt as described in Chapter 2B.*
  d) *On completion, fill the fluid reservoir and bleed the system as described in Section 22.*

22 Power steering system – bleeding
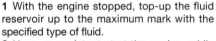

1 With the engine stopped, top-up the fluid reservoir up to the maximum mark with the specified type of fluid.
2 Have an assistant start the engine, while you keep watch on the fluid level. If the system has been drained during servicing work, be prepared to add more fluid as soon as the engine starts – the fluid level is likely to drop quickly.
3 Once the fluid level has stabilised, turn the engine off.
4 Check that the power steering fluid level is still up to the maximum mark, topping-up if necessary.
5 Start the engine and allow it idle for about 10 seconds, without turning the steering. Stop the engine, then check and top-up the fluid level if necessary.
6 Restart the engine, and turn the steering onto full left-hand lock, holding it there for a few seconds, and then onto full right-hand lock; check all steering hose/pipe unions for signs of leakage. **Note:** *Do not hold the steering at full lock for more than 10 seconds at a time, otherwise the hydraulic system may be damaged.*
7 Stop the engine, and top-up the fluid level if necessary.

8 Start the engine once more, and this time run it for about 2 minutes, turning the steering fully to the right and left.
9 Once all air is removed from the system, stop the engine, and check the fluid level as described in *Weekly checks*. Take the car for a journey of a few miles, then recheck the fluid level with the system fully up to operating temperature – repeat the bleeding process completely if there is any suggestion that air is still present (eg, excessive noise).

23 Track rod end balljoint – removal and refitting

Removal

1 Loosen the wheel bolts, apply the handbrake, then jack up the relevant front wheel and support on axle stands (see *Jacking and vehicle support*). Remove the front wheel.
2 Measure the exposed amount of adjustment thread showing on the inboard side of the track rod end locknut. This will act as a guide to the adjustment position when refitting the track rod end to the track rod.
3 Slacken the track rod end locknut **(see illustration)**.
4 Slacken and remove the track rod end balljoint-to-hub carrier locknut, and using a balljoint splitter, separate the balljoint from the hub carrier. Lift the track rod balljoint from the hub carrier. Unscrew the track rod balljoint from the track rod **(see illustration)**. Note that the track rod ends are marked R and L, to indicate right- and left-hand.
5 Carefully clean the balljoint/strut tapers and the track rod threads. Renew the balljoint if its movement is sloppy or too stiff, if it is excessively worn, or if it is damaged in any way; carefully check the stud taper and threads. If the balljoint gaiter is damaged, the complete balljoint assembly must be renewed; it is not possible to obtain the gaiter separately.

Refitting

6 Screw the track rod balljoint and locknut onto the track rod, until the amount of

exposed adjustment thread matches that noted on removal. Finger-tighten the locknut.
7 Fit the balljoint into the taper on the hub carrier, then fit a new nut and tighten it to the specified torque.
8 If the tracking is not going to be adjusted immediately the car is lowered, tighten the locknut to the specified torque now.
9 Refit the wheel, then lower the car to the ground and tighten the wheel bolt to the specified torque.
10 On completion, have the tracking (front wheel alignment) checked as soon as possible. A good indication of the need for this will be whether the steering wheel is centralised, but even this isn't foolproof.

24 Track rods – removal and refitting

Removal

1 Remove the relevant steering rack gaiter as described in Section 20.
2 Using a large open-ended spanner, unscrew the locking collar securing the track rod to the rack **(see illustration)**.

Refitting

3 Refitting is a reversal of removal, noting the following points:
  a) *Use a new track rod balljoint nut.*
  b) *Hold the track rods parallel to the rack when tightening the track rod locking collar.*

24.2 Unscrew the track rod locking collar

c) *Tighten all fasteners to the specified torque (where possible).*
d) *On completion, have the front wheel alignment checked at the earliest opportunity.*

25 Wheel alignment and steering angles – general information

1 Accurate wheel alignment is essential for precise steering and handling, and for even tyre wear. Before carrying out any checking or adjusting operations, make sure that the tyres are correctly inflated, that all steering and suspension joints and linkages are in sound condition, and that the wheels are not buckled or distorted, particularly around the rims. It will also be necessary to have the vehicle positioned on flat, level ground, with enough space to push the car backwards and forwards through about half its length.

2 Front wheel alignment consists of four factors:

Camber is the angle at which the roadwheels are set from the vertical, when viewed from the front or rear of the vehicle. 'Positive' camber is the angle (in degrees) that the wheels are tilted outwards at the top from the vertical.

Castor is the angle between the steering axis and a vertical line when viewed from each side of the vehicle. 'Positive' castor is indicated when the steering axis is inclined towards the rear of the vehicle at its upper end.

Steering axis or kingpin inclination is the angle, when viewed from the front or rear of the vehicle, between the vertical and an imaginary line drawn between the upper and lower front suspension strut mountings.

Toe setting is the difference, viewed from above, between lines drawn through the roadwheel centres and the car's centre-line. Toe-in is when the roadwheels point inwards, towards each other at the front, while toe-out is when the splay outwards from each other at the front

3 Camber, castor, steering axis inclination and 'thrust angle' are set during manufacture, and are not adjustable. Unless the vehicle has suffered accident damage, or there is gross wear in the suspension mountings or joints, it can be assumed that these settings are correct. If for any reason it is believed that they are not correct, the task of checking them should be left to a Ford dealer or tyre specialist, who will have the necessary special equipment needed to measure the small angles involved.

4 It is, however, within the scope of the home mechanic to check and adjust the front wheel toe setting. To do this, a tracking gauge must first be obtained. Two types of gauge are available, and can be obtained from motor accessory shops. The first type measures the distance between the front and rear inside edges of the roadwheels, as previously described, with the vehicle stationary. The second type, known as a 'scuff plate', measures the actual position of the contact surface of the tyre, in relation to the road surface, with the vehicle in motion. This is achieved by pushing or driving the front tyre over a plate, which then moves slightly according to the scuff of the tyre, and shows this movement on a scale. Both types have their advantages and disadvantages, but either can give satisfactory results if used correctly and carefully.

5 Many tyre specialists will also check toe settings free, or for a nominal charge.

6 Make sure that the steering is in the straight-ahead position when making measurements, and the vehicle is at normal kerb weight (ie, no-one inside, and no significant load or luggage carried).

Front wheel toe adjustment

7 If adjustment is necessary, apply the handbrake, then jack up the front of the vehicle and support it securely on axle stands. Slacken the track rod end locknuts, then rotate the adjuster threaded section using the nut provided to alter the length of the track rod (as necessary); shortening the track rod will reduce toe-in/increase toe-out. Ensure that the rack gaiter is not twisted during the procedure.

8 When the setting is correct, tighten both the locknuts to the specified torque setting. Check that the rack gaiter is straight.

9 Recheck the toe setting and, if necessary, repeat the adjustment procedure.

Chapter 11
Bodywork and fittings

Contents

Degrees of difficulty

Easy, suitable for novice with little experience	Fairly easy, suitable for beginner with some experience	Fairly difficult, suitable for competent DIY mechanic	Difficult, suitable for experienced DIY mechanic	Very difficult, suitable for expert DIY or professional

Specifications

Torque wrench settings	Nm	lbf ft
Bonnet hinge bolts	24	18
Bonnet lock bolts	12	9
Child's seat belt lower mounting bolt	20	15
Exterior mirror retaining screws	7	5
Front bumper mounting bolts	21	15
Rear bumper mounting bolts	21	15
Seat bolts	40	30
Seat belt anchor bolts	40	30
Seat belt, front pretensioner stalk locknut	20	15
Seat belt inertia reel bolt	40	30
Tailgate mounting nuts	24	18
Tailgate striker	10	7

1 General description

One body shape is available, with a with various seating permutations. The body is of all-steel construction, and incorporates calculated impact crumple zones at the front, and side impact protection beams, with a central safety cell passenger compartment.

During manufacture, the underbody is treated with underseal. The bumpers and wheelarch liners are plastic mouldings, for durability and strength.

2 Maintenance – bodywork and underframe

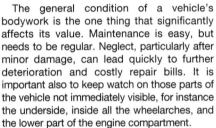

The general condition of a vehicle's bodywork is the one thing that significantly affects its value. Maintenance is easy, but needs to be regular. Neglect, particularly after minor damage, can lead quickly to further deterioration and costly repair bills. It is important also to keep watch on those parts of the vehicle not immediately visible, for instance the underside, inside all the wheelarches, and the lower part of the engine compartment.

The basic maintenance routine for the bodywork is washing – preferably with a lot of water, from a hose. This will remove all the loose solids which may have stuck to the vehicle. It is important to flush these off in such a way as to prevent grit from scratching the finish. The wheelarches and underframe need washing in the same way, to remove any accumulated mud which will retain moisture and tend to encourage rust. Paradoxically enough, the best time to clean the underframe and wheelarches is in wet weather, when the mud is thoroughly wet and soft. In very wet weather, the underframe is usually cleaned of large accumulations automatically, and this is a good time for inspection.

Periodically, except on vehicles with a wax-based underbody protective coating, it is a good idea to have the whole of the underframe of the vehicle steam-cleaned, engine compartment included, so that a thorough inspection can be carried out to see what minor repairs and renovations are necessary. Steam cleaning is available at many garages, and is necessary for the removal of the accumulation of oily grime, which sometimes is allowed to become thick in certain areas. If steam-cleaning facilities are not available, there are some excellent grease solvents available which can be brush-applied; the dirt can then be simply hosed off. Note that these methods should not be used on vehicles with wax-based underbody protective coating, or the coating will be removed. Such vehicles should be inspected annually, preferably just before Winter, when the underbody should be washed down, and any damage to the wax coating repaired. Ideally, a completely fresh coat should be applied. It would also be worth considering the use of wax-based protection for injection into door panels, sills, box sections, etc, as an additional safeguard against rust damage, where such protection is not provided by the vehicle manufacturer.

After washing paintwork, wipe off with a chamois leather to give an unspotted clear finish. A coat of clear protective wax polish will give added protection against chemical pollutants in the air. If the paintwork sheen has dulled or oxidised, use a cleaner/polisher combination to restore the brilliance of the shine. This requires a little effort, but such dulling is usually caused because regular washing has been neglected. Care needs to be taken with metallic paintwork, as special non-abrasive cleaner/polisher is required to avoid damage to the finish. Always check that the door and ventilator opening drain holes and pipes are completely clear, so that water can be drained out. Brightwork should be treated in the same way as paintwork. Windscreens and windows can be kept clear of the smeary film which often appears, by proprietary glass cleaner. Never use any form of wax or other body or chromium polish on glass.

3 Maintenance – upholstery and carpets

Mats and carpets should be brushed or vacuum-cleaned regularly, to keep them free of grit. If they are badly stained, remove them from the vehicle for scrubbing or sponging, and make quite sure they are dry before refitting. Seats and interior trim panels can be kept clean by wiping with a damp cloth. If they do become stained (which can be more apparent on light-coloured upholstery), use a little liquid detergent and a soft nail brush to scour the grime out of the grain of the material. Do not forget to keep the headlining clean in the same way as the upholstery. When using liquid cleaners inside the vehicle, do not over-wet the surfaces being cleaned. Excessive damp could get into the seams and padded interior, causing stains, offensive odours or even rot. If the inside of the vehicle gets wet accidentally, it is worthwhile taking some trouble to dry it out properly, particularly where carpets are involved. *Do not leave oil or electric heaters inside the vehicle for this purpose.*

4 Minor body damage – repair

Repairs of minor scratches in bodywork

If the scratch is very superficial, and does not penetrate to the metal of the bodywork, repair is very simple. Lightly rub the area of the scratch with a paintwork renovator or a very fine cutting paste to remove loose paint from the scratch, and to clear the surrounding bodywork of wax polish. Rinse the area with clean water.

Apply touch-up paint to the scratch using a fine paint brush; continue to apply fine layers of paint until the surface of the paint in the scratch is level with the surrounding paintwork. Allow the new paint at least two weeks to harden, then blend it into the surrounding paintwork by rubbing the scratch area with a paintwork renovator or a very fine cutting paste. Finally, apply wax polish.

Where the scratch has penetrated right through to the metal of the bodywork, causing the metal to rust, a different repair technique is required. Remove any loose rust from the bottom of the scratch with a penknife, then apply rust-inhibiting paint to prevent the formation of rust in the future. Using a rubber or nylon applicator, fill the scratch with bodystopper paste. If required, this paste can be mixed with cellulose thinners to provide a very thin paste which is ideal for filling narrow scratches. Before the stopper-paste in the scratch hardens, wrap a piece of smooth cotton rag around the top of a finger. Dip the finger in cellulose thinners, and quickly sweep it across the surface of the stopper-paste in the scratch; this will ensure that the surface of the stopper-paste is slightly hollowed. The scratch can now be painted over as described earlier in this Section.

Repairs of dents in bodywork

When deep denting of the vehicle's bodywork has taken place, the first task is to pull the dent out, until the affected bodywork almost attains its original shape. There is little point in trying to restore the original shape completely, as the metal in the damaged area will have stretched on impact, and cannot be reshaped fully to its original contour. It is better to bring the level of the dent up to a point which is about 3 mm below the level of the surrounding bodywork. In cases where the dent is very shallow anyway, it is not worth trying to pull it out at all. If the underside of the dent is accessible, it can be hammered out gently from behind, using a mallet with a wooden or plastic head. Whilst doing this, hold a suitable block of wood firmly against the outside of the panel, to absorb the impact from the hammer blows and thus prevent a large area of the bodywork from being 'belled-out'.

Should the dent be in a section of the bodywork which has a double skin, or some other factor making it inaccessible from behind, a different technique is called for. Drill several small holes through the metal inside the area – particularly in the deeper section. Then screw long self-tapping screws into the holes, just sufficiently for them to gain a good purchase in the metal. Now the dent can be pulled out by pulling on the protruding heads of the screws with a pair of pliers.

The next stage of the repair is the removal of the paint from the damaged area, and from an inch or so of the surrounding 'sound' bodywork. This is accomplished most easily by using a wire brush or abrasive pad on a power drill, although it can be done just as effectively by hand, using sheets of abrasive paper. To complete the preparation for filling, score the surface of the bare metal with a screwdriver or the tang of a file, or alternatively, drill small holes in the affected area. This will provide a good 'key' for the filler paste.

To complete the repair, see the Section on filling and respraying.

Repairs of rust holes or gashes in bodywork

Remove all paint from the affected area, and from an inch or so of the surrounding 'sound' bodywork, using an abrasive pad or a wire brush on a power drill. If these are not available, a few sheets of abrasive paper will do the job most effectively. With the paint removed, you will be able to judge the severity of the corrosion, and therefore decide whether to renew the whole panel (if this is possible) or to repair the affected area. New body panels are not as expensive as most people think, and it is often quicker and more satisfactory to fit a new panel than to attempt to repair large areas of corrosion.

Remove all fittings from the affected area, except those which will act as a guide to the original shape of the damaged bodywork (eg headlight shells etc). Then, using tin snips or a hacksaw blade, remove all loose metal and any other metal badly affected by corrosion. Hammer the edges of the hole inwards, to create a slight depression for the filler paste.

Wire-brush the affected area to remove the powdery rust from the surface of the remaining metal. Paint the affected area with rust-inhibiting paint; if the back of the rusted area is accessible, treat this also.

Before filling can take place, it will be necessary to block the hole in some way. This can be achieved with aluminium or plastic mesh, or aluminium tape.

Aluminium or plastic mesh, or glass-fibre matting, is probably the best material to use for a large hole. Cut a piece to the approximate size and shape of the hole to be filled, then position it in the hole so that its edges are below the level of the surrounding bodywork. It can be retained in position by several blobs of filler paste around its periphery.

Aluminium tape should be used for small or very narrow holes. Pull a piece off the roll, trim it to the approximate size and shape required, then pull off the backing paper (if used) and stick the tape over the hole; it can be overlapped if the thickness of one piece is insufficient. Burnish down the edges of the tape with the handle of a screwdriver or similar, to ensure that the tape is securely attached to the metal underneath.

Bodywork repairs – filling and respraying

Before using this Section, see the Sections on dent, deep scratch, rust holes and gash repairs.

Many types of bodyfiller are available, but generally speaking, those proprietary kits which contain a tin of filler paste and a tube of resin hardener are best for this type of repair which can be used directly from the tube. A wide, flexible plastic or nylon applicator will be found invaluable for imparting a smooth and well-contoured finish to the surface of the filler.

Mix up a little filler on a clean piece of card or board – measure the hardener carefully (follow the maker's instructions on the pack), otherwise the filler will set too rapidly or too slowly. Using the applicator, apply the filler paste to the prepared area; draw the applicator across the surface of the filler to achieve the correct contour and to level the surface. When a contour that approximates to the correct one is achieved, stop working the paste – if you carry on too long, the paste will become sticky and begin to 'pick-up' on the applicator. Continue to add thin layers of filler paste at 20-minute intervals, until the level of the filler is just proud of the surrounding bodywork.

Once the filler has hardened, the excess can be removed using a metal plane or file. From then on, progressively-finer grades of abrasive paper should be used, starting with a 40-grade production paper, and finishing with a 400-grade wet-and-dry paper. Always wrap the abrasive paper around a flat rubber, cork, or wooden block – otherwise the surface of the filler will not be completely flat. During the smoothing of the filler surface, the wet-and-dry paper should be periodically rinsed in water. This will ensure that a very smooth finish is imparted to the filler at the final stage.

At this stage, the 'dent' should be surrounded by a ring of bare metal, which in turn should be encircled by the finely 'feathered' edge of the good paintwork. Rinse the repair area with clean water, until all the dust produced by the rubbing-down operation has gone.

Spray the whole area with a light coat of primer – this will show up any imperfections in the surface of the filler. Repair these imperfections with fresh filler paste or bodystopper, and again smooth the surface with abrasive paper. If bodystopper is used, it can be mixed with cellulose thinners, to form a thin paste which is ideal for filling small holes. Repeat this spray-and-repair procedure until you are satisfied that the surface of the filler, and the feathered edge of the paintwork, are perfect. Clean the repair area with clean water, and allow to dry fully.

The repair area is now ready for final spraying. Paint spraying must be carried out in a warm, dry, windless and dust-free atmosphere. This condition can be created

artificially if you have access to a large indoor working area, but if you are forced to work in the open, you will have to pick your day very carefully. If you are working indoors, dousing the floor in the work area with water will help to settle the dust which would otherwise be in the atmosphere. If the repair area is confined to one body panel, mask off the surrounding panels; this will help to minimise the effects of a slight mismatch in paint colours. Bodywork fittings (e.g. chrome strips, door handles etc) will also need to be masked off. Use genuine masking tape, and several thickness of newspaper, for the masking operations.

Before starting to spray, agitate the aerosol can thoroughly, then spray a test area (an old tin, or similar) until the technique is mastered. Cover the repair area with a thick coat of primer; the thickness should be built up using several thin layers of paint, rather than one thick one. Using 400 grade wet-and-dry paper, rub down the surface of the primer until it is smooth. While doing this, the work area should be thoroughly doused with water, and the wet-and-dry paper periodically rinsed in water. Allow to dry before spraying on more paint.

Spray on the top coat, again building up the thickness by using several thin layers of paint. Start spraying at one edge of the repair area, and then, using a side-to-side motion, work until the whole repair area and about 2 inches of the surrounding original paintwork is covered. Remove all masking material 10 to 15 minutes after spraying on the final coat of paint.

Allow the new paint at least two weeks to harden, then, using a paintwork renovator or a very fine cutting paste, blend the edges of the paint into the existing paintwork. Finally, apply wax polish.

Plastic components

With the use of more and more plastic body components by the vehicle manufacturers (e.g. bumpers, spoilers, and in some cases major body panels), rectification of more serious damage to such items has become a matter of either entrusting repair work to a specialist in this field, or renewing complete components. Repair of such damage by the DIY owner is not feasible, owing to the cost of the equipment and materials required for effecting such repairs. The basic technique involves making a groove along the line of the crack in the plastic, using a rotary burr in a power drill. The damaged part is then welded back together, using a hot air gun to heat up and fuse a plastic filler rod into the groove. Any excess plastic is then removed, and the area rubbed down to a smooth finish. It is important that a filler rod of the correct plastic is used, as body components can be made of a variety of different types (e.g. polycarbonate, ABS, polypropylene).

Damage of a less serious nature (abrasions, minor cracks etc) can be repaired by the DIY owner using a two-part epoxy filler repair material which can be used directly from the tube. Once mixed in equal proportions, this is used in similar fashion to the bodywork filler used on metal panels. The filler is usually cured in twenty to thirty minutes, ready for sanding and painting.

If the owner is renewing a complete component himself, or if he has repaired it with epoxy filler, he will be left with the problem of finding a suitable paint for finishing which is compatible with the type of plastic used. At one time, the use of a universal paint was not possible, owing to the complex range of plastics met with in body component applications. Standard paints, generally speaking, will not bond to plastic or rubber satisfactorily, but professional matched paints, to match any plastic or rubber finish, can be obtained from some dealers. However, it is now possible to obtain a plastic body parts finishing kit which consists of a pre-primer treatment, a primer and coloured top coat. Full instructions are normally supplied with a kit, but basically the method of use is to first apply the pre-primer to the component concerned, and allow it to dry for up to 30 minutes. Then the primer is applied, and left to dry for about an hour before finally applying the special-coloured top coat. The result is a correctly coloured component, where the paint will flex with the plastic or rubber, a property that standard paint does not normally possess.

5 Major body damage – repair

Where serious damage has occurred, or large areas need renewal due to neglect, it means that complete new panels will need welding-in, and this is best left to professionals. If the damage is due to impact, it will also be necessary to check completely the alignment of the bodyshell, and this can only be carried out accurately by a Ford dealer using special jigs. If the body is left misaligned, it is primarily dangerous, as the car will not handle properly, and secondly, uneven stresses will be imposed on the steering, suspension and possibly transmission, causing abnormal wear, or complete failure, particularly to such items as the tyres.

6 Door rattles – tracing and rectification

1 Check first that the door is not loose at the hinges, and that the latch is holding the door firmly in position. Check also that the door lines up with the aperture in the body. If the door is out of alignment, adjust it as described in Section 22.
2 If the latch is holding the door in the correct position, but the latch still rattles, the lock mechanism is worn and should be renewed.
3 Other rattles from the door could be caused by wear in the window operating mechanism, interior lock mechanism, loose glass channels or loose wiring.

7 Bonnet – removal, refitting and adjustment

Removal

1 Fully open the bonnet, then place some cardboard or rags beneath the corners by the hinges to protect the bodywork.
2 Squeeze together the lugs of the retaining clips, and remove the bonnet insulator panel. There are 10 clips retaining the panel (see illustration).
3 Disconnect the windscreen washer tube from the connecting piece. Unplug the heated jet wiring connectors and release the hose/loom from retaining clips. Prise out the harness grommet adjacent to the hinge, and pull the harness/hose from the bonnet (see illustrations).
4 Prop the bonnet open using two stout lengths of wood, one positioned at each corner. Alternatively, enlist the help of an assistant to support the bonnet.
5 Mark the location of the hinges with a pencil, then loosen the four hinge-to-bonnet retaining bolts (see illustration).
6 Support the bonnet as the securing bolts

are unscrewed, then withdraw the bonnet from the car.

Refitting and adjustment

7 Refitting is a reversal of removal. Ensure that the hinges are adjusted to their original positions. Close the bonnet very carefully initially; misalignment may cause the edges of the bonnet to damage the bodywork. If necessary, adjust the hinges to their original positions and check that the bonnet is level with the surrounding bodywork. If necessary, adjust the height of the bonnet front edge by screwing the rubber buffers in or out.
8 Check that the bonnet lock operates in a satisfactory manner. In particular, check that the safety catch holds the bonnet after the bonnet release cable has been pulled.

8 Bonnet lock and release cable – removal and refitting

Removal

1 Open the bonnet and locate the bonnet lock mechanism, mounted in the crossmember at the front of the engine compartment. Use a marker pen or similar to make alignment marks between the lock and the mounting panel.
2 Release the bonnet cable from the retaining clips in the engine compartment.
3 Remove the radiator grille as described in Section 10.

7.2 Squeeze together the clips and pull them from the panel

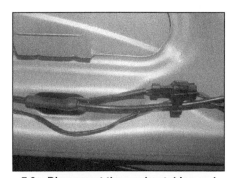

7.3a Disconnect the washer tubing and heated jet wiring connectors

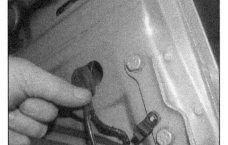

7.3b Prise out the grommet and pull the harness/hose from the bonnet

7.5 Undo the two bolts each side and remove the bonnet

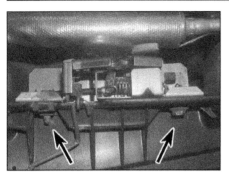

8.4 The bonnet lock is retained by two bolts (arrowed)

8.5 Disconnect the inner and outer cable from the lock

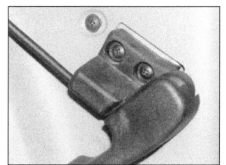

8.7 Undo the two screws and remove the release handle

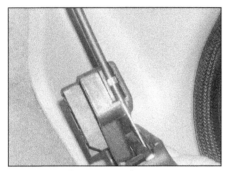

8.8a Disconnect the outer . . .

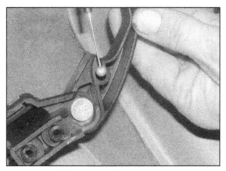

8.8b . . . and inner cable

4 Slacken and remove the two retaining bolts, and lift the bonnet lock from the crossmember **(see illustration)**.

5 Detach the release cable outer and inner, as the lock is withdrawn **(see illustration)**.

6 If required, the bonnet release cable can now be removed as follows.

7 Working in the driver's side footwell, undo the two screws and remove the release handle from the trim panel **(see illustration)**.

8 Disengage the outer cable, then the inner cable from the handle **(see illustrations)**.

9 Tie a length of cord to the inner end of the release cable in the driver's footwell, and

carefully pull the complete cable through the bulkhead and into the engine compartment, leaving the length of cord in place of the release cable. Undo the cord from the cable, and leave the cord ends exposed in the engine compartment and footwell.

Refitting

10 Refit in the reverse order of removal. Tie the inner end of the cable to the exposed cord in the engine compartment, carefully pull the cable through to the release handle, then untie the cord.

11 When positioning the cable in the engine

compartment, ensure that it is rerouted correctly to avoid kinks, sharp bends and chaffing. Check for satisfactory operation of the cable and the lock before closing the bonnet. Ensure that the bonnet locks properly when closed, and also that the safety catch operates correctly when the bonnet release cable is actuated.

9 Bumpers – removal and refitting

Front bumper

Removal

1 Working at each front wheelarch in turn, undo the three Torx screws each side to release the trailing edges of the bumper from the wheelarch liner **(see illustration)**.

2 Unscrew and remove the three retaining bolts at the centre, rear edge of the bumper from below.

3 Undo the retaining screws and remove the front number plate. Undo the two Torx screws in the number plate recess **(see illustration)**.

4 Carefully withdraw the bumper assembly by sliding it squarely away from the front of the

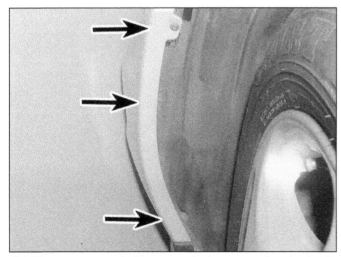

9.1 Three screws each side secure the bumper to the wheelarch liner (arrowed)

9.3 Remove the number plate and undo the two Torx screws

9.4a Pull the ambient temperature sensor from the bumper

9.4b Front bumper bar upper . . .

9.4c . . . and lower mounting bolts

vehicle and out from the guides beneath the headlamps. Disconnect the front lamp and ambient temperature sensor wiring plugs as the bumper is withdrawn. If required, the bumper bar can be removed by unscrewing the four bolts securing it to the chassis **(see illustrations)**.

Refitting

5 Refitting is a reversal of removal. Tighten the bumper retaining bolts to the specified torque.

Rear bumper

Removal

6 Pull the rubber tailgate weatherstrips from the flanges on the rear bumper **(see illustration)**.
7 On models fitted with a tow bar, remove the spare wheel, and pass the support bracket through it.
8 Working at each rear wheelarch in turn, undo the three screws each side to release the leading edges of the bumper from the wheelarches **(see illustration)**. **Note:** *Watch out for the screws behind each mudflap.*
9 Working up behind the rear bumper, slacken and remove the two bolts each side securing the chassis members to the bumper **(see illustration)**.

9.6 Pull the weatherstrip from the bumper flange

10 On models fitted with a tow bar, undo the screws securing the towing electrical socket to the bumper.
11 Carefully withdraw the bumper assembly by sliding it squarely away from the rear of the vehicle. If the bumper sticks in position, free the leading edges one at a time by grasping the lower edge of the bumper just to the rear of the wheelarch and pivoting it upwards and away from the wing, to release it from its securing bracket. If required, the cover can be separated from the bumper bar by undoing the upper and lower row of Torx screws **(see illustration)**.

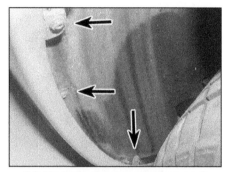

9.8 Undo the three screws (arrowed) securing the leading edge of the rear bumper

Refitting

12 Refit in the reverse order of removal. Loosely fit all retaining bolts and screws before fully tightening them. Tighten the retaining bolts to the specified torque.

10 Radiator grille –
removal and refitting

Removal

1 The radiator grille is secured at its top edge

9.9 Working from below, undo the two bolts each side securing the bumper to the chassis (arrowed)

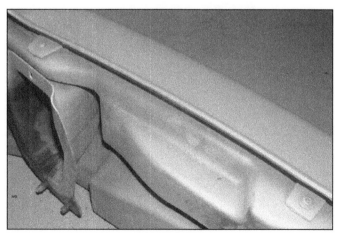

9.11 Undo the Torx screws and separate the cover from the bumper bar

10.1a Prise up the centre . . .

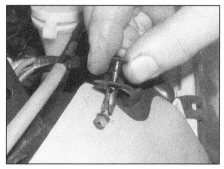

10.1b . . . and remove the clip

10.2 Slacken the indicator retaining bolt

by four plastic retaining clips. To release the clips, prise up the centre of each clip using a small screwdriver or similar **(see illustrations)**. Remove the clips.

2 Slacken the retaining bolt, slide the indicator forward and disconnect the wiring plug **(see illustration)**. Repeat this procedure on the remaining front indicator.

3 Working in the indicator lamp apertures, unscrew the retaining bolt each side **(see illustration)**.

4 Unclip and remove the front grille.

Refitting

5 Refitting is a reversal of removal, ensuring that the inner and outer clips are fully engaged **(see illustration)**. As the radiator grille is refitted, remember to align the bonnet safety catch release lever with the aperture in the grille.

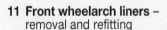

11 Front wheelarch liners –
removal and refitting

Removal

1 Chock the rear wheels, apply the handbrake, then loosen the relevant front wheel bolts. Jack up and support the front of the car on axle stands (see *Jacking and vehicle support*). Remove the relevant roadwheel.

2 The liner is secured by eight Torx screws. Remove the screws and manoeuvre the liner from under the front wing.

Refitting

3 Refitting is a reversal of removal.

12 Tailgate and trim –
removal and refitting

Removal

1 Open the tailgate, then unclip the upper trim screw covers (one each side). Undo the two upper trim screws, and remove each half of the upper trim by pulling each trim away from the tailgate **(see illustration)**.

2 Working on the lower edge of the tailgate, prise out the plastic caps, undo the two

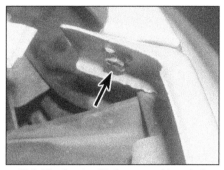

10.3 The front grille is secured by a bolt each side in the indicator aperture (arrowed)

retaining screws and carefully remove the pull-down handle **(see illustration)**.

3 Undo the seven screws, securing the trim panel to the tailgate. Pull the trim away from the lock end of the tailgate, then release the

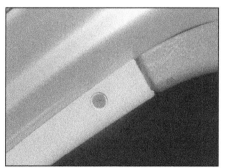

12.1 Prise out the cover and remove the upper trim screws

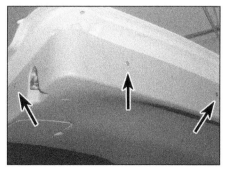

12.3a The tailgate trim is secured by seven screws around its edges (three arrowed) . . .

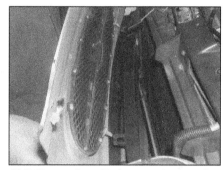

10.5 Ensure the grille inner and outer clips are engaged

four clips securing the trim to the panel below the window **(see illustrations)**.

4 With the trim removed, disconnect the wiring plugs to the rear lamps and wiper motor. Release the wiring harness from the

12.2 Undo the pull-down handle screws

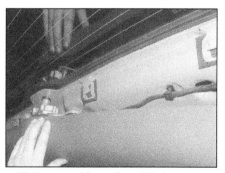

12.3b . . . and four clips at its top edge

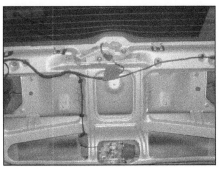

12.4 Release the wiring harness from the retaining clips

12.5 Remove the tailgate washer jet

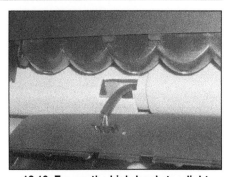

12.10 Ensure the high-level stop-light wires do not become trapped

retaining clips. Make a note of the fitted position of the harness **(see illustration)**.
5 Depress the retaining clip, and carefully prise out the tailgate washer jet. Disconnect the rubber hose from the jet **(see illustration)**.
6 Prise out the rubber grommet adjacent to the hinge, and pull the harness and washer tube from the tailgate.
7 Mark the relationship between the tailgate and its hinges using a felt tip pen.
8 Enlist the aid of an assistant to help support the tailgate, then detach the tailgate struts with reference to Section 13.
9 Unscrew and remove the tailgate-to-hinge securing bolts, and lift the tailgate clear of the vehicle.

Refitting

10 Refit in the reverse order of removal. Check that the tailgate is correctly aligned

before fully tightening the tailgate hinge bolts. When refitting the upper tailgate trim panels, ensure that the high-level stop-light wires do not become trapped **(see illustration)**.
11 The fit and closing tension of the tailgate can be adjusted by altering the positions of the rubber buffers at the upper and lower edges of the tailgate.

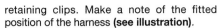

13 Tailgate support strut(s) – removal and refitting

Removal

1 Open the tailgate and support it with a prop (or with the aid of an assistant).
2 Undo the retaining bolts and separate the upper strut mounting plate from the tailgate **(see illustration)**.

3 Disconnect the strut(s) at the upper and lower balljoints by lifting the spring clips, and prising the joint free **(see illustration)**.
4 If a strut is defective in operation, it must be renewed. Do not attempt to dismantle and repair the strut. Note that the struts are filled with pressurised gas, and so should not be punctured or disposed of by incineration.

Refitting

5 Refit in the reverse order of removal. The thinner, piston rod end of the strut(s) must be attached to the bodywork. Ensure that the strut is securely engaged with the balljoints.

14 Tailgate lock, handle and cylinder – removal and refitting

1 Remove the tailgate lower trim panel with reference to Section 12. Disconnect the battery negative terminal as described in Chapter 5A.

Lock

Removal

2 Working at the lower edge of the tailgate, undo the three lock retaining screws **(see illustration)**.
3 Working inside the tailgate, manoeuvre the lock from position, and disconnect the wiring plugs as the lock assembly is withdrawn. If required, the lock motor can be removed from the lock, once the two lock motor screws have been removed **(see illustrations)**.

13.2 Undo the tailgate strut mounting plate bolts

13.3 Prise out the clip and remove the strut

14.2 The tailgate lock is secured by three screws

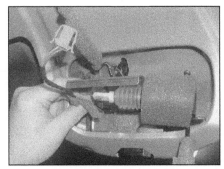

14.3a Disconnect the wiring plugs as the lock is withdrawn

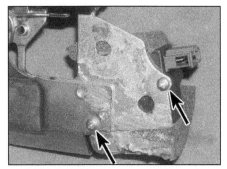

14.3b To remove the lock motor, undo the two screws (arrowed)

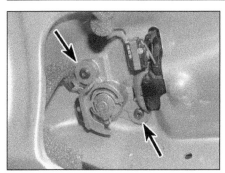

14.6 Undo the cylinder assembly screws (arrowed)

14.7 The handle is secured by one screw

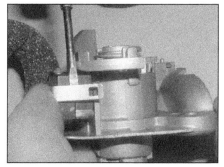

14.10 Prise off the retaining clip to remove the switch

Refitting

4 Refit in the reverse order of removal.

Handle

Removal

5 Remove the tailgate lock assembly, as described in Paragraphs 2 and 3.
6 Working inside the tailgate, unplug the lock cylinder assembly wiring plugs, undo the two Torx screws remove the cylinder assembly **(see illustration)**.
7 Unscrew the remaining Torx screw and remove the handle assembly **(see illustration)**.

Refitting

8 Refitting is a reversal of removal.

Cylinder assembly

Removal

9 Remove the lock cylinder assembly as described in Paragraphs 5 to 6 of this Section.
10 If required, the microswitches can be removed by prising off the retaining clip(s) with a small flat bladed screwdriver **(see illustration)**.
11 To remove the lock cylinder, insert the key, and prise off the circlip at the inner end of the cylinder **(see illustration)**.
12 Lift off the spring and the operating lever. The cylinder can now be withdrawn from the underside of the assembly. **Do not** invert the assembly as the cylinder sleeve and spacer will fall out **(see illustrations)**.

Refitting

13 The remainder of refitting is a reversal of removal.

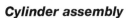

15 Door trim panel – removal and refitting

Front door trim

Removal

1 Open the door and insert a thin-bladed screwdriver between the door trim surround and the window switch panel. Gently prise the lower edge of the switch panel from the trim,

14.11 Slide out the lock cylinder circlip

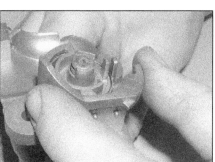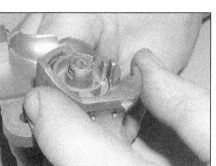

14.12b ... and operating lever ...

15.1 Prise up the lower edge and slide the switch panel down

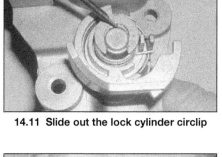

14.12a Remove the spring ...

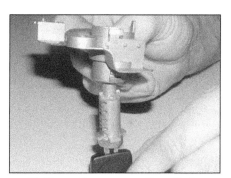

14.12c ... then remove the cylinder

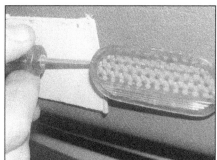

15.2 Take care not to damage the trim whilst removing the courtesy light

and then slide the panel downwards **(see illustration)**. Disconnect the switch wiring plugs as the switch panel is withdrawn. On models with manually-adjustable door mirrors, unscrew the collar from the control

surround, and push the control down through the door trim.
2 Carefully prise the courtesy light from the door trim **(see illustration)**. Disconnect the wiring plug as the lamp is removed.

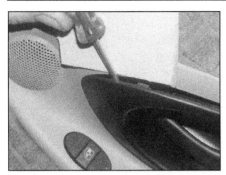

15.3 Starting in the centre, prise out the handle bezel

15.4 Undo the screw adjacent to the interior handle

15.5a Carefully prise the door trim clips from the frame

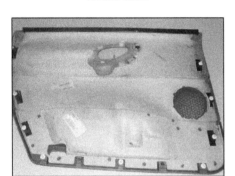

15.5b The door trim is retained by eleven clips

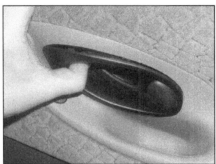

15.7 Pull the handle surround forwards, then prise it free with a small screwdriver

Disconnect the electric window switch (where applicable), speaker, and sill illumination lamp wiring plugs as the trim is withdrawn. If required the door membrane can be removed after undoing the four retaining screws and removing the speaker **(see illustration)**. Disconnect the speaker wiring plug as it is withdrawn. The door membrane is glued in place – if care is taken during its removal, it may be possible to re-use it.

Refitting

11 Refitting is a reversal of removal. Note that when refitting the interior handle surround engage the upper retaining clips first.

3 Prise out the interior handle bezel, starting in the centre **(see illustration)**.
4 Undo the trim retaining screw adjacent to the interior handle **(see illustration)**.
5 Starting with the clip at the lower rear corner of the trim, using a flat-bladed screwdriver, carefully prise the trim away from the door frame, releasing the eleven trim retaining clips, and remove the door trim panel **(see illustrations)**. **Note:** *When removing the driver's door trim, disconnect the flashing LED wiring plug as the trim is withdrawn.* If required, the plastic membrane can be removed by carefully cutting through the mastic holding it place and removing the door speaker (where fitted).

Refitting

6 Refit in the reverse order of removal.

Rear door trim

Removal

7 Insert a thumb into the interior handle recess, and pull the door handle surround forwards slightly. Using a small screwdriver, carefully prise out the door handle surround **(see illustration)**.
8 Remove the screw at the front of the interior handle recess **(see illustration 15.4)**.
9 On models with manually-operated rear windows, slide the collar behind the handle in the opposite direction to the handle, then pull the handle from the spindle **(see illustration)**.
10 Starting with the clip at the lower rear corner of the trim, using a flat-bladed screwdriver, carefully release the eleven trim retaining clips, and lift the trim away from the door frame **(see illustration 15.5a)**.

16 Door lock –
removal and refitting

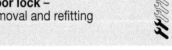

Removal

1 Fully close the door window. Disconnect the battery negative terminal as described in Chapter 5A.
2 Remove the door trim panel and speaker (see Section 15).
3 Using a plastic knife, cut through the sealant between the plastic membrane and the door frame. Carefully peel the membrane away from the door. **Note:** *Do not attempt to peel away the membrane without first cutting through the sealant.*
4 Prise out the rubber grommet in the end of the door frame, and undo the exterior handle retaining screw **(see illustration)**.

15.9 On models with manual rear windows, slide the collar out and pull the handle from the spindle

15.10 Undo the four screws and remove the door speaker

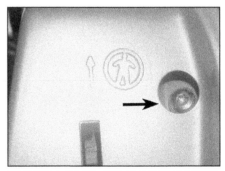

16.4 Prise out the rubber grommet (where fitted) and undo the exterior handle screw (arrowed) – rear door shown

16.5 The door lock is secured by three Torx screws

5 Slacken and remove the three Torx screws securing the door lock to the door frame **(see illustration)**.

6 To disengage the lock from the handle, carefully pull the lock inward and down from the handle as the exterior handle is pulled

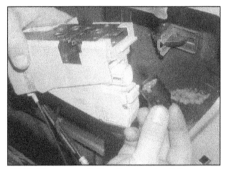

16.9 Disconnect the door lock wiring plug

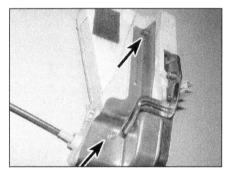

16.10 The metal lock shield is secured by two Allen screws (arrowed)

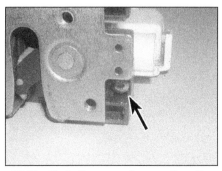

16.13a Undo the screw (arrowed) on the back . . .

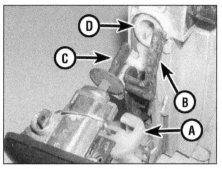

16.6 Shown removed, the exterior handle lug (A) engages with the lever (B), and where applicable, the cylinder rod (C) fits into the slot (D)

outwards **(see illustration)**.

7 Slide the exterior handle towards the front of the vehicle, and pull the key end of the handle out from the door. Now slide the handle towards the rear of the vehicle, and out from the door **(see illustration)**.

8 Working inside the door, undo the screw securing the interior door handle, unclip the handle cable from the retaining clips, and lift the handle up and out of the locating lug in the door **(see illustration 17.16)**.

9 Manoeuvre the lock from the door, disconnecting the wiring plug(s) as the lock is withdrawn **(see illustration)**.

10 Undo the two Allen screws and remove metal shield from the lock **(see illustration)**.

11 Release the two clips and remove the plastic lock shield cover from the lock **(see illustration)**.

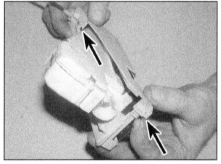

16.11 Release the clips and remove the plastic lock shield cover (arrowed)

16.13b . . . and end of the lock (arrowed)

16.7 Pull out the key end of the handle first

12 Slide the interior handle cable outer from the bracket on the lock, and disconnect the inner cable nipple from the operating lever **(see illustration)**.

13 Undo the two retaining screws, and remove the motor from the lock **(see illustrations)**.

Refitting

14 Refitting is a reversal of the removal procedure, ensuring that the exterior handle engages correctly with the lock actuating lever, and barrel lock rod.

15 It is possible to adjust the action of the exterior handle in relation to the lock. Prise out the grommet in the end of the door frame and slacken the lever positioning screw **(see illustration)**.

16 Position the actuating lever so that the handle lever is a one millimetre interference fit against it. Tighten the lever positioning screw, and refit the grommet.

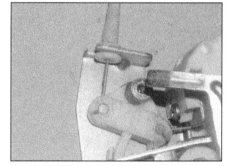

16.12 Slide the outer cable from the bracket, and disconnect the inner cable

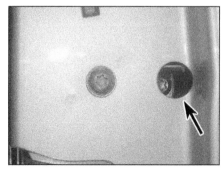

16.15 Prise out the grommet to expose the lock lever positioning screw (arrowed)

17.7 Pull the key end of the handle out, then slide it to the rear

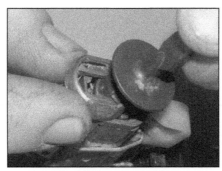

17.10a Slide out the circlip . . .

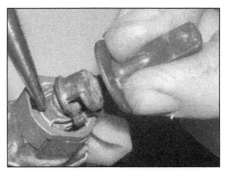

17.10b . . . remove the operating rod . . .

17.10c . . . and the spring . . .

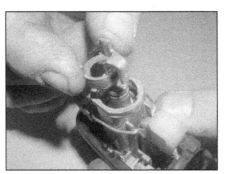

17.10d . . . then lift out the lever . . .

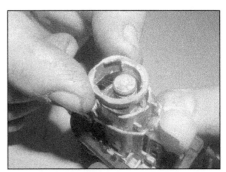

17.10e . . . followed by the collar

17 Door handles and lock cylinder – removal and refitting

Exterior door handle

Removal

1 Fully close the front door window. Disconnect the battery negative terminal as described in Chapter 5A.
2 Remove the door trim panel and speaker (see Section 15).
3 Using a plastic knife, cut through the sealant between the plastic membrane and the door frame. Carefully peel the membrane away from the door. **Note:** *Do not attempt to peel away the membrane without first cutting through the sealant.*
4 Prise out the rubber grommet in the end of the door frame, and undo the exterior handle retaining screw **(see illustration 16.4)**.
5 Slacken and remove the three Torx screws securing the door lock to the door frame **(see illustration 16.5)**.
6 To disengage the lock from the handle, carefully pull the lock inward and down as the exterior handle as pulled outwards **(see illustration 16.6)**.
7 Slide the exterior handle towards the front of the vehicle, and pull the key end of the handle out from the door. Now slide the handle towards the rear of the vehicle, and out from the door **(see illustration)**.

Refitting

8 Refitting is a reversal of removal. If required, refer to the lock adjustment procedure described in Paragraphs 15 and 16 of the previous Section.

Lock cylinder

Removal

9 Remove the exterior door handle as described in Paragraphs 1 to 7.
10 Slide out the cylinder retaining clip and remove the lock components. **Note:** *The components retained by the clip are spring pressurised. Slide out the clip, and release the components slowly (see illustrations).*
11 Insert the key into the barrel, turn the barrel through 90° anti-clockwise, and pull the key, complete with the barrel, from the housing **(see illustration)**.

Refitting

12 Refitting is a reversal of removal. If required, refer to the lock adjustment procedure described in Paragraphs 15 and 16 of the previous Section.

Interior door handle

13 Fully close the front door window. Disconnect the battery negative terminal as described in Chapter 5A.
14 Remove the door trim panel and speaker (see Section 15).
15 Using a plastic knife, cut through the sealant between the plastic membrane and the door frame. Carefully peel the membrane away from the door. **Note:** *Do not attempt to peel away the membrane without first cutting through the sealant.*
16 Unscrew the interior door handle retaining screw **(see illustration)**.

17.11 Turn the key a 90° anti-clockwise and remove the barrel

17.16 Undo the interior handle screw

17.18 Carefully remove the lever return spring

17.19a Slide out the plastic retainer . . .

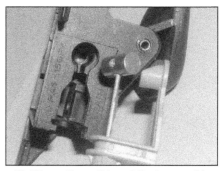

17.19b . . . then slide out the inner cable

17 Release the door handle cable retaining clips, and lift the interior handle from the locating lug in the door.
18 Using a screwdriver, remove the lever return spring (see illustration).
19 To disconnect the actuating cable, slide out the plastic retainer, place the lever in the locked position to align the inner cable with the release slot, then lift the cable from the handle (see illustrations).
20 Refitting is a reversal of removal.

18 Door window and regulator – removal and refitting

Door window glass

Removal

1 Remove the door trim and membrane as described in Section 15.
2 Temporarily reconnect the window switch and move the window until the clamps' securing Torx bolts are accessible. Mark the position of the clamps on the glass using tape or a permanent marker to record the relationship between the clamp jaws and the glass. This will aid alignment during refitting (see illustrations). On models with manual rear windows, temporarily refit the winder handle and position the window so that the clamps' Torx screws are accessible.

3 Slacken and remove the bolts, then release the window glass from the clamps. Lower the glass to the bottom of the door.
4 Starting at the front and rear edges, prise the outer weatherstrip from the door, and tilt the glass forward (see illustration).
5 Starting at the front and rear lower edges, carefully prise the window channel rubber from the door frame (see illustration).
6 With the channel rubber removed, carefully lift the glass from the door (see illustration).

Refitting

7 Refitting is a reversal of removal. On refitting the glass, align the previously made marks between the clamps and the glass, but do not fully tighten the clamp bolts until the glass is in the fully raised position.

Window regulator

Removal

8 Remove the door trim and membrane as described in Section 15.
9 Where applicable, temporarily reconnect the window switch and move the window until the clamps' securing Torx bolts are accessible. Mark the position of the clamps on the glass using tape or a permanent marker to record the relationship between the clamp jaws and the glass. This will aid alignment during refitting (see illustrations 18.2a and 18.2b).
10 Slacken and remove the bolts, then release the window glass from the clamps. Lift the glass to the top of the door, and tape or wedge it in place.
11 Where applicable, push the wiring plug upwards to disconnect it from the electric

18.2a Lower the window until both window clamps . . .

18.2b . . . are visible

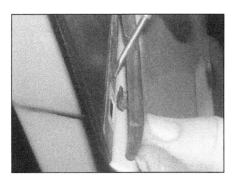

18.4 Prise the outer weatherstrip from the door

18.5 Pull the window channel rubber from the door frame

18.6 Lift the glass from the door

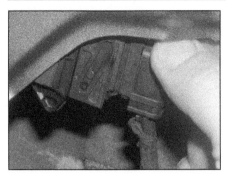

18.11 Push the connector up to unplug it

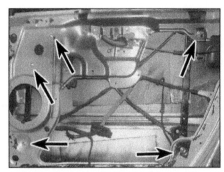

18.12a Undo the five bolts (arrowed) . . .

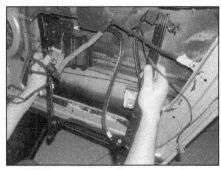

18.12b . . . and remove the regulator

window motor **(see illustration)**. Release any wiring harness cable ties secured to the regulator.

12 Slacken and withdraw the five retaining bolts, and release the two retaining clips, then manoeuvre the regulator from the door **(see illustrations)**.

13 If required, the electric window motor (where fitted), can now be removed as described in the next Section.

Refitting

14 Refitting is a reversal of removal.

19 Electrically-operated windows – general information and motor renewal

Window switches

1 Refer to Chapter 12, Section 6.

Window winder motors

Removal

2 Remove the window regulator as described in Section 18.

3 Remove two regulator-to-motor Torx bolts and screw them into the regulator casing **(see illustrations)**. This secures the baseplate to the regulator.

4 Undo the remaining Torx bolts and separate the motor from the regulator **(see illustration)**.

19.3a Remove two Torx bolts (arrowed) . . .

Refitting

5 Refitting is a reversal of removal.

6 Once the window operation is known to be correct, refit the inner trim panel as described in Section 15.

Rear side window motors

Removal

7 With reference to Section 31, remove the D-pillar trim.

8 Unclip the window opening rod from the motor **(see illustration)**.

9 Disconnect the motor wiring plug, undo the two retaining screws and remove the motor and bracket.

Refitting

10 Refitting is a reversal of removal, tightening all fasteners securely.

19.3b . . . and screw them into the holes (arrowed) to secure the regulator baseplate

20 Rear opening side window – removal and refitting

Removal

1 Remove the trim from the D-pillar with reference to Section 31.

2 On models with electrically-powered opening side window, undo the screw securing the motor operating arm to the window **(see illustration)**.

3 On models with manually-opened rear windows, undo the three countersunk screws securing the catch to the D-pillar.

4 Where fitted, disconnect the aerial connections. Carefully prise away the trim from the front inner edge of the glass, undo

19.4 Undo the remaining bolts and separate the motor from the regulator

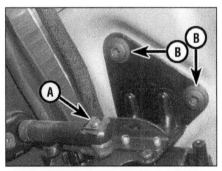

19.8 Unclip the rod (A), undo the screws (B) and remove the motor and bracket

20.2 Undo the operating arm screw

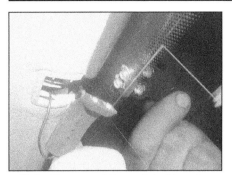

20.4a Disconnect the aerial wiring plug

20.4b Prise away the trim . . .

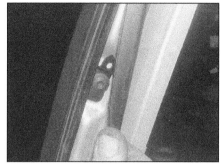

20.4c . . . and undo the two screws

the two retaining screws and remove the glass **(see illustrations)**.

Refitting
5 Refitting is a reversal of removal. Tighten all fasteners securely.

21 Front quarter light glass – removal and refitting

Removal
1 Remove the relevant A-pillar trim with reference to Section 31.
2 Undo the three retaining nuts, and remove the window and seal from the vehicle body **(see illustration)**.

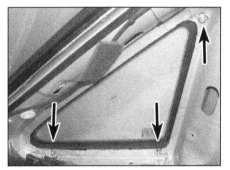

21.2 Undo the three nuts (arrowed) and remove the window

22.4 Undo the nut and bolt and disconnect the check strap

Refitting
3 Refitting is a reversal of removal.

22 Doors – removal and refitting

Removal
1 Disconnect the battery negative lead as described in Chapter 5A.
2 Where fitted, depress the retaining clip and remove the door check strap plastic shield.
3 Rotate the door harness wiring plug collar 90° anti-clockwise, and separate it from the pillar socket **(see illustration)**.
4 Undo the single nut and bolt, and

22.3 Rotate the connector anti-clockwise to unplug it

22.5 Slacken the locking screw and lift the door away

disconnect the door check strap **(see illustration)**.
5 Unscrew the door hinge locking screws, and lift the door from its hinges **(see illustration)**.

Refitting
6 Refitting is a reversal of the removal procedure.
7 On completion, shut the door and check it for closure and alignment. Check the depth at which the striker enters the lock. If adjustment is required, slacken the securing bolts and reposition the striker plate **(see illustration)**.

23 Windscreen and tailgate glass – general information

The windscreen and tailgate glass are directly bonded to the metalwork. Their removal and refitting requires the use of special tools not readily available to the home mechanic. This work should therefore be left to a Ford dealer, or a specialist glass renewal company.

24 Sunroof – general

1 Removal and refitting, and adjustments to the roof panel, are best entrusted to a Ford

22.7 If necessary, slacken the bolts and reposition the striker plate

24.2a The cranking tool is clipped to the motor casing (arrowed)

24.2b Insert the tool and wind the sunroof closed

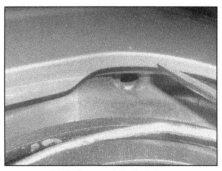

24.3 Sunroof drain tubes

garage, as specialised tools are required, and the complete headlining must be removed.

2 The sunroof panel motor can be removed and refitted as described in Chapter 12. If the motor malfunctions when the roof panel is in the open position, it can be wound shut manually. To do this, remove the entire interior light assembly, then pull the overhead panel to the rear and remove it. The cranking tool is clipped to the motor casing **(see illustrations)**. Insert the cranking tool into the hole at the end of the motor shaft. The tool can then be turned to close the sunroof as required.

3 If the sunroof water drain hoses become blocked, they may be cleared by probing them with a length of suitable cable (an old speedometer drive cable is ideal). Insert the cleaning tool into the top of the hoses,

accessible when the sunroof is fully open. The front drain tubes terminates just in front of the A-pillars, behind the wheelarch liners. The rear drain tubes terminate behind the leading edges of the rear bumper **(see illustration)**.

25 Door mirror – renewal

Complete mirror assembly

1 Remove the door trim as described in Section 15, and carefully peel back the door membrane in the corner adjacent to the mirror, and disconnect the wiring plug **(see illustration)**.

2 Prise out the two plastic covers from the door frame.

3 Unscrew the two Torx retaining screws, and withdraw the mirror **(see illustration)**.

4 Fit the new mirror housing using a reversal of the removal procedure.

Mirror

 Warning: Wear gloves and eye protection when carrying out this operation, particularly if the mirror glass is broken.

5 To remove the mirror, first press the lower edge of the mirror in, then using a wide flat-bladed tool, lever the top of the mirror out. Where applicable, disconnect the mirror wiring plugs **(see illustrations)**.

6 To refit, press firmly at the centre of the mirror glass to engage the retaining clips. On completion, check the operation of the mirror adjustment mechanism using the adjustment knob/buttons.

26 Centre console – removal and refitting

Rear section

Removal

1 Remove the cassette storage box from the rear of the console.

2 Free the edges of the handbrake lever

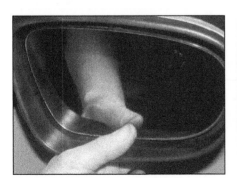

25.1 Disconnect the mirror wiring plug (arrowed)

25.3 Undo the Torx screws and remove the mirror

25.5a Press the lower edge in . . .

25.5b . . . then lever the top edge out . . .

25.5c . . . and disconnect any wiring plugs

gaiter from the console, and remove it from the lever.

3 Undo the two retaining screws at the front of the console, and the two screws in the recess under the cassette storage box **(see illustration)**.

4 Pull the console up from the rear and manoeuvre it over the handbrake lever.

Refitting

5 Refitting is a reversal of the removal procedure.

Front section

Removal

6 Prise out the storage tray/ashtray from the front of the console.

7 On manual transmission models, unscrew the gear knob. Carefully pull the rear edge of the gearshift gaiter surround towards the front, then lever up the rear edge and unclip it from the console **(see illustration)**.

8 On models with automatic transmission, undo the screw securing the selector grip, and pull the grip upwards with the lever trim. Carefully unclip the selector display trim from the centre console.

9 Undo the four retaining screws, and unclip the ashtray illumination bulbholder (where fitted), then lift out the console **(see illustration)**. Unclip the diagnostic socket as the console is withdrawn.

Refitting

10 Refitting is a reversal of removal.

27 Facia and associated panels – removal and refitting

Removal

1 Disconnect the battery negative lead (refer to Chapter 5A). **Note:** *If the vehicle has a security-coded radio, check that you have a copy of the code number before disconnecting the battery. Refer to your Ford dealer if in doubt.*

2 Open the fusebox on the driver's side of the facia, pulling the panel downwards, then outwards, and remove it from the vehicle.

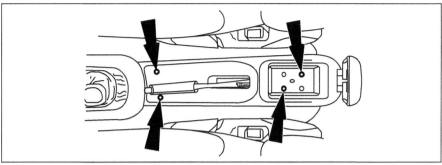
26.3 Undo the centre console screws (arrowed)

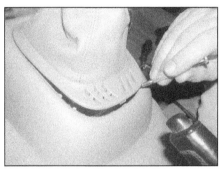
26.7 Lever up the rear edge of the lever trim

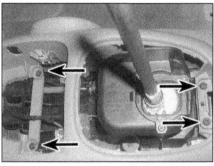
26.9 The centre console is secured by four screws (arrowed)

3 Pull the lower fusebox cover downwards, and remove it **(see illustration)**.

4 Undo the two screws securing the lower centre facia panel **(see illustration)**.

5 At the right-hand end of the facia, prise out the centre spreader pin, and remove the retaining clip **(see illustration)**.

6 Undo the five retaining screws and remove the driver's side lower facia panel. Make a note of their fitted positions, and disconnect the various wiring plugs as the panel is withdrawn **(see illustration 31.40)**.

7 Remove the audio unit as described in Chapter 12.

8 On models with electronic climate control, reach through the audio unit aperture, release the locking tab and gently pull the control unit from the centre panel. Disconnect the unit's wiring plugs as it is withdrawn from the panel **(see illustration)**.

9 On models with conventional heating/manual air conditioning, use a small screwdriver to gently prise out the storage compartment below the audio unit in the

27.3 Pull the lower fusebox cover down and remove it

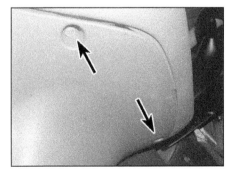
27.4 Undo the lower centre facia panel screws (arrowed)

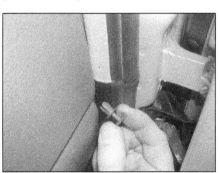
27.5 Prise out the centre pin and remove the clip

27.8 Release the locking tab (arrowed) and pull the climate control unit from the centre panel

27.10 Undo the screws (arrowed) and remove the bezel

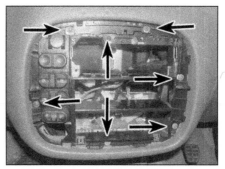

27.11 The centre panel is secured by seven screws (arrowed)

27.12 Release the retaining clips and pull the control panel from the dowels

centre control panel. Again with a screwdriver, gently prise out the heater control panel trim. Use a pad of soft material between the screwdriver and the panel to prevent any accidental damage.

10 Slacken and remove the five (four on vehicles with electronic climate control) heater control/audio unit bezel retaining screws **(see illustration)**. Carefully pull the bezel out, and disconnect the cigarette lighter wiring plug as it is withdrawn.

11 Unscrew the seven centre panel retaining screws, and starting at its lower edge, remove the panel from the facia **(see illustration)**. Note their fitted locations, and disconnect the switches wiring plugs as the unit is withdrawn.

12 On models with conventional heating/ manual air conditioning, release the two retaining clips at the top of the panel, and pull the rotary control panel from the locating

dowels. Disconnect the units wiring plugs as it is withdrawn **(see illustration)**.

13 Remove the instrument panel (see Chapter 12).

14 Remove both A-pillar trims as described in Section 31.

15 Remove the steering wheel, and column combination switches as described in Chapters 10 and 12 respectively.

16 Open the passenger side glovebox, and pull the lid out to detach it from the hinge pins.

17 At the left-hand end of the facia, prise out the centre spreader pin, and remove the retaining clip.

18 Undo the five retaining screws and remove the passenger side lower facia panel. Note their fitted positions, and disconnect the various wiring plugs as the panel is withdrawn **(see illustration 31.43)**.

19 Remove the passenger airbag with

reference to Chapter 12, or upper passenger side glovebox with reference to Section 28 of this Chapter.

20 Undo the six retaining bolts/screws, and remove the passenger airbag mounting bracket.

21 Starting at the opposite end of the surround to the light switch, carefully prise out the light switch surround from the driver's side of the facia. Use a pad of soft material between the screwdriver and the panel to prevent any accidental damage **(see illustration)**. Disconnect the switch wiring plugs as the unit is withdrawn.

22 Using a screwdriver and a pad of soft material between the screwdriver and the facia to prevent any accidental damage, carefully prise out the face level vents from the facia.

23 The facia is now retained by four screws on the passenger side, two bolts on the lower driver's side, two bolts in the instrument panel aperture, and one screw in the centre face level vent aperture. Remove the bolts/screws **(see illustrations)**.

24 Working in the engine compartment, pull up and remove the battery compartment upper panel (see Chapter 5A).

25 Undo the three retaining screws, and remove the bulkhead cover from the engine compartment. Slide the cover to the right-hand side and manoeuvre it from behind the coolant expansion tank.

26 Where fitted, unscrew the two retaining nuts and remove the alarm horn from the scuttle area. Disconnect the horn wiring plug as it is withdrawn.

27.21 Carefully prise the light switch from the facia

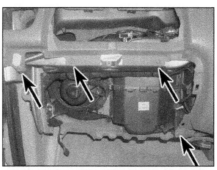

27.23a The facia is secured by four screw on the passenger side (arrowed) . . .

27.23b . . . two bolts (arrowed) on the lower driver's side . . .

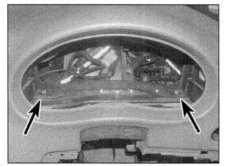

27.23c . . . two in the instrument panel aperture (arrowed) . . .

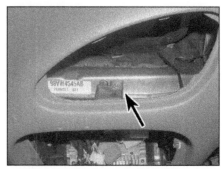

27.23d . . . and one in the centre face level vent aperture (arrowed)

27.27 Undo the bolt in the scuttle area

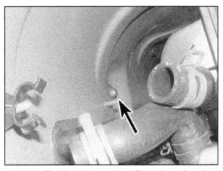

27.30 Behind the pollen filter housing is the remaining facia bolt (arrowed)

27.31 Prise out the sunlight sensor

27 Slacken and remove the facia bolt from the scuttle area **(see illustration)**.
28 Remove the pollen filter (see Chapter 1A or 1B).
29 Undo the three retaining nuts (one at each end, and one in the middle), and move the pollen filter housing as far forward as possible.
30 Remove the facia retaining bolt behind the pollen filter housing **(see illustration)**.
31 Where fitted, prise out the rear edge first and remove the sunlight sensor from the centre of the facia and disconnect the wiring plug **(see illustration)**.
32 With the help of an assistant, manoeuvre the facia from the vehicle, ensure that all clips securing the wiring harnesses to the facia have been released. Disconnect the audio

tweeters wiring plugs, and release their harness retaining clips as the facia is removed.
33 To remove the crossmember, undo the two bolts retaining the brace in the lower, centre position of the facia **(see illustration)**.
34 Drill out the two shear bolts securing the steering column to the crossmember. Once the steering column has been lowered, undo the two bolts securing the pedal bracket to the crossmember, and (on petrol models) the three nuts securing the ECM bracket **(see illustration)**.
35 Release the two retaining clips and carefully pull the top of the fusebox/central junction box to the rear, and lift it from the crossmember bracket.
36 The crossmember is then secured by two

bolts at either end, two bolts securing it to the heater box housing, and four bolts securing the bulkhead bracket on the driver's side **(see illustrations)**. If the crossmember is being removed to access the heater matrix, it is only necessary to move the crossmember 30 to 40 mm away from the bulkhead, and therefore not necessary to release any wiring harness clips providing care is taken. Otherwise, note the fitted positions of the various wiring harnesses/earth connections, and release the retaining clips. Remove the crossmember.

Refitting

37 Refitting is a reversal of the removal process. Ensure that the heater control cables (where fitted) and all wiring harnesses are correctly routed and clipped in position.

27.33 Undo the bolts and remove the brace (arrowed)

27.34 Pedal bracket-to-crossmember bolts

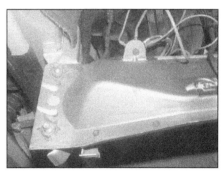

27.36a The crossmember is secured by two bolts at each end . . .

27.36b . . . two bolts . . .

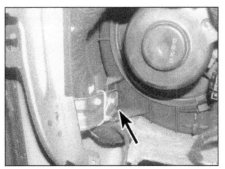

27.36c . . . on the heater box housing (arrowed) . . .

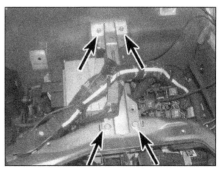

27.36d . . . and four bolts securing the bulkhead bracket (arrowed)

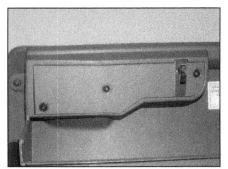

28.2a Undo the three screws . . .

28.2b . . . and prise the lock/handle from the glovebox

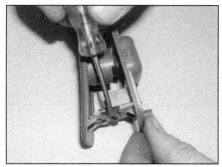

28.3a Prise the operating lever from the lock . . .

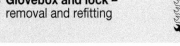

28 Glovebox and lock –
removal and refitting

Lower glovebox

Removal

1 Open the glovebox, and pull it to the rear to release the hinge pins from the hinges.
2 To remove the lock/handle assembly, undo the three retaining screws, and prise the lock/handle from the front of the glovebox **(see illustrations)**.
3 Prise the operating lever from the lock, and using a small screwdriver, remove the lock barrel **(see illustrations)**.

Refitting

4 Refit in the reverse order of removal.

Upper glovebox

Removal

5 Remove the passenger side lower facia panel as described in Section 31.
6 Open the glovebox and undo the three screws at its upper edge **(see illustration)**.
7 Undo the two screws at the lower edge and manoeuvre the glovebox from the facia. Where fitted, disconnect the glovebox light wiring plug. Removal of the lock assembly is as previously described in Paragraphs 2 to 3.

29.2 Position the support arm at 90° to the vertical, then twist it clockwise

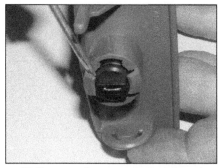

28.3b . . . and remove the lock barrel

Refitting

8 Refitting is a reversal of removal.

29 Interior mirror –
removal and refitting

⚠️ **Warning: Use extreme care whilst attempting this procedure. The windscreen is easily cracked.**

1 Twist the mirror support arm 90° anti-clockwise, and remove it from the mounting plate.
2 To refit, position the support arm at 90° to the vertical, then carefully turn it clockwise to the point where the lock spring is felt to engage **(see illustration)**.

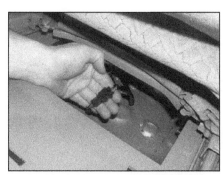

30.4 Disconnect the seat heater wiring plug, and where fitted, the side airbag connector

28.6 Undo the three screws at the glovebox upper edge

3 If the mirror mounting plate becomes detached, clean away the old glue, then apply a suitable glass-to-metal glue in accordance with the glue manufacturer's instructions, and refit the mounting plate into position. Ensure that the plate is correctly orientated, so that when the mirror is fully fitted to it, the mirror support arm is vertical.

30 Seats –
removal and refitting

Front seat

⚠️ **Warning: On models fitted with side airbags, prior to disconnecting the airbag wiring plug, it is essential you are electrostatically discharged by touching a door lock, or the vehicle body briefly.**

Removal

1 Move the seat forwards to the extent of its travel, and raise it to its maximum height.
2 Disconnect the battery negative cable (see Chapter 5A).
3 Behind the front seat, remove the storage compartment cover.
4 Where applicable, disconnect the seat heater wiring plug, and the side airbag connector **(see illustration)**.
5 Detach the side airbag wiring harness (where fitted) from the retaining bracket.

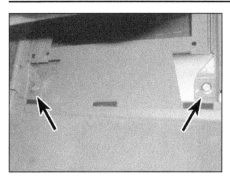

30.6 Undo the rear seat mounting bolts (arrowed)

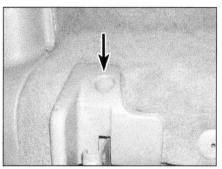

30.8 The outboard seat rail bolt cover is secured by a screw (arrowed)

30.9 Inboard front seat rail bolt

6 Unscrew and remove the rear seat rail mounting bolts **(see illustration)**.
7 Lower the seat and move it fully to the rear.
8 At the front of the seat, remove the inboard seat rail bolt cover. Undo the outboard cover retaining screw and remove the cover **(see illustration)**.
9 Undo the two front seat rail mounting bolts, and remove the seat **(see illustration)**. **Note:** *Due to the risk of injury or component failure, no further dismantling of the seats is recommended.*

Refitting

10 Refit the seat in the reverse order of removal. **Note:** *If after refitting the seat(s), the airbag warning light on the dash signals a fault, take the vehicle to a Ford dealer or suitably-equipped specialist, to have the self diagnosis system interrogated and the fault code erased.*

Rear seat

Removal

11 Due to the vehicle's design, the rear seats can be moved to give numerous seating configurations. To remove a seat, fold the seatback forwards, pull the lever at the side of the seat and lift the rear of the seat.
12 With the seat fully folded, squeeze together the release levers between the front mountings, and lift the seat from the floor.

Refitting

13 Squeeze together the release levers, and insert the front mountings into the desired location. Release the levers, and unfold the seat.

31 Interior trim – general information, removal and refitting

Trim panels

1 The interior trim panels are secured using either screws or various types of trim fasteners, usually studs or clips.
2 Check that there are no other panels overlapping the one to be removed; usually there is a sequence that has to be followed, and this will only become obvious on close inspection.

3 Remove all obvious fasteners, such as screws. If the panel will not come free, it is held by hidden clips or fasteners. These are usually situated around the edge of the panel and can be prised up to release them; note, however that they can break quite easily so new ones should be available. The best way of releasing such clips without the correct type of tool, is to use a large flat-bladed screwdriver. Note in many cases that the adjacent sealing strip must be prised back to release a panel.
4 When removing a panel, **never** use excessive force or the panel may be damaged; always check carefully that all fasteners or other relevant components have been removed or released before attempting to withdraw a panel.
5 The pillars at the front of the passenger cabin, level with the windscreen are known as the A-pillars. The subsequent pillars are

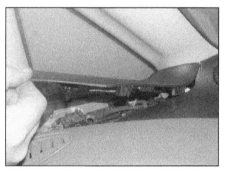

31.7 Unclip the panel at the end of the facia

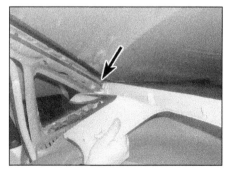

31.9 Pull the top of the trim away first, then lift it from the lug at the bottom (arrowed)

known as the B-, C- and D-pillars. The D-pillars are level with the tailgate.

A-pillar trim removal

6 Pull the weatherstrip from the door aperture in the area of the A-pillar.
7 Unclip and remove the facia trim panel adjacent to the pillar **(see illustration)**.
8 Remove the plastic cover and undo the pillar trim screw **(see illustration)**.
9 Unclip and remove the A-pillar trim **(see illustration)**.

B-pillar trim removal

10 Remove the front seat belt upper and lower mounting point covers, and remove the mounting bolts.
11 Undo the pillar trim retaining screw, and pull the door weatherstrips from either side of the trim **(see illustration)**.
12 Unclip and remove the pillar trims.

31.8 Uncover the trim retaining screw

31.11 Undo the B-pillar trim retaining screw

31.16a Remove the screw . . .

31.16b . . . and unclip the C-pillar trim

31.19 Unclip the D-pillar trim

C-pillar trim removal

13 Remove the second row seat belt upper mounting point cover, and remove the mounting bolt.

14 Pull the door weatherstrip from the door aperture adjacent to the C-pillar trim.

15 Where fitted, slacken and remove the luggage compartment cover bracket retaining bolt from the C-pillar.

16 Undo the C-pillar retaining screw, and unclip the trim from the pillar **(see illustrations)**.

D-pillar trim removal

17 Remove the rear seat belt upper mounting point cover and remove the mounting bolt.

18 Pull the weatherstrip from the tailgate aperture adjacent to the D-pillar trim.

19 Unclip and remove the D-pillar trim **(see illustration)**. On models with rear air conditioning, the pillar trim is secured by two retaining screws,

Luggage area side trim removal

20 Where fitted, remove the luggage compartment cover from the vehicle.

21 If the right-hand side trim is to be removed, detach the tool storage compartment cover from the side trim. Where fitted, undo the retaining screws, and remove the CD autochanger (see Chapter 12). Disconnect the autochanger wiring plug as the unit is withdrawn.

22 Again, if removing the right-hand side trim, open the storage compartment at the top of the side trim, and undo the retaining screws **(see illustration)**.

23 Undo the screw and remove the luggage compartment cover retaining hook **(see illustration)**.

24 Where fitted, undo the two retaining screws and remove the luggage compartment cover bracket from the front of the side trim **(see illustration)**.

25 Undo the screw and remove the plastic cover over the tailgate side striker plate. Mark the relationship of the tailgate side striker plate to the vehicle body, then undo the two retaining bolts, and remove the striker plate **(see illustrations)**.

26 Prise out the luggage compartment light(s), and disconnect the wiring plug(s).

27 Unscrew the plastic clip(s) at the base of the side trim **(see illustration)**.

28 Carefully prise out the rear seat belt guide from the side trim, then undo the rear seat belt

31.22 Viewed from inside the storage compartment after removing the CD autochanger, undo the retaining screws

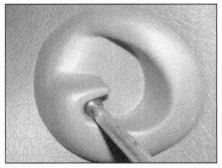

31.23 Where fitted, undo the luggage compartment cover hook screw

31.24 Undo the luggage compartment cover bracket screws

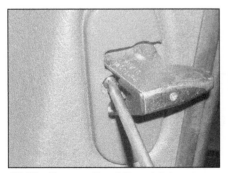

31.25a Remove the striker plate cover . . .

31.25b . . . then make alignment marks and remove the plate

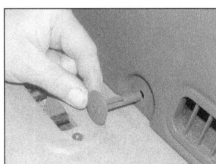

31.27 Unscrew the plastic fastener at the base of the trim

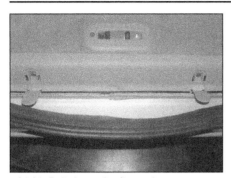

31.31 Pull down the flaps, then unscrew the sill scuff plate screws

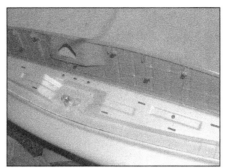

31.33 Unclip the tailgate load sill trim

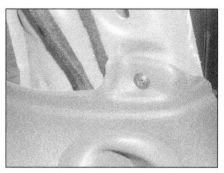

31.34 Remove the trim screw at the D-pillar

lower mounting bolt or unclip the belt from the lower mounting as applicable.

29 Remove the C- and D-pillars, as described in Paragraphs 13 to 19 of this Section.

30 Pull the weatherstrips from the door and tailgate apertures adjacent to the side trim, and across the load sill trim of the tailgate.

31 Prise open the two plastic flaps, undo the two retaining screws and remove the sill scuff plate from the relevant rear door (see illustration).

32 Slacken and remove the second row seat belt lower mounting bolt.

33 Prise up and release the clips securing the tailgate load sill trim (see illustration).

34 Unscrew the side trim retaining screw at the D-pillar (see illustration).

35 Using a flat-bladed screwdriver (or similar), carefully release the trim retaining clips along the front and rear edges of the luggage compartment side trim. With the edges released, lift the trim upwards to disengage the four retaining clips at the trim top edge (see illustrations). Disconnect the speaker wiring/power outlet sockets/ temperature sensor plugs as the trim is withdrawn.

Refitting all trim panels

36 Refitting is the reverse of the removal procedure; secure the fasteners by pressing them firmly into place and ensure that all disturbed components are correctly secured to prevent rattles.

Driver's side lower facia panel

37 Open the fusebox on the driver's side of the facia, pulling the panel downwards, then outwards, and remove it from the vehicle.

38 Pull the lower fusebox cover downwards, and remove it (see illustration 27.3).

39 At the right-hand end of the facia, prise out the centre spreader pin, and remove the retaining clip (see illustration 27.5).

40 Undo the five retaining screws and remove the driver's side lower facia panel. Make a note of their fitted positions, and disconnect the various wiring plugs as the panel is withdrawn (see illustration).

Passenger side lower facia panel

41 Remove the passenger side lower glovebox as described in Section 28 of this Chapter.

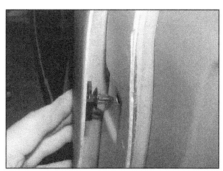

31.35a Unclip the front and rear edges of the trim . . .

42 At the left-hand end of the facia, prise out the centre spreader pin, and remove the retaining clip (see illustration).

43 Undo the five retaining screws and remove the panel. Note their fitted locations, and disconnect the various wiring plugs as the panel is withdrawn (see illustration).

Front carpet

44 The passenger compartment floor carpet is in one piece and is secured at its edges by screws or clips, usually the same fasteners used to secure the various adjoining trim panels.

45 Carpet removal and refitting is reasonably straightforward but very time-consuming because all adjoining trim panels must be removed first, as must components such as the seats, the centre console and seat belt lower anchorages.

31.35b . . . then lift the trim to release the clips at the top

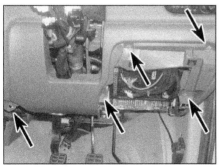

31.40 The driver's side lower facia panel is secured by five screws (arrowed)

31.42 Prise out the centre spreader pin and remove the clip

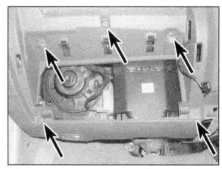

31.43 Undo the five screws (arrowed) and remove the passenger side lower facia panel

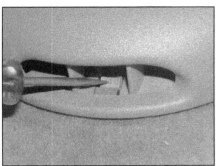

31.48a Depress the retaining clips and lift the centre floor cover . . .

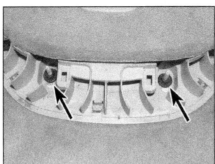

31.48b . . . then undo the two nuts (arrowed) and remove the vent

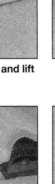

31.49 Unclip the trim at the front edges of the carpet

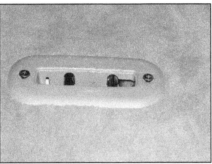

31.50 Undo the screws and remove the seat mounting covers

Rear carpet

46 To remove the rear carpet, remove all of the rear seats from the vehicle.
47 Remove both left- and right-hand luggage compartment side trims, as described in Paragraphs 20 to 35 of this Section.
48 Depress the retaining clips, lift the floor centre vent cover, undo the two retaining nuts, and remove the vent from the floor (see illustrations).
49 Carefully unclip the pieces of trim securing the carpet at its front edge (see illustration).
50 The rear seat mounting covers in the floor are held in place by two screws each. Undo all screws and remove the mountings from the floor (see illustration).
51 Remove the carpet from the vehicle.
52 Refitting is a reversal of removal.

Headlining

53 The headlining is clipped to the roof and can be withdrawn only once all fittings such as the grab handles, sun visors, sunroof (if fitted), windscreen, rear quarter windows and related trim panels have been removed, and the door, tailgate and sunroof aperture sealing strips (as applicable) have been prised clear.
54 Note that headlining removal and refitting requires considerable skill and experience if it is to be carried out without damage and is therefore best entrusted to an expert.

32 Seat belt pretensioning mechanism – general information

All models are fitted with front seat belt pretensioners. The system is designed to instantaneously take up any slack in the seat belt in the case of a direct or oblique frontal impact, therefore reducing the possibility of injury to the occupants. Each front seat is fitted with its own tensioner, which is situated behind the lower B-pillar trim panel/sill scuff plate.

The seat belt tensioner is triggered by a frontal impact above a predetermined force. Lesser impacts and impacts to the rear of the vehicle will not trigger the system.

When the system is triggered, the explosive

gas in the tensioner mechanism retracts and locks the seat belt through a cable which acts on the inertia reel. This prevents the seat belt moving and keeps the occupant firmly in position in the seat. Once the tensioner has been triggered, the seat belt will be permanently locked and the assembly must be renewed, together with the impact sensors.

There is a risk of injury if the system is triggered inadvertently when working on the vehicle, and it is therefore strongly recommended that any work involving the seat belt tensioner system is entrusted to a Ford dealer. Note the following warnings before contemplating any work on the front seat belts.

> ⚠ *Warning:*
> • *Do not expose the tensioner mechanism to temperatures in excess of 100°C (212°F).*
> • *If the tensioner mechanism is dropped, it must be renewed, even it has suffered no apparent damage.*
> • *Do not allow any solvents to come into contact with the tensioner mechanism.*
> • *Do not attempt to open the tensioner mechanism as it contains explosive gas.*
> • *Tensioners must be discharged before they are disposed of, but this task should be entrusted to a Ford dealer.*

33 Seat belts – general

Note: *Refer to the warnings in Section 32 before working on the seat belts.*
1 Periodically check the belts for fraying or other damage. If evident, renew the belt.
2 If the belts become dirty, wipe them with a damp cloth, using a little liquid detergent only.
3 Check the tightness of the anchor bolts, and if they are ever disconnected, make quite sure that the original sequence of fitting of washers, bushes, and anchor plate is retained.
4 Access to the front belt height adjuster and inertia reel units can be made by removing the trim from the B-pillar on the side concerned (see illustrations).

33.4a Front seat belt top mounting bolt

33.4b Front seat belt inertia reel

33.5a Rear seat belt top mounting bolt

33.5b Rear seat belt inertia reel

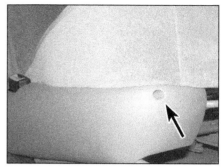

33.5c The seat base trim is secured by a screw at the front (arrowed) . . .

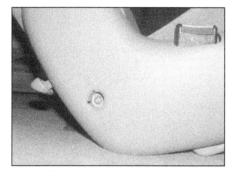

33.5d . . . and one at the side

33.5e Seat belt stalk mounting bolt

34 Sun visors – removal and refitting

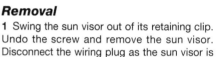

Removal

1 Swing the sun visor out of its retaining clip. Undo the screw and remove the sun visor. Disconnect the wiring plug as the sun visor is withdrawn **(see illustration)**.
2 To remove the sun visor retaining clip, prise out the plastic cap, undo the retaining screw.

Refitting

3 Refitting is a reversal of removal.

35 Grab handles – removal and refitting

Removal

1 Hold down the grab handle, and prise up the plastic covers. Undo the retaining screws and remove the handles **(see illustration)**.

Refitting

2 Refitting is a reversal of removal.

5 The rear seat belt anchorages/inertia reel units can be checked by removing the C-pillar trims (second row of seats), or the luggage compartment side trims – see Section 32 **(see illustrations)**. The rear seat belt stalks are fitted to the sides of the seat bases. Undo the trim screws and unscrew the stalk mounting bolt **(see illustrations)**.
6 The torque wrench settings for the seat belt anchor bolts and other attachments are given in the Specifications at the start of this Chapter.
7 Never modify the seat belts, or alter the attachments to the body, in any way.
8 Note that the front seat belt anchorages incorporate pyrotechnic pretensioners. If a pretensioner must be removed, the B-pillar trim and door sill scuff plate should be removed, and the tensioner and inertia reel removed at the same time. The tensioner is retained by one bolt **(see illustration)**. Take great care not to knock the tensioner against anything. Due to the risk of injury, we recommend removal and replacement of the pretensioners should be entrusted to a Ford dealer or specialist.

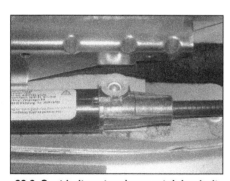

33.8 Seat belt pretensioner retaining bolt

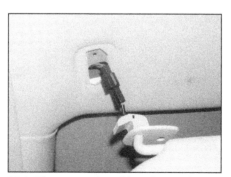

34.1 Disconnect the wiring plug as the sun visor is withdrawn

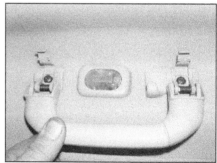

35.1 Prise up the covers and undo the grab handle screws

Notes

Chapter 12
Body electrical system

Contents

Degrees of difficulty

| **Easy,** suitable for novice with little experience | | **Fairly easy,** suitable for beginner with some experience | | **Fairly difficult,** suitable for competent DIY mechanic | | **Difficult,** suitable for experienced DIY mechanic | | **Very difficult,** suitable for expert DIY or professional | |

Specifications

System type . . . . 12 volt, negative earth

Bulbs   Power rating (watts)

Bulb	Power rating (watts)
Brake and tail lights	21/5 (bayonet)
Clock	1.2 (panel bulb)
Engine compartment light	5 (festoon)
Foglight:	
Front	55 (H1 type)
Rear	21 (bayonet)
Footwell, entrance lights	5 (festoon)
Glovebox light	3 (festoon)
Grab handle	5 (capless)
Headlights (halogen)	60/55 (H4 type)
High-level stop-light	5 (capless)
Indicators	21 (bayonet)
Instrument cluster	5 or 1.2 (capless)
Interior lights	10 (festoon)
Interior mirror light	3 (festoon)
Luggage compartment	5 (festoon)
Number plate light	5 (capless)
Reading lights	10 (capless)
Reversing light	21 (bayonet)
Separate tail lights	5 (bayonet)
Sidelights	5 (capless)
Side repeaters	5 (capless)
Vanity lights	3 (festoon)

Torque wrench settings

	Nm	lbf ft
Airbag control module	6	4
Driver's airbag securing plate-to-steering wheel screws	4	3
Headlamp screws	8	6
Passenger airbag unit-to-facia-screws	4	3
Seatbelt pretensioner locknut	20	15
Side impact sensor retaining bolts	9	7
Windscreen wiper arm nuts	20	15
Windscreen wiper linkage bolts	20	15
Windscreen wiper motor	6	4

1 General information and precautions

 Warning: Before carrying out any work on the electrical system, read through the precautions given in 'Safety first!' at the beginning of this manual, and in Chapter 5A.

1 The electrical system is of 12 volt negative earth type. Power for the lights and all electrical accessories is supplied by a lead-acid type battery which is charged by the alternator.

2 This Chapter covers repair and service procedures for the various electrical components not associated with the engine. Information on the battery, alternator and starter motor can be found in Chapter 5A.

3 It should be noted that prior to working on any component in the electrical system, the battery negative terminal should first be disconnected to prevent the possibility of electrical short-circuits and/or fires (see Chapter 5A). **Note:** *If the vehicle has a security-coded radio, check that you have a copy of the code number before disconnecting the battery. Refer to your Ford dealer if in doubt.*

2 Electrical fault finding – general information

Note: *Refer to the precautions given in 'Safety first!' and in Chapter 5A before starting work. The following tests relate to testing of the main electrical circuits, and should not be used to test delicate electronic circuits (such as anti-lock braking systems), particularly where an electronic control module is used.*

General

1 Typically, electrical circuit consists of an electrical component, any switches, relays, motors, fuses, fusible links or circuit breakers related to that component, and the wiring and connectors which link the component to both the battery and the chassis. To help to pinpoint a problem in an electrical circuit, wiring diagrams are included at the end of this Chapter.

2 Have a good look at the appropriate wiring diagram, before attempting to diagnose an electrical fault, to obtain a complete understanding of the components included in the particular circuit concerned. The possible sources of a fault can be narrowed down by noting if other components related to the circuit are operating properly. If several components or circuits fail at one time, the problem is likely to be related to a shared fuse or earth connection.

3 An electrical problem will usually stem from simple cause, such as loose or corroded connections, a faulty earth connection, a blown fuse, a melted fusible link, or a faulty relay (refer to Section 3 for details of testing relays). Visually inspect the condition of all fuses, wires and connections in a problem circuit before testing the components. Use the wiring diagrams to determine which terminal connections will need to be checked in order to pinpoint the trouble-spot.

4 The basic tools required for electrical fault-finding include a circuit tester or voltmeter (a 12 volt bulb with a set of test leads can also be used for certain tests); a self-powered test light (sometimes known as a continuity tester); an ohmmeter (to measure resistance); a battery and set of test leads; and a jumper wire, preferably with a circuit breaker or fuse incorporated, which can be used to bypass suspect wires or electrical components. Before attempting to locate a problem with test instruments, use the wiring diagram to determine where to make the connections.

5 Sometimes, an intermittent wiring fault (usually caused to a poor or dirty connection, or damaged wiring insulation) can be pinpointed by performing a wiggle test on the wiring. This involves wiggling the wiring by hand to see if the fault occurs as the wiring is moved. It should be possible to narrow down the source of the fault to a particular section of wiring. This method of testing can be used in conjunction with any of the tests described in the following sub-Sections.

6 Apart from problems due to poor connections, two basic types of fault can occur in an electrical circuit: open-circuit, or short-circuit.

7 Largely, open-circuit faults are caused by a break somewhere in the circuit, which prevents current from flowing. An open-circuit fault will prevent a component from working, but will not cause the relevant circuit fuse to blow.

8 Low resistance or short-circuit faults are caused by a 'short'; a failure point which allows the current flowing in the circuit to 'escape' along an alternative route, somewhere in the circuit. This typically occurs when a positive supply wire touches either an earth wire, or an earthed component such as the bodyshell. Such faults are normally caused by a breakdown in wiring insulation, A short circuit fault will normally cause the relevant circuit fuse to blow.

9 Fuses are designed to protect a circuit from being overloaded. A blown fuse indicates that there may be problem in that particular circuit and it is important to identify and rectify the problem before renewing the fuse. Always renew a blown fuse with one of the correct current rating; fitting a fuse of a different rating may cause an overloaded circuit to overheat and even catch fire.

Finding an open-circuit

10 One of the most straightforward ways of finding an open-circuit fault is by using a circuit test meter or voltmeter. Connect one lead of the meter to either the negative battery terminal or a known good earth. Connect the other lead to a connector in the circuit being tested, preferably nearest to the battery or fuse. Switch on the circuit, bearing in mind that some circuits are live only when the ignition switch is moved to a particular position. If voltage is present (indicated either by the tester bulb lighting or a voltmeter reading, as applicable), this means that the section of the circuit between the relevant connector and the battery is problem-free. Continue to check the remainder of the circuit in the same fashion. When a point is reached at which no voltage is present, the problem must lie between that point and the previous test point with voltage. Most problems can be traced to a broken, corroded or loose connection.

Finding a short-circuit

11 Loading the circuit during testing will produce false results and may damage your test equipment, so all electrical loads must be disconnected from the circuit before it can be checked for short circuits. Loads are the components which draw current from a circuit, such as bulbs, motors, heating elements, etc.

12 Keep both the ignition and the circuit

under test switched off, then remove the relevant fuse from the circuit, and connect a circuit test meter or voltmeter to the fuse connections.

13 Switch on the circuit, bearing in mind that some circuits are live only when the ignition switch is moved to a particular position. If voltage is present (indicated either by the tester bulb lighting or a voltmeter reading, as applicable), this means that there is a short-circuit. If no voltage is present, but the fuse still blows with the load(s) connected, this indicates an internal fault in the load(s).

Finding an earth fault

14 The battery negative terminal is connected to 'earth': the metal of the engine/transmission and the car body – and most systems are wired so that they only receive a positive feed, the current returning through the metal of the car body. This means that the component mounting and the body form part of that circuit. Loose or corroded mountings can therefore cause a range of electrical faults, ranging from total failure of a circuit, to a puzzling partial fault. In particular, lights may shine dimly (especially when another circuit sharing the same earth point is in operation), motors (eg, wiper motors or the radiator cooling fan motor) may run slowly, and the operation of one circuit may have an apparently unrelated effect on another. Note that on many vehicles, earth straps are used between certain components, such as the engine/transmission and the body, usually where there is no metal-to-metal contact between components due to flexible rubber mountings, etc.

15 To check whether a component is properly earthed, disconnect the battery and connect one lead of an ohmmeter to a known good earth point. Connect the other lead to the wire or earth connection being tested. The resistance reading should be zero; if not, check the connection as follows.

16 If an earth connection is thought to be faulty, dismantle the connection and clean back to bare metal both the bodyshell and the wire terminal or the component earth connection mating surface. Be careful to remove all traces of dirt and corrosion, then use a knife to trim away any paint, so that a clean metal-to-metal joint is made. On reassembly, tighten the joint fasteners securely; if a wire terminal is being refitted, use serrated washers between the terminal and the bodyshell to ensure a clean and secure connection. When the connection is remade, prevent the onset of corrosion in the future by applying a coat of petroleum jelly or silicone-based grease or by spraying on (at regular intervals) a proprietary ignition sealer or a water dispersant lubricant.

3   Fuses and relays –
general information

Central junction box

1 Vehicles from 1998 model year were equipped with a central junction box which incorporated not only the relays and fuses, but also an ECM (Electronic Control Module) known as a GEM (Generic Electronic Module). This module is the 'switching centre' of the vehicle. Depending on the vehicle trim level, it controls the windscreen wiper interval, front and rear window heating interval, windscreen washer system, central locking, electric windows, radio remote control, anti-theft warning system with ultrasonic monitoring, and the bulb failure monitoring system. The central junction box is located under the driver's side of the facia.

Main fuses

2 The fuses are located in the central junction box under the driver's side of the facia, and in an auxiliary fusebox in the left-hand corner of the engine compartment.

3 Access to the fuses is gained by pulling open the cover panel (central fusebox), or lifting the lid (auxiliary fusebox) **(see illustrations)**.

4 Each fuse is numbered; the fuses' ratings and circuits they protect are listed on the rear face of the cover panel.

5 On some models (depending on specification), some additional fuses are located in separate holders next to the relays.

6 To remove a fuse, first switch off the circuit concerned (or the ignition), then pull the fuse out of its terminals. The wire within the fuse should be visible; if the fuse is blown the wire will have a break in it, which will be visible through the plastic casing.

7 Always renew a fuse with one of an identical rating; never use a fuse with a different rating from the original or substitute anything else. Never renew a fuse more than once without tracing the source of the trouble. The fuse rating is stamped on top of the fuse; note that the fuses are also colour-coded for easy recognition.

8 If a new fuse blows immediately, find the cause before renewing it again; a short to earth as a result of faulty insulation is most likely. Where a fuse protects more than one circuit, try to isolate the defect by switching on each circuit in turn (if possible) until the fuse blows again.

9 Always carry a supply of spare fuses of each relevant rating on the vehicle, a spare of each rating should be clipped into the base of the fusebox.

Relays

10 The relays are mounted in the central junction box under the driver's side facia, and also in the auxiliary fusebox in the engine compartment **(see illustration)**. The seat heating relays are located under the relevant seat.

11 The relays are of sealed construction, and cannot be repaired if faulty. The relays are of the plug-in type, and may be removed by pulling directly from their terminals. In some cases, it will be necessary to prise the two plastic clips outwards before removing the relay.

12 If a circuit or system controlled by a relay develops a fault and the relay is suspect, operate the system; if the relay is functioning, it should be possible to hear it click as it is energised. If this is the case, the fault lies with the components or wiring of the system. If the relay is not being energised, then either the

3.3a Pull down the cover panel to access the main fusebox . . .

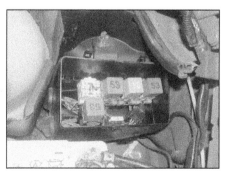
3.3b . . . or lift the lid on the auxiliary fusebox

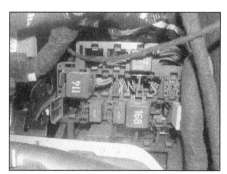
3.10 Relays on the central junction box (viewed with the facia removed)

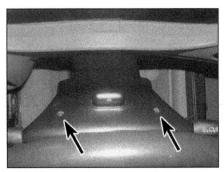

5.2 Remove the steering column upper shroud screws (arrowed)

5.3 Undo the steering column combination switch retaining screw

5.4 Lift the switch assembly from the column

relay is not receiving a main supply or a switching voltage, or the relay itself is faulty. Testing is by the substitution of a known good unit, but be careful; while some relays are identical in appearance and in operation, others look similar but perform different functions.

13 To renew a relay, first ensure that the ignition switch is off. The relay can then simply be pulled out from the socket and the new relay pressed in.

4 Ignition switch/steering column lock – removal and refitting

Refer to the information given in Chapter 10.

5 Steering column combination switch – removal and refitting

Removal

1 Disconnect the battery negative lead (refer to Section 1 and Chapter 5A).
2 With the steering column in its lowest and rearmost position, undo the retaining screws and remove the steering column upper shroud **(see illustration)**.
3 Undo the combination switch retaining screw **(see illustration)**.
4 Note their fitted locations and disconnect the switch wiring multiplugs. Note that the design of the plugs is such that it is impossible to reconnect them to the wrong

switches. Remove the switch **(see illustration)**. No further dismantling of the switch is recommended.

Refitting

5 Refitting is a reversal of removal.

6 Switches – removal and refitting

Facia-mounted light switch

1 Disconnect the battery negative terminal as described in Chapter 5A.
2 With a pad of soft material between the screwdriver and the facia, carefully prise the switch panel from the facia, starting at the opposite end of the panel to the main light switch **(see illustration)**.
3 Disconnect the wiring plugs as the switch panel is withdrawn. Note that the design of the plugs is such that it is impossible to refit any plug to the wrong switch.
4 Refit in the reverse order of removal.

Headlight range control/ dash illumination adjuster

5 Remove the facia mounted light switch as described in Paragraphs 1 to 3 of this Section.
6 Using a small screwdriver, release the locking mechanism and remove the switch retaining collar.
7 Slide the headlight range adjuster/dash illumination adjuster from the main light switch **(see illustration)**.
8 Refit in the reverse order of removal.

Door mirror adjuster

9 With a pad of soft material between the screwdriver and the surround to prevent any damage, gently prise the lower edge of the switch panel from the trim, and then slide the panel downwards. Disconnect the switch wiring plugs as the switch panel is withdrawn. Release the retaining clips and remove the switch from the panel **(see illustrations)**.
10 Refit in the reverse order of removal.

6.2 Starting at the dimmer switch end, carefully prise the switch from the facia

6.7 Slide the adjuster switch out

6.9a Prise the lower edge up, and slide the panel down . . .

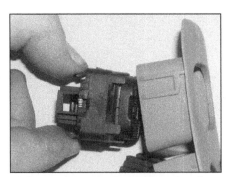

6.9b . . . then squeeze together the clips and remove the switch

6.11 Carefully prise the interior light/switch panel from the overhead console

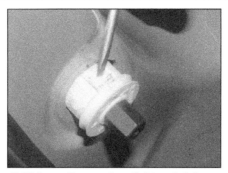

6.15 Lever the courtesy light switch from the door aperture

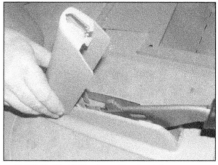

6.17 Pull off the handbrake trim cover

Sunroof control

11 With a pad of soft material between the screwdriver and the surround to prevent any damage, gently prise the interior light/sliding roof operating switch panel from the overhead console (see illustration).

12 Note their fitted positions, and disconnect the wiring plugs as the panel is withdrawn.

13 release the four retaining tabs, and pull the switch from the panel.

14 Refit in the reverse order of removal.

Courtesy light

15 The courtesy lights are controlled by switches fitted to the lower corners of the door apertures. The luggage compartment light is controlled by a switch incorporated into the tailgate lock (see Chapter 11). To remove a door switch, disconnect the battery negative terminal (see Chapter 5A), and carefully lever the switch from the door aperture. Disconnect the wiring plug as the switch is withdrawn (see illustration).

16 Refitting is a reversal of removal.

Handbrake warning

17 Remove the rear section of the centre console as described in Chapter 11. On models without a rear centre console, pull off the handbrake trim cover (see illustration).

18 Squeeze together the retaining clip lugs, and remove the switch from the bracket. Disconnect the wiring plugs as the switch is withdrawn (see illustrations).

19 Refit in the reverse order of removal.

Electric window

Door-mounted

20 On front doors, with a pad of soft material between the screwdriver and the surround to prevent any damage, gently prise the lower edge of the switch panel from the trim, and then slide the panel downwards (see illustration 6.9a). Disconnect the switch wiring plugs as the switch panel is withdrawn. Squeeze together the retaining clips and remove the switch (see illustration).

21 On rear doors, remove the door trim panel as described in Chapter 11.

22 Disconnect the wiring plug, squeeze together the retaining clips and remove the switch (see illustration).

23 Refitting is a reversal of removal.

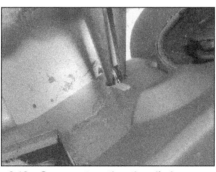

6.18a Squeeze together the clip lugs . . .

6.18b . . . and remove the handbrake warning switch

Facia-mounted

24 Remove the audio unit as described in Section 18.

25 On models with electronic climate control, remove the control unit from the centre panel.

26 On models with conventional heating/manual air conditioning, use a small screwdriver to gently prise out the storage compartment below the audio unit in the centre control panel. With a screwdriver, gently prise out the heater control panel trim. Use a pad of soft material between the screwdriver and the panel to prevent any accidental damage (see illustration).

27 Slacken and remove the heater control/audio unit bezel retaining screws. Using a screwdriver, carefully release the two right-hand tangs holding the bezel in place, followed by the single left-hand tang (see

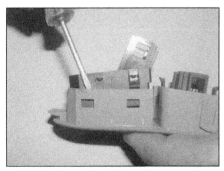

6.20 Release the clips and remove the switch

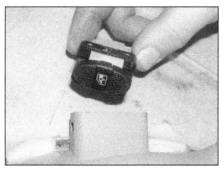

6.22 Squeeze together the clips and remove the switch

6.26 Carefully prise out the heater control panel trim

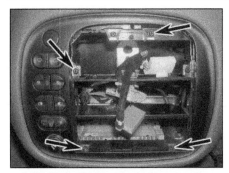

6.27 Undo the screws and remove the bezel (arrowed)

6.28 Push the switch from the panel

pull the switch from the panel. Disconnect the wiring plugs as the switch is withdrawn **(see illustration)**.

7 Exterior light units and bulbs – removal and refitting

1 Whenever a bulb is renewed, note the following points:
 a) *Ensure the ignition is turned off.*
 b) *Remember that if the light has just been in use, the bulb may be extremely hot.*
 c) *Always check the bulb contacts and holder, ensuring that there is clean metal-to-metal contact between the bulb and its live(s) and earth. Clean off any corrosion or dirt before fitting a new bulb.*
 d) *Wherever bayonet-type bulbs are fitted, ensure that the live contact(s) bear firmly against the bulb contact.*
 e) *Always ensure that the new bulb is of the correct rating and that it is completely clean before fitting it; this applies particularly to headlight/foglight bulbs (see below).*

Headlight

2 On the right-hand headlamp, slide up the plastic panel. Detach the cover cap from the rear of the headlamp unit by rotating it anti-clockwise **(see illustrations)**.
3 Unplug the wiring connector from the rear of the relevant bulb.
4 Release the metal retaining clip and withdraw the bulb **(see illustrations)**.

6.35 Release the retaining clip and remove the tailgate ajar switch (arrowed)

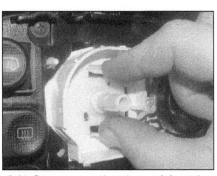

6.41 Squeeze together the retaining tabs and pull the blower motor switch from the panel

illustration). Remove the bezel, disconnect the cigarette lighter wiring plug as it is withdrawn.
28 Carefully push the switch from the control panel **(see illustration)**.
29 Disconnect the wiring plug as the switch is withdrawn.
30 Refitting is a reversal of removal.

Stop-light

31 Refer to Chapter 9.

Steering column combination

32 Refer to Section 5.

Luggage area light/tailgate ajar

33 Remove the tailgate trim panel as described in Chapter 11, Section 12.
34 Disconnect the switch wiring plug.
35 Release the retaining clip and remove the switch **(see illustration)**.
36 Refitting is a reversal of removal.

Heated window/ seat heating/auxiliary heater

37 The removal and refitting procedure for these switches is identical to that given for the facia-mounted electric window switches, in Paragraphs 24 to 30 in this Section.

Reversing light

38 Refer to Chapter 7A.

Heater blower motor

39 Use a small screwdriver to gently prise out the heater control panel trim. Use a pad of soft material between the screwdriver and the

panel to prevent any accidental damage.
40 Pull the knob from the switch.
41 Depress the two retaining tabs (one at the top, and one at the bottom of the switch), and

7.2a Slide up the plastic panel . . .

7.2b . . . and turn the cover cap 90° anti-clockwise

7.4a Squeeze together the ends of the metal clip . . .

7.4b . . . and remove the bulb

7.5 Make sure the lugs on the bulb align with the grooves in the reflector

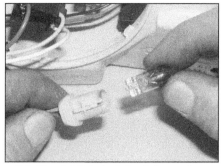

7.8 The sidelight bulb is of the capless type

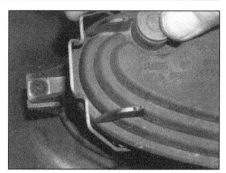

7.10 Release the metal clip and remove the foglight cover

5 Refitting is a reversal of removal. Insert the new bulb so that the lugs on the bulb plate align with the grooves in the reflector **(see illustration)**. Do not touch the glass of the new bulb with bare fingers. If the glass is accidentally touched, clean it with methylated spirit.

Sidelight

6 Remove the cover cap from the rear of the headlight by rotating it anti-clockwise **(see illustration 7.2b)**.
7 Pull the bulbholder from the rear of the light unit.
8 Pull the bulb to remove it from the bulbholder **(see illustration)**.
9 Refitting is a reversal of removal.

Front foglights

10 The front foglights are fitted into the front bumper. Release the spring clip and remove the cover from the rear of the unit **(see illustration)**.
11 Disconnect the wiring plug, release the retaining clip and remove the bulb from the unit **(see illustration)**.
12 Refitting is a reversal of removal.

Front direction indicator

13 Open the bonnet, and slacken the outer screw above the headlamp assembly **(see illustration)**. Pull the complete indicator from the vehicle.
14 Rotate the bulbholder anti-clockwise and withdraw it from the light unit.

15 Depress and rotate the bulb to remove it from the bulbholder **(see illustration)**.
16 Refitting is a reversal of removal. Engage the guide pegs at the lower inner edge of the direction indicator unit with those on the outer edge of the headlamp unit.

Direction indicator side repeater

17 Great care must be exercised when attempting to remove the side repeater lamps, as it is only possible to remove them in one direction (depending on the position in which they previously fitted), and impossible to recognise which side of the repeater the spring clip or the mounting sits. Push the lens towards the front or rear of the vehicle to compress the spring clip, then tilt it out at the rear or front to release the lens from the bodywork. Rotate the bulbholder anti-clockwise, extract the

7.11 Disconnect the wiring, release the clip, and remove the bulb

bulbholder from the lens, then pull the bulb from the bulbholder **(see illustrations)**.
18 Refitting is a reversal of removal.

7.13 Slacken the screw and slide the indicator assembly forward

7.15 Depress and twist the bulb anti-clockwise to remove it

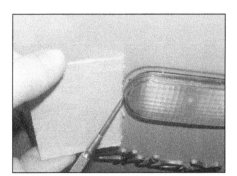

7.17a Push the lamp to compress the spring clip, and carefully lever out the mounting end

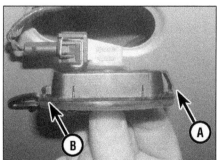

7.17b Side repeater spring clip (A) and mounting (B)

7.17c Rotate the bulbholder and pull the bulb out

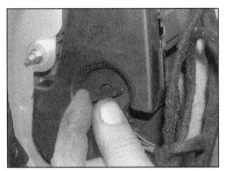

7.19 Rotate the screw to the vertical position

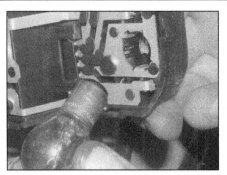

7.20 Push and twist the bulb to remove it

7.21 Undo the nuts and remove the light unit

Rear body-mounted lights

19 Open the tailgate, and open the access flap on the side trim. Turn the thumbscrew on the rear of the light unit to the vertical

7.24 Depress the retainer (arrowed)

7.25 Push and twist the bulb to remove it

position, and remove the bulbholder **(see illustration)**.
20 Press and twist the relevant bulb anti-clockwise, and withdraw it from the bulbholder **(see illustration)**.
21 To remove the light unit, remove the bulbholder unit as described above, then unscrew and remove the retaining nuts. Remove the light unit **(see illustration)**.
22 Refit in the reverse order of removal, ensuring that the seal is correctly positioned. On completion check for the satisfactory operation of all rear lights.

Rear tailgate-mounted lights

23 Open the tailgate, and remove the access flap on the rear of the trim.
24 Depress the spring retainer and remove the bulbholder assembly **(see illustration)**.
25 Depress and twist the bulb, then withdraw it from the bulbholder **(see illustration)**.

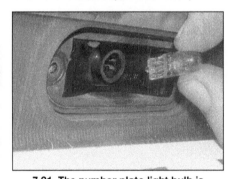

7.31 The number plate light bulb is capless

26 To remove the light unit, with reference to Chapter 11, Section 12, remove the tailgate trim panel.
27 Disconnect the wiring plug from the light unit on each side.
28 Slacken and remove the retaining nuts, and remove the light assembly from the tailgate. Note that the light assembly is also held in position by an adhesive compound. Take great care not to damage the assembly during removal.
29 Refit in the reverse order of removal, ensuring that the seal is correctly positioned. On completion check for the satisfactory operation of all rear lights.

Number plate lights

30 The number plate lights are located in the tailgate, just above the number plate. Undo the two retaining screws and remove the relevant lens and bulbholder from the light unit.
31 The bulb is a push-fit in the holder **(see illustration)**.
32 Refit in the reverse order of removal, and check the light for satisfactory operation.

High-level stop-light

33 Open the tailgate, depress the locking tabs at each end of the unit, and remove the bulbholder **(see illustration)**.
34 Pull the relevant bulb from the holder **(see illustration)**.
35 Refitting is a reversal of removal.
36 If required, the stop-light can be removed by sliding it towards the lower end of the tailgate **(see illustration)**.

7.33 Depress the retaining clips and remove the high-level stop-light bulbholder

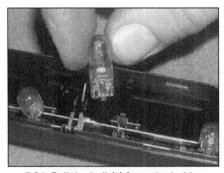

7.34 Pull the bulb(s) from the holder

7.36 Slide the high-level stop-light from its mountings

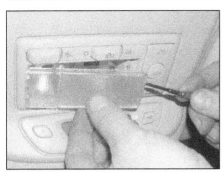

8.2 Carefully unclip the light lens

8.3 Manoeuvre the bulb from the spring contacts

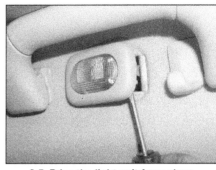

8.5 Prise the light unit from place

8 Interior light bulbs – renewal

1 Whenever a bulb is renewed, note the following points:

a) Remember that if the light has just been in use, the bulb may be extremely hot.

b) Always check the bulb contacts and holder, ensuring that there is clean metal-to-metal contact between the bulb and its live(s) and earth. Clean off any corrosion or dirt before fitting a new bulb.

c) Wherever bayonet-type bulbs are fitted, ensure that the live contact(s) bear firmly against the bulb contact.

d) Always ensure that the new bulb is of the correct rating and that it is completely clean before fitting it.

Interior/reading lights

Front/centre interior lights

2 Unclip the lens from the light unit (see illustration). Use a pad of soft material under the screwdriver to prevent damage to the surround.

3 Remove the bulb from its holder. The light is fitted with a festoon bulb which can be prised from its spring contacts (see illustration).

4 Refit in the reverse order of removal.

Reading lights

5 Using a screwdriver, carefully prise the light unit from it location (see illustration). Where a reading light is incorporated into the same unit as an interior light, the complete unit must be prised from position (see illustration 6.11).

6 With the unit removed, twist the bulbholder anti-clockwise, and pull the capless bulb from the holder (see illustrations).

7 Refitting is a reversal of removal.

Luggage area, engine compartment, passenger footwell and glovebox lights

8 Prise free the light unit and extract the festoon bulb from its holder. When removing the glovebox light unit, prise the top of the lens out first (see illustrations).

9 Refit in the reverse order of removal, and check for satisfactory operation.

Sun visor/vanity mirror light

10 Prise free the mirror frame from the sun visor. The festoon bulbs can be extracted from their holders (see illustrations).

11 Refit in the reverse order of removal.

8.6a Pull the bulb from the holder

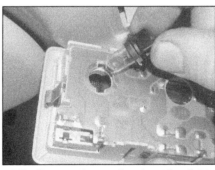

8.6b Remove the overhead reading light bulb from the back of the light unit

8.8a Manoeuvre the festoon bulb from the spring contacts

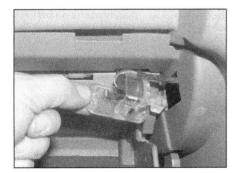

8.8b Prise out the top of the glovebox light first

8.10a Prise the mirror frame from the sunvisor . . .

8.10b . . . and remove the bulb(s)

8.13 Twist the bulbholder 90° anti-clockwise and remove it from the instrument cluster

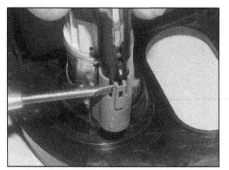

8.16 Lift the clip and pull free the bulbholder

8.25 Depress the clip and remove the bulbholder from the front of the heater control panel

Instrument panel bulbs

12 Remove the instrument panel as described in Section 10.

13 On some models the illumination and warning light bulbs are integral with their holders, whilst on others the bulbs are capless and can be pulled from the holders. To remove bulbholder, twist the bayonet-fit bulbholder through quarter of a turn anti-clockwise and withdraw it carefully **(see illustration)**.

14 Refit in the reverse order of removal.

Cigar lighter illumination

15 In order to access the cigar lighter illumination bulbholder, it is necessary to remove the heater control panel as described in Chapter 3.

16 Leaving the cigar lighter in the panel, lift

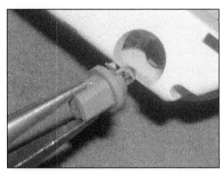

8.27 Remove the bulbholder from the rear of the clock

the clip and pull free the bulbholder from the rear of the lighter **(see illustration)**. The bulb is integral with the holder.

17 Refit in the reverse order of removal.

Switch illumination

18 Most switch illumination bulbs are usually built into the switch itself, and cannot be renewed separately. Refer to Section 6 and remove/renew the switch. The exception is the hazard warning light switch, the illumination bulb for which can be renewed independently of the switch.

19 Undo the two retaining screws and remove the upper steering column shroud **(see illustration 5.2)**.

20 Carefully prise the cover from the switch, and slide the bulb/holder from the switch. The bulb is integral with the holder.

21 Refitting is a reversal of removal.

Heater control illumination

22 Only models fitted with convention heating or manual air-conditioning systems and controls are equipped with renewable bulbs.

23 Remove the heater control panel as described in Chapter 3.

24 Disconnect the bulbholder wiring plug from the rear of the unit.

25 Using a small screwdriver, depress the retaining lug, and remove the bulbholder from the front of the unit **(see illustration)**. Note that the bulb is integral with the holder.

26 Refit in the reverse order of removal,

noting that the switch centre section will only fit in one position.

Clock illumination

27 Carefully prise the clock from the overhead console. Use a pair of pliers to unscrew the bulbholder from the rear of the unit. The illumination bulb is integral with the bulbholder **(see illustration)**.

28 Refitting is a reversal of removal.

---

9 Headlights – removal, refitting and beam adjustment

Headlight unit

Removal

1 Open the bonnet, and remove the front direction indicator lamps as described in Section 7.

2 Remove the radiator grille with reference to Chapter 11.

3 Disconnect the wiring plug from the rear of the relevant headlight unit.

4 Each headlight is secured by four screws **(see illustration)**. Undo the screws and remove the headlight. On the right-hand headlight, disconnect the wiring plug as the unit is withdrawn.

5 If required, the right-hand side headlight shield can be removed by lifting out the air inlet duct (petrol engines), and undoing the two retaining screws. Before the shield can be lifted from place, the two halves must be separated by pressing in the centre pins of the retaining clips **(see illustration)**.

Refitting

6 Refitting is a reversal of the removal procedure. On completion check for satisfactory operation, and have the headlight beam adjustment checked as soon as possible (see below).

Headlight lens

Removal

7 Remove the headlight assembly as described earlier in this Section.

9.4 The headlight is secured by four screws (arrowed)

9.5 To remove the clips, push the centres out

9.8 Prise off the lens retaining clips

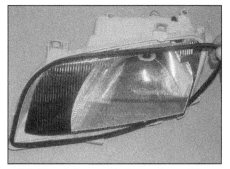

9.9 Check the seal is in good condition

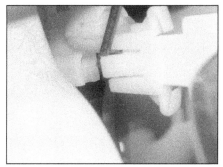

9.11 Reflector inner retaining clip

8 Carefully prise off the retaining clips, and pull the lens from the unit **(see illustration)**.

Refitting

9 Check that the seal between the lens and the shell is in good condition. Position the lens and seal against the headlight shell, and carefully push the retaining clips into place **(see illustration)**.

10 The remainder of refitting is a reversal of removal.

Headlight reflector

Removal

11 Remove the headlight lens as described in the previous sub-Section, and the headlight bulb as described in Section 7 of this Chapter. Using an Allen key, turn the inner beam adjustment screws (see Paragraph 20) clockwise until the reflector is pushed forward sufficiently to access the reflector inner retaining clip **(see illustration)**. Count the number of turns of the adjustment screw, so that the reflector can be returned to its original position.

12 Lift the reflector slightly to disconnect the range control motor. Turn the outer beam adjustment screw sufficiently to allow the reflector to move to the outside and disconnect the outer adjustment spindle **(see illustration)**. Again, count the number of turns of the adjustment screw, so that the reflector can be returned to its original position.

Refitting

13 Separate the range control motor adjustment spindle clip from the reflector, and position it on the motor spindle. Engage the outer spindle clip ball with its socket. Align the reflector with the spindle clips and push it into position. Turning the beam adjustment screws, return the reflector to its original position.

14 The remainder of refitting is a reversal of removal. If necessary have the headlight alignment checked by a suitably-equipped workshop.

Range control motor

Removal

15 Remove the headlight reflector as described in the previous sub-Section.

16 Undo the two range control motor retaining screws **(see illustration)**.

17 Separate the range control motor wiring from the headlamp unit wiring plug **(see illustration)**.

Refitting

18 Install the range control motor wiring into the headlamp unit wiring plug. The remainder of refitting is a reversal of removal. On completion, check for satisfactory operation, and have the headlight beam adjustment checked as soon as possible.

Beam adjustment

19 Accurate adjustment of the headlight beam is only possible using optical beam setting equipment, and this work should therefore be carried out by a Ford dealer or suitably-equipped workshop.

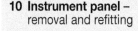

9.12 Reflector outer retaining clip

20 For reference, the headlights can be adjusted using the adjuster screws, accessible via the top of each light unit **(see illustration)**.

21 Some models are equipped with an electrically-operated headlight beam adjustment system which is controlled through the switch in the facia. On these models, ensure that the switch is set to the basic 0 position before adjusting the headlight aim.

10 Instrument panel –
removal and refitting

Removal

1 Disconnect the battery negative lead (refer to Section 1 and Chapter 5A).

9.16 Headlamp range control motor

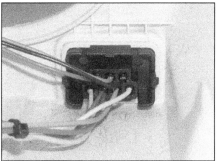

9.17 Separate the range control motor wiring from the plug

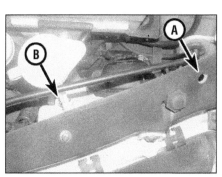

9.20 Vertical adjustment screw (A) and horizontal adjustment screw (B)

10.3 Undo the trim surround retaining screws (arrowed)

10.4a The instrument panel is secured by two screws (arrowed)

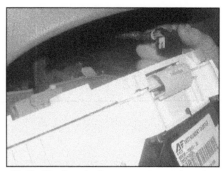

10.4b Unplug the instrument panel as the unit is withdrawn

2 Release the column adjustment handle, and position the steering wheel as far away from the instrument panel as possible.

3 Undo the two retaining screws and pull the trim surround from the facia. Note the retaining clip at the lower edge of the trim **(see illustration)**.

4 Slacken and remove the two retaining screws, tilt the top of the instrument panel towards the steering wheel, and manoeuvre it through the facia aperture. Disconnect the wiring plug(s) as the unit is withdrawn **(see illustrations)**. No further dismantling of the instrument panel is possible. If any of the instrument panel components are faulty (excluding bulbs – see Section 8), then the complete panel must be renewed.

Refitting

5 Refitting is a reversal of removal

11.3a Lift the cover . . .

11 Windscreen wiper components – removal and refitting

Wiper blades

1 Refer to *Weekly checks*.

Wiper arms

2 If the wipers are not in their parked position, switch on the ignition, and allow the motor to automatically park.

3 Before removing an arm, mark its parked position on the glass with a strip of adhesive tape. Prise off the cover and unscrew the spindle nut approximately two turns **(see illustrations)**. Ease the arm from the spindle by rocking it slowly from side-to-side, then completely unscrew the nut and remove the washer and the arm.

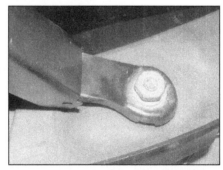

11.3b . . . then undo the nut and ease the arm from the spindle

4 Refitting is a reversal of removal, but before tightening the spindle nuts, position the wiper blades as marked before removal. If the original position of the arms has been lost, position the arm/blades as shown **(see illustration)**.

Wiper motor

Removal

5 Disconnect the battery negative terminal and remove the battery compartment upper panel (see Chapter 5A).

6 Release the three retaining screws and remove the bulkhead trim **(see illustration)**. Slide the trim to the right-hand side and manoeuvre it from behind the coolant expansion tank.

7 Unscrew the retaining nut and remove the linkage lever from the motor spindle. Use an extension bar to prevent the lever rotating whilst slackening the nut **(see illustration)**.

8 Mark the position of the wiper motor relative to the mounting bracket, then undo the three retaining bolts. Disconnect the wiper motor wiring plug as the motor is withdrawn.

Refitting

9 Refitting is the reverse of removal ensuring the mounting bolts are tightened to the specified torque. Also ensure that the cowl panel is correctly clipped in position.

Wiper linkage

Removal

10 Remove the wiper arms as described previously in this Section.

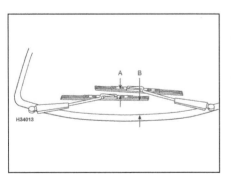

11.4 Position the wiper blades so that A = 15 to 20 mm, and B = 35 mm

11.6 Undo the screws (two arrowed) and remove the bulkhead trim

11.7 Use a socket extension bar to prevent the linkage turning whilst undoing the nut

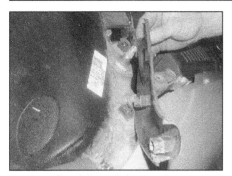

11.11 Carefully pull the scuttle corner trims from place

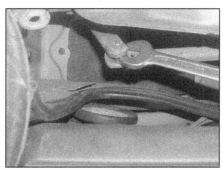

11.13 Prise the right-hand linkage rod from the balljoint

11.14 Use a small screwdriver to extract the spindle circlip

11 Carefully pull the two scuttle corner trims from place **(see illustration)**.
12 The bulkhead trim is retained by three screws. Release the screws and remove the trim. Slide the trim to the right-hand side and manoeuvre it from behind the coolant expansion tank.
13 Using an open-ended spanner, carefully prise the right-hand linkage rod from the balljoint **(see illustration)**.
14 Prise out the right-hand spindle circlip, recover the washer, and slide the spindle from the housing **(see illustration)**. Note the washers at the base of the spindle.
15 Unscrew the wiper spindle nuts, and recover the washers **(see illustration)**.
16 Undo the four retaining screws, then remove the linkage complete with the wiper motor. Disconnect the wiper motor wiring plug as the assembly is withdrawn **(see illustration)**.
17 The linkage rods can be removed by prising the balljoints apart using an open-ended spanner. Note their fitted positions.
18 If the motor is to be removed from the linkage, mark the position of the motor lever prior to undoing the retaining nut.

Refitting

19 Refitting is a reversal of removal.

12 Washer system – general information

1 All models are fitted with a windscreen and tailgate window washer system. Some models are fitted with headlight washers.
2 The fluid reservoir(s) for the windscreen washer (and where applicable, for the headlight washers) is/are located in the engine compartment on the left-hand side. The fluid pump is attached to the side of the reservoir body, as is the level sensor **(see illustrations)**. Access to the reservoir and pump is achieved by removing the front bumper assembly – see Chapter 11.
3 The tailgate washer is fed by the same reservoir and pump, operating in the reverse direction.
4 The reservoir fluid level must be regularly topped-up with windscreen washer fluid containing an antifreeze agent, but not cooling

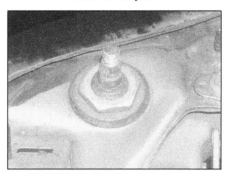

11.15 Undo the wiper spindle nuts

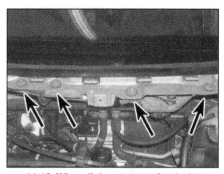

11.16 Wiper linkage mounting bolts (arrowed)

system antifreeze – see *Weekly checks*.
5 The supply hoses are attached by rubber couplings to their various connections, and if required, can be detached by simply pulling them free from the appropriate connector.
6 The windscreen washer jets can be adjusted by inserting a fine pin and pushing the jet up or down in the holder **(see illustration)**. When adjusted correctly, the jets should be aimed at a point just above the centre of the wiper swept area. To remove a washer jet, remove the bonnet insulation, pull off the hose, disconnect the wiring plug, and lever the rear edge of the jet out **(see illustration)**.

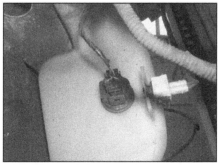

12.2a Washer fluid reservoir level sensor . . .

12.2b . . . and pump

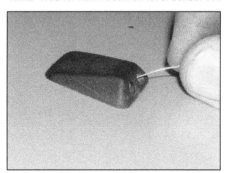

12.6a Adjust the washer jets using a fine pin

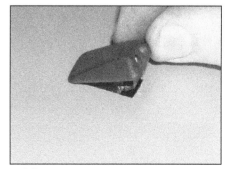

12.6b Lever the rear edge of the washer jet out first

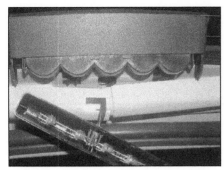

12.7 To access the tailgate washer jet, unclip the stop-light cover and tailgate trim

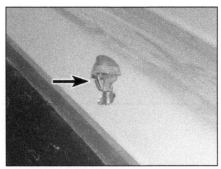

12.8 Compress the spring clip (arrowed) and push the jet from the tailgate

13.3 Undo the spindle nut and remove the cover

7 To remove the tailgate washer jet, open the tailgate unclip the high-level stop-light cover, and unclip the top of the tailgate trim **(see illustration)**.

8 Using a suitable screwdriver, press the jet from the tailgate, and disconnect the hose **(see illustration)**.

9 Access to the headlamp washer components is achieved by removing the front bumper cover (see Chapter 11). The headlight washer jets are best adjusted using the Ford tool, and should therefore be entrusted to a Ford garage to set.

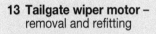

13 Tailgate wiper motor – removal and refitting

Removal

1 Disconnect the battery negative lead (see Chapter 5A).

2 Remove the wiper arm and blade as described in Section 11.

3 Undo the nut and remove the spindle cover **(see illustration)**.

4 Remove the tailgate trim panel as described in Chapter 11.

5 Detach the wiring connector from the wiper motor.

6 Undo the four bolts and remove the motor retaining plate, and the motor itself **(see illustration)**.

Refitting

7 Refit in the reverse order of removal. Refit the wiper arm and blade so that the arm is parked correctly.

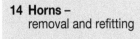

14 Horns – removal and refitting

Removal

1 Remove the front bumper as described in Chapter 11.

2 With the bumper removed, undo the horn unit retaining nut(s) and disconnect the wiring connector(s) **(see illustration)**.

Refitting

3 Refit in the reverse order of removal. Check for satisfactory operation on completion.

15 Bulb failure module – removal and refitting

Removal

1 Remove the instrument panel as described in Section 10.

2 Working through the instrument panel aperture, undo the retaining bolt, slide the module from the bracket, and disconnect the

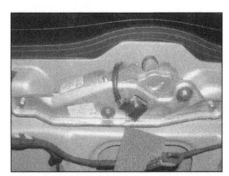

13.6 The wiper motor and mounting plate are secured by four bolts

wiring plugs as the module is withdrawn **(see illustration)**.

Refitting

3 Refitting is a reversal of removal.

16 Sunroof motor – removal and refitting

Closing sunroof manually

1 If the motor malfunctions when the roof panel is in the open position, it can be wound shut manually. To do this, carefully prise the interior light assembly from the roof console,

14.2 The horns are accessible after the front bumper had been removed

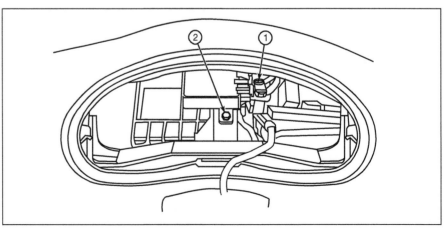

15.2 Disconnect the bulb failure mounting bolt (2) and disconnect the wiring plugs (1)

then undo the two console trim panel retaining screws, and push the trim panel to the rear. Release the manual cranking tool which is clipped to motor. Turn the cap on the lever hole in the direction of the arrow, insert the cranking tool into the hole at the end of the motor shaft. The tool can then be turned to close the sunroof as required – see Chapter 11, Section 24.

Motor

Removal

2 Ensure that the sunroof is fully closed – refer to paragraph 1 if the motor has failed. Disconnect the battery negative lead (refer to Section 1 and Chapter 5A).
3 Carefully prise the interior light assembly from the roof console, and disconnect the wiring plugs. Take care not to damage the light surround.
4 Prise the clock assembly from the console (see Section 26). Again, take care not to damage the console. Disconnect the wiring plug as the clock is withdrawn.
5 Undo the two console retaining screws in the interior light aperture, and slide the console to the rear and withdraw it from the roof panel **(see illustration)**.
6 Disconnect the motor wiring plug, undo the two retaining screws, and remove the motor **(see illustration)**.

Refitting

7 Refit in the reverse order of removal, noting the following points:
  a) *As with removal, it is important that the roof panel be in the closed position to ensure correct engagement. If the motor was activated whilst it was removed, or if a new motor is being fitted, it must be set for correct engagement before fitting. To do this, connect up the switch wiring to it and turn the switch to the closed position. This will activate the motor so that it is set at the closed position, ready for fitting.*
  b) *Check for satisfactory operation of the sunroof on completion.*

17 Central locking system – general information

1 All models are equipped with a central door locking system, which automatically locks all doors and the rear tailgate in unison with the manual locking of either front door. The system is operated electronically with motors/switches incorporated into the door lock assemblies. The system is controlled by an electronic control unit located under the front passenger's seat on models up to 1998 model year. After this date the function of the control unit is incorporated into the central junction box under the driver's side of the facia.
2 The control unit is equipped with a self-diagnosis capability. Should the system develop a fault, have the control unit

16.5 Undo the overhead console retaining screws

interrogated by a Ford dealer or suitably-equipped specialist. Once the fault has been established, refer to the relevant Section of Chapter 11 to renew a door lock or tailgate lock as applicable.

18 Radio/cassette player – removal and refitting

Note: *This Section applies only to standard-fit audio equipment.*

Removal

1 The radio/cassette player is fitted with special mounting clips, requiring the use of special removal tools, which should be supplied with the vehicle, or may be obtained from an in-car entertainment specialist.
2 Insert the removal rods in the holes provided on the upper and lower edges of the radio/cassette player unit.
3 Slide the removal tools fully into the slots until they locate **(see illustration)**.
4 Withdraw the radio/cassette player from the mounting case, then disconnect the loudspeaker, supply and aerial plugs. Note that some radio units also have a fuse fitted on the rear face.

Refitting

5 Refitting is a reversal of removal, but push the radio fully into its case until the spring clips are engaged. If the radio is of the security code type, it will be necessary to

18.3 Slide the removal tools into the slots, gently push them to the outside, and pull the unit from the centre panel

16.6 The sunroof motor is secured by two screws (arrowed)

enter the code number before switching on the radio.

19 Power amplifier – removal and refitting

Note: *This Section applies only to standard-fit audio equipment.*

Removal

1 In order to gain access to the power amplifier, the heater control panel must be removed, as described in Chapter 3. Note that on non-air conditioned models, there is no need to disconnect the control cables from the panel. Suspend the panel from the facia using a cable tie.
2 Note the routing of the amplifier wiring harness, and remove the three amplifier retaining screws **(see illustration)**.
3 Disconnect the two wiring plugs and remove the amplifier from the facia.

Refitting

4 Refitting is a reversal of removal. Tighten the amplifier retaining screws securely.

20 CD autochanger – removal and refitting

Note: *This Section applies only to standard-fit audio equipment.*

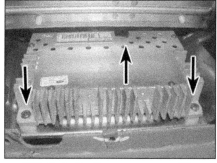
19.2 Undo the three power amplifier retaining screws (arrowed)

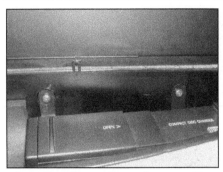

20.2 The CD autochanger is secured by two screws

Removal

1 Raise the right-hand rear storage compartment lid, and remove the foam packing piece.
2 Undo the two retaining screws, and lift the autochanger from the storage compartment (see illustration).
3 Depress the locking tab and disconnect the wiring plug.
4 If necessary, undo the Torx screws and remove the mounting brackets from each side of the unit.

Refitting

5 Refitting is a reversal of removal.

21 Radio aerial –
removal and refitting

1 The aerial is built into the right-hand rear side window. To remove the window, refer to Chapter 11, Section 20.

22 Speakers –
removal and refitting

1 The various audio system speakers are fitted into the interior trim panels. Mid-range speakers are fitted to the front and rear door trims and the luggage compartment side trim panels, whilst high-frequency 'tweeters' are fitted to the rear doors and the facia.

22.3 The door mounted mid-range speakers are retained by four screws

Door-mounted speaker

2 To remove a door-mounted mid-range speaker, remove the appropriate door trim as described in Chapter 11.
3 Undo the four retaining screws, and disconnect the wiring plug(s) as the speaker is withdrawn (see illustration).
4 Refit in the reverse order of removal.

Luggage area speaker

5 Remove the relevant luggage compartment side trim panel as described in Chapter 11, Section 31.
6 Disconnect the speaker wiring plug, undo the four retaining screws/nuts, and remove the speaker (see illustration).
7 Refitting is a reversal of removal.

Door-mounted tweeter

8 Remove the appropriate door trim as described in Chapter 11.
9 Disconnect the wiring plug to the speaker, release the four locking tabs with a small screwdriver, and remove the speaker (see illustration).
10 Refit in the reverse order of removal.

Facia-mounted tweeter

11 Using a small screwdriver, carefully prise the speaker from the facia. Use a pad of soft material under the screwdriver blade to prevent damage to the facia (see illustration).
12 Disconnect the wiring plug as the speaker is withdrawn.
13 Refitting is a reversal of removal.

23 Airbag system – general
information and precautions

Warning:
• *Before carrying out any operations on the airbag system, disconnect the battery negative terminal (see Chapter 5A), and wait at least 15 minutes before starting any operation. Ensure that the battery negative lead cannot accidentally be reconnected.*
• *Before working on the airbag(s) or seat belt pretensioners, ensure you are electrostatically discharged, by touching a suitable metal part. e.g. a metal bench, or mains water pipe.*
• *Do not use a 'code saver' device when working on the supplementary restraint system.*
• *When operations are complete, make sure no one is inside the vehicle when the battery is reconnected.*
• *Note that the airbag(s) must not be subjected to temperatures in excess of 90°C (194°F). When the airbag is removed, ensure that it is stored the correct way up to prevent possible inflation.*
• *Do not allow any solvents or cleaning agents to contact the airbag assemblies. They must be cleaned using only a damp cloth.*
• *The airbags and control unit are both sensitive to impact. If either is dropped or damaged they should be renewed.*
• *Disconnect the airbag control unit wiring plug prior to using arc-welding equipment on the vehicle.*

A driver's airbag is fitted as standard to the Galaxy range, whilst a passenger's airbag, and side airbags are available as options. The driver's airbag is fitted to the centre of the steering wheel. The passenger's airbag is fitted to the upper surface of the facia. The airbag system comprises of the airbag unit(s) (complete with gas generators), an impact sensor, the control unit and a warning light in the instrument panel. Seat-mounted side airbags are also fitted on certain models, as are seat belt pretensioners. These components are incorporated into the same

22.6 Luggage compartment side trim speaker

22.9 Release the clips and remove the speaker

22.11 Use a pad of soft material to prevent damage to the facia whilst prising out the speaker

airbag control system, the complexity of the removal and refitting procedures precludes their coverage in this manual.

The airbag system is triggered in the event of a direct or offset frontal impact above a predetermined force. The airbag is inflated within milliseconds, and forms a safety cushion between the driver and the steering wheel or (where applicable) the passenger and the facia. This prevents contact between the upper body and the steering wheel, column and facia, and therefore greatly reduces the risk of injury. The airbag then deflates almost immediately through vents in the side of the airbag.

Every time the ignition is switched on, the airbag control unit performs a self-test. The self-test takes approximately 5 seconds, and during this time the airbag warning light on the facia is illuminated. After the self-test has been completed, the warning light should go out. If the warning light fails to come on, remains illuminated after the initial 5-second period, or comes on at any time when the vehicle is being driven, there is a fault in the airbag system. The vehicle should then be taken to a Ford dealer for examination at the earliest possible opportunity.

24 Airbag system components – removal and refitting

Note: *Refer to the warnings in Section 23 before carrying out the following operations.*
1 Disconnect the battery negative terminal (see Section 1 and Chapter 5A), and wait at least 15 minutes before starting any procedure involving any airbag, control unit or sensor.

Driver's airbag

2 Set the steering wheel to straight-ahead, then turn it 90° to the left or right. Release the steering column adjustment lever, and pull the wheel out and down as far as possible.
3 Undo the recessed Torx screw, rotate the steering wheel 180° in the opposite direction, and undo the second recessed Torx screw **(see illustration)**.
4 Return the steering wheel to the straight-ahead position, then carefully lift the airbag assembly away from the steering wheel and

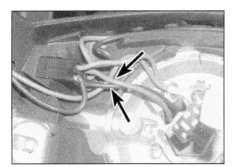
24.11 Disconnect the horn buttons wires (arrowed)

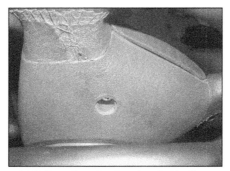
24.3 Turn the wheel and undo the Torx screws

24.7a Undo the two retaining bolts and the remove the passenger airbag

disconnect the wiring connector(s) from the rear of the unit **(see illustration)**. Note that the airbag must not be knocked or dropped, and should be stored the correct way up with its padded surface uppermost.
5 On refitting, reconnect the wiring connector(s) and seat the airbag unit in the steering wheel, making sure the wire does not become trapped. Tighten the Torx screws to the specified torque. Ensure the passenger compartment is unoccupied, then reconnect the battery negative lead.

Passenger airbag

6 The passenger side airbag is located under a cover above the glovebox. With reference to Chapter 11, remove the glovebox.
7 Slacken and remove the two retaining bolts and remove the passenger airbag from the facia. Disconnect the airbag wiring plug as it is withdrawn **(see illustrations)**. Note that the airbag must not be knocked or dropped, and

24.12 Undo the three screws securing the locking ring. Note the locking plunger (arrowed)

24.4 Disconnect the airbag wiring plug

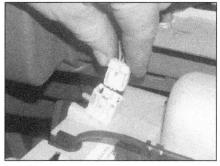
24.7b Disconnect the wiring plug as the airbag is withdrawn

should be stored the correct way up with its curved surface uppermost. Note that if the original airbag has been deployed, carefully check the facia for any signs of cracking, distortion, or whitening (indicating that the area has been stressed). If any of these defects are present, the facia must be renewed, as described in Chapter 11.
8 Refitting is a reversal of removal. Ensure that the wiring connector is securely reconnected.
9 Ensure that no-one is inside the vehicle, then reconnect the battery negative lead.

Airbag wiring contact unit

10 Remove the steering wheel as described in Chapter 10.
11 Disconnect the two horn buttons wiring plugs **(see illustration)**.
12 Undo the three retaining screws and remove the clockspring locking ring **(see illustration)**.

24.13 Withdraw the contact unit from the steering wheel

24.15 Apply a little molybdenum disulphide grease to the horn contact slip-ring

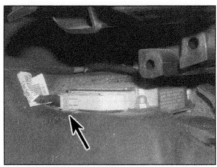

24.16 Release the locking tab (arrowed) and disconnect the airbag control unit connector

13 Carefully withdraw the contact unit from the steering wheel **(see illustration)**.
14 Refit the contact unit to the steering wheel, and carry out the following centralisation procedure: depress the locking plunger **(see illustration 24.12)**, and rotate the outer rotor anti-clockwise until it becomes tight. Rotate the outer rotor clockwise approximately 2.75 turns. Release the locking plunger, and make sure that the plunger locks the contact unit in this position.
15 The remainder of refitting is a reversal of removal. If a new contact unit has been fitted, apply a little molybdenum disulphide grease to the horn slip-ring **(see illustration)**.

Airbag control unit

16 The control unit is located beneath the heater housing. Remove the centre console, and lower centre panel trim as described in Chapter 11. Release the locking tab and release the two-stage locking connector from the unit. Stage one disengages the connector terminals, and stage two releases the connector from the control unit **(see illustration)**.
17 Undo the three retaining nuts and remove the control unit.
18 Refitting is a reversal of removal.

Side airbags

19 The side airbags are incorporated into the side of the front seats. Removal of the units requires the seat upholstery to be removed. This is a specialist task, which we recommend should be entrusted to a Ford dealer or specialist.

Crash sensors for side airbags

20 The sensors are located under each front seat. Slide the seat fully forward and raise it to its maximum height.
21 Note the wiring harness routing, and disconnect the sensor wiring plug.
22 Unscrew the two retaining Allen bolts. Remove the sensor.
23 Refitting is a reversal of removal. Ensure the passenger compartment is unoccupied prior to reconnecting the battery negative lead.

25 Anti-theft alarm system – general information

An engine immobiliser is fitted as standard, and a volumetric sensing perimeter alarm is available as an option.

Should the system(s) become faulty, the vehicle should be taken to a Ford dealer for examination. They will have access to a special diagnostic tester which will quickly trace any fault present in the system.

26 Clock – removal and refitting

Removal

1 Using a screwdriver, carefully prise the clock from the overhead console **(see illustration)**.
2 Disconnect the wiring plug as the clock is removed. If required the bulb can be renewed as described in Section 8 of this Chapter.

Refitting

3 Refitting is a reversal of removal.

27 Ambient air temperature sensor – removal and refitting

Removal

1 Remove the radiator grille as described in Chapter 11.
2 Disconnect the sensor wiring plug.
3 Depress the retaining clips at the front of the sensor, and pull it out of the mounting bracket **(see illustration)**.

Refitting

4 Refitting is a reversal of removal.

28 Fuel filler flap lock motor – removal and refitting

Removal

1 Working in the luggage compartment, remove the vehicle jack storage cover.

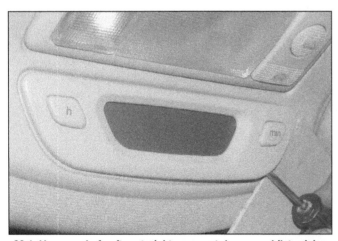

26.1 Use a pad of soft material to prevent damage whilst prising out the clock

27.3 Pull the ambient temperature sensor from the mounting bracket

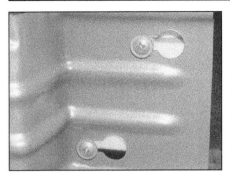

28.4a Slacken the screws . . .

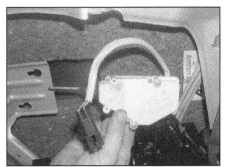

28.4b . . . and remove the fuel filler flap
motor (shown with the trim panel removed)

29.4 Disconnect the vacuum hose and
wiring plug from the switch

2 Prise out and remove the seat belt guide from the luggage compartment side panel.
3 Undo the retaining screws and remove the rear storage box.
4 Disconnect the lock motor wiring plug, slacken the two retaining bolts and remove the motor (see illustrations).

Refitting

5 Refitting is a reversal of removal.

29 Cruise control system – general information, and component renewal

General information

Both petrol and diesel versions of the Galaxy can be specified with cruise control. On petrol models, the system comprises an electronic control module (ECM), a vacuum pump, a brake pedal switch/vacuum valve, a clutch pedal switch/vacuum valve (manual transmission models only), an accelerator pedal vacuum servo, and the driver's control switches.

On diesel models, the cruise control system is purely electronic, comprising of brake and clutch pedal switches, and driver control switches. The system control is incorporated into the Electronic Diesel Control ECM, which regulates the amount of fuel injected into the engine to maintain the desired speed.

On both petrol and diesel models, the

existing vehicle speed sensor is used to provide input to the control units.

Component renewal

Driver's speed control switch

1 The driver's speed control switch is an integral part of the steering column combination switch – refer to Section 5.

Brake pedal switch/vacuum valve (petrol models)

2 Open the central fusebox cover on the driver's side of the lower facia. Hinge the cover down and pull it from the hinges.
3 Undo the six retaining screws and remove the lower facia trim panel (see Chapter 11, Section 31).
4 Disconnect the wiring plug and the vacuum hose from the switch/valve (see illustration).
5 Unscrew the switch from the mounting bracket.
6 To refit the switch, hold the pedal in the rest position, and screw the switch into the bracket until the plunger reaches its stop position (see illustration). Reconnect the wiring plug and the vacuum pipe. The remainder of refitting is a reversal of removal.

Clutch pedal switch/vacuum valve (petrol models)

7 The procedure for the clutch switch is identical to that given for the brake pedal switch earlier in this Section.

Brake pedal switch (diesel models)

8 Open the central electrical box cover on the

driver's side of the lower facia. Hinge the cover down and pull it from the hinges.
9 Undo the six retaining screws and remove the lower facia trim panel.
10 Disconnect the switch wiring plug, and turn the switch anti-clockwise to remove it.
11 Refitting is a reversal of removal.

Clutch pedal switch (diesel models)

12 The procedure for the clutch switch is identical to that given for the brake pedal switch earlier in this Section.

Speed electronic control module (ECM)

13 Remove the facia as described in Chapter 11.
14 Unscrew the retaining nut, and disconnect the wiring plug as the ECM is removed (see illustration).
15 Refitting is a reversal of removal.

Vacuum pump

16 On models with automatic transmission, remove the transmission ECM as described in Chapter 7B.
17 On all models, slacken the left-hand front indicator lamp retaining screw, slide the indicator forward and disconnect the wiring plug.
18 Working through the indicator aperture, carefully prise the vacuum pump rubber mountings from the inner wing panel (see illustration).
19 Pull the pump through the indicator aperture, and disconnect the vacuum pipe

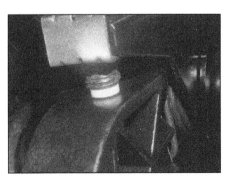

29.6 Screw in the switch until the plunger
is fully retracted

29.14 Disconnect the wiring plug as the
ECM is removed

29.18 Prise the vacuum pump rubber
mountings from the inner wing

and wiring plug as the pump is withdrawn **(see illustration)**.

20 To refit the pump, ensure all three rubber mountings are fitted to the pump mounting bracket.

21 Insert the pump and bracket through the indicator aperture, and pull the rubber mountings through the holes in the inner wing.

22 The remainder of refitting is a reversal of removal.

Accelerator pedal vacuum servo

23 Open the fusebox cover on the driver's side of the lower facia. Hinge the cover down and pull it from the hinges.

24 Undo the six retaining screws and remove the lower facia trim panel (see Chapter 11, Section 31).

25 Disconnect the vacuum pipe from the servo **(see illustration)**.

26 Using a screwdriver, carefully prise the servo actuating rod from the accelerator pedal.

27 Undo the retaining nut and remove the servo.

29.19 Disconnect the vacuum pipe and wiring plug as the pump is withdrawn

28 To refit the servo, position the unit in the mounting bracket and tighten the retaining nut securely.

29 Push the actuating rod back onto the accelerator pedal, and reconnect the vacuum pipe.

30 To reset the servo, turn the adjusting sleeve anti-clockwise, and pull it fully forward.

29.25 Disconnect the vacuum pipe from the servo unit

31 Check, and if necessary, adjust the accelerator cable (see Chapter 4A).

32 Push the servo adjusting sleeve backwards until all play at the pedal is eliminated. Turn the adjusting sleeve clockwise to lock it in position. Check the accelerator pedal for freedom of movement.

33 The remainder of refitting is a reversal of removal.

FORD GALAXY 1995 to 2000 wiring diagrams

Diagram 1

Key to symbols

Bulb

Switch

Multiple contact
switch (ganged)

Fuse/fusible
link and current
rating

F5
30A

Resistor

Variable
resistor

Connecting
wires

Plug and
socket contact

Item no.

2

Pump/motor

M

Earth point
and location

E12

Gauge/meter

Diode

Wire splice
or soldered
joint

Solenoid
actuator

Light emitting
diode (LED)

Wire colour and wire size
(brown with black tracer, 4mm²)

Br/Sw 4

Screened cable

Dashed outline denotes part of a
larger item, containing in this case
an electronic or solid state device.
2 - unspecified connector
         pin 2.
182 1 - Connector C182, pin 1.

182

Earth points

E1   LH engine compartment
E2   LH engine compartment
E3   RH engine compartment
E4   LH front engine compartment
E5   Tailgate
E6   Above rear view mirror
E7   LH engine bulkhead (pre 99)
E7   LH rear engine (post 99)

E8   Engine
E9   Under RH front seat
E10 Under LH front seat
E11 RH luggage compartment
E12 LH engine compartment
E13 LH front engine compartment
E14 LH luggage compartment
E15 Dash panel centre

E16 Dash panel
E17 LH rear engine
     compartment
E18 Under luggage
     compartment floor
E19 Under RH dash panel
E20 LH engine

Key to circuits

Diagram 1   Information for wiring diagrams
Diagram 2   Front and rear wash/wipe, airbag, ABS, cigarette lighter and horn
Diagram 3   Central locking, de-icing and sunroof
Diagram 4   Interior lights, headlights, sidelights, licence plate light and tail lights
Diagram 5   Headlight leveling, brake light, direction indicator lights,
               hazard warning, reverse lights, foglights and heated seats
Diagram 6   Electric mirrors, electric windows, electric rear quarter windows,
               heated rear window and mirrors
Diagram 7   Heater blower, air conditioning and radio
Diagram 8   Additional heater, rear heating, diagnostic connector, starting and charging
Diagram 9   Automatic transmission
Diagram 10   Engine management system (Petrol engines)
Diagram 11   Engine management system (Diesel engines)
Diagram 12   Instrument module
Diagram 13   Engine cooling fans

Central junction box

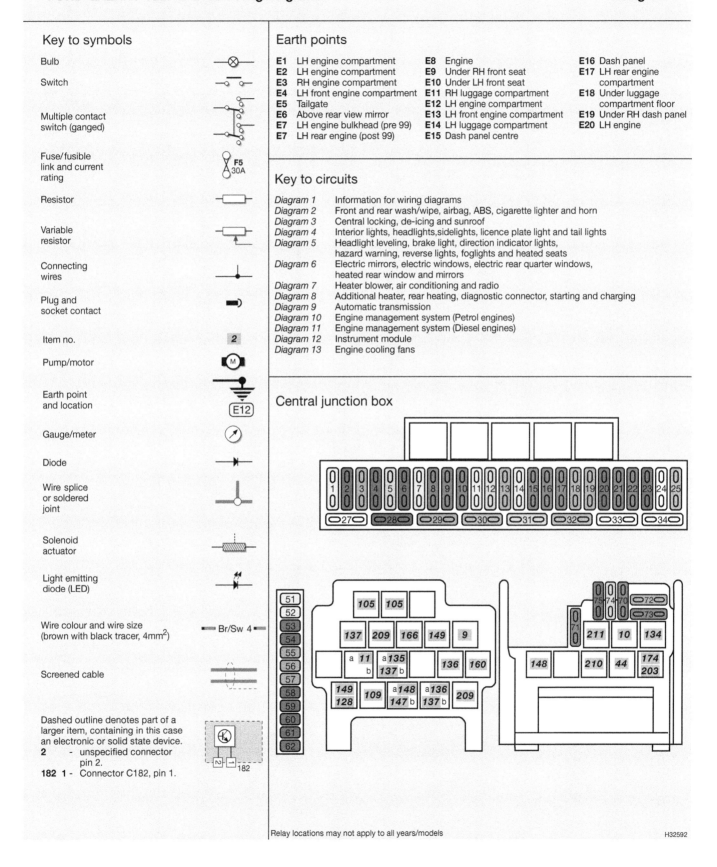

Relay locations may not apply to all years/models

H32592

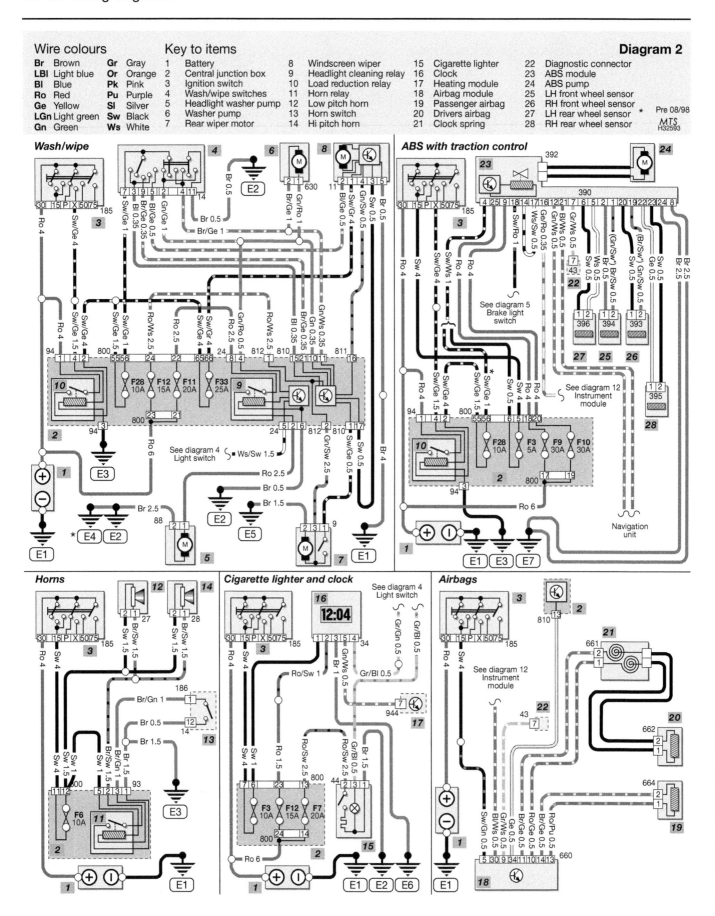

Wire colours

Br	Brown	**Gr**	Gray
LBl	Light blue	**Or**	Orange
Bl	Blue	**Pk**	Pink
Ro	Red	**Pu**	Purple
Ge	Yellow	**Sl**	Silver
LGn	Light green	**Sw**	Black
Gn	Green	**Ws**	White

Key to items

1 Battery
2 Central junction box
3 Ignition switch
4 Wash/wipe switches
5 Headlight washer pump
6 Washer pump
7 Rear wiper motor

8 Windscreen wiper
9 Headlight cleaning relay
10 Load reduction relay
11 Horn relay
12 Low pitch horn
13 Horn switch
14 Hi pitch horn

15 Cigarette lighter
16 Clock
17 Heating module
18 Airbag module
19 Passenger airbag
20 Drivers airbag
21 Clock spring

22 Diagnostic connector
23 ABS module
24 ABS pump
25 LH front wheel sensor
26 RH front wheel sensor
27 LH rear wheel sensor
28 RH rear wheel sensor

Diagram 2

Pre 08/98

MTS
H32593

Wash/wipe

ABS with traction control

Horns

Cigarette lighter and clock

Airbags

Wire colours

Br	Brown	**Gr**	Gray
LBl	Light blue	**Or**	Orange
Bl	Blue	**Pk**	Pink
Ro	Red	**Pu**	Purple
Ge	Yellow	**Sl**	Silver
LGn	Light green	**Sw**	Black
Gn	Green	**Ws**	White

Key to items

1	Battery	32	LH rear door lock unit	39	Tailgate switch (outside)
2	Central junction box	33	RH door lock switch	40	LH rear door switch
3	Ignition switch	34	LH door lock switch	41	LH front door switch
10	Load reduction relay	35	Tailgate lock switch	42	RH rear door switch
29	RH front door lock unit	36	Fuel flap filler motor	43	RH front door switch
30	LH front door lock unit	37	Tailgate motor	44	Heated windscreen relay
31	RH rear door lock unit	38	Tailgate switch (inside)	45	LH heated washer jet

46	RH heated washer jet
47	LH windscreen heater
48	RH windscreen heater
49	Windscreen/rear window heater switch
50	Sunroof switch
51	Sunroof motor unit

*   Pre 08/98
** 08/98 on

Diagram 3

MTS H32594

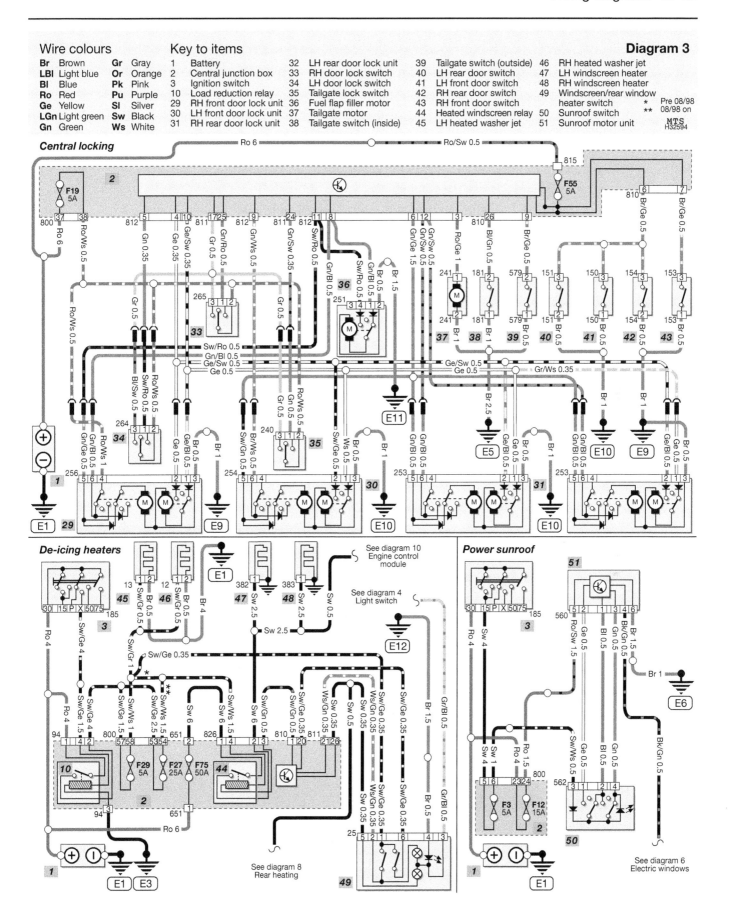

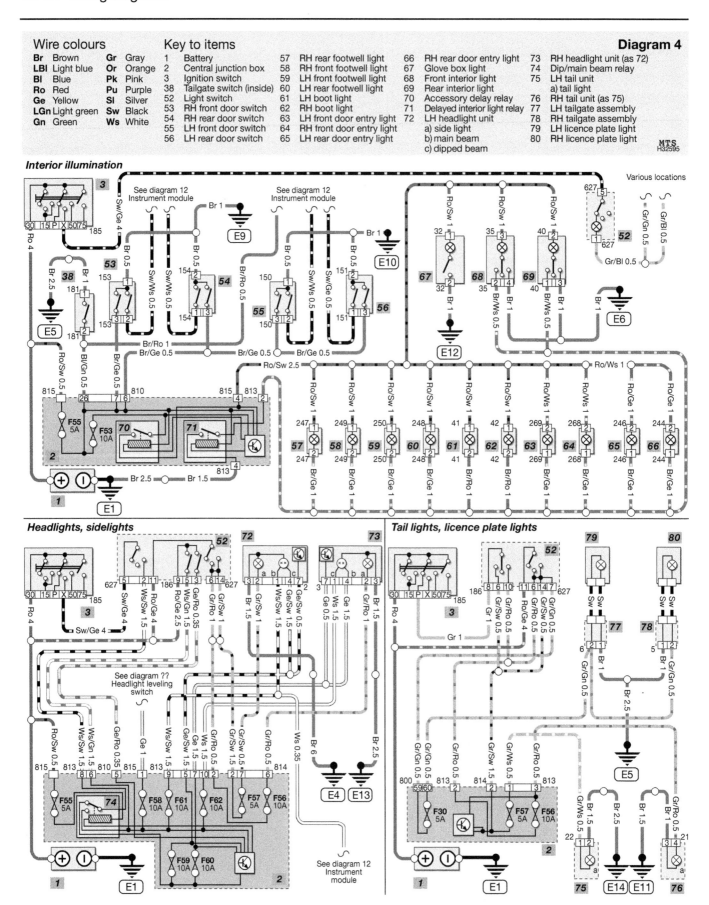

Wire colours

Br	Brown	**Gr**	Gray
LBl	Light blue	**Or**	Orange
Bl	Blue	**Pk**	Pink
Ro	Red	**Pu**	Purple
Ge	Yellow	**Sl**	Silver
LGn	Light green	**Sw**	Black
Gn	Green	**Ws**	White

Key to items

1 Battery
2 Central junction box
3 Ignition switch
38 Tailgate switch (inside)
52 Light switch
53 RH front door switch
54 RH rear door switch
55 LH front door switch
56 LH rear door switch
57 RH rear footwell light
58 RH front footwell light
59 LH front footwell light
60 LH rear footwell light
61 RH boot light
62 RH boot light
63 LH front door entry light
64 RH front door entry light
65 LH rear door entry light
66 RH rear door entry light
67 Glove box light
68 Front interior light
69 Rear interior light
70 Accessory delay relay
71 Delayed interior light relay
72 LH headlight unit
  a) side light
  b) main beam
  c) dipped beam
73 RH headlight unit (as 72)
74 Dip/main beam relay
75 LH tail unit
  a) tail light
76 RH tail unit (as 75)
77 LH tailgate assembly
78 RH tailgate assembly
79 LH licence plate light
80 RH licence plate light

Diagram 4

MTS
H32595

Interior illumination

Headlights, sidelights

Tail lights, licence plate lights

Wire colours

Br	Brown	**Gr**	Gray
LBl	Light blue	**Or**	Orange
Bl	Blue	**Pk**	Pink
Ro	Red	**Pu**	Purple
Ge	Yellow	**Sl**	Silver
LGn	Light green	**Sw**	Black
Gn	Green	**Ws**	White

Key to items

1	Battery
2	Central junction box
3	Ignition switch
52	Light switch
72	LH headlight unit
73	RH headlight unit
74	Dip/main beam relay
75	LH tail unit
	b) brake light

	c) direction indicator
76	RH tail unit (as 75)
77	LH tailgate assembly
	a) reversing light
	b) fog light
78	RH tailgate assembly
	(as 77)
81	Brake light switch
82	High level brake light

83	Gearbox switch
84	LH indicator relay
85	RH indicator relay
86	LH front indicator
87	RH front indicator
88	LH side indicator
89	RH side indicator
90	RH front foglight
91	LH front foglight

92	Rear foglight busbar
93	Heated seat control unit
94	LH seat control unit
95	RH seat control unit
96	LH seat heater
97	RH seat heater
98	LH seat back heater
99	RH seat back heater

Diagram 5

MTS
H32596

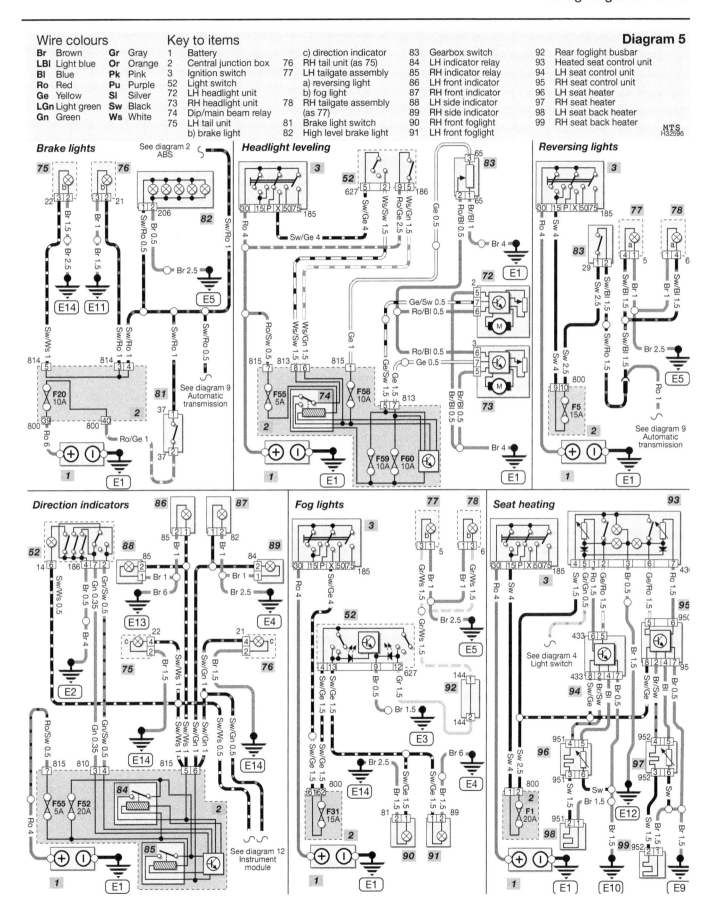

Wire colours

Br	Brown	**Gr**	Gray
LBl	Light blue	**Or**	Orange
Bl	Blue	**Pk**	Pink
Ro	Red	**Pu**	Purple
Ge	Yellow	**Sl**	Silver
LGn	Light green	**Sw**	Black
Gn	Green	**Ws**	White

Key to items

1 Battery
2 Central junction box
3 Ignition switch
100 Rear window heater relay
101 LH door mirror
102 RH door mirror
103 Rear window heater
104 Power mirror switch
105 Power mirror module
106 Rear quarter window switch
107 LH quarter window motor
108 RH quarter window motor
109 Quarter light relay
110 RH front window switch
111 LH front window switch
112 RH rear window switch
113 LH rear window switch
114 Rear window double switch
115 RH front window unit
116 LH front window unit
117 RH rear window unit
118 LH rear window unit

Diagram 6

MTS
H32597

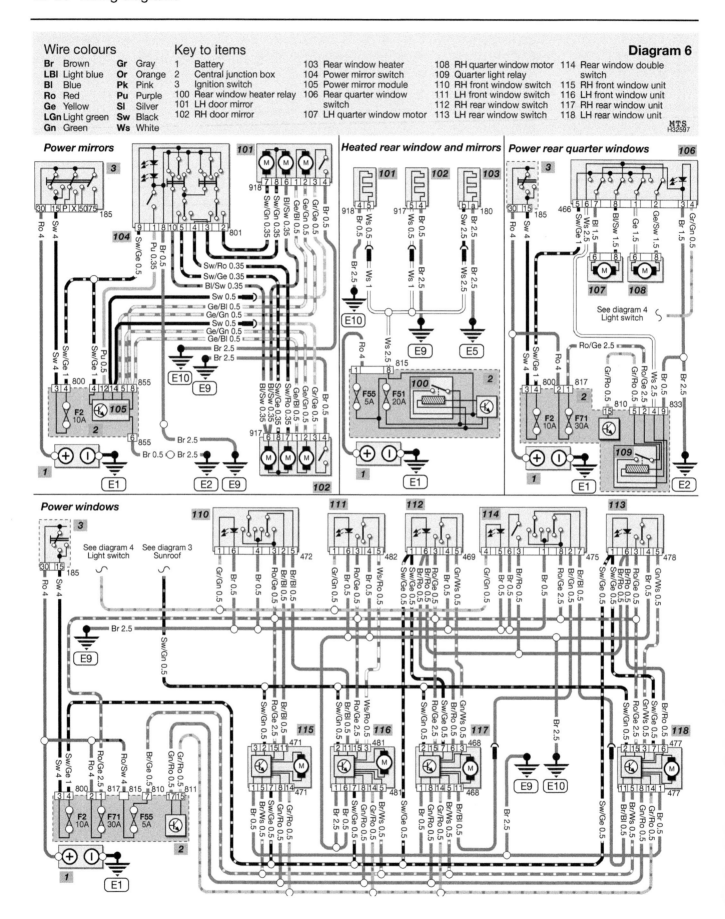

Power mirrors

Heated rear window and mirrors

Power rear quarter windows

Power windows

See diagram 4
Light switch

See diagram 3
Sunroof

Wire colours

Br	Brown	**Gr**	Gray
LBl	Light blue	**Or**	Orange
Bl	Blue	**Pk**	Pink
Ro	Red	**Pu**	Purple
Ge	Yellow	**Sl**	Silver
LGn	Light green	**Sw**	Black
Gn	Green	**Ws**	White

Key to items

1	Battery
2	Central junction box
3	Ignition switch
22	Diagnostic connector
119	Radio
120	LH dash speaker
121	RH dash speaker
122	LH front door speaker
123	RH front door speaker
124	LH rear door speaker
125	RH rear door speaker
126	LH third seat row speaker
127	RH third seat row speaker
128	Additional heater fan relay
129	Heater blower switch
130	Series resistor pack
131	Heater blower motor
132	A/C switch
133	De-icing switch
134	Power relay
135	A/C wide open throttle relay
136	Lo speed fan relay
137	Hi speed fan relay
138	Radiator fan control unit
139	Outside temperature thermo switch
140	3 way pressure switch
141	Thermo switch 3
142	A/C clutch diode
143	A/C clutch solenoid
144	Cooling fan motor
*	No additional heater
**	Additional heater only
***	A/C only

Diagram 7

MTS
H32598

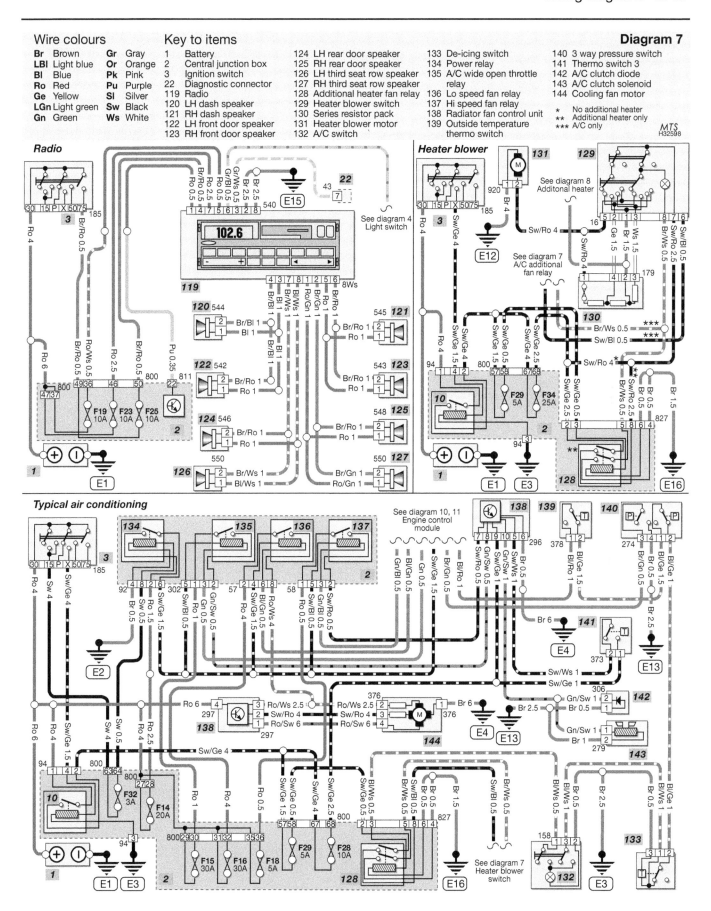

Wire colours

Br	Brown	Gr	Gray
LBl	Light blue	Or	Orange
Bl	Blue	Pk	Pink
Ro	Red	Pu	Purple
Ge	Yellow	Sl	Silver
LGn	Light green	Sw	Black
Gn	Green	Ws	White

Key to items

1 Battery
2 Central junction box
3 Ignition switch
17 Heating module
22 Diagnostic connector
145 Battery 2
146 In line fuse
147 Auxiliary battery heating cut-out relay
148 Independant heating control relay
149 Second speed blower relay
152 Outside temp thermo switch
151 Additional fuel heater pump
152 Additional water pump
153 Additional heater booster pump solenoid
154 Series resistor pack
155 Rear heater control
156 Rear blower motor
157 Auxiliary heater switch
158 Second heat exchanger motor
159 Second heat exchanger control unit
160 Alarm
161 Starter motor
162 Alternator
163 Booster heater
164 Petrol engine control module
165 Diesel engine control module

* No windscreen heater
** Windscreen heater only
*** Pre 08/98 only
**** Post 08/98 only
***** Not 2.0i or 2.3i

Diagram 8

MTS
H32599

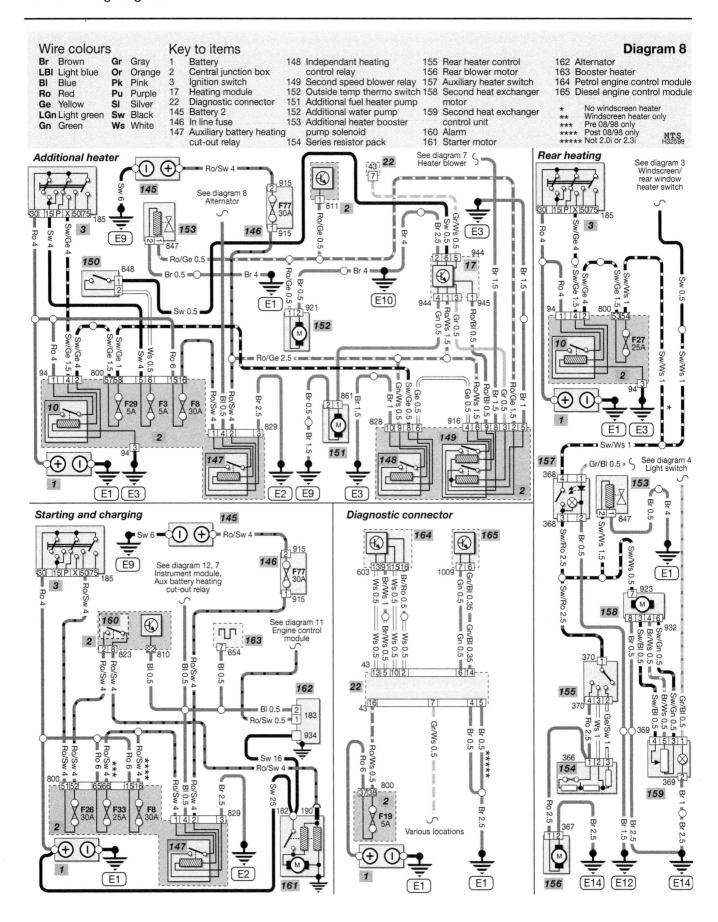

Additional heater

Rear heating

Starting and charging

Diagnostic connector

Wire colours

Br Brown
LBl Light blue
Bl Blue
Ro Red
Ge Yellow
LGn Light green
Gn Green

Gr Gray
Or Orange
Pk Pink
Pu Purple
Sl Silver
Sw Black
Ws White

Key to items

1 Battery
2 Central junction box
3 Ignition switch
22 Diagnostic connector
161 Starter motor

166 Automatic transmission relay
167 Transmission control module
168 Shift lock magnetic clutch
169 Gearshift lever
170 Transmission unit

171 Transmission speed sensor
172 Transmission range sensor
173 Kickdown switch

Diagram 9

*   2.8i only
**   Not 81kW TDi
*** 81kW TDi only

MTS
H32600

Automatic transmission and starting

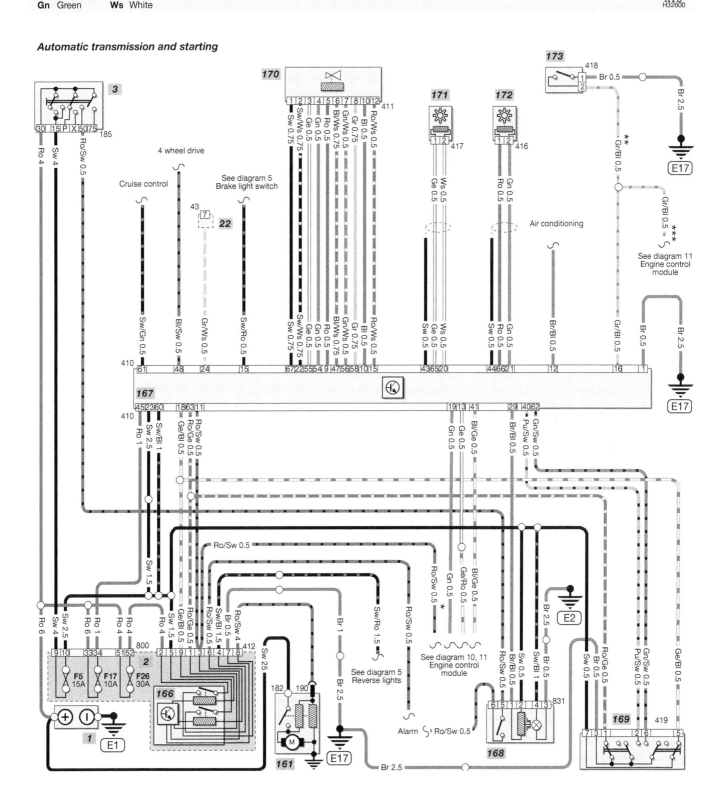

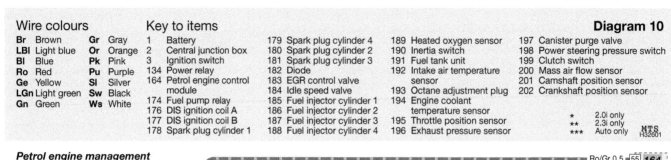

Wire colours

Br	Brown	Gr	Gray
LBl	Light blue	Or	Orange
Bl	Blue	Pk	Pink
Ro	Red	Pu	Purple
Ge	Yellow	Sl	Silver
LGn	Light green	Sw	Black
Gn	Green	Ws	White

Key to items

1 Battery
2 Central junction box
3 Ignition switch
134 Power relay
164 Petrol engine control module
174 Fuel pump relay
176 DIS ignition coil A
177 DIS ignition coil B
178 Spark plug cylinder 1
179 Spark plug cylinder 4
180 Spark plug cylinder 2
181 Spark plug cylinder 3
182 Diode
183 EGR control valve
184 Idle speed valve
185 Fuel injector cylinder 1
186 Fuel injector cylinder 2
187 Fuel injector cylinder 3
188 Fuel injector cylinder 4
189 Heated oxygen sensor
190 Inertia switch
191 Fuel tank unit
192 Intake air temperature sensor
193 Octane adjustment plug
194 Engine coolant temperature sensor
195 Throttle position sensor
196 Exhaust pressure sensor
197 Canister purge valve
198 Power steering pressure switch
199 Clutch switch
200 Mass air flow sensor
201 Camshaft position sensor
202 Crankshaft position sensor

* 2.0i only
** 2.3i only
*** Auto only

Diagram 10

MTS
H32601

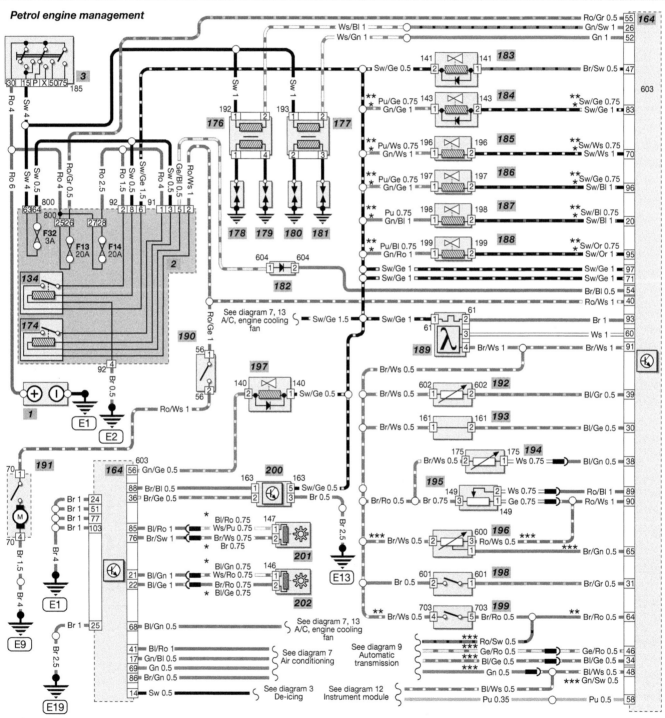

Petrol engine management

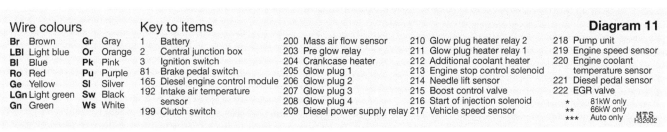

Wire colours

Br	Brown	**Gr**	Gray
LBl	Light blue	**Or**	Orange
Bl	Blue	**Pk**	Pink
Ro	Red	**Pu**	Purple
Ge	Yellow	**Sl**	Silver
LGn	Light green	**Sw**	Black
Gn	Green	**Ws**	White

Key to items

1 Battery
2 Central junction box
3 Ignition switch
81 Brake pedal switch
165 Diesel engine control module
192 Intake air temperature sensor
199 Clutch switch

200 Mass air flow sensor
203 Pre glow relay
204 Crankcase heater
205 Glow plug 1
206 Glow plug 2
207 Glow plug 3
208 Glow plug 4
209 Diesel power supply relay

210 Glow plug heater relay 2
211 Glow plug heater relay 1
212 Additional coolant heater
213 Engine stop control solenoid
214 Needle lift sensor
215 Boost control valve
216 Start of injection solenoid
217 Vehicle speed sensor

218 Pump unit
219 Engine speed sensor
220 Engine coolant temperature sensor
221 Diesel pedal sensor
222 EGR valve
* 81kW only
** 66kW only
*** Auto only

MTS
H32602

Diagram 11

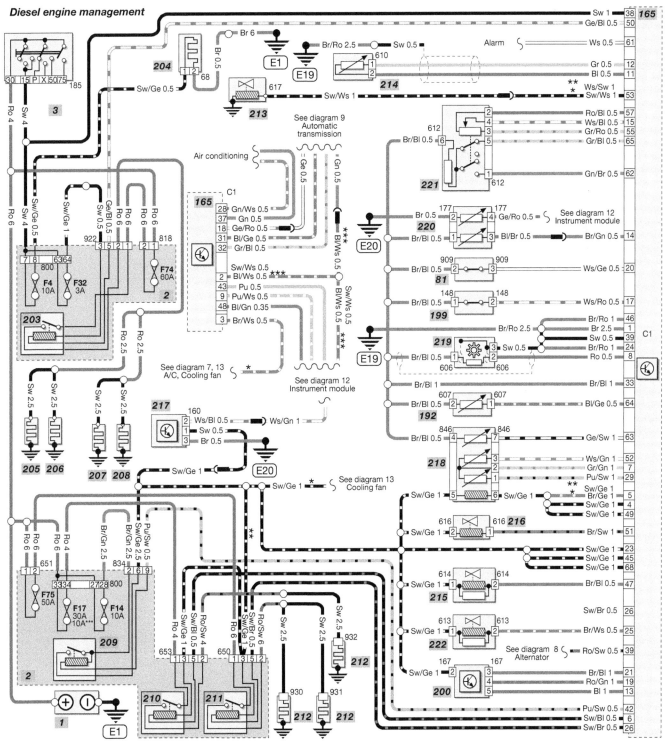

Wire colours

Br	Brown	**Gr**	Gray
LBl	Light blue	**Or**	Orange
Bl	Blue	**Pk**	Pink
Ro	Red	**Pu**	Purple
Ge	Yellow	**Sl**	Silver
LGn	Light green	**Sw**	Black
Gn	Green	**Ws**	White

Key to items

1 Battery
2 Central junction box
3 Ignition switch
22 Diagnostic connector
191 Fuel tank unit
217 Vehicle speed sensor
220 Engine coolant sensor
223 Instrument module
   a) illumination
   b) fuel gauge

c) low coolant level
d) trailer tell-tell light
e) luggage compartment open
f) RH front door open
g) LH front door open
h) LH rear door open
i) RH rear door open
j) main beam warning
k) LH indicator tell-tail
l) RH indicator tell-tail

m) ABS
n) Charge warning
o) airbag
p) temp gauge
r) glow warning
s) tachometer
t) speedometer
u) brake warning
v) oil pressure warning
224 Coolant level sensor

225 Oil temperature sensor
226 Hand brake switch
227 Brake fluid level switch
228 Low oil pressure switch
229 High oil pressure switch

* Petrol only
** Diesel only
*** 2.0i only
**** 2.3i only
***** 1.9 TDi only

Diagram 12

MTS
H32603

223

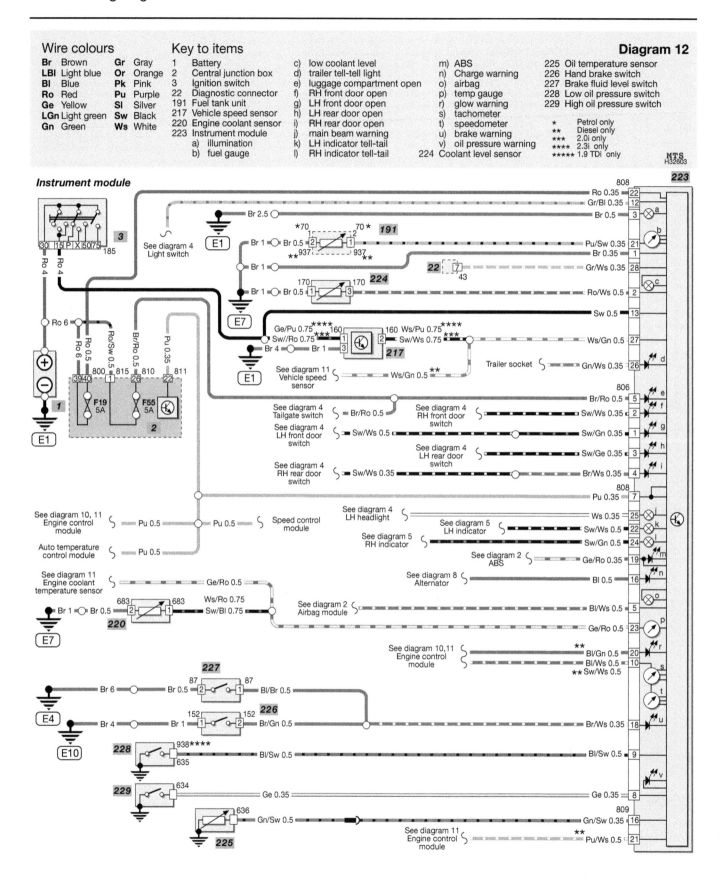

Wire colours

Br Brown
LBl Light blue
Bl Blue
Ro Red
Ge Yellow
LGn Light green
Gn Green

Gr Gray
Or Orange
Pk Pink
Pu Purple
Sl Silver
Sw Black
Ws White

Key to items

1 Battery
2 Central junction box
3 Ignition switch
136 Lo speed fan relay
137 Hi speed fan relay
138 Radiator fan control unit

144 Cooling fan motor
230 Engine cooling fan resistor
231 Cooling fan motor 2
232 Thermo switch

Diagram 13

MTS
H32604

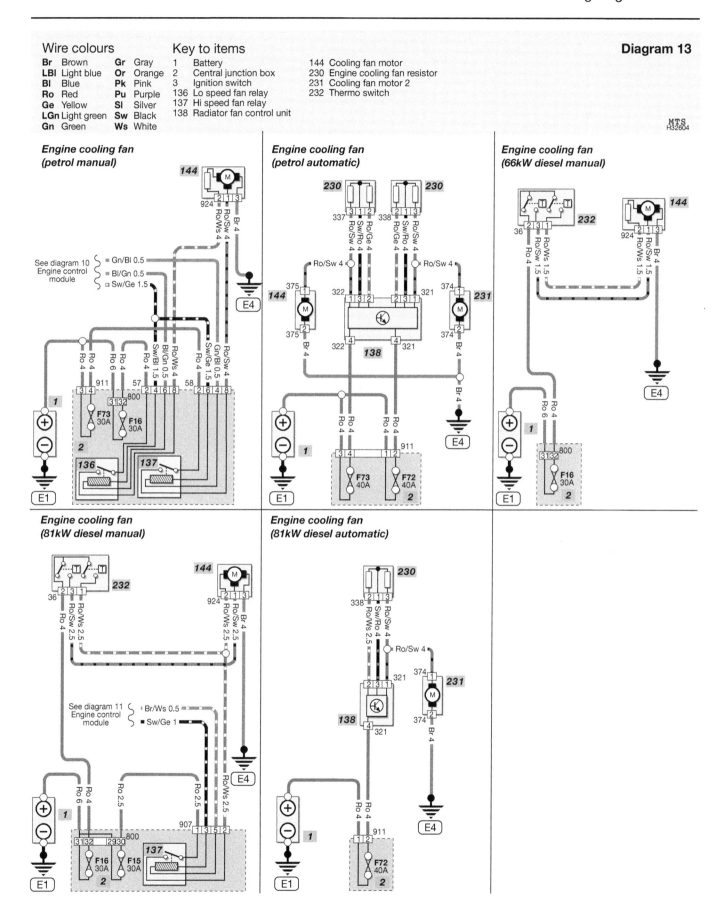

Engine cooling fan (petrol manual)

Engine cooling fan (petrol automatic)

Engine cooling fan (66kW diesel manual)

Engine cooling fan (81kW diesel manual)

Engine cooling fan (81kW diesel automatic)

Notes

Reference REF•1

Dimensions and weights

Note: *All figures are approximate, and may vary according to model. Refer to manufacturer's data for exact figures.*

Dimensions

Overall length	4620 mm
Overall width (excluding mirrors)	1810 mm
Overall height (unladen)	1730 to 1762 mm
Turning circle	11.7 m

Weights

Kerb weight:

Petrol engine models:	
2.0 litre	1665 to 1899 kg (manual)
2.3 litre	1670 to 1905 kg (manual) or 1700 to 1929 kg (automatic)
Diesel engine models	1666 to 1895 kg (manual) or 1696 to 1925 kg (automatic)
Permissible gross weight:	
2.0 litre	2400 kg
2.3 litre	2400 kg (manual) or 2450 kg (automatic)
Diesel engine models	2400 kg (manual) or 2450 kg (automatic)
Maximum roof rack load	75 kg

Conversion factors

Length (distance)
Inches (in)	x 25.4	= Millimetres (mm)	x 0.0394	=	Inches (in)
Feet (ft)	x 0.305	= Metres (m)	x 3.281	=	Feet (ft)
Miles	x 1.609	= Kilometres (km)	x 0.621	=	Miles

Volume (capacity)
Cubic inches (cu in; in³)	x 16.387	= Cubic centimetres (cc; cm³)	x 0.061	=	Cubic inches (cu in; in³)
Imperial pints (Imp pt)	x 0.568	= Litres (l)	x 1.76	=	Imperial pints (Imp pt)
Imperial quarts (Imp qt)	x 1.137	= Litres (l)	x 0.88	=	Imperial quarts (Imp qt)
Imperial quarts (Imp qt)	x 1.201	= US quarts (US qt)	x 0.833	=	Imperial quarts (Imp qt)
US quarts (US qt)	x 0.946	= Litres (l)	x 1.057	=	US quarts (US qt)
Imperial gallons (Imp gal)	x 4.546	= Litres (l)	x 0.22	=	Imperial gallons (Imp gal)
Imperial gallons (Imp gal)	x 1.201	= US gallons (US gal)	x 0.833	=	Imperial gallons (Imp gal)
US gallons (US gal)	x 3.785	= Litres (l)	x 0.264	=	US gallons (US gal)

Mass (weight)
Ounces (oz)	x 28.35	= Grams (g)	x 0.035	=	Ounces (oz)
Pounds (lb)	x 0.454	= Kilograms (kg)	x 2.205	=	Pounds (lb)

Force
Ounces-force (ozf; oz)	x 0.278	= Newtons (N)	x 3.6	=	Ounces-force (ozf; oz)
Pounds-force (lbf; lb)	x 4.448	= Newtons (N)	x 0.225	=	Pounds-force (lbf; lb)
Newtons (N)	x 0.1	= Kilograms-force (kgf; kg)	x 9.81	=	Newtons (N)

Pressure
Pounds-force per square inch (psi; lbf/in²; lb/in²)	x 0.070	= Kilograms-force per square centimetre (kgf/cm²; kg/cm²)	x 14.223	=	Pounds-force per square inch (psi; lbf/in²; lb/in²)
Pounds-force per square inch (psi; lbf/in²; lb/in²)	x 0.068	= Atmospheres (atm)	x 14.696	=	Pounds-force per square inch (psi; lbf/in²; lb/in²)
Pounds-force per square inch (psi; lbf/in²; lb/in²)	x 0.069	= Bars	x 14.5	=	Pounds-force per square inch (psi; lbf/in²; lb/in²)
Pounds-force per square inch (psi; lbf/in²; lb/in²)	x 6.895	= Kilopascals (kPa)	x 0.145	=	Pounds-force per square inch (psi; lbf/in²; lb/in²)
Kilopascals (kPa)	x 0.01	= Kilograms-force per square centimetre (kgf/cm²; kg/cm²)	x 98.1	=	Kilopascals (kPa)
Millibar (mbar)	x 100	= Pascals (Pa)	x 0.01	=	Millibar (mbar)
Millibar (mbar)	x 0.0145	= Pounds-force per square inch (psi; lbf/in²; lb/in²)	x 68.947	=	Millibar (mbar)
Millibar (mbar)	x 0.75	= Millimetres of mercury (mmHg)	x 1.333	=	Millibar (mbar)
Millibar (mbar)	x 0.401	= Inches of water (inH$_2$O)	x 2.491	=	Millibar (mbar)
Millimetres of mercury (mmHg)	x 0.535	= Inches of water (inH$_2$O)	x 1.868	=	Millimetres of mercury (mmHg)
Inches of water (inH$_2$O)	x 0.036	= Pounds-force per square inch (psi; lbf/in²; lb/in²)	x 27.68	=	Inches of water (inH$_2$O)

Torque (moment of force)
Pounds-force inches (lbf in; lb in)	x 1.152	= Kilograms-force centimetre (kgf cm; kg cm)	x 0.868	=	Pounds-force inches (lbf in; lb in)
Pounds-force inches (lbf in; lb in)	x 0.113	= Newton metres (Nm)	x 8.85	=	Pounds-force inches (lbf in; lb in)
Pounds-force inches (lbf in; lb in)	x 0.083	= Pounds-force feet (lbf ft; lb ft)	x 12	=	Pounds-force inches (lbf in; lb in)
Pounds-force feet (lbf ft; lb ft)	x 0.138	= Kilograms-force metres (kgf m; kg m)	x 7.233	=	Pounds-force feet (lbf ft; lb ft)
Pounds-force feet (lbf ft; lb ft)	x 1.356	= Newton metres (Nm)	x 0.738	=	Pounds-force feet (lbf ft; lb ft)
Newton metres (Nm)	x 0.102	= Kilograms-force metres (kgf m; kg m)	x 9.804	=	Newton metres (Nm)

Power
Horsepower (hp)	x 745.7	= Watts (W)	x 0.0013	=	Horsepower (hp)

Velocity (speed)
Miles per hour (miles/hr; mph)	x 1.609	= Kilometres per hour (km/hr; kph)	x 0.621	=	Miles per hour (miles/hr; mph)

Fuel consumption*
Miles per gallon, Imperial (mpg)	x 0.354	= Kilometres per litre (km/l)	x 2.825	=	Miles per gallon, Imperial (mpg)
Miles per gallon, US (mpg)	x 0.425	= Kilometres per litre (km/l)	x 2.352	=	Miles per gallon, US (mpg)

Temperature
Degrees Fahrenheit = (°C x 1.8) + 32   Degrees Celsius (Degrees Centigrade; °C) = (°F - 32) x 0.56

It is common practice to convert from miles per gallon (mpg) to litres/100 kilometres (l/100km), where mpg x l/100 km = 282

Spare parts are available from many sources, including maker's appointed garages, accessory shops, and motor factors. To be sure of obtaining the correct parts, it will sometimes be necessary to quote the vehicle identification number. If possible, it can also be useful to take the old parts along for positive identification. Items such as starter motors and alternators may be available under a service exchange scheme – any parts returned should be clean.

Our advice regarding spare parts is as follows.

Officially appointed garages

This is the best source of parts which are peculiar to your car, and which are not otherwise generally available (eg, badges, interior trim, certain body panels, etc). It is also the only place at which you should buy parts if the vehicle is still under warranty.

Accessory shops

These are very good places to buy materials and components needed for the maintenance of your car (oil, air and fuel filters, light bulbs, drivebelts, greases, brake pads, touch-up paint, etc). Components of this nature sold by a reputable shop are of the same standard as those used by the car manufacturer.

Besides components, these shops also sell tools and general accessories, usually have convenient opening hours, charge lower prices, and can often be found close to home. Some accessory shops have parts counters where components needed for almost any repair job can be purchased or ordered.

Motor factors

Good factors will stock all the more important components which wear out comparatively quickly, and can sometimes supply individual components needed for the overhaul of a larger assembly (eg, brake seals and hydraulic parts, bearing shells, pistons, valves). They may also handle work such as cylinder block reboring, crankshaft regrinding, etc.

Tyre and exhaust specialists

These outlets may be independent, or members of a local or national chain. They frequently offer competitive prices when compared with a main dealer or local garage, but it will pay to obtain several quotes before making a decision. When researching prices, also ask what extras may be added – for instance fitting a new valve and balancing the wheel are both commonly charged on top of the price of a new tyre.

Other sources

Beware of parts or materials obtained from market stalls, car boot sales or similar outlets. Such items are not invariably sub-standard, but there is little chance of compensation if they do prove unsatisfactory. In the case of safety-critical components such as brake pads, there is the risk not only of financial loss, but also of an accident causing injury or death.

Second-hand components or assemblies obtained from a car breaker can be a good buy in some circumstances, but this sort of purchase is best made by the experienced DIY mechanic.

Vehicle identification numbers

Modifications are a continuing and unpublicised process in vehicle manufacture, quite apart from major model changes. Spare parts manuals and lists are compiled upon a numerical basis, the individual vehicle identification numbers being essential to correct identification of the component concerned.

When ordering spare parts, always give as much information as possible. Quote the car model, year of manufacture, body and engine numbers as appropriate.

The *vehicle identification plate* is situated at the base of the left-hand side B-pillar **(see illustration)**. The *vehicle identification number* is also repeated in the form of plate visible through the windscreen on the passenger's side and on the bulkhead panelling in the centre-rear of the engine compartment **(see illustration)**.

The *engine number* is stamped on the front side of the cylinder block, adjacent to the transmission joint. Diesel engine models also have a sticker on the timing belt cover. *Other identification numbers* or codes are stamped on major items such as the gearbox, etc. These numbers are unlikely to be needed by the home mechanic.

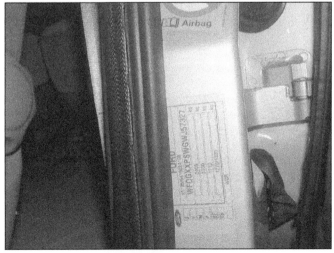

Vehicle identification plate

Vehicle identification number

Whenever servicing, repair or overhaul work is carried out on the car or its components, observe the following procedures and instructions. This will assist in carrying out the operation efficiently and to a professional standard of workmanship.

Joint mating faces and gaskets

When separating components at their mating faces, never insert screwdrivers or similar implements into the joint between the faces in order to prise them apart. This can cause severe damage which results in oil leaks, coolant leaks, etc upon reassembly. Separation is usually achieved by tapping along the joint with a soft-faced hammer in order to break the seal. However, note that this method may not be suitable where dowels are used for component location.

Where a gasket is used between the mating faces of two components, a new one must be fitted on reassembly; fit it dry unless otherwise stated in the repair procedure. Make sure that the mating faces are clean and dry, with all traces of old gasket removed. When cleaning a joint face, use a tool which is unlikely to score or damage the face, and remove any burrs or nicks with an oilstone or fine file.

Make sure that tapped holes are cleaned with a pipe cleaner, and keep them free of jointing compound, if this is being used, unless specifically instructed otherwise.

Ensure that all orifices, channels or pipes are clear, and blow through them, preferably using compressed air.

Oil seals

Oil seals can be removed by levering them out with a wide flat-bladed screwdriver or similar implement. Alternatively, a number of self-tapping screws may be screwed into the seal, and these used as a purchase for pliers or similar device in order to pull the seal free.

Whenever an oil seal is removed from its working location, either individually or as part of an assembly, it should be renewed.

The very fine sealing lip of the seal is easily damaged, and will not seal if the surface it contacts is not completely clean and free from scratches, nicks or grooves. If the original sealing surface of the component cannot be restored, and the manufacturer has not made provision for slight relocation of the seal relative to the sealing surface, the component should be renewed.

Protect the lips of the seal from any surface which may damage them in the course of fitting. Use tape or a conical sleeve where possible. Lubricate the seal lips with oil before fitting and, on dual-lipped seals, fill the space between the lips with grease.

Unless otherwise stated, oil seals must be fitted with their sealing lips toward the lubricant to be sealed.

Use a tubular drift or block of wood of the appropriate size to install the seal and, if the seal housing is shouldered, drive the seal down to the shoulder. If the seal housing is unshouldered, the seal should be fitted with its face flush with the housing top face (unless otherwise instructed).

Screw threads and fastenings

Seized nuts, bolts and screws are quite a common occurrence where corrosion has set in, and the use of penetrating oil or releasing fluid will often overcome this problem if the offending item is soaked for a while before attempting to release it. The use of an impact driver may also provide a means of releasing such stubborn fastening devices, when used in conjunction with the appropriate screwdriver bit or socket. If none of these methods works, it may be necessary to resort to the careful application of heat, or the use of a hacksaw or nut splitter device.

Studs are usually removed by locking two nuts together on the threaded part, and then using a spanner on the lower nut to unscrew the stud. Studs or bolts which have broken off below the surface of the component in which they are mounted can sometimes be removed using a stud extractor. Always ensure that a blind tapped hole is completely free from oil, grease, water or other fluid before installing the bolt or stud. Failure to do this could cause the housing to crack due to the hydraulic action of the bolt or stud as it is screwed in.

When tightening a castellated nut to accept a split pin, tighten the nut to the specified torque, where applicable, and then tighten further to the next split pin hole. Never slacken the nut to align the split pin hole, unless stated in the repair procedure.

When checking or retightening a nut or bolt to a specified torque setting, slacken the nut or bolt by a quarter of a turn, and then retighten to the specified setting. However, this should not be attempted where angular tightening has been used.

For some screw fastenings, notably cylinder head bolts or nuts, torque wrench settings are no longer specified for the latter stages of tightening, "angle-tightening" being called up instead. Typically, a fairly low torque wrench setting will be applied to the bolts/nuts in the correct sequence, followed by one or more stages of tightening through specified angles.

Locknuts, locktabs and washers

Any fastening which will rotate against a component or housing during tightening should always have a washer between it and the relevant component or housing.

Spring or split washers should always be renewed when they are used to lock a critical component such as a big-end bearing retaining bolt or nut. Locktabs which are folded over to retain a nut or bolt should always be renewed.

Self-locking nuts can be re-used in non-critical areas, providing resistance can be felt when the locking portion passes over the bolt or stud thread. However, it should be noted that self-locking stiffnuts tend to lose their effectiveness after long periods of use, and should then be renewed as a matter of course.

Split pins must always be replaced with new ones of the correct size for the hole.

When thread-locking compound is found on the threads of a fastener which is to be re-used, it should be cleaned off with a wire brush and solvent, and fresh compound applied on reassembly.

Special tools

Some repair procedures in this manual entail the use of special tools such as a press, two or three-legged pullers, spring compressors, etc. Wherever possible, suitable readily-available alternatives to the manufacturer's special tools are described, and are shown in use. In some instances, where no alternative is possible, it has been necessary to resort to the use of a manufacturer's tool, and this has been done for reasons of safety as well as the efficient completion of the repair operation. Unless you are highly-skilled and have a thorough understanding of the procedures described, never attempt to bypass the use of any special tool when the procedure described specifies its use. Not only is there a very great risk of personal injury, but expensive damage could be caused to the components involved.

Environmental considerations

When disposing of used engine oil, brake fluid, antifreeze, etc, give due consideration to any detrimental environmental effects. Do not, for instance, pour any of the above liquids down drains into the general sewage system, or onto the ground to soak away. Many local council refuse tips provide a facility for waste oil disposal, as do some garages. If none of these facilities are available, consult your local Environmental Health Department, or the National Rivers Authority, for further advice.

With the universal tightening-up of legislation regarding the emission of environmentally-harmful substances from motor vehicles, most vehicles have tamperproof devices fitted to the main adjustment points of the fuel system. These devices are primarily designed to prevent unqualified persons from adjusting the fuel/air mixture, with the chance of a consequent increase in toxic emissions. If such devices are found during servicing or overhaul, they should, wherever possible, be renewed or refitted in accordance with the manufacturer's requirements or current legislation.

OIL CARE
FOLLOW THE CODE

OIL BANK LINE
0800 66 33 66
www.oilbankline.org.uk

Note: It is antisocial and illegal to dump oil down the drain. To find the location of your local oil recycling bank, call this number free.

The jack supplied with the vehicle tool kit should only be used for changing the roadwheels – see *Wheel changing* at the front of this manual. When carrying out any other kind of work, raise the vehicle using a hydraulic trolley jack, and always supplement the jack with axle stands positioned under the vehicle jacking points.

When using a trolley jack or axle stands, always position the jack head or axle stand head under, or adjacent to one of the relevant wheel changing jacking points under the sills **(see illustration)**. Use a block of wood between the jack or axle stand and the sill.

Do not attempt to jack the vehicle under the front crossmember, the sump, or any of the suspension components.

The jack supplied with the vehicle locates in the jacking points on the underside of the sills – see *Wheel changing* at the front of this manual. Ensure that the jack head is correctly engaged before attempting to raise the vehicle.

Never work under, around, or near a raised vehicle, unless it is adequately supported in at least two places.

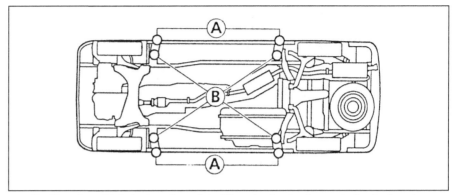

Position the vehicle jack under points (A), and axle stands or a trolley jack under points (B)

Radio/cassette unit anti-theft system – precaution

The radio/cassette unit fitted as standard equipment by Ford is equipped with a built-in security code to deter thieves. If the power source to the unit is cut, the anti-theft system will activate. Even if the power source is immediately reconnected, the radio/cassette unit will not function until the correct security code has been entered. Therefore, if you do not know the correct security code for the unit, do not disconnect the battery negative lead, or remove the radio/cassette unit from the vehicle.

Introduction

A selection of good tools is a fundamental requirement for anyone contemplating the maintenance and repair of a motor vehicle. For the owner who does not possess any, their purchase will prove a considerable expense, offsetting some of the savings made by doing-it-yourself. However, provided that the tools purchased meet the relevant national safety standards and are of good quality, they will last for many years and prove an extremely worthwhile investment.

To help the average owner to decide which tools are needed to carry out the various tasks detailed in this manual, we have compiled three lists of tools under the following headings: *Maintenance and minor repair, Repair and overhaul*, and *Special*. Newcomers to practical mechanics should start off with the *Maintenance and minor repair* tool kit, and confine themselves to the simpler jobs around the vehicle. Then, as confidence and experience grow, more difficult tasks can be undertaken, with extra tools being purchased as, and when, they are needed. In this way, a *Maintenance and minor repair* tool kit can be built up into a *Repair and overhaul* tool kit over a considerable period of time, without any major cash outlays. The experienced do-it-yourselfer will have a tool kit good enough for most repair and overhaul procedures, and will add tools from the *Special* category when it is felt that the expense is justified by the amount of use to which these tools will be put.

Maintenance and minor repair tool kit

The tools given in this list should be considered as a minimum requirement if routine maintenance, servicing and minor repair operations are to be undertaken. We recommend the purchase of combination spanners (ring one end, open-ended the other); although more expensive than open-ended ones, they do give the advantages of both types of spanner.

☐ *Combination spanners:*
  Metric - 8 to 19 mm inclusive
☐ *Adjustable spanner - 35 mm jaw (approx.)*
☐ *Spark plug spanner (with rubber insert) - petrol models*
☐ *Spark plug gap adjustment tool - petrol models*
☐ *Set of feeler gauges*
☐ *Brake bleed nipple spanner*
☐ *Screwdrivers:*
  Flat blade - 100 mm long x 6 mm dia
  Cross blade - 100 mm long x 6 mm dia
  Torx - various sizes (not all vehicles)
☐ *Combination pliers*
☐ *Hacksaw (junior)*
☐ *Tyre pump*
☐ *Tyre pressure gauge*
☐ *Oil can*
☐ *Oil filter removal tool*
☐ *Fine emery cloth*
☐ *Wire brush (small)*
☐ *Funnel (medium size)*
☐ *Sump drain plug key (not all vehicles)*

Repair and overhaul tool kit

These tools are virtually essential for anyone undertaking any major repairs to a motor vehicle, and are additional to those given in the *Maintenance and minor repair* list. Included in this list is a comprehensive set of sockets. Although these are expensive, they will be found invaluable as they are so versatile - particularly if various drives are included in the set. We recommend the half-inch square-drive type, as this can be used with most proprietary torque wrenches.

The tools in this list will sometimes need to be supplemented by tools from the *Special* list:

☐ *Sockets (or box spanners) to cover range in previous list (including Torx sockets)*
☐ *Reversible ratchet drive (for use with sockets)*
☐ *Extension piece, 250 mm (for use with sockets)*
☐ *Universal joint (for use with sockets)*
☐ *Flexible handle or sliding T "breaker bar" (for use with sockets)*
☐ *Torque wrench (for use with sockets)*
☐ *Self-locking grips*
☐ *Ball pein hammer*
☐ *Soft-faced mallet (plastic or rubber)*
☐ *Screwdrivers:*
  Flat blade - long & sturdy, short (chubby), and narrow (electrician's) types
  Cross blade – long & sturdy, and short (chubby) types
☐ *Pliers:*
  Long-nosed
  Side cutters (electrician's)
  Circlip (internal and external)
☐ *Cold chisel - 25 mm*
☐ *Scriber*
☐ *Scraper*
☐ *Centre-punch*
☐ *Pin punch*
☐ *Hacksaw*
☐ *Brake hose clamp*
☐ *Brake/clutch bleeding kit*
☐ *Selection of twist drills*
☐ *Steel rule/straight-edge*
☐ *Allen keys (inc. splined/Torx type)*
☐ *Selection of files*
☐ *Wire brush*
☐ *Axle stands*
☐ *Jack (strong trolley or hydraulic type)*
☐ *Light with extension lead*
☐ *Universal electrical multi-meter*

Sockets and reversible ratchet drive

Brake bleeding kit

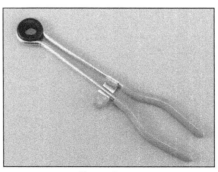

Hose clamp

Angular-tightening gauge

Torx key, socket and bit

Special tools

The tools in this list are those which are not used regularly, are expensive to buy, or which need to be used in accordance with their manufacturers' instructions. Unless relatively difficult mechanical jobs are undertaken frequently, it will not be economic to buy many of these tools. Where this is the case, you could consider clubbing together with friends (or joining a motorists' club) to make a joint purchase, or borrowing the tools against a deposit from a local garage or tool hire specialist. It is worth noting that many of the larger DIY superstores now carry a large range of special tools for hire at modest rates.

The following list contains only those tools and instruments freely available to the public, and not those special tools produced by the vehicle manufacturer specifically for its dealer network. You will find occasional references to these manufacturers' special tools in the text of this manual. Generally, an alternative method of doing the job without the vehicle manufacturers' special tool is given. However, sometimes there is no alternative to using them. Where this is the case and the relevant tool cannot be bought or borrowed, you will have to entrust the work to a dealer.

☐ *Angular-tightening gauge*
☐ *Valve spring compressor*
☐ *Valve grinding tool*
☐ *Piston ring compressor*
☐ *Piston ring removal/installation tool*
☐ *Cylinder bore hone*
☐ *Balljoint separator*
☐ *Coil spring compressors (where applicable)*
☐ *Two/three-legged hub and bearing puller*
☐ *Impact screwdriver*
☐ *Micrometer and/or vernier calipers*
☐ *Dial gauge*
☐ *Stroboscopic timing light*
☐ *Dwell angle meter/tachometer*
☐ *Fault code reader*
☐ *Cylinder compression gauge*
☐ *Hand-operated vacuum pump and gauge*
☐ *Clutch plate alignment set*
☐ *Brake shoe steady spring cup removal tool*
☐ *Bush and bearing removal/installation set*
☐ *Stud extractors*
☐ *Tap and die set*
☐ *Lifting tackle*
☐ *Trolley jack*

Buying tools

Reputable motor accessory shops and superstores often offer excellent quality tools at discount prices, so it pays to shop around.

Remember, you don't have to buy the most expensive items on the shelf, but it is always advisable to steer clear of the very cheap tools. Beware of 'bargains' offered on market stalls or at car boot sales. There are plenty of good tools around at reasonable prices, but always aim to purchase items which meet the relevant national safety standards. If in doubt, ask the proprietor or manager of the shop for advice before making a purchase.

Care and maintenance of tools

Having purchased a reasonable tool kit, it is necessary to keep the tools in a clean and serviceable condition. After use, always wipe off any dirt, grease and metal particles using a clean, dry cloth, before putting the tools away. Never leave them lying around after they have been used. A simple tool rack on the garage or workshop wall for items such as screwdrivers and pliers is a good idea. Store all normal spanners and sockets in a metal box. Any measuring instruments, gauges, meters, etc, must be carefully stored where they cannot be damaged or become rusty.

Take a little care when tools are used. Hammer heads inevitably become marked, and screwdrivers lose the keen edge on their blades from time to time. A little timely attention with emery cloth or a file will soon restore items like this to a good finish.

Working facilities

Not to be forgotten when discussing tools is the workshop itself. If anything more than routine maintenance is to be carried out, a suitable working area becomes essential.

It is appreciated that many an owner-mechanic is forced by circumstances to remove an engine or similar item without the benefit of a garage or workshop. Having done this, any repairs should always be done under the cover of a roof.

Wherever possible, any dismantling should be done on a clean, flat workbench or table at a suitable working height.

Any workbench needs a vice; one with a jaw opening of 100 mm is suitable for most jobs. As mentioned previously, some clean dry storage space is also required for tools, as well as for any lubricants, cleaning fluids, touch-up paints etc, which become necessary.

Another item which may be required, and which has a much more general usage, is an electric drill with a chuck capacity of at least 8 mm. This, together with a good range of twist drills, is virtually essential for fitting accessories.

Last, but not least, always keep a supply of old newspapers and clean, lint-free rags available, and try to keep any working area as clean as possible.

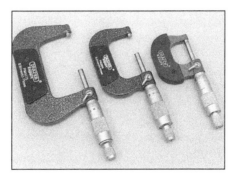

Micrometers

Dial test indicator ("dial gauge")

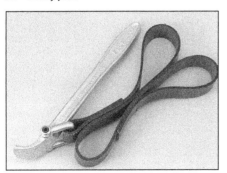

Strap wrench

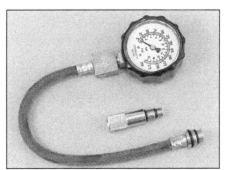

Compression tester

Fault code reader

This is a guide to getting your vehicle through the MOT test. Obviously it will not be possible to examine the vehicle to the same standard as the professional MOT tester. However, working through the following checks will enable you to identify any problem areas before submitting the vehicle for the test.

Where a testable component is in borderline condition, the tester has discretion in deciding whether to pass or fail it. The basis of such discretion is whether the tester would be happy for a close relative or friend to use the vehicle with the component in that condition. If the vehicle presented is clean and evidently well cared for, the tester may be more inclined to pass a borderline component than if the vehicle is scruffy and apparently neglected.

It has only been possible to summarise the test requirements here, based on the regulations in force at the time of printing. Test standards are becoming increasingly stringent, although there are some exemptions for older vehicles.

An assistant will be needed to help carry out some of these checks.

The checks have been sub-divided into four categories, as follows:

1 Checks carried out **FROM THE DRIVER'S SEAT**

2 Checks carried out **WITH THE VEHICLE ON THE GROUND**

3 Checks carried out **WITH THE VEHICLE RAISED AND THE WHEELS FREE TO TURN**

4 Checks carried out on **YOUR VEHICLE'S EXHAUST EMISSION SYSTEM**

1 Checks carried out **FROM THE DRIVER'S SEAT**

Handbrake

☐ Test the operation of the handbrake. Excessive travel (too many clicks) indicates incorrect brake or cable adjustment.

☐ Check that the handbrake cannot be released by tapping the lever sideways. Check the security of the lever mountings.

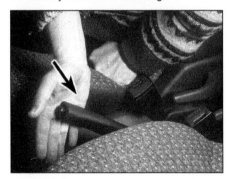

Footbrake

☐ Depress the brake pedal and check that it does not creep down to the floor, indicating a master cylinder fault. Release the pedal, wait a few seconds, then depress it again. If the pedal travels nearly to the floor before firm resistance is felt, brake adjustment or repair is necessary. If the pedal feels spongy, there is air in the hydraulic system which must be removed by bleeding.

☐ Check that the brake pedal is secure and in good condition. Check also for signs of fluid leaks on the pedal, floor or carpets, which would indicate failed seals in the brake master cylinder.

☐ Check the servo unit (when applicable) by operating the brake pedal several times, then keeping the pedal depressed and starting the engine. As the engine starts, the pedal will move down slightly. If not, the vacuum hose or the servo itself may be faulty.

Steering wheel and column

☐ Examine the steering wheel for fractures or looseness of the hub, spokes or rim.

☐ Move the steering wheel from side to side and then up and down. Check that the steering wheel is not loose on the column, indicating wear or a loose retaining nut. Continue moving the steering wheel as before, but also turn it slightly from left to right.

☐ Check that the steering wheel is not loose on the column, and that there is no abnormal

movement of the steering wheel, indicating wear in the column support bearings or couplings.

Windscreen, mirrors and sunvisor

☐ The windscreen must be free of cracks or other significant damage within the driver's field of view. (Small stone chips are acceptable.) Rear view mirrors must be secure, intact, and capable of being adjusted.

☐ The driver's sunvisor must be capable of being stored in the "up" position.

Seat belts and seats

Note: *The following checks are applicable to all seat belts, front and rear.*

☐ Examine the webbing of all the belts (including rear belts if fitted) for cuts, serious fraying or deterioration. Fasten and unfasten each belt to check the buckles. If applicable, check the retracting mechanism. Check the security of all seat belt mountings accessible from inside the vehicle.

☐ Seat belts with pre-tensioners, once activated, have a "flag" or similar showing on the seat belt stalk. This, in itself, is not a reason for test failure.

☐ The front seats themselves must be securely attached and the backrests must lock in the upright position.

Doors

☐ Both front doors must be able to be opened and closed from outside and inside, and must latch securely when closed.

2 Checks carried out WITH THE VEHICLE ON THE GROUND

Vehicle identification

☐ Number plates must be in good condition, secure and legible, with letters and numbers correctly spaced – spacing at (A) should be at least twice that at (B).

☐ The VIN plate and/or homologation plate must be legible.

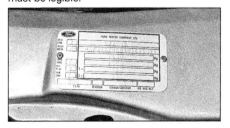

Electrical equipment

☐ Switch on the ignition and check the operation of the horn.

☐ Check the windscreen washers and wipers, examining the wiper blades; renew damaged or perished blades. Also check the operation of the stop-lights.

☐ Check the operation of the sidelights and number plate lights. The lenses and reflectors must be secure, clean and undamaged.

☐ Check the operation and alignment of the headlights. The headlight reflectors must not be tarnished and the lenses must be undamaged.

☐ Switch on the ignition and check the operation of the direction indicators (including the instrument panel tell-tale) and the hazard warning lights. Operation of the sidelights and stop-lights must not affect the indicators - if it does, the cause is usually a bad earth at the rear light cluster.

☐ Check the operation of the rear foglight(s), including the warning light on the instrument panel or in the switch.

☐ The ABS warning light must illuminate in accordance with the manufacturers' design. For most vehicles, the ABS warning light should illuminate when the ignition is switched on, and (if the system is operating properly) extinguish after a few seconds. Refer to the owner's handbook.

Footbrake

☐ Examine the master cylinder, brake pipes and servo unit for leaks, loose mountings, corrosion or other damage.

☐ The fluid reservoir must be secure and the fluid level must be between the upper (A) and lower (B) markings.

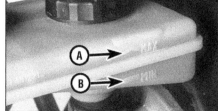

☐ Inspect both front brake flexible hoses for cracks or deterioration of the rubber. Turn the steering from lock to lock, and ensure that the hoses do not contact the wheel, tyre, or any part of the steering or suspension mechanism. With the brake pedal firmly depressed, check the hoses for bulges or leaks under pressure.

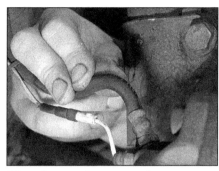

Steering and suspension

☐ Have your assistant turn the steering wheel from side to side slightly, up to the point where the steering gear just begins to transmit this movement to the roadwheels. Check for excessive free play between the steering wheel and the steering gear, indicating wear or insecurity of the steering column joints, the column-to-steering gear coupling, or the steering gear itself.

☐ Have your assistant turn the steering wheel more vigorously in each direction, so that the roadwheels just begin to turn. As this is done, examine all the steering joints, linkages, fittings and attachments. Renew any component that shows signs of wear or damage. On vehicles with power steering, check the security and condition of the steering pump, drivebelt and hoses.

☐ Check that the vehicle is standing level, and at approximately the correct ride height.

Shock absorbers

☐ Depress each corner of the vehicle in turn, then release it. The vehicle should rise and then settle in its normal position. If the vehicle continues to rise and fall, the shock absorber is defective. A shock absorber which has seized will also cause the vehicle to fail.

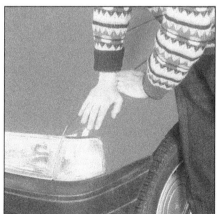

Exhaust system

☐ Start the engine. With your assistant holding a rag over the tailpipe, check the entire system for leaks. Repair or renew leaking sections.

3 Checks carried out
WITH THE VEHICLE RAISED AND THE WHEELS FREE TO TURN

Jack up the front and rear of the vehicle, and securely support it on axle stands. Position the stands clear of the suspension assemblies. Ensure that the wheels are clear of the ground and that the steering can be turned from lock to lock.

Steering mechanism

☐ Have your assistant turn the steering from lock to lock. Check that the steering turns smoothly, and that no part of the steering mechanism, including a wheel or tyre, fouls any brake hose or pipe or any part of the body structure.
☐ Examine the steering rack rubber gaiters for damage or insecurity of the retaining clips. If power steering is fitted, check for signs of damage or leakage of the fluid hoses, pipes or connections. Also check for excessive stiffness or binding of the steering, a missing split pin or locking device, or severe corrosion of the body structure within 30 cm of any steering component attachment point.

Front and rear suspension and wheel bearings

☐ Starting at the front right-hand side, grasp the roadwheel at the 3 o'clock and 9 o'clock positions and rock gently but firmly. Check for free play or insecurity at the wheel bearings, suspension balljoints, or suspension mountings, pivots and attachments.
☐ Now grasp the wheel at the 12 o'clock and 6 o'clock positions and repeat the previous inspection. Spin the wheel, and check for roughness or tightness of the front wheel bearing.

☐ If excess free play is suspected at a component pivot point, this can be confirmed by using a large screwdriver or similar tool and levering between the mounting and the component attachment. This will confirm whether the wear is in the pivot bush, its retaining bolt, or in the mounting itself (the bolt holes can often become elongated).

☐ Carry out all the above checks at the other front wheel, and then at both rear wheels.

Springs and shock absorbers

☐ Examine the suspension struts (when applicable) for serious fluid leakage, corrosion, or damage to the casing. Also check the security of the mounting points.
☐ If coil springs are fitted, check that the spring ends locate in their seats, and that the spring is not corroded, cracked or broken.
☐ If leaf springs are fitted, check that all leaves are intact, that the axle is securely attached to each spring, and that there is no deterioration of the spring eye mountings, bushes, and shackles.

☐ The same general checks apply to vehicles fitted with other suspension types, such as torsion bars, hydraulic displacer units, etc. Ensure that all mountings and attachments are secure, that there are no signs of excessive wear, corrosion or damage, and (on hydraulic types) that there are no fluid leaks or damaged pipes.
☐ Inspect the shock absorbers for signs of serious fluid leakage. Check for wear of the mounting bushes or attachments, or damage to the body of the unit.

Driveshafts (fwd vehicles only)

☐ Rotate each front wheel in turn and inspect the constant velocity joint gaiters for splits or damage. Also check that each driveshaft is straight and undamaged.

Braking system

☐ If possible without dismantling, check brake pad wear and disc condition. Ensure that the friction lining material has not worn excessively, (A) and that the discs are not fractured, pitted, scored or badly worn (B).

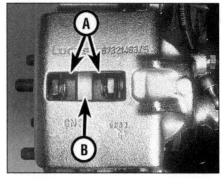

☐ Examine all the rigid brake pipes underneath the vehicle, and the flexible hose(s) at the rear. Look for corrosion, chafing or insecurity of the pipes, and for signs of bulging under pressure, chafing, splits or deterioration of the flexible hoses.
☐ Look for signs of fluid leaks at the brake calipers or on the brake backplates. Repair or renew leaking components.
☐ Slowly spin each wheel, while your assistant depresses and releases the footbrake. Ensure that each brake is operating and does not bind when the pedal is released.

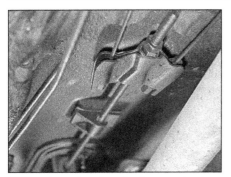

☐ Examine the handbrake mechanism, checking for frayed or broken cables, excessive corrosion, or wear or insecurity of the linkage. Check that the mechanism works on each relevant wheel, and releases fully, without binding.

☐ It is not possible to test brake efficiency without special equipment, but a road test can be carried out later to check that the vehicle pulls up in a straight line.

Fuel and exhaust systems

☐ Inspect the fuel tank (including the filler cap), fuel pipes, hoses and unions. All components must be secure and free from leaks.

☐ Examine the exhaust system over its entire length, checking for any damaged, broken or missing mountings, security of the retaining clamps and rust or corrosion.

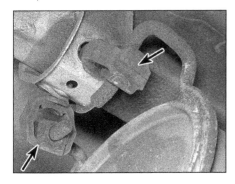

Wheels and tyres

☐ Examine the sidewalls and tread area of each tyre in turn. Check for cuts, tears, lumps, bulges, separation of the tread, and exposure of the ply or cord due to wear or damage. Check that the tyre bead is correctly seated on the wheel rim, that the valve is sound and properly seated, and that the wheel is not distorted or damaged.

☐ Check that the tyres are of the correct size for the vehicle, that they are of the same size and type on each axle, and that the pressures are correct.

☐ Check the tyre tread depth. The legal minimum at the time of writing is 1.6 mm over at least three-quarters of the tread width. Abnormal tread wear may indicate incorrect front wheel alignment.

Body corrosion

☐ Check the condition of the entire vehicle structure for signs of corrosion in load-bearing areas. (These include chassis box sections, side sills, cross-members, pillars, and all suspension, steering, braking system and seat belt mountings and anchorages.) Any corrosion which has seriously reduced the thickness of a load-bearing area is likely to cause the vehicle to fail. In this case professional repairs are likely to be needed.

☐ Damage or corrosion which causes sharp or otherwise dangerous edges to be exposed will also cause the vehicle to fail.

4 Checks carried out on **YOUR VEHICLE'S EXHAUST EMISSION SYSTEM**

Petrol models

☐ Have the engine at normal operating temperature, and make sure that it is in good tune (ignition system in good order, air filter element clean, etc).

☐ Before any measurements are carried out, raise the engine speed to around 2500 rpm, and hold it at this speed for 20 seconds. Allow the engine speed to return to idle, and watch for smoke emissions from the exhaust tailpipe. If the idle speed is obviously much too high, or if dense blue or clearly-visible black smoke comes from the tailpipe for more than 5 seconds, the vehicle will fail. As a rule of thumb, blue smoke signifies oil being burnt (engine wear) while black smoke signifies unburnt fuel (dirty air cleaner element, or other carburettor or fuel system fault).

☐ An exhaust gas analyser capable of measuring carbon monoxide (CO) and hydrocarbons (HC) is now needed. If such an instrument cannot be hired or borrowed, a local garage may agree to perform the check for a small fee.

CO emissions (mixture)

☐ At the time of writing, for vehicles first used between 1st August 1975 and 31st July 1986 (P to C registration), the CO level must not exceed 4.5% by volume. For vehicles first used between 1st August 1986 and 31st July 1992 (D to J registration), the CO level must not exceed 3.5% by volume. Vehicles first

used after 1st August 1992 (K registration) must conform to the manufacturer's specification. The MOT tester has access to a DOT database or emissions handbook, which lists the CO and HC limits for each make and model of vehicle. The CO level is measured with the engine at idle speed, and at "fast idle". The following limits are given as a general guide:

> *At idle speed -*
> CO level no more than 0.5%
> *At "fast idle" (2500 to 3000 rpm) -*
> CO level no more than 0.3%
> (Minimum oil temperature 60°C)

☐ If the CO level cannot be reduced far enough to pass the test (and the fuel and ignition systems are otherwise in good condition) then the carburettor is badly worn, or there is some problem in the fuel injection system or catalytic converter (as applicable).

HC emissions

☐ With the CO within limits, HC emissions for vehicles first used between 1st August 1975 and 31st July 1992 (P to J registration) must not exceed 1200 ppm. Vehicles first used after 1st August 1992 (K registration) must conform to the manufacturer's specification. The MOT tester has access to a DOT database or emissions handbook, which lists the CO and HC limits for each make and model of vehicle. The HC level is measured with the engine at "fast idle". The following is given as a general guide:

> *At "fast idle" (2500 to 3000 rpm) -*
> HC level no more than 200 ppm
> (Minimum oil temperature 60°C)

☐ Excessive HC emissions are caused by incomplete combustion, the causes of which can include oil being burnt, mechanical wear and ignition/fuel system malfunction.

Diesel models

☐ The only emission test applicable to Diesel engines is the measuring of exhaust smoke density. The test involves accelerating the engine several times to its maximum unloaded speed.

Note: *It is of the utmost importance that the engine timing belt is in good condition before the test is carried out.*

☐ The limits for Diesel engine exhaust smoke, introduced in September 1995 are:
Vehicles first used before 1st August 1979:
> Exempt from metered smoke testing, but must not emit "dense blue or clearly visible black smoke for a period of more than 5 seconds at idle" or "dense blue or clearly visible black smoke during acceleration which would obscure the view of other road users".
Non-turbocharged vehicles first used after 1st August 1979: 2.5m-1
Turbocharged vehicles first used after 1st August 1979: 3.0m-1

☐ Excessive smoke can be caused by a dirty air cleaner element. Otherwise, professional advice may be needed to find the cause.

Engine

- ☐ Engine fails to rotate when attempting to start
- ☐ Engine rotates, but will not start
- ☐ Engine difficult to start when cold
- ☐ Engine difficult to start when hot
- ☐ Starter motor noisy or excessively-rough in engagement
- ☐ Engine starts, but stops immediately
- ☐ Engine idles erratically
- ☐ Engine misfires at idle speed
- ☐ Engine misfires throughout the driving speed range
- ☐ Engine hesitates on acceleration
- ☐ Engine stalls
- ☐ Engine lacks power
- ☐ Engine backfires
- ☐ Oil pressure warning light illuminated with engine running
- ☐ Engine runs-on after switching off
- ☐ Engine noises

Cooling system

- ☐ Overheating
- ☐ Overcooling
- ☐ External coolant leakage
- ☐ Internal coolant leakage
- ☐ Corrosion

Fuel and exhaust systems

- ☐ Excessive fuel consumption
- ☐ Fuel leakage and/or fuel odour
- ☐ Excessive noise or fumes from exhaust system

Clutch

- ☐ Pedal travels to floor – no pressure or very little resistance
- ☐ Clutch fails to disengage (unable to select gears)
- ☐ Clutch slips (engine speed increases, with no increase in vehicle speed)
- ☐ Judder as clutch is engaged
- ☐ Noise when depressing or releasing clutch pedal

Manual transmission

- ☐ Noisy in neutral with engine running
- ☐ Noisy in one particular gear
- ☐ Difficulty engaging gears
- ☐ Jumps out of gear
- ☐ Vibration
- ☐ Lubricant leaks

Automatic transmission

- ☐ Fluid leakage
- ☐ General gear selection problems
- ☐ Transmission will not downshift (kickdown) with accelerator pedal fully depressed
- ☐ Engine will not start in any gear, or starts in gears other than Park or Neutral
- ☐ Transmission slips, shifts roughly, is noisy, or has no drive in forward or reverse gears

Driveshafts

- ☐ Vibration when accelerating or decelerating
- ☐ Clicking or knocking noise on turns (at slow speed on full-lock)

Braking system

- ☐ Vehicle pulls to one side under braking
- ☐ Noise (grinding or high-pitched squeal) when brakes applied
- ☐ Excessive brake pedal travel
- ☐ Brake pedal feels spongy when depressed
- ☐ Excessive brake pedal effort required to stop vehicle
- ☐ Judder felt through brake pedal or steering wheel when braking
- ☐ Pedal pulsates when braking hard
- ☐ Brakes binding
- ☐ Rear wheels locking under normal braking

Steering and suspension

- ☐ Vehicle pulls to one side
- ☐ Wheel wobble and vibration
- ☐ Excessive pitching and/or rolling around corners, or during braking
- ☐ Wandering or general instability
- ☐ Excessively-stiff steering
- ☐ Excessive play in steering
- ☐ Lack of power assistance
- ☐ Tyre wear excessive

Electrical system

- ☐ Battery will not hold a charge for more than a few days
- ☐ Ignition/no-charge warning light remains illuminated with engine running
- ☐ Ignition/no-charge warning light fails to come on
- ☐ Lights inoperative
- ☐ Instrument readings inaccurate or erratic
- ☐ Horn inoperative, or unsatisfactory in operation
- ☐ Windscreen/tailgate wipers inoperative, or unsatisfactory in operation
- ☐ Windscreen washers inoperative, or unsatisfactory in operation
- ☐ Electric windows inoperative, or unsatisfactory in operation

Introduction

The vehicle owner who does his or her own maintenance according to the recommended service schedules should not have to use this section of the manual very often. Modern component reliability is such that, provided those items subject to wear or deterioration are inspected or renewed at the specified intervals, sudden failure is comparatively rare. Faults do not usually just happen as a result of sudden failure, but develop over a period of time. Major mechanical failures in particular are usually preceded by characteristic symptoms over hundreds or even thousands of miles. Those components which do

occasionally fail without warning are often small and easily carried in the vehicle.

With any fault-finding, the first step is to decide where to begin investigations. Sometimes this is obvious, but on other occasions, a little detective work will be necessary. The owner who makes half a dozen haphazard adjustments or replacements may be successful in curing a fault (or its symptoms), but will be none the wiser if the fault recurs, and ultimately may have spent more time and money than was necessary. A calm and logical approach will be found to be more satisfactory in the long

run. Always take into account any warning signs or abnormalities that may have been noticed in the period preceding the fault – power loss, high or low gauge readings, unusual smells, etc – and remember that failure of components such as fuses or spark plugs may only be pointers to some underlying fault.

The pages which follow provide an easy-reference guide to the more common problems which may occur during the operation of the vehicle. These problems and their possible causes are grouped under headings denoting various components or systems, such as Engine, Cooling system, etc. The general Chapter which deals with the problem is also shown in brackets; refer to the relevant part of that Chapter for system-specific information. Whatever the fault, certain basic principles apply. These are as follows:

☐ *Verify the fault.* This is simply a matter of being sure that you know what the symptoms are before starting work. This is particularly important if you are investigating a fault for someone else, who may not have described it very accurately.

☐ *Don't overlook the obvious.* For example, if the vehicle won't start, is there fuel in the tank? (Don't take anyone else's word on this particular point, and don't trust the fuel gauge either!) If an electrical fault is indicated, look for loose or broken wires before digging out the test gear.

☐ *Cure the disease, not the symptom.* Substituting a flat battery with a fully-charged one will get you off the hard shoulder, but if the underlying cause is not attended to, the new battery will go the same way. Similarly, changing oil-fouled spark plugs for a new set

will get you moving again, but remember that the reason for the fouling (if it wasn't simply an incorrect grade of plug) will have to be established and corrected.

☐ *Don't take anything for granted.* Particularly, don't forget that a new component may itself be defective (especially if its been rattling around in the boot for months), and don't leave components out of a fault diagnosis sequence just because they are new or recently-fitted. When you do finally diagnose a difficult fault, you'll probably realise that all the evidence was there from the start.

Engine

Engine fails to rotate when attempting to start

☐ Battery terminal connections loose or corroded (see *Weekly checks*).
☐ Battery discharged or faulty (Chapter 5).
☐ Broken, loose or disconnected wiring in the starting circuit (Chapter 5).
☐ Defective starter solenoid or switch (Chapter 5).
☐ Defective starter motor (Chapter 5).
☐ Starter pinion or flywheel/driveplate ring gear teeth loose or broken (Chapter 2 and 5).
☐ Engine earth strap broken or disconnected (Chapter 5).

Engine rotates, but will not start

☐ Fuel tank empty.
☐ Battery discharged (engine rotates slowly) (Chapter 5).
☐ Battery terminal connections loose or corroded (see *Weekly checks*).
☐ Ignition components damp or damaged – petrol models (Chapters 1 and 5).
☐ Broken, loose or disconnected wiring in the ignition circuit – petrol models (Chapters 1 and 5).
☐ Worn, faulty or incorrectly-gapped spark plugs – petrol models (Chapter 1).
☐ Preheating system faulty – diesel models (Chapter 5).
☐ Fuel injection system fault – petrol models (Chapter 4).
☐ Stop solenoid faulty – diesel models (Chapter 4).
☐ Air in fuel system – diesel models (Chapter 4).
☐ Major mechanical failure (e.g. timing chain/belt) (Chapter 2).

Engine difficult to start when cold

☐ Battery discharged (Chapter 5).
☐ Battery terminal connections loose or corroded (see *Weekly checks*).
☐ Worn, faulty or incorrectly-gapped spark plugs – petrol models (Chapter 1).
☐ Preheating system faulty – diesel models (Chapter 5).
☐ Fuel injection system fault – petrol models (Chapter 4).
☐ Other ignition system fault – petrol models (Chapters 1 and 5).
☐ Low cylinder compressions (Chapter 2).

Engine difficult to start when hot

☐ Air filter element dirty or clogged (Chapter 1).
☐ Fuel injection system fault – petrol models (Chapter 4).
☐ Low cylinder compressions (Chapter 2).

Starter motor noisy or excessively-rough in engagement

☐ Starter pinion or flywheel ring gear teeth loose or broken (Chapter 2 and 5).
☐ Starter motor mounting bolts loose or missing (Chapter 5).
☐ Starter motor internal components worn or damaged (Chapter 5).

Engine starts, but stops immediately

☐ Loose or faulty electrical connections in the ignition circuit – petrol models (Chapters 1 and 5).
☐ Vacuum leak at the throttle body or inlet manifold – petrol models (Chapter 4).
☐ Blocked injector/fuel injection system fault – petrol models (Chapter 4).
☐ Air in fuel system – diesel models (Chapter 4).

Engine idles erratically

☐ Air filter element clogged (Chapter 1).
☐ Vacuum leak at the throttle body, inlet manifold or associated hoses – petrol models (Chapter 4).
☐ Worn, faulty or incorrectly-gapped spark plugs – petrol models (Chapter 1).
☐ Uneven or low cylinder compressions (Chapter 2).
☐ Camshaft lobes worn (Chapter 2).
☐ Timing chain/belt incorrectly fitted (Chapter 2).
☐ Blocked injector/fuel injection system fault – petrol models (Chapter 4).
☐ Air in fuel system – diesel models (Chapter 4).
☐ Faulty injector(s) – diesel models (Chapter 4).

Engine misfires at idle speed

☐ Worn, faulty or incorrectly-gapped spark plugs – petrol models (Chapter 1).
☐ Faulty spark plug HT leads – petrol models (Chapter 1).
☐ Vacuum leak at the throttle body, inlet manifold or associated hoses – petrol models (Chapter 4).
☐ Blocked injector/fuel injection system fault – petrol models (Chapter 4).
☐ Faulty injector(s) – diesel models (Chapter 4).
☐ Uneven or low cylinder compressions (Chapter 2).
☐ Disconnected, leaking, or perished crankcase ventilation hoses (Chapter 4).

Engine misfires throughout the driving speed range

☐ Fuel filter choked (Chapter 1).
☐ Fuel pump faulty, or delivery pressure low – petrol models (Chapter 4).
☐ Fuel tank vent blocked, or fuel pipes restricted (Chapter 4).
☐ Vacuum leak at the throttle body, inlet manifold or associated hoses – petrol models (Chapter 4).
☐ Worn, faulty or incorrectly-gapped spark plugs – petrol models (Chapter 1).
☐ Faulty spark plug HT leads – petrol models (Chapter 1).
☐ Faulty injector(s) – diesel models (Chapter 4).
☐ Faulty ignition coil(s) – petrol models (Chapter 5).
☐ Uneven or low cylinder compressions (Chapter 2).
☐ Blocked injector/fuel injection system fault – petrol models (Chapter 4).

Engine (continued)

Engine hesitates on acceleration

- ☐ Worn, faulty or incorrectly-gapped spark plugs – petrol models (Chapter 1).
- ☐ Vacuum leak at the throttle body, inlet manifold or associated hoses – petrol models (Chapter 4).
- ☐ Blocked injector/fuel injection system fault – petrol models (Chapter 4).
- ☐ Faulty injector(s) – diesel models (Chapter 4).

Engine stalls

- ☐ Vacuum leak at the throttle body, inlet manifold or associated hoses – petrol models (Chapter 4).
- ☐ Fuel filter choked (Chapter 1 and 4).
- ☐ Fuel pump faulty, or delivery pressure low – petrol models (Chapter 4).
- ☐ Fuel tank vent blocked, or fuel pipes restricted (Chapter 4).
- ☐ Blocked injector/fuel injection system fault – petrol models (Chapter 4).
- ☐ Faulty injector(s) – diesel models (Chapter 4).

Engine lacks power

- ☐ Timing chain/belt incorrectly fitted or tensioned (Chapter 2).
- ☐ Fuel filter choked (Chapter 1 and 4).
- ☐ Fuel pump faulty, or delivery pressure low – petrol models (Chapter 4).
- ☐ Uneven or low cylinder compressions (Chapter 2).
- ☐ Worn, faulty or incorrectly-gapped spark plugs – petrol models (Chapter 1).
- ☐ Vacuum leak at the throttle body, inlet manifold or associated hoses – petrol models (Chapter 4).
- ☐ Blocked injector/fuel injection system fault – petrol models (Chapter 4).
- ☐ Faulty injector(s) – diesel models (Chapter 4).
- ☐ Injection pump timing incorrect – diesel models (Chapter 4).
- ☐ Brakes binding (Chapters 1 and 9).
- ☐ Clutch slipping (Chapter 6).
- ☐ Air filter element clogged (Chapter 1).

Engine backfires

- ☐ Timing chain/belt incorrectly fitted or tensioned (Chapter 2).
- ☐ Vacuum leak at the throttle body, inlet manifold or associated hoses – petrol models (Chapter 4).
- ☐ Incorrect HT firing sequence – petrol models (Chapter 5)
- ☐ Blocked injector/fuel injection system fault – petrol models (Chapter 4).

Oil pressure warning light illuminated with engine running

- ☐ Low oil level, or incorrect oil grade (*Weekly checks*).
- ☐ Faulty oil pressure switch (Chapter 2).
- ☐ Worn engine bearings and/or oil pump (Chapter 2).
- ☐ High engine operating temperature (Chapter 3).
- ☐ Oil pressure relief valve defective (Chapter 2).
- ☐ Oil pick-up strainer clogged (Chapter 2).

Engine runs-on after switching off

- ☐ Excessive carbon build-up in engine (Chapter 2).
- ☐ High engine operating temperature (Chapter 3).
- ☐ Fuel injection system fault – petrol models (Chapter 4).
- ☐ Faulty stop solenoid – diesel models (Chapter 4).

Engine noises

Pre-ignition (pinking) or knocking during acceleration or under load

- ☐ Ignition system fault – petrol models (Chapters 1 and 5).
- ☐ Incorrect grade of spark plug – petrol models (Chapter 1).
- ☐ Vacuum leak at the throttle body, inlet manifold or associated hoses – petrol models (Chapter 4).
- ☐ Excessive carbon build-up in engine (Chapter 2).
- ☐ Blocked injector/fuel injection system fault – petrol models (Chapter 4).

Whistling or wheezing noises

- ☐ Leaking inlet manifold or throttle body gasket – petrol models (Chapter 4).
- ☐ Leaking exhaust manifold gasket or pipe-to-manifold joint (Chapter 4).
- ☐ Leaking vacuum hose (Chapters 4 and 9).
- ☐ Blowing cylinder head gasket (Chapter 2).

Tapping or rattling noises

- ☐ Worn valve gear or camshaft (Chapter 2).
- ☐ Ancillary component fault (coolant pump, alternator, etc) (Chapters 3, 5, etc).

Knocking or thumping noises

- ☐ Worn big-end bearings (regular heavy knocking, perhaps less under load) (Chapter 2).
- ☐ Worn main bearings (rumbling and knocking, perhaps worsening under load) (Chapter 2).
- ☐ Piston slap (most noticeable when cold) (Chapter 2).
- ☐ Ancillary component fault (coolant pump, alternator, etc) (Chapters 3, 5, etc).

Cooling system

Overheating

- ☐ Insufficient coolant in system (*Weekly checks*).
- ☐ Thermostat faulty (Chapter 3).
- ☐ Radiator core blocked, or grille restricted (Chapter 3).
- ☐ Electric cooling fan or thermostatic switch faulty (Chapter 3).
- ☐ Inaccurate temperature gauge sender unit (Chapter 3).
- ☐ Airlock in cooling system.
- ☐ Expansion tank pressure cap faulty (Chapter 3).

Overcooling

- ☐ Thermostat faulty (Chapter 3).
- ☐ Inaccurate temperature gauge sender unit (Chapter 3).

External coolant leakage

- ☐ Deteriorated or damaged hoses or hose clips (Chapter 1).

- ☐ Radiator core or heater matrix leaking (Chapter 3).
- ☐ Pressure cap faulty (Chapter 3).
- ☐ Coolant pump internal seal leaking (Chapter 3).
- ☐ Coolant pump-to-housing seal leaking (Chapter 3).
- ☐ Boiling due to overheating (Chapter 3).
- ☐ Core plug leaking (Chapter 2).

Internal coolant leakage

- ☐ Leaking cylinder head gasket (Chapter 2).
- ☐ Cracked cylinder head or cylinder block (Chapter 2).

Corrosion

- ☐ Infrequent draining and flushing (Chapter 1).
- ☐ Incorrect coolant mixture or inappropriate coolant type (see *Weekly checks*).

Fuel and exhaust systems

Excessive fuel consumption

☐ Air filter element dirty or clogged (Chapter 1).
☐ Fuel injection system fault – petrol models (Chapter 4).
☐ Faulty injector(s) – diesel models (Chapter 4).
☐ Ignition system fault – petrol models (Chapters 1 and 5).
☐ Brakes binding (Chapter 9).
☐ Tyres under-inflated (see *Weekly checks*).

Fuel leakage and/or fuel odour

☐ Damaged fuel tank, pipes or connections (Chapter 4).

Excessive noise or fumes from exhaust system

☐ Leaking exhaust system or manifold joints (Chapters 1 and 4).
☐ Leaking, corroded or damaged silencers or pipe (Chapters 1 and 4).
☐ Broken mountings causing body or suspension contact (Chapter 1).

Clutch

Pedal travels to floor – no pressure or very little resistance

☐ Faulty master or slave cylinder (Chapter 6).
☐ Faulty hydraulic release system (Chapter 6).
☐ Broken clutch release bearing or arm (Chapter 6).
☐ Broken diaphragm spring in clutch pressure plate (Chapter 6).

Clutch fails to disengage (unable to select gears)

☐ Faulty master or slave cylinder (Chapter 6).
☐ Faulty hydraulic release system (Chapter 6).
☐ Clutch disc sticking on gearbox input shaft splines (Chapter 6).
☐ Clutch disc sticking to flywheel or pressure plate (Chapter 6).
☐ Faulty pressure plate assembly (Chapter 6).

Clutch slips (engine speed increases, with no increase in vehicle speed)

☐ Faulty hydraulic release system (Chapter 6).

☐ Clutch disc linings excessively worn (Chapter 6).
☐ Clutch disc linings contaminated with oil or grease (Chapter 6).
☐ Faulty pressure plate or weak diaphragm spring (Chapter 6).

Judder as clutch is engaged

☐ Clutch disc linings contaminated with oil or grease (Chapter 6).
☐ Clutch disc linings excessively worn (Chapter 6).
☐ Faulty or distorted pressure plate or diaphragm spring (Chapter 6).
☐ Worn or loose engine or gearbox mountings (Chapter 2).
☐ Clutch disc hub or gearbox input shaft splines worn (Chapter 6).

Noise when depressing or releasing clutch pedal

☐ Worn clutch release bearing (Chapter 6).
☐ Worn or dry clutch pedal pivot (Chapter 6).
☐ Faulty pressure plate assembly (Chapter 6).
☐ Pressure plate diaphragm spring broken (Chapter 6).
☐ Broken clutch friction plate cushioning springs (Chapter 6).

Manual transmission

Noisy in neutral with engine running

☐ Input shaft bearings worn (noise apparent with clutch pedal released, but not when depressed) (Chapter 7A).*
☐ Clutch release bearing worn (noise apparent with clutch pedal depressed, possibly less when released) (Chapter 6).

Noisy in one particular gear

☐ Worn, damaged or chipped gear teeth (Chapter 7A).*

Difficulty engaging gears

☐ Clutch fault (Chapter 6).
☐ Worn or damaged gear linkage (Chapter 7A).
☐ Worn synchroniser units (Chapter 7A).*

Jumps out of gear

☐ Worn or damaged gear linkage (Chapter 7A).

☐ Worn synchroniser units (Chapter 7A).*
☐ Worn selector forks (Chapter 7A).*

Vibration

☐ Lack of oil (Chapter 1).
☐ Worn bearings (Chapter 7A).*

Lubricant leaks

☐ Leaking oil seal (Chapter 7A).
☐ Leaking housing joint (Chapter 7A).*
☐ Leaking input shaft oil seal (Chapter 7A).

Although the corrective action necessary to remedy the symptoms described is beyond the scope of the home mechanic, the above information should be helpful in isolating the cause of the condition, so that the owner can communicate clearly with a professional mechanic.

Automatic transmission

Note: *Due to the complexity of the automatic transmission, it is difficult for the home mechanic to properly diagnose and service this unit. For problems other than the following, the vehicle should be taken to a dealer service department or automatic transmission specialist. Do not be too hasty in removing the transmission if a fault is suspected, as most of the testing is carried out with the unit still fitted.*

Fluid leakage

☐ Automatic transmission fluid is usually dark in colour. Fluid leaks should not be confused with engine oil, which can easily be blown onto the transmission by airflow.
☐ To determine the source of a leak, first remove all built-up dirt and grime from the transmission housing and surrounding areas using a degreasing agent, or by steam-cleaning. Drive the vehicle at low speed, so airflow will not blow the leak far from its source. Raise and support the vehicle, and determine where the leak is coming from.

General gear selection problems

☐ Chapter 7B deals with checking and adjusting the selector mechanism on automatic transmissions. The following are common problems which may be caused by a poorly-adjusted mechanism:
 a) *Engine starting in gears other than Park or Neutral.*
 b) *Indicator panel indicating a gear other than the one actually being used.*
 c) *Vehicle moves when in Park or Neutral.*
 d) *Poor gear shift quality or erratic gear changes.*
☐ Refer to Chapter 7B for the selector mechanism adjustment procedure.

Transmission will not downshift (kickdown) with accelerator pedal fully depressed

☐ Low transmission fluid level (Chapter 1).
☐ Incorrect selector mechanism adjustment (Chapter 7B).

Engine will not start in any gear, or starts in gears other than Park or Neutral

☐ Incorrect selector mechanism adjustment (Chapter 7B).

Transmission slips, shifts roughly, is noisy, or has no drive in forward or reverse gears

☐ There are many probable causes for the above problems, but unless there is a very obvious reason (such as a loose or corroded wiring plug connection on or near the transmission), the car should be taken to a franchise dealer or automatic transmission specialist for the fault to be diagnosed. The transmission control unit incorporates a self-diagnosis facility, and any fault codes can quickly be read and interpreted by a dealer or specialist with the proper diagnostic equipment.

Driveshafts

Vibration when accelerating or decelerating

☐ Worn inner constant velocity joint (Chapter 8).
☐ Bent or distorted driveshaft (Chapter 8).

Clicking or knocking noise on turns (at slow speed on full-lock)

☐ Worn outer constant velocity joint (Chapter 8).
☐ Lack of constant velocity joint lubricant, possibly due to damaged gaiter (Chapter 8).

Braking system

Note: *Before assuming that a brake problem exists, make sure that the tyres are in good condition and correctly inflated, that the front wheel alignment is correct, and that the vehicle is not loaded with weight in an unequal manner. Apart from checking the condition of all pipe and hose connections, any faults occurring on the anti-lock braking system should be referred to a Ford dealer or specialist for diagnosis.*

Vehicle pulls to one side under braking

☐ Worn, defective, damaged or contaminated front or rear brake pads on one side (Chapters 1 and 9).
☐ Seized or partially-seized front or rear brake caliper (Chapter 9).
☐ A mixture of brake pad lining materials fitted between sides (Chapter 9).
☐ Brake caliper mounting bolts loose (Chapter 9).
☐ Worn or damaged steering or suspension components (Chapters 1 and 10).

Noise (grinding or high-pitched squeal) when brakes applied

☐ Brake pad friction lining material worn down to metal backing (Chapters 1 and 9).
☐ Excessive corrosion of brake disc – may be apparent after the vehicle has been standing for some time (Chapters 1 and 9).
☐ Foreign object (stone chipping, etc) trapped between brake disc and shield (Chapters 1 and 9).

Excessive brake pedal travel

☐ Faulty master cylinder (Chapter 9).
☐ Air in hydraulic system (Chapter 9).
☐ Faulty vacuum servo unit (Chapter 9).
☐ Faulty vacuum pump – diesel models (Chapter 9).

Braking system (continued)

Brake pedal feels spongy when depressed

- ☐ Air in hydraulic system (Chapter 9).
- ☐ Deteriorated flexible rubber brake hoses (Chapters 1 and 9).
- ☐ Master cylinder mountings loose (Chapter 9).
- ☐ Faulty master cylinder (Chapter 9).

Excessive brake pedal effort required to stop vehicle

- ☐ Faulty vacuum servo unit (Chapter 9).
- ☐ Disconnected, damaged or insecure brake servo vacuum hose (Chapters 1 and 9).
- ☐ Faulty vacuum pump – diesel models (Chapter 9).
- ☐ Primary or secondary hydraulic circuit failure (Chapter 9).
- ☐ Seized brake caliper (Chapter 9).
- ☐ Brake pads incorrectly fitted (Chapter 9).
- ☐ Incorrect grade of brake pads fitted (Chapter 9).
- ☐ Brake pads contaminated (Chapter 9).

Judder felt through brake pedal or steering wheel when braking

- ☐ Excessive run-out or distortion of brake disc(s) (Chapter 9).
- ☐ Brake pad linings worn (Chapters 1 and 9).
- ☐ Brake caliper mounting bolts loose (Chapter 9).
- ☐ Wear in suspension or steering components or mountings (Chapters 1 and 10).

Pedal pulsates when braking hard

- ☐ Normal feature of ABS – no fault

Brakes binding

- ☐ Seized brake caliper piston(s) (Chapter 9).
- ☐ Incorrectly-adjusted handbrake mechanism (Chapter 9).
- ☐ Faulty master cylinder (Chapter 9).

Rear wheels locking under normal braking

- ☐ Rear brake pad linings contaminated (Chapters 1 and 9).
- ☐ Rear brake discs warped (Chapters 1 and 9).

Steering and suspension

Note: *Before diagnosing suspension or steering faults, be sure that the trouble is not due to incorrect tyre pressures, mixtures of tyre types, or binding brakes.*

Vehicle pulls to one side

- ☐ Defective tyre (see *Weekly checks*).
- ☐ Excessive wear in suspension or steering components (Chapters 1 and 10).
- ☐ Incorrect front wheel alignment (Chapter 10).
- ☐ Accident damage to steering or suspension components (Chapters 1 and 10).

Wheel wobble and vibration

- ☐ Front roadwheels out of balance (vibration felt mainly through the steering wheel) (Chapter 10).
- ☐ Rear roadwheels out of balance (vibration felt throughout the vehicle) (Chapter 10).
- ☐ Roadwheels damaged or distorted (Chapter 10).
- ☐ Faulty or damaged tyre (*Weekly checks*).
- ☐ Worn steering or suspension joints, bushes or components (Chapters 1 and 10).
- ☐ Wheel bolts loose (Chapter 1 and 10).

Excessive pitching and/or rolling around corners, or during braking

- ☐ Defective shock absorbers (Chapters 1 and 10).
- ☐ Broken or weak coil spring and/or suspension component (Chapters 1 and 10).
- ☐ Worn or damaged anti-roll bar or mountings (Chapter 10).

Wandering or general instability

- ☐ Incorrect front wheel alignment (Chapter 10).
- ☐ Worn steering or suspension joints, bushes or components (Chapters 1 and 10).
- ☐ Roadwheels out of balance (Chapter 10).
- ☐ Faulty or damaged tyre (*Weekly checks*).
- ☐ Wheel bolts loose (Chapter 10).
- ☐ Defective shock absorbers (Chapters 1 and 10).

Excessively-stiff steering

- ☐ Seized track rod end balljoint or suspension balljoint (Chapters 1 and 10).

- ☐ Broken or incorrectly adjusted auxiliary drivebelt (Chapter 1).
- ☐ Incorrect front wheel alignment (Chapter 10).
- ☐ Steering gear damaged (Chapter 10).

Excessive play in steering

- ☐ Worn steering column universal joint(s) (Chapter 10).
- ☐ Worn steering track rod end balljoints (Chapters 1 and 10).
- ☐ Worn steering gear (Chapter 10).
- ☐ Worn steering or suspension joints, bushes or components (Chapters 1 and 10).

Lack of power assistance

- ☐ Broken or incorrectly-adjusted auxiliary drivebelt (Chapter 1).
- ☐ Incorrect power steering fluid level (*Weekly checks*).
- ☐ Restriction in power steering fluid hoses (Chapter 10).
- ☐ Faulty power steering pump (Chapter 10).
- ☐ Faulty steering gear (Chapter 10).

Tyre wear excessive

Tyres worn on inside or outside edges

- ☐ Incorrect camber or castor angles (Chapter 10).
- ☐ Worn steering or suspension joints, bushes or components (Chapters 1 and 10).
- ☐ Excessively-hard cornering.
- ☐ Accident damage.

Tyre treads exhibit feathered edges

- ☐ Incorrect toe setting (Chapter 10).

Tyres worn in centre of tread

- ☐ Tyres over-inflated (*Weekly checks*).

Tyres worn on inside and outside edges

- ☐ Tyres under-inflated (*Weekly checks*).
- ☐ Worn shock absorbers (Chapter 10).

Tyres worn unevenly

- ☐ Tyres/wheels out of balance (*Weekly checks*).
- ☐ Excessive wheel or tyre run-out (Chapter 10).
- ☐ Worn shock absorbers (Chapters 1 and 10).
- ☐ Faulty tyre (*Weekly checks*).

Electrical system

Note: *For problems associated with the starting system, refer to the faults listed under 'Engine' earlier in this Section.*

Battery will not hold a charge for more than a few days

- [ ] Battery defective internally (Chapter 5).
- [ ] Battery electrolyte level low – where applicable (*Weekly checks*).
- [ ] Battery terminal connections loose or corroded (*Weekly checks*).
- [ ] Auxiliary drivebelt worn – or incorrectly adjusted, where applicable (Chapter 1).
- [ ] Alternator not charging at correct output (Chapter 5).
- [ ] Alternator or voltage regulator faulty (Chapter 5).
- [ ] Short-circuit causing continual battery drain (Chapters 5 and 12).

Ignition/no-charge warning light remains illuminated with engine running

- [ ] Auxiliary drivebelt broken, worn, or incorrectly adjusted (Chapter 1).
- [ ] Internal fault in alternator or voltage regulator (Chapter 5).
- [ ] Broken, disconnected, or loose wiring in charging circuit (Chapter 5).

Ignition/no-charge warning light fails to come on

- [ ] Broken, disconnected, or loose wiring in warning light circuit (Chapter 12).
- [ ] Alternator faulty (Chapter 5).

Lights inoperative

- [ ] Bulb blown (Chapter 12).
- [ ] Corrosion of bulb or bulbholder contacts (Chapter 12).
- [ ] Blown fuse (Chapter 12).
- [ ] Faulty relay (Chapter 12).
- [ ] Broken, loose, or disconnected wiring (Chapter 12).
- [ ] Faulty switch (Chapter 12).

Instrument readings inaccurate or erratic

Fuel or temperature gauges give no reading

- [ ] Faulty gauge sender unit (Chapters 3 and 4).
- [ ] Wiring open-circuit (Chapter 12).
- [ ] Faulty gauge (Chapter 12).

Fuel or temperature gauges give continuous maximum reading

- [ ] Faulty gauge sender unit (Chapters 3 and 4).
- [ ] Wiring short-circuit (Chapter 12).
- [ ] Faulty gauge (Chapter 12).

Horn inoperative, or unsatisfactory in operation

Horn operates all the time

- [ ] Horn contacts permanently bridged or horn buttons stuck down (Chapter 12).

Horn fails to operate

- [ ] Blown fuse (Chapter 12).
- [ ] Cable or cable connections loose, broken or disconnected (Chapter 12).
- [ ] Faulty horn (Chapter 12).

Horn emits intermittent or unsatisfactory sound

- [ ] Cable connections loose (Chapter 12).
- [ ] Horn mountings loose (Chapter 12).
- [ ] Faulty horn (Chapter 12).

Windscreen/tailgate wipers inoperative, or unsatisfactory in operation

Wipers fail to operate, or operate very slowly

- [ ] Wiper blades stuck to screen, or linkage seized or binding (*Weekly checks* and Chapter 12).
- [ ] Blown fuse (Chapter 12).
- [ ] Cable or cable connections loose, broken or disconnected (Chapter 12).
- [ ] Faulty relay (Chapter 12).
- [ ] Faulty wiper motor (Chapter 12).

Wiper blades sweep over too large or too small an area of the glass

- [ ] Wiper arms incorrectly positioned on spindles (Chapter 12).
- [ ] Excessive wear of wiper linkage (Chapter 12).
- [ ] Wiper motor or linkage mountings loose or insecure (Chapter 12).

Wiper blades fail to clean the glass effectively

- [ ] Wiper blade rubbers worn or perished (*Weekly checks*).
- [ ] Wiper arm tension springs broken, or arm pivots seized (Chapter 12).
- [ ] Insufficient windscreen washer additive to adequately remove road film (*Weekly checks*).

Windscreen washers inoperative, or unsatisfactory in operation

One or more washer jets inoperative

- [ ] Blocked washer jet (Chapter 12).
- [ ] Disconnected, kinked or restricted fluid hose (Chapter 12).
- [ ] Insufficient fluid in washer reservoir (*Weekly checks*).

Washer pump fails to operate

- [ ] Broken or disconnected wiring or connections (Chapter 12).
- [ ] Blown fuse (Chapter 12).
- [ ] Faulty washer switch (Chapter 12).
- [ ] Faulty washer pump (Chapter 12).

Electric windows inoperative, or unsatisfactory in operation

Window glass will only move in one direction

- [ ] Faulty switch (Chapter 12).

Window glass slow to move

- [ ] Regulator seized or damaged, or in need of lubrication (Chapter 11).
- [ ] Door internal components or trim fouling regulator (Chapter 11).
- [ ] Faulty motor (Chapter 11).

Window glass fails to move

- [ ] Blown fuse (Chapter 12).
- [ ] Faulty relay (Chapter 12).
- [ ] Broken or disconnected wiring or connections (Chapter 12).
- [ ] Faulty motor (Chapter 12).

Central locking system inoperative, or unsatisfactory in operation

Complete system failure

- [ ] Blown fuse (Chapter 12).
- [ ] Faulty relay (Chapter 12).
- [ ] Broken or disconnected wiring or connections (Chapter 12).

Latch locks but will not unlock, or unlocks but will not lock

- [ ] Faulty switch (Chapter 12).
- [ ] Broken or disconnected latch operating rods or levers (Chapter 11).
- [ ] Faulty relay (Chapter 12).

One lock fails to operate

- [ ] Broken or disconnected wiring or connections (Chapter 12).
- [ ] Faulty motor (Chapter 11).
- [ ] Broken, binding or disconnected lock operating rods or levers (Chapter 11).
- [ ] Fault in door lock (Chapter 11).

A

ABS (Anti-lock brake system) A system, usually electronically controlled, that senses incipient wheel lockup during braking and relieves hydraulic pressure at wheels that are about to skid.

Air bag An inflatable bag hidden in the steering wheel (driver's side) or the dash or glovebox (passenger side). In a head-on collision, the bags inflate, preventing the driver and front passenger from being thrown forward into the steering wheel or windscreen.

Air cleaner A metal or plastic housing, containing a filter element, which removes dust and dirt from the air being drawn into the engine.

Air filter element The actual filter in an air cleaner system, usually manufactured from pleated paper and requiring renewal at regular intervals.

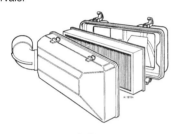

Air filter

Allen key A hexagonal wrench which fits into a recessed hexagonal hole.

Alligator clip A long-nosed spring-loaded metal clip with meshing teeth. Used to make temporary electrical connections.

Alternator A component in the electrical system which converts mechanical energy from a drivebelt into electrical energy to charge the battery and to operate the starting system, ignition system and electrical accessories.

Ampere (amp) A unit of measurement for the flow of electric current. One amp is the amount of current produced by one volt acting through a resistance of one ohm.

Anaerobic sealer A substance used to prevent bolts and screws from loosening. Anaerobic means that it does not require oxygen for activation. The Loctite brand is widely used.

Antifreeze A substance (usually ethylene glycol) mixed with water, and added to a vehicle's cooling system, to prevent freezing of the coolant in winter. Antifreeze also contains chemicals to inhibit corrosion and the formation of rust and other deposits that would tend to clog the radiator and coolant passages and reduce cooling efficiency.

Anti-seize compound A coating that reduces the risk of seizing on fasteners that are subjected to high temperatures, such as exhaust manifold bolts and nuts.

Asbestos A natural fibrous mineral with great heat resistance, commonly used in the composition of brake friction materials.

Asbestos is a health hazard and the dust created by brake systems should never be inhaled or ingested.

Axle A shaft on which a wheel revolves, or which revolves with a wheel. Also, a solid beam that connects the two wheels at one end of the vehicle. An axle which also transmits power to the wheels is known as a live axle.

Axleshaft A single rotating shaft, on either side of the differential, which delivers power from the final drive assembly to the drive wheels. Also called a driveshaft or a halfshaft.

B

Ball bearing An anti-friction bearing consisting of a hardened inner and outer race with hardened steel balls between two races.

Bearing The curved surface on a shaft or in a bore, or the part assembled into either, that permits relative motion between them with minimum wear and friction.

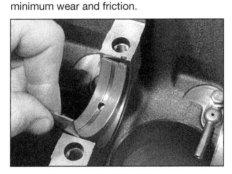

Bearing

Big-end bearing The bearing in the end of the connecting rod that's attached to the crankshaft.

Bleed nipple A valve on a brake wheel cylinder, caliper or other hydraulic component that is opened to purge the hydraulic system of air. Also called a bleed screw.

Brake bleeding Procedure for removing air from lines of a hydraulic brake system.

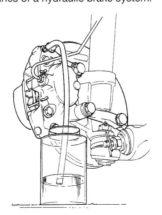

Brake bleeding

Brake disc The component of a disc brake that rotates with the wheels.

Brake drum The component of a drum brake that rotates with the wheels.

Brake linings The friction material which contacts the brake disc or drum to retard the vehicle's speed. The linings are bonded or riveted to the brake pads or shoes.

Brake pads The replaceable friction pads that pinch the brake disc when the brakes are applied. Brake pads consist of a friction material bonded or riveted to a rigid backing plate.

Brake shoe The crescent-shaped carrier to which the brake linings are mounted and which forces the lining against the rotating drum during braking.

Braking systems For more information on braking systems, consult the *Haynes Automotive Brake Manual*.

Breaker bar A long socket wrench handle providing greater leverage.

Bulkhead The insulated partition between the engine and the passenger compartment.

C

Caliper The non-rotating part of a disc-brake assembly that straddles the disc and carries the brake pads. The caliper also contains the hydraulic components that cause the pads to pinch the disc when the brakes are applied. A caliper is also a measuring tool that can be set to measure inside or outside dimensions of an object.

Camshaft A rotating shaft on which a series of cam lobes operate the valve mechanisms. The camshaft may be driven by gears, by sprockets and chain or by sprockets and a belt.

Canister A container in an evaporative emission control system; contains activated charcoal granules to trap vapours from the fuel system.

Canister

Carburettor A device which mixes fuel with air in the proper proportions to provide a desired power output from a spark ignition internal combustion engine.

Castellated Resembling the parapets along the top of a castle wall. For example, a castellated balljoint stud nut.

Castor In wheel alignment, the backward or forward tilt of the steering axis. Castor is positive when the steering axis is inclined rearward at the top.

Catalytic converter A silencer-like device in the exhaust system which converts certain pollutants in the exhaust gases into less harmful substances.

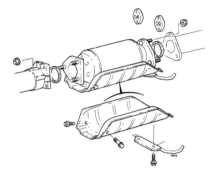

Catalytic converter

Circlip A ring-shaped clip used to prevent endwise movement of cylindrical parts and shafts. An internal circlip is installed in a groove in a housing; an external circlip fits into a groove on the outside of a cylindrical piece such as a shaft.

Clearance The amount of space between two parts. For example, between a piston and a cylinder, between a bearing and a journal, etc.

Coil spring A spiral of elastic steel found in various sizes throughout a vehicle, for example as a springing medium in the suspension and in the valve train.

Compression Reduction in volume, and increase in pressure and temperature, of a gas, caused by squeezing it into a smaller space.

Compression ratio The relationship between cylinder volume when the piston is at top dead centre and cylinder volume when the piston is at bottom dead centre.

Constant velocity (CV) joint A type of universal joint that cancels out vibrations caused by driving power being transmitted through an angle.

Core plug A disc or cup-shaped metal device inserted in a hole in a casting through which core was removed when the casting was formed. Also known as a freeze plug or expansion plug.

Crankcase The lower part of the engine block in which the crankshaft rotates.

Crankshaft The main rotating member, or shaft, running the length of the crankcase, with offset "throws" to which the connecting rods are attached.

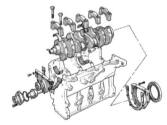

Crankshaft assembly

Crocodile clip See Alligator clip

D

Diagnostic code Code numbers obtained by accessing the diagnostic mode of an engine management computer. This code can be used to determine the area in the system where a malfunction may be located.

Disc brake A brake design incorporating a rotating disc onto which brake pads are squeezed. The resulting friction converts the energy of a moving vehicle into heat.

Double-overhead cam (DOHC) An engine that uses two overhead camshafts, usually one for the intake valves and one for the exhaust valves.

Drivebelt(s) The belt(s) used to drive accessories such as the alternator, water pump, power steering pump, air conditioning compressor, etc. off the crankshaft pulley.

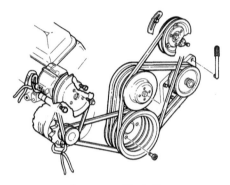

Accessory drivebelts

Driveshaft Any shaft used to transmit motion. Commonly used when referring to the axleshafts on a front wheel drive vehicle.

Drum brake A type of brake using a drum-shaped metal cylinder attached to the inner surface of the wheel. When the brake pedal is pressed, curved brake shoes with friction linings press against the inside of the drum to slow or stop the vehicle.

E

EGR valve A valve used to introduce exhaust gases into the intake air stream.

Electronic control unit (ECU) A computer which controls (for instance) ignition and fuel injection systems, or an anti-lock braking system. For more information refer to the *Haynes Automotive Electrical and Electronic Systems Manual*.

Electronic Fuel Injection (EFI) A computer controlled fuel system that distributes fuel through an injector located in each intake port of the engine.

Emergency brake A braking system, independent of the main hydraulic system, that can be used to slow or stop the vehicle if the primary brakes fail, or to hold the vehicle stationary even though the brake pedal isn't depressed. It usually consists of a hand lever that actuates either front or rear brakes mechanically through a series of cables and linkages. Also known as a handbrake or parking brake.

Endfloat The amount of lengthwise movement between two parts. As applied to a crankshaft, the distance that the crankshaft can move forward and back in the cylinder block.

Engine management system (EMS) A computer controlled system which manages the fuel injection and the ignition systems in an integrated fashion.

Exhaust manifold A part with several passages through which exhaust gases leave the engine combustion chambers and enter the exhaust pipe.

F

Fan clutch A viscous (fluid) drive coupling device which permits variable engine fan speeds in relation to engine speeds.

Feeler blade A thin strip or blade of hardened steel, ground to an exact thickness, used to check or measure clearances between parts.

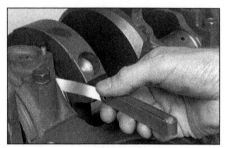

Feeler blade

Firing order The order in which the engine cylinders fire, or deliver their power strokes, beginning with the number one cylinder.

Flywheel A heavy spinning wheel in which energy is absorbed and stored by means of momentum. On cars, the flywheel is attached to the crankshaft to smooth out firing impulses.

Free play The amount of travel before any action takes place. The "looseness" in a linkage, or an assembly of parts, between the initial application of force and actual movement. For example, the distance the brake pedal moves before the pistons in the master cylinder are actuated.

Fuse An electrical device which protects a circuit against accidental overload. The typical fuse contains a soft piece of metal which is calibrated to melt at a predetermined current flow (expressed as amps) and break the circuit.

Fusible link A circuit protection device consisting of a conductor surrounded by heat-resistant insulation. The conductor is smaller than the wire it protects, so it acts as the weakest link in the circuit. Unlike a blown fuse, a failed fusible link must frequently be cut from the wire for replacement.

G

Gap The distance the spark must travel in jumping from the centre electrode to the side electrode in a spark plug. Also refers to the spacing between the points in a contact breaker assembly in a conventional points-type ignition, or to the distance between the reluctor or rotor and the pickup coil in an electronic ignition.

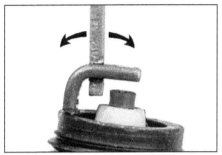

Adjusting spark plug gap

Gasket Any thin, soft material - usually cork, cardboard, asbestos or soft metal - installed between two metal surfaces to ensure a good seal. For instance, the cylinder head gasket seals the joint between the block and the cylinder head.

Gasket

Gauge An instrument panel display used to monitor engine conditions. A gauge with a movable pointer on a dial or a fixed scale is an analogue gauge. A gauge with a numerical readout is called a digital gauge.

H

Halfshaft A rotating shaft that transmits power from the final drive unit to a drive wheel, usually when referring to a live rear axle.

Harmonic balancer A device designed to reduce torsion or twisting vibration in the crankshaft. May be incorporated in the crankshaft pulley. Also known as a vibration damper.

Hone An abrasive tool for correcting small irregularities or differences in diameter in an engine cylinder, brake cylinder, etc.

Hydraulic tappet A tappet that utilises hydraulic pressure from the engine's lubrication system to maintain zero clearance (constant contact with both camshaft and valve stem). Automatically adjusts to variation in valve stem length. Hydraulic tappets also reduce valve noise.

I

Ignition timing The moment at which the spark plug fires, usually expressed in the number of crankshaft degrees before the piston reaches the top of its stroke.

Inlet manifold A tube or housing with passages through which flows the air-fuel mixture (carburettor vehicles and vehicles with throttle body injection) or air only (port fuel-injected vehicles) to the port openings in the cylinder head.

J

Jump start Starting the engine of a vehicle with a discharged or weak battery by attaching jump leads from the weak battery to a charged or helper battery.

L

Load Sensing Proportioning Valve (LSPV) A brake hydraulic system control valve that works like a proportioning valve, but also takes into consideration the amount of weight carried by the rear axle.

Locknut A nut used to lock an adjustment nut, or other threaded component, in place. For example, a locknut is employed to keep the adjusting nut on the rocker arm in position.

Lockwasher A form of washer designed to prevent an attaching nut from working loose.

M

MacPherson strut A type of front suspension system devised by Earle MacPherson at Ford of England. In its original form, a simple lateral link with the anti-roll bar creates the lower control arm. A long strut - an integral coil spring and shock absorber - is mounted between the body and the steering knuckle. Many modern so-called MacPherson strut systems use a conventional lower A-arm and don't rely on the anti-roll bar for location.

Multimeter An electrical test instrument with the capability to measure voltage, current and resistance.

N

NOx Oxides of Nitrogen. A common toxic pollutant emitted by petrol and diesel engines at higher temperatures.

O

Ohm The unit of electrical resistance. One volt applied to a resistance of one ohm will produce a current of one amp.

Ohmmeter An instrument for measuring electrical resistance.

O-ring A type of sealing ring made of a special rubber-like material; in use, the O-ring is compressed into a groove to provide the sealing action.

Overhead cam (ohc) engine An engine with the camshaft(s) located on top of the cylinder head(s).

Overhead valve (ohv) engine An engine with the valves located in the cylinder head, but with the camshaft located in the engine block.

Oxygen sensor A device installed in the engine exhaust manifold, which senses the oxygen content in the exhaust and converts this information into an electric current. Also called a Lambda sensor.

P

Phillips screw A type of screw head having a cross instead of a slot for a corresponding type of screwdriver.

Plastigage A thin strip of plastic thread, available in different sizes, used for measuring clearances. For example, a strip of Plastigage is laid across a bearing journal. The parts are assembled and dismantled; the width of the crushed strip indicates the clearance between journal and bearing.

Plastigage

Propeller shaft The long hollow tube with universal joints at both ends that carries power from the transmission to the differential on front-engined rear wheel drive vehicles.

Proportioning valve A hydraulic control valve which limits the amount of pressure to the rear brakes during panic stops to prevent wheel lock-up.

R

Rack-and-pinion steering A steering system with a pinion gear on the end of the steering shaft that mates with a rack (think of a geared wheel opened up and laid flat). When the steering wheel is turned, the pinion turns, moving the rack to the left or right. This movement is transmitted through the track rods to the steering arms at the wheels.

Radiator A liquid-to-air heat transfer device designed to reduce the temperature of the coolant in an internal combustion engine cooling system.

Refrigerant Any substance used as a heat transfer agent in an air-conditioning system. R-12 has been the principle refrigerant for many years; recently, however, manufacturers have begun using R-134a, a non-CFC substance that is considered less harmful to the ozone in the upper atmosphere.

Rocker arm A lever arm that rocks on a shaft or pivots on a stud. In an overhead valve engine, the rocker arm converts the upward movement of the pushrod into a downward movement to open a valve.

Rotor In a distributor, the rotating device inside the cap that connects the centre electrode and the outer terminals as it turns, distributing the high voltage from the coil secondary winding to the proper spark plug. Also, that part of an alternator which rotates inside the stator. Also, the rotating assembly of a turbocharger, including the compressor wheel, shaft and turbine wheel.

Runout The amount of wobble (in-and-out movement) of a gear or wheel as it's rotated. The amount a shaft rotates "out-of-true." The out-of-round condition of a rotating part.

S

Sealant A liquid or paste used to prevent leakage at a joint. Sometimes used in conjunction with a gasket.

Sealed beam lamp An older headlight design which integrates the reflector, lens and filaments into a hermetically-sealed one-piece unit. When a filament burns out or the lens cracks, the entire unit is simply replaced.

Serpentine drivebelt A single, long, wide accessory drivebelt that's used on some newer vehicles to drive all the accessories, instead of a series of smaller, shorter belts. Serpentine drivebelts are usually tensioned by an automatic tensioner.

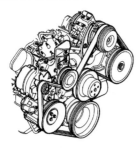

Serpentine drivebelt

Shim Thin spacer, commonly used to adjust the clearance or relative positions between two parts. For example, shims inserted into or under bucket tappets control valve clearances. Clearance is adjusted by changing the thickness of the shim.

Slide hammer A special puller that screws into or hooks onto a component such as a shaft or bearing; a heavy sliding handle on the shaft bottoms against the end of the shaft to knock the component free.

Sprocket A tooth or projection on the periphery of a wheel, shaped to engage with a chain or drivebelt. Commonly used to refer to the sprocket wheel itself.

Starter inhibitor switch On vehicles with an automatic transmission, a switch that prevents starting if the vehicle is not in Neutral or Park.

Strut See MacPherson strut.

T

Tappet A cylindrical component which transmits motion from the cam to the valve stem, either directly or via a pushrod and rocker arm. Also called a cam follower.

Thermostat A heat-controlled valve that regulates the flow of coolant between the cylinder block and the radiator, so maintaining optimum engine operating temperature. A thermostat is also used in some air cleaners in which the temperature is regulated.

Thrust bearing The bearing in the clutch assembly that is moved in to the release levers by clutch pedal action to disengage the clutch. Also referred to as a release bearing.

Timing belt A toothed belt which drives the camshaft. Serious engine damage may result if it breaks in service.

Timing chain A chain which drives the camshaft.

Toe-in The amount the front wheels are closer together at the front than at the rear. On rear wheel drive vehicles, a slight amount of toe-in is usually specified to keep the front wheels running parallel on the road by offsetting other forces that tend to spread the wheels apart.

Toe-out The amount the front wheels are closer together at the rear than at the front. On front wheel drive vehicles, a slight amount of toe-out is usually specified.

Tools For full information on choosing and using tools, refer to the *Haynes Automotive Tools Manual.*

Tracer A stripe of a second colour applied to a wire insulator to distinguish that wire from another one with the same colour insulator.

Tune-up A process of accurate and careful adjustments and parts replacement to obtain the best possible engine performance.

Turbocharger A centrifugal device, driven by exhaust gases, that pressurises the intake air. Normally used to increase the power output from a given engine displacement, but can also be used primarily to reduce exhaust emissions (as on VW's "Umwelt" Diesel engine).

U

Universal joint or U-joint A double-pivoted connection for transmitting power from a driving to a driven shaft through an angle. A U-joint consists of two Y-shaped yokes and a cross-shaped member called the spider.

V

Valve A device through which the flow of liquid, gas, vacuum, or loose material in bulk may be started, stopped, or regulated by a movable part that opens, shuts, or partially obstructs one or more ports or passageways. A valve is also the movable part of such a device.

Valve clearance The clearance between the valve tip (the end of the valve stem) and the rocker arm or tappet. The valve clearance is measured when the valve is closed.

Vernier caliper A precision measuring instrument that measures inside and outside dimensions. Not quite as accurate as a micrometer, but more convenient.

Viscosity The thickness of a liquid or its resistance to flow.

Volt A unit for expressing electrical "pressure" in a circuit. One volt that will produce a current of one ampere through a resistance of one ohm.

W

Welding Various processes used to join metal items by heating the areas to be joined to a molten state and fusing them together. For more information refer to the *Haynes Automotive Welding Manual.*

Wiring diagram A drawing portraying the components and wires in a vehicle's electrical system, using standardised symbols. For more information refer to the *Haynes Automotive Electrical and Electronic Systems Manual.*

Note: *References throughout this index are in the form "Chapter number" • "Page number"*